Donovan
America's Master Spy

This painting of Maj. Gen. William J. Donovan
greets the visitor to CIA headquarters in
Langley, Virginia. Donovan is considered the
father of American centralized intelligence.

Donovan
America's Master Spy

Richard Dunlop

Skyhorse Publishing

Skyhorse Publishing books may be purchased in bulk at special discounts for sales promotion, corporate gifts, fund-raising, or educational purposes. Special editions can also be created to specifications. For details, contact the Special Sales Department, Skyhorse Publishing, 307 West 36th Street, 11th Floor, New York, NY 10018 or info@skyhorsepublishing.com.

Skyhorse® and Skyhorse Publishing® are registered trademarks of Skyhorse Publishing, Inc.®, a Delaware corporation.

Visit our website at www.skyhorsepublishing.com.

10 9 8 7 6 5 4 3 2 1

Library of Congress Cataloging-in-Publication Data is available on file.
ISBN: 978-1-62636-539-1

Printed in the United States of America

Contents

Foreword

On the day in May 1940 that Winston Churchill became prime minister, he telephoned me at my London home to say that he was dining with Max Beaverbrook and suggested that I join them. The dinner party was a serious affair. Other guests included Boom Trenchard of RAF and Scotland Yard fame, General Weygand of France, and Bill Hughes, prime minister of Australia. With the port and cigars Winston rose from his seat and beckoned to me. We walked over to the dining room window, heavily draped because of the blackout. Winston said quietly to me, "Bill, you know what you must do at once. We have discussed it most fully, and there is a complete fusion of minds. So off you go. You will have the full support of every resource at my command, and God will guide your efforts as He will ours. This may be our last farewell, so au revoir and good luck."

It may be that at this late date I am thought of mainly as having been a regional representative of British Intelligence in the United States. My original charter went beyond that and indeed, under the master code name of Intrepid, was soon expanded to include representation in America of all the British secret and covert organizations, nine of them, and also security and communications. In fact, the communications division of my organization was by far the largest of its type in operation, handling more than a million message groups a day. In addition, there was the responsibility of acting as a go-between for Winston Churchill and Franklin Roosevelt. My work as British Security Coordinator became an all-encompassing secret service.

I must enlarge a bit upon what were my principal concerns when I arrived in New York in late May 1940. Obviously, the establishment of a secret organization to investigate enemy activities and to institute adequate wartime security measures in the Western Hemisphere in relation to British interests in a neutral territory were of importance, and American assistance in achieving this goal was essential. The procurement of certain supplies for Britain was high on my priority list, and it was the burning urgency of this requirement that made me instinctively concentrate on the single individual who could help me. I turned to Bill Donovan.

By virtue of his independence of thought and action, Donovan inevitably had his critics. But there were few among them who would deny that he reached a correct appraisal of the international situation in the summer of 1940. At that time the United States government was debating two alternative courses of action. One was to endeavor to keep Britain in the war by supplying her with material assistance of which she was desperately in need. The other was to give Britain up for lost and to concentrate exclusively on American rearmament to offset the German threat. That the former course was eventually pursued was due in large measure to Donovan's tireless advocacy of it.

Immediately after the fall of France, not even President Roosevelt himself could feel assured that aid to Britain would not be wasted in the circumstances. I need only remind today's readers that dispatches from the U.S. ambassadors in London and Paris were stressing that Britain's cause was hopeless. The majority of the President's cabinet was of the same opinion. American isolationism was given vigorous expression by such men as Charles Lindbergh and Sen. Burton K. Wheeler. Donovan on the other hand was convinced that, granted sufficient aid from the United States, Britain could and would survive. It was my task first to inform Donovan of Britain's most urgent requirements so that he could make them known in appropriate quarters, and second to furnish him with concrete evidence in support of his contention that American material assistance would not be improvident charity but a sound investment.

Very shortly after I arrived in the United States, Donovan arranged for me to attend a meeting with Secretary of the Navy Knox, Secretary of War Stimson, and Secretary of State Hull, where the main subject of discussion was Britain's lack of destroyers. The way was explored for finding a formula for the transfer of 50 overage American destroyers to the Royal Navy without a legal breach of U.S. neutrality and without affront to American public opinion. It was then that I suggested that Donovan pay a visit to Britain with the object of investigating conditions at first hand and assessing for himself the British war effort. Donovan conferred with Knox, and they jointly conferred with the President. Donovan left by Clipper July 14, on one of the most momentous missions ever undertaken by any agent in the history of western civilization.

I arranged that he should be afforded every opportunity to conduct his inquiries. I endeavored to marshal my friends in high places to bare their breasts. He was received in audience by the king. He had ample time with Churchill and members of his cabinet. He spoke with industrial leaders and with representatives of all classes in Britain. He learned what was true—that Churchill, defying the Nazis, was no mere bold facade but the very heart of Britain, which was still beating strongly.

Donovan flew back to America in early August, and shortly after his arrival I was able to inform London that his visit had been everything I had hoped for. Donovan and Knox pressed the destroyers-for-bases case with the President despite strong opposition from below and procrastination from above. At midnight of August 22, 1940, I was able to report to London that the destroyer deal was agreed upon, and that 44 of the 50 ships were already commissioned. It is certain that the destroyers-for-bases deal would not have eventuated when it did without Donovan's intercession, and I was instructed to convey to him the warmest thanks of His Majesty's Government.

My work with Donovan could be described as covert diplomacy. There were other supplies that he was largely instrumental in obtaining for Britain during the same period. Among them were 100 Flying Fortresses for RAF Coastal Command and a million American rifles and 30 million rounds of ammunition for the British Home Guard, who were then mock training with broomsticks. During the early winter of 1940 His Majesty's Government was especially concerned to secure the assistance of the U.S. Navy in convoying British merchant shipping across the Atlantic. This was a measure of intervention that the U.S. government was understandably reluctant to take. Donovan pleaded the case for us at a meeting with Knox, Stimson, and Hull in December 1940. This conference led to Donovan's second trip. There was more to it than that, since Churchill wanted an influential American to apply some subtle delaying tactics in Bulgaria and Yugoslavia, which might affect the timetable of Hitler's expected attack on Russia.

Donovan's achievements in Britain and in the Mediterranean and Middle East were highly significant. When he returned to Washington on March 18, 1941, he brought with him a very comprehensive situation report with which to enlighten the President. At breakfast with President Roosevelt, he was assured of active support for a step that, as far as we British were concerned, was as water to a parched man dying of thirst—direct transportation of war materials to the Middle East. Two weeks later the ships were loading. These are only some of the highlights of Donovan's accomplishments during this critical time.

From the beginning I had discussed with Donovan the necessity for the United States to establish an agency for conducting secret activities throughout the world, an agency with which I could collaborate fully by virtue of its being patterned after my own organization. He early agreed in principle, and on his first two visits to England he spent some time with British Intelligence, Special Operations Executive, and other similar agencies, both at headquarters and field training stations. Upon his return from his second visit, he discussed with the President the need for expanding the scope of American secret activities.

The idea that Donovan himself should direct the new agency that we envisaged did not at first appeal to him, nor was it by any means a foregone conclusion that he would be offered the appointment. Yet I was convinced that he was the obvious man for the job. In the first place, he had the confidence of the President, the secretary of state, and of the civilian heads of the service departments. In the second place, he had been involved in intelligence work for most of his adult life and he had given considerable thought to the conduct of secret activities. Third, Donovan had all the requisite vision and drive to build swiftly an organization of sufficient size and competence to play an effective part in the war. Last, he had already shown his willingness to cooperate fully with the British Security Coordinator and the worth of his cooperation had been abundantly proved. On June 18, 1941, Donovan informed me that he had seen the President and had accepted the appointment of coordinator of all forms of intelligence. The directive was necessarily vague in its terminology, but in fact Donovan had been entrusted with responsibility not only for collecting intelligence but for coordinating this work with preparations to conduct special operations and subversive propaganda. That night I could sleep.

DONOVAN: AMERICA'S MASTER SPY chronicles Bill Donovan's entire life of service to his nation. Richard Dunlop, a former OSS agent who knew Donovan well during World War II and afterward, has brought to his work the very investigative flair and determined scholarship which his mentor, Bill Donovan, fostered in his aides. I worked closely with Donovan throughout the war, and my confidence in him proved to be fully justified. He was one of the most significant men of our century. It can be said for certain that before the war ended, Donovan's OSS was comparable quantitatively with the combined efforts of British Intelligence and Special Operations Executive, in itself a commendable accomplishment. When it is remembered how little time he had to build his organization and how many serious obstacles he faced at the outset, this is truly remarkable. Qualitatively too, much of OSS's work was without doubt of first-class importance by any standard.

Sir William Stephenson
Bermuda
May 1, 1982

Preface

When Dutch sculptor Kees Verkade was chosen to create a bronze tribute to Maj. Gen. William J. Donovan, he sculpted a 14-foot-tall figure of a tightrope walker. OSS men and women who attended the presentation ceremony in front of Columbia University Law School on May 24, 1979, thought that this was an appropriate figure to represent a man whose life had been an astonishing balancing act between a public career of soldier, statesman, lawyer, and humanitarian, and the clandestine life of an intelligence master.

Speaking at the presentation ceremony, John J. McCloy, assistant secretary of war when Bill Donovan was director of the Office of Strategic Services during World War II, remarked, "To class yourself as a colleague of Bill Donovan borders on the presumptuous. It carries connotations that may well not be deserved." What is true of John McCloy's relations to Donovan is many times over true of my own relations to him; but at the same time I can claim his friendship, and I still carry within me the extraordinary example of his life.

I had served Bill Donovan in a number of ways both abroad and in this country when one day he invited me to visit him at his law offices in New York. He commented that although I showed a certain aptitude for intelligence work, my talents were more suited to a career in journalism, for, he said, "You have an irresistible tendency to tell everything you know." I was discomfited even though I immediately realized he was entirely correct. He went on to tell me about his own writing. He was then finishing an article for the *Atlantic*, which he asked me to revise for him. Later he interested me in his enormous research project to lay the basis for a history of intelligence in the western world.

And then he began to give me documents and material that, without his ever saying so, clearly were intended to help me to write his own life's history. At breakfast in his apartment on Sutton Place, in his law office, or whenever we met on other business in Washington, Chicago, or New York, he invariably told stories drawn from his colorful past or discussed events in which he had played a pivotal if often secret part. Sometimes I would take notes, until he once remarked, "You should be able to remember things without scribbling on a piece of paper." I put away my pen and notepad.

When Donovan was asked by President Eisenhower to go to Thailand as American ambassador, he asked me to accompany him, because of my knowledge of Southeast Asia in general and of neighboring Burma in particular. It proved impossible for me to go, and I have always had the nagging feeling that I let the General down. No matter, he was just as much my friend when we next met, and he was just as candid in his remarks about his experiences in Southeast Asia.

Bill Donovan himself made it possible for me to write this book, but he would not have expected me to write from his viewpoint alone. My wife, Joan, and I interviewed upward of 200 people who knew the General, and we worked in more than 40 archives. I traveled to France, the United Kingdom, Germany, Greece, and Thailand following Bill Donovan's track. I talked to members of the Greek underground, and the French Resistance, who knew him well, and I met Thais who still hope that his concept of an American foreign policy toward underdeveloped nations might yet be implemented. Everyone with whom I spoke at home and abroad appreciated that in Donovan they had known a most uncommon man.

Prologue

JUST WITHIN THE MAIN ENTRANCE of the Central Intelligence Agency headquarters at Langley, Virginia, a lifelike painting of a man in the uniform of a major general looks down on the comings and goings of CIA men and women. The four ribbons above the left breast pocket represent the highest awards the United States can confer, among them the Congressional Medal of Honor. His right hand is hooked in the pocket of his uniform, and his blue eyes seem to search the passing faces. There is no guile in his expression, only a disarming candor. Above all, the face gives the appearance of resolve, a manly purposefulness tempered by an innate gentleness of spirit. The painting is a portrait of William Joseph Donovan, lawyer, statesman, heroic soldier, diplomat, father of American intelligence, and America's master spy—an enigma masked by charisma.

Thomas E. Stephens, the New York City painter admired for his more or less official portrait of President Dwight D. Eisenhower, painted Donovan's portrait as well. It is judged an excellent likeness, even though Stephens had only two sittings before Donovan was stricken by a cerebral hemorrhage in the spring of 1957. The artist had to finish the work from a photograph that was a favorite of his subject, a picture Donovan countless times fondly inscribed to faithful members of his Office of Strategic Services (OSS) and resistance leaders who have since come in from the cold. Even now not all these former agents may feel it safe or politic to display the photo, given a world in which yesterday's clandestine history and today's behind-the-scenes events have a way of intertwining.

When Stephens finished the portrait, it was first hung within the entrance of CIA headquarters, then in the old South Building at 25th and E streets in Washington, D.C., on a hill overlooking a brewery and an indoor skating rink in the bottoms along the Potomac River. There Donovan once had his office. Although Donovan lay stricken at Walter Reed General Hospital, his brilliant mind a shambles, CIA Director Allen Dulles wanted him to be brought to headquarters to see the painting and the honor it did him. It was an act of sentiment since Dulles had learned his trade under the director of the OSS.

Lawrence Houston, CIA's general counsel and another of Donovan's onetime aides, set out with a car and driver to bring his former chief from the hospital. When he walked into Donovan's sickroom he found him sitting up. Donovan's nurse had dressed him in his army uniform and had seen to it that his ribbons were in place and his thinning white hair neatly brushed.

Supported by Houston, Donovan managed to walk to the car. He gazed around him as the auto started down 16th Street toward the city. Even in the last months of his life it sometimes seemed as if the indomitable old hero would come back, that the fog would lift from his mind, and that he would again play a critical role in the day's events. To Houston this seemed to be one of those times. But as they drove on, it was only the children playing along the street that Donovan watched. His eyes sought them out eagerly, and if a roller-skating girl came scooting too near the curb or a boy pursuing a ball ran toward the car, he cried out. A man who had lost the power of speech for months found words to express his fear that a youngster might be hurt.

"Look out!" he cried at the driver. "Look out!"

"He was terrified that the car might hit a child," remembered Houston, "all the way to headquarters."

Donovan walked into the South Building entrance unaided, his step almost as brisk as when he had directed his vast intelligence net. When he saw the portrait within the door, his eyes brightened. He drew himself to full attention, his still powerful torso supported by enfeebled legs trembling with the strain. Aides said that the director of intelligence was hurrying from his office to welcome the man who had already become more myth than reality. Younger men, who had never seen Donovan and never expected to do so, stared at him. Somebody started a rattle of applause, but it was cut off when Donovan turned, a confused look on his face, his knees beginning to buckle.

"The clouds rolled in over his mind," said Houston. "He would have fallen, except we sustained him. He could not wait for the director, and we helped him from the building to the waiting car."

By the time Allen Dulles reached the lobby, Donovan was gone. There was no last chance for a beneficent smile from Donovan to erase the bitter memory that Dulles carried of the quarrels that had broken their friendship on an angry day in France as Hitler's Reich crumbled.

On the way back to Walter Reed, Donovan seemed to awaken. He drew a folded envelope from one pocket and a pencil from the other. His face took on its old resolve as he placed the envelope on his knee and began a note to the President. The Franklin Roosevelt archives at Hyde Park, New York, contain more than 7,500 pages of once top-secret notes and memos from intelligence chief Bill Donovan. Now, more than a dozen years after Roosevelt's death, Donovan began one more report. "Memorandum for the President," he wrote, and then the pencil trailed off the paper and fell from his hand. Donovan sank back in his seat. The remainder of the drive back to the hospital he was silent.

As Donovan lay ill in the hospital those last two years before his death in February 1959, men and women from the OSS came to see their onetime chief. The men clasped his hand and talked to him. He often understood and smiled at their reminiscences and jokes. Sometimes he tried to talk and with the help of his nurse, a woman devoted to him, he made his meanings clear.

The OSS women sat on the edge of his bed, and he beamed at them with the charm that had always drawn women to him. They held back the tears for his sake and because even in his long-drawn-out illness, he remained cheerful. "There were always his blue eyes, his wonderful eyes," said Elizabeth Heppner McIntosh, one of the scores of women who were devoted to both the OSS and its chief.

One day when nobody was watching him, Bill Donovan got out of his bed, drew his hospital robe around his pajamas, and put on his slippers. He somehow got out the door, down the corridor, and out of the building. Perhaps in his mind he was fleeing Nazi enemies, escaping from their prison. He set off down 16th Street beside the traffic until at last a motorist, seeing the old man in hospital garb, his legs stepping along in a brisk military pace, stopped and phoned to let Walter Reed know that a patient was on the loose. When the medical orderlies came for him, Donovan was ready to return to his bed, his determination gone.

David Crockett, old friend and OSS man, came to see Donovan in early February 1959. When Crockett had been in the OSS field headquarters at Caserta, Italy, in January 1944, Donovan had flown in from a confrontation with Soviet intelligence chiefs in their dread Lubyanka headquarters. Donovan was exhausted and sick with a virus contracted in the Moscow winter. Yet he would not go to a hospital. "I don't trust doctors," he told Crockett. "I don't like doctors, and I'm too busy to be ill."

All that night Crockett sat by his friend's sickbed and listened to his fevered ravings. In the morning Donovan thanked him with that special warmth he saved for OSS members who served him well.

Now at Walter Reed General Hospital, Donovan recognized Crockett, although it had been weeks since he had apparently recognized anybody. He nodded his head and tried to speak. "He had the same expression on his face as he had that morning in Caserta," Crockett remembered. When Crockett got up to leave, the nurse explained that the general wanted him to come back the next day. In the morning Crockett returned to Walter Reed only to be told by the nurse that Donovan was too sick to see him.

William J. Donovan never feared death, as he had demonstrated on battlefield after battlefield in World War I; his reckless courage had helped to make him known as Wild Bill Donovan, one of America's most famous heroes. The story is told of how, as he led a charge in France on seemingly impregnable German positions, Donovan turned to find not one of his men following him. As bullets spatted about him and shells burst nearby, he shouted, "What's the matter with you? Do you want to live forever?"

They had followed him then, rushing at the Germans to win a precious victory. Now it seemed that Donovan, hopelessly ill, was himself condemned to live forever. But at last, two days after David Crockett's visit, on February 8, he died. His wife, Ruth, no longer estranged, and his son, David, were at his bedside.

Allen Dulles sent a message to all CIA stations around the world:

> America has lost a soldier, a diplomat, an outstanding intelligence officer, a patriot dedicated to the welfare of our Nation.
>
> Bill Donovan was the father of "central intelligence." To him belongs the credit for organizing and directing the Office of Strategic Services during World War II. I was proud to be associated with him then and later to have the benefit of his experience and advice in my work as head of the Central Intelligence Agency.
>
> Our country honored his military heroism and leadership by awarding him America's three highest military decorations: the Medal of Honor, the Distinguished Service Cross, and the Distinguished Service Medal. He also earned the National Security Medal, the highest award in the field of intelligence relating to our national security. He was a great leader.

It is said that there are no bugles and flags for spies, but for Bill Donovan there was a funeral mass at St. Matthew's Cathedral in Washington, and his flag-draped casket rode on a caisson drawn by six black horses to Arlington National Cemetery. There, as a bugle sounded taps, he was buried with full military honors among America's heroes. Newspapers editorialized about Donovan's bravery and patriotic service.

Admiral Wilhelm Canaris, German intelligence chief during World War II, once remarked that of all the Allied leaders, he most would have liked to meet and know William J. Donovan. Adolf Hitler, who in 1923 had met and confided in Donovan, always feared and hated him more than he did any other American. As might be expected, the intelligence chiefs of friendly nations expressed their sorrow at the passing of the man acknowledged to be one of the great spymasters of the 20th century. Sir William Stephenson, Britain's "Intrepid," who had always been "Little Bill" to Donovan's "Big Bill," inseparable friend and partner in intelligence, was one of the pallbearers. Even top Soviet authorities sent word that they too mourned his passing. He had been a worthy enemy. It remained for Carleton S. Coon, a renowned social anthropologist and an OSS agent in the Mediterranean, to speak for OSS men and women when he wrote "On Learning of the Death of 'Wild Bill' Donovan":

Wild, people called him, who had heard of his fame
And wild he was in heart and in feyness.
But more than wild was the man with the wile of Odysseus.
Like the King of Assassins he welded together
An army of desperate, invisible soldiers,
Each as bold as himself in single deeds
But none as keen as himself, the leader of all, commander
of men
Who could ask, "Jim, will you limpet that ship?"
Knowing the answer, for none would refuse him, or
"Carl, a free ride to Albania? Yes? Then you're off,
Ten minutes to Zero," and we would all die for him.
Die for him some of us did, but he died for us all.
Some who are left would burn him whole, like a Viking jarl
in his ship.
Others would cover his bones with a colossal marble cross.
Each to his taste, say I, Yankee, Irishman, Italian.
As many tombs will he have in our hearts as the scattered
remains of Osiris.
How lucky we were that he came when he did in the long tide
of history.
Hail to Wild Bill, a hero of men and a name to hang
myths on.
As American as chowder, Crockett, and Putnam.
A free fighter's hero, may God give him peace.

PART ONE

The Making of a Hero

1883–1918

1

The Boy from the Irish First Ward

WILL DONOVAN UNDERSTOOD as a boy what a secure hiding place could mean to a hunted man. He lived much of his childhood in what he was to know later as a safehouse. He was accustomed from a very early age to finding strange men at breakfast, usually young and always pale, clothed in dark suits shiny with wear. Nobody had to caution the five Donovan children not to talk about the strangers, even to their playmates in the Irish First Ward on the Buffalo, New York, waterfront. The men stayed a few days at the most and then disappeared just as suddenly as they had come.

In the last decades of the 19th century, many Irish refugees who had left the troubles in their homeland and immigrated to Canada crept across the border into the United States. Buffalo Irish, sympathetic to their compatriots, took them into boats at night on the Ontario shore and ferried them over the dark waters of Lake Erie or the Niagara River to the sandy lakefront. Will Donovan early realized that when his father and mother, usually so cheerful and bantering, fell silent at dinner, men were even then gathering in some secret place on the Canadian shore. The boy noticed that his good-night hug from his father and mother would be more affectionate than usual. Ever afterward the calm before a storm was a time to show love or to declare friendship, for there might never be such a chance again; things might go awry and everything might be swept away. Will would fall asleep knowing that his mother would tiptoe into the attic room where he slept with his two younger brothers, Tim and Vincent, to see that her sons were quiet in their beds.

No matter how deeply he slept, Will would awaken to the muffled sound of the heavy brogans of the men, walking up Michigan Avenue and then pausing at the stoop of the brick house at number 74. There were five steps to climb, each step sounding in the boy's ears, and then the secret rap on the door, not too loud. When Grandfather Donovan, who lived on the first floor, opened the door, a few soft words were spoken, the men would enter, and the door would close with a light thud. Will would fall asleep again to the sound of voices talking and to an occasional snatch of laughter, nervous with relief.

The refugees usually slept on the first floor, where Will's grandfather and grandmother lived, or sometimes on the second floor, where Mother and Father Donovan and Will's sisters, Mary and the baby Loretta, had their bedrooms. Then one night a boy about Will's age came. There was no room for him below, so Mother Donovan brought him upstairs and put him to bed next to her oldest son. Will awoke to the odor of stale sweat, which suddenly meant fear to him. The strange boy lay beside him, unwashed, exhausted, and already fast asleep. Even in his sleep, fright clung to him. Will drifted back to sleep.

In the morning he awakened and raised up on his elbows to look at a pale face topped with carroty hair on the pillow beside him. Even a young lad could be a refugee from Ireland then. When the boy's eyes opened, they clouded with apprehension. Will smiled to reassure him.

"Are you from Canada?" he asked.

The boy nodded.

"You're safe in America now," said Will.

Already his voice carried more than a boy's conviction, and the strange boy smiled back. Will and Tim stayed indoors to play with the refugee boy for a day or two, and then he too was gone. He left behind him the sweaty smell of fear that Will was never to forget. The man at whose death the *New York Times* was to editorialize "No one can forget that he was always brave" became determined that he would never smell of fear.

Donovan relatives say that William J. Donovan had his ancestry traced back to 12th-century Ireland, but if so, the genealogy has been lost. At least there is no question that Donovan's forebears came from Cork, that southern county where people believe, like St. Augustine, that an ounce of honey attracts more flies than a gallon of vinegar. A Cork man is adept at "soothering," the fine knack of soothing ruffled spirits with gentle words. Blarney Castle is in Cork, and the Blarney Stone casts its spell not only upon those who kiss it but upon the people of the entire county. A Cork man is lighthearted and eloquent by disposition, and Will's grandfather Timothy, who was born in Cork at Skibbereen, was no exception.

There is little information about Tim Donovan's parents. He was raised not by his mother and father but by his uncle, the parish priest. Cerebral and well educated, Tim became a teacher in the parish school. In Skibbereen a teacher was expected to be as poor as the proverbial church mouse, which the better families of the community expected him to resemble in many other ways as well. When Timothy Donovan fell in love with Mary Mahoney, whose family lived in a substantial house, her parents were disturbed. They were appalled when she returned his love. Timothy and Mary stood up for another young couple at their wedding in the parish church, and swept away by the romantic occasion, they decided to get married too. When Timothy and Mary announced that they intended to emigrate to America, the Mahoneys, far from objecting, bitterly told them to be on their way. Most likely they contributed to the newlyweds' finances. At least when Tim and Mary did set out for America, they, unlike most emigrants, did not travel penniless.

In the middle of the 19th century Buffalo was the greatest inland immigrant port in the United States, and most of the immigrants were Irish. The Irish settled on the Flats, where Little Buffalo Creek flowed into Lake Erie. It was an area so often flooded by Lake Erie storms that its residents were said to live "down where the geese wear rubber boots."

As the golden flood of grain from the Midwest was carried eastward over the Great Lakes to Buffalo, it was up to the Irish workers to shovel it out of the holds of the ships and carry it ashore in bags and baskets to warehouses along the waterfront. The laborers were called scoopers because they scooped up the grain. They tied their pants legs tight to their legs to keep out the grain, and it was always easy to spot a scooper on the streets of the Irish First Ward by the way he tied his pants.

By the time Mary and Tim Donovan arrived on the Buffalo waterfront, 2 million bushels of grain from the West were being carried ashore every day of the year. Irish labor was cheap, and when Joseph Dart, a Buffalonian, invented the world's first steam grain elevator, he was assured that it could never compete with the Irish. "An Irishman's back is the cheapest elevator ever built," he was told.

Dart persisted, and his first elevator building erected on the shore of Buffalo Creek was able to raise 2,000 bushels an hour instead of the previous 2,000 bushels a day. Over the next decades elevator after elevator was built. Soon the waterfront of the Irish First Ward, which extended from the foot of Main Street to the present Elk Street and South Park Avenue, was lined with the enormous structures, each serviced by railroad tracks, along which the busy locomotives chuffed and shunted their strings of grain cars. Buffalo grew rich, and handsome mansions sprung up along Delaware Avenue. The Irish stayed poor, and they built their cottages along the streets blocked off from the lake by the grain elevators on both banks of Buffalo Creek.

Here and there, rising above the cottages of what more fortunate Buffalonians called the shanty Irish, were a few larger brick or frame houses left from the days before the immigrants occupied the area. Tim and Mary Donovan bought such a brick house on Michigan Avenue, and there they raised their family. Their son Timothy, born in 1860, was the fourth of ten children, five boys and five girls. He found the waterfront, its lake boats, its switching locomotives and freight cars, its sailors and railroaders and their stories far more interesting than his classes at school. This disturbed his scholarly father and his mother, who fancied her son a priest-to-be, but when the boy's absences from school became more and more regular, Timothy and Mary acquiesced in what appeared to be the inevitable. Tim dropped out of school and went to work in the railroad yards that straddled the foot of Michigan Avenue. In time he became the yardmaster.

At 21 Tim Donovan had become a tall young man, thin but with broad shoulders that stood him in good stead in a rough-and-ready neighborhood where saloon fistfights broke out on payday, which for scoopers and railroaders alike was every Friday. When Mark Twain came to Buffalo in 1869 to edit the *Buffalo Express,* in which he had a one-third interest, he looked with wonder on the hard-drinking Irish of the First Ward. An Irishman, he observed, never touched beer when he could drink whiskey. "Give an Irishman lager for a month and he's a dead man," he noted. "An Irishman is lined with copper, and the beer corrodes it. But whiskey polishes the copper and is the saving of him."

On Fridays, Irishmen bent on polishing their copper tarried late into the evening before they finally sauntered or stumbled home. Tim Donovan was not a drinking man, but he liked to stand at the bar in the Swanee House at Michigan and Ohio or at Belgian Mary's, still closer to home on Michigan, sip ginger ale, argue politics, and declaim Irish poetry. Now that he was no longer confined to school, he developed the scholarly ways of his father, and in his room in the big brick house on Michigan Avenue he began to fill shelf after shelf with books. There were works by Shakespeare, Dickens, other popular English novelists, and the Irish poets, and biographies of men who had helped to shape democracy both in Great Britain and in the United States. The books that Tim Donovan collected on his shelves were to prove fascinating to his son Will, and many years later would hold a place of honor in the large library in Donovan's New York apartment.

Young Tim, as he was called to distinguish him from his father, met and fell in love with Anna Letitia Lennon, whose carefully brushed long brown hair, fresh prairie complexion, and lively ways set her apart from the other girls in the First Ward. Anna's parents also were immigrants, from County Monaghan in the north of Ireland. They too had come to Buffalo and the Irish First Ward, but one of the periodic epidemics that swept through the poor neighborhoods took both their lives, so that Anna was left an orphan when still very young. Cousins took her to the Kansas prairies, where she was raised at Leavenworth. The Kansas relatives were comfortable, middle-class people, and Anna was to enjoy later in life telling her children of sunlit days in small-town Kansas, riding in her own pony cart. Anna also was given a good schooling. At the age of 18 she returned to Buffalo, where she met Tim.

It did not take Anna long to discover that the handsome youth with a railroad worker's strength was gentle and considerate of other people's feelings and concerns, and was as intrigued by the world of books as she was. Let there be an argument in the saloon, on the street, or around the Donovan family Sunday dinner table, to which Anna was often invited, and Tim Donovan would always champion the underdog. When it came to politics on the Buffalo waterfront, this meant that Tim backed the Republicans, whose policies scarcely were calculated to win friends among the Irish immigrants. Eventually Tim became the Republican leader in the ward, although it sometimes seemed as if he were both the leader and the entire Republican constituency. He was an easy man for Anna to love, and in 1882 Tim and Anna were married.

Tim and Anna Donovan's first child, a boy, was born on January 1, 1883. The baby was baptized William at the font of St. Bridget's Parish Church. At his confirmation he was to take the middle name of Joseph. A year later Anna gave birth to a second son, Timothy. The senior Donovans had kept the downstairs of the house on Michigan Avenue for themselves and their still young children, and Tim and Anna had moved upstairs to the second floor.

It was a happy family, made happier still by the birth of Mary, the first daughter, named for her grandmother. Four more babies followed in the next few years as Will and Tim and Mary tumbled about at play, grew stronger, and first walked the few blocks to St. Bridget's Parish School at the corner of Fulton and Louisiana streets. Tragically, infectious meningitis was endemic on the Buffalo waterfront, and each of the four new babies in turn sickened with fever, headache, nausea, and then the fatal drowsiness and stupor. Their necks and backs stiffened, and the stricken children died.

To Will, death became a shadowy thing that lurked in the dark corners of the old brick house and crept out at night to take away small children. He mourned the loss of each baby and sometimes would throw his arms around the knees of his father or mother where they sat in the living room, reading their newspapers or books, and bury his head in their laps. Will did not cry. He was a solemn boy who rarely smiled but looked at his parents and teachers with a blue-eyed intensity that was almost disturbing. It was not easy to be the oldest son at the age of 6, 7, or 8 and to feel a big brother's responsibility for the family when tragedy never seemed far away. He had learned at an early age that the deepest love could not keep back death. Then Vincent was born and lived. When Will was 15 years old, Loretta, the last of the Donovan children, arrived. It was shortly after Loretta's birth that the first of the Irish immigrants appeared at the house. From then on muffled footsteps in the night were a part of the growing family's life.

The Irish First Ward was hardworking and friendly. "Lace curtain" Irish families with more means, who could afford to hang Victorian lace at their windows, had settled along the Niagara riverfront. Many of them worked as governesses, cooks, and servants in the fine mansions that were being erected by wealthy people along Delaware Avenue and looked down on the inhabitants of the First Ward of Will Donovan's boyhood, but there was no denying the close bonds that tied together the working people of the waterfront. Each of the cottages along the dirt streets was surrounded by a white picket fence, a kitchen garden, and flowers blooming about the doorway. The neighbors, who had come mostly from the rural regions of Ireland, kept chickens as well as geese, ducks, and even cows and pigs in backyard sheds.

The housewives kept their homes scrubbed clean and tidy even if they could afford to hang only muslin or net curtains at their windows. They draped their laundry in the backyards on wash days and gossiped across the fences. There was no room for juvenile delinquency, for let a rough boy begin some mischief and there was always an alert mother to bring him around with appropriate remarks. Every mother's son of the Irish boys knew that it was the Irish mothers who were the disciplinarians both in the family and the neighborhood. The Donovan family was no exception. Will Donovan grew up loving both his parents, but while he looked to his father for understanding and companionship, he was in awe of his mother's authority.

> *The Erie is a-risin',*
> *The gin is gittin' low.*
> *I scarcely thought I'd git a drop*
> *'Til I git to Buffalo!*

Boatmen barging the long miles of the Erie Canal to the entrepôt on Lake Erie, and Great Lakes mariners sailing from such western lake ports as Chicago and Milwaukee arrived in Buffalo parched and thirsty. The two groups came together on the waterfront and were not exactly restrained in their behavior. When Will Donovan was a boy, the district lying just across Main Street possessed 93 saloons, 15 so-called concert halls, and a large number of dance halls. The women of the district might keep boarding houses, work as laundresses or seamstresses, or tell fortunes, but the sailors and boatmen found that they were equally available for night employment at other age-old tasks.

Will was warned by both his father and mother never to cross Main Street into this sinful neighborhood, particularly after dusk. "Only scamps and hooligans go over there," Donovan later in life remembered his mother telling him. Then one day he vanished into Buffalo's waterfront jungle. "The family looked for him to go to a funeral, which the whole family was obliged to attend," recalled an aunt, Mary Duggan. "He was nowhere to be found. Later they discovered he had got himself a job over on Garrison Street near the docks so he could watch the boats."

Will's father was not one of the scoopers and railroaders who chose to do their drinking and fighting with the boatmen and sailors. Tim

Donovan was a family man, and often he would take his oldest son with him to a neighborhood saloon at noon on Saturdays. Will would stand beside his father, sip a glass of ginger ale, and help himself to the free lunch set out on the counter. Around the boy raged impassioned discussions of politics, Irish history, poetry, and any other subject that occurred to the eloquent drinkers. A scooper who might heft bags of grain on weekdays became a bard or a master political strategist on Saturdays, and the boy listened eagerly. He would smile his small but delighted smile when his father scored a point off his opponents, who generally included all the other men in the saloon. Sometimes the conversation would come to a sudden halt.

"What do you think of that, boy?" somebody would demand, and Will, having grasped not only the sense of the discussion but often a solution to the problem under consideration, would reply. As he spoke sense, even the warring factions would conciliate, somebody would order "another glass for the lad," and Will's father would clap his arms around his shoulders and give him an affectionate squeeze. In this way the precocious boy practiced soothering, and it is scarcely a wonder that by the time he grew to manhood he was a master of the art.

The saloons of the Buffalo waterfront were an integral part of Will Donovan's boyhood. He learned that among the roughest men who frequented them was a code of honor and courtesy. Later in life he told how a man's drink was always respected if he were called away from the bar. "He need only attach a note to his unfinished drink, and he could be confident that when he returned, the drink would be waiting for him," he recounted. "That is, except for the time when an enormous scooper attached a note to his libation that read, 'The man who owns this drink weighs in at 250 pounds and has the muscles of a prize fighter. He will be back.'

"A skinny leprechaun of a man winked at the saloon crowd, quaffed the drink, and wrote out a note which he left beneath the empty glass: 'The man who drank this weighs 90 pounds and can run like the wind. He won't be back.'"

Sometimes the men would be overcome by a fit of nostalgia for old Ireland or an attack of tenderness and fall to singing ballads and love songs. Will sang along with them, and all his life he was to be fond of singing.

To young Will, the ward, as old-timers called it, was the sort of place in which you could not throw a stone for fear you might hit a cousin. He was the acknowledged leader of the neighborhood boys, cousins or not, even those who were one or two years older and consequently stronger than he was, because he had a thoughtful and determined way about everything he did, and he was always selfless in his decisions.

None of this kept him from often being the butt of many of the boys' pranks. On hot summer days, the boys walked down to the Michigan Avenue bridge over Buffalo Creek, stripped off their clothes beneath the bridge, and plunged into the murky waters that only a boy would dare swim in. Invariably Will would emerge naked and dripping from the water to find that grinning boys had knotted his corduroy knickers in a way that defied untying. One day when he knew his mother waited anxiously for him at home, he lost his temper and in a fury threw some half-dozen or so whooping, partly clothed youngsters into the creek. Will Donovan was a quiet boy who seldom took offense, but he had uncommonly strong muscles and was a match for any of them if he decided to fight. To his credit, Will's fighting was almost always in defense of a child being bullied by a bigger boy. He would even champion a "narrow back," which is what the broad-backed Irish boys, accustomed to working hard from early childhood, called a more slender native American boy.

The Irish author Liam O'Flaherty once remarked that "the Irish respect the poet, the warrior, and the priest. The poet's sense of beauty, the warrior's courage, and the priest's immortality." Ward mothers never disparaged a son's sense of beauty or his courage, but to a woman they were determined to achieve immortality for him. Whether a boy had a pleasing voice or sang like a crow, they urged that he be allowed in the choir of the parish church, and they importuned the priests to let their offspring serve as altar boys. Anna Donovan was no different from the other women, and she was proud and delighted when the Reverend James Edward Quigley at St. Bridget's selected both Will and Tim to serve as altar boys. Will, who early developed a firm religious belief, was among the most faithful of the altar boys, but Tim, impatient with the lengthy masses, became adept at excuses for not being able to serve.

On December 12, 1896, the Reverend Mr. Quigley was named third bishop of Buffalo. The newly selected bishop took both Tim and Will, 13 and 14 years old, with him to St. Joseph's Cathedral, where they carried his train during his solemn consecration on February 24, 1897. Bishop Quigley kept the two boys on as altar boys at St. Joseph's, and Will and Tim either trudged to the cathedral or rode there on the jangling trolley cars that ran on South Park Avenue.

Encouraged by his mother, Will could think of no better life than that of a priest, and he determined to get an education that would make an ecclesiastical career possible. When he served at the altar in the cathedral, the organ seemed to rumble of sacred things, and the pipes spoke to his Gaelic heart and soul. The boys in the cathedral choir had been carefully chosen and were well trained. When they sang, their voices rose thrilling against the high, vaulted roof. Will listened, and the age-old mysteries of his church stirred within him.

As he grew up in the church, Will formed a close and affectionate relationship with James Edward Quigley. Born on October 15, 1855, in Oshawa, Ontario, Quigley was the sort of clergyman who could inspire a vigorous youngster from the Buffalo waterfront. He had first tried to gain entrance to the U.S. Military Academy at West Point but then decided on the priesthood. Quigley was a learned man with an insatiable appetite for knowledge, and a brilliant pulpit speaker, but he was equally at home on a corner lot playing baseball with parish boys. The priest was Will's boyhood idol, and Will took a boy's delight in showing his hero that he was one of the best ballplayers in the parish.

Most likely Father Quigley smiled at Will's youthful efforts to demonstrate his athletic prowess, but he was more impressed by his mind. It was Father Quigley who instructed Will in his catechism and who officiated at his confirmation when the boy chose the name Joseph from the roll of the saints as his middle name. Father Quigley also encouraged the boy to enter Nardin Academy, and he very likely helped to arrange financial assistance so that Will could continue in school.

Nardin Academy shaped Will's young mind, and he was always appreciative of this. The Daughters of the Heart of Mary, who founded the school, had their origins in 1790, during the French Revolution, when the anticlerical terror raged in France. Many convents and monasteries were burned, and monks and nuns were tortured and put to death. Marie-Adelaide de Cice, a young noblewoman, determined to establish an order for women whose members would live in the world without wearing habits, secretly if necessary to escape persecution, and yet go about their religious life. To this day the Daughters of the Heart of Mary may serve Christ within the community without identifying themselves with an order. A Daughter of the Heart of Mary is often a professional woman, a lawyer or a doctor, who carries on her work in the community but is a secret member of the order.

"If you ask me if I'm a member, I may not answer and tell you I'm a religious," explained Irene Murphy, who is the principal of Nardin Academy today. "It depends on the work we're doing."

It is conceivable that an intelligent and perceptive boy, whose mind was trained by a sisterhood who do good works in the world while literally living cover lives, might have learned from them some of the attitudes and skills that were to serve well in the world of international intrigue.

The sisters at Nardin Academy encouraged scholarship, daily attendance, and exemplary conduct. Miss Nardin lectured the boys of Will Donovan's time. "You may one day be a leader among men. How sad if at the supreme moment or in a case of urgency you would lose control of self."

She might well have had Will in mind. His quiet ways concealed a violent temper that his brother Tim, his opposite in personality, was gifted at arousing. An angry Will would lunge at Tim, and the boys would flail at one another with bare fists until they could be separated. Finally their father bought two pairs of boxing gloves, which he hung in the barn behind the house. If the boys grew angry with one another, Tim Donovan seized each by an arm and led them to the barn, where he bid them put on the gloves and settle their differences. "Go to it, boys," Will Donovan recalled his saying.

Will and Tim would punch at one another with all their might until at last, exhausted, they would grudgingly shake hands and try again to be good brothers. Gradually Will conquered his temper because his father and the sisters at the academy convinced him it was a weakness. He learned that even when he was angry he could keep his voice soft and measured. Still, as any OSS man who had erred could testify, he never managed to keep the flash of anger from his eyes.

Will Donovan's classmates remembered him as having a quiet sense of humor and as being proud, sensitive to slight and injustice, and easily the most determined youngster in the ward. One classmate remembered, "The thing that impressed me was that Will was not bright in the ordinary sense of the word. Studies never came easy to him, but he had the tenacity of a bulldog, and when he once got a fact in his mind, nothing in the world could ever pry it out."

Will showed the same tenacity on the football field. When his passing arm failed in accuracy and strength, he persuaded his brother Tim to go with him to the beach at the foot of Michigan Avenue, where, for hours on end, afternoon after afternoon, he practiced throwing a forward pass until a tired Tim was near sobbing in his anger and bafflement at such monumental determination. Will hefted dumbbells in the barn and ran on the beach to develop his strength. On Saturdays he prowled the railroad yards, the waterfront, and the farmers' market, walking for hours, lone and observant, watching the people. He boxed and wrestled any boy who would go to the barn with him, and he read everything he could find by or about Theodore Roosevelt, who was his boyish idea of what a man should be. Will tried with what almost became desperation to make himself like the New York City aristocrat whose self-made good health and rugged life captured the imagination of a whole generation of American boys.

James Clarence Mangan wrote scores of poems fervent with his love for Ireland. His patriotic poems were the sort that a man could recite in a saloon on the Buffalo waterfront, and by the time the last stirring phrase had been uttered there would not be a dry eye in the place. Will had often heard Mangan's ballads in the saloons of the ward and, when he competed in Nardin Academy's annual declamation contest at age 12, he chose one of Mangan's most stirring poems.

"'Twas there I first beheld, drawn up in file and line, / The brilliant Irish hosts; they came, the bravest of the brave!" began the boy before the large audience of parents and friends of the schoolchildren. His blue eyes flashed with the meaning of the words; his shoulders were straight and proud. When he was finished there was silence and then tumultuous applause. Will inclined his head slightly as if he were a handsome young prince acknowledging the acclaim of his people instead of a poor boy on the waterfront. There was no question that he had won the contest, and when the last child had recited, Will stood before the crowd again as the public-speaking teacher awarded him a shiny medal in a box. The teacher held up her hand to silence the cheering crowd, and everybody waited for Will to say something. For a moment he stared dismayed at all the waiting adults, his father and mother among them, their faces flushed with pride and concern for what he might now say.

"Medals don't mean anything," Will at last said, his voice strong and confident for a 12-year-old, "and things don't mean anything after they've passed; it's doing the thing that matters."

When Will was 14, with the financial aid of Bishop Quigley he entered St. Joseph's Collegiate Institute, which had been founded by the Christian Brothers. He was by then a handsome boy of about average height who always seemed taller because of his confident manner. He appears in a picture of the St. Joseph's junior football team, taken in 1897, as a solemn boy with a shock of unruly hair staring somewhat wistfully at the camera. He was the quarterback and the first football captain of the St. Joe Juniors, and when the team won the 115-pound championship of Buffalo, he felt a happy glow of pride. At the same time, when other boys or adults complimented him on his leadership, he would invariably smile and say something like, "Anyone could do it with the other fellows playing such fine football." Later in life he said similar things when anybody complimented him on his extraordinary leadership of either the Fighting 69th in World War I or the OSS in World War II.

Will had always taken his studies seriously, but at St. Joseph's he concentrated with new determination. When he was reading a Shakespeare play or a Dickens novel from his father's library, even his mother could not get his attention. He was restless and moody now, and he would sometimes walk to the cathedral and kneel before a side altar and pray. People who came upon him took one look at his almost haunted face and went away in silence. Clearly, Tim Donovan's oldest son was not an ordinary boy. To the devout Irish this could mean only one thing—he would be a priest and a great credit to the ward.

By now Tim was writing plays, and Will and Tim would act them out for friends and family. Everybody agreed that though Tim could write the plays, it was Will who had a flair for acting. There were also family musical evenings. Tim played the violin, Will the piano, and all the Donovans had good voices.

As teenagers, Will and Tim became good friends, but even so, Will was partial to his youngest brother, Vincent, and he was to remain so all his life. He called him the Rock because Vincent was always a dependable listener, even as a small child. When he was discouraged, Will would sit at his sleepy brother's bed at night and pour out his heart. Vincent listened patiently and sympathized with his oldest brother, whom he idolized. Vincent, now a pupil at Nardin Academy, was thought to be the brightest of all the Donovan children. He was also judged to have the kindest and most affectionate heart, and it was believed throughout the ward that he too would be a priest. Aunt Mary Duggan remembered that he would often put on a makeshift priest's attire and parade around the house. One day Tim went his younger brother one better and announced that he would not be just a priest; he'd be a bishop. Will informed his brothers that he would reserve judgment, but whatever the other two wound up as, he'd be the head boss.

At the age of 16 Will, tired of wearing a boy's knickers, bought his first pair of long pants from money he had earned at odd jobs. Anna took one look at her oldest son's purchase and laughingly threatened to cut them off at the knees. Will was growing tall. Soon he would be wanting to leave home. She looked at her son with a mixture of love and regret. That night he carefully placed the pants beneath his mattress and slept on them so that she could not slip into his room and cut off the legs. His new pants were a claim on a man's estate.

The 20th century arrived, and Will Donovan turned 17. His father had given up his work in the railroad yards and was now the secretary of the Holy Cross Cemetery Corporation, his office in a room at the cathedral. The Donovan family moved to 74 Prospect Avenue, which was nearer to the cathedral. They still lived in the Irish First Ward, but they no longer need look down Michigan Avenue from their front window at the great grain elevators that blocked a view of the lake, nor listen at night to the switching locomotives or the Albany Express roaring by. Will Donovan gave the family even more cause for a happy beginning to the new century: He had been accepted as a student by Niagara University at Niagara Falls.

2

Donovan the Young Lawyer

ON WILLIAM J. DONOVAN'S registration form, preserved in the archives of Niagara University, the address 74 Michigan Avenue, Buffalo, New York, has been crossed out and 74 Prospect Avenue written in. The student's bills, a note penned on the form says, were to be sent to 50 Franklin Street, which was the address of St. Joseph's Cathedral. There they were paid in part by Will's father and in part by Bishop Quigley, who remained interested in the schooling of his young protégé.

Will Donovan's academic records are also preserved in the archives. They show that he was at first a mediocre student. Slow to make friends, he took long, solitary walks along the Niagara Gorge, through which the Niagara River boiled on its headlong descent from the Falls to Lake Ontario. When he had done poorly on a test or feared that he had, he stood on the brink looking down on the whirling waters of the rapids and threw stone after stone off into the void, almost as he had once thrown a football to his brother on the Lake Erie beach.

Will at least made a friend in Father Egan, a Vincentian who was the prefect of discipline at Niagara University from 1896 to 1905. Egan, an earnest man, was ten years older than Will, had been born and raised in New York City, and was popular with the students. He taught Latin, English, and Greek, as well as elocution. On March 6, 1900, his loyal students presented a program in honor of the Irish patriot Robert Emmet and "complimentary to Father Egan." To the surprise of the other students and the delight of Father Egan, Donovan won third prize in rhetoric.

As Will became popular at school, he began to invite friends home to spend the weekend with him. Anna Donovan now would find herself preparing meals for an additional four or five college boys who were hungry for home cooking after their dormitory fare. Sometimes Will and his friends would act out parts of Shakespeare plays for the family, or guests and family would sing the popular songs of the turn of the century, as well as the old Irish and English ballads.

One of the songs bound to bring out the best in these mainly Irish youths was "My Wild Irish Rose," written by Chauncey Olcott, a Buffalo Irish-American who had gone to New York City to make a reputation as an Irish tenor. All Buffalo loved Olcott. When he returned to his hometown and sang "My Wild Irish Rose" at the Star Theater, with his mother sitting in a front box, the Irish audience cheered and wept. Whenever they had the price of admission, Will and his friends walked over to the Star, only a few blocks away from the Donovan home, and sometimes Will thought seriously of a career in the theater. His fine tenor voice would then stand him in good stead.

That first summer of his three years at Niagara University, Will Donovan worked on a road crew. His hard muscles were put to good use, but he used his head too, and before the end of the summer he was the project surveyor. During his years at Niagara, Will Donovan made striking gains in scholarship. In subjects as diverse as algebra, music, Greek, Spanish, Latin, rhetoric, history, and elocution he won medals as either the leading student of his class or a close runner-up. At the same time he had become socially confident; there were fewer long agonized walks beside the river and more good times with other students.

When the young man who seemed destined to begin his studies in the seminary at Niagara University decided to enroll in the school of law at Columbia University, friends and family in Buffalo's First Ward were surprised. Father Egan, however, was not, for he had come to believe that his most promising student was better suited for the law than for the priesthood. In the autumn of 1902 Will set out on the train for New York City, where he would have to complete his undergraduate degree at Columbia College before entering the law school. The train rolled through the Buffalo yards, where his father had once been the yardmaster, and out past the cottages of the Irish First Ward and the old brick house standing among them. The Donovan house, which only a few years before had sheltered Irish refugees; St. Bridget's Parish Church, where Will and Tim had served Father Quigley as altar boys; Nardin Academy, where Will had won his first medal and been acclaimed in public; the beach with its lapping waves; the shunting trains; and the great elevators filled with grain all faded away behind the train. Will Donovan, not yet 20, was on his way to his first encounter with a city in which he was one day to be famous.

From the start, Donovan was known at Columbia as Bill, not Will. He brushed his brown hair back straight, dressed neatly, and had a ready smile and a cheerful greeting for the students and faculty members he encountered as he strode across South Field on his way to class. He pledged Phi Kappa Psi fraternity and became the house manager, for which he received his room and board. He had saved enough money from his summer employment to get by financially. Later at Columbia he worked in a baking-powder factory and tutored children to augment his funds.

John Giraud Agar, a prominent New York City attorney at the time, took a fatherly interest in young Bill Donovan, who had come to the Agar house to tutor the three oldest sons. Once Agar had taken the measure of the threadbare student, he overpaid him so that Bill would not have to go on doing the factory and road-gang work that had so far made his college career possible. John Agar's friendship came at the right time in the life of Bill Donovan.

At the same time, Bill more than earned his pay as a tutor. The three boys, bright and personable, won his affection. He not only tutored them in the subjects at hand but shared his experiences at Columbia with them, much as he had once shared his thoughts and activities with his younger brother Vincent.

John Giraud Agar, Jr., the oldest of the Agar children, was killed in France during World War I, and Donovan always felt that with his death America lost a future leader of stature. The second son was William Macdonough Agar, who became an outstanding geologist and shared enough of his mentor Bill Donovan's concern with the Catholic church and its place in 20th-century life to write the book *Catholicism and the Progress of Science*. The third son, then 9 years old, was Herbert Sebastian Agar, later a diplomat, poet, author, editor, and Pulitzer Prize winner for his history *The People's Choice*.

Bill Donovan's friendship with the Agar family and John Agar's generosity made it possible for him to drop all his other jobs and to concentrate on his studies. Even so, he never neglected his family. He wrote long letters to his mother, whose cooking he sadly missed. For his little sister Loretta he bought what to a poor student was an expensive Christmas present—a teddy bear. Theodore Roosevelt, Donovan's boyhood hero, had been sworn in as President of the United States on September 14, 1901, after William McKinley was assassinated in Buffalo. The new President's vigorous good health, high idealism, and zest for living had captured the national imagination. His determined fight to create a national park system so that future generations of Americans would be able to enjoy wilderness and wildlife had struck an answering chord on college campuses. A toy bear cub, which came to be called the teddy bear after Teddy Roosevelt, symbolized the President's dedication to the wilderness.

Tim Donovan was now studying at medical school in Buffalo. Vincent was growing up. One day Bill took the Delaware, Lackawanna, and Western Railroad ferry across the Hudson River to Hoboken, New Jersey, where at the Lackawanna Station he met 14-year-old Vincent, still in a small boy's knickers, who had come to visit his big brother in the fascinating but undoubtedly wicked city. Bill took the boy to the LaSalle Academy on 59th Street. There he spent the night, while Bill returned to Columbia. In the morning the two brothers rode the subway to Herald Square, where at the Rogers Peet store Bill bought Vincent his first pair of long pants.

The brothers went on to Coney Island, where among the rides and arcades they found a photographic concession. Bill paid the photographer to take a picture of Vincent, proudly wearing his new pants. Once he was back in his room at the Phi Kappa Psi house, Bill wrote a letter home, enclosing Vince's picture. He remembered his own boyhood fear that his mother might shorten his long pants while he slept, and he wanted her to know in advance that her youngest son was growing up and that she might as well get accustomed to it.

Now that Bill did not have to work every spare moment, he took to running around the reservoir in Central Park each day to get into shape. He went out for the cross-country track team, he boxed and wrestled, and he joined the rowing team. Ed Hanlon, who had been the Australian sculling champion, was then coaching the crew. Donovan and the other seven men of his crew sometimes took the train up to Poughkeepsie, where they rowed on the Hudson.

In his last year at Columbia College, Bill Donovan went out for football. He became the second string quarterback and a tackle, soon known throughout the Ivy League for the power with which he hit an opposing player. Bill won his letter, but he was never able to replace another Irish-American youth as quarterback. His rival and friend was Edward Trowbridge Collins, who had enrolled at Columbia College in 1903 at the age of 16 and, although he weighed only 140 pounds, was an incomparable player.

Bill Donovan received his bachelor of arts degree in 1905. The Columbia College yearbook printed a picture of an intense young Donovan and asked, enigmatically enough, "Is he quiet or always making a fuss?" His fellow classmates voted Donovan both the "most modest" and "the second handsomest" man. Donovan also served on the debating team, and he won the George Curtis Medal for Public Speaking with the oration "The Awakening of Japan."

In the fall of 1906 Donovan began his studies in the law school. The school might have been small enough to share a building with the department of political science, but the faculty was extraordinary, and each member helped to shape Donovan's mind. There was Professor Harlan F. Stone, who had obtained his own Columbia Law School degree in 1898 and who later was to be dean of the law school, U.S. attorney general under President Coolidge, and Chief Justice of the Supreme Court. He spoke before his students entirely without notes. Stone never raised his voice and, as Donovan was quick to learn, disapproved of lawyers who did. He evidenced kindly good humor, and his personal integrity was obvious in every well-considered statement. Harlan Stone was the first of the 20th century's major figures whom Donovan was to know, and this New England crab apple of a man whose motto was "Eat it up; wear it out; make it do; do without" impressed the young man from the Buffalo waterfront.

William O. Douglas, who studied under Stone at Columbia in the early 1920s, described the professor as standing "behind the desk and against the blackboard, twirling his tortoiseshell glasses in his hand, his casebook usually closed on the desk before him. He did not often lecture but used the Socratic method, which he had developed to a high degree of perfection. His questions seldom referred to cases, but to problems raised or suggested by them." Above all, according to Douglas, Stone believed that "there is no possible teaching without blessed friendship, which is the best conductor of ideas between man and man." Bill Donovan basked in the warmth of his favorite professor's friendship. At the time he had no idea how important that friendship was to prove to be in Washington, D.C., almost 20 years later.

Immensely impressive as he was, Harlan Stone was not the only great law professor at Columbia. Another was Jackson E. Reynolds. "I had some rather famous students among my classes," he said. "General 'Wild Bill' Donovan was a student of mine, and Franklin Delano Roosevelt. The last-named was not much of a student and nothing of a lawyer afterward. He did later exert a tremendous influence on the law of the country by the hundreds of appointments he made to the federal bench, good, bad, and indifferent. General Donovan was a good student, industrious, quick and alert, his work—practical, adaptable to any problem."

Franklin Roosevelt had entered Columbia in 1904. From the start Roosevelt, as handsome and rich a young man as there was in the school, showed little serious interest in the study of law. By the end of his first year he had failed two courses and passed others with B minuses. Nor was he friendly toward the other students on the campus. Later he maintained that he had known Bill Donovan at Columbia, but Donovan only laughed at this. "I would meet Franklin Roosevelt walking across the campus almost every day, but he never once even noticed. His eyes were always fixed on some other object."

Donovan, who saw in a Columbia law degree freedom from the life he had known in the Buffalo First Ward, had time only for his studies, while Roosevelt was in the middle of his campaign to win the hand of his cousin Eleanor in marriage. He was far more interested in the balls and parties of upper-crust New York than he was in the dull classrooms of Columbia.

Donovan and Roosevelt, two men who were to work together so

closely in World War II, contrasted sharply in other respects at Columbia. In the autumn of 1904, Franklin Roosevelt walked into Tiffany's on Fifth Avenue and selected a diamond ring for his fiancée, Eleanor. Bill Donovan danced with a few girls at law school dances but had no time for romance. Both Donovan and Roosevelt voted the Republican ticket for Theodore Roosevelt over Judge Alton B. Parker in the elections of 1904, but the following March 4, Franklin and Eleanor Roosevelt rode to Washington in the private railroad car of their cousin George Emlen Roosevelt. They stayed with the President's sister, Mrs. W. Sheffield Cowles, and during the inauguration they sat on the steps of the U.S. Capitol immediately behind Theodore Roosevelt. They lunched at the White House, and running America seemed to be something of a cozy family affair. Bill Donovan, meanwhile, read about the inauguration in the newspapers. His hero, Teddy Roosevelt, an aristocrat who had the good instincts of the common man, was in the White House, and Donovan was filled with hope for his country.

In the spring of 1907, Franklin Roosevelt took New York's bar examination, but when he passed, decided not to bother with his law degree. Once Bill Donovan received his law degree, in the same year, he took the train back to Buffalo.

Just as Professor Harlan Stone never raised his voice when he argued a legal point, so Bill Donovan, now 24 years old and a lawyer with the small Buffalo firm of Love and Keating, never raised his voice in the courtroom. Just as Professor Stone carefully considered each statement he made and each position he took, so Donovan exerted himself to be judicious and deliberate both in word and action. In the courtroom he was friendly and unassuming. His blue eyes beamed good will, and he was unperturbable and courteous despite the most frantic ravings of opposing counsel. Harlan Stone would have been proud of him.

The young lawyer had learned at Columbia to prepare each case with great care. Even in his early 20s he had developed the ability to read at a rapid rate, a trait that was later to amaze his OSS aides, and he was able to discern quickly the essential features of a case. His legal briefs were both short and complete, which is not usually the case with a young lawyer just entering the profession. In two years, Donovan was made a junior partner of the firm. He resigned in 1911 to form a partnership with Bradley Goodyear, a scion of one of Buffalo's leading families. That same year Donovan and Goodyear merged with the city's leading law firm, headed by the redoubtable John Lord O'Brian and Chauncey Hamlin. Donovan's name went up on the glass doors of suite 604 of the Iroquois Building. The firm was then known as O'Brian, Hamlin, Donovan, and Goodyear.

Most of Bill Donovan's clients were drawn from the Buffalo business community, but he also found time to take care of the legal interests of individuals who came to him. One such case was a woman who desperately needed his legal advice. On the morning they were scheduled to meet, Donovan was stricken by a terrible pain in his abdomen. A doctor called to the scene prodded his stomach. Donovan winced. "You must have bed rest," said the doctor.

No sooner had the physician left than Donovan got out of bed, dressed, and hurried to his office. Smiling despite the pain, he counseled the woman and set her fears at rest. When she left, Donovan collapsed in agony. An ambulance rushed him to the hospital, where a surgeon removed his gangrenous appendix. As Donovan came out of the anesthetic, he discovered a bunch of flowers in his hand and thought he had died. Then he heard a muffled sobbing and, turning his head, saw his client sitting by his bed. She was weeping for the handsome young lawyer who had endangered his life to keep an appointment with her because he knew how confused and afraid she had been.

Within a week Donovan was back at his office. As the story went around Buffalo, people agreed that young Bill Donovan was not only a brilliant attorney but also a man with compassion and heart, who cared as much for a lonely woman with a legal problem as he did for the most important client. All his life Donovan was to find time for a woman and her problems, particularly if the woman was attractive.

During the years that Bill Donovan was becoming established as a Buffalo lawyer, his brother Tim completed his medical studies and began a medical career that in time was to make him one of Erie County's leading endocrinologists. Vincent completed his studies at St. Joseph's Collegiate Institute and was studying to be a priest. He had his father's introspective turn of mind.

The Buffalo in which Bill Donovan was making his way as a lawyer was at its zenith. In the heart of the city was Niagara Square, where the traffic circled the McKinley Monument. The mansions of the well-to-do and privileged lined Delaware Avenue, and Donovan made every effort to win friends among them and gain access to their drawing rooms. Donovan, a strong oarsman, rowed for the Celtic Rowing Club, pride of the First Ward Irish, for which his father had once rowed, and on occasion he stroked the team to victory over a Canadian club in a 15-man war canoe event. Then Donovan changed his allegiance and became captain of a war canoe crew at the Buffalo Canoe Club at Crystal Beach, Ontario, some 25 miles away from Buffalo by road but in plain sight of Buffalo's downtown towers across Lake Erie. The Buffalo Canoe Club, then and now a haunt of Buffalo's blue bloods, still keeps one of the old war canoes in its boathouse, although the club no longer enters a team in water events.

Theodore Roosevelt had ridden to fame as a Rough Rider, and Bill Donovan was delighted to hear early in 1912 that the State of New York had decided to increase the cavalry units of the National Guard. When Col. Oliver B. Bridgeman of the First Cavalry of the New York National Guard and Capt. Lincoln G. Andrews of the Second Cavalry, U.S. Army, called a meeting of interested young men from the Buffalo area at the University Club on Delaware Avenue, Donovan was among them. So were many other members of the Buffalo Canoe Club who, listening to Donovan's enthusiastic talk about military service, had decided to come along.

On May 7, 1912, the first 42 men of Troop I, Donovan included, were mustered into service at the 74th Regimental Armory. Captain Sherman S. Jewitt of Company C, 74th Infantry, New York National Guard, was put in temporary command, and the new troop was designated Troop I, First Cavalry. From the start Troop I, whose membership had grown within a month to 60 men, was in the main made up of socially prominent young Buffalonians with a zest for adventure.

At that time it was up to the volunteer members of a cavalry troop in the New York National Guard to equip themselves, which included buying their own horses. Each citizen trooper in Troop I subscribed a sum of money to the fund, and the unit bought its first six mounts so that the men could begin their riding practice on Humboldt Parkway. The horses were kept in the old livery stable on the parkway, which was rented for them by Erie County. For the first month after the horses were purchased, Bill Donovan, who until then had never been on a horse in his life, got out of bed at five o'clock every morning and hurried to the stables to saddle up and ride out on the parkway. With his usual determination, he cantered through rain or shine, ignoring his sore buttocks, every day becoming more sure of himself on horseback until he was as fine a rider as any of the young socialites who had been riding horses when he was riding the streetcar to his classes at St. Joseph's.

Dismounted drills were held regularly, first at the 74th Regiment Armory and then at the 65th Regiment Armory, where the men were given locker space and the use of the drill hall one night a week. Headquarters were also at the 65th Regiment Armory, and Donovan rarely failed to be there on drill night. Within a month he was made a corporal. Evenings at home, Donovan studied cavalry tactics and strategy. He was delighted when in July the troop was ordered to its first encampment on a farm owned by Troop D, First Cavalry, at Manlius, a small town southeast of Syracuse. Captain Andrews was in charge of the week of field instruction.

Donovan returned to Buffalo with Troop I more enthusiastic than ever about military life. In October, when orders came for the troop to choose its first officers, he was elected captain. Davis T. Dunbar became first lieutenant, and George B. Walbridge was made second lieutenant. The men had elected a stern taskmaster as their captain, but Donovan also demonstrated a thorough willingness to surpass each man in his command when it came to work. In the following months Troop I's weekly meetings were devoted to dismounted drill and elementary horsemanship. Discipline was firm, and when Captain Andrews returned to inspect the troop in the spring, he congratulated Captain Donovan and his men on their excellence.

Donovan's law practice continued to grow, but he still found time for Troop I. In June 1913, the troop's officers and sergeants entrained for Long Island, where at Montauk Point they underwent a course of instruction run by the New York National Guard. Since the enlisted men of the troop had not made the trip and no training was scheduled for them by the National Guard during the summer of 1913, Donovan organized a week's march. In July the entire troop, taking time from civilian pursuits, set off on horseback for a ride that took them from Buffalo to Orchard Park, Springville, Plato, Lake View, and then back to Buffalo. All week Donovan and the other officers put into action what they had learned at Montauk Point. Camping at night, living in the open, developing a close bond with their mounts, the men began to feel more and more like real cavalrymen.

In the spring of 1914, a strike at the Gould Coupler Works in industrial Depew, on the southeastern outskirts of Buffalo, turned violent, and the governor ordered the 74th Infantry of the National Guard to patrol the town and maintain law and order. In April Donovan received orders to relieve the 74th in Depew and to serve "in aid of Civil Authorities." When Donovan and the 60 men of his command reached Depew, they paraded up the main street in a show of strength. Wearing their dress uniforms and holding drawn sabers at the ready, the men cantered past hostile crowds of strikers. Donovan, at the head of the column, swung past a saloon that was the strikers' command post, and his horse stumbled. While he fought to stay in the saddle, he dropped his saber with a ringing clatter on the cobblestone pavement. A strike ringleader dashed from the curb, seized the saber, and raced into the saloon.

"Take command," ordered Donovan, and Lieutenant Dunbar spurred into place before the troop.

Donovan wheeled his horse back to the saloon, tied it to a post, and shouldered his way through the swinging door into the dingy interior. The man with his saber froze as the angry captain strode up to where he was standing at the bar. He seized the man's arm, wrenched the saber from him, and grabbing him by the neck, marched him to the entrance, where he booted him into the street. Troop I cheered, and so did citizens who had been watching from the sidewalks. Even strikers applauded the young officer's courage.

Donovan mounted his horse in silence and resumed his place at the head of the column, leading the troop down the street. Over the next few days, strikers and strikebreakers alike and the citizens of Depew learned that Captain Donovan was strictly impartial but would not permit violence and lawlessness of any kind. Captain Andrews inspected the troop while it was on duty in Depew. Once again he complimented Captain Donovan and his men on their high degree of efficiency and morale. Troop I plainly benefited from the experience of patrolling a town in which law and order had broken down.

Bill Donovan might be the captain of Troop I, which was beginning to be recognized as one of the top cavalry units of the New York National Guard, and a busy young attorney, but he also found time to make speeches on behalf of the Republican Party. He displayed the same ready grasp of the political essentials that had distinguished the saloon orators of his First Ward boyhood. At the same time the flair for the theater that he had shown as a boy brought him into the Studio Club, where well-to-do Buffalonians put on amateur theatricals for charity. There he met Ruth Rumsey, a tall girl with blue eyes who was counted among the most beautiful of Delaware Avenue's young women. The daughter of the city's first citizen, the late Dexter Rumsey, she had an air of assurance that might have been a trifle overpowering, except that it was lightened by a certain genial charm and wit. Being fond of riding and fox hunting, she had an outdoorswoman's complexion. Bill Donovan was drawn to this girl, who was not only beautiful but had both intellect and his zest for the active life.

In 1914, the celebrated English-born actress Eleanor Robson, who in 1910 had become Mrs. August Belmont, came to Buffalo to attend a Studio Club production of Robert Browning's *In a Balcony*. A few years before, the actress had played Constance in the New York production of the same drama. Immediately taken with Bill Donovan, who was the Studio Club's male lead, she went backstage and invited him to come to New York City where, she promised, she would coach him in dramatics. Eleanor Robson Belmont was a woman of both theatrical talent and great spirit. She may have had only a professional interest in the handsome and gifted young Donovan, but hardly any of Donovan's friends in Buffalo believed that. He took a weekly train to New York City.

At the same time he made frequent visits to the Rumsey house at 742 Delaware Avenue. From his law office downtown or the University Club on Delaware, Donovan would walk down the street to the yellow brick mansion. He would arrive at the door, his fresh face beaming

Irish good cheer, be admitted by the butler, and stride into the large Gothic drawing room to the right of the central hall. When the other guests had gathered and conversation was at its best, dinner would be announced, and everybody would enter the dining room with the formality that might be expected of Buffalo's first family.

Important visitors to Buffalo from all over the world often stayed with the Rumseys, or at least came to dinner. Then there might be a party with the furniture pushed back and an orchestra engaged to play in the conservatory adjoining the dining room so that guests could dance from one room to another, making a circuit of the mansion's interior. Donovan made a point of impressing each important guest in one way or another, and he jotted down their names and addresses for future attention. The pick of Buffalo's eligible bachelors were guests at the Rumsey house, but Mrs. Rumsey soon realized that her daughter seemed to notice only Bill Donovan.

Sometimes on a quiet Sunday afternoon, Donovan played billiards with Ruth's brother Dexter, or the two young men sat in the library and talked enthusiastically. Here Donovan was at his best, because this was the world of books and ideas.

There was also a music room, and at Rumsey "at homes" Donovan sang the popular ballads of the day while Ruth accompanied him on the piano. It was all very romantic, and Mrs. Rumsey found herself drawn to the young Irishman. At the same time there were obstacles to the romance. The Rumseys were staunch Presbyterians who attended regular services in the Westminster Presbyterian Church next to their home, and Bill Donovan was Catholic. When Donovan proposed marriage and Ruth readily accepted, the young couple kept their engagement secret at Ruth's wish. First she wanted Mrs. Rumsey and the Rumsey relatives and friends to realize that Bill Donovan was not a social climber but a young man of such great talent and promise that he would be a welcome addition to any family, no matter how distinguished.

From the start there were wealthy Protestant Buffalonians who disapproved of Bill Donovan. He was a Catholic, and he came from the waterfront First Ward, a neighborhood at the very bottom of the social ladder. Most people could forgive him being a Catholic. Confronted by his charm and his intellectual and professional attainments, people in time also forgave him the misfortune of his social background. But to this day in Buffalo, and at Nonquitt on the Massachusetts South Shore, where the Rumseys and other prominent Buffalo families had summer homes, it is said that Bill Donovan began to philander even before his wedding. His presumed affair with Eleanor Robson Belmont was widely talked about, and when people heard about Ruth Rumsey's engagement, they felt she had made a dubious choice.

Bill Donovan's heart might be in the Rumsey mansion, but he often found time to go to dinner at his parents' house on Prospect Avenue. One day after dinner, Bill's brother Tim took him aside and explained that their mother's heart had been gravely weakened by a continuing attack of rheumatic fever and that she could be expected to die at any time. But Anna Donovan went about her busy life as if there were nothing the matter with her, and she was full of joy when, in the spring of 1914, Mrs. Rumsey announced that her daughter Ruth was to be married in July to Bill.

Only a short time later Anna Donovan died. On her deathbed she insisted that Vincent, then a seminarian at the Dominican Novitiate in Somerset, Ohio, not come home. She feared that, in those days of slow travel, the trip might set him back in his studies. It was a great satisfaction to the dying woman that at least one of her beloved sons had chosen to go into the priesthood. She also requested that Bill and Ruth go ahead with their wedding on the date set for it.

In that early summer of 1914, when death darkened his romance, only Ruth could make him happy. Then, only ten days before the wedding was to take place, Ruth was rushed to the hospital for an emergency appendectomy. Bill was distraught. He stayed at the hospital, grieving for what he feared would be his second terrible loss, until at last it was apparent that his fiancée was going to be all right.

The wedding, held on July 15, was small. Fifty relatives and close friends of both families came to the Rumsey mansion. Monsignor John Biden, the Donovan family pastor from St. Bridget's, performed the ceremony. Bill Donovan, now 31, was married. He gave up his drama lessons in New York City. The young couple went off on a honeymoon to the Lake Erie shore.

While Bill Donovan's life was undergoing so many changes, Europe was moving toward war. Preoccupied as he was with his personal problems, Donovan still regularly drilled Troop I at the armory, and realizing that conditions in Europe were becoming increasingly grave, he sought out visitors to Buffalo from across the Atlantic to learn what he could about the likelihood of war. The events that had begun in Sarajevo in Bosnia on June 28 with Gavrilo Princip's assassination of the Archduke Francis Ferdinand and his wife led inexorably from one fatal development after another to the British declaration of war on Germany on August 4.

Ruth and Bill were on their honeymoon during the last part of July and early August, and each day the newspapers told of such dire things as Austria-Hungary's declaration of war on Serbia on July 28, the Russian mobilization of July 30, and the German declaration of war on Russia August 1 and on France August 3. All of this was scarcely conducive to a happy honeymoon. No doubt Ruth acquiesced with a sigh when her husband suggested that they break off their stay on the lakeshore and return to Buffalo.

Back in Buffalo, Donovan drilled Troop I in rifle and dismounted maneuvers. He studied the military and economic strengths of each of the warring European powers. Most people in Buffalo believed that the war in Europe would be over soon and would end in an overwhelming Allied victory. Donovan was far less sanguine, and he felt certain that if the war went on long enough, the United States would be drawn into it. If his country did indeed go to war, Donovan was determined that Troop I would be ready.

Near Derby, on the Lake Erie shore southwest of Buffalo, Lieutenant Stryker of the National Guard had a farm that in future years was to become the Lake Shore Hunt Club. Since the State of New York failed to authorize a camp for Troop I that summer, the men volunteered to pay their own expenses to camp on Stryker's farm. By then Troop I had more than 50 horses and was as well equipped a force as the state could mobilize. At camp Donovan made sure that the men had plenty of rifle practice. He saw to it later that fall and winter that the cavalrymen practiced on the outdoor Kenilworth Range when weather permitted or at the indoor range in the 65th Regiment Armory. All this rifle training paid off in 1914, when Troop I, the youngest National Guard organization in the state, placed third in marksmanship.

Having failed to muster its National Guard for training in the summer of 1914, the State of New York decided to hold an important camp at Fishkill Plains in the Hudson Valley the following July. For the first time Troop I would be thrown together with the rest of the cavalry regiment, which would include men from Manhattan, Brooklyn, Syracuse, and Rochester. This was the first time since the Civil War that the state would bring together a cavalry regiment for maneuvers. Donovan was resolved that his men would look good in comparison with other units, and winter and spring he drilled them in mounted work.

At Fishkill, Donovan's Troop I was complimented highly by cavalry officers from the Regular Army who attended maneuvers. The troop compared favorably in all respects with the old troops of the First Regiment. Donovan had a feeling of contentment that lasted all the long rail miles back to Buffalo, but once home, he became dissatisfied again. It was one thing to lead a troop of men in maneuvers in the Hudson Valley. It would be another if necessity forced him to lead Troop I against the formidable German cavalry in France.

After the early return from their honeymoon, Bill and Ruth Donovan had moved into the Rumsey mansion, where they lived happily with Mrs. Rumsey. Just about a year after their marriage, Ruth gave birth to their first baby, a boy, whom they named David. The young couple's happiness in their son was chilled because Bill's father was very ill. It was hard to say exactly what was the matter with him; he simply wasted away. He had shown little interest in living since the death of his wife.

About a week before his father's death, Bill Donovan went to tell him about the birth of his grandson, David. It seemed only yesterday that a small boy had sat on the stool next to his father in a First Ward saloon and listened to the political wrangling or joined in the Irish songs. Now the son stood tall and confident, and the father was a weak old man lying forlorn in his sickbed. But when he heard about his grandson, the old man brightened. He looked wistfully at his son, who had already accomplished so much.

"I hope you'll be as proud of him as I've always been of you," he said.

3

Relief Mission to Europe

AS 1915 DREW TO A CLOSE, the war in Europe was a stalemate. The successes of the Allies and Central Powers alike had turned to disaster. Beginning in December, the British withdrew from their dismal Gallipoli expedition. The German generals August von Mackensen and Paul von Hindenburg had driven the Russians out of Galicia and most of Russian Poland the previous summer and autumn, inflicting upward of 2 million casualties on the czar's ill-equipped and poorly led troops and taking 750,000 prisoners. Bulgaria, which had joined the Central Powers in October with a declaration of war on Serbia, had assisted Germany and Austria in the conquest not only of Serbia but also of Montenegro and Albania. The Central Powers also defeated Romania.

Superior Central Powers tactics and leadership, combined with their central position, had darkened the outlook for an Allied victory in Europe. Even in France, the British and French were hard put to hold their positions. On the other hand, British command of the seas made it possible for the Allies to bring additional forces, principally from the British Empire, to France, and at the same time to deny supplies from abroad to their enemies. German submarine warfare might harass Allied shipping, but Britain and France were still able to transport vital foodstuffs and other imports from around the world.

As the British North Sea blockade of the Central Powers grew increasingly effective, Germany and her allies suffered. The civilians of German-occupied Belgium, Poland, Serbia, Albania, and Montenegro suffered far more. The fighting had devastated many cities and towns and destroyed a good part of the autumn harvest. Already Herbert Hoover and other Americans were at work in Belgium providing food for the Belgian people.

The Rockefeller Foundation, in New York City, had been endowed by John D. Rockefeller with $101 million for the relief of human suffering in all parts of the world. Shortly after the outbreak of the war, the foundation trustees had appointed a War Relief Commission. Made up of men drawn from business and professional life, who served without pay, the commission undertook to advise the foundation on how the suffering of noncombatants might be alleviated. The commission would also supervise and carry out any measures of relief that might be decided upon by the foundation and approved by the appropriate Allied and Central Powers authorities.

On February 23, 1916, William Donovan received a telegram at his office in the Iroquois Building in Buffalo:

"Could you arrange come here conference Saturday morning, February twenty-sixth. After conference, if mutually agreed between you and foundation that you go abroad in its service, could you arrange your affairs, leave Rotterdam sailing New York March seventh. Warwick Greene."

Only four days earlier, Greene had been appointed director of the War Relief Commission. He had heard about the Buffalo attorney, now 33, who was as personable as he was brilliant. The next day he received a return wire:

"Will be in New York Friday on business. Will phone you and if convenient would like to meet you. W. J. Donovan."

On Friday afternoon Bill Donovan walked into Warwick Greene's office at the Rockefeller Foundation. The two men got along well from the start. Both were oarsmen; both were patriots and keenly aware of the significance to Americans of the events in Europe. As soon as he left Greene, Donovan put in his application for a passport. On March 7, the original date set for departure, the foundation received a telegram from Robert Lansing, President Woodrow Wilson's secretary of state:

"Department has rec'd application of Wm J Donovan for passport for nearly all European countries including all belligerent countries. States he is going in service of Relief Commission, Rockefeller Foundation. Department desires avoid issuance passports belligerent countries on both sides. Please state which countries Relief Commission desires Donovan visit. He sails eleventh."

Greene wired back the next day:

"Replying your telegram March seventh. Contemplated sphere of war relief activity of William J. Donovan is area controlled by Teutonic countries, especially Poland. Probably no occasion for him to visit Allied countries except in transit."

The department issued a passport to Donovan, and at last, on March 14, Greene, Donovan, and two more War Relief Commission aides, R. C. Foster and H. D. Topping, sailed aboard the liner *St. Paul*. Ruth and their baby were to stay with Mrs. Rumsey in the big house on Delaware Avenue until Donovan could make arrangements for her to join him in Europe. The Greene party sailed not for Rotterdam as originally planned but for Southampton, England.

Southampton, the busiest port in the British Isles, was crowded with great ships bringing supplies and recruits from all over the English-speaking world. The *St. Paul* docked there on March 18, and the War Relief Commission members boarded a train that took them 70 miles to London's Waterloo Station. They hurried to the American Embassy at number 14 Grosvenor Gardens. Greene was anxious to get his relief team into the field, and his aides were equally impatient.

While the *St. Paul* was still a day out of Southampton, Greene had written to William Phillips, under secretary of state in Washington, about his plans for the War Relief Commission:

"I am strongly impressed with the necessity of maintaining the spirit of neutrality on the part of the men to whom the State Department has granted these general passports. I feel that our usefulness will depend on the maintenance of an impartial attitude that would carry conviction to all with whom we come in contact, so I shall see to it that they feel in honor bound to conduct themselves in such manner that no Government will ever regret having given permission to any member of our party to cross their boundaries."

In June Bill Donovan, by then in Berlin, explained the operations of the commission in more detail in a letter to the German humanitarian Professor Dr. Ludwig Stein, also in Berlin:

"Members of the Commission who are sent to countries at war or to neighboring countries are required to devote themselves exclusively to the objects of their mission. They are obliged to observe strict neutrality in word and act, to refrain from expressions of opinion on the issues of the war and to preserve in the strictest confidence any knowledge as to facts of actual or potential military significance of which the correct performance of their purely neutral functions may make them cognizant."

Walter Hines Page, ambassador to the Court of St. James, and his first secretary, Irwin Loughlin, did their best to be of assistance, although at the very time the War Relief Commission was in London, the embassy was involved in a diplomatic crisis. Page, acting under directions from President Wilson, had been doing his best to preserve some semblance of neutrality in the face of Germany's unrestricted submarine warfare on North Atlantic shipping. On March 24 a German U-boat sank the unarmed French channel steamer *Sussex,* and 80 persons, including American citizens, were killed or injured. Wilson, soon to be campaigning for reelection, did not want to lose German-American and neutralist votes by adopting too harsh a policy toward Germany. With the sinking of the *Sussex,* however, he felt he had no choice but to threaten to sever diplomatic relations with Germany if the government of Kaiser Wilhelm II did not "immediately declare and effect an abandonment of its present methods of warfare against passenger and freight carrying vessels."

The diplomatic crosscurrents in London were intriguing to a young man who was having his first close look at an international crisis, but Bill Donovan was anxious to cross the Channel to Europe. First, however, Greene had to establish a fund of £200 at the London office of Herbert Hoover's Commission for Relief in Belgium. Donovan would be able to draw upon this sum for his expenses. Soon after their arrival in London, Donovan and Greene went to Hoover's office in the London Wall buildings. They not only made necessary financial arrangements but accepted Hoover's invitation for Donovan to visit Commission for Relief operations in Belgium before he undertook his own mission in Poland.

"On the 9th of April, 1916, I left London under instructions to proceed to Holland, arrange there for the purchase of milk for shipment to Warsaw," Bill Donovan noted in a report to Warwick Greene. Once in the Netherlands, Donovan lost no time. On April 12 he drove an auto to the plant of the Nutricia Company, a few miles outside The Hague. "This plant is owned by a Hollander named Chris Hodjes," he reported. "He is a man who dislikes the Germans and whose custom is almost solely with England and her colonies. He has a neat-appearing and seemingly well-organized plant. With him I arranged for the purchase of 100 metric tons of milk powder per month, contingent upon approval of the German Government for its importation."

Donovan was elated at his apparent initial success. On the same day that he drove to the Nutricia Company, the German authorities gave him permission to enter Belgium, and he prepared to leave immediately. Then he learned that the Germans had regulations that limited his chances to ship supplies to the hungry Poles. There were more than 200 German agents at work in the Netherlands purchasing supplies for the use of the German people and armed forces. The Imperial Government refused to give Donovan a permit to export any foodstuffs for occupied nations if this meant denying provisions to the Germans.

Next, he hurried to see Dr. Richard Kuhlmann, the German minister at The Hague. Surely the German nation would not block the shipment of milk powder to hungry Poland, he argued; it would be a callous act. Donovan also pointed out that the pro-British Nutricia Company had refused to ship milk powder to Germany anyway, and it would not cut into German supplies if the company sent milk powder to Poland. The minister gravely nodded his head and promised to advise his government.

Donovan also called upon Dr. Henry Van Dyke, American minister to the Netherlands and Luxembourg, to enlist his assistance in persuading the Dutch government not to place any obstacles in the way of the delivery of milk powder. Van Dyke had early taken an interest in war relief and had made the arrangements to ship the first two cargoes of supplies to Belgium for Herbert Hoover's commission. He had the confidence of the German minister to the Netherlands, and he was determined to keep the door open for relief shipments.

When Donovan reached the American Legation, he was ushered directly into the library to see Van Dyke, who immediately agreed to do everything he could to expedite German permission for the export to Poland. Later in the day Donovan called upon C. A. Young, director in Holland for the Commission for Relief in Belgium, who promised that he would take care of the actual shipping of the milk powder. The War Relief Commission could pay for the milk through the existing offices of the Commission for Relief in Belgium.

The same day that he called on Van Dyke and Young, Donovan also met with Caspar Whitney. Whitney had traveled and explored in North and South America, Mexico, Siam, Malaya, and India for ten years. He had been a war correspondent in Cuba in 1898, and now he was working for Herbert Hoover's group in the Netherlands. Whitney, at 51 a veteran of many intrigues, was taken with young Donovan and agreed to carry messages for him to Warwick Greene in London. On the next day, April 13, he crossed the North Sea to England, a trip that German submarines and airplanes had made hazardous.

As Donovan waited for word from the Rockefeller Foundation as to how he should proceed in Europe, he spent the next five weeks observing food and health conditions in Belgium, as well as the way in which the Belgian Commission for Relief operated. He studied the detailed reports of the negotiations, conferences, and agreements between the commission and the German government, and he went down to the Brussels waterfront to spend several days, as he reported to Greene at the American Embassy in London, "viewing the unloading of lighters, the storing of supplies and more particularly the office system of the shipping department."

He was impressed with the work, which was directed by a Mr. Boltens, a Belgian who before the German invasion had been a banker. "His department, to my mind," wrote Donovan, "is the real heart of the entire commission because upon its proper functioning depends the successful operation of the entire system of distribution." He reported that "the next two weeks I devoted to a study of conditions in Brussels. Here the Belgian people had evidenced the best of their tendency to organize committees. The poor were well taken care of in the soup kitchens which were maintained, the food substantial, well-prepared and quickly served."

Toward the end of May, Donovan received a wire from Greene directing him to continue his efforts for shipments to Poland in Berlin, where he arrived on May 26. He checked into the elegant Hotel Esplanade on the Bellevuestrasse, which was favored by diplomats, and immediately went to see James W. Gerard, the American ambassador, in his grand house on the Wilhelm Platz, directly opposite the Chancellor's Palace and the Foreign Office. Donovan found that long tables had been set up in the ballroom for the use of relief workers. He soon learned that the Polish people were suffering even more than the Belgians.

The Rockefeller Foundation had agreed to fund the relief work and to send representatives to carry it out. When General von Hindenburg approved of the plans, Dr. Oscar F. T. Lewald of the Department of the Interior signed for the German government. Donovan learned from Ambassador Gerard through American diplomatic channels that the British government was concerned that the shipments actually reach the Poles and not be diverted to the German military. Gerard had already submitted certain British prerequisites to the Foreign Office and arranged for conferences with both Prince Franz Xavier von Drucki-Lubecki and Dr. Lewald.

On May 28, Donovan met with Prince Lubecki to discuss the British position. Prince Lubecki, a German nobleman with Polish blood and sympathies, hoped to establish a Polish kingdom between Germany and Russia when the war was over. He was anxious to cooperate fully with Donovan to prevent starvation in Poland.

Donovan then met first with Lubecki and Lewald at the Department of the Interior. His first significant conference on a matter of international interest lasted two hours.

Lewald was of the opinion that no reply should be sent to England's demands, since he thought they were "unreasonable and meant not to be accepted," reported Donovan. "I, however, stated to him that it seemed to me very foolish on the part of the German Government to let this answer go by default; that if it were true that this British document were political, it would carry great weight with the neutral world and it was incumbent upon the German Government to make some answer."

Donovan's quiet reasonableness influenced the German officials. He urged the Germans not to let Britain put them in a bad light. That afternoon the whole thing was thrashed out at a conference, and the Germans agreed to the various British points.

Donovan left for Stockholm, where on June 2 he met Warwick Greene to discuss the availability of supplies from neutral countries for Poland. He also urged Greene to arrange for Ruth to join him in Berlin. He had dined in the German capital with William C. Bullitt, foreign correspondent for the *Philadelphia Ledger.* Bullitt, who later was to serve the United States as ambassador in France and the Soviet Union, was accompanied by his wife, and Donovan saw no reason why Ruth shouldn't be at his side during the negotiations with the Germans.

Greene agreed and cabled the Rockefeller Foundation in New York, "Heartily approve Donovan's wife coming. Can you secure same passport."

On June 4, Donovan returned to Berlin, where he discovered that the Germans were not willing to endanger the shipment of supplies to their own troops and constabulary in Poland in order to ship foodstuffs for the Poles. He reported to Greene, who was back in London, that Lewald was firm in his refusal, "it being evident that in this he was influenced by the military department." Lewald did agree to obtaining milk from Holland for the Poles. Donovan wired C. A. Young in The Hague to confirm arrangements with the Nutricia Company. He received no reply, but two days later both Young and Herbert Hoover arrived in Berlin and appeared at the Hotel Esplanade. When Young told him that he was too busy to make the arrangements, Donovan left the next night for Holland, where he called upon Hodjes of the Nutricia Company. Just an hour before his arrival, a German agent had seen Hodjes and bought his surplus for the month of 100 tons. Nutricia had only ten tons in stock, which they could send to Poland in July.

To Donovan's dismay, he learned from the Deutsche Bank that the funds earmarked for the purchase of the milk had not been transferred to Berlin. He had no alternative but to return to Berlin and reason with the German government not to block shipments of milk to Poland simply because their own purchasing agents had managed to force the Nutricia Company to sell to them. He traveled with two German purchasing agents, named Jancquel and Joseph, whom he persuaded to give him the name of another Dutch firm that would be permitted by the German government to furnish milk for Polish relief.

The negotiations in Berlin were repeated in Vienna, where Donovan now traveled. He called upon the Austrian Foreign Office and presented the Rockefeller Foundation proposal. "It was not our purpose to beg to be admitted into the nations under their military control for the purpose of administering relief," Donovan reported. He told the Austrians "that if their Government was anxious to have such relief administered, we would be glad to cooperate and put up the money."

The Austrians said they were willing. The greatest need was in Montenegro and Albania. The American Red Cross was providing relief in Serbia, but Macedonia, which had been conquered by the Bulgarians, was greatly in need of relief. The Austrians undertook to make arrangements for Donovan to go into the occupied countries to investigate conditions. They agreed to inform him in Berlin, to which he returned, as to precisely what they would be willing to have done.

Back in Berlin, Dr. Lewald told Donovan of a Jewish committee that had been formed to assist the Jewish hungry in Poland and suggested that he go to see them. Donovan saw Dr. Friedman, the committee head. "I made clear to them the nonsectarian position of the Rock-efeller Foundation," Donovan wrote Greene, "and that its representatives were here not to align themselves with one side or the other in any racial or religious controversies, but simply to feed those who were hungry." The Jewish committee maintained that the Poles were discriminating against Jews in administering any relief that reached the country. Donovan agreed to have his agent in Holland purchase supplies for the committee; the Jews in turn were to send funds to Holland to pay for the supplies. The Rockefeller representative in Poland would supervise distribution.

The following month saw similar negotiations in Berlin and Vienna. Donovan met Greene again in Switzerland. He outlined proposals for the purchase of foodstuffs in neutral countries and their distribution both in Poland and the Balkans. In Vienna he called upon the Bulgarian queen and the minister of war to discuss arrangements for relief measures in Occupied Serbia. He also conferred with Dr. Harry Plotz, the American virologist with the Red Cross Typhus Commission. Dr. Plotz had just arrived from the Balkan fronts, where he had been delousing the Bulgarian Army as a means of stopping typhus. Plotz had also been in Siberia, and he talked about that barren land, where in a few years Donovan was to carry out his first important intelligence assignment. Bill Donovan was already gathering information, seemingly just for the excitement of learning, but with an eye for what was significant.

Donovan was in Berlin on June 21 when cables arrived from Washington that abruptly brought his work for the Rockefeller Foundation to an end. He wrote to Greene in London:

> Word came in to the Embassy today that the entire National Guard has been mobilized and there is imminent danger of war with Mexico. I am well aware that you and I agreed long ago that in an event such as this it was my obligation to return home.
>
> I want to take this opportunity of telling you that this news has not stampeded me and that I am keeping my mind on the job. It does seem to me, however, that as soon as I can line up this work for someone else to take over, I should return. I have cabled to the General that I will be back as soon as I can have matters adjusted here.

Donovan already had in mind a replacement, someone who was taking an active role in the relief work for both Poland and the Balkans. On June 27, he received a cable from Warwick Greene, who hoped Donovan could remain until July 8.

Donovan, representing the Rockefeller Foundation, endeavored to extend relief not just to women and children but to the 4 million prisoners of war held by the warring powers under often brutal conditions.

Caught between Allied and Central Powers policies, both of which placed the relief for conquered civilian populations well beneath the demands of war, neither Donovan nor any other Rockefeller official was able to achieve what he had hoped.

Bill Donovan had participated in relief measures that meant not only the shipment of powdered milk from the Netherlands to Poland but also the movement of cocoa from Berlin to Warsaw, and the provision of used clothing from Paris for refugees. Several other times in the decades to come he was to take a personal role in alleviating the misery of refugees from wars and political persecution. He also had met Herbert Hoover and made him his friend. That friendship would have great importance to both men.

Although he had fully intended to preserve the neutrality that the spirit of the War Relief Commission intended, Donovan, a competent army officer, could not help but make observations about the armed forces of the warring powers. He had been given the opportunity to observe the German government at work. When after a brief stay in London he boarded a ship for the voyage home to New York, he carried with him the terrible certainty that the United States would be drawn into the European war.

Donovan had badly mixed up his expense accounts, something that he was to do all his life. It took the Rockefeller Foundation several months of correspondence and investigation to straighten them out. Characteristically, Donovan had drawn far less money than he was entitled to. And, as was also to happen repeatedly over the years, by the time Ruth Donovan was prepared to join her husband in Europe, he was already on his way home.

4

Joining Up with the Fighting 69th

ON JUNE 18, 1916, Newton D. Baker, secretary of war, issued a proclamation calling up the National Guard:

> In view of the disturbed conditions on the Mexican border, and in order to assure complete protection for all Americans, the President has called out substantially all the State militias, and will send them to the border wherever and as fully as General Funston determines them to be needed for the purpose stated.
>
> If all are not needed, an effort will be made to relieve those on duty from time to time so as to distribute the duty.
>
> This call for militia is wholly unrelated to General Pershing's expedition and contemplates no additional entry into Mexico, except as may be necessary to pursue bandits who attempt outrages on American soil.

Pancho Villa, the Mexican revolutionary, had become embittered against Americans because the United States had recognized the government of his rival, Gen. Venustiano Carranza. In January 1916, his men captured a train in Chihuahua, hauled 19 U.S. citizens from it, and peremptorily shot them. Villa led 1,500 of his soldiers across the border on March 9 and attacked Columbus, New Mexico. The attack killed nine citizens of the town before U.S. troopers arrived and drove off the raiders. President Wilson sent Gen. John J. Pershing with 4,000 Regular Army soldiers into Mexico to pursue Villa. Carranza protested the American pursuit and threatened war. At the same time, U.S. intelligence had proof of the extensive activity of German agents in Mexico, and it seemed a sensible precaution to send the National Guard to the border in support of Pershing's expedition. About 110,000 National Guardsmen took up positions along 1,200 miles of border reaching from Brownsville, Texas, to Yuma, Arizona.

Troop I had moved into the new armory at 1015 West Delavan Avenue in Buffalo in May, and it was still getting settled when, on June 19, orders were received by Western Union telegram. The Buffalo cavalrymen mobilized and headed down to the Mexican border, where they set up their tents near the border town of McAllen, Texas. The tents were ranked in a trim military row with the officers' tents followed by the men's tents. The mess shed was to the left, and picket lines extended to the corrals.

As soon as Donovan's ship reached New York, he hurried to see his wife and son, and then caught the first train he could for Texas. When he reached McAllen, he took command of Troop I. He strode down Buffalo Street and the men set up a loud shout of welcome. Galloping Bill, as some of the troopers called him, had arrived, and soon the troop would be up to snuff.

For most of the National Guard units called to the border, the entire experience was tedious at best, for scarcely a shot was fired in anger. The men rolled craps, tossed each other aloft in blankets, and built sandbag forts along the Rio Grande just in case the Mexicans decided to carry out another raid. But for Troop I, the border experience was a different matter altogether. Galloping Bill led his men on 25-mile dismounted hikes. With their broad-brimmed campaign hats keeping off the desert sun and their tight puttees chafing their calves, they hiked and hiked some more. Troop I also took long rides, some of 250 miles, and participated in maneuvers with other units.

"After snaking their way through a two-mile cloud of dust for 170 miles across the southern tip of the United States, the New York Cavalry returned to camp at McAllen after an eleven-day hike, full of dust, sand, salt water, and sympathy for Mr. Pershing," wrote Edward Streeter in the *Rio Grande Rattler,* which the National Guardsmen published at Hidalgo, Texas.

The men practiced at the rifle range, and they drilled. While the morale of other units with less zealous commanders plummeted, Troop I's morale soared. Carl Dickey of the *New York Times* wrote in the *Rio Grande Rattler* how Donovan's men were "picking cactus out of their hides, while they are telling lies about how much they enjoyed sleeping with rattlesnakes, how much they revelled in these Texas once-in-a-century rains, how good Texas gumbo mud felt in a fellow's ears, how much fun it was to see just how much space there was between the front of a person's commissary department and his backbone by going without rations for a couple of days."

Milton Klein of the Buffalo Cavalry Association was only 16 years old when he was with Bill Donovan on the Mexican border. In 1980, sitting with Gen. Ed Hogan, another old Donovan friend, in their room at the Connecticut Street Armory in Buffalo, beneath the Troop I guidons that had been carried on the border, he remembered what it was like.

"The elite of Buffalo belonged to Troop I," he recalled. "It was a silk stocking troop, but this didn't keep Bill Donovan from giving the boys a hell of a working over. If anybody complained, he gave him a glance, which while both mild and sympathetic, expressed such incredulity that anybody might possibly malinger, that every man of us shaped up. He drove us hard because he figured America's entry into war in

Europe was inevitable and that not only our effectiveness as a military unit was at stake, but whether or not each of us would ever return from battle depended upon our training."

Off duty, Donovan and his men rode into McAllen and walked along its dusty main street, two blocks long, where they could take a bath and get a shave in a bathhouse, dine in a restaurant or lunchroom, purchase trinkets in souvenir shops, and take aim at the targets in a shooting gallery. Donovan took a certain satisfaction in hitting the targets with greater accuracy than most of the men he commanded.

One by one, as the troubles with Mexico quieted down, the National Guard units were withdrawn from the border. Troop I stayed on and Donovan, writing to Warwick Greene on October 20 about his still snarled War Relief Commission expense account, commented, "Here we have no ideas of our release. Everything points to preparation for departure. Yet, Secret Service men say that conditions in the interior are as bad as they have ever been. As captain, acting major, judge advocate and regimental athletic director, I manage to keep very much engaged."

Back in Buffalo, A. Conger Goodyear, a brother of Donovan's law partner, had been placed in command of a custodial troop at the Delavan Street Armory. Donovan wrote to him to urge that Buffalo raise a squadron of cavalry as part of a division that Theodore Roosevelt, Jr., was assembling. War with Germany might break out at any time. In previous wars patriotic Americans had raised and equipped military units at their own expense to go to the support of their government. There was some talk in 1916 about a possible draft if America went to war, but to men like Donovan, Goodyear, and Roosevelt, a true patriot did not wait to be asked to serve.

"As we look at the matter here," Goodyear wrote to Donovan on February 12, "there seems to be very little prospect of this country sending over any large force; in fact, most people think it is very doubtful if we send any force at all. If a regiment were organized here, I think that it would have practically no chance to see any active service. In other words, it would not be ready for service until the spring of 1918. I do not believe that the war will last until that time."

Donovan pointed out that the necessary steps to raise the regiment might be speeded up if Roosevelt, who knew Army Chief of Staff Gen. Leonard Wood well, would only talk to the general and enlist his support. In such a regiment, Donovan was to be a major and Goodyear was to command a squadron. The total cost of arming and equipping the regiment was to be about $750,000. Another $250,000 would be spent to purchase horses. The gentlemen soldiers of Buffalo corresponded among themselves and with Theodore Roosevelt, Jr., but nothing came of the proposal. The War Department politely refused their aid. Things had changed, and if the United States went to war, the battles were to be fought in the main with conscripts.

Finally Troop I was ordered home. Donovan wired to Goodyear a few days before their departure: "We leave March 5th, entire Regiment destined Buffalo. Transhipped there. If Regiment in town that evening will entertain officers personally Buffalo Club. Will want you there and such as you can select. Can you suggest entertainment enlisted men. Regiment can't parade. Will wire later. Our men do not wish tickets of admission nor standing luncheon nor Billy Sunday."

The troop reached Buffalo on March 12. Lieutenant Charles Pearson could boast with some satisfaction, "So well were its papers prepared that it was inspected and mustered out of service of the United States the following day, March 13, 1917, after serving nine long months."

Mayor Louis P. Fuhrmann ordered a civic celebration to honor the return of the Buffalo troop from the Mexican border. Donovan and his men mounted their horses and, despite his previous dismissal of the idea, paraded down Main Street while crowds cheered. Afterward he entertained his fellow officers at the Buffalo Club. As he sat among the "silk stocking" troopers in one of the city's most prestigious clubs, he must have been pleased at the progress of events that had carried him from the rough waterfront of his city to such public esteem.

More important for his future, Bill Donovan had observed the 69th Infantry, New York, in service on the Mexican border, and he now intended to join the "Fighting 69th" if America found itself at war in Europe. The Fighting 69th had had an opportunity to observe him as well. Father Francis P. Duffy, the regimental chaplain, noted that "on the Border when he was Captain of Troop I of the 1st Cavalry, he was the best known man of his rank in the New York Division." For a few months Bill Donovan settled down in Buffalo with his wife and child. He practiced law, and he drilled Troop I at the Delavan Street Armory. He also studied French and German. There was no doubt in his mind that war with Germany was at hand.

It was Douglas MacArthur who suggested that the new 42nd Division formed from National Guard units from many states be called the Rainbow because, as he put it, it was "spreading like a rainbow across the country." MacArthur was pleased to serve in the division headquarters since from the start the Rainbow Division was intended to be the first National Guard unit to see action in France.

War was declared on Germany on April 6, 1917. On July 15, the Fighting 69th Regiment of the New York National Guard, made up mainly of Irish-Americans, was incorporated into the division, as Father Francis Duffy said, "to put a green in the rainbow." Regular Army numbering required that the regiment now be called the 165th, but the men still referred to their historic outfit as the Old 69th, and the regimental flag of the Fighting Harps continued to fly 11 streamers as proof that it had fought in 11 Civil War battles, including Bull Run, Antietam, Bloody Ford, and Marye's Heights. Its history reached back through the Mexican War and the War of 1812 to the Revolution. A total of 50 furls, representing 50 engagements, flew from its flag. Most recently the regiment had seen service on the Mexican border. With the outbreak of war, the 69th had started a recruiting campaign in New York City with the slogan "Don't join the 69th unless you want to be among the first to go to France."

Young men and boys from all over the New York City metropolitan area volunteered, so that by the end of July the ranks were filled. On Monday, August 24, the 165th Infantry was mobilized at its armory on Manhattan's Lexington Avenue. It paraded north on Fifth Avenue, the regimental band blaring "Garry Owen," while a cordon of police kept back crowds of cheering New Yorkers.

Sobbing mothers, wives, and sweethearts tried to break through the police to kiss the boys a last good-bye. The regiment marched to 48th Street and then to the East River, where it boarded the 34th Street Ferry for the trip to Long Island City. There a train waited to carry the men to Mineola, Long Island. The regiment was to be trained at Camp Mills, a vast array of tents that covered the level fields adjoining the Mineola Aviation Field and that in time would house 27,000 soldiers.

When America declared war, Bill Donovan, learning that former President Theodore Roosevelt had offered to raise four volunteer divisions to go to France, got in touch with his boyhood hero and asked to serve under his command. Roosevelt had heard of the commander of Troop I who had made his unit one of the crack cavalry outfits in America. The old Rough Rider saw that Donovan was a man after his own heart. Donovan would serve as a lieutenant colonel.

Congress voted to authorize Roosevelt to raise his volunteers, but President Wilson refused to allow him to do so. He claimed that Roosevelt's divisions would attract too many capable Regular Army officers and would undercut the draft, which was Wilson's answer to America's manpower needs. He also accused Roosevelt, who had opposed him in the 1912 election, of seeking to advance his political fortunes through a military adventure. Wilson sent Roosevelt a blunt notice that he was to halt his efforts to raise the force.

On May 21, Roosevelt consulted with Bill Donovan and 19 other proposed leaders of the divisions by telephone and wire, and decided to give up his plan. He sent a message to each of his commanders. "I now release you and all your men," Donovan read with anger and disappointment.

I wish to express my deep sense of obligation to you and to all those who had volunteered under and in connection with this division.

As you doubtless know, I am very proud of the Rough Riders, the First Volunteer Cavalry, with whom I served in the Spanish-American War. I believe it is a just and truthful statement of the facts when I say that this regiment did as well as any of the admirable regular regiments with which it served in the Santiago campaign. It was raised, armed, equipped, drilled, mounted, dismounted, kept two weeks aboard transports, and put through two victorious aggressive fights in which it lost one third of the officers and one fifth of the men; all within sixty days from the time I received my commission.

If the President had permitted me to raise the four divisions, I am certain that they would have equaled this record, only on a hundredfold larger scale. They would have all been on the firing line before or shortly after the draft army had begun to assemble; and moreover they could have been indefinitely reinforced, so that they would have grown continually stronger and more efficient.

I regret from the standpoint of the country that your services were not utilized. But the country has every reason to be proud of the zeal, patriotism, and businesslike efficiency with which you came forward.

Bill Donovan was not to serve in the Great War under the command of his boyhood hero, but he intended at least to serve. He accepted an assignment as assistant chief of staff of the 27th Division, a safe berth that would insure a man of his military acumen ready advancement. He was offered the rank of colonel, and Buffalonians, meeting him on the street or at the Buffalo Club, congratulated him. One evening Donovan spoke at a war rally held in Buffalo's Convention Hall.

"The test of citizenship is our willingness to affix our signatures to an oath of enlistment and delivering that oath to a recruiting officer," he stated. "Our flag has meant a country of peace and comfort and happiness, but now it stands as a symbol of service and of sacrifice."

Even as he was talking, Donovan was intriguing to get himself transferred from the 27th Division headquarters, where life promised to be much too quiet for a man of his temperament and ambition. He had observed the Fighting 69th on the Mexican border, and he was convinced that the regiment's spirit was bound to carry it into the hottest of the fighting in France. The 69th was Irish, and within the now successful Buffalo lawyer still beat the heart of the 12-year-old boy who had won a medal for his declamation of a poem about leading Irish hosts into battle.

Father Duffy wrote of Donovan in his journal, "Everybody knew that he could get higher rank by staying with the 27th Division, but he preferred to join our Regiment, especially now that it is to be the first in the fray, and he would rather be Major than Colonel, for in battles, as now conducted, it is Majors who command in the actual fighting."

John Cassidy, then a 16-year-old private, remembered the day that Major Donovan arrived to take command of the First Battalion of the 165th. Donovan walked the company streets with Capt. Tom Riley, who was six feet six inches tall. The new commanding officer was shorter than his companion, but to the watching men he appeared a good half-foot taller.

"Tom, what the hell is this?" Donovan demanded, looking about him at the new recruits. "A regiment or a mob?"

Donovan had brought along several dozen pairs of boxing gloves, and he soon had the men in his command squaring off in a boxing tournament. He led the soldiers on 4-mile cross-country runs, in which he invariably returned to camp fresher than any of the men, who were mostly in their teens or early 20s.

Duffy noted that Donovan, now in his mid-30s, was "very attractive in face and manner, an athlete who always keeps himself in perfect condition. I like him for his agreeable disposition, his fine character, his alert and eager intelligence. But I certainly would not want to be in his battalion."

Sergeant Mike Donaldson, a redoubtable giant of a man, was acknowledged the boxing champion of the regiment. One day he asked the First Battalion's CO to put on the gloves with him. Donovan smiled in a gentle sort of way and demurred, but when he saw that dozens of men had clustered around and were expecting him to take up the challenge, he slipped on a pair of gloves. Those angry hours of boxing his brother in the barn behind his boyhood home made him confident. As the big man flailed and slugged at him, Donovan danced lightly about, jabbing him in the face. Finally a blow struck the sergeant full on the jaw, and he sank to his knees.

"Holy Christ," remembered a soldier who watched the battle between the regiment's champion and the officer. "Donovan put the gloves on with him one time. Donaldson couldn't touch him."

Reveille for the 165th Infantry at Camp Mills was at 4:50 A.M., and in Donovan's regiment there were no slugabeds. "All right, men!" he'd shout, sometimes bursting right into their tents. "Three minutes to make up your cots, and then out here on the double. Full packs today!"

After an hour of exercises there would be a strenuous hike or run before breakfast. There were drill at formations, bayonet practice with dummies, and sitting-up exercises, the latter considered the very latest in physical conditioning. Sometimes the men played baseball or football or boxed, and when there was nothing else to do, Donovan led his battalion on another cross-country run. Evening mess was at 6:00 P.M.

"Our gathering place was Camp Mills, Long Island," Sgt. Dick O'Neill, later to earn the Congressional Medal of Honor, said after the war. "It was here that they started to turn us into a division. And it was here that I got to know our battalion commander, Major William

Joseph Donovan. Now, let me point out that my son is named William Donovan O'Neill; that should tell you what I thought about him. He surely worked us that summer at Mills. But I ask you, was there any other way to get us ready for what was coming?"

Donovan had rented a tiny house close by the camp, and Ruth and young David lived there. Usually he spent the night with his family. On September 17, Vincent Donovan was ordained a priest at the Catholic University of America in Washington, D.C., a matter of great pride and satisfaction to his brother. When soon afterward Ruth gave birth to a girl, Bill Donovan hoped that his brother could christen her. Instead Father Duffy baptized the infant, with holy water sprinkled from an army canteen. To Father Duffy, the 69th was "Irish by adoption, Irish by conviction, Irish by association," since only 5 percent of the men enlisted in it were not of Irish ancestry. He had dedicated the regiment to St. Patrick, and it made the men of Donovan's command proud that their CO had chosen the name Patricia for his child, whom they adopted as a daughter of the regiment.

Back in New York City the celebrated Irish tenor John McCormack sang a concert at the Hippodrome and the New York Giants played an exhibition game at the Polo Grounds to raise money for the Fighting 69th's recreation fund. McCormack came to sing for the boys at the camp too, and there was scarcely a dry eye as he sang Irish song after Irish song.

One day Joyce Kilmer, one of America's best-known poets, joined Donovan's battalion. He had two sons and two daughters, and with his gentle ways hardly seemed the sort of man who would volunteer to be among the first overseas. But he too had responded to the wave of patriotism sweeping New York City.

Lieutenant Oliver Ames reported for duty with Donovan's battalion in September. A member of the Harvard University Regiment, Ames had attended the 1916 Plattsburg, New York, camp for young officers, finishing his training in May. On October 6, Ames married Caroline Lee Fessenden, to whom he was to write some of the most deeply moving accounts of the events that awaited the regiment in France.

The 165th New York was combined with the 166th Ohio to make up the 83rd Brigade, commanded by Brig. Gen. Michael J. Lenahan. After the war, General Lenahan recalled that it was "urgent to land another combat division in France as soon as possible to augment Regular Army troops. The men selected were those of the highest caliber and those nearly ready for immediate field service, the elite of the National Guard."

How prepared were these men? Bill Donovan was not so sure. "There was no rifle range at Camp Mills," he said later, "and none of the men had any real training as marksmen."

In early September, former President Theodore Roosevelt came to

Camp Mills to visit General Lenahan, an old friend. When the soldiers discovered the unmistakable bulk of one of America's most popular figures coming out of their leader's tent, they set up a loud cheer. Donovan found himself cheering with the rest. The men shouted for a speech, and Roosevelt silenced them with a jaunty wave of his hand. He said that he wished he could go with them. Donovan shook his hand, and Roosevelt asked that he bring his four captains in the First Battalion out to his home in Oyster Bay to dine with him. On September 8, Roosevelt wrote a letter to his son Archibald Bulloch Roosevelt, already serving in France.

> Last evening Major Donovan of the 165th (who would have been a lieutenant colonel in my division) and his four captains dined here. They hope to go abroad in two or three weeks; and then I hope they will see you. They have good fighting stuff in them. Their regiment was at Mineola where I visited it; it is built around the old 69th N.Y.N.G. as a nucleus. They are having difficulties not only with their multitude of raw recruits but with some of the elderly regular officers; for the War Department is paying an amount of attention to seniority that inevitably means much slurring of merit and promotion of demerit.

Roosevelt could well have been writing about Donovan, who had been recommended by a board of officers to serve as a colonel of the 165th Infantry but did not receive the post because army regulations required that it be given to a Regular Army officer.

Donovan, fresh from dining with the vigorous Roosevelt, renewed his efforts to shape his battalion into a fighting force. The autumn weeks were passing, and Donovan expected to receive his marching orders almost any day. In Europe the Allies awaited the arrival of American troops to break the stalemate.

The men also knew that their marching orders would soon be issued, and fear and excitement spread through the camp. There were last farewells with loved ones, and then, when the orders did not come as expected, still more last farewells. Bill Donovan spent as much time as he could with Ruth and the children. He held his new baby on his knee and put his arm around his son's slender waist as if he could never hug his children enough. Ruth watched and suppressed her tears.

In the battalion streets between the tents, Father Duffy walked, his hands folded behind him in meditation. When his eyes met those of a worried young soldier, he gave him what Alexander Woollcott, then a correspondent for the army newspaper, *Stars and Stripes,* called "the heart-warming benediction of Father Duffy's smile. I seem to remember it more often that not as a mutinous smile, the eyes dancing, the lips puckering as if his conscientious sobriety as a priest was once more engaged in its long, losing fight with his inner amusement at the world."

His smile was infectious, but after Father Duffy had passed by, the men felt fear return. Joyce Kilmer noted in his journal: "Twice secret orders to sail were received at Regimental Headquarters, and twice these orders were hastily countermanded. The suspense began to tell on officers and men, to tell even more, perhaps, on those to whom they had again and again to say good-bye."

At last, on the night of October 25, 1917, Major Donovan led the First Battalion through the dark camp and down the silent lanes to the long train that was to take them to Montreal. "And now there were no crowds, there was no music," wrote Kilmer. "It was a journey more momentous, greater in historical importance, than its flower and flag decked setting forth for Camp Mills. But it was not like those memorable events, a time for music and pomp. The feeling of the officers and men was one of stern delight, of that strange religious exaltation with which men of Celtic race and faith go into battle."

Donovan at last was leading his fellow Irish-Americans in war. As the troop train rumbled through the night on its way to the Canadian border, Father Duffy passed from car to car, hearing confessions and giving absolution. He blessed rosaries and crucifixes presented to the young soldiers by their mothers. Donovan's battalion was the first unit of the 165th to leave for France. The rest of the regiment remained at Camp Mills, preparing to sail on November 11.

When the train reached Montreal, it proceeded to the waterfront over tracks usually reserved for freight shipments. Tight security was observed as the men went aboard the rust-streaked SS *Tunisian*. German submarines operating in the North Atlantic must not learn that a troopship was about to sail from Montreal for England. At eight o'clock on the morning of October 27, the *Tunisian* dropped down the St. Lawrence River with the men hiding below decks so that German spies could not see them. Once the ship was out on the wide Gulf of St. Lawrence, far below Quebec City, the men crowded up on deck to get their last look at North America. Few of them had ever been on the ocean, and their first sight of its rolling vastness filled them with dismay that at least lessened their preoccupation with the German army or even the U-boats that might be lurking ahead.

One day before the *Tunisian* docked in Liverpool, England, Oliver Ames wrote to his parents in Boston: "If you ever want to appreciate your family and friends, just try a 3,000-mile trip across the ocean in a rotten little tub, a huge life preserver with you every minute, and a feeling every minute that you may have to swim for it, and the water looking oh, so cold, to say nothing of the glorious future of participating in an Allied drive in the spring which may bring you glory and martyrdom; I wonder how I'll like to be a martyr; my chief occupation on the trip has been one long attempt to persuade myself I'll like it."

On November 10, with a year and a day of war still to go, the *Tunisian* docked at Liverpool. The men, toting their packs, went ashore and boarded a waiting train that rolled across the rain-soaked English countryside to Southampton. When the battalion reached Southampton, it was quartered in a bleak rest camp. In his war diary, Donovan noted that at Southampton there was a "three mile march through a dark, dirty seaport town to a rest camp—rest would be too complimentary—wooden floors, tents, no fires, a very poor night." The men shivered through the following day until it was dark enough on the night of November 11 to go aboard the boat for the Channel crossing to Le Havre.

"That boat ride was not soon to be forgotten," wrote Donovan. "Neither moon nor stars. Boat so crowded that it was like walking on a floor of faces to get through the ship. Then the landing. Marching through a strange city with queer names in an unknown tongue on all the shop windows. And our men truly overwhelmed. They seemed stunned with the new tongue and quite at a loss."

The men hiked 5 miles to another rest camp, this one, in Donovan's words, "well kept, clean with bathing facilities. A good place for officers' mess, but very tiresome sleeping on the hard tent floors."

The battalion spent an anxious day awaiting the arrival of one company that had been forced to take a later Channel boat. That night the men marched, according to Donovan, "through a heavy fog along dark, unlighted, narrow, muddy streets to our station. Loading the men, thirty-five or forty in horse cars, officers in third class carriages, which were much like the slabs in a morgue and quite as cold. The entire battalion in one train."

This was the battalion's first encounter with what the men called "side-door Pullmans," the French freight cars designed to hold either 40 men or eight horses. "The main objection to the 40-and-8s," said one soldier, "being that the horses had been sleeping in them the night before and somebody had forgotten to get them ready for the troops, who were bundled into them in a pitch-black night."

The men spread their blankets on the filthy floors and draped them over the open doors to keep off the blasts of freezing wind. They dined on hardtack and canned corned beef as they jolted for four days across France to Lorraine. Donovan remarked on the lack of sanitary arrangements and discovered that it was impossible to keep the men on the train whenever it stopped at some small town. There was a weary day, a cold and sleepless night, and then, on November 15, the battalion detrained at Savoie.

There was nobody at the station to meet the battalion, and Donovan had to discover where his command was to go as best he could. Their legs stiff from being cramped in a cold boxcar, the men hiked over the frozen roads to Naives-en-Blois, which Father Duffy described as "a group of forty houses along the slopes of a crinkled plain." There they established regimental headquarters in the town that the men's fumbling tongues called Blooey. The officers were billeted in the houses lining two muddy streets. The men spread their blankets on the straw of stables and barns, ten, 15, or 30 to a building, depending on its size.

"There are three classes of inhabitants in the houses—" read Father Duffy as he censored a letter a soldier had written home, "first, residents; second, cattle; third, soldiers."

"It was here that our troubles really began," wrote Joyce Kilmer. "The hell of it was the foulup in clothing. Here we were in the Vosges Mountain area, with what was to be one of the worst winters in French history beginning, and half the men didn't have their overcoats. Can you imagine that? Hardly any of them had winter brogans—many were walking around in those light shoes you'd wear in a dress parade during the summer. Why, the next thing you knew a lot of the boys had rags on their feet. And the blankets—we had lightweight summer ones until the first of the year."

"It does not seem real that I should be here in the land of chivalry," Donovan wrote, "and battle seems highly improbable. I live with Madame Depuis, whose husband died during the war and whose son is now at Verdun. She is very agreeable and old and motherly. She has given me a pleasant room."

Donovan was concerned by the failure of winter uniforms to arrive and by the lamentable sanitary conditions in the town. "The last soldiers were French, and they departed some time ago. I believe that no cleaning has been done since that time. The important thing is cleaning of the streets and the adoption of sanitary and hygienic measures." The water, at least, he thought to be quite good, "but for the present we boil it for all purposes." He also observed that it grew dark at four and at six a heavy mist began to descend. "It is droll here," he said, "with no telephone and no means of transportation. Yet surprising how soon one is accustomed to the lack."

Donovan went boar hunting with the mayor of the town. "The scheme was to have a group go in at one end with dogs and chase them toward the other end. When one is caught sight of, a great shout is set up by the beaters so that the men waiting may be ready. Rustled up three, and one of villagers killed one of them. These boars are the real thing and when wounded are quite ugly. Just now the Mayor came in person to invite me to a great feast of boar eating. They think me quite a linguist. In fact, I seem to be quite amusing to them."

5

Rehearsal for War

WHILE THE BATTALION was getting settled in France, Donovan was ordered to a Field Officers' School for a course that would acquaint him with the French Army's hard-won knowledge of trench warfare. He soon missed Madame Depuis's comfortable house. Observed Donovan,

> This field officers' school should be good to teach humility. We come here from fairly comfortable billets to a different arrangement altogether. We are on the side of a high hill. Mud, just as tenacious and much more abundant and long-staying, predominates. We are in barracks, much on the style of the officers' camps, only without floors. No light but candle and lanterns. Cots, muddy floors, and dampness. I am rather glad of it all myself because it means a little taste of inconvenience, and I was beginning to think it was a war de luxe. I am looking forward to the work with real pleasure and hope it is hard. I want to get it into my fibre and be able to impart it to the battalion.

Twenty-five percent of the officers at the school were permitted to go to Paris each week, but Donovan did not put his name in for leave. "I have not put my name in, as I have no desire to go there," he said.

Theodore Roosevelt's son Archie came to see Donovan. Another of the former President's sons, Ted, was stationed only 5 miles away, but Bill Donovan was too preoccupied with learning the military lessons of his French mentors to go and see him. He found the meals "quite good and almost too abundant. Exercise is what I need most." He wrote,

> A hundred different human frailties now assert themselves. Jealousies and pettiness and selfishness. And then out of it all stand a few strong figures who are true and patriotic and unselfish.
>
> There are many doleful expressions around here, homesick and blue. Many of these young married fellows are down and out. What I contemplate is far different and far more amusing than you see at home. There are now over fifty crowded into this barracks. It is muddier than outdoors; the fires won't burn. Constantly you hear coughing through the room. In spite of it all, my health is good, and I am getting in some good hours of studying.

Curiously, Donovan does not say if he himself were sometimes "doleful, homesick and blue," missing Ruth and the children. Yet he wrote regularly to Ruth, telling about his life in France.

In Naives-en-Blois, Donovan had begun to study French with the villagers. Now he complained that he was living entirely with Americans, none of whom seemed interested in learning the language of the country in which they found themselves. One day he went to the French hospital to beg a hot bath. When he had finished a long soak in water as hot as he could get it, Dr. Wilbert, a young French physician, asked if Donovan would like to meet with him for an hour every day. The doctor would teach the American French, and Donovan would teach him English. Donovan readily agreed. He soon made a close friend of the doctor, who before the war had been a children's specialist in Paris.

On a typical Sunday, Donovan reported, he arose at 7:00 A.M. "Great variety of weather in the past two hours, sun, rain, hail, and snow," he wrote to Ruth. He read maps, went to Mass, and wrote to Ruth that "the town dates from the 12th century and looks as if it has tried to save the accumulation of dirt for all these years." Despite the bad weather, Donovan occupied his spare time with muddy walks through the countryside. He wore out his shoes and socks and had to buy more from the quartermaster. He wrote to Ruth to send socks. He confessed to a yen for candy and hoped that she would send him some in a Christmas box.

The day that Gen. John Pershing came to the Field Officers' School a cold snap froze the mud. The sun sparkled as Donovan and his fellow officers demonstrated before the commander of the American Expeditionary Force how to lead a bayonet charge, control the firing line, launch rifle grenades, raid a trench, aim trench mortars, and direct artillery fire. Live ammunition was used throughout the day.

Four fashionably dressed ladies, as well as President Wilson's friend Col. Edward M. House, had accompanied the general. "I think the ladies scarcely knew what it was all about," Donovan wrote to Ruth.

As for Pershing, Donovan described him as "short of six feet. Thick through the chest; not so well set up in the legs; exceedingly well dressed, tan shoes, spurs, leather puttees laced in English fashion up the front, a dark, olive drab overcoat, very snappy—and a nice fitting hat. His face is softer than his pictures, and he has not the grim expression seen in them. He looks like a real he-man."

Soon afterward Donovan and five other officers moved from the barracks into a tiny Swiss-style chalet with a wooden floor and a stove. The stove seemed to them the most marvelous invention achieved by mankind. Nor was the chalet crowded, since three of the men assigned to it were on the sick list. Donovan felt pampered, and his conscience began to trouble him. How could he be living so comfortably when the men of his battalion were undoubtedly shivering in the cold? He felt better about things when he was chosen to referee a French Army maneuver in the field for three days with only his bedroll to keep off the chill. The French soldiers impressed him—they were not as big as the Americans, but they were tough and wiry. Some of them, apaches from the Parisian slums, particularly interested him. "To me they have a certain air that is quite attractive," he wrote in his journal.

Possibly he was missing his own command of young New Yorkers. He did not have long to wait to see the First Battalion of the 69th, for he soon completed his course and returned to Naives-en-Blois. The men groaned when the man some called Blue-Eyed Billie came back. They had reason to groan. The cruel weather did not keep Donovan from leading the First Battalion on long marches. Kilmer noted in his diary:

"December 7, hiked 10 kilometers. Food—coffee like water, luke-warm—a few strips of bacon—all we had that day.

"December 10, hiked 10 kilometers—many of the men without shoes—weather freezing. One meal, some kind of stew."

The front was close enough so that when the wind was right the men could hear the boom of the big guns at St. Mihiel. The stalemate on the front continued, but there were frequent exchanges of artillery fire. Donovan and his men feared that German planes might appear overhead and drop bombs, so at night it was counted too dangerous to light a cigarette outdoors.

Exultant at being back in command, Donovan drilled his men and conditioned them to the hardships of a winter campaign. The men complained bitterly, but he paid no attention. One day Father Duffy overheard three doughboys discussing their CO. One thought he was a prince of good fellows and should, in fact, be the king of Ireland. One of the others agreed.

"He's a son-of-a-bitch!" announced the third.

They argued furiously, with Donovan's defenders maintaining that he was no easier on himself than on the men he led.

The third soldier finally gave in. "He's a son-of-a-bitch," he said, "but he's a game one."

When Father Duffy told Donovan of the incident, he laughed. "Father, that's what I want on my epitaph," he said.

Some of the men took to calling Donovan Galloping Bill, as the troopers of Troop I had named him down on the Mexican border; others nicknamed him Hard-Boiled Bill. One day Donovan led the men on a wild 3-mile run, vaulting over walls, plunging down embankments, leaping over ditches, writhing through barbed-wire entanglements. They ended up gasping for breath in a windswept field. Donovan glared at the men. "What's the matter with you guys?" he demanded. "I've got the same fifty pounds on my back as you men, and I'm ten years older."

There was silence broken only by the sound of panting men. Then from the rear of the group came an anonymous reply: "But we ain't as wild as you, Bill."

Donovan was to bear the name Wild Bill for the rest of his life, even though his leadership was believed by both his fellow officers and his command to be as quiet and analytical as it was bold and strenuous.

While the battalion was in training at Naives-en-Blois, big Mike Donaldson went AWOL. Marine MPs caught up with him in Paris and clapped him in a guardhouse. When he was returned to the 165th, Donovan put him to work digging a hole ten feet by ten feet. It took the muscular giant all day. When he was told that Donaldson had completed the hole, Donovan said, "All right, now make him fill it up."

As Christmas approached, the mess sergeants scoured the French countryside for chickens and any other edibles that could be bought. The 165th was resolved to celebrate the day with religious fervor and with a dinner, which many were convinced might be their last good meal on earth. Major Hugh W. Ogden, the judge advocate for the Rainbow Division, noted in his diary that the temperature on Christmas Eve dropped to 5 degrees Fahrenheit. The men shivered in their ramshackle billets and waited for the Christmas Eve services to begin in the 700-year-old village church with its seven-foot-thick tower, in which slits had been cut for bowmen, soldiers of a faraway time.

Forty men were billeted in a barn near where Lt. Oliver Ames was housed in a village dwelling. "I can hear them singing," he wrote on Christmas Eve to his wife, "and the most mournfully sentimental songs."

Joyce Kilmer, his fingers cramped with the cold, also wrote to his wife on Christmas Eve. "We may have Christmas Mass in the church here tonight. Father Duffy has had a choir practicing for it, and we possess a tenor soloist. He is an Italian, a barber when not singing or soldiering."

The men walked through the dark village streets to the church and crowded inside with the villagers, until Cpl. Martin Hogan thought that the sides would be pushed out. Bill Donovan waited with General Lenahan for the church services to begin.

"We sat in my room until 11:30," Lenahan wrote in his journal, "and then went to the old village church. Father Francis P. Duffy, chaplain of the 165th Infantry, had made arrangements for Solemn High Mass, having secured the services of the Curé and of several other French priests from nearby towns. The church was filled to capacity with townspeople, chaplains, and soldiers of the French Army, home from the front on Christmas leave. Father Duffy met me at the church door and escorted me through the church to the Bishop's seat, which I occupied during the mass."

The band of the 165th, located on the Epistle side of the sanctuary, played. The regimental officers stood with Lenahan on the Gospel side. Standing on the flooring of cold stone, Donovan listened to the band play "Adeste Fideles," and the choir sing "Noël" in French. Father

Duffy preached in English. The flickering candlelight, the music, the shining faces of the men made a strong impression on everyone there. "It was the most inspiring religious service I had ever witnessed," wrote Lenahan, back in his warm room.

The men walked to their stables, their hearts at peace for the moment. By 2:00 A.M. all was quiet in the village and in the surrounding countryside, where the other battalions of the regiment were sheltering as best they could in farm outbuildings.

It began to snow and continued all night. Snow fell on the ice-glazed roads, on the fields, and on the ancient houses. It sifted through the chinks in stable walls and roofs, and covered the blankets of the sleeping men. Christmas breakfast turned out to be bacon sandwiches with hot coffee, but the plain fare was entirely acceptable to the men because the first real mail from home had arrived. Midday mess was more impressive. There were turkey, chicken, cranberries, mashed potatoes, carrots, bread pudding, nuts, figs, and coffee. The men gorged themselves and trooped into the market shed, where the band played Christmas carols and they sang. There were no presents.

"It is just as well," observed Father Duffy, "for we depart tomorrow on a four-day hike over snowy roads, and the less we have to carry the better."

The men charged with transport doubtless would have agreed with their chaplain. On Christmas Eve the mules had arrived. Most of them were unbroken and unshod, and getting them ready for departure on December 26 proved a nearly impossible task. Shouts and cursing seemed out of keeping with the spirit of Christmas, so the men tried patience and gentle words on the recalcitrant beasts without any notable success. The wagoners had to throw the mules down on stable floors to put on the unfamiliar harnesses.

The snow fell all day and throughout the night. The men awoke the next morning to a gray sky. A gusting wind whirled the still falling snow across the roads, over which they set off after a hasty breakfast, straining beneath their 50-pound packs.

"It was still snowing when we broke camp at nine o'clock," Corporal Hogan recalled later, "and a head-on wind blew the sharp crystals into our faces and eyes."

The 83rd Brigade, made up of the Ohioans and the New Yorkers, marched off over different roads to their evening destinations, some 15 miles away at eight different billeting areas. The snow was often thigh-deep on the roads, which twisted up into the foothills of the Vosges Mountains. Beneath the snow was glare ice, and the soldiers often slipped and fell.

The men were still in their summer uniforms, some had no overcoats, and only a few had gloves. Just as George Washington's men, their shoes worn out, had trudged through the snow of Valley Forge in bare feet, leaving bloody marks behind them, so did the men of the 165th Regiment on the march that day in the Vosges. Some men whose shoes had worn through bought or begged wooden sabots from the peasants past whose mountain farms the weary column straggled. Others wrapped their feet in gunnysacks.

Donovan trudged along at the end of the column to pick up stragglers. He came upon an 18-year-old youth who had sunk down into the snow, too tired to get up. He regarded the boy's bloody feet with compassion.

"I think I'm going to die," the youth whimpered.

"You can't die without my permission," Donovan asserted, "and I don't intend to give it. I'll take your pack, but you've got to hike."

With his commanding officer shouldering his pack, the boy limped down the road.

"On a hike the Infantry will get through," Father Duffy wrote in his journal at the end of the first day's march. "There is never any doubt of that. They may be footsore, hungry, broken-backed, frozen, half-dead, but they will get through."

The problem, as the chaplain saw it, was the supplies. He accompanied the supply wagons, which stuck on the steep icy roads. "Again and again they came to hills where every wagon was stalled," Duffy wrote. "The best teams had to be unhitched and attached to each wagon separately until the hill was won. Over and over the toil-worn men would have to cover the same ground till the work was done, and in tough places they had to spend their failing strength tugging on a rope or pushing a wheel. Wagoners sat on their boxes with hands and feet freezing and never uttered a complaint. The wagons were full of food, but no man asked for a mite of it—they were willing to wait till the companies ahead would get their share."

That night the men huddled together for warmth in barns and other outbuildings. Many could look up through broken roofs to see the stars now twinkling down from a sky as cold as it was clear. There were no fuel and no fires, and the wagons were still stuck in the snow far behind. When they did roll into the billet area in the middle of the night, the fresh meat and vegetables were frozen solid. The men refused to crawl from their blankets to cook. By morning a man lucky enough to have shoes found they were frozen so stiff that he could not put them back on his cracked and swollen feet. He burned paper and straw in them to thaw them out.

The men ate a substantial breakfast and set off on the second day's march. Donovan seemed to be everywhere on the road. Sometimes he spoke in a kind and affectionate way to his young soldiers so that they responded as a boy does to his father. Sometimes his words had a sharp bite to them, and men responded just as quickly to this. By some intuition he always seemed to know what manner to assume toward each of his suffering men. Always he appeared a man of resolution, cheerful and unbowed despite the fact that his pack too was piled high with the still falling snow and that he too, by the end of the afternoon, could not hide the utter fatigue that was engulfing the entire command.

At noon, Father Duffy noted, the bugle blew mess call, but there was nothing at all to eat. The men slumped in the snow and failed to make even the sardonic remarks that soldiers usually delight in. Toiling through the drifts, the hungry men begged food from farms and villages, even though they risked a stiff fine if Donovan saw them. The French, impoverished by the war, gave them raw potatoes. That night the men again slept hungry and cold in cattle sheds.

Kilmer wrote about the third day to his wife. "We had hiked seventeen miles that stormy December day—the third of a four days' journey. The snow was piled high on our packs, our rifles were crusted with ice, the leather of our hob-nailed boots was frozen stiff over our lamed feet."

On the evening of December 29, the 165th floundered through the snow into Longeau, their destination. French girls cheered the soldiers, and the men blew them kisses. They broke into "In the Good Old Summertime" and, standing knee-deep in the snow, with the bandsmen blowing through frozen instruments, they entertained the French girls with some good old American songs. Donovan grinned. He had brought his men through their first ordeal.

The 32nd Battalion of French Chasseurs had been selected to instruct the 69th in open and trench warfare at Longeau. The regiment would join the French for their baptism of fire at Lunéville in the middle of February. A weary stalemate continued on the western front, and the Allies planned to use the lull in the fighting to train the fresh American troops so that, when the decisive spring battles began, they would be ready.

The French and American commanders of the Field Officers' School where Donovan had trained had been deeply impressed by his keen mind and quick command of the information learned. They now put in a request to transfer him to a new school that was to be formed. It would mean an advance in rank, but Donovan wanted no part of it. First he sent Lt. Oliver Ames to see Gen. Douglas MacArthur at division headquarters to try to prevent such a transfer. Ames reported that there was indeed such an order; in fact, it had been issued ten days before but had been held up because the Rainbow did not want to lose such an effective field officer.

Donovan went to see MacArthur, who confirmed what he had told

Ames. MacArthur listened to Donovan's complaint. "Let's go, Bill," he cried. "Don't let them get you away from the line. Fighting men are the real soldiers."

MacArthur and Donovan jumped into MacArthur's staff car and drove the 40 or so miles to general headquarters at Chaumont, where the two men strode in unannounced on General Pershing. MacArthur did the talking. He told Donovan's story and urged that Pershing keep Donovan in his command. Pershing nodded approval, and Donovan was free to rejoin his men at Longeau.

"Perhaps I am foolish to stay here," he wrote in his diary upon his return to Longeau. "Perhaps I should seize the opportunity of getting in that new school where I know both the commandant and the director. But I want to stay by these men here and finish the job. I told the colonel that I did not expect promotion, that I was content to serve as a major, and that I was going to turn out the best battalion in the entire army."

Donovan's men were issued steel helmets, hand grenades, and two gas masks apiece, one English and the other French. They were now housed in the red-roofed village of Percey, south of the old fortress town of Langres in the Haute Marne. The officers were billeted in houses and the men slept in haylofts. Despite the chill winter, Donovan soon had his men running over the roads again. He encouraged them to box and himself put on the gloves with soldiers who challenged him. The Chasseur officers charged with training the 165th thought Donovan an odd sort of officer, but then he was an American, and Americans were indeed curiously democratic. There was no doubting the immense hold he had on his command.

At Percey many a young American accustomed to throwing a baseball overhand learned the English overhead bowling delivery that seemed appropriate for hurling grenades with accuracy. They tossed the grenades into a pit, where they exploded with a satisfying roar. The men dug trenches for practice, and learned how to fire French machine guns, the Stokes mortars, and one-pound cannon. They lunged with fixed bayonets at targets.

"I went out on the rifle range with a few delinquents and some prisoners as well as two or three officers," Donovan wrote. "Prepared the field for tomorrow. I now have a string of eighty targets, half for auto rifles and half for ordinary rifles. The range sets in a little arroyo between two hills and makes an excellent place. We have completed a throwing place for grenades, and the men are now getting the idea. Most of them do exceedingly well."

Donovan rehearsed combat skills himself. One day as he practiced with his pistol, he made believe he was attacking a German position. "You must do that in this kind of work to get anything out of it at all," he wrote to his brother Vincent. "I played at the defense of a shell hole, at killing a German while running towards him, and all kinds of things I used to do as a youngster on the stairway on dark nights."

Donovan now lived in the old château overlooking Percey. "Begin at my feet and move up," he wrote to Ruth one night. "A pair of felt slippers, army socks, flannel trousers and the inside of a trench coat. That is real luxury. A blazing fire, a real oil lamp, and you have all the conveniences."

He also now had an orderly, John Patrick Kayes, a soldier who used to be Col. Vincent Astor's valet. Other officers were quick to accept Donovan's invitation to lunch or dinner, served in his room by the attentive Kayes. One evening Donovan gave a sumptuous dinner in honor of the commander of the Chasseurs.

When fellow officers dropped in to see him, they found Donovan hospitable and talkative. "I called on Donovan this evening and found him sitting in a big, chilly chamber in the old chateau in front of a fire that refused to burn," Duffy wrote in his journal on February 2.

> He had had a hard day and was still busy with orders for the comfort of men and animals.
>
> "Father," said Donovan, "I have just been thinking that what novelists call romance is only what men's memories hold of the past, with all realization of the discomforts left out, and only the dangers past and difficulties conquered remaining in the imagination. What difference is there between us and the fellow who has landed at the Chateau in Stanley Weyman or Robert Stevenson's interesting stories, who has come in from a hard ride, and is giving orders for the boarding of his horse or the feeding of his retinue, as he sits with his jack boots pulled down, before the unwilling fire and snuffs his candle to get sufficient light to read his orders for the next day's march."

Duffy and Donovan talked long, with Donovan doing most of the talking. "I get much comfort from the Major's monologue," the chaplain further jotted in his journal. "It supplies an excellent romantic philosophy with which to face the sordid discomforts which are the most trying part of war."

Duffy called on Donovan often, as did Lieutenant Ames. Ames, who had served Donovan well on his mission to General MacArthur, had won his commander's friendship and confidence. Donovan made him his adjutant. On January 27, an exuberant Ames wrote to his parents:

> What do you think the Major then did? He made me his adjutant, which is the greatest honor I've ever had; it couldn't be so great with any other major but Bill Donovan, but he, to my mind, and in fact to every officer who really knows him, is the "livest" officer in the American Expeditionary Force; and some day when people at home begin to hear

about him you ought to be proud that your son was once his adjutant. Perhaps you wonder why, if he is such a "live wire" he is not more than a major; the answer is that for the last two months, general headquarters have been trying to get him on the staff, but he hates the staff and has his heart set on having the best battalion in the United States Army, and with the most wonderful management has succeeded in "ducking it," at the same time keeping in good graces. I'm awfully afraid, however, we'll lose·him soon, which would be a calamity.

Ames soon realized that being Donovan's adjutant was not going to be a sinecure. He wrote home, "After the first four days, I was really all in. I was so unused to the speed. Donovan has a wonderful mind, the result of years of training, has energy, is untiring, his personality is the strongest I've ever come in contact with, and with it all he combines the most consummate tact."

For a short time Donovan rode a horse as he went about his duties. "Have been riding a Government borrowed horse for the last few days, and he was terrible," he wrote. "He had a head, four legs, and a tail. That was his nearest resemblance to a horse."

The men went on maneuvers, took long marches, and repaired their clothes, now of winter issue. "The spirit of the men was wonderful," said their commander. "They are all believing that they are in the best battalion in the army. Last night we practiced men in the relief of trenches. We were on a high hill, and down in the valley we could see the thin light of passing trains and hear the faint rumble of cannons in the distance. The men were quite impressed, and some a little frightened. All of them went quietly. I stood near the front line trenches they had built, and some of them were keenly observing the wheat field in front of them as if it were sown with Germans. They played the game."

One day Donovan's brother Tim, now a military surgeon, rode 6 miles on horseback to visit him. He arrived more than a little sore. "It will probably be my last chance to see him," Donovan noted.

In the middle of February, Donovan led his men, some wearing new English shoes too large for them, away from Percey. They hiked about 10 miles to the train. "I marched at the rear of the column and kept men from straggling," he wrote. "Men in addition to their packs had musettes of automatic ammunition. These weighed at least thirty pounds each."

When Thomas Johnson, war correspondent for the *New York Sun*, happened along in his car, Donovan persuaded him to load the ammunition in the back seat and trunk and carry it to the railroad station toward which the column was laboring.

The battalion boarded a train of 40-and-8s and started on their way. Corporal Hogan wrote, "Cooties seemed to become especially restless in the close atmosphere of the boxcars, and each little cootie had a way of protesting all his own. Now when forty men roll around the hard floor of a dark boxcar, all scratching violently together, the resulting medley is not an inspiring one."

Some of the men cursed and some sang as the train went swaying and jouncing through the night. In the morning the men ate a ration of canned "Willie" and hardtack. They arrived at 6:30 A.M. in Lunéville. German observer planes flew overhead as they disembarked. The men marched to a nearby village, where they found billets. On February 21, the regiment paraded in the main square of Lunéville and was reviewed by Major General Bassiliere, commander of the 17th French Army Corps.

"In the midst of it, an aeroplane," wrote Donovan in his diary, "but it was driven off. It is strange how these Dutchmen get word of these things."

Bombers were expected every night. "In my house there is a nice large cellar," said Donovan, "to which I know the way without a guide."

On February 27, the First Battalion moved out for the front.

6

A Wood Called Rouge Bouquet

THE FIGHTING 69TH RELIEVED a French unit on a quiet sector near Lunéville. Donovan's First Battalion was the first into the trenches. He set up his command post beneath a road culvert near Rouge Bouquet. Duckboards led to damp trenches cut through a woods to the jagged front line. Beyond, tangled with barbed wire and swept by gunfire, no-man's-land extended to the German lines, perhaps 2 miles away. It was a quiet sector and the trenches were not well kept up.

"Off duty the men lived in mean little dugouts, thinly roofed, poorly floored, wet and cold," noted Father Duffy.

Situated some 3 miles behind the trenches, the support area, which the men called Camp New York, was to Corporal Hogan "the muddiest camp in France. It oozed, quivered, and trickled. It slipped down our backs, matted our hair, got into our eyes, and savored our food. We floundered and splashed and clunked through its wallows."

Duckboard walks ran through Camp New York, but they were so narrow that when two men met, one of them had to step off into the muck.

Donovan rotated the companies in the trenches so that at first companies A, B, and D were in the lines and C Company was kept in a support position. At night the men ventured out into no-man's-land on patrols. They cut the wire and scouted for enemy raiding parties.

"At daybreak this morning," Donovan wrote to Ruth, "a patrol returned, bringing only a bouquet of tulips and forget-me-nots gathered in no-man's-land. Incredible, isn't it?"

Sometimes the Germans, for no particular reason, peppered the American line with machine-gun and rifle fire. American artillery in back of the Fighting 69th, impatient with waiting, would open up on the German rear, and the Germans would shoot back. They fired huge aerial torpedoes, called minenwerfers, that came wobbling through the sky to blast enormous holes wherever they hit. At first Donovan's men derided what they called flying G.I. cans, but when they heard the terrifying roar of their explosion and saw the destruction that they wrought, their ridicule stilled.

Privates Arthur Trager and John Lyons of Company D were wounded in a fusillade, becoming the first casualties of the First Battalion. On the whole, however, there was so little fighting that Donovan led his men on cross-country runs, leaping streams and climbing over barbed wire, just to keep them trim. He also set up a blackboard in his command post and lectured his officers about the terrain and strategy.

On March 1, two officers and 50 men of the First Battalion advanced through no-man's-land and drove the German defenders out of a strong point in advance of their lines. Four men were killed, three wounded, and one missing, but the point was held against German counterattacks. Although a minor action, it was the first permanent gain made by American troops in France, making their first appearance in the lines.

The German troops raided the trenches held by the First Battalion. They attacked seven times in one night and were driven off seven times. Tim O'Rourke, standing next to Lt. Thomas Young, caught a German sniper in his rifle sights and fired. "Boys, I got my first German," he announced with satisfaction. The next instant a grenade, lobbed into the trench, exploded and killed him. Death was not yet such a commonplace that the men were not deeply shocked. An officer attempted to quiet the fears that rose up in each man.

"Boys, we have two and a half million men behind us," he said.

"But they are a hell of a long ways behind," replied an ashen-faced young soldier.

The Germans, having grown weary of the unseemly disrespect the Americans showed for the informal truce in this quiet sector, opened up one night with a massive barrage. "High explosives, gas shells, shrapnel, and machine gun bullets made the night a hideous inferno," wrote Corporal Hogan. "The earth around us boiled and churned and groaned and shivered. The air above us hissed and roared and snapped."

Wild Bill was everywhere in the trenches, rallying his men. With Donovan's strong arm around his shoulders, his firm and confident voice in his ear, a young soldier about to break felt his courage renew.

Sergeant O'Neill remembered later, "Actually, he was the calmest man under fire I ever saw. Oh, you'd think he was standing at the corner of Broadway and Forty-second Street, not in the middle of a barrage. And he was always in the middle of everything. Bill was not a dugout officer. That's why he was such a great leader. Once the men realized that the major was going to keep calm no matter what happened, they began to count on him to do the right thing."

On March 5, the Second Battalion relieved the First Battalion in the trenches, and Donovan's men withdrew to the relative security of Camp New York. Donovan did not retire with his men but stayed on in the line to give the commanding officer of the Second Battalion the advantage of his experience in the fighting.

The Second Battalion's baptism of fire was not long in coming. The

Germans fired a devastating barrage. One minenwerfer landed squarely on the top of a ramshackle dugout, exploded, and dumped tons of rock and clay down on a lieutenant and 24 enlisted men. Donovan, standing with the Second Battalion's commanding officer in the command post beneath the road culvert, listened to the first report of the calamity brought by a frightened soldier. The officer in command was almost as shaken as the man who brought the grim news. When Donovan realized that the officer was not going to hurry to the trenches to find out for himself what had happened, he asked for permission to go in his place.

"No," he replied. "Majors are not expendable."

Donovan waited for a moment, his temper rising, and then demanded that he be given permission to go. Confronted with Donovan's flashing blue eyes, the commanding officer mumbled his permission, and Donovan was out the door on the run, slipping on the wet duckboards.

"Major Donovan found the men in line contending with a desperate condition," wrote Father Duffy in his diary. "The trenches were in places leveled by the bombardment and though the enemy were no longer hurling the big torpedoes, they kept up a violent artillery attack on the position. The only answer that we could make to this was from the trench mortars and one-pounders. One of these guns was blown clean out of position."

Donovan was anxious to get to the cave-in and the trapped men, but he knew that the first duty of a soldier is to hold his position. He quickly saw to it that the front-line defense was organized. Next, as he wrote to Ruth,

> Went around to each man on post, talked to him and straightened him out. It was just getting dark; flares were going up from the French and Germans, and there was tenseness in the air. I went down myself into this dugout where the men were working, got them organized a little better, and picking up ten men who had lost their way and wanted to get back with these two officers, started with them.
>
> This was about 8:30. I stopped for a minute to put my arm around a youngster who was on guard and asked him if he were going to let those damned Dutchmen get his goat, in response to which he smiled and said, "No," grasped his gun a little more firmly and resumed his watch more intently. [The boy was 17-year-old Eddie Kelly.]
>
> I was not more than two minutes away from him and had left the trench and got into a little path leading back through the woods, when a terrible bombardment commenced. We were out of all shelter, so I made the little detachment lie down in the woods while those large minenwerfers and shrapnel scattered around in a terrifying manner.
>
> Most of them were passing over the trench system with a whistling, penetrating noise and seemed to be seeking us out individually. They

were striking around us and lighting up the dead trees. In the blaze of the explosions you could see the twigs and branches and sometimes trees crash down. It did not last long and seeming to me that the trench system had not been touched, I gathered these ten men, who by this time were thoroughly frightened, together, and started out through the dark, very lonely muddy trail back to the post of command.

The party had not gone very far when the Klaxon that indicated a gas attack sounded. Donovan continued,

> We all put on our gas masks and grabbing one another's arms, hands, or sticks, resumed the march. After going about a quarter of a mile, I lifted my mask to test the gas, and feeling that the air was clean, took it off. I made the rest of them keep theirs on for a few minutes until I made certain.
>
> We then all took them off, and when we got about half way another gas alarm sounded. By that time these poor micks with me were scared to death. They got ploughing around—making so much noise that I thought we would have had the whole German artillery firing on us. Went back to one man who was particularly obnoxious and handed him a good punch in the jaw. That quieted all of them. Then I put one lieutenant in front, one in the middle, and I took up the rear and marched them back.

Donovan gave a few directions to the now completely demoralized commander. The second bombardment had scattered the men attempting to dig out those trapped in the collapsed dugout. The officer in charge came to Donovan.

"He was shaken and frightened," wrote Donovan to Ruth, "and no one seemed to know what to do, so I jumped up and said I was damned if I was going to see these men stay there without a chance, so I started out and picked up two of the lieutenants who had been with me before and whom I myself had trained, so I knew I could depend on them, and we went back."

The barrage had caved in part of the trench, through which the three men hastened. "As I entered the trench, I fell over the dead body of a soldier," Donovan wrote, "and found that it was the youngster whom just a few minutes before I had been talking to, and telling him what his duty was. It appears that after I left him and the shelling commenced, they had yelled to him to seek cover, but he refused to leave his post. He had been hit in the head with a piece of shrapnel and killed instantly. I hope, Ruth, that if my day should come here, I would be lucky enough to die as he did."

Donovan at last reached the shattered dugout. He ripped off his gas mask and coat and jumped into the hole, where the earth was still falling. "Thought again of you and the youngsters," he wrote, "wished I had finished my letter to you, and then made up my mind that the thing to do was to go to work. Had only a little entrenching tool. I started in digging after I knew that one man had been partly uncovered just before the last bombardment and had been talking and that his face must be somewhere near where I was. After a while, I made a hole leading to his face because I could hear the breathing, but the breathing was that of a man about to die. I talked to him and yelled to the others, but got no response."

Seven men who had been freed from the suffocating debris joined Donovan and the rescue party. The earth kept slipping and shifting around the diggers, threatening to bury them in turn. Close to where Donovan dug, a muddy hand, cold and lifeless, appeared in the muck.

Deep down to Donovan's left, a buried boy was shouting in his delirium. "Come on, come on, fellows!" he would cry. Then he would lower his voice to a poignant murmur. "Mother," he would beg.

"I wish I could give you the picture," Donovan wrote. "The winding stairway shattered, covering held by a few broken posts, one candle lighting our work, two young officers on the stairway tense and white and tired, and while willing to face all personal dangers rapidly losing their nerve at the cries of the poor devils and the absolute futility and hopelessness of it all.

"As I looked at that mass of earth it was brought home to me that nothing more could be done and that this must be their tomb. I did not want to go then, so I sent up a message to bring up the engineers. I almost wished that the rest of the covering would fall and bury me."

Donovan finally went up above and put three sergeants of his own battalion, who had been helping to orient the Second Battalion to trench warfare, to work on the front-line trench that had been smashed. He went up and down the trench, "saw these youngsters standing at their posts and told them what to do and quieted them down, and then, having sent away all the lieutenants and sergeants, I found myself alone. It was then two o'clock in the morning, and as I stumbled across the broken trenches, ran into those poor kids who were shivering, they didn't know whether from cold or fire. I did not know the way very well. I had no rifle, no revolver, nothing but a fancy cane, so I had to have some one with me. I caught hold of one husky youngster who had a rifle, and he undertook to guide me out."

The boy crouched low beneath the German fire and crawled along so slowly that Donovan pressed his cane against the seat of his breeches to keep him moving.

"When we got to the trail leading to the woods, he was in despair, and did not like the idea of starting out," Donovan continued, "so I had to get ahead of him and lead him. Luckily my bump of direction held good, and I went into our line instead of the Germans'."

By then it was 4 A.M. There was no transport, so Donovan hiked 4 miles to the regimental headquarters to report to the colonel. He then hiked back to the Second Battalion command post.

"I did not like the shell fire," he later wrote to Ruth, "but I found that the danger and responsibilities quickened my instincts and decisions so that I was able to do a lot of things which in reality I had no authority to do. But you would be surprised at the fear of the dark that men have, and you would wonder how the mere fact that a man is an officer and is standing with them has a guiding effect upon an enlisted man. These men did not know me. I was not their battalion commander, but all they needed was someone to talk to them."

The Rainbow Division cited Donovan as a "superior officer who has shown brilliant military qualities, notably on the seventh and eighth of March, 1918, by giving during the course of a violent bombardment an example of bravery, activity, and remarkable presence of mind."

French authorities awarded Donovan the coveted Croix de Guerre. "I told them that while I would like to have it for the sake of my wife and youngsters one day," he wrote to Ruth, "I did not think in this case I was entitled to one because I did only what I should have done—that I was not only a Major of a battalion, but an officer of the regiment and because of my rank more was expected of me."

Donovan finally accepted the award on the condition that the medal also be given to the three sergeants and the lieutenants who had worked under his direction. French General Gaucher pinned the Croix de Guerre on the chest of Maj. William J. Donovan in a ceremony on March 16. When other officers congratulated him on being awarded such a high honor for valor in his very first engagement, Donovan had little to say.

"All of which seems absurd to me," he wrote to Ruth, "because why am I here except to look out for those youngsters who are with us?"

Warwick Greene, proud of his aide of War Relief Commission days, learned of Donovan's Croix de Guerre and wrote to his mother, "Did you know that Donovan has won the Croix de Guerre? And with very, very complimentary remarks from the French. He should make a wonderful officer, that fellow, and I hear good things about him from everybody. He ought to go far if he doesn't get killed first. There should be a marvelous opportunity for men with a natural gift for military command in our Army. And I should say that Donovan has very great gifts for handling and leading men. I am delighted to hear that he has won distinction so soon."

General Charles Menoher brought Gen. James G. Harbord and Secretary of War Newton D. Baker to the sector. General Harbord and Baker were touring the battlefront. They came, as Harbord put it in his war diary, "to inspect a battalion of the old 69th, New York, now wearing a higher number in a greater army. The battalion was commanded by a nice-looking New York Irishman named Donovan, wearing a bright, new-looking Croix de Guerre conferred on him by the French the day before. General Menoher called the attention of the Secretary to it, saying, 'This officer is wearing this without warrant of law or regulations, Mr. Secretary.' The Secretary said to Donovan, 'I give you executive authority to wear that cross. If anyone questions your right to wear it, refer them to me.' "

Not all the officers in the Rainbow Division were proud of Donovan's Croix de Guerre, won in his very first engagement. Some at headquarters scoffed at a safe distance from the front and averred that nobody could be that brave or distinguished in conduct under fire.

Eddie Kelly was buried in Croismare in a plot near a roadside calvary. Donovan stood by, his face solemn, his blue eyes tearful. It hardly seemed to him then that he had done a good job of looking out for his youngsters. A marble tablet was affixed to the ruins of the dugout beneath which brave men had been crushed. "Here on the field of honor rest" began the inscription, followed by a list of the men entombed. Joyce Kilmer had intended to write a book about his life in the Fighting 69th. Now he wrote the poem "Rouge Bouquet," his first attempt at versification in a dugout.

> *In a wood they call the Rouge Bouquet*
> *There is a new made grave today,*
> *Built by never a spade nor pick*
> *Yet covered with earth ten metres thick.*
> *There lie many fighting men,*
> *Dead in their youthful prime,*
> *Never to laugh nor love again*
> *Nor taste the Summertime,*
> *For Death came flying through the air*
> *and stopped his flight at the dugout stair,*
> *Touched his prey and left them there,*
> *Clay to clay....*
> *Let your rifles rest on the muddy floor,*
> *You will not need them any more,*
> *Danger's past,*
> *Now at last,*
> *Go to sleep!*

Three days later the Germans sent a choking cloud of poisonous gas over the lines held by the 165th Infantry. Donovan immediately rejoined his First Battalion in Camp New York. Spring found the battalion recuperating in a village overlooking the Vosges Valley. To Donovan the view from the village resembled the Genesee Valley in his native New York just as it began to turn green, except that the fields were studded with French and German graves from the earlier fighting.

"Stretching for miles was the rich green meadowland and winding river," he wrote to Ruth. "Dusty red ploughed fields were splashed on the upper rim, and at intervals—much as David might set his building blocks on a green carpet—were dotted with many villages. You would be surprised to see how eagerly the men drank in the picture. Your soldier man is a sentimental person, and when he is happiest he is singing some lonesome melody of home or mother."

On St. Patrick's Day, a Sunday, Donovan and his men went to Mass. There were games during the day, and that night the regimental band played Irish airs. Father Duffy read Kilmer's "Rouge Bouquet" to the men for the first time.

"The last lines of each verse are written to respond to the notes of 'Taps,' the bugle call for the end of the day, which is also blown ere the last sods are dropped on the graves of the dead," he noted in his diary. "Sergeant Patrick Stokes stood near me with his horn and blew the tender plaintive notes before I read the words, and then from the deep woods where Egon was stationed came a repetition of the notes."

Egon was a bugler who played from the heart, and the men wept for their lost comrades. Donovan stood with his head bowed, tears welling from his eyes. Father Duffy looked about him at the regiment. "We can pay tribute to our dead," he said softly, "but we must not lament for them overmuch."

Donovan lifted his head and transfixed the chaplain with a steady gaze.

7

Taking Hell with Bayonets

AFTER ST. PATRICK'S DAY, Donovan's men, back in the trenches, prepared to carry out a raid. Donovan drilled his officers before the blackboard in the command post, and he exercised the men to be sure they were in condition for the attack. Donovan also studied a stone tablet by the roadside that commemorated the Duke of Lorraine's 400-year-old victory over the Duke of Burgundy on the same terrain.

Then on the morning of March 21, 1918, the American artillery laid down a barrage. Donovan and his men went over the top at 7:35 A.M. The previous night he had sent scouts out to cut the wire, and now the men poured through the gaps and ran zigzagging toward the German lines. At 7:50 the American artillery struck the German lines again, and when the men reached the enemy trenches they found that the Germans had pulled back. Then the German artillery opened up on their abandoned trenches, and the Americans in turn fell back to their own lines.

Two days later the entire 165th Infantry was withdrawn from the lines for a rest. They marched through Lunéville as German shells fell, speeding them on their way with the threat of death or dismemberment.

In March Father Duffy found Donovan and his men staying in the Haxo Barracks at the north end of Baccarat, a town in the gentle Meurthe Valley that had been partly destroyed by the Germans in 1914, its famous glass factory gutted by fire. "Dropped over in the morning to call on the First Battalion," he noted. "I found them in the field, where Donovan had had them lined up for a cross-country run. I prudently kept out of his way, until he was off with his wild youngsters."

Off went Donovan, still bent on keeping his men in the peak of condition, running over hills and through the woods, splashing through brooks, climbing over barbed-wire fences. A few hours later he burst back into sight, still running strong, followed by his boys, who now ran as strongly as he did.

"Oh, Father," he said as he stopped before Duffy, who had spent the time chatting with a Donovan aide. "Why didn't you get here earlier? You missed a fine time."

"My Guardian Angel was taking care of me, William, and saw to it that I got here late," replied Father Duffy.

That afternoon the regimental band came over to play for the men, and there was a vaudeville show. The men gave a loud cheer at Donovan's appearance and demanded that he make a speech. Donovan would have none of it, insisting that Father Duffy talk in his stead, which Duffy did.

"I got square by telling the story of a Major who had been shot at by a German sniper while visiting one of his companies in the trenches," he wrote. "He made a big fuss about it with the Captain who in turn bawled out an old sergeant for allowing such things to happen. The sergeant went himself to settle with the Heinie that was raising all the trouble. Finally he got sight of his man, took careful aim and fired. As he saw his shot reach home, he murmured, 'Take that, confound you, for missing the Major.' "

Donovan studied the top of his boots while the men of his command roared their approval of the chaplain's story. Later he was prevailed upon to sing for the men. He favored them with an Irish tenor's version of "The Heart of the Gas House District."

More familiar now with the qualities of his men, Donovan made command changes. He named Joyce Kilmer a sergeant and placed him in charge of field intelligence. He reasoned that the poet's fine eye for detail would enable him to make careful and accurate observations of enemy dispositions on midnight forays into no-man's-land.

"By the way, I'm a sergeant now," Kilmer wrote to Father Daly, a friend back in New York, on April 5. "I'll never be anything higher. To get a commission I'd have to go away for three months to a school, and then—whether or not I was made an officer—I'd be sent to some outfit other than this, and I don't want to leave this crowd. I'd rather be a sergeant in the 69th than a lieutenant in any other regiment in the world." Kilmer also refused a staff assignment on *Stars and Stripes* in his desire to remain with Donovan.

While the Fighting 69th rested in and around Baccarat, the Ohioans, who made up the other half of the brigade, held the line. On April 23, orders came for the New Yorkers to relieve the Ohio troops on the left of the Rainbow Division's sector. Donovan and his men marched over a road that led east of town across the Meurthe Valley and up into a gap in the high hills, beyond which the American line defended a string of villages. The First Battalion was once again first into the trenches that ran along the edge of the Bois Boubroux.

From the sheltering trees, Donovan and his men peered across no-man's-land for any sight of the Germans. To their right the trenches twisted over open ground to the eastern tip of Ancerville, where the regiment set up their machine guns in broken cellars and half-fallen walls. To the rear was a bivouac area where the regiment's supporting battalion lived in what the men christened Camp Mud. By then they were accustomed to what Alexander Woollcott called the sound of France: "Rain pattering on a steel helmet, while its wearer stands ankle-deep in the mud of trenches."

The First Battalion so dominated no-man's-land that the men boasted they could hang their wash to dry on the barbed wire. Almost every night Sergeant Kilmer and a few men scouted close to the German lines because Donovan, already an officer who understood the vital importance of knowing what his enemy was up to, had an insatiable appetite for information. Sergeant Major Lenist Esler, wounded and home from the front, told a *New York Times* reporter, "I was supply sergeant at the time, and Joyce Kilmer was a perfect trial to me. He would always be doing more than his orders called for—that is, getting much nearer to the enemy's position than any other officer would ever be inclined to send him. Night after night he would be out in no-man's-land, crawling through barbed wires, in an effort to locate enemy positions and enemy guns, and tearing his clothes to shreds. On the following day he would come to me for a new uniform."

On the night of April 28, Kilmer and his men scouted as far as a ruined church. Within the church Kilmer worked out a defense in case the Germans surprised the party, and he made mental notes about its location in case it became a possible strong point in battle.

As the party was about to leave, he said to the others, "I never like to leave a church without saying a prayer." The sergeant and his men knelt in the broken vault, prayed silently, and then slipped out of the church and into no-man's-land so they could be back in the American lines by dawn.

On another scouting expedition into the night, Donovan, Kilmer, and John Kayes crept through the woods to where they had heard a suspicious sound. They captured a German who was attempting to infiltrate the American lines wearing an American uniform. Woollcott visited the Fighting 69th on his journalistic rounds, and he wrote in a letter about Kilmer, "He had become quite an institution, with his arms full of maps as they used to be full of minor poetry, and his mouth full of that imperishable pipe."

Woollcott also marveled at Donovan, the commanding officer who would take risks to scout no-man's-land himself. But at division headquarters, General Menoher was outraged by the commander of the First Battalion, whose conduct endangered his life. When Father Duffy expressed the general's viewpoint to Donovan, he grimaced. He knew what the soldiers in the trenches thought of generals safe at headquarters. "Donovan says," wrote Duffy in his diary, "it would be a blamed good thing for the Army if some General got himself shot in the front line."

When things were quiet, Duffy found that there was an entirely different Donovan from the man who courted danger and whose men had come to look upon him as their greatest shield against death. Donovan, Ames, Duffy, Kilmer, and other soldiers talked together in the trenches and at the battalion command post, and there was much laughter.

"Books and fighting and anecdotes and good fellowship and things to eat and religion," wrote Duffy on May 15, "all the good old human interests are common to us, with a flavor of literature, of what human-minded people have said in the past to give them breadth and bottom."

At the time, Donovan's command post was in what Oliver Ames wrote home was a beautiful place. "Going out of the back door you came into this trench with apple trees and apple blossoms dropping over you, and lilac bushes also," he told his wife.

German snipers hiding in houses up on the hills picked off men just outside the headquarters door, but this did not suppress the delight that Donovan and his men took in the natural beauty of the world around them. They did, however, take a dim view of matters when a party of bold Germans invaded a company kitchen and made off with the beef intended for supper.

On June 10, the Fighting 69th took over a new sector from a French regiment adjoining an area called Rendezvous des Chasseurs, held by the Iowa regiment of the Rainbow Division. A high ridge reached out between two deep valleys choked with woods that led toward the German lines. The French had planted flower beds and strawberries around what now became Donovan's command post. When the lines were quiet, Donovan and his staff dined alfresco under the trees. An intact generating plant operated in the vicinity, and at night Donovan could lie in his bunk and read a French translation of Caesar's *Commentaries* with notes by Napoleon Bonaparte.

"I enjoy being with Donovan," wrote Duffy after a night chat in the command post. "He is so many-sided in his interests, and so alert-minded in every direction, and such a gracious attractive fellow besides, that there is never a dull moment with him."

Father Duffy also observed how devoted Ames and Weller, Donovan's two lieutenants, were to their superior. He wrote,

> Ames takes me aside periodically to tell me in his boyish, earnest way that I am the only man who can boss the Major into taking care of himself and that I must tell him that he is doing entirely too much work and taking too great risks and must mend his evil ways. I always deliver the message, though it never does any good.
>
> Just now I am not anxious for Donovan to spare himself, for I know that he has been sent here because in spite of its sylvan attractiveness, this place is a post of danger, so situated that the enemy could cut it off from reinforcements and bag our two companies unless the strictest precautions are kept up.

When a German gas attack struck neighboring French troops, Donovan visited the French to observe how effective the attack had been and how the French had countered it. He was indeed doing all he could to take precautions against anything the Germans might do. For the moment, his command's most formidable foe was Spanish influenza, which struck in epidemic force on June 15. Donovan went about sympathizing with his sick soldiers as if he were a father of a group of boys back home.

Sergeant O'Neill, 20 years old, found himself commissioned and placed in command of a company. Donovan congratulated him.

"O'Neill," he said, "these are great soldiers; they'll take hell with bayonets if they're properly led."

The long stalemate on the western front was about to end. German Gen. Erich Ludendorff had massed 200,000 men for a last offensive, and the 42nd Division was withdrawn from Chasseurs to become part of Gen. Henri Gouraud's Fourth French Army, which was fated to meet the onslaught. The 77th Division, which had been raised in New York City, was to replace the 42nd. As the men of the Fighting 69th, marching by night over moonlit roads to escape German observation, met units of the relieving troops, they recognized old friends from home, and traded insults and badinage. One of Donovan's men saw his brother among the troops heading for the front. The two men rushed into each other's arms, sobbing and laughing at the same time.

"Take care of yourself, you old son-of-a-bitch!" cried the soldier in the 69th as his brother went swinging away toward the Germans.

The soldier stood there as his fellows marched through the night, until Donovan, who had watched the emotional encounter, put an arm around his shoulders. "Come on, son," he said in the soft voice that never failed to strike home to the hearts of his men, "the Germans would not dare to harm a hair of an Irish lad's head."

The men from New York marching both to and from the front sang together in soft voices as they passed each other: "East Side, West Side, / All around the town. / The tots sing 'Ring-a-Rosie,' / 'London Bridge is falling down.' "

On the first day, the 69th hiked to Noyement over hilly Lorraine roads. By June 22 they were at Marieville, and then at Châtel-sur-Moselle they took a train. The next day they transferred to another train and continued their circuitous route around the German salient, transferring from one train to another to Nancy and down to Neufchâteau, and northwest again to Bar-le-Duc. On June 24 they detrained at Coalus, south of Châlons-sur-Marne. They were quartered in five villages along the River Coole in the province of Champagne, where white stone houses roofed with gray tile stretched along shady roads.

Only two nights later they left the villages to hike along the dusty road. The men jested and sang as they marched into Châlons with its cathedral and houses of chalk stone. Cobblestones were hard beneath feet used to mud. Soon they were out of town, marching through villages to Bois de la Lyre, situated on a plain and seeming too open to enemy attack to men who had grown accustomed to the hills of Lorraine.

Blue skies in the days that followed looked down on violets and poppies. For the time being, Donovan's battalion was being held in support. On July 4 he stood on the ancient Roman road that led toward the battle line and thought about his nation's independence and of the fate of nations whose time had come and then gone. The man who read Caesar's *Commentaries* in search of age-old insights into battle was deeply moved. He knew that one of the Great War's most decisive battles was about to begin and that his battalion would be in the thick of it.

"I don't expect to come back," he wrote to Ruth, "and I believe that if I am killed it will be a most wonderful heritage to my family."

It is probably just as well that Ruth had no opportunity to reply to such a grim letter as she waited in her Buffalo home, stricken by the terrifying events in Europe in which her husband was playing such a dangerous role. And it is just as well she did not know that French commanders expected only token resistance from the still green American troops. They anticipated that the Americans would stand against Ludendorff's veterans only a few hours and then would fall back shattered. The pursuing Germans would lunge after them and fall into a trap to be sprung by the French. The Americans were to serve as little more than the bait to tempt the Germans into the trap.

Donovan studied his maps and the terrain. He read General MacArthur's orders with considerable anger. MacArthur, who understood the French strategy, had instructed the regimental commanders to post only a few men in the first trench line, which would easily fall. Most were to be positioned in the second line, from where they were also expected to withdraw as the Germans swept ahead.

On July 15 at 12:04 A.M., the German artillery commenced one of the war's most tremendous barrages. When at 4:30 A.M. the artillery stopped firing as suddenly as it had started, the silence over no-man's-land was dreadful. The first Germans appeared wraithlike, running toward the American lines through the morning mist. Minenwerfers suddenly rained down on the defending Americans, and machine guns chattered death. The Americans who escaped the first charge scrambled back to the second line.

The Germans found themselves in full possession of the American first trenches; they thought they had won. They shouted and cheered and broke into song. Then the American barrage opened up on the trenches. Since each piece of artillery had been carefully zeroed in on

the trenches when they were still in American hands, the accuracy of the gunfire was uncanny. Some of the crack Prussian Guards still managed to reach the second line of trenches, but they too were repulsed, after bloody hand-to-hand encounters. The Germans broke off the attack.

To Donovan's disgust, the Germans resorted to subterfuge. Four Germans, each with a red cross emblazoned on his arm, carried a stretcher up to the lines held by the 69th. When they were close, they yanked a blanket from the stretcher to reveal a machine gun, with which they opened fire. The Americans shot them dead. Still another group tried to infiltrate the American lines one night wearing French uniforms. They too were shot. All told, some breakthroughs were made, but the German attack had been halted by the Americans. They had not been defeated as the French battle plans had expected they would be. After three days of battle, the Germans began to pull back, except from the Château-Thierry salient.

Donovan was jubilant, and he wrote to Ruth, who could scarcely believe her good fortune in having escaped widowhood: "America is now magnificent—beyond anything I expected. Her ideals clearer, her purpose higher than all the others. Another thing. Have you considered that before long America will be the strongest nation, with her fleet, her industries, her Army, all organized? I wonder if, as these increase, envious eyes may be cast upon her. I hope the war won't end that way."

After a week, the Fighting 69th was moved to the vicinity of Château-Thierry in the now familiar 40-and-8s. When they arrived in Château-Thierry, they discovered that the town had been wrecked by the fighting only a few days before. Donovan and his men knew that they had been pulled out of a victorious battle to spearhead an attack on the German salient, which still thrust deep into the French countryside. It promised to be a bloody business. The night of July 24, Donovan and Ames walked out into the country along the Marne to a place called La Fère, where Donovan waited patiently for his adjutant to write a letter to his wife.

"We missed our automobile ride and had to walk home," Donovan wrote later on. "We knew that it was going to be a hard fight that we were going into, and that our battalion would be picked for the most difficult job. I told him that we both had to consider that we might finish there."

Because of the First Battalion's superior conditioning and lightweight equipment, upon which Donovan insisted, it was counted upon to drive ahead in battle. Donovan's fighting spirit was already a legend in the American Expeditionary Force, and his superiors knew he would lead his battalion against the Germans with a dash that would be essential if the Fourth Imperial Prussian Footguard were to be defeated.

On July 25, the battalion climbed into French trucks driven by Vietnamese, brought from Asia by the French. The trucks wound their way among the ruins and out into the country. "The road was crammed with all kinds of marching troops," wrote Donovan to Oliver Ames's wife, "huge artillery and supply trains, and the air was filled with airplanes and balloons. It was like a country circus, and Oliver was like a youngster at it, enjoying every minute. That night he and I crawled in under the bare boards of an old ambulance and managed to get two hours' sleep."

Donovan and his four company commanders made a reconnaissance toward the German lines while Ames marched the battalion into its billets and prepared it for action. The First Battalion was to lead the American attack, and Donovan, true to character, wanted to know what the tactical situation was. Upon their return to the American lines, Donovan and his officers found themselves under heavy shelling.

"In the afternoon," he wrote, "we ran into a terrific fight, very hot and bloody. Two of my commanders were wounded, and a shell mixed with high explosives and gas hit the roof over my head. A rain of rocks and dirt and tiles fell about me, and I got a beautiful mouthful of gas. Back at the chateau a doctor gave me some sniffs of ammonia and fixed up my eyes with boric acid and laid me down on a billiard table to rest."

With Lieutenant Buck wounded and Lieutenant Hutchinson gassed, Donovan, suffering from the gas himself, remained at his command post in the château. Conflicting orders came from General MacArthur at division headquarters directing him to advance, then to wait, then to advance. When he was told that the original orders were to stand, Donovan got up from the billiard table, buckled on his helmet and gear, and went out to lead his men into action. The battle was fierce.

That night Donovan and Ames, as Donovan put it, "made relief, finishing about three o'clock in the morning of the 27th, and at eight o'clock, we found the Germans retiring. Of course there was a great scramble and very much to do and a general pushing forward of the line."

Ames and Donovan, despite their sleepless nights, led the pursuit of the Germans. On the afternoon of July 27 they passed east through a thick forest and came out on a hill crest overlooking the tiny Ourcq River. As they advanced, German artillery laid down heavy fire to cover the withdrawal of their infantry from the woods. Donovan, realizing how exposed his men now were, quickly extended his lines to make contact with the Iowans on the right.

"After a day of pursuit, we came in front of Sergy about seven o'clock that night," wrote Donovan after the battle. "We sustained a heavy bombardment and some losses." Ames was all over the field, he continued, "spreading cheerfulness wherever he went, and brave—

very brave. That night on the edge of the wood, we managed to lean against a tree together and got an hour or two of sleep."

Between nine and ten on the next morning, Donovan, with Ames at his side, advanced his entire battalion of a thousand men down a hill and across the Ourcq River on a narrow plank. He had been ordered to come to the relief of Company K, which, having followed the retiring Germans across the river, had encountered deadly resistance. He lost no time.

A young soldier, looking at the sluggish little stream beneath the plank, spat into it. "It needs all the help it can get," he explained.

Donovan's men never did get the hang of the French name and persisted in calling the plashy little stream the O'Rourke. Six men were killed during the crossing. Father Duffy came upon young Jack Finnegan, dying beside the river, and offered him his canteen.

"And what do ye have, Father?" the boy asked.

"Well, water, my boy."

"Water, sure, give it to the Ourcq. It needs it more than I do."

Once across the river, the men charged up a steep hill in Bois Colas and routed its German defenders. Donovan made no effort to hold the entire hill but contented himself with keeping the Germans from establishing it as a machine-gun position. He spotted his automatic riflemen and sharpshooters in a nearby wheatfield to harass the Germans, and positioned most of his men under the lee of a high inner bank of the river road.

"We held that hill all that day and night," wrote Donovan, "although we had nothing on either of our flanks, and Oliver and I managed to get one hour's refreshing sleep in a hole that he and my orderly Kayes dug out."

Beyond the meadow where Donovan had placed his sharpshooters, the Germans had established a machine-gun post at the Meurcy Farm. The stone house, connected to a stone barn and sheds by a stone wall, made a sturdy fortress from which the Germans could fire down into the meadows along the Ourcq. The morning of July 29, Donovan directed attacks on the farm from his command post on a little knoll at the edge of the forest, despite the murderous German machine-gun fire.

Sergeant Dick O'Neill found himself involved in the fighting from the start of the day. He wrote in his diary, "Donovan had sent me out in charge of a mission of great importance. The success or failure of this mission would determine, in all probability, if or if not a good many of my buddies would be alive at day's end. This was uppermost in my mind when the scrap began. As for the action itself, it all happened so fast I can't really tell you what I was thinking. But I can tell you one thing: I had no desire to get killed. Who the hell does?"

Lieutenant H. D. Scott, in command of a battery of 155 pieces, found Donovan at his command post. Scott had gone forward from Forêt de Fère to establish liaison with the 165th so as to support the infantry more effectively with his fire. He was not too happy about the very good possibility of getting shot; tucked in his pocket were fresh orders for home.

"After some plain and fancy ducking and driving," he wrote after the war, "we reached the infantry dug in on the hill of Bois Colas, under fire of small arms and shrapnel. They were firing from the forward edge of the woods on Meurcy Farm, Bois Brûlé, and a wheatfield between, at range of about four hundred meters. In command was Major William Donovan, who ever since has been my hero ideal of a soldier."

During a lull, Scott crawled back to Donovan's post of command and had a drink of French whiskey. About that time a very young soldier came running up. "Major, sir, the Germans are coming around the corner of the hill—there's a thousand of them," cried the boy.

"Oh, Lord," thought Scott, "here's where we get captured, and me with that order for home in my pocket." Scott loosened up the Colt .45 he had never yet fired in anger.

Donovan glared at the young soldier and remarked, "very calmly and emphatically," as Scott put it, "Why the hell come and tell me about it? Get your bayonets fixed and go out and get 'em!"

Soldiers around Donovan jumped up and trotted off through the trees with their equipment rattling. There was a burst of small arms fire, a few shouts. Then the men came back and took cover around their leader, ready for the next alarm. Harold Henderson, a youth who only a year before had been a student in a New York City high school, brought a message to Donovan through the German fire "as if he were an A.D.T. messenger on Broadway," according to Father Duffy. Donovan remarked on his bravery and then moved forward with his men up a creek bed that afforded some cover. Duffy later described what happened:

"Major Donovan, never happy unless in the middle of things, had gone up the bed of the brook so as to keep ahead of the advance of C on the left and A on the right. Lieutenant Ames, his adjutant, was with him, led by devotion as well as duty, for the Major was his ideal leader. They lay half in the brook, resting on the bank, when a sniper's bullet from the farmyard whizzed past Donovan's ear and struck Ames in the head, liberating for larger purposes a singularly attractive and chivalrous soul."

Another bullet struck Donovan on the hand. When others came up, they discovered Donovan, his hand bleeding, still half in the water, cradling the dead youth in his arms. Private Pat Gillespie swore, and when he saw a flicker of movement behind a dead horse lying in the farmyard, he fired and killed the sniper who most likely had killed Oliver Ames.

Donovan wrote to Caroline Ames about her husband's last morning:

> Early again the next morning we started out to advance. The elements on our right and left failed to move forward, and we pushed on, driving the Germans back slowly. I shall always be glad for one thing that I did. Our forward lines were held up, and I called to your husband who was a little behind me and had him lie down behind a little mound of earth. I then told him what fine work he had been doing and that he had saved a good many lives for the battalion, and that I was not going to forget it. We were together from that time on until I heard that an officer in charge of the first group of troops had been wounded. I told your husband to take charge of headquarters, that I was going forward. I went forward alone. As I ran through machine gun fire, I heard a running behind me and turned and saw Oliver coming. I told him to go back. He said, "no," that he was going to take care of me. I lay down by a little creek, and he came over beside me. A sniper, undoubtedly trying for me, hit him in the right ear. He died at once, painlessly.
>
> I would gladly that I had been the one, and he had been spared to you.

That night Oliver Ames's body was buried near where he had fallen. A corporal made a wooden cross from an empty ammunition box and placed it over the grave. "A courteous kindly gentleman and a true soldier," somebody carved on the cross, together with the name and "Killed in action on July 29, 1918."

Colonel Frank R. McCoy, commanding the 165th Infantry, summed up the fighting that led to Ames's death:

> My Third Battalion, commanded by Major McKenna, went over at daybreak and reached their objective without great loss, but their fighting Irish got the better of them, and they streamed up the open slopes to take Boche machine guns with their hands and teeth and as a battalion were soon finished; so that the First Battalion was ordered to make a passage of the lines. Ames came to my Post of Command under very heavy fire for final orders and took them back to Donovan, who with him soon appeared and led that battalion over the open valley so skillfully—he and Ames never handled a football eleven better—that with comparatively small losses they reached the heights around the Meurcy Farm and the following day the Bois Colas beyond the farm, where they were the arrow point of the whole Franco-American drive for four days and nights of bitter fighting.
>
> I worked my way out that afternoon and found Donovan determinedly planning and fighting, but feeling as though he had lost his right hand.

Donovan waited for a few weeks to write to Caroline Ames: "I have no desire to intrude upon your grief. I have refrained until you should be in receipt of your husband's citation for the Distinguished Service

Cross. It was the one thing I could do to very inadequately obtain some recognition of his magnificent work. Now I must hasten to get you word, because one cannot tell when one's own time is coming. More than my feeling of respect and admiration for his qualities as a soldier and a gentleman, there was between us an even deeper relation. To me he was like a younger brother."

Donovan had lost Oliver Ames, but he still had Joyce Kilmer, who took Ames's place as the battalion adjutant. "The Major placed great reliance on his coolness and intelligence," wrote Father Duffy, "and kept him by his side. That suited Joyce, for to be at Major Donovan's side in a battle, is to be in the center of activity and in the post of danger. To be in a battle, a battle for a cause that had his full devotion, with a regiment he loved, under a leader he admired, that was living at the top of his being."

The morning of July 30 dawned over the beautiful French countryside with a perfection totally out of keeping with the brutal events taking place. German artillery were dropping shells upon the First Battalion's positions when Dick O'Neill came upon Donovan, who was grieving for his lost friend. Donovan immediately told him that he must know how many machine guns the Germans had and exactly where they were placed. Then the artillery could zero in on them.

"Dick," he said, "it would be a lot better if your boys could knock out those guns. We could move faster."

"Dick," said O'Neill to himself, "this is a hell of a morning to pick to get killed."

O'Neill took 35 men and moved toward the German lines. Just as he located the guns, the Germans opened up. A bullet knocked the rifle out of O'Neill's hands. He still had his pistol, so he rushed forward and tumbled into a gravel pit where, to his dismay, 25 Germans and several machine guns were hidden. He threw his grenade and fired his pistol until it was empty. When the firing stopped, he had suffered five flesh wounds, and there were five dead Germans. The remainder surrendered, and O'Neill, bleeding from his wounds, had 20 prisoners to escort back to the American lines. He hadn't gone far when the German machine guns opened up. He was hit again, and several of the captives were shot dead by their own countrymen's fire.

When O'Neill brought the remainder of his captives into the lines, soldiers wrapped him in a blanket and started to carry him to a dressing station. O'Neill cursed them feebly and demanded that they instead take him to Donovan so he could tell him exactly where the German guns were located. The men, having seen his many wounds, argued that he must get to a doctor quickly.

"I'm not going anywhere until I tell the major where those machine guns are," he insisted.

The soldiers carried him to Donovan, who listened intently to his report and began to give orders. His mission accomplished, O'Neill fainted and was carried to the dressing station.

Donovan then went forward through Bois Colas to observe across open fields Bois Brûlé, which he knew must be taken. Kilmer, unbidden, followed. Both men lay at the north edge of the woods, from where they could study the enemy positions. Donovan moved ahead in order to see better, but Kilmer remained behind. When Donovan, having made his observation to his satisfaction, returned to Kilmer, he found him lying as if still scouting, his eyes looking over a little ridge at the edge of the copse. A bullet had struck him in the head, and he was dead.

"His body was carried out and buried by the side of Ames," said Duffy. "God rest his dear and gallant soul."

Private Edwin J. Stubbs, an A Company sniper, and Pvt. Walter Collins, a sniper from B Company, carried Kilmer in from the battlefield in a shelter half. Fourth Division engineers helped Donovan's men dig the grave.

"I remember distinctly," Stubbs said after the war, "finding a stout wooden stake and driving it into the ground at the head of the grave, then securely fastened one of Kilmer's identification tags thereto; later a wooden cross replaced the stake.

"I recall very clearly that after I had driven the stake home and when several of us paused to observe the work, a single 77 shell fell and exploded near our midst which caused us to scatter and hit the ground."

On July 31, First Battalion attacked Meurcy Farm. Donovan led the attack across the open fields from Bois Colas. John Kayes, Colonel Astor's former gentleman's gentleman, had until now kept well out of the battle, but with both Kilmer and Ames dead he was determined not to let his beloved major out of his sight. He followed Donovan on his rounds as the commanding officer prepared for the attack, and he disregarded instructions to go to the rear.

"The little stream running through the farm land was the point of division between the assaulting companies," Donovan noted, "A and C Companies being on the right of the advance, B and D on the left. Before we advanced, some of the regiment had been in the farm and in the farm house. As I was coming up, I saw a German detachment creeping back into position. As we advanced against the farm there were several members of our own regiment lying dead, which is proof to me that our outfit had already been there."

During the charge across the fields, Kayes was at Donovan's heels, his angular figure, stoop-shouldered and elderly, presenting an easy target. A German machine-gun slug hit him in the ankle, and as he pitched forward, other bullets hit him in the thigh, arm, and face.

Stricken, he still found strength to protest when Donovan swooped him up in his arms and carried him through the machine-gun fire back to the safety of Bois Colas. Kayes was evacuated to a hospital but died a few weeks later.

Donovan's men captured Meurcy Farm later that day. Fighting on August 1 was bloody. Donovan was concerned that the Germans might retake the farm, which had cost him so dearly to capture. "I kept everyone out of the farm building itself," he wrote in his war diary, "for fear of its being destroyed by shell fire, although we sent patrols into the building from time to time to be sure that no Germans were hidden in there."

All told in the fighting on the Ourcq, the 165th Infantry had lost 250 dead and 1,250 wounded. Donovan's casualties were high, since First Battalion had led the attack for six days. On August 2 at 4:00 A.M. Donovan sent patrols scouting forward, and they returned to report that, finally, the enemy had vanished. The Prussian footguard had fallen back to a ridge south of the Vesle River. Their division had lost 184 officers and 5,450 men in the battle.

Now that the fighting was over, the Fighting 69th could bury its dead. A pebble's toss from the Ourcq, Oliver Ames and Joyce Kilmer rested in fresh graves side by side. At the graveside services, a bugle sounded taps and "Rouge Bouquet" was read aloud. Alexander Woollcott reported, "The lines were read by Joyce's own beloved Father Duffy, and those who were there told me the tears streamed down the face of every boy in the regiment. They just blubbered."

Donovan, his hand wrapped in a bandage, one leg bloody from shrapnel, wept with the others. He had lost three of the finest friends he was ever to know, and all his life he was to live with an aching regret.

From the field hospital, Donovan wrote Ruth:

> In every day of that fight, our Battalion had participated. It had never retired, it had gone the farthest and stayed the longest. I hope that my name on the casualty list did not worry you. My wounds amounted to nothing. The one on the hand simply made a little bone bruise, for as luck would have it my hand was going away when the bullet struck. By the way I had been previously hit on the chest with a piece of shell which ripped my gas mask, and another fragment had hit me on the left heel, tearing my shoe and throwing me off balance. I think perhaps there is a little shrapnel in my leg, but I hope to have some pretty Red Cross nurse hold my hand while they take it out. I guess I have been born to be hanged.

8

Wild Bill Leads the Charge

ON SEPTEMBER 7, 1918, Donovan stood at stiff attention together with other officers and men of his command while General Pershing awarded them the Distinguished Service Cross. Donovan was cited for being "in advance of the division for four days, all the while under shell and machine gun fire from the enemy, who were on three sides of him, and he was repeatedly and persistently counter-attacked, being wounded twice."

"Pershing has been here and given us the crosses," he wrote to Ruth. He could also now sign his name "Lieutenant Colonel." There was talk about making him a full colonel and putting him in command of the regiment. "Oh, hell, Father," he told Duffy, "I don't want to be Colonel. As Lieutenant Colonel, I can get into the fight, and that's what I'm here for."

Donovan wrote to Ruth,

> One thing I am glad of, and that is that the system which I used in the training of the men justified itself. Their discipline and above all their spirit held them full of fight in a position which had previously been given up by two other outfits. Physical endurance will give one control of one's nerves long after the breaking point. Courage is the smallest part of it. These men who all along thought me too strict, and felt I had made them work when others did not work, are now convinced that I was right, and that I would ask them to do nothing that I myself would not do. This tribute is greater than any honor my superior officers can give me.

Although he remained in command of his troops, every few days in August Donovan made a trip to the field hospital to have his wounds cared for. There he saw his brother Tim, who was a surgeon with a Buffalo unit.

Only five days after Pershing had pinned the Distinguished Service Cross on his chest, Donovan was in action again. The German-held St. Mihiel salient thrust 30 miles into France from the town of St. Mihiel, crossing the Meuse River and cutting communications from Paris and Verdun to the Lorraine front. It was a barrier to the invasion of southern Germany. An attack on the salient by 450,000 American troops was scheduled, and in the vanguard was the Rainbow Division. The 165th Infantry was picked to lead the Rainbow's attack, and it fell to Lieutenant Colonel Donovan to spearhead the regiment's attack with his First Battalion.

On the night of September 11, Donovan and his men were at the southeast of the salient at Pont-à-Mousson on the Moselle River, 30 miles south of Verdun. Rain swept down on the river valley with nightfall, and the men kept to their billets. Only a few wet and chilled soldiers held the trenches until a few hours before the attack was to begin. The attackers filed into the trenches with a gloomy air that made Donovan apprehensive. His battalion had suffered heavy casualties on the Ourcq, and three out of every four officers and 65 percent of the men were replacements. Plainly the Germans were in a strong defensive position, and casualties were bound to be high.

At 1:00 A.M., with the rain still swirling about the trenches, the French and British artillery opened up with a mighty salvo. All along the front 3020 guns roared. Although the Germans had expected the American attack for days, the onslaught in the dark and rainy night caught them off guard. To Donovan's surprise no German guns fired back. Allied commanders did not know that the Germans had decided to give up the salient and were already moving valuable war materials out and beginning to withdraw their troops. One German commander of the 77th Reserve Division had misunderstood his instructions to withdraw and had kept two thirds of his men in position opposing the 165th, even though his artillery support had already withdrawn through St. Mihiel.

The rain stopped, but the dawn was cold and windy. Donovan moved through the trenches, smiling unless he noticed some preparation that was not exactly right. Then, either with a sharp command or a sorrowful look, he required the mistake to be corrected.

"There's nothing to it," he said. "It will be a regular walk-over. It will not be as bad as some of the cross-country runs I gave you in your training period."

Most of the men had never had that training period. They were young recruits fresh from the States, and they looked at this confident officer with amazement. They had heard about him long before arriving in the regiment, but here was the living reality, moving up and down the trenches, an officer unlike any other they had met.

"There's nothing to it," he said again and again. "It will be a regular walk-over."

The young soldiers began to believe him. Five o'clock in the morning was H hour. Four-inch Stokes mortars laid down a smoke screen and, behind a rolling barrage, the battalion started forward in a skirmish line through the barbed wire. Donovan raced back from the front

Top: As a boy William Donovan swam beneath the Michigan Avenue bridge on Buffalo's waterfront, where grain elevators rose beside turgid waters.
(Buffalo and Erie County Historical Society)
Bottom: In the 1890s young Donovan often sauntered along Elk Street in the Irish First Ward, only a few blocks from his home.
(Buffalo and Erie County Historical Society)

Donovan entered
St. Joseph's Collegiate
Institute at the age of 14.
He was captain of the
school's first football team
and an altar boy at nearby
St. Joseph's Cathedral.
(St. Joseph's Collegiate Institute)

Captain William J.
Donovan, the commander
of Troop I, First Cavalry,
New York National Guard,
shown here in dress
uniform. Although he grew
up on the Irish waterfront,
Donovan became the
leader of Buffalo's
adventurous blue-blood
troopers.
(Buffalo Cavalry Association)

Below: Seated before his tent, Donovan (center) and his aides study field maps near McAllen, Texas, during the crisis with Mexico in 1916.
(Buffalo Cavalry Association)

Right: In 1917, after the United States declared war on Germany, Donovan volunteered to serve as an officer in the 165th Infantry, better known as the historic Fighting 69th. To keep his men in trim, he led them on long runs over rough terrain, earning the lasting sobriquet of Wild Bill.
(Buffalo and Erie County Historical Society)

Donovan showed dauntless courage and keen military judgment under fire in action on the western front. Coupled with his charismatic leadership, these qualities made him one of the most admired field officers in the American Expeditionary Force.
(National Archives)

During a lull in the fighting, Donovan welcomes a French lieutenant whose patrol has just made contact with one of the 165th's battalion outposts.
(National Archives)

The war over, Colonel Donovan (left), now commander of the 165th Infantry, stands with Father Francis Duffy, regimental chaplain, outside headquarters at Remagen, Germany.
(National Archives)

Donovan (right) looks on while Gen. John J. Pershing awards Brig. Gen. Douglas MacArthur with the Distinguished Service Cross at Bulligny, France, September 7, 1918. MacArthur never forgave Donovan for winning more combat awards than he did in World War I.
(MacArthur Memorial)

French General Gaucher pins the Croix de Guerre on the chest of William J. Donovan on March 16, 1918. When other officers congratulated him, Donovan with characteristic modesty had little to say. He wrote home to his wife that receiving such a high award for simply doing his duty seemed "absurd to me."
(National Archives)

When the first caucus of the American Legion was held in Paris in March 1919, Donovan was an outspoken advocate of the enlisted man's views.
(American Legion)

wave when he saw that the support companies were moving too slowly through the wire. "Get moving!" he shouted. "What the hell do you think this is, a wake?"

Back at the head of the advance, Donovan led his men on a sweep to the left of Bois de Remieres. German machine guns fired with deadly effect, but the assault troops coolly deployed and fired back. The automatic teams crawled ahead. Donovan shouted for action, urging his men forward, standing erect as the Germans shot at him. "What's the matter with you?" he cried. "Do you want to live forever?"

Burdened with their ammunition and machine guns, crews got up and ran forward, stumbling beneath the heavy loads. They took new positions and fired point-blank at the astounded Germans. The infantry pushed ahead behind their leader at such a speed that they outran the rolling barrage, which had been set to advance 100 meters every four minutes. Snipping with wire cutters and blasting holes with bangalore torpedoes, the men charged through the old, rusty barbed wire that had held back the Allies for years. British and French tanks trying to assist them mired in the rain-sogged ground and were left far behind. The Germans fled, but Donovan and his men were on their heels, shouting, taking prisoners.

St.-Baussant fell to a bayonet charge. The next strong point was Maizeray. German troops firing from its walls pinned down Donovan's battalion. He led 30 of his men down the Meuse River and crossed the shallow Rupt de Mad River out of sight of the German machine gunners and artillery. The attackers slipped through the woods around the enemy flank and opened fire. Enemy machine gunners fired back, and a battery of artillery only 500 yards away opened up. But they could not stop the attack.

"Kamerad!" cried the German infantry and gun crews, and threw up their arms in surrender. By the afternoon of September 12, the attack had gone beyond the first day's objectives. French civilians crawled out of cellars in farmhouses and villages and stared at the Americans. Donovan's men overran paneled dugouts fitted with electricity, running water, and dining and recreation rooms that had kept the Germans comfortable for several years. They ate food left in German field kitchens.

The Rainbow Division was moving up in force on all sides, and Donovan pressed forward. He established a prisoner park on a road into the village of Essey, where tanks helped to crush resistance. "Prisoners began to come back to us in droves," wrote Donovan. "We had to press forward so fast that we could not keep track of them, but gave them a kick in the backside and sent them on their way."

By one o'clock in the afternoon of the second day, Donovan and his men were in the town of Pannes. The First Battalion command post was in a dugout. Donovan sat within, giving orders to his men and taking reports as officers and noncoms came in and out of a drizzle that had begun. The officers debated whether to move the artillery forward with the assaulting infantry, something that had not yet been done. Donovan cut off the talk.

"Well, we have not done it before, but we'll give it a whirl this time," he said.

The Germans reeled from the shock of the 42nd Division's attack, but they recovered and fought back. The battle line rolled back and forth, and the outcome of the war had come to depend on this terrible struggle.

Donovan's next headquarters was in a forester's house on the road to Haut-Mont. Sergeant Moore of B Company brought in a German prisoner to be interrogated. The prisoner said he was a sentinel at a machine-gun post manned by an officer and eight men. He offered to lead the Americans to the post and promised that all would surrender but the officer and a noncommissioned officer. Donovan distrusted the man, but he finally suggested that a rope be put around his neck and he be allowed to guide a patrol to the machine-gun position. So restrained, the man led the Americans to the post, which did indeed surrender, except for the officer, who died rather than give up.

Donovan advanced his headquarters to a hut near Hassavant Farm. Lieutenant Richard Allen came off of a patrol, hungry and tired. Donovan's orderly put a roast beef sandwich and cup of coffee on the table before him. Before he could eat it, a soldier brought in two prisoners, a Romanian boy of 16 and a tall old German soldier, who had become lost in the woods during the German retreat. They had surrendered to a patrol. Donovan grabbed the sandwich with one hand and the coffee with the other. He handed the sandwich to the surprised boy and the coffee to the old soldier.

Lieutenant Allen was dismayed. "Colonel, it is against regulations to feed prisoners," he protested, "before they have been questioned at Division. You should not feed these men."

"Allen, you ought to be ashamed of yourself. This poor little boy has been wandering around in the woods for two days with nothing to eat," said Donovan.

"Besides, that was my sandwich," insisted Allen.

"And you, a great big healthy man, would take his meal away from him!" finished Donovan.

The Rainbow Division's advance drove the Germans out of villages, forests, and ridges. Other U.S. divisions attacked in support. After two days the Germans withdrew behind the Hindenburg Line. Three days after Donovan led the first skirmish line into action, the St. Mihiel salient, held since 1914 as a dagger thrust at Paris, had ceased to exist.

Donovan's last objective was St.-Benoît. The Germans had set fire to the town before they fled. "One group discovered the church ablaze," Donovan wrote in his journal, "and ran in to save what they could. They carried out pictures of St. Anthony of Padua and of the Holy Virgin, as well as some sacred vessels. A scout found a bag of potatoes which the Germans had left behind, so while the men worked in relays putting out the fire, those off duty roasted their potatoes in the embers."

The Rainbow Division was kept in the line until September 17, when it was relieved. Orders soon arrived for Lt. Col. William J. Donovan to report for duty at the Staff College. There would be a promotion. At Donovan's insistence General Menoher, commander of the 42nd Division, and General MacArthur did their best to keep him with the 165th Infantry. Because the provost marshal general of the division wanted a soldier and lawyer with a knowledge of French at headquarters, they could only win assurances that Donovan would not be transferred until after the next battle. The American Army was getting primed for the Argonne offensive, and it was agreed that nothing should be done to weaken the assault. Donovan was undeniably the most impressive combat officer in the division.

"The outstanding figure in the mind of every officer and man was Lt. Colonel William J. Donovan," Father Duffy wrote in his diary. "Donovan is one of the few men I know who really enjoys a battle. He goes into it in exactly the frame of mind that he had as a college man when he marched out on the gridiron before a football game, and his one thought throughout is to push it through."

The German Kriemhilde Stellung consisted of three lines of trenches, each defended by barbed wire that ran east and west past the villages of St. Georges and Landres-et-St.-Georges in the Argonne Forest.

"We were suddenly ordered forward to relieve another Division, the First," Donovan wrote to Ruth. "The same old jumble of troops and caissons and trains on the road, only now the roads more slippery and more in need of repair. Our way led past freshly killed and yet unburied Germans, through unmistakable smell of dead horses to a farm in a valley where we parked our wagons and disposed of our men. The farmhouse had been used as a dressing station for one of the regiments of the other division. Outside was a huge collection of torn and bloody litters, broken salvaged equipment, reddened underclothing and discarded uniforms, all of our own men—the cast off of the dead and wounded."

A "nice fat Y.M.C.A. man in a suit of blue overalls and a sombrero" served hot cocoa from a big cauldron and beef on bread. "There could have been no better meal," said Donovan.

He slept that night in an ambulance. In the morning Donovan

established the regimental commander in a cellar. Since he had been chosen to lead the assault when the battle began, he then went to the front to survey the position that the 165th was going to occupy.

> The division preceding us had a terrific fight just three days before, and the ground was a stew of dead—Boche and American. One attack had evidently been made in the morning mist and as it cleared an entire company was caught on a little rise. The bodies were laid out in rows. It was easy to determine the formation and the plans of the different leaders. In one hole we found a wounded German who had lain there three days afraid to come out—in another, a wounded German and wounded American who had crawled in the same hole, shared their water and cigarettes, and then, rolling into the German's blanket, had gone to sleep.
>
> The support line was in rear of a long ridge running some three kilometers. This was the ridge the Germans had held commanding the valley. I went to their machine gun positions. Gun after gun was there with the gunners lying beside them, dead. From these positions I could look back across the valley and then it was easy to see how heavy a toll could be demanded for entrance there. Over this ridge and into the next valley. Here the Germans had a prison camp. The shacks of the officers had been on the northern slope of the ridge and had evidently been well equipped. Now they were shell broken, full of gas, and in pitiful disorder. Near some of them were the bloody torn bodies of what were evidently orderlies. In the valley itself were the prison buildings similar to all such in all armies. The wooden shacks with bunks and small bit of land enclosed with barbed wire some ten feet high. On the other side of the valley were two knolls which were the westerly continuation of the ridge. This was our advanced position.

Donovan observed more American dead than German, showing the determination of the Americans to go forward regardless of cost. He reported his findings to his own regiment and went with the First Battalion when the Rainbow relieved the First Division.

"I decided to occupy the whole of the Côte de Maldah so as to prevent the Germans from getting any part of it and thereby perhaps making the reverse slope untenable." Donovan recognized that the Côte de Maldah was the key to the whole situation and must be firmly in American hands.

It rained for a week, making the front a morass of mud, but on October 12 Donovan moved into an attack position. He established his command post on the long ridge that was called the Côte de Châtillon.

"I slept two hours that night under a shelter tent," he wrote, "and except for a few telephone interruptions had a good rest. With the telephone lying beside you, it is not bad. I was on, as were all the men, the reverse slope, well under the top. Our only danger was from splinters."

On the morning of October 14, very early, he received orders that the attack would be made at dawn.

"There were a multitude of things to do, and the orders coming so late they could not be done properly," he complained to Ruth.

"Instead of taking off all signs of rank, as officers are supposed to do to avoid being made a mark for sharpshooters," Father Duffy noted, "he had donned a Sam Brown belt with double shoulder straps so that none of his men could miss knowing who he was; that the enemy also would pick him out was a matter of serene indifference."

"Another thing I did was to provide for extra bandoleers of ammunition and extra canteens of water," Donovan wrote.

> Besides having both sent up from the rear, I arranged to have men collect the bandoleers from the dead and wounded after the advance began, and the canteens from the dead. Much to our disgust, some of the canteens sent up from the rear were uncovered French ones, the metal of which reflected the sun, so that, of course, no one wanted one of them anywhere near him.
>
> That night I sent out a patrol to look over the sunken road we had chosen for a jumping off point. Their leader, whom, as I remember, was Knolles, reported to me on his return that he had gone beyond the sunken road and found nothing on the way out, but that on the way back they had fallen over a small German outpost. His patrol fired at the outpost and the outpost fired at them. However, he ran into no other Germans than this one outpost. From this I concluded that the Germans had no position south of the sunken road.

German shells thundered down on the sunken road as Donovan prepared to take the 165th Infantry into action. "Come on, fellows!" he cried when zero hour came. "It's better ahead than it is here." To the right and left, commanders new to fighting and green troops still clung to cover. "Come on, we'll have them on the run before long!" he shouted.

Donovan put a strong arm around a scared boy. "Come on, old sport, nobody in this regiment was ever afraid!"

He leaped from the trench, and the men followed him on a wild charge into no-man's-land, where the machine-gun bullets were spitting and shells bursting. Reaching a jumble of shell holes, Donovan waved his men to take cover in them. Nonchalantly he stood before them in the open, unfolding a map of the terrain and studying it while machine-gun bullets rattled and spattered. His demonstration of cold nerve broke his men's fear.

"Come on now, men," he said at last. "They can't hit me, and they won't hit you."

Donovan recounted how he sent men to get a platoon of machine guns whose fire he hoped would keep down the German fire. "We moved further forward, going across the stream on which were the little woods and up the slope on the other side. Some of the leading men got into the wire at the top of the hill. Men were dropping all over. It was a pretty difficult place. Those who got into the wire were killed or wounded. The rest finally came to a halt on the slope running up from the stream along which there was some cover here and there but not much."

German shells began to spray shrapnel on the Americans. By now it was noon of the first day, and at last the machine guns were brought up and put into action. When night came, Donovan ordered his officers to have their men collect all the wounded and carry them back.

He kept his command post on a hillside even though it was exposed to enemy fire. "I decided to stay where I was," he explained, "because while it was not the position from which I could best command the assault and support battalions, I did not want any of the men to think that I was quitting them when they were in such a difficult position. The telephone worked some of the time so that I was not entirely out of communication with the rest of the troops under my command."

During the night Donovan ordered scouts to establish contact with the 167th Alabama on the right and the 166th Ohio on the left. Donovan reasoned that since the Germans could no longer see an attacking party, he might be able to break through in the dark. He sent Captain Bootz and his company into action. The American casualties were heavy, and Bootz returned to report.

"We have got too many green replacements to do this sort of work," he said. "All day long we have been trying to keep them from bunching up, but they will do it and are even worse at night, when they can't see each other unless they are bunched up. The Germans are jittery and at the slightest noise bring down a heavy fire. I think we had better wait until morning, as you can see all we have done so far is to thoroughly wake up the Germans. Look at the rockets going up along their whole line."

Some Americans were captured in the night fighting. One escaped and came back to tell Donovan that there were Germans in front of the barbed wire only about 100 yards away. More waited behind the wire, and still others were coming up. A counterattack seemed certain.

"I was so damned tired," Donovan admitted later. "I had about reached the point where I didn't give a damn if they did counterattack."

In the morning Donovan's old First Battalion, now commanded by Major Kelly, attacked. Wrote Donovan,

> I knew all the older men in it. Just before Kelly started, I walked around amongst them telling them that we had to go through and that they were the fellows to do it. When they started forward I went with them. I had hardly started when I was shot in the knee. I always thought it was a rifle bullet, but the men near me said it was a machine gun one. At any rate down I went. Just as I did so, I saw the tanks coming back. I

was told that one of them had gotten into the wire, but where they had attacked was on the other side of a slight fold in the ground so I did not personally see it. Also I was lying on the ground so my vision was limited. I sent Wheatley over to one of the tanks. He came back and said the driver was shot in the eye. I then asked for artillery fire. My request was promptly complied with, but the fire was not heavy enough to keep the Germans down and give our men a chance to break through.

The Germans counterattacked from just south of Landres-et-St.-Georges, but Stokes mortar and machine-gun fire turned them back.

"This counterattack," continued Donovan, "convinced me that Kelly's position invited enemy attempts to cut him off. Also he was suffering badly from direct fire from the German artillery in the Bois Hazois, to say nothing of fire into his right flank and rear from the Côte de Châtillon.

"I therefore sent word for him to retire. He sent back the reply that he would do so with a written order. Therefore, lying on the ground, I wrote out an order and sent it by one of my runners, Mack Rice."

When Donovan was hit, he later wrote Ruth, "I fell like a log, but after a few minutes managed to crawl into my little telephone hole. A machine gun lieutenant ripped open my breeches and put on the first aid. The leg hurt, but there were many things to be done."

Major Anderson, commanding the reserve battalion, came up. "I had heard that Donovan had been shot through the leg," he said after the war, "so started up to see him. It was then about seven o'clock in the morning. It was broad daylight by the time we got to where we could see him. He was lying in a foxhole on the reverse slope of the hill just in front of the German position. His position was not only isolated but an extremely dangerous one."

Captain Fecheimer also arrived on the scene. "How in hell is anybody going to get him out of here?" he asked himself.

Anderson and Fecheimer lay down on the ground.

"Hello," Donovan said. Shrapnel and bullets winged about them.

"You'd better get in here with me," he told Anderson. "Fecheimer, you get over in that foxhole over there," he said to the captain.

"I looked at it," Fecheimer remembered later, "and there were already two men in it, so I looked for another one. Seeing an empty one just behind the one Donovan had pointed out, I got in it. Shortly after, a shell landed in the one with the two men in it, blowing them both to pieces."

"The situation was bad," Donovan wrote. "There was more defense than we thought, and the battalion was held up. Messengers I sent through were killed or wounded and messages remained undelivered. We were shelled heavily. Beside me three men were blown up, and I was showered with the remnants of their bodies. No communication with the rear as the telephone was still out. Gas was then thrown at us, thick and nasty. Five hours passed. I was getting very groggy."

Kelly, having received his written orders, fell back with the First Battalion to a little stream and dug in on the night of October 15. The front was now stable. Donovan, propped up against the bank of his foxhole, his leg swathed in a bloody bandage, was growing too weak from loss of blood to continue much longer and at last had to allow his men to wrap him in a blanket. He had continued in command for a long day after being wounded. When shock wore off, he had been in great pain. Four men picked him up and started back across the open terrain. A shell burst nearby.

"Take cover and leave me, boys," Donovan weakly demanded. "You can never make it."

"We can go anywhere you can, Colonel," said one.

They carried him safely back to the regimental dressing station set up by surgeon George Lawrence. There he was met by Father Duffy. Donovan weakly shook his fist at the chaplain. "Father, you're a disappointed man," he said. "You expected to have the pleasure of burying me here."

"I certainly did, Bill, and you are a lucky dog to get off with nothing more than you got," Duffy replied.

Donovan's wound was dressed in the first-aid station, and he was placed in an ambulance for a 2-mile ride over shell-torn roads to the Field Hospital. He was placed on the ground while it was determined that no immediate operation was needed. Again he rode in a lurching ambulance, this time for 4 miles to a mobile unit.

"At this hospital I was taken in during a pounding rain," he wrote to Ruth. "They took a complete record of my name, regiment, rank, nature, and date of wound. Then they stripped me and rubbed me over with a warm sponge. It being the first in many days, it was very welcome. Then the anti-tetanus injection. Then on a stretcher and put in a row in the waiting room off the operating room awaiting my turn."

Donovan closed his eyes and tried to sleep. "Hello, Colonel!" he heard someone say. It was a runner from his old battalion who had been wounded after he had.

In the operating room the surgeons decided that no operation was needed, so with his leg splinted, Donovan was put into a ward. He luxuriated between clean sheets.

> Beside me was an officer shot through the stomach and dying, across two officers coming out of ether and asking the nurse to hold their hands or smooth their brows. In the next ward a bedlam of delirium. Early in the morning the man next to me died, still calling for his wife and children.
>
> Pancakes for breakfast and then prepared for evacuation. Our cards

containing our history were attached, and we were loaded into ambulances and sent to Evacuation No. 10. It was in a pouring rain, and the road was terrific. I had with me several badly wounded officers who groaned the whole time, and I was not very comfortable myself, so that on the road things were not happy.

At the Evacuation Hospital we were handled like pieces of freight. Put on a rack, and when your turn came put in front of a checker who carefully noted your record. Then to bed. I was given a room. I was in an old French barracks hospital. The nurse was a sister of Rose, the hammer thrower, and looked to me husky enough to handle any of us.

The hospital was filled to overflowing as casualties came in from the bloody Argonne. Donovan and 15 others were put on a French train.

"The stretchers and slings were most uncomfortable," he wrote. "We had coffee without milk, canned corned beef heated, and nothing else. I passed it all and dug up some Y.M.C.A. crackers I had been saving. We had a French orderly on the train. An old Breton, most obliging. He knew no French yet always knew what the men wanted. All night long this patient fellow worked, always awake, and always smiling."

In Paris, Donovan was placed in the Latin Quarter in a building that before the war had housed American girls studying art. There he convalesced as the war came to an end.

9

The Men We Left Behind

COLONEL WILLIAM J. DONOVAN'S extraordinary heroism at Landres and St. Georges, France, October 14–15, 1918, won him a bronze oak leaf cluster to his Distinguished Service Cross. He was also awarded two Purple Hearts and the nation's highest honor, the Congressional Medal of Honor, which entitles its holder to receive a salute from any person in the military services and to walk out on the floors of Congress at any time.

The citation in the Congressional Record reads:

> Before Landres and St. Georges in the Argonne on October 14 and 15 the positions were known to be strong. The artillery preparation was brief. It was evident that the attack could be carried through only by desperate resolution. This resolution Lt. Colonel Donovan determined to reinforce by his own example. When the Third Battalion moved out to the assault, he went forward in the rear of the first wave, deliberately wearing the marks of his rank so as to be easily recognized by his men though it also rendered him conspicuous to the enemy.
>
> The assaulting battalion met with a terrible reception as it crossed the open ground and moved up the slopes toward the trenches. Machine guns and artillery ravaged it from the front and flanks.
>
> Officers and many of the best non-commissioned officers were hit and some platoons began to be disorganized. Then Colonel Donovan, moving erect from place to place in full view of the enemy, reorganized and heartened his men. As spurts of dust went up around him and shells broke in the vicinity, "See," he said, "they can't hit me and they won't hit you."
>
> Officers and men of this battalion say that it would have been impossible for them to have made the advance they did had it not been for the cool resolution, indifference to danger, and personal leadership of Colonel Donovan. It is the general opinion that his conduct on this occasion was of the highest type of courage witnessed by anybody in this regiment during the four major actions in which it has been engaged.

Donovan's reaction was much like that of the 12-year-old boy who had won a medal for elocution in a grammar school on the Buffalo waterfront. "It doesn't belong to me; it belongs to the boys who won it," he said.

America's allies also gave high awards to the hero of the Argonne as he regained his strength in the Paris hospital. The French had already given him the Croix de Guerre. Now the Italian government conferred the Croce al Merito di Guerra on him. The French added a palm and a silver star to his Croix de Guerre and awarded him the Légion d'Honneur, with the rank of commander, and the Italians countered with the Order of the Crown. The king of England made him a knight commander of the Order of the British Empire. Leopold, king of the Belgians, named him to the Order of Leopold with the rank of grand officer, Belgium's highest award, with a palm denoting heroism in action. Poland gave Donovan the Commander's Cross with Star, Polish Order of Polonia Restituta, and Norway the Commander's Order with Star, Order of St. Olav. William J. Donovan received more awards than any other American in the 42nd Division, including Gen. Douglas MacArthur, and most likely in the entire American Expeditionary Force.

On October 2, former President Theodore Roosevelt wrote to Bill Donovan. "I see you have been cited again and promoted to a Lieutenant Colonelcy. I wish to tell you how proud I am of you and with what interest I follow all that you have done." Later, on October 25, he wrote again, "Ted has just written me saying he would give anything if only he could be made a Lt. Colonel in a regiment under you as Colonel and under Frank McCoy as Brigadier General. My boys regard you as about the finest examples of the American fighting gentleman."

Doubtless Bill Donovan, remembering how as a little boy he had tried to live the virile life of challenge as exemplified by the Rough Rider, was more pleased with the letters from Roosevelt than with the awards that kings now competed in giving him.

Years later, John J. McCloy told an audience of former OSS men how in 1918 he had gone with his commanding officer to see General Menoher, commander of the 42nd Division. "My chief greeted him with, 'Minnie, how are you getting along?' Menoher's nickname at West Point had been 'Minnie.'

"His reply was, 'Fine, except that I have two extraordinary characters in this division, neither of whom I can control. The enemy I can deal with, but these two win more medals than I have to give out. One is Bill Donovan and the other is Douglas MacArthur."

A short time after that McCloy met Donovan himself at the front.

"I have now in my library a picture taken of him at that time with his steel hat just a little cocked, his tunic muddy, and his Irish eyes aflash," he told the OSS men. "He had the mark of bravery and leadership written all over him. I remember how much I then envied him, his élan, his spark, and his record."

While Donovan was still in the hospital, the provost marshal had him transferred to his department, and when he was well enough,

Donovan set about his duties. He toured France by car. In his position of inspector instructor in the provost marshal's department, he was entitled to the best billets and the best food. On Thanksgiving Day the Old 69th was at Useldingen Castle in Luxembourg, still scarcely believing that the war had ended. It was only a few weeks before, on November 11, that they had seized Engineer and Signal Corps supplies of rockets and flares to celebrate the armistice. Bonfires had burned along the lines, and in the chill of a French November, Allied and German soldiers had warmed themselves together at the fires. Now Father Duffy was celebrating Mass in the courtyard of the castle, using a breach in the fortifications as his pulpit. Glancing to the side of the soldiers, he saw a familiar figure on crutches. It was Bill Donovan. The men, catching sight of him, set up a mighty cheer.

"I want to be back with my old outfit," Donovan confided to Duffy.

"For Donovan's sake, I shall omit the pathos," Duffy wrote in his diary. "When that young man wants anything very bad, he gets it. I expect to see him back on duty with us in a very, very brief time."

Duffy was right. But Donovan continued at his work for the provost marshal long enough to reorganize the administration with such efficiency that he was given still another top award, the Distinguished Service Medal.

On December 3, the Fighting 69th marched across a bridge over the Sauer River into the village of Bollendorf. They had at last arrived in Germany. The men tramped over rough roads through the Eifel Mountains and rested in Wershofen for five days, going over equipment and patching shoes. They were there when Lt. Col. William J. Donovan caught up to them and took command of the Old 69th by direct order of general headquarters.

Things were different now. The men marched in easy stages through the valley of the Ahr River to Altenahr, where they were billeted in luxurious resort hotels. They passed through the walled town of Ahrweiler and reached the Rhine at Remagen, which was to be their home for the next four months. They moved into homes and hotels, and every soldier had a bed. As the regiment approached the town, Bill Donovan and Father Duffy went ahead to arrange the billet for headquarters. They called on the Burgermeister, as Duffy said, "a kindly, gentlemanly, educated man, who was anxious to do everything to make our stay in town a harmonious one."

The regiment celebrated Christmas at Remagen amidst a defeated enemy who seemed to want only peace and friendship. When the soldiers sang "Take Me Back to New York Town," German girls looked properly pensive. Little girls learned to skip rope to "The Sidewalks of New York." Each of the companies gave dinners at the Remagen hotels with the money they had saved from their pay when they were far too busy fighting to spend it. Donovan attended every dinner and was always asked to make a speech.

"He got in many a strong word of spirit and discipline," recalled Duffy, "which had better results in that environment than could have been produced on a more formal occasion."

When Bill Donovan's promotion to full colonel came through, he used his higher rank to advance the other officers and noncoms of his command. He too gave dinners, and invited the officers of other regiments stationed in the occupation forces nearby to participate in what he called "our Metropolitan Hibernian hospitality."

On March 16, General Pershing drove to Remagen to review the Rainbow Division. When he came to the 165th, all drawn up proudly before him, he saw the silver battle furls that covered the flag staff from the silk of the colors to the lowest tip. The staff had been stretched beyond the regulation length to make room for an extra foot of furls.

"What regiment is this?" demanded Pershing.

"The 165th Infantry, sir."

"What regiment was it?"

"The 69th New York, sir."

"The 69th New York. I understand now."

Almost every evening Father Duffy and Colonel Donovan walked along the river road beside the Rhine. They strolled to the place Lord Byron had described in *Childe Harold's Pilgrimage*. There was a magnificent view of villages and vineyards where the Rhine swung to the right to pass through the Siebengebirge Gorge. "The companionship makes it all the more attractive," Duffy wrote in his diary.

> This young Buffalo lawyer who was suddenly called into the business of war, and has made a name for himself throughout the American Expeditionary Force for outstanding courage and keen military judgment, is a remarkable man. As a boy he reveled in Thomas Francis Meaghen's "Speech on the Sword" and his dream of life was to command an Irish brigade in the service of the Republic. His dream came true, for the 69th in this war was larger than the Irish Brigade ever was. But it did not come true by mere dreaming. He is always physically fit, always alert, ready to do without food, sleep, rest, in the most matter of fact way, thinking of nothing but the work in hand. He has mind and manners and varied experience of life and resoluteness of purpose. He has kept himself clean and sane and whole for whatever adventure life might bring him, and he has come through this surpassing adventure with honor and fame. I like him for his alert mind and just views and ready wit, for his generous enthusiasms and his whole engaging personality. The richest gain I have gotten out of the war is the friendship of William J. Donovan.

That was what Duffy wrote in his diary, but when he was talking with Donovan, as often as not they had heated differences of opinion about things as varied as the merits of Tolstoi's novels and whether the Hudson or the Rhine was the more beautiful river. Said Duffy,

> Those infernal youngsters of ours have been telling stories about both of us, most of which, at least those that concern myself, attest the loyalty of my friends better than their veracity. There is only one way to take it—as a joke. If either of us gets a clipping in which his name is mentioned, he brandishes it before company under the nose of the other, challenging him to produce small proof of being as great a hero. The other day Captain Ryan gave Donovan an editorial about him from a paper in Watertown, New York. It was immediately brought to mess, and Donovan thought he had scored a triumph, but I countered with a quotation from a letter, which said that my picture, jeweled with electric lights, had a place of honor in the window of a saloon.

Donovan continued his study of French and went to Paris to represent the Rainbow Division at a meeting to organize the American Legion. Occupation duty after the excitement of war had resulted in a lowering of morale. America's citizen soldiers wanted only one thing— to go home, or as one man put it, "to see the Statue of Liberty looming up on the horizon." Donovan, the citizen-soldier hero of the American Expeditionary Force, was one of the men called upon to make suggestions on how to improve morale. He met with Theodore Roosevelt, Jr., Ogden Mills, and Col. Ralph Van Deman. Donovan wrote later,

> I suggested a practical thing to do was to call a group of officers from all over the AEF who knew conditions, that group of officers to meet with representatives of the General Staff. I was called upon as sort of prosecuting attorney to state the case to the General Staff. Previously, Mills and Roosevelt and myself, who may be considered the first three members of the Legion, had agreed to take up the project with these twenty members. This was done. At the time of the meeting, it was decided to have Teddy Roosevelt call a meeting in the United States, and that Bennett Clark would preside at the meeting in Paris.

The 20 citizen soldiers met for dinner at a French military club in Paris on the night of February 15. Theodore Roosevelt, Jr., presided, and once dinner was over he explained the need for a veterans' organization.

"It is a nervy thing for us, as a self-appointed committee, to set about such a thing," he concluded, "but someone has got to do it, and it ought to be done as soon as possible for the good of the men and for the good of the country."

One general immediately wanted to know where everybody in the room stood on the question of universal training and a bigger army. Unless he could be sure the new organization would back such purposes, he announced, "I don't want to have anything to do with the movement."

Bill Donovan arose, and his eyes flashed. He announced that it was presumptuous enough even to issue a call for a soldiers' organization, and that it would be "unthinkable to try to wish any pre-thought-out policies on the unborn babe."

"After a heated argument, in which the Colonel was all alone in his contentions," wrote George A. White, who was present, "it was decided that after the child had been duly born and reared, it could decide for itself whether it wanted mush or hot cakes for breakfast and also what variety of military policy it preferred."

It was by then after midnight, and Donovan had managed to win the others to his side. He had spoken up for the enlisted man's viewpoint.

Among the other officers present at the Paris meeting was Ned Buxton, who was to be a lifelong friend of Donovan's. Between the wars, he was a correspondent and a textile manufacturer. During World War II he served in OSS headquarters. He was also Sgt. Alvin York's commanding officer in World War I. It was Buxton who convinced York, a pacifist, that it was possible to kill German soldiers and be a good Christian. Said York, "He was the first New Englander I ever knowed. I was kinder surprised at his knowledge of the Bible. It made me happy my battalion commander was familiar with the word of God."

Orders came for the 165th Infantry to return home. Donovan, back at Remagen, took his final stroll along the Rhine with Father Duffy. Talk returned to what they would do when home in the United States. Donovan said that after his final duties with the regiment, he was going to "run away from it all and go off with my wife on a trip to Japan."

On April 2, the Fighting 69th boarded trains for Brest, where they remained for a few days. Then they sailed aboard two ships for Hoboken. Donovan sailed in the former *City of Paris*, renamed the *Harrisburg*. On April 21, he could look out at the southern shore of Long Island and at last glimpse the Statue of Liberty. A flotilla of small boats, tugs, and ferries came down the bay to welcome the regiment. As the ship tied up at a Hoboken pier, a pretty girl on shore shouted, "Hello, Mike!" She was answered by 300 voices. The Fighting 69th was home at last.

A week after their tumultuous welcome in New York Harbor, the Fighting 69th fell in at the foot of Fifth Avenue. Donovan stood at their head. When somebody suggested that he ought to ride in an open car over the 5-mile length of the parade, he snapped, "It was good enough to go on foot in Europe. It's good enough now."

Donovan's staff fell into place behind him. Young girls passed out roses, which the men tucked into their web belts.

A huge crowd had gathered the length of the avenue, a jubilant crowd that laughed and cheered at every little thing—a tot waving an American flag, a young boy with a placard that read "Welcome Dad. The ice man never came to our house all the time you were with Wild Bill!"—anything that lent humor to the festive mood. Near the triumphal arch at the foot of the avenue, where the 69th had gathered, the crowd was having a boisterous good time. Then Col. William J. Donovan drew himself erect to give a command, and the crowd suddenly grew still.

"Forward, march!" Donovan ordered.

Bandmaster Henry Zitzmann's band swung into "Killarney," and the men who had survived the holocaust in France stepped off smartly. A great cheer went up. The 69th passed up Fifth Avenue to the music of "Garry Owen," to other Irish and American marches and songs, and to Victor Herbert's new march, which Father Vincent Donovan had asked the Irish-American to write using Joyce Kilmer's "When the 69th Comes Home" as the lyrics. (Herbert signed over the royalties from the march to Kilmer's widow.) Confetti rained from the tall buildings. Wounded men unable to make the march rode in cars at the end of the parade. Will Rogers spoke for New York and most of America when he commented, "If they really want to honor the boys, why don't they let them sit in the stands and have the people march by?"

Then what may have been Bill Donovan's proudest day was over. After the parade concluded, Donovan went to Camp Mills with his brother Vincent. There, in the old campsite where he had first taken command of the First Battalion, he wept. "I can't forget the men we left behind," he told his brother.

In the days that followed, there were other events to show New York's pride in the 69th. An official reception was held by Mayor John Hylan on the steps of City Hall, and the mayor conferred the freedom of the city on Donovan and his officers. The mayor and a committee headed by Commissioner Rodman Wanamaker gave a dinner in Donovan's honor, and the entire regiment was honored at a Hotel Commodore dinner. The Lamb's Club and the Press Association feted Donovan.

On April 19 the *New York World* had announced that $150,000 had been raised by the wealthy trustees of the regiment to help find jobs for the returning men and to assist those who might find themselves in need. "All the funds on hand to be turned over to Father Duffy and Colonel Donovan to be used as their experience dictates," stated the newspaper. Donovan was delighted with this financial help to his men, for he already knew of hardship cases. The Fighting 69th had lost 644 men killed and 2,857 wounded in France, and there were widows and orphans to worry about and men whose injuries would long keep them from earning a living. The nine World War I silver furls to the regiment's battle flag had not been won easily.

On Thursday, May 15, it was Father Duffy Day at the Polo Grounds. A band played a concert at 1:30 P.M. while the crowd gathered. The New York Giants were to play the Chicago Cubs at 3:30, but for once it was not the ball game that the crowd had come to cheer. They roared their approval of Father Duffy when the 69th's chaplain stood up to bless them, and when Wild Bill Donovan arose to speak, there was a cheer that shook the stands.

Donovan took this moment to say good-bye to his men. "There can be no keener regret than the parting of men who have fought together in a common cause and where friendship has been sealed by the blood of comrades," he said in the hush that had fallen upon the stadium. "Throughout this war, sustained by the trust of its people at home, inspired by the ancient tradition, this regiment has carried the fight to the foe without faltering."

The crowd waited for more, but Donovan sat down, having said what he had to say. There was a silence and then renewed applause for this valiant commander and his men. Bill Donovan, now a national hero, was mustered out of the army.

PART TWO

The President's "Secret Legs"

1919–1941

10

Siberian Adventure

FOR THE FIRST 20 MILES out of Vladivostok, the train ran north along the coast of Peter the Great Bay. Smoke belched from the locomotive and drifted in a cloud out over the water. Soot blew in the coach windows, opened to catch the breeze from the Sea of Japan.

The date was July 11, 1919, and the train was an extraordinary one. In several of the cars and on the locomotive itself, soldiers of America's Siberian Expeditionary Force, their rifles and machine guns at the ready, kept a sharp eye on the tracks ahead and on the forests and fields through which the railroad ran. Under strict orders from President Wilson, the American Army was neutral in the struggle between the Whites and the Bolsheviks for control of what had once been the czar's Far Eastern empire. Both partisans and Bolsheviks wrecked trains, regardless of what flag flew from the front of the boiler.

A Cadillac automobile rode on a flatcar. It belonged to Maj. Gen. William S. Graves, commander of the U.S. forces in Siberia. The general himself rode in a bare compartment with two companions. He stared moodily out the window from time to time, for he was a blunt soldier, not at all pleased to be making the political journey upon which the train had started. One of the other men was Roland Morris, American ambassador to Japan, and charged by the State Department in Washington with handling the Russian question in the Far East. Beside him sat a stocky 36-year-old colonel in neat, almost natty, civilian clothing. He had a guileless face and a gentle voice, both seemingly out of keeping with his reputation as one of America's premier war heroes. This was William J. Donovan on his first important intelligence mission.

The roots of America's World War II Office of Strategic Services and the Central Intelligence Agency, which was to succeed it, run deep through the tangled history of the 20th century. It may be said that the taproot reached back to this train and this man on that hot day along the shores of an Asian sea. In the weeks that lay ahead, Donovan was to learn a great deal of lasting importance, not only about what was happening in Siberia but about how interdepartmental rivalries both in Washington and in the field made it possible for foreign interests to manipulate American policy. What he learned was going to stand him in good stead when, more than two decades later, he was made director of his country's first comprehensive strategic intelligence service.

Bill Donovan had returned to Buffalo from his military service in Europe in early May. His restless mind was already preoccupied with affairs far across the Pacific, where he was convinced the seeds of another war were being sown. One day he talked to John Lord O'Brian, one of his law partners, who had gone to Washington to serve as an intelligence aide in the Justice Department when America declared war. O'Brian, who had since become an intelligence adviser to President Wilson, was looking for somebody to go to Siberia as a secret presidential agent. Conflicting reports were reaching the President from State Department and military representatives in Siberia, and such an agent was needed to provide objective information on conditions in the Russian Far East.

Walking beside the Rhine with Father Duffy in early April, Donovan had planned to take Ruth on a long-delayed honeymoon trip to Japan. He told O'Brian that they would make the trip now. Then he would go on to Siberia for the President. Donovan was told that under no circumstances should he inform General Graves, Ambassador Morris, or the consul general in Vladivostok that he was on a confidential mission.

Ruth was delighted at the prospect of a trip to the Far East. The children's grandmother took care of David and Patricia, and the Donovans set off on what seemed to be a romantic journey. The trip across America by train and across the sea on a luxury liner was indeed a restful and happy one.

As soon as he reached Tokyo, Donovan had gotten in touch with Morris, who had been directed to make a fact-finding trip to Omsk, and asked if he might accompany the ambassador to Siberia. He mentioned nothing of his confidential mission. Morris wired the acting secretary of state on July 7:

> Colonel Donovan of the 165th (formerly 69th) New York Regiment, Rainbow Division, is extremely anxious to go to Omsk with me in a purely private capacity and at his own expense. He is deeply interested in the situation in the Orient, and I have valued my talk with him as he brings to these problems a refreshing point of view, representative, I think, of our younger Americans who were privileged to fight in France. I believe it would be helpful in many ways if he could take back to America his own direct impressions. I am sure he would also be of assistance to me both by his personality and in testing my own impressions and conclusions. While not asking you to assume any responsibility if I should take him, I would appreciate an expression of your views. Please reply to Vladivostok.

Donovan and Morris left Japan by boat for Vladivostok on July 10 and were at the American consulate there when Morris received a reply to his cable: "For Morris, yours, July seventh, nine P.M./confidential, for the Acting Secretary of State. I can see no objection to your taking Colonel Donovan if you wish to do so."

Left behind in Tokyo, Ruth was upset. She had understood why her husband had interrupted their honeymoon to return to Buffalo when World War I began, and she had understood as well why he went to Europe for the War Relief Commission and then served on the Mexican border before returning to Europe with the Fighting 69th. The world was at war, and other women also had given up their husbands. This was different. America was not at war, and she had set out with Bill on what was to be a second honeymoon. Now he was leaving her in Tokyo, telling her that he and Ambassador Morris were going to Siberia. The ambassador had requested that he go, he said, and it was his patriotic duty to make the trip. They were going to investigate the White Russian government of Adm. Aleksandr Kolchak. He had no idea how long he would be gone. Ruth could either return to America or wait for him in Japan. She chose to go home to Buffalo and her children.

Roland Sletor Morris, with whom Donovan crossed the Sea of Japan, was a prominent Philadelphia lawyer who had risen through Democratic politics until in 1917 President Wilson sent him as ambassador to Japan. From Tokyo he kept a close eye on the increasing signs of Japanese imperialism while striving to foster better relations between the United States and Japan. With the outbreak of civil war in Russia, President Wilson asked Morris to handle the Russian question in the Far East.

In Vladivostok, Donovan and Morris met General Graves, who had received a message from Washington: "If the American Ambassador to Japan, Mr. Roland S. Morris, goes to Omsk, you will go with him." Graves had sent a message back to Washington objecting to the trip. He did not want to depart from the strict neutrality demanded of him by the President and feared that to go to Omsk would imply his support of Admiral Kolchak and the White Russians. On July 7 he received a second cable from the War Department. "If Morris goes to Omsk, it is desired you accompany him."

America's Siberian intervention had begun in August 1918, while the war was still raging in Europe. Graves, commanding the Eighth Division in training at Camp Fremont near Palo Alto, California, received an encoded message in July from the War Department ordering him to take the first and fastest train from San Francisco to Kansas City. There he was to proceed to the Baltimore Hotel and ask for the secretary of war. If the secretary was not there, Graves was to wait for him. Newton D. Baker, secretary of war in Wilson's cabinet, was waiting at the hotel.

Baker informed the general that the President had picked him to head an American expedition to Siberia. He handed him a sealed envelope and remarked, "This contains the policy of the United States in Russia, which you are to follow. Watch your step; you will be walking on eggs loaded with dynamite. God bless you and good-bye."

Wilson himself had had a hand in drafting the contents of the envelope. American troops were to go to Siberia to safeguard military stores gathered there for the war against Germany. With the collapse of the czar's regime, there was a considerable risk that German and Austrian prisoners released in Siberia would be able to capture the supplies. The American troops were also to assist the Czech Legion, which had broken away from the Austrian Army on the Russian front and was attempting to reach Siberian ports from which its 40,000 men could reenter the war on the Allied side. Finally, the Americans were to help the Russian people as they established their own political institutions out of chaos. They would aid in the operation of the railroads so that vital food and clothing could move to isolated towns and villages, but they were to remain strictly neutral in the civil war between the White and Bolshevik factions.

When Graves arrived in Vladivostok in September 1918, the British and French found him intractable and stubborn and unwilling to oppose the Bolsheviks as they desired. The Japanese, who had also sent a strong contingent of troops to Siberia, were even more critical of Graves. They were not only opposed to the Bolsheviks, but they hoped to annex part of the former czar's territory in Asia. Siberia was a cockpit of contending Russian and Cossack armies and an arena of political conflict among the Allies.

On July 14, 1919, the *North China Star,* which circulated throughout the Orient, printed a report from its Paris correspondent asserting that Wilson had ordered Morris to make inquiries at Omsk about the competence of the Kolchak government. The report went on to say that Morris was to discuss the military and political situation with the Kolchak cabinet and observe conditions in the White capital. Morris had the power, the article said, to recommend or deny U.S. recognition of the White Russian regime.

When the *North China Star* story appeared, Graves, Donovan, and Morris were already on their way to Omsk. On a seat beside them in the train compartment, they kept handy a National Geographic map of North Asia and "Stanford's Map of the Siberian Railway, the Great Land Route to China and Korea," published in London. From Vladivostok to Nikolsk their train chuffed slowly down the tracks, which had been allowed to fall into wretched condition. Beyond Nikolsk the train rolled through prosperous villages and fields of wheat, untouched by the civil war being fought for their control. It was a fruitful land, and Donovan jotted in his journal: "The difficulty in Russia is not absence of money, or resources, but of management. With stable government, can live within herself and produce everything. Situation here must be grappled with."

The train crossed into Manchuria on the Chinese Eastern Railroad and headed west to Harbin (Haerhpin), a city built by the Russians from a fishing village on the Sungari River when the southern section of the Chinese Eastern Railroad was completed in 1898. The three men in the compartment looked out on a typical provincial Russian city, lying to the east of the tracks. Tree-lined streets radiated from the Orthodox cathedral in front of the railroad station, simmering in the July heat, proof of the expansive colonialism of the Russian people in Asia. After Japan's victory in the Russo-Japanese War in 1905, the city had been transferred from the Russian-owned railroad's administration to that of a Chinese- and Japanese-dominated council; but the impress of the Russians was clear 14 years later. If the Russians could settle their political problems, they would certainly remain a major force in the Far East.

On July 15, the Asiatic News Agency carried a dispatch from Harbin that Roland Morris, his secretary, and an American general had arrived during the night from Vladivostok. Donovan must have been amused to be identified in print as the ambassador's secretary. "The fact that Ambassador Morris is accompanied by a high military officer shows that the United States government pays great attention to the existing military situation in Siberia as a result of the Bolshevik advance on the Ufa and Perm fronts," concluded the dispatch.

The train climbed among the Greater Khingan Mountains as it continued on its 920-mile run through Manchuria to where it reentered Siberia and joined the Trans-Siberian Railroad. From time to time, camel caravans plodded beside the tracks, the camels snorting at the puffing locomotive. Two Russian-speaking interpreters were assigned to the men in the compartment, and whenever the train stopped at a station they swung down off the cars to talk with the people crowded on the platform. Many were refugees fleeing the fighting in western Siberia. The interpreters questioned them about the struggle and about the degree of support for the Bolsheviks and for Admiral Kolchak's regime in Omsk. Whenever possible they talked to women, for they had quickly learned that Russian women were outspoken and direct in their replies, while men were guarded.

The refugees told of the pistol-and-whip recruiting of village men and boys by Bolshevik commanders, of the vindictive murder of educated people. The Reds plundered wherever they went, for their ill-supplied army lived off the land. Donovan was appalled at the stories he heard about the Bolsheviks, but then he began to gather even crueler reports about the conduct of the White Army.

White Army commanders based in the towns strung along the railroad sent their soldiers out to raid villages accused of helping the Reds. They rounded up men, women, and children, put them in corrals, and demanded indemnities of supplies and money. If the payments were not forthcoming, village leaders were shot or burned. Men and women were strung by their ears to the fronts of their houses. With the Siberian winter temperatures dropping down to −50 degrees Fahrenheit, White soldiers cut holes in the ice of ponds and plunged leaders into the frigid waters, much as if they were dipping candles. Covered by layer after layer of ice, the frozen victims were placed in the center of their village to stand like statues until the spring thaw. Supplies taken from villages by the soldiers were sold across the Chinese border to enrich the commanders.

After hearing these stories, the three Americans traveling through Siberia were not surprised that men and boys were taking to the forests to fight back against both the Whites and the Reds. When American soldiers first came to Siberia, there had been little for them to do but to fish in the streams for trout and salmon. Now detachments were being attacked by bands of partisans, who in their fury struck at Russians and foreigners alike. Americans were killing and being killed.

Morris cabled to the State Department from Chita on July 15: "Hope to report from Irkutsk my observations on present conditions on Chinese Eastern and in territory controlled by Semionoff."

On July 17, he sent his lengthy report on the Cossack leader, Grigori Semionoff, which Donovan helped him to compose. Morris discussed the activities of the Japanese soldiers who garrisoned the towns in Manchuria and their support for the Cossacks. His cable continued:

> From Manchuria Station to Verkhne Udinsk the railway is dominated by Semionoff with the open support of the Japanese Military authorities. His relations with the Kolchak Government are merely nominal. His strength is wholly Japanese. He has constantly interfered with the Allied inspectors who have again and again sought and have been refused the support of the Japanese Military, supposedly guarding the railway in this section. I arrived at Chita just after Semionoff's bandits in one of their armoured cars had seized the office car and equipment of Major Gravis, an American engineer and the Allied Divisional Inspector. I am using this incident to bring the general question to definite issue. At Chita I saw General Oba, the Japanese Divisional Commander, and discussed the entire situation for several hours. Later under Japanese pressure Semionoff promised to return the car but has not yet done so. During

our interview, General Oba frankly expressed to me his profound admiration for Semionoff, his confidence in Semionoff's purposes and motives, and the close relation which existed between them.

Parts of the railroad, reported Morris, were controlled by the Americans or the Czechs, but the Japanese were in the strongest position.

From Vladivostok to Irkutsk, excepting only two sectors guarded by American troops, the military control of the railways is in the hands of the Japanese who are using the Cossack organization subsidized and supported by them to discredit Allied operation. Kolchak is powerless to withstand this influence which has gone as far as to force the appointment of the bandit Kalmykoff as the representative of Dutoff, the Kolchak commander of all military operations in the East.

To my mind the Japanese plan is perfectly clear. Baffled by the Railway Agreement in their organized attempt to take possession of the Chinese Eastern and Trans-Siberian Railways as far as Chita, and thus dominate Eastern Siberia and Northern Manchuria, the Japanese Government is countenancing a less obvious but a more insidious scheme of operating through the Cossack organization which is the only support Kolchak has east of Chita. It will not be difficult for Japan to dispose of the Eastern Cossacks when they have served the purpose.

The tragedy of a nation at war with itself was all around the three Americans. There were also reminders of the inhumanity of the czars. At Irkutsk, 20 czarist prisoners still could be seen with balls and chains fastened to their ankles. They cradled the balls in their arms as they trudged beside the tracks. Beyond Irkutsk were the deep forests around Krasnoyarsk, where German and Austrian prisoners were starving in a prison camp. The Russians refused to release the men, although they no longer could feed them. Donovan obtained a copy of a directive issued to his troops by Rozanoff, one of Admiral Kolchak's top generals:

1. In occupying the villages which have been occupied by bandits (partisans), insist upon getting the leaders of the movement and where you cannot get the leaders, but have sufficient evidence as to the presence of such leaders, then shoot one out of every ten people.

2. If when the troops go through a town, and the population will not inform the troops, after having a chance to do so, of the presence of the enemy, a monetary contribution should be demanded of all, unsparingly.

3. The villages where the population meet our troops with arms should be burned down, and all the full-grown male population should be shot; property, homes, carts, etc., should be taken for the use of the army.

Donovan learned that Rozanoff kept hostages. If one of his men was killed, he killed ten hostages. Yet when he was introduced to the three Americans, Rozanoff was all smiles and observed that he was handling the situation in his district with gloves on. He had heard that conditions in Vladivostok called for more stringent measures, and if he were transferred there, he assured the Americans, he would certainly take his gloves off.

The Americans were disgusted with General Rozanoff. When later in Omsk they learned from British Gen. Sir Alfred Knox that he had urged that Rozanoff, "a bully fellow," be sent to Vladivostok as Kolchak's liaison with Graves, the American general icily replied that he was not interested in individuals and only hoped that Kolchak would send to Vladivostok a man "who would follow the practices of civilized nations."

At Tomsk, the Americans met the governor of the province, who had been appointed by Kolchak. When they asked him what people in the area thought of the White government, he said that they had no confidence in the officials around Kolchak.

Donovan, who had gone to Europe for the War Relief Commission to relieve human distress and who as a fighting commander in France had always given his men the best care he could manage, never forgot the cruel indifference that Russian commanders showed for their miserable soldiers. He had seen nothing like it in France, and his first impression of what he came to think of as Oriental despotism was an indelible one.

Finally, late at night on July 21, the train arrived at Omsk, located where the Om River flows into the Irtysh. The city was originally built as a Russian fort against the marauding Kirghiz tribesmen. It was here that Russian novelist Dostoevski had been imprisoned in the fortress and had written about his experience in *The House of the Dead*. In August 1919 refugees fleeing the war zones crowded every building to bursting, devoured the remaining supplies, and were dying of disease. This was Kolchak's capital.

No sooner had the train reached Omsk than Morris received a telegram from the State Department ordering him to support Kolchak. He turned to Graves. "Now, General, you will have to support Kolchak."

Graves said he had received nothing from the War Department.

"The State Department is running this, not the War Department."

"The State Department is not running me."

Donovan was learning that other governments might have a consistent policy determined for all services, but not the United States. To Graves it seemed questionable that even the President could order him to take sides in the Russian Civil War.

On July 22 Morris cabled to the State Department:

> I find the situation here extremely critical. Complete demoralization of Kolchak's Siberian Army. It is estimated that there are 35,000 cars filled with refugees, proceeding east from Ekaterinberg, Chiligbinsk, and the surrounding country. Railway east of Omsk already badly. con-

gested and any additional burden may tie up entire system. After conferring with Colonel Emerson, Major Slaughter, Harris, and Dr. Manget of
the Red Cross, I have directed that the fifty or more American nurses in
this district be sent east as soon as cars can be obtained for them. It is
possible that the Siberian Army may be reorganized on a line running
through Kinyan and Tuswan, but while I regret the abandonment of the
Red Cross work here, I thought it unwise to run the risk of having all
the American women stranded in Siberia.

Despite Morris's reports, in Washington and Paris the diplomats
and agents who favored Kolchak carried the day, and the State Department recommended aid to his government. In Omsk Donovan realized that Kolchak's army was a retreating mob. What could be expected
of soldiers serving under such generals as Semionoff, who boasted that
he could not sleep at night when he had not killed someone during the
day?

"Bolshevists making strong effort in Siberia because of internal
strife," Donovan wrote in his journal. "Workers in Siberia are yearning
for Bolshevism. Red Army has mobilized most of peasants with trained
fanatical Communists distributed among them, one mounted man to
every five others. The whip and the pistol get them."

Donovan saw that the White Russian forces had become disorgan-
ized. The officers were taking to their heels, and the soldiers were
throwing down their arms, discarding their ammunition, and shuffling
out of their heavy clothing to flee. Even the Cossacks were giving up.
Donovan and an interpreter used Graves's car to drive out into the
country around Omsk. They picked up refugees from the fighting front
and interrogated them as they rode to the city.

On August 1, Donovan wrote in his journal:

> Inspection of sick and wounded trains near Omsk. Indescribable. . . .
> The trains come in bearing about 600–1,000 patients daily. They have
> inadequate personnel for caring for the sick and wounded. The wounds
> are gangrenous—worms can be seen crawling about the wounds. The
> dead lie in the cars—wagons bearing coffins come up, and thirty or forty
> dead per day are carried away. The typhus patients relieve themselves
> under the cars, beside the cars, and when too weak, even in the cars.
> Their efforts to climb in are pitiful. They are undernourished. They are
> fed irregularly. No provision to feed them at this point. They are lousy.
> They get no water except at unstated intervals. Sometimes piteous, flesh-
> covered skeletons in loose, foul, filthy garments can be seen crawling to
> the stream for a drink. Wounded and dysentery and typhus all together.
> They are all in boxcars.

The next day Donovan reported, "Visited German and Austrian
prison camp. Men here who have had the same uniforms for four five
years. Food consists of bread and coffee for breakfast, a sort of rye or

barley for lunch, and meat for dinner. Those in hospital get the same except for milk."

Donovan also collected intelligence of another sort in Omsk. On August 4, he recorded in his journal: "Dinner with Japanese mission at Hotel Russe. Heavy food, much wine and night very hot. Major General Takinagi said oldest generation of officers speak French, his generation German, youngest generation English. Japanese Consul next to me spoke French, Russian, English, and German. Said that there were 12,000 Chinese in the Bolshevik forces, that they were good troops. Lenin and Trotsky used them as personal guard."

On August 10 Donovan wrote in his journal: "Fate of government will be decided in a few months. The question is not of fighting spirit of Bolsheviks, but lack of fighting quality of Whites."

He visited the bazaar at Omsk on August 13. Donovan already understood the value of what agents of every Oriental country know of as "bazaar intelligence."

The situation in Omsk continued to deteriorate. On August 20 Morris cabled the State Department to advise Bill Donovan's wife, as well as his own, that "their party was well protected and that they must not be alarmed if they should hear of unsettled conditions here." Donovan and Morris left Omsk in a few days to return over the chaotic railroad to Vladivostok. On the return trip, the train stopped at Chita, where Lt. John J. McDonald of the American Russian Railway Service Corps told how Semionoff's soldiers only a few days before had taken prisoners from a train and slaughtered them with a machine gun. Donovan recorded the story. To read it today is to look back through time at the tragedy of the Russian people in Siberia.

"I had heard of these killings that Semionoff was having at different points along the line of the railroad, but I really couldn't believe it," Lieutenant McDonald told Donovan.

> It didn't seem possible that such things could be true even here in Siberia, so I said to myself that it was just some more Russian lies. One day I went down to Adrianovka. I arrived there the evening of the 18th of August. Lieutenants McNutt and Griggs, of the Railway Corps, were there, and they told me about the killing of the Bolshevik prisoners. They said that that day they had tramped over a large part of the country a verst [about 1 km] or two east of Adrianovka, trying to locate the place of killing, but hadn't found anything. They said there was a train in the yards then, with about 400 prisoners in cars, and that indications were that there would be a killing in the next day or two.
>
> I knew the stories about Macavievo, and I knew they handled the prisoners rough. One morning I had seen a prison train with two cars filled with women, one boxcar and one regular prison car. As I was going by, an old woman looked out between the bars and hailed me. Then she pulled a young girl up to the window, a sick-looking redhaired girl, who

spoke to me in very good English. I then asked her where she was going, and she answered, "I only wish I knew." The train pulled out almost immediately, and I could not find out more.

Just the same, I found it hard to believe they were as bad as the stories made out. Early next morning, however—that was the nineteenth—we saw a bunch of Semionoff's soldiers walking in from the east, carrying long-handled shovels. The boys—I mean Lt. McNutt and Griggs—said they had seen the same kind of a gang come in previous to other killings.

Shortly afterwards we saw them loading soldiers on the prisoners' train, and taking a machine gun from an armoured car that was standing there, and putting it on the train. They took ten carloads—about a half—of the prisoners and started east from the yards. They left at 9:50.

It was then I decided to find out what I could about the killing, so I footed it east after them. About two versts out, I finally came in sight of the train (I call it the murder train) standing near a curve of the railroad. I kept on, hoping to reach the place, but was stopped by a guard. I was then about a hundred yards from the train, but because of the topography of the country, I couldn't see anything of the soldiers or the prisoners. I pretended not to understand Russian when the guard stopped me, but he put a shell into his rifle to assist my understanding. I understood; I knew I was near where the killing had been, and I wasn't quite sure when I walked away whether I'd get one from that guard or not.

I had only been back at the station a few minutes when that train came back empty. It had gone out full. It had been gone just one hour and fifty-five minutes. I noticed they had not brought the machine gun back. Then they loaded the second batch. By the way, Stepanoff, Semionoff's colonel in charge, just as the first load was leaving, went out and got a rifle for himself. There were Kolchak guards on the train, for they had on British uniforms. The second train was gone one hour and fifty minutes, and brought the machine gun back with it.

I didn't go out again that day, but the next morning McNutt and Griggs and I, three of us, went out. On the way, we met peasant women carrying boots and socks and clothing. At the place where the train had been standing the day before, we saw that the roadbed had marks of a large number of people getting off and moving about. The ground was littered with torn clothing, worn-out puttees, and papers of all kind, including a Bolsheviki rouble-note. Just a short distance from the track—about fifteen feet—we found one body, shot through the lower jaw, left, and through the cheek. Thirty feet further on we found another body. The weeds and ground by the bodies seemed to indicate struggles. The poor devils had evidently tried to escape. We walked on toward some mounds of fresh earth we saw, and found three large holes, two filled up and covered over, and one only about half filled, with just a little covering of earth over the bodies. I picked up several shells at the edge of the grave: of two different calibres, partly a large calibre, but mostly a smaller one. There was nothing to indicate what they were or where they were made. A short distance eastward, possibly a hundred yards from the three holes, we found another, that had evidently been there much longer. It was filled, but there was such a thin layer of earth on top that dogs or other animals had dragged some of the bodies out. Some had had the feet cut off, one had no head, one had the genitals cut off. Of course, dogs might have done it, but it didn't look like the work of dogs. At another hole we found just the trunk of a body lying on some fresh earth. It was all black and ugly.

It had been raining for some time, so we turned and went back to Adrianovka. It rained all the next day, but the day after that it cleared up in the afternoon. So at about five o'clock I went out with my camera to see if I could not get some pictures for evidence. The other boys didn't come with me; they had had enough. When I got there I found that the bodies had been buried. There were some little boys there, digging around after loot, and they told me that the section hands of the railway had done the burying. The boys showed me where six other bodies had been found on the other side of the tracks—shot evidently when they were trying to escape. It seemed to me the big killing had been done by lining the prisoners up along the edge of the hole, and firing at them catercornered across it. An old peasant woman that lived nearby told me they had had to give up getting in their grain because of the stench. . . . I told her they'd better get gas masks and go to it—they might need the grain. But I didn't get any pictures.

That night Semionoff went thru on his way east. There were a number of Japanese on the train, and women. They stopped at Adrianovka and had a celebration—a big banquet. Stepanoff was there. They had music and plenty of booze. Then Semionoff went on east, to Vladivostok.

"That night we saw the train of Semionoff," Donovan jotted in his diary on September 1.

Donovan's train reached Vladivostok on September 6, 1919, and his first intelligence mission was at an end. He helped Morris draft a report, which recommended against American support for the Kolchak government. Donovan and Morris found themselves forced to wait in Vladivostok to satisfy the Japanese quarantine regulations against cholera before they could continue on to Japan. Donovan also had trouble getting steamer space, but at last he sailed for Japan. He brought with him a copy of the *Tokyo Shimbun* of August 25, which accused Roland Morris of negotiating with Admiral Kolchak for an American base on the Kamchatka Peninsula.

The Japanese correspondent quoted "a certain report" as saying, "Ostensibly a lease on the coast of Kamchatka is for the acquisition of fishing rights. That, however, is a pretext. For naval purposes the United States is not satisfied with the Aleutian Islands. Again, to secure Petropavlovsk Bay on the southern coast of Kamchatka which is highly suitable for a naval base is undoubtedly the intention of the United States. This is without doubt the first step in the coercion of Japan by the United States. Japan cannot be indifferent."

In Tokyo, Donovan found that the Japanese talked about little but the American plot to establish a naval base on Kamchatka, while in reality there had been no negotiations whatsoever between Ambassador Morris and Admiral Kolchak on that question. On the other hand, the Japanese government was plotting in the most cynical way to take eastern Siberia away from Russia while the Russians were preoccupied with their bloody civil war. The western Allies had sent token forces into Siberia, but there were at least 120,000 Japanese troops in the country, and Japanese intrigue was pervasive.

At the request of Ambassador Morris, then Lt. Col. Robert L. Eichelberger, General Graves's intelligence officer, had completed an exhaustive study of Japanese actions and plans in Siberia. "The Japanese High Command managed to achieve for itself a record of complete perfidy, of the blackest and most heinous double-dealing," Eichelberger wrote.

Donovan was of the same opinion. He was very disturbed by what he had learned in Siberia and alarmed by the mounting anti-American attitude of the Japanese militarists. He made another entry in his Siberian journal: "There are those who believe that there can be no permanent and helpful solution to the Far Eastern tangle so long as Japan preserves the ideals of Germany and remains an aristocracy. You cannot name a single salient feature of Germany's psychology and method that cannot be duplicated in Japan.

"The sooner there takes place a radical change in Japan and the ideals of democracy come to the front of that country, the better for the Far East and for the whole world."

President Wilson did not send men into the field to find out the facts and then disregard their reports. He ordered American troops out of Siberia and exerted pressure on America's allies to remove their troops as well. On December 31, 1919, America's Siberian Expeditionary Force received orders to withdraw. The withdrawal began on January 17, 1920, and by April 1, the last American soldier had sailed from Vladivostok. The Russians were to solve their problems by themselves without foreign interference. Even the Japanese belatedly and reluctantly withdrew from Siberia. Admiral Kolchak's forces were defeated before the Allies left. In the spring of 1920, he was captured by the Bolsheviks and put to death.

Thirty years afterward, seated at his desk in his law office at 2 Wall Street in New York, Bill Donovan reminisced about his train ride across Siberia, and his impressions of the Kolchak government. "Admiral Kolchak was an honest and patriotic Russian," he said, "and it was a pity that he surrounded himself with men whose attitude toward the Russian people was little more than criminal. How could America help Kolchak when to do so would not help the Russian people?"

11

Fact-Finding in Europe

ONCE BACK IN the United States, Donovan took a train to Washington to report to John Lord O'Brian and to Secretary of War Baker. He wrote to Roland Morris, who was in Tokyo, "I dodged all the newspapermen until I was able to reach Washington and then passed through various departments."

Donovan experienced his first inquisition at the hands of the Washington press corps, which had sensed that the army officer who was so famed for his bravery and leadership in France was now the bearer of confidential information. "Baker first gave out an interview," he told Morris, "and then I asked them how far they wanted me to talk, and they replied I could state what I felt should be said." Donovan met with the press at the War Department and answered the questions put by the reporters with apparent candor. He told them only what it was in the national interest to say. It may have been his maiden performance before the press at the end of a fact-finding trip overseas, but he proved to be both compelling and effective.

The reports Donovan made to official Washington were received somewhat less enthusiastically. John Lord O'Brian and, through him, President Wilson might understand, but other government officers were less likely to listen. "I know you would have been greatly disappointed in the attitude of the State Department," he told Morris.

> There is a feeling there that the troops would be withdrawn, and that we would take no further action in Siberia excepting simply to say that Japan had been a naughty boy. They said they appreciated the position you had taken in regard to the Japanese menace in eastern Siberia but felt they could do nothing further, because they could not be backed by public opinion. I asked them how they could ever be backed unless they set out to enlighten public opinion.
>
> There has been in the last two months a great access of interest in the entire Eastern question, and if the administration were only wise enough even politically it could in its turn at least bring the great mass of the people behind it. I am afraid that the great trouble with both parties now is that they are pussy-footing. The election is too near.

The propensity for American political leaders to play domestic politics with even the most critical international issues was already apparent to Donovan. The timidity and indecision he found in the Wilson administration depressed him. Was Japan to be given a free hand in Siberia? Was nothing to be done about the suffering Russian people?

Donovan left for Buffalo, where he was disturbed to find crowds demonstrating in downtown streets in support of Russian Bolsheviks. "There is undoubtedly a sympathy, even though an unreasonable sympathy for the Bolsheviks, among a great many of the well-to-do pseudo-intellectual group," he wrote to Morris.

Pro- and anti-Bolsheviks alike went to see Donovan in Buffalo because, unlike most people interested in the Russian question, he had seen the civil war. He spoke with an authority that grew out of field experience. This was to become the hallmark of Donovan's approach to future foreign issues. Others might talk about the situation abroad, but he would base his views on observations he himself had made in the field.

Donovan, now living comfortably with Ruth and the children on Delaware Avenue and practicing law with the firm of O'Brian, Donovan, Goodyear, and Hellings, took an active interest in what was happening in Western Europe. On November 15, he met with a trade mission from Italy, Belgium, France, and England. The mission was headed by a Mr. Seiner, a French steel man whose factories had made the vaunted 75s and 155s, artillery pieces that had played such an important role in defeating Germany. Seiner informed Donovan that American banks must give huge credits to the devastated European nations or else they would be obliged to deal with their erstwhile enemy Germany. Conger Goodyear, brother of Donovan's law partner Bradley Goodyear, had just returned from Europe and had observed that Germany was "to his mind the strongest country economically on the continent."

Goodyear also reported a formidable pro-Kaiser group that, judging from its public acceptance, indicated that the new German Republic would not last very long. Goodyear had also visited Vienna, Prague, and Warsaw, and he informed Donovan that "conditions were pitiful in Vienna and Austria generally, that the people there seemed to have no hope, that the Czechs, while ignorant in the establishment of government, had enough capable men to really put their program through, and the Poles had a tremendous project and much of its success would be dependent upon the character of [Ignace] Paderewski." Cardinal Mercier, whom Donovan had met in 1916 when he was in Belgium for the War Relief Commission, stayed with Donovan for two days at the big house on Delaware Avenue and shared his views on the social and political situation in his own country.

Throughout the 1920s and 1930s Donovan was to keep himself informed about what was taking place outside his country's boundaries.

He made dozens of trips abroad. He talked with every foreign visitor or American traveler he could find who was capable of making useful observations on events. Just as he had once prepared himself for the practice of the law and military leadership, he now was preparing himself for a career in intelligence and foreign affairs. When John Lord O'Brian asked Donovan to go to Siberia, he had brought him into the informal circle of men who learned what they could about what was going on behind the scenes in the world and kept one another up-to-date. They also kept responsible officials of the American government informed. They were motivated by patriotism and by the conviction that the American government, which had virtually no intelligence service, must have accurate information and insight into the complicated world beyond the nation's boundaries.

At the same time Bill Donovan studied America's domestic affairs. He wanted to know such things as why the steel strike earlier in 1919 had been a failure. What effect was the coal strike then going on in December likely to have on the economy? He wondered whether American unions were going to be controlled by a radical element or by leaders with more traditional views. He wrote that "too many of our businessmen are attributing all of the trouble to the reaction after the emotional stimulus of the war and will not realize that a great economic change is being effected all over the world." He found his fellow Buffalo Club members to be singularly obtuse about economic and social issues.

Donovan took an interest in politics. The presidential sweepstakes was on, and he first supported Republican Gov. Frank Lowden of Illinois, "the businessman governor." Later he switched his allegiance to Maj. Gen. Leonard Wood, with whom he entered into a correspondence. It seemed to Donovan that Leonard Wood would make the best Republican candidate. He further believed that the Democrats would be well advised to nominate William McAdoo, who as Wilson's secretary of the treasury had done a remarkable job of financing the war through Liberty Loan drives and who had been director general of the nation's railroads when the government took them over during the war emergency.

Whenever Donovan's law practice took him to New York or Washington, he looked up men active in public affairs in his spare time, so that he soon became acquainted with such people as Bernard Baruch, "the adviser of presidents," who listened with interest to the lawyer from Buffalo. Donovan lamented that there was a dearth of leadership in the nation. "Everyone is talking, but no one seems to be thinking," he complained.

Donovan also took the leadership in organizing the first American Legion post in Buffalo. He became the first member in New York State of the national executive committee and in December chaired the New York delegation to the founding national convention in Minneapolis. Donovan was, in short, a very busy man—exuberant, fascinated by the world around him, his mind digging deep into all manner of subjects. Still he found time to remember Father Duffy, who had become very much involved in Irish politics. That year he sent Father Duffy a Christmas check. "Will you buy yourself the most vivid green pyjamas for Christmas, and think of me when you wear them," he wrote.

On New Year's Day, 1920, Bill Donovan was 37 years old. He was approaching middle age. Everybody who wished him a happy New Year at a party on New Year's Eve was impressed with what the young Irishman from the Buffalo waterfront had accomplished in the world, and many said so. But he was dissatisfied. Precious years had slipped away from him, and there was so much to be done in a world that had been turned topsy-turvy by the war.

The new year began happily for Bill and Ruth Donovan and their children, who were together at last. Ruth and Bill went everywhere in Buffalo society, their views were asked on everything, their opinions quoted, their social leadership followed. At the same time, Bill Donovan did not forget his old friends in the First Ward. Buffalo's mayor, James D. Griffin, grew up in the Irish First, and he remembered his father playing baseball for the Willdon Club, which William Donovan's old neighbors had named for the Irish boy who had made good. Sometimes Bill Donovan would saunter down from his law office in the Iroquois Building to the sandlot at Hayward and Elk, where the boys played ball. He also turned up in the old neighborhood to shoot off a blank pistol to start the annual footraces for the young boys. The boys always ran their best when they saw Buffalo's war hero holding the starting gun and eyeing them with a look of kind attention that seemed to single out each and every one. Donovan also judged the frequent horsemanship competitions held at the armory by his old Troop I. In February 1920 he became secretary of the District Republican Club.

In March Donovan sailed for Europe on a fact-finding mission. He traveled through the Low Countries, Germany, Poland, France, and Italy to observe conditions. He looked up old German friends from his 1916 stay in Berlin. He found the defeated Germans in a mood of self-pity; many felt deserted by their leaders, who had surrendered an army that was still unbeaten. Politicians, particularly those who were trying to make the new republic function, were scorned, and the military caste was praised as the last hope of the German people. The economy was in chaos, but already many Germans were talking about rearming.

In Paris, Donovan attended the peace conference as an observer.

The previous year the Treaty of Versailles had been signed with Germany; the Treaty of Saint-Germain had been concluded with Austria. The Treaty of Neuilly had ended the war with Bulgaria, but the victorious Allies were still wrangling about what to do with Hungary and Turkey. Donovan had no actual role to play in the discussions, but he was on intimate terms with the members of the American delegation, and his views were taken into account. As the spring faded into summer, a feeling of boredom and frustration had seized on the conference, and Donovan was far from sanguine about the results. He had already seen firsthand the mood in Germany, in part induced by the Treaty of Versailles, and he already held the view that the peace treaties had laid the foundation for a second world war.

Journalist Oswald Garrison Villard, who covered the tortuous negotiations, often talked with Donovan. In 1932 Villard wrote in *The Nation,* "I was so impressed with the man at the Peace Conference in Paris that I ventured to prophesy that he had a considerable career ahead of him." Many others attending the conference or covering it for the press were impressed with Colonel Donovan, who had come to Paris directly from an extensive tour of both defeated Germany and the victorious Allied nations. Donovan returned to America toward the end of May. He was fascinated by what he was learning in Europe, but he had a commitment at home.

That spring, before leaving for Europe, Donovan had been chosen as a delegate to the Republican National Convention in Chicago. Back in Buffalo he learned that the entire delegation was pledged to Nicholas Murray Butler, president of Columbia University, as a native-son candidate. It was understood that after the first ballot each of the delegates could vote his preference, and Donovan, together with most upstate New Yorkers, favored Leonard Wood. On Saturday, June 5, the New York delegation set out for Chicago on a special New York Central train. Donovan boarded in Buffalo late that evening. As the train rolled along the shores of Lake Erie, the delegates talked excitedly of Republican prospects for victory in the autumn, the qualities of the various candidates, and the platform issues. Chauncey M. Depew, 86 years old and as urbane and witty a politician as there was in America, dominated the talk. He had already attended a dozen GOP conventions. Donovan listened attentively but had little to say. There was a sense of history in the making.

Early the next afternoon, the train passed through the smoky Indiana suburbs, pulling into Chicago's LaSalle Street Station at 3:50 P.M. Senator James W. Wadsworth, who had taken an interest in young Donovan, had arrived in Chicago on an earlier train. Two New Yorkers, George Henry Payne and Lafayette R. Gleason, had adventurously driven west in an auto. The early arrivals met the special train, and there was a backslapping reunion on the station platform. Donovan and most of the other New Yorkers stayed at the Congress Hotel on South Michigan Avenue.

When they arrived at the hotel, they found General Wood standing in the lobby, shaking hands with incoming delegates so that they could get a close-up look at him. Wood proved to be an exemplary hand-shaker, but he could not compete, at least in volume, with his rival Sen. Hiram Johnson who, according to the *Chicago Tribune,* that day shook hands at the rate of 65 a minute for eight minutes. The New Yorkers roamed up and down Peacock Alley in the hotel, where Chicagoans traditionally went to see and be seen, and they talked late in their rooms. They read the New York newspapers, specially flown out to them.

Monday morning at 11:00 A.M. the delegation caucused in the hotel's Gold Room. Then they tramped up and down Michigan Avenue, where, from the University Club at Monroe to the Auditorium, each hotel had its own presidential candidate waiting in his suite to shake hands and explain in a few well-chosen words why the delegates should support him. Donovan ended the day still impressed with Wood, whom he believed to be the most impressive of America's soldiers-turned-politicians, with the exception of George Washington.

Donovan was up early on Tuesday morning and rambled off to walk through Grant Park. Then he fell in with the other 1,600 delegates and 13,000 guests who converged upon the Chicago Coliseum at 15th and Wabash, where the doors opened at 9:00 A.M. Young Ben Hecht, writing for the *Chicago Daily News,* reported: "Republicans marched upon the Coliseum today with pink feathers tucked behind their ears, lapels alive with badges, medals and streamers, hands swarming with banners and slogans.

"Michigan Avenue filled up. Wabash Avenue filled up. The side streets looked like little carnivals. The coppers at the door of the Coliseum began to perspire. The elegantly mannered colored gentleman assisting visitors to alight in front of the main entrance lost his gold-braided hat."

By 10:30 A.M. Donovan sat with the New York delegation on hard wooden kitchen chairs and listened as William Weil's Chicago Band played patriotic music. Henry L. Stimson joined the 88-man New York delegation. In years to come, when Donovan was to guide America's intelligence organization, Stimson, as Franklin Roosevelt's secretary of war, would be a close associate. Will H. Hays of Indiana, chairman of the Republican National Committee, called the convention to order. Donovan concentrated on the ringing speeches and on the wrangling and political infighting that were to be so much a part of his future life.

His first national convention was one of the hardest fought and hottest in American history. Chicago's weather turned out to be stifling. A late spring heat wave sent the thermometer into the middle 90s, and the delegates sweltered in the Coliseum. Events dragged on until, on Friday, the nominations were made. Leonard Wood led in all the early balloting, but he could not draw enough support from Governor Lowden to insure his nomination. Even on the first ballot, the New York delegation broke and gave 18.5 of its 88 votes to candidates other than Nicholas Murray Butler. To Donovan's regret, strong sentiment arose among the New Yorkers for Governor Lowden, whose reorganization of the state administration and businesslike performance in office had made him the darling of the conservatives. Each defection from the New York delegation, supposedly pledged to Butler, seemed to help Lowden.

With the Wood and Lowden supporters neck-and-neck in the voting, roll call after roll call droned on in the heat. At the end of the fourth ballot, Wood had 314.5 votes and Lowden had 289; Sen. Hiram Johnson had 140 votes, Pennsylvania Gov. W. E. Sproul had 79.5, and Sen. Warren G. Harding of Ohio had 61.5. Harding was far behind, but he had the advantage of a campaign manager, Harry M. Daugherty, who was a political infighter without peer at the convention. He also had the support of a coterie of U.S. senators, among which New York's Wadsworth was prominent, who wanted a nominee who would be "of the U.S. Senate, by the U.S. Senate, and for the U.S. Senate." They preferred a candidate who would be easy to dominate once he was in the White House, and handsome Warren Harding, who had never caused so much as a ripple in Congress, seemed ideal. Certainly both Wood and Lowden, and probably Johnson too, were far too able and headstrong.

On Saturday morning Lowden and Wood were still locked in combat, and the perspiring delegates could well imagine that they might be in Chicago all summer. What most delegates didn't know was that on Friday evening George Harvey, publisher of the *North American Review* and *Harvey's Weekly,* a member of the New York delegation, and a close friend of Senator Wadsworth, had invited a number of key delegates to a meeting in his suite 408–410 at the Blackstone Hotel. The delegates arrived at 10:00 P.M. and were met by Harry Daugherty, who proposed that Harding be the "dark horse" to break the deadlock between Wood and Lowden.

Key delegates were routed out of bed by phone calls and loud pounding on their doors and brought to the room to get their instructions for the next day's balloting. At four o'clock in the morning the coterie of senators in the suite sent for Warren Gamaliel Harding, who was soundly sleeping at the Auditorium Hotel. When he walked into the room, he was asked if there was anything in his background that would embarrass the Republican Party if he were nominated for the presidency. Harding went into the adjoining bedroom and thought for ten minutes. He came out and said, "No." ("Nobody thought to ask Harry Daugherty to search his own conscience," remarked Bill Donovan in 1952.)

After the eighth ballot on Saturday morning, it became obvious that political lightning had struck the convention. Delegations began to defect from the leading candidates to favor Warren G. Harding. On the tenth ballot, New York and Pennsylvania, both large contingents, declared for Harding, and he won with 674.7 votes. The convention exploded into wild celebration. Donovan watched his fellow delegates with disgust at the surrender that even he in the last ballot had been forced to join.

When the final vote was tallied, reporters asked Harding how the "deal" had been made. He grinned through his fatigue. "We were forced to stay with a pair of deuces and drew to a full house," he honestly replied.

Donovan rode the train back to Buffalo, where he angrily told Ruth about his first venture into Republican national politics.

Bill Donovan stayed at home for only a few weeks. On Friday, July 9, he sailed from New York aboard the SS *Olympic* in the company of Grayson M. P. Murphy. He had gotten to know Murphy in the Rainbow Division when Murphy had been a lieutenant colonel in charge of Operations. Prior to his military service Murphy, a New York banker, had been the first European commissioner of the American Red Cross. Now he was one of Donovan's intelligence friends. The two men represented a consortium in investments abroad. At the same time, they intended to learn what they could about political and economic developments in Europe.

In the days before air transport lent a casual quality to travel, ship passengers, particularly in first class, accepted one another socially and carried on extended conversations as they lounged in deck chairs, sipped a drink at the bar, or dined in full dress in the dining salon. The shipboard situation was made to order for Donovan, who was well versed in conversational chess.

Every day Donovan searched his fellow passengers for new insights, new viewpoints, new information. He and Murphy fell into conversation with Thomas Fortune Ryan, a New York financier, who was involved in everything from his city's street railways to mining diamonds in the Congo and Angola. Having spent the morning chatting about international finance with Ryan, Donovan turned to Foster Kennedy, a leading New York City neurologist. Kennedy had served in the British Army in the war, and the two men spoke of the psychological factors that affect men as they go into battle.

Some of Donovan's time was spent preparing a memorandum of corporation laws in Holland for Murphy, who was interested in Netherlands trade with China. A group of Murphy's associates were so impressed with Donovan during a shipboard conference that they suggested he be sent to China for two years to represent an international banking group.

The SS *Olympic* was now powered by oil rather than coal. Donovan investigated the advantages of the changeover. He talked with an Antwerp ivory merchant. He explored the cotton business. He delved into the virtues of the consortium's establishing a European headquarters. He discussed. He questioned. He listened. He watched. And he recorded conversations and observations in his diary.

Donovan's diaries and journals, kept on and off throughout his life, show much the same kaleidoscope of ideas and activities, the constantly searching mind, the rare combination of thinker and doer, the unusual blend of pragmatic idealism, gregarious friendship, and enlightened self-interest. Even in what was apparently casual conversation, his mind probed and dug, and he tucked ideas and facts away for future consideration.

The man with the easygoing charm was prized by all who came to know him on the ship for the incisive qualities of his mind, but he puzzled them. Why didn't he accept the opportunities that were offered to him to take his place among the top financiers and legal minds of the postwar period? They had not seen him on his previous trip in the spring, walking the streets of Warsaw, gazing at the pinched faces of cold and hungry children. They had not listened with him to embittered German aristocrats who refused to admit that their nation had lost the war. Nor had they watched the delegates at the Paris peace conference endlessly chattering and not understanding what dragon's teeth they were sowing. Aboard the *Olympic,* Donovan talked; but he listened more than he talked, and in so doing prepared himself still further for what was to be an enigmatic role in the future events, a role that in 1920 he already anticipated. Donovan arrived in London on the evening of Thursday, July 15.

Arthur Hamilton Lee, Lord Lee of Fareham, minister of agriculture, was married to an American woman, Ruth Moore, daughter of New York banker J. G. Moore. He had lived an adventurous life as a special correspondent for the *Daily Chronicle* of London during the Klondike gold rush in the Yukon, had made a military survey of the Canadian frontier, and had served as a military attaché with the U.S. Army during the Spanish-American War. Theodore Roosevelt had made him an honorary member of his Rough Riders. When Lord Lee heard that Colonel Donovan was in London, he invited him and Murphy to Chequers Court, his country estate.

On Sunday the two Americans drove 40 miles northwest of London into the Chiltern Hills of Buckinghamshire to one of England's most historic great houses. Donovan, with his fascination for ancient things, was intrigued to learn that the estate adjoined the Icknield Way, a road that had been constructed even before the arrival of the Romans and was most likely the oldest road in England. As Donovan was ushered into the Stone Hall, with its self-portrait of Sir Joshua Reynolds, he stepped for the first time into a great house that he was to visit often two decades later, when it was the official country residence of Prime Minister Winston Churchill. Lord Lee had presented Chequers to the British nation in 1917, together with an endowment for maintenance, but he was still in residence.

"This house, which is Tudor in style, had on its site a home as far back as 1100," Donovan wrote in his journal. "It is most tastefully arranged. It is low, built of old red brick, and has the old English leaded windows. It is rich in its collection of paintings, there being Rubens, Reynolds, Rembrandt, among the others. They also have some very rare mementoes, including the key of the room in which Napoleon was born, a lock of his hair, and a lock of the hair of his young son, also a locket of Queen Elizabeth, the top of which raised on a small hinge, inside being a very small worked likeness of Elizabeth and her mother. There was also a watch of Lord Nelson." Donovan, who always responded romantically to his brushes with history, also noted, "The most interesting thing was the life mask of Oliver Cromwell. Only one copy of this had been made, and that was given by Lord Lee to Roosevelt. This life mask showed Cromwell to be much fuller faced than I ever thought. He had a large nose and a wart on his right eyebrow."

Donovan was not impressed with Lord Lee. "He is a man of medium height, dark, rather bright looking," he observed, "but gives the impression of narrowness and selfishness."

In less than a year Lord Lee was to become first lord of the Admiralty, and until his death in 1947 was to play an important role in his nation's affairs. He was to become for Donovan a valued acquaintance during the years of World War II.

"I talked with Lee about the League of Nations," wrote Donovan. "He does not believe in it. I asked him if Lloyd George believes in it. This proved an embarrassing question, but I judged from the evasiveness of the answer that Lloyd George does not believe in it." During World War I, Lord Lee had been personal military secretary to David Lloyd George, and Donovan had reason to think that Lee had discovered the British prime minister's true feelings.

"I suppose that England and Germany will now play ball together," Donovan said to his host.

"Certainly, why not?" replied Lord Lee.

"I suppose that both of you will exploit Russia," remarked Donovan.

"I certainly hope so," said Lord Lee.

The subject changed to France. "I asked him what was the feeling towards France," Donovan wrote in his journal, "and he allowed that any feeling that had been whipped up in England during the war had since been lost; that one could not expect the Englishmen to think anything of the French."

Out of countless such conversations with political leaders, in and out of office, in every nation he visited over the next two decades, Donovan was to shape his shrewd insights into important individual and national attitudes.

Donovan and Murphy drove back to London that evening, since they had important appointments in the morning. "As we came home the whole countryside was flooded with people who had been on their day's outing. Every available field was crowded with those engaged in sports," wrote Donovan. The healthy interest the British showed in recreation and sports was clearly a source of their continued national vigor. Donovan observed the well-organized, well-uniformed Salvation Army holding meetings, and in Hyde Park he paused to listen to the orators who ranged throughout the political spectrum, each haranguing his own little knot of listeners. This too was a source of continued national vigor.

The next week was crammed with business discussions concerning potash and phosphate markets in Europe and the Far East, the Chinese market for power plants and textile machinery, and plans for the development of the Australian woolen industry. Donovan also found time to lunch on Tuesday with Lincoln Eyre, a foreign correspondent for the *New York World,* who had just arrived in London from a conference charting Europe's coal and steel future. Eyre also had with him motion-picture footage showing the tragic conditions in Bolshevik Russia. That afternoon Donovan attended the British Institute of Industrial Art Exhibition to study the latest in British technology, as well as the progress the British were making in putting their disabled ex-servicemen to productive work. There was still an hour of the afternoon left when he walked out of the exhibition, so he went immediately to the National Gallery to study a current exhibition of fine art.

During meetings over the next few days, Donovan learned about Chinese coal resources, efforts being made in South China to produce rubber, British factories being built in Shanghai to supply the Asiatic market, British automobile exports, and the establishment in Dusseldorf of a new German bank that would specialize in trade with and across Holland and in the import of basic raw materials into Germany.

On Friday he spent the day with an Italian financier visiting in London, who told him how Italian economic conditions were darkening the nation's future. "There is discontent in every class with the Government," Donovan wrote at the end of the day. "With the bourgeoisie because of the heavy impost of taxes; with the nationals because of what they consider a weak foreign policy in regard to Fiume; and with the workmen because of the heavy hand that has been placed on the striking of labor. In his opinion, however, while there are many isolated fires, there is no great conflagration. He would not be surprised, though, if the King should abdicate, but evolution, not revolution, would follow."

There also was a long talk with an expert on Spain. The key Spanish leather industry was facing bankruptcy, and the Spanish government had embargoed rice, which was in short supply. "It is a badly governed country," Donovan noted. "There are no constructive measures taken to perpetuate the prosperity of the war. There are strikes among the farm laborers, but due to the fact that the unions are not financially strong enough to take care of the men for more than six days, these strikes last for not longer than that period."

Donovan also found it significant to note that before the outbreak of the war, 200,000 people had emigrated from Britain to her colonies every year.

When his business discussions in London were concluded, Donovan continued on to the Continent. He made another tour of European nations, each of which was trying to repair the terrible damage done by the war not only to its cities and towns and their factories and shops, but also to the social fabric. He particularly valued a stay in Berlin, where Ellis Loring Dressel of the American Commission made it possible for him to see what was happening in Germany from the inside out. He visited the old battlefields of northern France where the Rainbow Divison had fought. He stood again at the graves of Joyce Kilmer and Oliver Ames. He could not help wondering if all the suffering and death, the heroism of the Fighting 69th had been for nothing. His sense of foreboding grew.

When Donovan returned to America, his report to John Lord O'Brian was anything but optimistic.

12

Racket-Busting DA

FRANK RAICHLE, a premier Buffalo attorney for more than 60 years, remembered the day back in 1920 that he first met Bill Donovan. "Back from Europe, Donovan talked to the dean of the University of Buffalo law school about getting a law clerk. The dean recommended me. I was a 1919 graduate, only twenty at the time, but I still had not passed my bar exams when I went down to Donovan's law offices for an interview. Donovan took a great interest in encouraging youth, and I was no exception."

Raichle saw the law office expand with the passing months. New men kept joining the firm. Among these was Ganson Depew, the brilliant nephew of Chauncey Depew, whom Donovan had come to know at the Republican convention in Chicago. Donovan went off to Europe on confidential business of his own from time to time, but he was, in the main, in Buffalo during 1921. It was a happy family time for Ruth and Bill and the children, an idyll that Ruth at least, knowing the mettle of her husband, recognized could not last.

Frank Raichle could also see that Bill Donovan—lawyer, clubman, Buffalo civic leader, husband, father—was restless. "He was ambitious but not offensively ambitious," he remembered of those years, as he himself became a junior partner and then a partner in the firm, which was emerging as one of the most important in western New York. Donovan was by then counted among the state's foremost trial lawyers.

In early 1922 the nation's coal miners went out on strike, and fuel rationing proved necessary in New York State. All sorts of legal problems arose, and on September 6, Gov. Nathan L. Miller appointed Bill Donovan counsel to William H. Woodin, the New York State fuel administrator. Donovan was to prosecute coal dealers who tried to profiteer in the emergency. The rich were not to stock their cellars with more coal than they needed while the poor went cold. He received no salary, but the job appealed to him.

Governor Miller was not the only man in public life who had his eye on the war hero, who was as able and honest as he was popular. Stephen T. Lockwood, U.S. district attorney for western New York, for the last eight years had been accused by the New York State Anti-Saloon League of a lack of zeal in enforcing Prohibition in the Buffalo area. Buffalo, being close to the Canadian border, was notorious both for rum-running and opium and heroin smuggling. Lockwood refused to resign under fire, but the Harding administration believed that he had become a political embarrassment. Senator James Wadsworth, who had come to appreciate Bill Donovan's qualities when they were together in Chicago, suggested to the attorney general and the President that Donovan would be a fine choice for the job, once Lockwood could be eased out of it.

Donovan was first approached about the matter in late autumn 1921, but he refused even to consider the post. He was, he claimed, entirely happy to be in private law practice. By December 20, reports came out of Washington stating that Donovan was not only willing but eager to accept the office. On February 7, 1922, President Harding appointed Donovan U.S. district attorney for western New York.

"I'm going to do whatever is my job," Donovan replied when newspapermen demanded to know what he was going to do as the DA.

Wets and dries alike applauded the new appointment, because each group felt that the new DA was bound to look upon its position with favor. On February 15 Donovan was sworn in at the Federal Building in Buffalo. Although a teetotaler himself, he did not believe in Prohibition. Yet after he had taken his oath, he informed the crowd that had gathered for the occasion, "The Prohibition law, as well as all other laws, will be strictly upheld." Donovan called attention to his oath of office to uphold the Constitution. When newspapermen pressed him on his position on Prohibition, he snapped, "This office is neither the side door of a saloon nor the anteroom of the Anti-Saloon League."

Donovan surrounded himself with capable young lawyers. At the same time, he paid close attention to the viewpoints of senior lawyers. He would sit late at night listening to leaders of the bar reminisce. "He was making an intellectual pattern, in which coming experiences would fall into their relationships," an older lawyer later told Anne Hard of the *New York Herald Tribune*, "and not be, as for so many young minds, entirely new. He had worked at war. Now he was working at law."

Frank Raichle had a burning desire to be a trial lawyer. "I wanted to be Bill's assistant," he remembered. "He only appointed Depew from our office."

Donovan's five young assistants were devoted to him. "There's no such thing as passing the buck with the Colonel," one told a reporter from the *Buffalo Times*. "So long as you do your best, it is always the right thing to do."

From his office in the Federal Building on Washington Street, Donovan set out to enforce the law without reservation. He reorganized the district attorney's office. He decided to start his reforms with the mayor of Buffalo.

Mayor Frank X. Schwab owned a brewery. When the Volstead Act was passed, forbidding the manufacture, sale, and transportation of alcoholic beverages, he ignored it. Buffalonians applauded, bought his beer, and elected him mayor, despite charges brought against him by Donovan's predecessor. Donovan moved Mayor Schwab's case to trial.

"It'll be political suicide to prosecute," he was advised. "If guilty, let him be given the extreme penalty," Donovan told the press. Schwab raged. Buffalo newspapers asserted that his indictment by the former district attorney had helped rather than hindered his election. Now confronted with Donovan, the mayor blustered but finally pleaded nolo contendere and accepted punishment. Donovan, who appreciated the legal tangle that would result from the conviction of the mayor on federal charges, accepted the plea.

Schwab agreed to a civil penalty of $10,000 and a criminal fine of $500. After he lost the next election, Buffalo's bootlegger mayor never forgave Donovan. Donovan's view on the matter was made clear in a letter to his friend Alexander Woollcott. "I think you agree with me that we do not want people in this country to think that they are above the law, and if you and I sweated and sloughed around France we did not do it in order to establish a 'Mandarin' government."

Donovan enforced the Prohibition laws against big and small rum-runners and bootleggers with impartiality. Rumrunners used the same routes across Lake Erie and the Niagara River from Canada that his grandfather had once used to smuggle Irishmen into the country, and from boyhood he had known exactly how things were done. Night interceptions by the Coast Guard were easy for him to arrange, and the flood of liquor across the Niagara frontier soon was reduced to a trickle.

"Are these men and is the invisible power behind these defendants, which is disclosed by their very attitude on the stand, to be the government of America?" Donovan demanded as he confronted bootleggers in court. "Are they to be able to invade our very courts of justice and there to break down by fraud, by intimidation, and by bribery the principles on which the entire structure of our government rests? Or are they to be made to feel that the forces of law have the courage to stand up and say that a reign of this kind—such a reign of terror as this—is at an end?"

The new district attorney cracked down even harder on narcotics smuggling. The narcotics ring for 17 western New York counties was controlled from Buffalo. The ring had bought protection from the Buffalo police and had so far been immune to prosecution.

A few hundred Chinese then lived in Buffalo on lower Michigan Avenue. Harry Chinn, known as the mayor of Chinatown, ruled over them with patriarchal authority. He was chief of the narcotics ring and openly operated an opium den on Michigan near William Street. He claimed that he could effect the transfer of any policeman who threatened to interfere. Donovan persuaded a police lieutenant, Austin J. Roche, to assist in cracking down on the narcotics ring, but Roche was soon transferred to a remote part of the city where he could do no damage. Despite his transfer, Roche continued to work in plain clothes during his off-duty time. He gained evidence that Chinn not only dealt in opium but also trafficked in morphine and cocaine.

Dissatisfied with the slow pace of the inquiry, Donovan telephoned Ralph Oyler, a nationally known federal narcotics agent in New York City, and asked him to come to Buffalo. He urged Oyler to bring Raphael Ray Connelly with him, because Connelly had ferreted out drugs in New York's Chinatown. Donovan also secretly brought a young Chinese named Chung Su to Buffalo. In the Buffalo Chinatown the youth claimed to be from San Francisco, and nobody guessed he was Donovan's man. He lost no time in working himself into Chinn's confidence. Chung Su discovered that Chinn not only headed the dope ring, but he also operated the fan-tan gambling network and smuggled Chinese aliens into the country.

Chung Su came to Donovan's office late one evening to report that Chinn was expecting a large shipment of opium from across the border. When Donovan directed him to try to buy a large portion of it, Chung Su succeeded in setting up the purchase at Harry Chinn's opium den. On the night of the deal, with opium and cash on the table before them, Chung Su and Chinn talked about future plans. At 6:00 P.M. Donovan and his men left the Federal Building and walked through a drizzling rain, their coat collars drawn up against the chill. They sauntered into Donovan's old neighborhood, attracting little attention as they blended in with the workmen from the railroad yards and the grain docks, who were going home from work.

When they reached Chinn's opium den, Donovan shouldered the door open and burst into the room, followed by his men. Chinn tried unsuccessfully to escape through a trapdoor that led underground through a secret tunnel.

The raid cracked the narcotics ring. Donovan's investigators had done such a thorough job that it proved possible to obtain indictments not only against Harry Chinn but also against Joe DiCarlo, who Donovan established was the actual leader of the gang. DiCarlo was also linked to the gangland slaying of "Busy Joe" Pattituccio at the Niagara Street Cafe some months before and was sentenced to a jail term in the U.S. Penitentiary at Atlanta. Chinn too went to jail. Bill Giallela and Lester Cameron, gangland chieftains, were convicted as well. The drug racket in Buffalo had come to an abrupt end.

For years a ring of burglars had looted the Buffalo freight yards of the New York Central Railroad. The railroad police and the Buffalo police refused to stop the thievery because they shared in the profits, which every year amounted to $2 million to $3 million. When Donovan's men began to investigate, a ringleader dropped in to see the DA. He pointed out that a minister who had spoken out against the racket had been repaid for his sermon: One night a blast had wrecked his house and seriously injured his children. The hoodlum threatened that Donovan's children would be kidnapped, his house dynamited, and he himself murdered.

"You fellows need a good adviser," Donovan replied. "You can't threaten me. I'll see you in jail." That day, Donovan characteristically worked late, ate a snack in a nearby beanery, and then walked the 3 miles home along Delaware Avenue. He refused to change his habits despite the threat.

"I'd much rather have had those criminals shoot me down than to hurt Ruth and the kids," he said later, "so I made myself an easy target." Nothing happened, not then or later.

Donovan drew up indictments of 36 men—including railroad policemen, yardmen, engineers, and fences—for having conspired to steal large quantities of goods from the railroad. Among the ringleaders was a prominent Buffalo Catholic. As the Jersey City lawyer Peter Bentley, who was in Buffalo at the time, reported, "When one of the representatives of the highest standing in the community or the Church approached Colonel Donovan on the subject of releasing this man, he was promptly shown the door and told never to return upon such a mission."

One of Ruth's maids also attempted to intercede with Donovan on behalf of the same defendant. "The Colonel asked the domestic what he ought to do if someone stole the money which the domestic had in a bank," wrote Bentley. "The reply was that the Colonel should send the criminal to jail. Colonel Donovan thereupon replied that that was what he was going to do to the man in question."

Donovan did send the gang to jail. Thirty-two in all went to the penitentiary.

Throughout 1922 Donovan attacked crime in western New York with a zeal that drew national attention. He broke up a crooked labor union, and he prosecuted the Rochester and Pittsburgh Coal and Iron Company for accepting rebates on freight rates from the Buffalo, Rochester and Pittsburgh Railway Company in violation of the Elkins Act. Each company paid a fine of $40,000. Donovan also prosecuted the New York Central, the Erie, and the Lehigh Valley railroads for violating the extension-of-credit provisions of the Interstate Commerce Commission.

That summer, workers struck the International Railway Company, which then operated high-speed electric trolley cars to Niagara Falls. On August 17, just as a train was crossing a trestle, a charge of dynamite went off and a number of passengers, including women and children, were maimed. Local authorities were slow to arrest the responsible strikers, and the nation's newspapers editorialized about the lack of law enforcement in western New York. Donovan entered the case and in a few days had the ringleaders and the actual "dynamitards" behind bars. He prosecuted them, and they were given sentences.

District Attorney Donovan forced an investigation of the Buffalo Police Department, and he prosecuted a state senator for perjury because of his false testimony about the train dynamiting. When the senator chose to run for reelection despite his conviction, Donovan asked President Harding to pardon him so that he would be eligible for office. "I don't want him to claim to be a martyr," he said. "I want the voters to defeat him."

The senator lost the election.

Donovan was himself a candidate for public office in the fall of 1922. Republican Gov. Nathan L. Miller, up for reelection, decided that he wanted Bill Donovan as his running mate for the office of lieutenant governor. When the party convention met in Albany at the end of September, the delegates judged that Donovan the war hero would lend strength to the ticket. On September 29, former Justice John Woodward of Buffalo arose on the convention floor to nominate Donovan. "I say that Colonel Donovan is the best equipped man in the state of his years," he orated.

Senator Wadsworth arose to loud cheers to second the nomination. "Donovan believes in being prepared to perform any service that comes to him," he remarked. "No lawyer in Buffalo has worked so hard to prepare himself for his profession. He fitted himself for service for the defense of his country in case of need long before the Great War. He is always ready."

Bill Donovan was nominated unanimously. On October 11 the *Buffalo Commercial* editorialized:

> It looks as though the Republican State Convention made no mistake when it put Colonel William J. Donovan on the ticket for Lieutenant Governor. If it were not for the overshadowing prominence of Nathan L. Miller and the imperative necessity of continuing him in office to carry out his plans and policies, Colonel Donovan might easily have secured first place on the ticket.
>
> The popularity of the man is boundless. He sprang from the common people. He is a self-made man in every sense of the word. Although he does not care to be exploited upon his record as a soldier, he nevertheless did his duty so strikingly and so effectively as to attract public notice. He is likeable and talented, level-headed and conservative.

Buffalonians were dismayed when the next month Alfred E. Smith defeated Nathan Miller. Miller had run a frugal administration and had killed popular programs in order to balance his budget. Al Smith promised a more openhanded approach to the governor's office. Donovan lost alongside his running mate, but he did attract 100,000 more votes than did Governor Miller. At the end of the year, Donovan and William Woodin both resigned from the Fuel Administration.

Donovan continued his gangbusting in western New York through the next two years, even when it meant raiding the Saturn Club, the leading blue-blood club in Buffalo. "Of course, Bill Donovan, Ganson Depew, Bradley Goodyear, and I were all members," recalled Frank Raichle. "Members had private lockers in which we kept our private booze. When Donovan hauled [gangland chief] Lester Cameron into court, he testified that one of his customers was the Saturn Club, and Bill warned club members time and again that they could not get around the Prohibition laws simply by keeping their liquor in lockers."

"What kind of man would raid his own club?" scoffed Bradley Goodyear, Donovan's friend and law partner.

Goodyear would have been well advised not to scoff. Newspaperman George G. Sher was in Donovan's office the night of the Saturn Club raid. "Go ahead, boys," Sher remembered Donovan telling the government agents. "I've warned these fellows three times. For all their prestige, they are no better than eastside saloons."

Recalling the evening in a letter to Herbert Hoover in 1929, Sher, by then managing editor of the *Philadelphia Record,* wrote, "Even now, the spirit of his enthusiasm sweeps over me as I recall the picture of him standing over the switchboard in his shirt sleeves waiting to give the word 'go' to a little band of government agents. And that at midnight when many men of Colonel Donovan's social standing would be enjoying some function or at home with their charming families."

"Dry Chief Michael H. Stapleton and his Merrie Men," as the *Buffalo Evening News* editor emeritus Alfred H. Kirchhofer labeled them, struck in the middle of the night. They broke into the lockers, each of which had the name of its owner on the door, and determined who was in violation of the law. When the story hit the morning papers, the Who's Who of Buffalo were identified as lawbreakers. The stories detailed exactly what was in each socialite's locker.

"The locker of Seymour H. Knox, Sr., for example, held a mere pint of whiskey," Kirchhofer noted. "One of the best stocked lockers at the Saturn Club was charged jointly to Shelton Weed and 'an eminent local jurist' whose name was covered up. Mr. Weed claimed entire ownership, thus absolving his brother-in-law . . . Louis B. Hart, a genial host and bon vivant, as well as surrogate of Erie County, and deeply embarrassed by the incident because of his judicial office."

The uproar was still mounting when Donovan's men raided the Buffalo Country Club, another lair of the socially prominent, where he was also a member. If somehow a leading citizen had escaped the Saturn Club raid, he now was incriminated in the country club raid. Committees of outraged club members were formed to fight Donovan. Club members took a pledge never to speak to him again, and Bradley Goodyear, who resigned in anger from the Donovan law firm, was one who never again spoke to him. Donovan's prominent brother-in-law, Dexter Rumsey, told everybody that it was exactly what might be expected from a moralistic Irishman with no sense of the proprieties. It is said that Ruth Donovan also never forgave him for embarrassing her family and their friends. Proper Buffalo had been revealed as amusingly improper.

"The Affair of the Lockers touched many eminent, respectable pillars of society," reported *Buffalo Magazine* six years later, "brought some of them unwelcome notoriety, which they felt Donovan was responsible for, broke up long-standing friendships and disrupted Donovan's own law firm, and left scars in his personal relations which have not yet healed."

A wag lampooned Donovan with a story that went around Buffalo: There was once a top sergeant known for his picturesque language. One day a private came to him grousing about a certain lieutenant who was making life miserable for him because of his insistence on the meticulous performance of certain unnecessary tasks. The sergeant listened to the complaints and then burst out, "That blankety-blank looie is just plain dooty struck!"

"Duty struck" Donovan was praised by his admirers for his devotion to his office and scorned by most of his own social set in Buffalo as a traitor to his class. What had happened, asked his critics, to the engaging young Irishman who had formed and led Troop I, had gone off to France and returned a war hero, and had shown such brilliance at the bar?

When a reporter from the *Buffalo Times* asked Donovan why he had raided the Saturn Club, he said, "Just as the crowd takes the cut of its clothes from its leaders, so also does it take its moral tone from them."

Donovan's remaining friends maintained that he had had no choice in the matter. He could not refrain from the raids without violating his oath of office, and he could not withhold the names from the newspapers. To do so would have meant one law for the poor and another for the rich, one law for strangers and another for his friends. His enemies insisted that he had engineered the whole thing to grab headlines and further his political ambitions. They also spread a rumor that Bill Donovan, the moralistic public official, had an immoral side to his private life. Some of his late hours, they said, weren't spent at the office at all but in the company of young women. When this gossip reached Ruth Donovan, her embarrassment and anger increased. She was left with a lasting wound when it became clear that there was more than a little truth to the rumors.

"I've heard the affair of the lockers discussed from California to Paris," Frank Raichle stated, "and there is no doubt that to this day Buffalo has still not forgiven Bill Donovan. When Herbert Hoover was considering Bill Donovan as attorney general or secretary of state, Buffalonians, instead of helping him to achieve high office, did everything they could to defeat him."

Ganson Depew stood by Donovan, but later in the year he died as a result of a polo accident. Bill Donovan, once the darling of the Buffalo Establishment, was now persona non grata. All the rest of his life, he was to feel the bitterness of this first serious reversal in his fortunes, but to all appearances he paid no attention. He traveled to Ottawa and talked to Canadian government officials about the feasibility of an international customs convention, which would help to close the Niagara border to illegal drugs and liquor. He persuaded Washington to take up the matter, and later in 1923 when a conference was held in Ottawa, he was the leading member of the American delegation. With the signing of an agreement, customs officers of the United States and Canada joined to combat smuggling. The convention would help catch violators of both countries' laws.

Donovan may have lost ground in his political career, but he was still a much admired soldier. In 1922 he had been elected national president of the Rainbow Division Veterans Association. More satisfying to Bill Donovan, early the following year he took the train down to New York City where, on January 17, 1923, at the jam-packed Lexington Avenue Armory, Maj. Gen. Robert L. Bullard presented the Congressional Medal of Honor that Donovan had been awarded in 1918 for his gallantry in France. General Bullard spoke eloquently and concluded, "I congratulate you on not having to die on the field of battle to get this medal as many have in our wars."

Fourteen hundred survivors of the regiment's campaign in France roared their approval until the armory shook. They shouted even louder when Donovan handed the medal over to the regiment for custody.

"A regiment lives by its traditions," said Donovan. "The noble tradition we have inherited impels me to ask that this medal remain in the Armory, there to serve as a recognition of the valor of our regiment, as an incentive to those who enlist under its standard, but most of all as a memorial to our brave and unforgotten dead."

In January 1923, Ruth and Bill Donovan sailed for Europe, where they stayed for three months. They enjoyed themselves thoroughly, looking up old friends and making new ones. At the same time, Donovan's investigations into what was happening and going to happen in Europe continued.

In Berchtesgaden he met a young political activist, six years his junior, who in 1919 as an agent of the German Army had enlisted in the obscure German Workers' Party to spy on it from within. He had become something other than an agent; in fact, he was soon a member of· the party's executive committee and had been instrumental in changing its name to the National Socialist German Workers' Party. Radical ideas were flourishing in the depressed Germany of 1923, and the new party trumpeted a jingoistic pride in the German people and a hatred for the bumbling Weimar Republic.

There were rumors that the party leader planned a march on Berlin. His name was Adolf Hitler, and Donovan was never to forget his meeting with him at the Pension Moritz, where Hitler lived at the time.

The Adolf Hitler that Bill Donovan met that March evening in the Bavarian Alpine resort confided in him as people were likely to do throughout his life. Hitler talked about his gentle Czech mother, Klara, and about his father, a brutal man who had struck him as a boy, and had beaten his pet dog until it wet on the carpet. "*I* never wet the carpet," Hitler told Donovan.

The evening was a monologue. Hitler told of his injury by a gas attack in 1918 and said that his eyes had never been right since. He talked about music: He disliked the music of Bach, Beethoven, and Brahms and preferred to listen to Wagner. He sipped his beer and whistled the "Swan Song" from *Lohengrin,* breathing in and out in a strange way so that the whistle never ceased. He was, Hitler said, like Christ driving the Jewish moneylenders from the temple. He was damp with perspiration when he finished talking. When it was time for the sympathetic American to leave, Hitler clasped Donovan's hand and shook it warmly.

Was Adolf Hitler merely a strange young man twisted by a sordid childhood? Donovan did not think so. Germany was a nation in profound trouble, and Hitler had a curious magnetism. As for Hitler, he was never to forget Donovan.

On April 18, Ruth and Bill Donovan returned to New York on the White Star liner *Majestic*. When shipboard reporters asked him what he thought of conditions in Europe, Donovan said that things were much improved but that the people were depressed. He did not mention the overwhelming problems he saw confronting the Weimar Republic in Germany.

13

With the Department of Justice

WHILE DISTRICT ATTORNEY DONOVAN was racket-busting in western New York, Harry Daugherty, attorney general of the United States, was bringing notoriety to the Harding administration with his poker and liquor parties at Howard Mannington's little green house on K Street, his stock market speculations, and the sale of Department of Justice liquor permits. With the death of President Harding on August 2, 1923, the Teapot Dome scandal erupted. At the Senate hearings that began in October, Daugherty's involvement in the sale of naval oil lands also became evident.

On March 1, 1924, on a return trip to Buffalo from Florida, Donovan stopped off in Washington to confer with Republican leaders about what was to be done with Daugherty. Newspapers printed stories that President Calvin Coolidge was about to remove Daugherty and put Donovan in his place, but Daugherty refused to resign his position in the face of the Senate inquiry. To do so, he claimed, would be to admit guilt.

"Daugherty's determination to stay in the cabinet until a thorough investigation of his department is made by the Senate Committee affects Donovan's nomination," reported the *Chicago Tribune*.

Donovan returned to Buffalo. When on March 28 Daugherty changed his mind and resigned at Coolidge's insistence, it was not Donovan but Harlan F. Stone, dean of the Columbia University Law School, who took his place. Stone went to Washington to meet with the President on April 9. When he left the White House, he asked a policeman, "Where is the Department of Justice?" Stone followed the officer's directions to the office on Vermont Avenue, where he set about cleaning up the accumulated mess left by what was one of the most corrupt administrations in American history.

Harlan Stone had followed with pride and approval the career of his prize student, William J. Donovan, and he asked him to come to Washington to take charge of the criminal division of the Department of Justice. Stone explained to Donovan that he wanted him to enforce the laws of the United States on a national level as vigorously as he had enforced them in western New York.

At Sunday dinner in Buffalo, Bill and Ruth Donovan told their children that they were moving to Washington. By then David was 9 and Patricia, 7. David was beginning to wonder if having a famous and dynamic father was an ideal arrangement for a boy. "Gee, Dad," he said. "Don't you think you could get a job as a bus driver instead?"

The Donovans moved to Washington, where they bought a handsome house at 1637 30th Street, Northwest, in Georgetown. Within a few days 41-year-old Bill Donovan had his first confrontation with 29-year-old John Edgar Hoover, acting director of the Federal Bureau of Investigation. Both men had been born on New Year's Day. But from the start they decided not to send one another birthday cards.

Under Harry Daugherty, Hoover had done much as he pleased; now he had to report to Donovan. Both Donovan and Hoover were ambitious, and Hoover resented the glamorous war hero's having authority over him, particularly when Donovan appeared to suspect that Hoover might well have been deeply involved in the skulduggery of the previous administration. Donovan learned that Hoover was tapping the telephones of private citizens, and he told Attorney General Stone. Stone called Hoover into his office and dressed him down.

Even at this early date in his career, J. Edgar Hoover was a law unto himself. He kept every one of his wiretaps in place. He also let it be known that he expected to be appointed director of the FBI by the attorney general, and he was furious when Donovan urged Stone not to give Hoover the job but instead to fire him.

"Hoover responded by making it clear to Stone that there was enough in his files to effectively sink the Republican Party in the upcoming presidential election," wrote William R. Corson in his book *The Armies of Ignorance*.

Donovan was disappointed when his onetime professor yielded in the face of Hoover's threat and appointed him FBI director on December 19, 1924. Donovan felt a great dislike for Hoover, a feeling that Hoover more than reciprocated. The enmity between the two men was to have serious results during World War II, when Hoover, the director of the FBI, continued his vendetta against Donovan, the director of the OSS.

The confrontation with Hoover was scarcely Donovan's only problem. He was responsible for prosecuting the Alien Property Custodian and other officials of the preceding administration. At Stone's request he also investigated the conduct of Sen. Burton K. Wheeler of Montana. Wheeler had been charged by Daugherty with practicing law before a government agency while being a public official, with the intent of defrauding the government. Americans believed at the time that Daugherty had concocted the charges with the aid of the FBI to harass Wheeler, whose Senate committee was in turn investigating Daugherty's conduct in office. On April 8 a federal grand jury at Great

Falls, Montana, had indicted Wheeler. Senator Tom Walsh of Montana acted as Wheeler's counsel. Felix Frankfurter considered the charges ludicrous and told Stone so, but the attorney general did not think it proper simply to drop the case without an effort to determine whether it had any validity. Donovan began his work on the case on September 24 and turned in his report to Stone on December 1. He recommended that Wheeler be prosecuted, and early in 1925 Stone obtained a second indictment from a District of Columbia grand jury.

When the case came to trial in Great Falls, the jury deliberated for ten minutes and acquitted Wheeler on the first ballot. H. L. Mencken wrote in the *Baltimore Sun*, "After filling the newspapers with fulminations for weeks on end, all the Daugherty gang could produce at Great Falls was a lot of testimony so palpably nonsensical and perjured that the jury laughed at it." In Washington a judge quashed the second indictment after hearing the legal arguments by Wheeler's defense.

Donovan and J. Edgar Hoover, who had made the initial investigations, were both blamed for the fiasco, and such powerful senators as Burton K. Wheeler, Tom Walsh, and William Borah held a lasting grudge against Donovan. Felix Frankfurter also felt that Donovan had behaved badly in the matter. For his part, Donovan always insisted that he had pushed the matter simply so that Wheeler would have every opportunity to demonstrate his innocence. "Senator Wheeler always got a fair break from me, and he knows it," he said later.

Much of Donovan's time during his first year at the Department of Justice was devoted to criminal cases. He cracked down on U.S. district attorneys who were lax in enforcing the laws. "He exercised discipline in a very forceful way," said longtime Donovan associate James Murphy, at the time a law student and later a prominent Washington attorney. "He called a DA from Washington and really tore the man to pieces. Then at the end he was gentle and sympathetic." Because Donovan had been one of the most successful crime-busting district attorneys in the nation, he knew what he was talking about. One way or another, he demanded results.

At the same time that he sent FBI agents into the field to probe wrongdoing, Donovan himself sometimes took to the field. Once, for example, reports reached him that bootleggers Willie Haar, Mannie Kessler, and George Remus had bribed Warden A. C. Sartain of the Atlanta Penitentiary to let them live in his house instead of in prison cells. Drugs and liquor were reportedly being smuggled into the jail. Donovan took a train to Atlanta. The bootleggers and the warden were enjoying their nightly game of poker above the warden's garage while another convict, known as Cincinnati, mounted guard at the foot of the stairs. The game was about to break up when a burly man pushed past Cincinnati and leaped up the stairs. To their amazement, the poker players found themselves being placed under arrest by the assistant attorney general of the United States. Donovan interrogated his prisoners, carried out an early-morning inspection of the penitentiary, prepared his case at breakfast, and went before the grand jury that morning. The jury indicted the warden and other officials. Donovan caught the first train to Washington and was there before the Washington newspapers had the story. Warden Sartain was convicted and locked up in his own prison, and Washington had another Bill Donovan yarn to tell.

Newspaper and magazine reporters sought out Bill Donovan for stories since he could always be counted on for a colorful interview. Mabel Willebrandt might go soberly about the task of enforcing Prohibition, but it was Bill Donovan who boarded the dirigible *Los Angeles* to fly with Vice Adm. Emory Scott Land and Assistant Secretary of the Navy Theodore Robinson to the West Indies to check on rum smugglers. They landed in Haiti and in the Virgin Islands. When they went aboard the battleship USS *Colorado,* Donovan climbed into a Vought seaplane beside the pilot and hitched a ride as the plane was catapulted into the air. In one interview, he was quoted as saying, "Everyone should learn to take a punch on the nose, to give one, and be in shape to give and take." On another occasion, he told a reporter, "The fellow who gets used to the soft seat of an automobile is liable to look for the soft side of popularity."

Donovan was asked to give advice to youth. "Do your job fearlessly without favor," he pronounced. "Don't ask your subordinate to do what you cannot do first. If you can do your task in a friendly way, by all means do it; but if you have to fight, hit first. Fight with your head; don't just get excited. And always be ready for the next step."

Middle-class America had found a champion in Washington. Hugh Fullerton, writing in the *Chicago Tribune,* said that Donovan "is the sort of human being God planned when he decided to create a man!" Still, J. Edgar Hoover didn't like Donovan, an increasing number of congressmen didn't like him, and such intellectuals as Felix Frankfurter didn't like him either. Politicians began to fear him as a dangerous rival.

Before he went to Washington, Donovan had been one of the front-running candidates for the Republican nomination for governor of New York. Instead he chose to throw his political weight behind his friend Col. Theodore Roosevelt, Jr., at the convention in Rochester. Roosevelt was nominated.

On October 2, 1924, Donovan led a delegation of Republican officials aboard a special Long Island Railroad train in New York and traveled out to Oyster Bay. At the railroad station, a band played "Hail, Hail, the Gang's All Here," while the officials got into 100 autos and moved in a procession to Roosevelt's Cove Neck home. The massed autos played their headlights on the porch, and then the assembled crowd marched to the house, carrying flares. When Roosevelt stepped out on the porch, there was a great cheer from the thousand people who had gathered on the lawn. Donovan informed Roosevelt that the convention had picked him to campaign against Al Smith, the Democratic candidate. Fireworks were set off, and again there was a loud cheer. Many of the Republicans there that night thought Bill Donovan would have made the best candidate for the governorship. They were even more certain of this when Al Smith won the election, a victory that made him the first Catholic presidential candidate four years later.

On March 2, 1925, Attorney General Stone resigned to become a Supreme Court justice, and Bill Donovan became the acting attorney general. The Law Enforcement Committee of 1000 urged President Coolidge to appoint Donovan attorney general, but the President instead named John Garibaldi Sargent, a fellow New Englander. If Donovan was disappointed at being passed over, he gave no indication. He cheerfully accepted Coolidge's decision on March 24 to put him in charge of the antitrust division as assistant to the attorney general. He moved into a flatiron-shaped office and set about enforcing the Sherman and Clayton acts.

"Government must not rely on its authority," said Donovan to the business community, "but upon its quality and character. . . . The Department of Justice in its enforcement of the law should be firm, but it should also be fair."

It was Donovan's view that the American businessman was not by nature a criminal. He remarked that business needs "a traffic policeman rather than a detective." American businessmen, he said, "should not be treated as though they were narcotics peddlers." He urged that business leaders who were contemplating plans that might result in possible infringements of the antitrust laws come to see him and get his opinion in advance. In this way he managed to head off violations of the law.

"Donovan was firmly convinced that individual freedom was vitally linked to our system of free enterprise," commented Allen Dulles, later closely associated with Donovan in the OSS. "He attacked restraints and monopoly with effective enthusiasm. In the Trenton Potteries case, the Supreme Court agreed that price fixing, per se, among dominant competitors was illegal. Brought under legal attack were such diverse industries as oil, sugar, harvesting machinery, motion pictures, water transportation, and labor unions."

Robert Choate, Washington correspondent of the *Boston Herald,* interviewed Donovan in his office and found him wearing a vested suit and a high collar, with his watch fob showing in just the right way.

> He was seated at his desk signing his mail and dictating to a secretary at the same time. He did not look like a trust-buster. He lacked the proverbial austerity of the lawyer. His light blue eyes radiated a warm personality, yet somehow, on entering the room, one was filled with a sense of intense activity.
>
> He was the least professional, yet the most businesslike of men. There were no formalities about him, no pomposity, none of the great and small pretenses with which men in public life invariably surround themselves as food for their vanities.

Donovan's energy and talents reached far beyond the antitrust division, and the saying went around Washington, "Donovan is the Department of Justice, and the Department of Justice is Donovan." He was given the authority to reorganize the department from top to bottom, and he did so. In 1925 he reduced his division's budget from $500,000 to $200,000, while at the same time collecting $600,000 in fines. To Washington insiders it seemed that when they approached the Department of Justice with any problem at all they'd be told, "Donovan has charge of that," or, "You had better see Donovan about that." They came to know that if they called Main 195, Branch 186, Donovan himself would pick up the phone and they would get action.

Anne Hard of the *New York Herald Tribune* watched Donovan argue a case before the Supreme Court. "His large, ingenuous blue eyes, unwinking, the quiet smile which frequently plays over his face, the softness of his voice, are deceptively disarming," she wrote. "He chooses very simple words. He speaks to the court as one gentleman to another by a fire in a library."

The courtroom victories won by Donovan became legendary. By the time of his resignation in 1929 he had pleaded and won more cases before the Supreme Court than any other man in history. One of his most important victories was in the Trenton Potteries case. Although he was opposed by Charles Evans Hughes, later Chief Justice of the Supreme Court, he persuaded the court to lay down the principle that an agreement on prices by manufacturers controlling an industry was illegal whether or not the prices agreed upon were high or low.

Donovan also turned out to be an effective spokesman for the Department of Justice at Senate hearings. Probably the most dramatic occasion was Donovan's confrontation with Sen. Tom Walsh, who still bore him a grudge. Harlan Stone had originally brought antitrust action against the Aluminum Company of America (ALCOA), in which the Mellon family of Pittsburgh had a large stake. After conferences with Coolidge and Andrew W. Mellon, Donovan announced on January 2, 1926, that the case against ALCOA was insubstantial. However, because Mellon was treasury secretary, the Senate Judiciary Committee decided to investigate the matter.

When the hearings began on January 8, Senator Walsh attacked Attorney General Sargent. He accused him of inattention to duty, of doing nothing about the case for eight months after he took office. Sharply questioned, Sargent insisted that the case was entirely in Donovan's hands. Donovan was the second witness, and he stepped into what was described as "an amphitheatre strung with leased telegraph wires and radio aerials" with a jaunty smile.

"Now, Senator," remarked Donovan at the outset. "I want this clearly understood, that I assume you and I are trying to analyze this as a couple of lawyers from the standpoint of evidentiary value, and not from the standpoint of any defense of the aluminum company."

"What a combat!" wrote Anne Hard. "On the one hand that fighting Irishman, Tom Walsh, of Montana, investigating, cross-examining. On the other hand that fighting Irishman of New York, answering, retorting.

> Usually in Washington almost any Democrat can chase almost any Republican by just waving an investigatory carving knife at him. Most Republicans in Washington when it comes to answering and retorting are dumb, driven cattle. Donovan turned on Walsh and gave him rapiers and poniards and battle axes for every carving knife he had.
>
> This was the best personal battle that any Senatorial investigation in Washington within my memory has exhibited. It was one of the few occasions upon which Walsh was obliged to leave the field unvictorious. That result required a man of Donovan's realistic preparedness plus his delight in the exchange of blows.

Donovan tied Walsh up in legal knots over the difference between evidence, hearsay, and "double hearsay." When he differed with the senator, he remarked with a smile, "I do not so understand it." He pointed out that J. E. P. Dunn, the Department of Justice's special investigator on the case, had found no evidence against ALCOA. The investigation was still going on, however. Walsh was sputtering with rage as the encounter drew near its end, and he angrily questioned Donovan's integrity in office. "I have learned the obligations to my country in other places than around this table," Donovan retorted, realizing that everybody in the room knew that he was one of the most highly decorated Americans in the history of the republic.

After the hearing had concluded, Donovan remarked, "A man in Washington who does not fear political consequences is a fool." Yet within a few months he was telling Robert Choate of his philosophy of law enforcement, "Diligence without recklessness. Strike with speed and summarily; don't be influenced by those with political affiliations."

Donovan may have decided that there was no case against ALCOA, but he prosecuted and won more antitrust cases than had any previous head of the antitrust division. He considered long-drawn-out cases a hardship and an expense for both the concerned businesses and the government, so he moved with speed. Of five cases he started in early 1926, four were terminated by July. He paid particular attention to industries concerned with the necessities of life, because he considered that they had the greatest impact on the average American.

These were good family years for Bill and Ruth Donovan. There were games of squash and tennis, hiking in Rock Creek Park, and boating on the Potomac or on Chesapeake Bay. Donovan found time to cultivate such people as Harlan Stone, whom he provided with occasional tickets for the Army–Navy game or sent such books as the *Life of Benjamin Franklin*. Stone was pleased with the book, and Donovan and he corresponded about Franklin throughout 1926. When Stone later decided to drive to the West, Donovan suggested an auto route and provided him with pamphlets about Yellowstone Park. Donovan also corresponded with William Howard Taft about points of legal scholarship and invited Taft to be a guest at the Donovan home in Buffalo when Taft attended the American Bar Association meetings there. Taft declined.

14

The Parade Passes By

DURING HIS YEARS in the Department of Justice, Bill Donovan curtailed his fact-finding trips to Europe, but he kept his finger on what was happening there. He took a direct interest in the Paris spy trial of Jules César and Joseph Laperre, and asked Secretary of State Frank Kellogg to obtain for him the official French report on the case. He made friends of foreign diplomats, scholars, and businessmen who came to Washington. Father Kornikowicz of Lublin University in Poland was his house guest when he came to America to arrange for the exchange of books and periodicals. Donovan learned a great deal about conditions in Poland from Kornikowicz. Charles Dewey, financial adviser to the Polish government in Warsaw, also informed him about events in Poland, and Polish Ambassador Jan Ciechanowski was a frequent Sunday afternoon visitor to Donovan's Georgetown home. The ambassador sipped Donovan's wine before the living-room fire and answered Donovan's questions about his country. Donovan was convinced in the late 1920s that Poland would be the first European nation to be torn apart by the next war in Europe.

Whatever country in Europe or the Far East came under his scrutiny, Donovan had well-placed contacts there. Italian Ambassador Augusto Rossi was a frequent dinner guest. Stanton Griffis, roving U.S. ambassador in Europe, was close to Donovan, and when Griffis returned from Europe, he invariably conferred with Donovan, giving him the latest information and asking his opinions before he reported to the President.

In the summer of 1927 President Coolidge announced, "I do not choose to run for President in 1928," and the race was on. Vice-President Charles G. Dawes and Secretary of Commerce Herbert Hoover were the principal candidates. Since Dawes had defeated Hoover by a vote of 682.5 to 234.5 for the nomination for vice-president at the Republican convention of 1924, he was the favorite, but Bill Donovan favored Hoover. They had known one another since meeting in London in 1916 when both were in war relief work. In the spring of 1927, Hoover had been Donovan's sponsor for the select Cosmos Club in Washington, and in July Hoover, a member of San Francisco's Bohemian Club, had invited Donovan to attend the club's August encampment in Bohemian Grove north of San Francisco. Later in the summer Hoover was Donovan's guest at his Buffalo home. Donovan spent the Christmas holidays with his family in Buffalo, and announced on the day after Christmas his support for Herbert Hoover for president.

By May of 1928, most of the Republican politicians in New York State, led by Charles D. Hilles, GOP national committeeman, favored Dawes. When the party gathered in convention in Kansas City in June, Donovan found himself estranged from the remainder of the New York delegation. The political bosses might dislike Hoover because they felt he would be hard to control, but Donovan admired his integrity and moral approach to politics. Donovan was with Hoover at his headquarters during the political infighting. "I sat across the desk from him from early morning till late at night," he wrote to Alfred H. Kirchhofer, the Buffalo editor who was Hoover's press chief, "and with him went through every phase of the activities. I came out of it with a finer conception of his character as well as of his quality of leadership, than I ever had before."

When it appeared that Dawes could not win, his supporters tried to persuade Coolidge that he should change his mind and run. When Coolidge would have none of it, they then attempted to get Hoover to at least make a deal over the nomination for vice-president. Donovan, whose friends had been booming him for the vice-presidency, was convinced that an open convention was not only good democracy but was in his own interest. A group of young idealists supported Donovan, but the political bosses who would control a closed convention rejected him as being too unmanageable.

"He was subjected to terrific pressure to indicate his choice," wrote Donovan of Hoover. "Perhaps I lent him some aid in refusing to yield and in insisting upon a free and open convention. I believed if he did this, the break would come. He would be in a much stronger position than if he had entered into any deal with anyone. The result justified that opinion."

Dawes withdrew, and Hoover was nominated on the first ballot. Senator Charles Curtis of Kansas was picked to be the candidate for vice-president.

"I think that the great significance of this nomination is something that the newspapers have missed," concluded Donovan. "It is retributive justice. The same gang that eight years ago emerged from a smoke-filled room victorious, this time had to go to the same kind of a room to surrender."

Hoover symbolized the swelling American prosperity and support for Prohibition, which he called the "noble experiment." Al Smith, the Democratic candidate, espoused repealing the 18th Amendment. Also, he was opposed by most rural American Protestants because he was a

Roman Catholic. On July 27, Hoover was given a tumultuous welcome home by his neighbors in Palo Alto, California, and immediately got to work with Bill Donovan's assistance in writing his acceptance speech. Once the speech was written, Hoover practiced it before a critical Donovan, who recommended taking this phrase out and adding that one or emphasizing this word or that. Finally with some old Stanford friends, 13 newspapermen, and Hoover's son Allan, the candidate and his speech writer went on a five-day fishing trip to relax. Donovan and Hoover put the finishing touches on the speech, which Hoover delivered on August 11 before a cheering crowd in the Stanford University football stadium.

"Given a chance to go forward with the policies of the last eight years, we shall soon, with the help of God, be in sight of the day when poverty will be banished from this nation," concluded Hoover.

During the campaign, Donovan was Hoover's strategist. "The political fight is on," he wrote Kirchhofer, "and I think it will be a hard one. You see, Smith, relying on the continued loyalty of the Southern Democrats, slapped them in the face with his 'wet' statement. There are many who claim that he will cut into the East."

Donovan sent men out to take confidential polls of key voting areas in the East. When influential people came to Washington to see Hoover, Donovan entertained them at his Georgetown home. When New York Republican Catholics threatened to bolt the party to campaign for Smith, Donovan called upon them to stay with Hoover. After all, he pointed out, he himself was a Catholic who was devoted to Hoover's candidacy.

Several years before the campaign, Donovan and other prominent Catholics in public life had formed Calvert Associates to publish and distribute accurate information about the Catholic Church. Early in October, when the campaign was at its height, Calvert Associates ran an advertisement in the *Commonweal* supporting Al Smith. Donovan was angry at what he considered reverse bigotry. "In my view the whole question of religious bigotry extended beyond this immediate campaign, and the only way to meet hysteria was by sanity, patience, and good example," he wrote to Michael Williams, editor of the *Commonweal*. "Bigotry is deplorable. To use it for political purposes is reprehensible."

Candidate Hoover's calendar shows that Bill Donovan was present at most of the important campaign meetings. He was not only the principal strategist for the Hoover campaign, but he also undertook to keep the candidate healthy. He persuaded Hoover to get out of bed every morning at 7:00 A.M. to perform exercises under the direction of John P. Macklen of the Buffalo Tennis and Squash Club. Macklen, who was Donovan's own trainer, saw to it that Hoover got in his exercise at home in Palo Alto, in hotels, and aboard campaign trains. "Mr. Hoover was never a minute late," reported Macklen. "At first we had light exercises, but later they became more rigorous calisthenics, a full hour a day followed by a bath or a swim if possible."

Donovan worked for Hoover's victory with night-and-day enthusiasm. Hoover won in a landslide, and he telegraphed Donovan to come and see him in Palo Alto. Newspapers predicted that the President-elect would name his old friend and campaign strategist attorney general. Perhaps instead, some newspapers suggested, Hoover would make Donovan secretary of war because of his heroic military record. Hoover's wire reached Donovan at the Blackstone Hotel in Chicago, and he left that afternoon by airplane for California. Not many people were flying in November 1928, and the flight captured the public imagination.

Donovan spent November 13 at Hoover's home. Mabel Willebrandt had come from her Los Angeles home also to be with Hoover that day. The President-elect asked her to write a report on several people who were under consideration for attorney general. Donovan was one of them.

At Hoover's request, Donovan drew up a memorandum about various possible appointments to the cabinet, together with how the press and the Congress might react to them. Hoover took the memo with him on a good-will trip to South America that had been scheduled for him. When Donovan returned east, he had every reason to believe Hoover would appoint him attorney general.

The President-elect would not take office until March 4, 1929. This left several months for speculation as to who would serve in his cabinet. Political pundits agreed that Bill Donovan would be among those picked. "You have to appreciate who this man is," wrote one journalist. "He is a war hero who has won all the medals, good looking, colorful, dashing, magnetic. He has everything."

This is not how Donovan looked to the Ku Klux Klan and extremist Protestant clergymen, who opposed him because he was a Catholic, or to the Anti-Saloon League, which opposed him because he lacked enthusiasm for the Volstead Act. Donovan, who had enforced the act with uncompromising diligence in western New York, believed that the "noble experiment" had failed and should be brought to an end.

Herbert Hoover, back from South America, set up his headquarters in Washington's Mayflower Hotel in early January. A steady stream of office-seekers came to visit him. Donovan had his advocates, but they were far outnumbered by his foes. Bishop James Cannon, Jr., who had led militant antiwet and anti-Catholic forces in Virginia to help break the old Democratic Solid South for Hoover, vehemently attacked Donovan. The pastor of the church where George Washington was baptized spoke out against the Romanist Donovan, and Otto V. Myers of the

United Guards of America, "A Pure Protestant Organization for Men and Women," objected to him as well.

"Most people of intelligence were much disgusted with the religious bitterness of the last campaign," wrote Frank R. Kent of the *Baltimore Sun*. "It was pretty generally hoped when the election was over that never again would a man's faith figure in the politics of the country. That is why the present drive of the Klan to prevent Colonel William J. Donovan from being named Attorney General is particularly sickening."

James L. Wright, a newspaperman who was close to both Donovan and Hoover, talked with Donovan on January 9. "I will never be in the cabinet," Donovan said. "I could not go in there without giving up my independence, and I will not give that up for any man or place. I am afraid Hoover is going to be another Taft. I have no doubt that the drive of the Ku Klux and others against me and their insistence upon a Protestant dry are having their influence. It looks as though he would be afraid to appoint a Catholic and a wet."

Two days later Wright wrote another letter in "great confidence" to his editor, Alfred Kirchhofer of the *Buffalo News*, concerning Hoover's position on Donovan. "After saying that when he [Hoover] was away some of Bill's foolish friends started a boom for him that resulted in all his potential as well as active enemies shooting at him, he said that Bill had become a sort of 'religious symbol,' that the Catholics took it for granted that they were to have the office of Attorney General, and that the 'dry' Catholics then insisted that a member of their church who is really dry be appointed to the place. This, so the Chief said, raised the religious issue in a way that will hurt Donovan as well as himself."

On January 12, Kirchhofer wrote to Hoover urging that Donovan be made attorney general. "He has given proof of his fidelity to the dry law by his personal conduct and official discharge of his duties in Buffalo and Washington. For his work here he still is being penalized by some who believe that money and influence outweigh the law, but he enforced it and if we had more men like him there would be greater respect for law. He would bring to the work vigor, intelligence, ability to get results and determination—qualities, among others, which are needed. Of his loyalty to the Constitution and law I know there can be no doubt."

Kirchhofer argued that to appoint Donovan would vindicate the principles of religious tolerance. He summed up, "If he [Donovan] doesn't become Attorney General, he certainly has nothing to lose, but I do feel that your administration would suffer the loss of a man who had a grip on the imagination of the country; whose courage and fidelity to public duty are accepted as a criterion; who has the ability and determination to carry out any duty imposed upon him, and who would be a constant friend and ally of his chief."

Other politicians opposed Donovan to seek revenge. Senator Burton K. Wheeler was still smarting from the charges brought against him in 1925, and his friends senators Tom Walsh and William Borah told Hoover that they would lead an attack on Donovan's nomination in the Senate. Borah informed Hoover that he had made a close personal study of the Senate and felt confident that Donovan's nomination would be disapproved. On the other hand, said Borah, there would be little opposition to Donovan as secretary of war.

As Hoover agonized over his decision concerning Bill Donovan, a crowd of reporters clustered about the entrance to his house at 2300 S Street. One afternoon Hoover sent for James Williams, a trusted confidant. Williams shoved a newspaper into his overcoat pocket and turned up his collar in an effort to resemble a reporter, so that he could get by the press without undergoing questions. F. Trubee Davison, the assistant secretary of war for air, had also been called in. As they waited, Davison asked, "What do you suppose he's sent for you about?"

"Well," said Williams, "he's probably sent for me to discuss Colonel Donovan. He's not going to give Donovan the attorney general's portfolio. He's probably going to offer him some other job and try to talk me into saying that's really more important than the attorney generalship."

Williams went in to see Hoover, and Hoover asked, "You've been to the Philippines?"

"Yes."

"You know that that job of governor general is in some respects more important than any cabinet job. I want to know what you think of Colonel Donovan for that job."

"Of course, I thought you were going to make him attorney general," said Williams.

Hoover said he had not decided. He had considered Donovan for that cabinet post, but this might be "more important."

The next day Williams got a telephone call from Donovan. "Mr. Hoover tells me that you are in favor of my going to the Philippines," said Donovan, "and wants me to talk with you. I think we'd better take an automobile ride, don't you?"

"Yes, that's the best way," agreed Williams.

Donovan and Williams did not want to be watched. "So he picked me up with his chauffeur at the Anchorage," said Williams.

> We went out to the end of Massachusetts Avenue. He told the chauffeur that he'd call him when he needed him. The chauffeur walked out of hearing and lit a cigarette, while I spelled out to Colonel Donovan exactly what happened, repeating the conversation.

I knew that Donovan wasn't going to accept the Governor Generalship of the Philippines after I had talked to him. Shortly after he declined it, he left for New Mexico. Of course, it had got out in the papers then that he was not going to be Attorney General. Trubee Davison and I went to the station to see him off.

Six months later, Donovan told me—he had a law office in Washington—that Trubee and I and the others who went to the station to see him off were duly reported to the President by a secret service man, or some other spotter.

Nor had the auto ride out Massachusetts Avenue gone unobserved. A second car had followed them, and the driver later told Donovan about it. Donovan checked with his chauffeur, who said, "Yes, there was an empty car. I remember it now. It was down below. I thought they had punctured a tire or something."

"That was the kind of clandestine atmosphere in which the administration started," said Williams. "Donovan was very bitter about it."

About this time Frank Knox, another Donovan friend, went to see Hoover. "Knox told me a revealing story about Hoover," noted Harold L. Ickes in his *Secret Diary*.

William J. Donovan of Buffalo was devoted to Hoover and had actively supported him in 1928. He was the most prominent Catholic who did support Hoover and perhaps the only outstanding Catholic who opposed Al Smith. Hoover had promised to make him Attorney General. Then, after the election, Donovan told Knox that Hoover was apparently not going through with his promise. Knox, as general manager of the Hearst papers, had kept Hearst, with a great deal of effort, in line for Hoover, despite the fact that Hearst hated Hoover personally. So Knox went to Hoover, who received him graciously and expressed deep gratitude for the support that Knox had given him. Knox told Hoover that he had nothing to ask for himself, but he did want to know whether reports he heard in New York that Donovan was not to be appointed Attorney General were true. He couldn't believe that such a dastardly thing could be in the mind of the President-elect. He took Hoover right down the line, to Hoover's great embarrassment. Hoover said that considerable pressure had been brought to bear against the proposed appointment, and with a final expression of contempt Knox left.

When Hoover told Donovan that he was not to be attorney general, he said he could instead be secretary of war, and the nation's press on February 26 reported that Donovan was to be secretary of war. Then Hoover changed his mind again and decided to offer Donovan the post of governor general of the Philippines. Donovan was angry when he went to see Hoover to tell him that he was unwilling to go out to the Pacific.

"Well, you will stay in public life, won't you?" asked Hoover.

"Yesterday you offered me the secretary of war if I did not want to go to the islands," replied Donovan.

"We will have to talk about that at length," said Hoover.

"No, it does not take me long to make up my mind," said Donovan. "If you meant that offer when you made it, I accept. If you didn't mean it, it is your privilege to withdraw it."

"Well, I don't want you to leave public life," Hoover replied.

"Mr. Hoover, the man who has kept me in public life for the past two years is yourself. You know the place that I am willing to accept if you want me to remain. I shall be at my home if you want to reach me today."

That afternoon at six o'clock, Donovan phoned Calvin Coolidge's private secretary. Coolidge was supporting Donovan for a cabinet post. Since there was little love lost between Coolidge and Hoover, this was not of much benefit. Donovan read the secretary a note he had just sent to Hoover. "Associate Justice Stone and Mr. Mark Sullivan have told me of the troubles you find yourself in with reference to the Secretaryship of War. Please let my name give you no further concern. I am planning to leave tonight for Santa Fe." (Donovan was chairman of the Rio Grande River Commission, which met in Sante Fe to allocate Rio Grande River rights.) Hoover phoned that evening as soon as he received the note and asked Donovan not to leave Washington but to come see him in the morning.

There was nothing much to be said when the two men met at Hoover's S Street house early the next day. Hoover stood in the doorway to tell Donovan good-bye, his hands in his pockets. Reporters waiting for Donovan to come out fired questions at him. "Did he ask you to become attorney general?"

"No."

"Did he ask you to be secretary of war?"

"No, we sat there rather embarrassed, and finally he asked me what I thought of the Philippines. I told him I wasn't interested. By that time it was most embarrassing, and I left."

Donovan stopped again to see Hoover that afternoon on his way to the train.

"It was a sad and strained parting," said Kirchhofer, "this breakup of the partnership. One who was close to the scene said Hoover had tears in his eyes."

Hoover appointed William D. Mitchell attorney general. He was a dry and a Protestant, so he was acceptable to Donovan's foes. Ironically, Donovan's old job, assistant to the attorney general, went to John Lord O'Brian. James W. Good, Hoover's western political manager, became secretary of war, and Dwight F. Davis, the secretary of war under Coolidge, became governor general of the Philippines.

Senator Royal Copeland of New York spoke his mind on the floor of the Senate. "There is in my state," he said, "an outstanding citizen, a distinguished lawyer, a brave soldier, a man who has served his country, Mr. Donovan; and now we learn that he cannot be appointed to the office of Attorney General because he is a Catholic or a 'wet,' I am not sure which. It is an outrageous thing that this man should be deprived of the privilege of serving his country, and serving it well, because he does not happen to conform to the standard fixed by those who dominate the next President."

Many years later, Herbert Hoover was asked by Alfred Kirchhofer to explain his actions for the record. Hoover wrote:

> Bill Donovan deserved a place on my administrative team. His contribution to the campaign of 1928 was worthy of recognition, but not as great as many others.
>
> He demanded the Attorney Generalship. I discussed with him both the Secretary of War and the Governorship of the Philippines. While he continued to insist upon his heart's desire, I had need to fill the War Department post.
>
> The religious issue intruded into the problem but not because he was a Catholic. The facts were Bill was opposed to prohibition and to appoint him to that post would bring protests from every religious group in the country, including many Catholics. The religious leaders had a remedy which was more vigorous prosecution of the violations of the law, and they had a propaganda machine working on it. Moreover, the Deep South voted for me. It was in a frenzy (including the Catholics) of determination to keep the negroes from having a drop of alcohol. Bill would not have had the confidence of any of these groups.

Some of Bill Donovan's supporters for a cabinet post in the Hoover administration had been confident that this would have been a stepping-stone in his ascent to the presidency. Bill Donovan, they were certain, would be the first Catholic president of the United States. As J. W. H. deBelleville put it, "In the opinion of many patriotic Americans at the present time nothing better could happen to the country than the election, at the close of Mr. Hoover's tenure of office, of a Catholic President of the high type of Col. Wm. J. Donovan. There are two O's also in the Colonel's name."

Donovan always considered his treatment at Hoover's hands the greatest disappointment of his life. Shortly after Hoover's inauguration, Donovan went with Leland W. Cutler to the Gridiron dinner in Washington. "Donovan was lampooned in a sketch at the dinner," said Cutler, "as a soldier who had gotten all the decorations the War Department could give. He was given a new one by his Commander in Chief, 'The Order of the Boot.' Donovan was very popular; he was loudly applauded and seemed sincerely affected, while the President, who sat directly in front of us, was plainly uncomfortable."

Hoover was even more uncomfortable a few moments later, when a man impersonating both the President and a bystander carried on a dialogue.

"What is Bill Donovan doing now, Mr. President?"

"Oh, he is sitting in the window, watching the parade go by."

"You had better look out, Mr. President, or he might start a parade of his own."

Donovan leaned close to Cutler and asked, "Le, would you join my parade?" Cutler said he would. Many of Donovan's fellow Americans were ready to join his parade during the spring of 1929 when Hoover threw him over.

15

Politics and Foreign Affairs

DONOVAN HAD BEEN so successful with the Rio Grande River Commission that President Coolidge also appointed him U.S. commissioner to the Colorado River Commission. Seven states had been squabbling about the water rights to the master river of the Southwest, and now on February 14, 1929, their representatives, together with Bill Donovan, met to reconcile their differences. They elected Donovan chairman.

James Murphy, still a law student at George Washington University, accompanied Donovan to Reno, Nevada, to attend a meeting of the commission. "The first session went on for weeks," he recalled years later. "Reno was then a small town. The first thing that Bill Donovan did was to get acquainted with a manicurist in the barber shop at our hotel."

The manicurist was attractive, which didn't detract from Donovan's interest in her, but the tidbits of information that she gave him about the other people attending the conference were what really mattered. "It's always important to find out all you can about people, to know who they are, and how they behave," Donovan explained to Murphy. "Then you can have a better chance of bringing them together."

Donovan made friends with the political leaders of the Southwest. "Governors, secretaries, political people, I saw them all with Donovan," said Murphy. "They were brilliant people in their fields, but Donovan was the most brilliant of them all. He could measure their thoughts and get them into agreement. He worked hard, day and night, met different elements to conciliate, persuade. He never compromised a principle.

" 'You may be right, and I respect your view,' Donovan would say, 'but I think I'm right and I'm going to have to insist on it.' "

Donovan was at his best when he could meet with one or two of the delegates at a time. He could draw them out, charm them so that they made compromises just to please him. He showed a formidable understanding of the history and geology of the area and of the engineering and agricultural problems involved.

During each recess in the negotiations, Donovan hurried back to Washington, because this was at the time he was being considered for the Hoover cabinet. By April most of the points at issue had been settled, but the Imperial Valley people still were reluctant to approve any upriver dams or irrigation projects that might siphon away water that they needed for their irrigation canals.

Finally, on June 14 Donovan could report to President Hoover that the conference was near agreement. Donovan convened the delegates in Washington for a final session. The Colorado River Compact made possible the construction of Boulder Dam, which Hoover was able to announce later in 1929.

At the same time that Donovan was chairing the Colorado River Commission, he was planning a new law firm. Henry Rerrick Bond had been assistant secretary of the treasury under Coolidge, in charge of internal revenue. Donovan and Bond announced their partnership on October 9.

"They had a balanced firm from the start," according to Jim Murphy. "Bond was the firm's tax expert, and antitrust was Donovan's specialty."

The Washington offices were in a 23-room suite on the tenth floor of the new Shoreham Building. Donovan had made Frank Raichle his New York City partner, and the offices of Donovan and Raichle were in the Lee Higgins Building at 41 Broad Street. Donovan and Raichle also had offices in Buffalo's Marine Trust Building. When soon afterward Donovan's New York landlord went bankrupt, he moved the firm to 2 Wall Street, where his own corner office overlooked Trinity Church and Broadway. Donovan placed a walnut bust of George Washington in his office as an inspiration, and he often gazed out the window at Trinity Church, where Alexander Hamilton, whose brand of conservative patriotism he admired, lay buried.

"Sometimes at night I think I can see the ghosts of the early American patriots rising from their graves to look with wonder at what their descendants have done with this island of Manhattan," he once told a visitor.

When a visitor came into the room, Donovan waved him to a dark green leather couch along one wall. He rarely conversed from behind his desk but perched on the other end of the couch or sat in a nearby red leather armchair, which he once said was his favorite chair in all the world. It was his "think chair." Sometimes he would ask Jane Smith or Walter Berry, his secretaries, to take all phone calls and keep callers away, and he would lean back in this chair and ponder his problems, which ranged from law cases to the latest intelligence on events in Europe. Occasionally also he stretched out on the couch and catnapped.

In the spring Raichle had told Donovan that he was going to get married. "Very interesting," said Donovan. "I have a piece of advice for you. Don't give up your woman friends. They'll tend to improve your manners."

Raichle helped to set up the New York offices, but after his marriage he preferred to live in Buffalo. Carl Newton and George Leisure, the latter a highly skilled trial lawyer who had been trained by Clarence Darrow, were among the other early New York partners. Over the years the firm kept changing partners and growing until it metamorphosed into Donovan, Leisure, Newton, Lumbard, and Irvine, one of the foremost law firms on Wall Street. Donovan and his partners were to handle some of the major cases of the 1930s.

"Donovan's law work was built on antitrust cases," said Jim Murphy. "He devoted the minimum time to his law practice, since he had no interest in accumulating a fortune, in making money for money itself. His interest was in world affairs."

When Murphy wanted to set up his own office, Donovan permitted him to take with him any cases he was working on. The Donovan law firm paid his salary for six months to help him get started. Murphy moved down one floor to the ninth floor, but Donovan still gave him special assignments. "His own office might be losing money," said Richard Greenlee, a young Donovan partner, "but he sent business to Jim Murphy."

During those years of his greatest legal success, Donovan was a lawyer's lawyer, an expert in appellate litigation as well as antitrust work. He argued a number of landmark cases before the Supreme Court.

"He had the ability to reduce complex problems to simple terms," explained Greenlee. "Instead of being content to see a corporate problem on paper, he would go to see factories and plants to observe concrete details. He then could understand the situation better, make pictures with words, and convince his listeners."

"He was intuitively brilliant," added Guy Martin, also a Donovan partner.

Donovan was always after the truth, determined to get at the facts and exhausting every conceivable way of unearthing them. On some cases he amassed incredible mountains of facts and figures and marshaled all of his evidence in clear and logical ways. This approach foreshadowed his vast intelligence undertakings of the future.

In the Humphrey case in 1935, Donovan argued before the Supreme Court that the President of the United States did not have the right arbitrarily to remove the chairman of the Federal Trade Commission. "The power to fire is the power to control," he claimed.

The Supreme Court agreed with Donovan, and it is generally believed that this decision played an important role in President Franklin Roosevelt's later attempt to pack the court. Roosevelt also believed that the power to fire is the power to control, and he had no intention of letting an uncooperative Supreme Court balk his complete control of the federal government.

During the Depression, producers of bituminous coal in Appalachia drew close to bankruptcy, and miners were being laid off in vast numbers. The mine owners came to Donovan with a plan to organize a joint selling agency representing 73 percent of the Appalachian coal producers. When John Lord O'Brian's antitrust division attacked the organization as being monopolistic and in restraint of trade, Donovan insisted that the organization was a necessary measure of "economic self-defense." O'Brian won the case in a federal court in Asheville, North Carolina, but Donovan appealed to the Supreme Court and won. Chief Justice Charles Evans Hughes wrote the opinion supporting Donovan.

"I think that it is a healthy sign to see that the Court is ready to approve a plan for the correction of abuses in industry when the industry itself shows the honesty and intelligence to try to work out a solution," Donovan wrote.

In 1929 Donovan served without fee as counsel to an investigation of bankruptcy scandals in New York. As the Great Depression deepened, bankruptcies increased, and by the time unscrupulous lawyers had finished with a case, creditors were lucky to get eight cents on a dollar of a debt. A federal judge, Francis A. Winslow, resigned in disgrace, a lawyer killed himself, and 12 other attorneys were indicted. Donovan's task was to investigate what was wrong with bankruptcy procedures and recommend reforms. A Yale Law School staff helped Donovan study 1,000 separate court files and listen to the testimony of 4,000 witnesses. The report filled 12 volumes covering bankruptcy proceedings not only in the United States but in foreign countries as well. The enormous fact-finding effort, depending as it did upon the work of so many people, all coordinated by Donovan, also foreshadowed some of the huge intelligence-gathering enterprises of the future OSS years.

The final 358-page summary was submitted by Donovan to Judge Thomas D. Thacker of the U.S. Court, Southern New York District, in April 1930. Donovan urged the creation of a federal bankruptcy administrator to take the burden off the federal judges. The administrator would be appointed by and responsible to the President. This would speed up cases, save time and money, and eliminate the opportunities for legal cupidity. Donovan's work became the basis for congressional reform of the federal bankruptcy laws.

Donovan also served without remuneration as counsel to a New York State legislative committee that investigated the Public Service Commission. This too led to reforms. In 1931 he was New York State chairman of the American Legion's drive to find jobs for the increasing armies of unemployed, and his committee found work for 100,000 men. He was chairman of the Emergency Unemployment Relief Committee's Morale Committee, and he was a member of the board of arbitration in the labor controversy between the American Train Dispatchers Association and the Boston and Maine Railroad. He served in all these capacities without pay.

The busy Donovan commuted back and forth between New York and Washington on the Pennsylvania Railroad. On Fridays he often took the Congressional Limited with Jim Murphy from Washington to New York, where he kept a suite at the St. Regis Hotel and later an apartment on Beekman Place. He'd work on the train or bring along somebody with whom he had business to discuss.

"He knew a lot of artists, writers, and performers," recalled Murphy, "and sometimes one of these people would ride with us. Alexander Woollcott came down from New York several times just to ride back on the train to New York with him. He would phone me to find out on what train Bill had a reservation, and he'd either meet Bill in the station or on the train."

Donovan would often carry a huge stack of books aboard the train. He read at great speed.

"You can't possibly know what you've just read," Murphy said one day.

"You check me," replied Donovan.

"I'd pick out a book, and he'd dictate a complete synopsis of the book, together with any detail that I asked for," remembered Murphy.

In New York City on a Saturday night, Donovan and Murphy often dined together and then went to Brentano's bookstore. There Donovan would browse through the latest titles and buy volumes on politics, foreign affairs, and biography. He read everything but novels, which he considered a waste of time. He did, however, have a deep affection for 18th-century poetry. As he read, he would mark passages in the book with a pencil, because this helped the information sink deep into his memory. He kept a lectern in his office so that if he grew tired of reading at his desk, he could read standing up.

Donovan's interests were wide-ranging and his ability to concentrate incredible. Ned Putzell, another friend, remembered going to see Donovan at his New York apartment and finding him stretched out on a cot, reading a book and listening to a news report from abroad on the short-wave radio, while his masseur kneaded his back. He studied the German language, because he was convinced that he would need to speak German in the future, and he learned everything he could about intelligence problems all the way back to biblical times. The intelligence services of the Byzantine Empire held a special fascination for him.

Both in New York and Washington, even in the winter, Donovan often kept the windows open in his office. "He wore a three-piece suit of wool," said Van Halsey, Donovan's stockbroker. "You'd have to put on a fur coat to go and see him in his office."

Murphy was a frequent guest in the Donovan home in Georgetown. He dined with him, and sometimes worked with him after dinner so late that Donovan would ask him to stay the night. "He wouldn't go to bed until three," said Murphy. "Then he'd be up at six."

Donovan would walk into Murphy's bedroom. "Come on, Jim!" he would say. "It's time for breakfast."

On most nights Donovan slept only three or four hours, but then he catnapped for ten minutes or so if he felt drowsy during the day.

He seemed to hunger for companionship. He loved parties, particularly if beautiful women were present, and on such occasions he was witty and charming. Since he was solicitous of the ladies, he always had his pick of them, married or unmarried, and he took full advantage of this. Women usually found him much more understanding than their husbands, and many asked his advice and counsel on all kinds of problems.

What Ruth Donovan thought of his dozens of feminine admirers and his affairs can only be surmised. Jim Murphy remembered only that from time to time Ruth and Bill Donovan would quarrel over money. She had been born wealthy, and her husband had been born poor. She seemed to have a much greater appreciation of the value of wealth than he did, and she found his life-style extravagant. Usually during these years she either kept to their summer home on the Massachusetts South Shore, where she had the sympathetic and friendly support of old friends, or stayed in New York at their Beekman Place apartment. Yet let Ruth have any trouble or illness, and Donovan rushed to her side.

Donovan spent as much time as he could with his teenage children. "Patricia had her father's energy and intelligence," said Guy Martin, "David his mother's shyness." Donovan found himself trying to rein his daughter in. When she talked about going on a round-the-world cruise on the schooner *Yankee*, an adventure that would have appealed to him when he was a youth, he refused to approve (he finally relented a few years later). On the other hand, he tried to spur his son on.

Van Halsey handled Donovan's stock investments. "He had no more idea of financial deals than a cat," he recalled. "It was also hard to catch him when a decision had to be made."

Donovan would phone Halsey with an order to buy this stock or that. "I want you to buy some National City Bank," he said one day.

"Why, Bill? Why?"

"Charlie Mitchell says that it's going sky high."

On the morning that the stock market crashed, Bill Donovan phoned Halsey. "I want you to buy some more National City."

"Bill, your account won't stand it. You've got too much already, Bill. We just can't do it."

"Charlie says you've got to."

"We'll have to get more collateral."

National City Bank went up to $550 a share, and then fell to $55. "We were able to rescue Bill's account," said Halsey, "and he was able to climb out of it."

Within a few months after the stock market's fall, Donovan was ready to plunge into stocks again, and Halsey had to remind him rather grimly that there are four words in the English language that an investor couldn't use—"if only" and "next time."

Throughout these hectic years of public service and private law practice in Washington and New York, Donovan continued to think of himself as a Buffalonian. He gave the Buffalo Club as his voting address, and he stayed there when he returned to the city without Ruth.

"He had a room on the top floor," said Phil Impelliteri, the club manager. "He would have breakfast at the club and then be gone all day, return for dinner, and then go for a long walk."

Bill Donovan would walk up Delaware Avenue past the big Rumsey house, where he had courted Ruth, or down to the waterfront and the grain elevators that he had known as a boy. At Christmastime Ruth and Bill and their children would arrive in Buffalo for the holidays. They stayed in the house on Delaware Avenue, and there was much good cheer and singing around the piano. Then the children would return to school, Ruth would go back to New York, and Bill more often than not would go to Washington.

The deepening world economic depression was causing fearful strains on the nations of Europe, and from time to time Donovan crossed the Atlantic to observe firsthand the unfolding crisis. Sometimes he had legal business to attend to as well, and sometimes he claimed to be traveling for pleasure.

Usually Donovan managed to make his trips without attracting public attention, but when he returned on June 4, 1931, on the *Île de France,* he had to be brought ashore in an ambulance. While he was playing tennis on the sports deck of the liner, his right leg suddenly collapsed under him. When the ship's surgeon examined him, he discovered torn ligaments around the knee that had been injured by a bullet in World War I. Donovan spent the remainder of the crossing in bed. When shipboard reporters flocked into his stateroom to interview him, he deprecated his injury. When they asked what he had been doing in Europe, he replied that he was not in government service and now had only a common garden variety of law practice. Not many of the reporters believed him.

In September 1931 Donovan went on a more significant trip, which he managed to keep so secret that even today there is little record to be found of it. On September 18, a bomb blew apart the tracks of the South Manchurian Railway near Mukden. The Japanese, who controlled the railroad under the terms of a lease forced upon China, blamed the Chinese for the incident; the Chinese in turn blamed the Japanese. Donovan intended to find out exactly who was to blame. The tracks were repaired in a few hours, but the Japanese found the explosion sufficient excuse for launching an invasion.

Donovan found himself in the same part of Manchuria that he had crossed with Ambassador Morris on the Siberian trip of 1919. He also found that some of the young Japanese officers he had met 12 years before were now in high command positions. They bluntly told him that China was destined to be part of Japan's necessary sphere of influence, and the United States would do well to accommodate itself to this. Chinese contacts told Donovan that not only the bombing but other incidents had been manufactured by the Japanese. In the summer of 1931, Manchurian soldiers in the pay of the Japanese pushed a Japanese officer off a sidewalk in Mukden. When he objected, they drew their knives and cut him to pieces. The Japanese government demanded to know what had happened. The soldiers announced that they had been picked by their superiors in the Chinese Army to murder Japanese officers.

Donovan listened to both the Chinese and Japanese, and he watched the Japanese Army as it swept aside futile Chinese resistance. The Chinese Army and civilian authorities were driven out of Manchuria. In 1932 Japan was to establish the puppet state of Manchukuo on Manchurian soil. China appealed to the League of Nations, but instead of withdrawing its forces, Japan withdrew from the League and occupied additional Chinese territory, in Jehol and Mongolia. Donovan returned to the United States convinced that the Japanese military jingoists, whom he had first observed at work in Siberia, were bound to bring their nation into conflict with his own. He shared his findings with other members of America's informal intelligence network.

Donovan continued to follow events in Manchuria with apprehension while taking a leading role in finding jobs for the unemployed in New York State. In that dark year of the Great Depression there were 12 million unemployed in the United States. On February 22, 1932, he spoke to a giant Prosperity Rally at Buffalo's Teck Theater and called the Depression "a greater disaster than war."

"We are now up against something that we were not asked to face in war," he told his audience, many of whom had fought in France.

"Over there we could plan for certain happenings, but now we are bucking up against the great unknown—and our fighting it is handicapped to a great extent by fear that has gripped many of our citizens."

Governor Franklin D. Roosevelt of New York seemed very likely to be the Democratic candidate for President, and Herbert Lehman, his lieutenant governor, promised to be the Democratic candidate for governor of New York. Whenever Republican leaders met to discuss a possible candidate to oppose Lehman, Bill Donovan's name came up. He continued to make speeches throughout the state but did not admit to being a candidate.

On June 26, Father Duffy died of an intestinal ailment that he had first suffered in France. Donovan was at the funeral in St. Patrick's Cathedral in New York. Six horses drew the caisson with its casket down Fifth Avenue. Captain, Father Duffy's horse, followed in the procession with the fighting padre's boots reversed in the stirrups. Then came Bill Donovan leading a column of veterans of the Fighting 69th. Thousands of people lined the avenue. Donovan became chairman of a committee to raise money for a memorial to Father Duffy, which was to be a statue of the priest erected in the middle of Broadway, close to Times Square.

By July Donovan had decided to run for governor, provided that strong support for his candidacy developed, but he did not underestimate the difficulty of defeating Roosevelt's candidate, Herbert Lehman. He wrote to Edward Tracy Clark, former President Coolidge's private secretary, for advice. Clark wrote back, "If you are ambitious to be Governor of New York, that is one thing, but I don't believe you are. If ambition is lacking, then the only other reason for taking the nomination is your duty to your party or to your President.

"The last is a compelling motive and doubtless will determine your course. Seriously, I do not believe that this year, with everything against us, any man can be elected who does not have the driving force which comes from ambition rather than duty."

On the Fourth of July, Melvin C. Eaton, the Republican leader of Chenango County, announced the Win with Donovan Committee. Across the state, Donovan committees sprang up. A Donovan office opened in Buffalo in the Rialto Building. His political enemies, some of whom still smarted over his Saturn Club raid, struck upon former State Supreme Court Justice Daniel J. Kenefick of Buffalo to stop Donovan. The Erie County party organization chose to portray Donovan as a supporter of the by now unpopular President Hoover and at odds with the state GOP committee. The rest of the state watched the two Buffalo candidates square off against each other.

Even while the Win with Donovan Committee boomed his candidacy, Donovan tried to slip away to Europe on a fact-finding journey to

Germany, where Hitler's Nazis were attempting to take advantage of the political chaos to seize power. On July 9 he sailed with Cornelius F. Kelly, president of the Anaconda Copper Company, aboard the *Île de France*. Kelly and Donovan were chatting in a corner of the promenade deck when a platoon of reporters happened upon them.

"How did you fellows ever find me?" asked Donovan. "Just going over for business reasons, and that's all." He complained that he had wished to depart without publicity. He denied that he was a candidate at this time. And he admitted that Kelly and he would go directly from Le Havre to Germany.

Once he was in Germany, Donovan studied the discontent of the people and the threat of a Nazi takeover. In April Paul von Hindenburg had been reelected president, but his opponent, Nazi leader Adolf Hitler, had polled more than 13 million votes. In July elections the Nazis had captured the largest number of seats in the Reichstag, and Chancellor Franz von Papen was now attempting to keep them from taking over the government. Donovan met with Papen, who explained that Germany was on the edge of civil war. The Nazi right and the Communist left, financed by Moscow, were at one another's throats. Germany must have a strong ruler, but Papen, who had been accused in the American press of seeking to become a dictator, denied any such desire. He assured Donovan that he would be able to prevent Hitler from coming into the government. Donovan was not so sure.

"Papen was a political typhoid Mary," Donovan later said, "who brought ruin to both his enemies and his friends."

When Donovan landed in New York on the Hamburg American liner *New York* on the evening of July 29, he was glad when shipboard reporters seemed interested only in his gubernatorial candidacy. On the pier Ruth Donovan, Melvin C. Eaton, and his law partner George Leisure, backed up by a deputation of World War I veterans, greeted him.

"If they can show a real demand, and I can be of real use," said Donovan, "I would accept the nomination, and if elected I would carry out the duties of the office to my best ability."

"The mere nomination of Colonel Donovan means his election," said Eaton.

"That sounds optimistic," remarked Donovan.

Nothing was said about the grave situation in Germany At home on Beekman Place, Bill Donovan practiced French and German with his family at breakfast. He took Patricia into his book-lined study and talked to her by the hour about the crisis in Europe. In the meantime he watched the Donovan-for-governor boom grow. There did not seem to be much that an American could do about Germany, and Donovan, who had not yet won an elected office despite his great popularity, was intrigued with the idea of becoming governor.

On August 16 in Buffalo, Donovan finally announced his candidacy. The New York State Republicans met in the old Broadway Auditorium in Buffalo on October 3, and Hamilton Fish, Jr., delivered the keynote speech on the theme of "Hold on to Hoover." The platform favored Prohibition and advocated tax reduction and retrenchment in government expenses.

Edward L. Bernays, a New York public relations counsel, went to Buffalo to advise Donovan on his campaign. He arrived the night the convention began. "I went first to the Colonel's suite at the Statler," he wrote, "where I fought my way through a mass of people; county chairmen were shaking both his hands and pledging their constituents' vote to him. The receptionist finally smuggled me into an adjoining room, where the crowd was smaller. Donovan, a well set-up figure, had a broad smile and exuded sincere charm. He was enjoying this spontaneous adulation."

"I am delighted you came up," said Donovan. "Missy has told me so much about you. I have been looking forward to talking to you. But you see how utterly impossible it is to do anything like that here and now. These are committee and county chairmen. I have to shake their hands and talk to them. I have an idea. Won't you and your wife come to lunch with me at my mother-in-law's home, Mrs. Rumsey, at 12:30 tomorrow? I want to see you; I want to talk to you, I need you."

At lunch the next day there was more of the same confusion. Donovan broke off shaking hands long enough to whisper in Bernays's ear, "I do want you to come to see me this afternoon at the Statler at three. Please see me."

That afternoon he was still shaking hands with well-wishers and asked Bernays to come and see him the next day. The next day turned out to be nomination day. Bands played, crowds cheered, and Bill Donovan put his arm around Bernays's shoulder and whispered, "Mr. Bernays, this is really no time or place to confer on serious matters. Why don't we postpone our meeting to my home, 1 Beekman Place, in New York?"

Amid the political hoopla Mayor Frank Roesch of Buffalo nominated Donovan, and on October 5 he won the nomination to oppose Lehman, who already had been picked by the Democrats. Assistant Secretary of War F. Trubee Davison of Nassau County, an old Donovan friend, was nominated for lieutenant governor. In his acceptance speech Donovan said, "I have stated and I do state now that I am for repeal of the 18th Amendment." This put him in direct conflict with his party's platform. Donovan also needled Franklin Roosevelt. "I make no pretense to being a farmer," he said. "I run no estate on the Hudson which I pretend is a farm."

Donovan marched through the streets of Buffalo in an old-fashioned political parade, behind men carrying red flares. Buffalo crowds gave the greatest ovation in the city's history to the candidate who had been born in the First Ward waterfront. Delaware Avenue was also caught up in the enthusiasm for Donovan, and on the afternoon before the parade Ruth Donovan and her mother gave a tea at the Rumsey home for the convention delegates. Newspapermen came to see the "quiet, gracious woman who may be the next hostess in the Albany Executive Mansion."

Ruth Donovan and her mother stood for two hours shaking hands with the delegates, giving each the rapt attention expected from a candidate's wife and mother-in-law. One reporter thought Ruth's simple remark that she was "very, very proud of him" spoke volumes when it came "from so naturally reticent a person."

The same reporter continued, "Apparently she never wearied and she never lost a certain charm of manner that blended with her perfect poise in the midst of tremendous excitement, especially when Colonel Donovan himself appeared, and the women crowded about him to utter congratulations."

Ruth Donovan, said the newspaper, was "naturally intensely interested in her husband's career, and she confines her own to homemaking and the care of their two children, seventeen-year-old David and fifteen-year-old Patricia."

The Donovan family came together in loving unity according to the best American political custom.

While Bernays was finding it impossible to advise candidate Donovan, a public relations man was counseling candidate Lehman, "Now look here. You're going to have a terrific battle to win. You can't overlook the fact that Donovan is a colorful figure, a very colorful figure, and you're not."

Lehman agreed that Donovan "was in the eyes of the public very colorful. He had made a fine war record, won the Medal of Honor, had been a colonel of a favorite regiment here in New York, the Old 69th. He was a handsome man and a good speaker."

Both Lehman and Donovan expected that the election would be close. "There was little realization of how strong the Democratic Party was," said Lehman many years later, "and how weak the Republican Party was that it affected my thinking about my own candidacy and my own campaign, and affected the thinking of my friends."

Donovan decided to strike directly at New York City, the Democratic stronghold. Tammany Hall was going through one of its periodic scandals, which promised to divide the Democratic Party in the city, and Donovan was assured that he could count on the support of his fellow war veterans. Donovan went to New York to deliver his first speech, at Jamaica in Queens. The next day he spoke at a huge rally at Madison Square Garden; former President Calvin Coolidge was there to give him support. The candidate spoke in New York nationality neighborhoods, making sure to address the Italians on Columbus Day, and then headed upstate for a whistle-stop campaign.

The issues were public utilities, Prohibition, labor, agriculture, and economy in government. Donovan claimed that Lehman's financial policies were ruinous, and Lehman said that Donovan was tied to the utility interests, lacked social imagination, and was a "semidry."

"Everyone knows that Donovan has been a Wet since he came marching home from the war," asserted the *New York Post*.

Donovan attempted to tie Lehman to Roosevelt and Al Smith. He demanded in an Albany speech whether Lehman "will report to Roosevelt if Roosevelt goes to Washington? Or will he have to call up the Empire State Building to know whether or not he can report to Roosevelt?"

Both Smith and Roosevelt joined the fray. When Roosevelt claimed to know Bill Donovan well when both were at Columbia Law School, Donovan replied, "Roosevelt said in the course of that speech, 'I'm going to talk about Bill Donovan. He is a good friend of mine,' which is not true. I happened to be in the same class in law school that he was, but I was a youngster earning my way through law school. He never knew me."

Donovan's speeches were drawing blood, and the *New York Post* remarked, "In Bill Donovan, Al Smith has met his match."

When Roosevelt emissaries approached Donovan with the suggestion that if he won, Roosevelt in Washington would be happy to cooperate with Donovan in Albany, Donovan replied, "Well, if that is the kind of cooperation he wants, he is not going to get it from Donovan, and it goes back to what he said when he endorsed the candidate for governor, this gentleman whom he picked to take his place as his successor, and whom he then called his own right arm. I said several weeks ago that my arm belongs to me."

Donovan assailed Roosevelt in a Watertown speech: "Are we going to lose our sovereignty as a state and surrender it into the lap of one man who simply wants to elect a pro-consul to govern one of the provinces of these forty-eight states? Now we begin to see a man with delusions of grandeur: that he is going to encompass a continent, and that he is going to be a new kind of red, white, and blue dictator."

When Lehman spoke of Donovan's great military record and suggested that this was about all there was to the man, Donovan replied, "I claim to have done no more than four million other men did. For me the war ended in 1918. I know better than anyone else that I was an ordinary guy, with a couple of lucky breaks, because I belonged to a great regiment; and I never tried to exploit the traditions of that regiment for my benefit and I am not going to do it now, and I am not going to let anyone else penalize me for belonging to that regiment."

Strikingly, Donovan's campaign leaflets pledged a New Deal in Albany several months before Roosevelt struck upon the concept of a New Deal in Washington.

On election day Herbert Lehman was elected in the Democratic sweep that saw Franklin Roosevelt take the presidency. "Somehow or other, Donovan's campaign never took fire," charitably remarked Lehman, "any more than Hoover's campaign did."

Edward Tracy Clark wrote to Donovan, "You made a great fight and you made it alone. Down underneath we will in later years finally find the real cause for this overwhelming defeat. I cannot bring myself to believe that it was either necessary or inevitable because of the depression."

"I think you are right in saying that we haven't yet learned the real cause of this defeat," Donovan conceded.

On January 5, 1933, Calvin Coolidge died, and his death seemed to end the Republican era once and for all. President Hoover asked Donovan to meet the presidential train at Penn Station, New York, at 5:25 A.M. on January 7 for the sad trip up to New England. "I went up to Coolidge's funeral on the President's train, and I sat with the President, Hughes and Stimson," wrote Donovan to diplomat Arthur Bliss Lane after the funeral. "None of them very exciting on that occasion at least."

Donovan was depressed, not only by his defeat at the polls and the election of a Democratic administration, but also by a report he received early in January from a well-placed German source, saying that Adolf Hitler was bound to become chancellor of Germany. On January 30, Hitler did indeed become chancellor, and on March 5, 1933, Germany held its last free election until after the war, and the Nazis and their rightist allies won a majority of the seats in the Reichstag. On March 21 the Third Reich was proclaimed, and as far as Donovan was concerned, the die was cast for World War II. He was convinced that the world was rushing toward one of history's great crises, and he feared he would not be involved in the events to come.

16

The Unfolding Crisis

"COLONEL DONOVAN has played an active part in American political life and is one of the leading lawyers of the country, but he has a hobby and that hobby is war," wrote Hugh R. Wilson, who represented the United States at the League of Nations in Geneva during the Italian invasion of Ethiopia. "Bill is not happy if there is a war on the face of the earth, and he has not had a look at it."

In reality Donovan's interest in the conflicts that erupted in Asia, Africa, and Europe in the 1930s was that of an intelligence man. He had come to play the leading role in the community of American citizens who, for patriotic reasons, kept abreast of crucial developments abroad. At the same time he enjoyed the excitement and danger that a close look at war represented. Donovan's sharpened intelligence instincts told him that the rush of events overseas sooner or later would compromise the interests of his own country, and he was determined to discover the military qualities, methods, and purposes of the opposing powers.

Several years later he wrote, "During the 1930s as a private citizen I visited Ethiopia, Spain, and other European countries to see what modern war would mean. All other nations, even the little ones, had capable secret intelligence agencies. We had only the conventional intelligence service of the Department of State, with its military and naval attachés, and the agencies attached to the War and Navy Departments, which limited themselves narrowly to items of purely military information."

During the summer of 1935, Donovan became increasingly concerned by the buildup of Italian military power in Eritrea. He knew from his friend Italian Ambassador Augusto Rossi that Italy's dictator, Benito Mussolini, was determined to conquer a new market for Italian exports and solve southern Italy's critical unemployment problem. Il Duce was avid to avenge the 1896 Italian defeat at Aduwa and above all to prove to the world that Fascism would be victorious in battle. In September Donovan traveled to England and the Continent; he returned to America convinced that Mussolini was not bluffing and fully intended to invade Ethiopia regardless of what the League of Nations threatened to do.

At a reunion of Rainbow Division veterans, Donovan and his old comrade-in-arms Douglas MacArthur, now chief of staff of the U.S. Army, talked over the idea of Donovan's going to Africa to learn exactly what was going on. On September 17, he wrote to MacArthur that he was "impressed with the fact that this little adventure of Italy may resolve itself into something that could include us all." He added that "a close view of the situation at this time might help us later," and he asked for the general's suggestions as to how he might arrange the necessary trip with the War Department. There was no response from MacArthur.

"Donovan scared MacArthur and other military men," remarked Jim Murphy. "They considered him just too brilliant. They were afraid he might show them up. Let him get started, and he'd soon be running everything."

In October MacArthur finished his tour of duty as chief of staff and went to the Philippines at the request of President Manuel Quezon to create and train an army for the commonwealth, which was to become independent in another ten years. On September 30, Deputy Chief of Staff Gen. George S. Simonds agreed with Donovan that he should "go abroad and look over the situation in the Mediterranean." Simonds said that he was "most sympathetic with your desire to get a look-in on this impending fracas," but that he could not provide funds for the trip. Donovan assured him that he was not thinking of making "any charge against the government at all."

On October 3, Marshal Pietro Badoglio led Mussolini's armies into Ethiopia. The expeditionary force was made up of more than 200,000 men and 7,000 officers, 6,000 machine guns, 700 cannon, 150 tanks, and 150 pursuit planes and bombers. When General de Bono in Africa asked him for more men, Mussolini wrote, "You ask for three divisions by the end of October. I mean to send you ten, repeat ten; five divisions of the regular army, five formations of Blackshirts. For the lack of a few thousand men, we lost the day at Aduwa. We shall never make that mistake. I am willing to commit a sin of excess, but never a sin of deficiency."

The European powers and the United States damned the invasion as a sin of another sort. The League of Nations members were convinced that economic sanctions would so cripple the Italian war machine that it would not be able to sustain its attack. The Ethiopians, it was confidently reported in the French, British, and American press, would surely prove too wily and difficult for the Italians. Optimistic reports circulated in the corridors of the League of Nations, and Italian delegates were themselves certain that their country was likely to suffer a disaster in Africa.

When Donovan went to see friends in the State Department, he found that they shared the optimism of their colleagues in Europe. They were sure as well that Mussolini would never give him permission to go to Badoglio's field headquarters. They pointed out that the British and American military attachés in Rome had been denied permission to visit Africa. British Foreign Secretary Anthony Eden had even gone to Rome to see Mussolini and learn about his plans: If Italy completed the conquest of Ethiopia, did he intend to strike at Egypt? Did he plan to advance from Libya to seize the Suez Canal? How strong was his army, and what was its temper?

"Eden tried to find out, and Mussolini had treated him like a child. Miffed, Eden and his entourage had flounced home," Donovan said later.

When the State Department refused to accredit Donovan as an observer, he went directly from the department to the Italian Embassy, where he called on Ambassador Rossi. The ambassador obliged him by writing a letter introducing Col. William J. Donovan, distinguished lawyer, who wished to understand the progress of affairs in the Mediterranean and Africa in order to advise his clients, who were among the most important corporations in the United States. Mussolini was also informed that Donovan wore the Croce di Guerra for his heroism in World War I.

Donovan reached Rome on December 23, 1935, and called on the foreign minister. "I am traveling as a private American citizen," he said, "and I want to understand the Italian situation because it affects business at home."

The minister said that Mussolini was very busy and could not see him.

"I am just as busy in America," replied Donovan. "I cannot wait indefinitely. If Mussolini cannot see me, I want to know so that I can leave at once."

Donovan returned to his hotel. In only a few minutes a message arrived from the minister, who said that Il Duce had granted him an interview at three o'clock the next afternoon. On December 24, Donovan pinned on his Croce di Guerra.

"I went to the Venetian Palace at 2:50," he wrote in his diary. "At the door were two sentries, not particularly smart. Inside the corridor was a major domo, dressed like a Park Avenue doorman. I gave him my letter, and he went to the telephone. A moment later a plainclothesman arrived with a paper, and compared it with the name on my letter. I tried to get my letter back, but they confiscated that. We climbed two flights of stairs, he pressed a button, a door opened, and a footman in livery ushered me into a waiting room."

While he waited, Donovan studied the room. Later he recalled the paintings that hung on the velvet walls. There were a Van Dyck, an anonymous 17th-century Italian, a Van Ploem, a Giovanni Pini of the early 16th century. At precisely three o'clock the plainclothesman returned, saluted Donovan, and ushered him into the council chamber, which was fitted with tables of dark wood covered by blue damask. Donovan and his guide paused at a door at the far end.

"The door was opened by an older usher in a black Prince Albert coat," wrote Donovan. "I entered a large room, bare and high. At the far end was a plain table, a few papers on it, a desk light. Behind the desk was Mussolini."

When Il Duce wished to make a visitor feel ill at ease, he customarily looked down at his papers as if preoccupied with their contents. The visitor was left shifting from one foot to another until Il Duce felt he had been kept waiting long enough. Catching Mussolini's glance as he entered, Donovan held it with his own as he walked the length of the room.

"I walked as if I were leading my regiment," he remarked later.

Mussolini stepped from behind the desk and shook hands. The Italian dictator and the American made small talk.

"Mussolini asked me how long I had been in France during the war," Donovan said later. "I told him nineteen months."

"Wounded?" asked Mussolini.

"Three times," Donovan replied.

Mussolini seemed impressed. "And now you wish to go to Eritrea?"

"I would be interested in seeing the spirit of your soldiers," replied Donovan. "I did not think much of your troops in the World War—neither the discipline of the men nor the quality of the officers. After the war I saw your officers chased by crowds through the streets of Milan."

"It is different now," Mussolini snapped. "You will see a vast change."

"I would like to see that change, and I would like to be where the men are because, to judge of their power and strength, one must see how they take care of their feet, of their middle, and their heads. If Italy is to have a new empire, she must have a new Tenth Legion."

Mussolini clapped his hands and smiled with pleasure at Donovan's mention of the crack Roman unit. "Tenth Legion, that is right." He regarded Donovan with a shrewd expression. "Your country will aid Britain? Are you in favor of the oil embargo?"

"I am in favor of a foreign policy that is our own, and not one that makes us an instrument of someone else," Donovan replied.

Again Mussolini clapped his hands in delight. "You will go to Africa. First to Libya and then to Abyssinia. You will see our colonization. You will see our soldiers, and you will see that Italy has a new Tenth Legion." Mussolini summoned an aide. "See that Colonel Donovan is put on the next plane and cable Marshal Badoglio that he personally must escort the colonel on a tour of the front."

Donovan went to Ethiopia as a representative of Benito Mussolini.

"Mussolini offered not only to let Bill see anything he wanted to see, but gave orders that all forms of transportation—horse, mule, camel, or airplane—should be made available to him," wrote Hugh Wilson. "All this under the one condition that Colonel Donovan promise to return straight to Rome and tell him what he thought of the show."

Donovan flew to Cairo. He traveled by air by way of Luxor and Khartoum in the Sudan to Ethiopia, where he spent ten days at the fighting front. He slept in a striped tent set up next to Marshal Badoglio's. He had a chance to see firsthand the thrust of modern tanks and aircraft against poorly armed if brave men. He spent time not only with Badoglio, with whom he formed a soldier's friendship for another soldier whose professional ability was evident, but also at corps, division, and brigade levels. He filled his daily diary with comments on battle positions, motor transport, and the S-81, which he described as "a huge bomber, much like the new Boeing the Army is getting out." Indefatigably he jotted down camp layouts, the soldiers' diet and morale, the apparent condition of army mules and horses. He analyzed Italian military strategy and talked about Italy's foreign policy with Badoglio. He concluded that Italy would easily win the war.

On his way back to Rome from Ethiopia, Donovan stopped off at Bengasi in Libya, where he interviewed the commissioner of the province, and at Tripoli, where he discussed Italy's plans for the Mediterranean with Gen. Italo Balbo, who had been pro-American since he led a flight of Italian warplanes to the Chicago World's Fair in 1933. Balbo liked Americans for their open ways, and he readily confided in Donovan.

Back in Rome, Donovan reported to Mussolini and gave him his candid views on the undoubted prowess of the Italian Army in Ethiopia. He went to see the American ambassador and told him that the Italian "service of supplies was excellent, that morale was high, that health and sanitation were splendid, efficiency first-rate, and that the military positions now occupied were secure and could be easily held." The ambassador informed Secretary of State Cordell Hull.

From Rome, Donovan went on to Paris, where he telephoned Hugh Wilson in Geneva on January 14. "Bill told me over the phone that he had just been to Ethiopia and asked whether I would like him to fly down and tell me about it," wrote Wilson. "Since Ethiopia was the one subject that was present with us day and night, I accepted enthusiastically and Bill duly arrived the next day."

Donovan briefed Wilson about the Italian war effort, the road construction, the health of the army, and how a great advance was being organized. "It would not be launched until it was ready, but when it was launched it would be irresistible," Wilson reported Donovan said. "We could count with certainty on the Italians' entry into Addis Ababa in good season before the rain commenced."

Significant to Wilson was that Donovan's views contradicted the optimistic reports still circulating in Geneva and in the other capitals of European diplomacy.

> The news brought by Donovan was of overwhelming importance; the whole of the League policy and, especially, British policy was predicated on the effectiveness of the sanctions in preventing an Italian victory. If the sanctions had no such effect it was obviously the better part of wisdom to alter radically the policy which depended on sanctions for success. Bill's story carried absolute conviction to me. I knew he was a competent observer. I knew he was completely unprejudiced, and I knew he submitted to me his observations only because he was convinced of their complete soundness.

In the morning Wilson walked with British Foreign Secretary Anthony Eden along the lake to the Old Disarmament Building, where the day's council session was to be held. He told Eden about Donovan and about some of his views.

"Eden was deeply perturbed," remembered Wilson later. "He recognized the importance of the report and asked me to send Donovan to see him at six o'clock that evening."

"Wilson wanted me to talk with Eden," Donovan wrote in his diary for January 16, "but I thought it was a mistake to go to Eden's hotel." After all, he had just been a guest of Benito Mussolini, Eden's foe, and Italian spies would certainly be watching and would report to Rome. He preferred to meet Eden in some clandestine fashion.

At five o'clock Wilson's phone rang. It was Eden. King George V had just died, and he had been ordered to return to London by the first airplane. He hoped that Colonel Donovan would be able to see him in London and asked for his address there.

Within a few days Donovan arrived in London and notified Eden's private secretary. But the funeral of the king and the ceremonies attending the coming to power of a new monarch and a new cabinet prevented Eden from seeing Donovan. These events apparently did not keep him from talking about Donovan's observations on the Ethiopian war, however. When Wilson arrived in London two weeks later he found that at dinner party after dinner party, people were telling the story of the American observer who had the "temerity to question the judgment of the best military opinion on the Continent."

Donovan briefed Eden's aides, but Eden took no action. Within a few weeks the worst happened in Ethiopia. The Italian advance indeed proved irresistible, and Addis Ababa fell. Italian soldiers, having destroyed most of Emperor Haile Selassie's army in the field, now wantonly slaughtered the imperial lions kept in a pound at his palace. The emperor fled to Britain.

"If I had been able to tell Eden that the Italians were sure to overrun Ethiopia, there might have been a shift in British policy that would have kept Italy in the League and prevented the birth of the Axis between Rome and Berlin," said Wilson.

"The history of mankind is the history of men," he wrote. "Sudden unpredictable decisions sometimes dictated by nothing more serious than indigestion have changed the fate of history. In this case an infinitely more serious factor, true, the death of a king, may have been that fortuitous event which kept Europe on the steady path to disaster."

At least if either London or Washington had realized the validity of Donovan's report on the competence and leadership of the Italian Army, the mounting danger in the Mediterranean might have been curtailed. Donovan returned to the United States and made a personal report to President Roosevelt. Setting political differences aside, Roosevelt appreciated that Donovan was America's leading intelligence expert and valued what he had to say. Donovan told the President that Italy's army was vastly improved and that if the army could be taken as an expression of the people's will, the Italians were possessed of a spirit of determination to the point of desperation. The Italian people knew the danger of their advance in Africa, but they would go through with it, pulling down the rest of Europe if it tried to block them.

Donovan also reported to the War Department, and on February 24, Major General Simonds commended him for the "pertinent and valuable information" that could not have been obtained through any other channel.

His Ethiopia mission may have been successful, but Donovan's law partners rebuked him. The government had brought suit against American Telephone & Telegraph Company just before his departure, and the Donovan firm had been retained to defend the case.

"We were fighting for our place in the Wall Street sun," recalled John Howley, then a junior partner. "Our success in the AT&T case all depended upon Donovan, and there he was running around in the wilds of Africa."

Donovan plunged back into the affairs of his law office. He also supported Frank Knox for the Republican nomination for president. It was inevitable that Col. Frank Knox, publisher of the *Chicago Daily News,* and Bill Donovan should become friends and political allies, for both were Republicans in the vigorous image of Teddy Roosevelt. Knox was close to Roosevelt in thought, manner, and appearance, for he had ridden with him in the First U.S. Volunteer Cavalry at San Juan Hill. Knox, a Rough Rider to the heart, had supported Roosevelt's Bull Moose campaign for the presidency. By late spring 1936, Donovan was holding a series of dinners at his Beekman Place duplex to win support from prominent politicians for Knox. When the Republican convention picked Gov. Alfred Landon of Kansas as the nominee for president,

Donovan and his friend Albert Lasker were instrumental in obtaining the vice-presidential nomination for Knox. Donovan was an adviser to Knox during the campaign, which President Roosevelt easily won.

Events in Europe had taken a tragic turn. The Spanish Civil War began on July 17, 1936, when Francisco Franco and a group of generals led their forces in revolt against the republic both in Spanish Morocco and in Spain. Rightists and leftists fought in the streets of Spain. Hitler and Mussolini had both promised to support Franco, and they lived up to their pledge not only with arms and supplies but with military personnel.

The Neutrality Act of 1935, which President Roosevelt had espoused in an effort to block American assistance to Italy during the Ethiopian invasion, could not be applied to the struggle in Spain since it was a civil war. Not until May 1, 1937, was new legislation passed and signed into law to prohibit the shipment of arms, munitions, and the tools of war to Spain. This had little effect in cutting off arms for Franco since nations other than the United States were providing men and arms. By this time Italy had sent upward of 60,000 men to Spain to help the rightist insurgents, and was employing its air force and navy. Germany had contributed between 10,000 and 20,000 men with tanks, artillery, planes, and communications equipment. Russia was dispatching men and arms to help the leftist Popular Front government.

Donovan kept one eye on affairs in Spain and the other on his law practice. Guy Martin, at that time a new member of the firm, remembered years later that, "Donovan was an indefatigable traveler on the shortest notice. At the same time he knew what the cases were about and exactly what I was doing. I don't remember his tossing a case and going off and leaving it."

The years that saw Europe sinking into the crucible of war were good years for Donovan's law practice. Among his clients were important German concerns, descendants of Prussian General Helmuth von Moltke, and the Viennese Rothschilds. From these people he learned a great deal about what was going on behind the scenes in Hitler's Reich. After the German occupation of Czechoslovakia, the Rothschilds engaged him to try to win back their holdings in Bohemia, which the Nazis had seized. Donovan went to Germany to argue with the Nazis on behalf of the Rothschilds. He also took advantage of the opportunity to talk to anti-Hitler friends, who then and later continued to hold high positions in Berlin. Donovan already had informants within Hitler's upper echelons.

In October 1937, the federal government brought to trial 18 U.S. oil companies, five subsidiaries, three oil trade journals, and 57 top oilmen at Madison, Wisconsin, for violating the Sherman Antitrust

Act. The defendants were accused of having "combined and conspired beginning in February, 1935, to raise and fix prices of gasoline sold in ten states of the Middle West."

Donovan, the nation's foremost antitrust lawyer, was chosen to head a defense force of 57 attorneys. He rented a big house in Madison's Shorewood Hills, installed Madge, his stocky English cook, and his Danish butler, and commuted by plane from New York City. The oilmen claimed that they were following Roosevelt's National Recovery Act directives, and Donovan collected 18 tons of documents in an effort to prove that they were right.

The proceedings against the oilmen were criminal in nature, which led Donovan to argue: "Since they [the government] have chosen to institute a criminal case, they must be bound by the rules that our Constitution has prescribed in order to protect the defendants when they are accused of crime. Now, an essential element in this case is the question of intent; did these men have a guilty intent in what they did? And it isn't sufficient alone to show that there was written approval or statutory approval. There is the question of instigation; there is the question of inducement; there is the question of approval."

Lawyer Donovan quoted Secretary of Interior Harold Ickes and President Roosevelt to show that they had both approved of the oil companies' conduct. When Judge Patrick Thomas Stone demanded that he stop quoting the President, Donovan produced a letter from Secretary Ickes to Charles E. Arnott, vice-president of Socony-Vacuum Oil Company, urging that the "companies combine to stabilize prices and authorizing them to do so."

The trial lasted until January 1938 before a jury of farmers who were totally unsympathetic to the machinations of big companies. In an effort to keep the jury objective, the book *The Life of Emile Zola* was banned from their sight because of its courtroom scenes, which were presumed to be inflammatory. John Steuart Curry, artist in residence at the University of Wisconsin, sketched Bill Donovan in court as he "made his voice ring with pathos and indignation" to make the final plea, concluding, "It is unthinkable that these men should be punished for doing the very thing the government asked them to do."

Costing $3 million, the trial ended in nominal fines for the defendants, which was considered a victory for the defense.

Even as the trial ground along, Donovan remained in touch with events in Europe. On May 21, 1937, he journeyed to Germany to watch the German Army try out the new Panther tank and artillery in maneuvers. In 1938 he was in Czechoslovakia to study the Sudetenland defenses then threatened by Hitler; he came away with admiration for the tough Czech Army, its morale and equipment, and its plans to fight off a German attack. At the same time he became convinced that European statesmen did not have the political courage to stand up to

Hitler. From Prague Donovan went on through the Balkans, meeting men who were to help him on future missions and observing conditions. He stopped off in Italy to talk to Italian sources about their nation's growing involvement in the Spanish Civil War and then crossed the western Mediterranean to Spain.

Donovan accompanied the Fourth Spanish Army in attacks on the Ebro River front. He watched German Panther tanks and Stuka dive-bombers in action against the government forces and saw firsthand what devastation they caused. "I believed Spain to be, ideology aside, a laboratory for the weapons of the next war," he later said, "and I went there to observe their performance. I met no other American observer."

From Spain Donovan traveled to Germany, where the German General Staff had invited him to observe the maneuvers at Nuremberg. He saw how the German Army was putting the lessons learned in Spain to work in the Bavarian exercises, which suggested that if a great war broke out in Europe, Germany planned to fight a war of movement. This clearly outmoded the Maginot Line and placed France in jeopardy.

When he returned to America, Donovan addressed the Army War College:

> We are facing a new kind of war, not so much in point of principle, because in war the fundamental principles remain the same, but new in respect of machines and weapons. More than that, this is war moving to a new tempo. The speed of attack has no precedent. Out of that speed come certain new characteristics of warfare. One is that which makes for greater decentralization of command. What struck me in observing the German Army was that this totalitarian state, through the necessity of the new war, had gone farther than any other country in decentralizing its command. It placed greater responsibility upon the junior officers and noncommissioned officers. And this requires training. It cannot be done overnight. Responsibility must be guided.
>
> The second characteristic of the new warfare is more perfect coordination between the air arm and the land arm.

On the flight home from Europe, Donovan briefed himself on a case that was paramount in his law office and upon his arrival presented his argument before the Supreme Court. Then he called upon Army Chief of Staff Gen. Malin Craig. Donovan reported to Craig on the German and Italian tactics in Spain, and the German Army maneuvers in Bavaria. "The German 88-millimeter cannon was a truly redoubtable weapon," he said. "It could shoot down Loyalist planes with ease, could fire against ground troops, and at point-blank range could blast huge holes in Russian tanks."

Craig expressed a polite interest, and he informed U.S. Army Ordnance of Donovan's report. Ordnance commented that no such gun as Donovan had described existed or could possibly prove practicable.

Donovan also reported to the White House. The political polarization of the totalitarians of the right and the left in Europe and the uncertainty and lack of preparation of the democracies opened the way to further military adventures. Donovan informed Roosevelt that Hitler meant war. There could be no other meaning to the "dress rehearsal" in Spain.

The President listened to Donovan's comments and began a reassessment of American policy, but General Craig and his ordnance staff refused to take his accounts of the 88-millimeter gun seriously. When the 88 came up against U.S. soldiers in North Africa four years later, it smashed American armor and slaughtered American soldiers exactly as Donovan had seen it destroying the enemies of fascism in Spain.

On October 5, 1937, at the dedication of Chicago's new Outer Drive bridge, Franklin Roosevelt made what has since been known as his Quarantine speech. He warned the American public that what was happening in Spain and in China, where Japan's aggression continued unabated, was a direct threat to their own country:

> Let no one imagine that America will escape, that America may expect mercy, that this western hemisphere will not be attacked and that it will continue tranquilly and peacefully to carry on the ethics and the arts of civilization. If we are to have a world in which we can breathe freely and live in amity without fear, the peace-loving nations must make a concerted effort to uphold laws and principles on which peace can rest secure.
>
> War is a contagion, whether it be declared or undeclared. It can engulf states and peoples remote from the original scene of hostilities. We are determined to keep out of war, yet we cannot insure ourselves against the disastrous effects of war and the dangers of involvement. We are adopting such measures as will minimize the risk of involvement, but we cannot have complete protection in a world of disorder in which confidence and security have broken down.

Those who listened to the President in the Indian summer day on Chicago's lakefront felt a dread chill. For the most part they listened in silence. Perhaps the President was wrong; after all, the Germans, the Japanese, and the Italians were civilized people, and they could not be planning Armageddon. In the weeks that followed, scores of important American leaders attacked the President for what they said was a warmongering speech. Some of the men who spoke out against him were members of his own party; most were Republicans who saw an opportunity to even scores with the man who had defeated them so overwhelmingly in two presidential elections and who had so drastically altered the fabric of American life. Three important Republicans spoke out in support of the President. They were Henry Stimson, Frank Knox, and William Donovan.

17

Contagion of War

IN THE LATE SPRING of 1939, Donovan wrote in his journal that "war was imminent" and that "the Germans would attack through the Low Countries." In June and July he visited the Netherlands and Belgium to learn whether the Dutch and Belgian armies would be able to oppose the German war machine. He studied economic conditions too and also toured France, Germany, Norway, Sweden, and Denmark. Everywhere he went he talked to his friends in the various governments and among the opposition parties. He met with professors at universities, industrial leaders, businessmen, labor leaders, and journalists.

The contagion of war that President Roosevelt had warned about in Chicago was spreading through Europe. In 1938 the Nazi legions extinguished the independence of Austria and in so doing also outflanked the defense line that Donovan had observed in Czechoslovakia along its mountain frontier with Germany. Hitler almost immediately began to agitate for annexation to the Reich of the Sudeten Germans along Czechoslovakia's borders. Donovan was shocked at the seizure of Austria, but he rationalized that after all the Austrians were a German people and that not much could be done about it. Czechoslovakia was another matter. That nation had virtually been planned as a state at the University of Chicago, and it was a bastion of democracy in Central Europe. When French Premier Edouard Daladier and British Prime Minister Neville Chamberlain surrendered the Sudetenland to Hitler at Munich on September 29 because Germany was ready to fight and France and Britain were not, Donovan was appalled. It seemed to him that now World War II was not only inevitable, but that it might be lost before it began.

March 15, 1939, saw the abject surrender of what remained of Czechoslovakia. Within a week Hitler had also taken the Memel district of Lithuania and was demanding that Poland agree to the annexation of Danzig and the cession of a strip of territory across the Polish Corridor to East Prussia. Mussolini invaded Albania on April 7, and Franco's victory in Spain was complete by midspring. Great Britain and France were at last feverishly arming.

When Donovan reached London, he studied British rearmament. He met with R. E. Butler of the foreign office, who described him as "an active man, of attractive temperament, who has visited Balbo in Libya, Mussolini in Rome, and has many contacts in Berlin with the Foreign Office and General Staff. He has just flown around Europe and renewed contacts, particularly in Berlin. His main impression is that the German Army, as he put it, is 'set for a fight' to achieve their aims at all costs."

Donovan warned his London friends that Britain would have "an exciting summer."

The year 1939 was a prosperous one for Bill Donovan's law practice, although he now spent less and less time on it. Both his Georgetown house and his New York duplex on Beekman Place were the settings for lively dinner parties, which included such diplomats as Dwight Morrow and Secretary of State Cordell Hull, political leaders such as Henry Stimson and Frank Knox, and journalists David Lawrence and Vincent Sheean, as well as a miscellany of friends, among them Albert Lasker, Eve Curie, John Golden, Bernard Gimbel, Andrew Meyers, Mrs. Anna Rosenberg, Dorothy Draper, Margaret Sanger, Lois Mattox Miller, Irene Dunne and her husband, and Greta Garbo. Ruth Donovan, quiet but poised, joined her husband at the New York gatherings except when she was in their summer home in Massachusetts. Conversation ranged through the world of theater and books to the situation in Europe. Donovan could always be counted upon for some trenchant remarks about Europe.

When he was in New York, Donovan frequently lunched or dined at the 21 Club, where he was instantly recognized by the maitre d' and given a prime table among the hobnobbing celebrities of the time. Albert Lasker remembered him at the 21 Club, "bland of eye, butter-soft in voice, and composed of equal parts of fire, iron, and pink leather." To some at 21 he was the war hero of World War I, to others the rich Wall Street lawyer or the popular public figure who might one day be the first Catholic president of the United States. To a few he was a man of mystery, whose comings and goings through the world's trouble spots had not gone unnoted.

To many of the women whom Donovan entertained at home or met in such places as 21, he proved irresistible.

"Bill preferred worldly women," remembered Guy Martin. "Sometimes he'd make two or three engagements that overlapped. He'd cope. 'Guy, you take Mrs. X to dinner,' he'd say. 'I'll get there.' He'd show up, and I would chase out. 'I have to go back to work,' I'd say."

Donovan, fresh from one dalliance, would devote himself to another. He brought the same sleepless energy and stamina to his relations with women that he showed in every other aspect of his life. Among the beautiful women who admired him was Diana Sheean. "She was infatuated with Bill," said Martin. "She talked to me about him. Bill was a puzzle. He pursued women with avidity, but he backed off emotionally when the relationship promised to become too close or permanent."

To Martin, this meant that Donovan was "deeply influenced by Catholic tradition." To others it simply meant that intriguing as he found attractive women to be, he loved Ruth.

Patricia Donovan and Mary Grandin were school friends at Rosemary Hall in Greenwich, Connecticut. Both were chestnut-haired girls, with similar attractive features and warmth. Both were witty, both rode horseback with grace and verve, and to their classmates it seemed natural that they would be the best of friends. Both had plenty of money, too. Mary's father was from one of the richest of the Pennsylvania oil families. Patricia often invited Mary home to spend vacations with the Donovans, and Mary soon found herself in love with David. David, who had finished prep school at St. George's School in Providence, was studying agriculture at Cornell University. Some friends of the Donovan family say that Mary first fell in love with David's father, whose reputation was well known, but when Bill Donovan made it evident that she was nothing more to him than a lovely young woman, she decided to marry the son. She could then at least be close to the fascinating father.

Elaborate dinners, luncheons, and teas for Mary Grandin enlivened the late spring of 1939 in Warren, Pennsylvania. In June, David Donovan finished his studies at Cornell, and on June 17, 1939, the couple were married. Patricia Donovan was the maid of honor, and the Reverend Vincent Donovan and the Reverend Pinkney Wroth, rector of Warren's Trinity Memorial Episcopal Church, officiated. Warren people remember that the Donovan chauffeur drove the Donovan family from New York City.

The Grandins had a huge tent erected over the backyard of their mansion on Conewango Avenue, and neighborhood children peeked inside to watch the guests at the reception dancing to an orchestra. When David Donovan signed his name on the registry, he gave "farmer" as his occupation, and after a honeymoon trip to Buck Hill Falls in Pennsylvania, and Bermuda, David and Mary made their home at Chapel Hill Farm, Virginia.

The summer brought war to Europe. On September 1 Hitler and Stalin united to attack Poland, and so the conflict was joined. Great Britain and France declared war on Germany on September 3. With the outbreak of war in Europe, Franklin Roosevelt summoned Congress into special session. He called for the repeal of the arms embargo, and in November Congress enacted legislation permitting the Allies to buy war goods in the United States. As 1939 drew to a close, Roosevelt also decided to create a bipartisan cabinet because of the critical situation abroad. He would take in some Republicans, and in early December Washington rumor suggested that Bill Donovan was to replace Secretary of War Harry Woodring.

"I don't think it is likely that the President will put a Republican in as a member of his cabinet," said Stephen T. Early, Roosevelt's press secretary. Even as Early was denying the President's intentions, Roosevelt was asking Frank Knox to a meeting at the White House on December 10, the next day. All that afternoon Roosevelt and Knox talked about the situation in Europe and Asia. During the course of the discussion, FDR asked the Chicago publisher and onetime vice-presidential candidate to be secretary of the navy. Knox demurred because he did not want his fellow Republicans to call him a "political Benedict Arnold." Furthermore, he did not consider the American situation grave enough. When Roosevelt did find it necessary to appoint a Republican to his cabinet, Knox said, he should appoint more than one. He argued that "a strong man be found for the War Department."

Roosevelt asked Knox who this should be—perhaps Herbert Hoover, Arthur H. Vandenberg, Henry Cabot Lodge, Thomas E. Dewey, or Alf Landon.

"Knox said that Landon was a 'nice' fellow but that he was not heavy," noted Harold Ickes in his diary. "He felt that it would be much better if the President would take Bill Donovan into the cabinet as another Republican."

Roosevelt asked Ickes for his views on the subject. "I pointed out two difficulties in the way of this. One, that it would mean another member of the cabinet from New York State, which is already over-represented; and two, that Donovan probably would not be interested in anything except the Attorney-Generalship, with respect to which there was a promise out to Bob Jackson as soon as there was a vacancy."

On December 15 Knox, having thought the matter over, wrote to the President from Chicago:

> I know Bill Donovan very well, and he is a very dear friend. He not only made a magnificent record in the world war, but he has every decoration which the American government can bestow for bravery under fire. Frankly, if your proposal contemplated Donovan for the War Department and myself for the Navy, I think the appointments could be put solely upon the basis of a nonpartisan, nonpolitical measure of putting our national defense departments in such a state of preparedness as to protect the United States against any danger to our security that might come from the war in Europe or in Asia.

"Bill Donovan is also an old friend of mine," Roosevelt wrote back two weeks later. "We were in law school together—and frankly, I should like to have him in the cabinet, not only for his own ability, but also to repair in a sense the very great injustice done him by President Hoover in the winter of 1929. Here again the question of motive must be considered, and I fear that to put two Republicans in charge of the armed forces might be misunderstood in both parties."

Roosevelt did not tell Knox so, but he already was contemplating another role for Donovan than that of secretary of war. He would become instead what the paraplegic Roosevelt was to call "my secret legs." It was Felix Frankfurter who, with the New York lawyer Grenville Clark, suggested that Henry Stimson, who had served in the cabinets of four Republican presidents, would be a good choice for secretary of war, even if he too came from New York.

As the year ended Bill Donovan paid little heed to Knox's indications that he might become secretary of war. "I'd get down on my hands and knees and scrub the Capitol's steps if that is what the President asked me to do," Donovan told a friend, "but I'm not pushing myself forward for any job."

Ruth and Bill Donovan and their children gathered for the Christmas holidays. This was the last Christmas they were all to spend together.

By January 1940 the law books on the shelves of Bill Donovan's private office had almost entirely been replaced by books on world affairs. Donovan left the day-to-day law practice to his partners.

In Europe the so-called Phoney War dragged on. The only winter fighting was in Finland. The Russians, having cowed the other Baltic states of Latvia, Lithuania, and Estonia into submission, had had their ultimatum to Finland go unanswered. On November 30, 1939, the Russian Air Force commenced hostilities by bombing Helsinki. Russia's armies attacked Finland, and to the amazement and applause of the western world, the Finns not only fought back but won victory after victory. Repulsed with heavy losses at Lake Ladoga, routed by Finnish ski troops at Salla, and devastated at the battle of Suomussalmi, the Russians seemed no closer to success than when they first attacked. Military analysts throughout the world gave the Soviet forces low ratings for efficiency and morale. Even when late in January the Russians threw a vast army into action and rolled over the fierce Finns to victory, they lost as many as 500,000 men, killed and wounded. Hitler helped Joseph Stalin arrange a peace on favorable terms to Russia, but he also expressed open contempt for the Soviet war machine. In time he was to act upon this contempt.

Donovan closely followed the events in Europe. He became president of the Paderewski Fund for Polish Relief and worked for Finnish relief as well. He brought to New York 80-year-old Ignace Paderewski, the famous Polish pianist, patriot, and statesman. Paderewski, who headed the Polish government in exile, would lend prestige to the nationwide campaign. Donovan mobilized a committee of distinguished Americans ranging from Eleanor Roosevelt to General Robert E. Wood, who was soon to lead the isolationist America First movement. Donovan and his friend Greta Garbo persuaded Leopold Stokowski to conduct a benefit concert for his native Poland. Unfortunately, when Stokowski's manager learned that the popular clarinetist Benny Goodman was also to be featured on the program, he withdrew the maestro; to appear with a pop musician would lower Stokowski's dignity. Both former President Hoover and President Roosevelt lent support to the campaign.

Donovan was convinced that the United States should not intervene in the war in Europe. The country must build up its political, economic, and military strength.

"I know too much about war to glory in it," he said. "But wars are made by politicians who neglect to prepare for it."

He made speeches and wrote articles opposing the draft, because he claimed it was antiquated. "This system assumes (1) that the country can better afford to lose a youth than an adult; and (2) that a stripling of eighteen is better prepared to defend his country than a vigorous man of forty-five. Both assumptions are false," he wrote in *Reader's Digest.*

Donovan regretted bitterly the loss of so many young men in World War I and the social and economic tragedy it represented. He pointed out that the nation's falling birthrate and the cessation of immigration at the time were placing a premium on youth. "We must economize on youth in the next war," he said, "if we are to survive even victory."

His battlefield observations of the European war machines caused Donovan to state, "I have followed the mechanization of war from Château-Thierry to the present, and have seen less and less emphasis placed on a soldier's brawn, and more and more on his brain. Instead of marching to war, today's soldier rides."

When it came to bravery, he believed that "the courage of youth and of older men strikes a rough balance," and that in "tight spots under fire I have seen older men become rallying points for young troops on the verge of panic."

Draft proponents fumed, but when one of the nation's foremost citizen soldiers spoke out in this fashion, America listened.

After her trip around the world in 1937, Pat Donovan had returned to Wellesley for a year, and then transferred as a junior to George Washington University in Washington, where in the spring of 1940 she was majoring in American thought and civilization. She lived at home in Georgetown, and Bill Donovan spent every evening he could with her, talking, arguing about politics and American history. Western civilization seemed to be bent on self-destruction, but to Donovan and his daughter the great past could only promise a great future. In the long tides of history, Hitler and Mussolini were only aberrations.

In late winter Ruth set out on Irving Johnson's yacht, *Yankee,* on a round-the-world trip, and by early April she was at sea between Honolulu and Samoa. On Saturday, April 6, Bill Donovan was in New York City. He was haunted by the recollection that it was exactly 23 years ago to the day that America had declared war on Germany in the World War. Now he wondered how long it would be before America might declare war again. Friends of his in Europe had alerted him to German plans to invade neighboring Denmark and strike at Norway, and even as he moodily ate breakfast at his Beekman Place duplex, he knew that Hitler's army, navy, and air force were preparing to strike. Donovan felt a curious dread.

Pat Donovan had driven down to Durham, North Carolina, to visit her friend Dorothy Wiprud, daughter of Georgetown neighbors, who was a student at Duke University. She was to drive back to Washington on Monday to resume her classes. An early spring storm swept down on the entire East Coast on Monday morning. Pat put up the top of her convertible to keep off the drenching rain and drove north through North Carolina and Virginia on Route 1. She passed through Richmond. The rain streamed against the windshield and washed the red mud of the Virginia fields down onto the road. Rounding a curve about 30 miles south of Fredericksburg, the car struck a patch of slippery mud. The wheels spun, and the automobile whirled out of control and into a tree. With the impact Pat was hurled from the car and thrown to the ground 14 feet away. A few minutes later a motorist stopped and hurried her to Mary Washington Hospital in Fredericksburg. But Pat never regained consciousness. She died of shock and internal injuries five hours after the accident.

The hospital telephoned both Bill Donovan and his son, David, who was at Chapel Hill Farm. David jumped in a car and sped to his sister's side. He got there before she died. In New York, Donovan could not get a plane because of the weather and had to take a train. One of his Washington law partners met the train at Washington's Union Station and told him that his daughter was dead. To Donovan the world seemed a senseless and mean place where a mad dictator ranted and threatened civilization itself and a young girl's life could be snuffed out. Bill Donovan never recovered from his daughter's death, although he was to come to feel for David's wife, Mary, some of the love that he had always given to Pat.

On the day that Pat Donovan died, Germany invaded Denmark, and within an hour Copenhagen capitulated. On the next day, while Bill Donovan was preoccupied with his grief, Germany invaded Norway. Over the next few weeks the British forces that had landed in

Norway were routed, and German control of Scandinavia was assured. The British were still enmeshed in Norway when on May 10 the Germans unleashed a devastating blitzkrieg through the Low Countries, just as Donovan had long before predicted they would. The onslaught of Hitler's mechanized forces on the ill-prepared and poorly led Allied forces resulted in the fall of France. England, her army badly beaten, stood alone, and only the narrow Channel barred the Germans from complete victory.

On June 20, Franklin Roosevelt responded to the European military crisis that darkened the future of the United States by taking two Republicans into his cabinet. Stimson was to be secretary of war, and Knox was to be secretary of the navy in a bipartisan government. Knox immediately phoned Donovan from Chicago and asked him to be under secretary of the navy; Donovan declined and the job went to James Forrestal. It was a post of importance, but Donovan had already made a commitment.

18

Confidential Mission to Britain

FOR YEARS BILL DONOVAN had been acquainted with British Adm. Blinker Hall, and on May 29, 1940, a slightly built Canadian in the service of British Secret Intelligence had arrived in New York with a letter from Hall to Donovan. The Canadian's name was William Stephenson. Winston Churchill, the new prime minister whom military disaster had brought to office, had given Stephenson a critical mission to the United States. He was to attempt to obtain destroyers, aircraft, and military equipment and supplies to replace those that the British Expeditionary Force had left behind on the beaches of Dunkirk. Stephenson knew that Donovan had been one of the key figures in America's clandestine intelligence net for a generation. In fact, he may have met Donovan in London as long ago as 1916, when both were young men just beginning to learn their trade. Stephenson got to the point. Could Donovan help him approach the President? Could Donovan influence the President? Realizing that without American support, England would quickly fall and that this would leave America isolated in an increasingly hostile world, Donovan assured Stephenson he would do all he could to help.

As June drew to a close, Donovan went to Philadelphia as part of the New York delegation to the Republican National Convention. The New Yorkers were pledged to support Gov. Thomas Dewey, and Donovan did not join in the raucous chants of "We Want Willkie" that reverberated through the convention hall. Actually, he was not sympathetic toward Dewey's candidacy but secretly favored Wendell Willkie, who shared his views on aiding the British. On June 28 the GOP grass roots delegates took over the convention from the political professionals and on the sixth ballot nominated Willkie.

Afterward, Donovan met his fellow New York delegate Allen Dulles in the crowded lobby of his hotel. He clapped Dulles on the back. "Let's go into the bar and talk," he said.

Allen's brother, John Foster Dulles, had been an ardent Dewey supporter, but Allen could see much merit in Willkie's candidacy. In the bar Donovan expressed his satisfaction that now both candidates for the presidency would have the same attitude toward the war in Europe. "We'll be in it before the end of 1941," Donovan told Dulles, "and when we are, there are certain preparations which should already have been made. That's where you come in."

Dulles had done intelligence work in Europe in World War I, and now Donovan, long before he himself had official status as America's master spy, considered Dulles a potential lieutenant in an overseas intelligence net that America would surely need before long.

When Frank Knox arrived in Washington on July 5 for his Senate confirmation hearings, Donovan met his train and took him to his Georgetown house, where Knox was to stay throughout the hearings. Donovan explained the British situation and asked Knox to assist him in approaching the President. Democratic Sen. Scott Lucas of Illinois came to lunch, and Donovan and Lucas spent the afternoon drilling Knox for his appearance before the Senate Naval Affairs Committee.

Intelligence from Great Britain was scarcely reassuring. The German Luftwaffe was systematically destroying both military targets and English cities, and the badly outnumbered Royal Air Force seemed unlikely to be able to turn aside the crushing blows. German submarines were sinking ship after ship at sea, and it appeared that Britain must inevitably be cut off from vital war materials and food supplies and starved into submission. From London, U.S. Ambassador Joseph P. Kennedy sent despairing reports about Britain's chances for survival. He seemed to welcome Britain's impending demise and applauded Hitler's new order with an enthusiasm that appalled most people in Washington.

"Democracy is finished in England," Kennedy told a reporter from the *Boston Globe*. He informed the reporter that democracy was nearly dead in the United States too. Kennedy was drawn temperamentally and socially to the coterie of highly placed Englishmen who were defeatist in mood and preferred an accommodation with Hitler to the mounting horror of what seemed to them a losing war.

Kennedy was not the only American advising Roosevelt that the British would not last much longer. U.S. Army Intelligence estimated that the Royal Air Force could survive as an effective fighting force for only a week or two. Even Britain's ambassador in Washington, Lord Lothian, was telling American officials that if Germany won the Battle of Britain, the king and queen would flee to Canada. The British fleet would retreat across the Atlantic to New World bases and carry on the struggle so that America and the British Commonwealth countries would have a last chance to fight for their freedom.

On July 1 Rear Adm. Walter S. Anderson, chief of U.S. Naval Intelligence, had testified before the Senate Naval Affairs Committee and presented such a conflicting picture of events in Europe that he left the senators completely confused. Anderson could only suggest that Knox, once confirmed, either go to England to find out what was really going on or send an observer in his place. This observer must be independent of Kennedy and other defeatist officials. Anderson was a good friend of Bill Donovan, but he did not mention him as the man to undertake this vital mission. Some senators immediately thought of Donovan as the man for the job; others suggested Bernard Baruch or Fiorello La Guardia, the feisty mayor of New York City.

Events in Europe had forced Donovan to realize how important the enactment of draft legislation had become, and in the late spring and early summer of 1940 he made several speeches in favor of the Burke-Wadsworth Selective Service Training bill. He still insisted that middle-aged men must register for the draft too. He testified before the Senate Committee on Military Affairs.

"Ask yourself what is the obligation that a government owes to the men it calls upon to fight its wars?" he said to the senators. "I think it owes him, first, a fair chance for his life, so that, prepared as he is to sacrifice his life, he shall not throw it away uselessly. To give him that fair chance, he must not only be physically conditioned, but he must be trained in the use of those new and complex weapons with which he must fight."

Even as Donovan testified, a messenger was hurrying to Capitol Hill from the White House. Some weeks before, John Lord O'Brian had urged that Franklin Roosevelt send Donovan to England to clear up the intelligence muddle. That very morning Frank Knox, now confirmed as navy secretary, suggested to the President that he send Donovan without delay. Roosevelt agreed, and when Donovan stepped outside the committee room, he was handed a note from the President summoning him to an urgent meeting at the White House.

At the White House Donovan joined the President, Secretary of State Hull, Secretary of the Navy Knox, and Secretary of War Stimson. The usually jovial President was grim-faced. He had summoned not only Donovan but the members of his cabinet with whom he shared the immediate responsibility for America's reaction to the collapse of France, the nation's oldest ally, and what promised to be the collapse of Great Britain, the nation's closest friend. He confessed that the government was in the dark as to exactly what was happening across the Atlantic. If Ambassador Kennedy was to be believed, there was no point in trying to aid Britain to resist the common enemy. But Kennedy was a notoriously unreliable observer, and perhaps Winston Churchill would succeed in infusing new spirit into the British. Would Britain fight on as Churchill was saying? Did Britain have the means to defend itself? What would be the best way to help? Exactly how did the Nazi fifth column operate in Europe, and how could the United States prevent a fifth column from operating within its own borders? These were the questions that Roosevelt and his top cabinet officers raised in the meeting.

It was Knox who asked Donovan if he would make the trip. When

Donovan agreed, it was decided that publicly he should claim to be making the trip on private business. This obviously would not appear to be the case to any half-knowledgeable observer; therefore insiders were to be told that an investigation of the Nazi fifth column was the reason for his journey. Secretly, however, he was to explore the entire situation in England. Kennedy was not to be told the true purpose of the mission, because he was considered untrustworthy. The nature of the trip was to be kept from J. Edgar Hoover as well, because with his great capacity for self-serving intrigue he might very easily disrupt things. Above all, a press leak could be serious because it might play into the hands of the isolationists, who already were raising a political storm over any possible American interest in aiding England. Donovan was instructed to call on other cabinet officers before he left to learn any questions that they would like to have answered concerning England.

Hull wired Kennedy on July 11 that Donovan would be making the trip, but that he would make his own arrangements. It would not be necessary for Kennedy to set up briefings and meetings for him. That evening Donovan and Knox dined at the Willard Hotel in downtown Washington. After dinner they sat late, the waiters keeping a respectful distance despite the hour, while they talked about Donovan's mission.

On July 12, Hull received Kennedy's reply: "I will render any service I can to Colonel Donovan whom I know and like. Our staff I think is getting all the information that possibly can be gathered and to send a new man in here at this time, with all due respect to Colonel Knox, is to me the height of nonsense and a definite blow to good organization."

Kennedy also telephoned Sumner Welles, under secretary of state, and told him he could not understand how Donovan could learn anything of value "except through our existing military and naval attachés." He added that the mission would "simply result in causing confusion and misunderstanding on the part of the British."

When Hull informed Roosevelt of Kennedy's cable and phone call, Roosevelt remarked to Knox, "Somebody's nose seems to be out of joint."

Unbeknown to Kennedy, Naval Intelligence Chief Anderson and Army Intelligence Chief Gen. Sherman Miles had already sent messages through secret channels to Capt. Alan G. Kirk, naval attaché, and Brig. Gen. Raymond E. Lee, military attaché, in London requesting that they help Donovan in his mission. They were instructed not only to brief Donovan but to set up meetings with top British intelligence officers. Roscoe H. Hillenkoetter, the naval attaché in Paris, was also directed to meet Donovan in London.

In the meantime, Donovan was calling upon concerned officials to obtain their list of queries to be answered. Edward Stettinius, Jr., who had taken over the post of adviser to the Council of National Defense, posed a tough group of questions:

1. What were found to be the main choke points in the British rearmament program?

2. To what extent was the shadow plant idea for obtaining reserve capacity found useful? What were the defects in this system that should be guarded against?

3. To what extent were machine tools found to be a choke point and what methods were utilized for overcoming it?

4. To what extent were mass-production operations in ammunition manufacture broken down into simple operations by semiskilled labor as compared to utilization of special high-production machine tools of a complicated character?

5. What methods were employed for overcoming the shortage in highly skilled workmen, leading men, designers, and other semitechnical classifications?

6. To what extent was the dilution of labor caused in munitions plants by the introduction of unskilled workers, male and female? What method was used in training this unskilled labor?

7. To what extent were educational or trial orders used as a preliminary to production orders?

8. Were the designs for armament frozen at the beginning of production or were frequent changes permitted in the hope of increasing output? To what extent had designs been previously proven to show their acceptability from a quantity production standpoint?

These were vital matters upon which America's own industrial mobilization might come to depend. Other government officials handed Donovan equally difficult questions: "What was the best defense against air attack? Could the war be won by air power and the blockade alone? Which types of ordnance were proving effective, and which types ineffective? How could intelligence operations be improved? What were the principal problems the British had encountered in mobilizing economically for war? The British were expanding their armed forces with the greatest possible speed, and the United States would probably have to undertake a similar expansion; in what ways could we profit by England's experience?"

Donovan's lifetime of mental conditioning, his legal training, and his experience as an intelligence observer uniquely qualified him for this demanding mission. As he went about Washington gathering the dozens of essentials for his mission, he knew that he was undertaking one of the most momentous assignments ever given to an American citizen. When he next returned to see Roosevelt, he was also informed that he must at the same time be a confidential presidential ambassador at the highest level, assuring Churchill and his government of the great concern felt by the President of the United States and his administration. Upon the outcome of Donovan's mission rested not only the fate of Great Britain but also that of his own country. Donovan left the White House in a very sober state of mind.

On Saturday, July 13, Navy Secretary Knox took his first trip in his official yacht, *Sequoia*. Bill Donovan and Jim Forrestal were his guests. They lunched on board and cruised down the Potomac until about six o'clock, talking over the situation in England and how Donovan might go about his task. Knox and Donovan returned to Donovan's Georgetown home, got into dinner clothes, and went to dine with Lord Lothian at 8:00 P.M. Lothian promised to arrange for Donovan to see Churchill.

Various government officials handed Donovan letters to people in Great Britain who could help him with his mission. A letter from Secretary Hull advised all American diplomatic and consular officers to extend "such courtesies and assistance as you may be able to render, consistent with your official duties." There were numerous letters to British business and government leaders, and Knox wrote to Lord Beaverbrook, Britain's minister of aircraft production:

> This letter will be presented to you by Colonel William J. Donovan, an intimate friend of mine at whose house, you will remember, we met some time ago. Colonel Donovan is abroad on an official mission for me, with the full approval of the President of the United States.
>
> I shall deeply appreciate anything you can do to promote the purpose of Colonel Donovan's mission, and I hope you will be as frank in talking to him as you might be in talking to me if I were able to go over myself.

On Sunday, July 14, a stocky, ruddy-faced man, athletic in bearing, boarded the Lisbon Clipper on the Baltimore waterfront. Alert reporters recognized William J. Donovan. "I'm on a personal business trip," he announced. "I am on my way to London via Bermuda and Lisbon."

Customs officials told reporters that Donovan was carrying a special passport that would allow him to fly on a British plane from Lisbon to beleaguered London. The Neutrality Act forbade American citizens from flying aboard the planes of the warring powers, but an exception had been made. When newsmen in Washington asked a State Department spokesman about Donovan's trip, he confirmed that Donovan was indeed on a mission for the government but that he knew nothing more about it. Earlier in the day Donovan had been handed a message that attachés Kirk and Lee were awaiting him in London and were prepared to cooperate with him without informing Ambassador Kennedy as to the true nature of his trip.

In Lisbon Donovan boarded a British plane for the hazardous flight to England. He flew northward along the coast of German-occupied Europe, while in London British officials were preparing to welcome him. In New York, British Security Coordinator William Stephenson helped too. He sent a secret radio message from his office in Rockefeller Center to Sir Stewart Menzies, head of the Secret Intelligence Service, to let Donovan have access to secret material. On July 15, Stephenson cabled to Churchill, "Colonel William Donovan personally representing President left yesterday by clipper. . . . United States Embassy not Repeat not being informed."

Another eyes-only cable from Stephenson, to King George VI, read, "Donovan by virtue of his very independence of thought and action inevitably has his critics but none will deny credit that is his due for reaching correct appraisal of international situation. The American government is debating two alternative courses of action. One would keep Britain in the war with supplies now desperately needed. Other is to give Britain up for lost. Donovan is President's most trusted personal adviser despite political differences, and I urge you to bare your breast to him."

Claridge's on Brook Street in London's Mayfair is the hotel where foreign royalty and chiefs of state usually find lodging when visiting the British capital, and it was there that Donovan was accustomed to stay. At the time of his arrival in London on July 17, a German air attack was in full fury. Donovan was exhilarated, for even as he checked into the hotel, its lobby seemingly unchanged since his last visit, he could hear the crunch of bombs falling not far away. He noted with approval that the hotel manager, who welcomed him as a frequent guest, seemed totally unperturbed.

Within a few hours of his arrival, Donovan went to Buckingham Palace to see the king. George VI welcomed him cordially and held out a paper to him; it was a deciphered message from Adolf Hitler to his field commanders. The king gave Donovan the message, but he did not disclose that the cipher had been broken by Britain's top-secret Ultra method, which Churchill was to call "my most secret source." (Without knowing the exact cryptanalytic method used, Donovan himself concluded over the next two weeks that since the British seemed to know the most intimate details of the German high command's plans, they had managed to break the most enigmatic of the German ciphers. He kept this knowledge to himself, because he realized the king had deliberately let him in on this secret.) The message was dated July 16.

"Since England, in spite of her hopeless military situation, shows no sign of being ready to come to an understanding," said Hitler, "I have decided to prepare a landing operation against England to eliminate England as a base for the prosecution of the war against Germany.

"First, the English Air Force must be so reduced morally and physically that it is unable to deliver any significant attack against the German crossing."

The king assured Donovan that the Germans would press the air attacks on Britain, and that Buckingham Palace was among the targets. As for the invasion itself, British Intelligence had concluded that it would be made on the east and south coasts. The Germans had the planes to drop up to 15,000 paratroopers on Norfolk, Suffolk, and Kent in one day.

"Donovan's plan of action was to see as many people as he could manage," said Conyers Read, an OSS aide in later years. "He brought together all the American military and naval observers in London at a series of informal breakfasts and luncheons and plied them with questions. He talked also with many other Americans, bankers, businessmen, newspaper correspondents, engineers, scholars. But his main business was with the British."

Captain Kirk and Brigadier General Lee proved particularly helpful. They briefed Donovan without informing Kennedy. Kirk told Donovan about the situation on the Continent and in Europe. In response to Donovan's questions about the ability of the Royal Air Force to stand off the Germans, Kirk replied that common sense said the Germans would win, but the young RAF flyers had such amazing morale they probably would be the victors. Lieutenant Colonel Carl Spaatz, an assistant military attaché at the embassy, who later was to command the air force, also informed Donovan that he was confident the Germans could not defeat the RAF. Donovan, knowing from the king that Hitler did not think he could successfully invade Britain until the RAF was destroyed, felt a first small hope that England might yet survive.

Lee, who had spent a frustrating six months as military attaché at an embassy headed by an ambassador entirely repugnant to him, reported in his journal of July 20, " 'Wild Bill' Donovan came in to make his presence known. I like him. My theory is that I welcome anyone who gets the intelligence and sends it home."

"Breakfasted with Donovan at Claridge's," Lee wrote on July 23. "He wanted to tell me what he is trying to do. He is really over here to gain firsthand knowledge of how the Conscription Law is working and of what sort of legislation is required successfully to operate a counterespionage organization. He expects to be heard by Congress on these two things. He feels that we will have conscription soon and as he phrases it, 'Our attitude toward it will be a test of our soul.' "

Donovan, true to his intelligence calling, told Lee only what he preferred him to know. Roscoe Hillenkoetter, naval attaché in Paris, came to London at Kirk's request with information for Donovan on long-range German aims for the French people and how the fifth column had been utilized to prepare the way for the Nazi panzers. American and British intelligence sources briefed him on the German exploitation of the fifth column in Poland, Denmark, Norway, Belgium, the Netherlands, Luxembourg, and France.

Admiral John H. Godfrey, the British director of naval intelligence, was given a more accurate idea of Donovan's purposes. "The object of Bill Donovan's mission was to discover if we were in earnest about the war," he wrote in his memoirs, "and if we were worth supporting, to enquire into our methods in adopting conscription, the difficulties we experienced, and how they were overcome, our anti–fifth columnist methods and to establish intimate collaboration with the British Navy both in the spheres of technical development and intelligence."

On another occasion, the admiral added: "I was one of the first people to meet him, and, without the help of the American Ambassador, he quickly established contacts with important people in this country. Donovan sensed the general air of defeatism at the Embassy and felt it to be more marked among the Naval than among the Army representatives. Undeceived by appearances he quickly became aware of the spiritual qualities of the British race—the imponderables that make for victory but had evaded Mr. Ambassador Kennedy, for whom he seemed to have very little use."

Soon after Donovan's arrival in London, Edgar Ansel Mowrer reached England. Considered one of the top foreign correspondents of the time, Mowrer had been based in Paris for the *Chicago Daily News,* and he had seen the Nazi blitzkrieg firsthand. He had retreated with the French Army to Bordeaux.

"My wife and I had been compelled to flee from Bordeaux by no less a person than Tony Biddle, our Ambassador, who told me he would not want to have me hiding under his bed," Mowrer later told Allen Dulles.

> One Dr. Joseph Paul Goebbels had said over the radio that he would give a division to lay hands on those two American SOBs, Mowrer and Knickerbocker. Hence I got out of Bordeaux and made my way with I don't know how many hundred thousands of other refugees to Lisbon.
>
> After a few days in Lisbon, quite unexpectedly I got a long message from Colonel Knox telling me that instead of returning to the United States, which had been my intention, I was to fly to London and put myself at the disposal of Colonel Donovan. This seemed rather cryptic, but I realized we were at war and not necessarily fully informed; so in due time, my wife and I fought our way on to a plane (and several other thousand tried to get on the same plane) and got to London, and I went to Colonel Donovan's hotel.

Mowrer found Donovan easy to get along with.

"Edgar," said Donovan, "Frank Knox told me that you would help me in any way you can."

"Sure, what do we do?"

"Well," said Donovan, "frankly, President Roosevelt is disturbed by the dispatches which he has received from London, and he wants to know whether or not the British are going to be able to hold out or are going to try to hold out against a German invasion.

"Now, as a news correspondent, you can ask any sort of impertinent questions which as a businessman. . . ." Donovan paused and then went on. "Furthermore, Knox tells me you have very close personal relations with the Minister of Information Alfred Duff Cooper, husband of Diana Manners."

"That is correct, we are fellow conspirators against Hitler," said Mowrer. He explained to Donovan that "all fellow conspirators against Hitler are locked in a freemasonry. We almost know each other by this kind of business."

"So," concluded Donovan, "now let's scatter out, and find out. You see the people you see, and I'll see the people I see, and we'll meet every three or four days and pool what we have."

Thanks to Bill Stephenson, Donovan had no difficulty in talking to Stewart Menzies, known simply as C in British intelligence circles. Menzies briefed Donovan on how the Secret Intelligence Service (SIS) worked with the British military. He kept in frequent touch with Donovan and made certain that other high officials in British Intelligence cooperated with him. Donovan was permitted to see the commandos in training, and he met with Colin Gubbins, who was readying guerrilla forces, not only to oppose the Germans in case they landed in Britain, but to carry the war back to the Continent. One day Donovan called on Gen. Frederick Beaumont-Nesbitt, the head of military intelligence. Beaumont-Nesbitt explained how the changes in German military equipment and tactics had forced a radical alteration in Britain's intelligence requirements. Economic warfare was more important than in any other war in history, but it had to be directed at specific targets, for example, the denial to the Axis of a certain type of carburetor employed in a tank's engine. Donovan went to see Sir Desmond Morton, director of the Industrial Intelligence Centre, who explored in more detail the relationship between the armies in the field and economic warfare.

Donovan was shown everything there was to see about British Secret Intelligence as well as Special Operations (SO), which, appropriately enough, had its headquarters on Baker Street in London, a street made famous by Sherlock Holmes. The Chief of the Special Operations Executive, Air Commodore Sir Frank Nelson, made certain that Donovan was welcomed at SO stations throughout Britain.

"Probably from the point of view of COI-OSS [U.S. central intelligence], the most important consequence of this visit to England was the development of close personal ties between Donovan and the most influential figures in British public life," said Conyers Read years after the war. "It marks the beginning of close cooperation with the British which was to characterize the whole history of COI-OSS. When Donovan later undertook to organize his secret intelligence . . . and his subversive operations . . . he turned frankly to British models."

Beneath the British treasury chambers in Whitehall, the British government had in 1936 converted a labyrinth of centuries-old tunnels and dungeons into an underground command post. Although the cabinet war room itself was beneath the treasury, passages extended to Downing Street, Trafalgar Square, Whitehall, the Home Office, even to Waterloo Station. Here Churchill held his late-night cabinet meetings dubbed "Midnight Follies," and here it was that Churchill remarked upon entering the room for the first time as prime minister, "If the invasion comes, that's where I'll sit. I'll sit there until the Germans are driven back or they carry me out—dead."

Donovan paid a visit to Churchill in his underground headquarters. He descended a spiral staircase into the war room where Churchill, wearing his boiler suit, talked to him candidly of Britain's future. The prime minister assured Donovan of his government's complete cooperation on his mission. Donovan and Churchill toted their own trays of food from the underground mess and dined together.

"In these dungeons under Whitehall, you step into a Shakespearean play," Donovan later told William Stephenson, "with stage directions like 'Army Heard in Distance, Sound of Trumpets!' . . .You know there isn't an army, but it's hard to be sure, down there in the theatre."

Donovan went about England visiting RAF bases and inspecting shore defenses hastily erected against the expected invasion. He learned how the British intended to turn their innocent-looking sandy beaches into a hell of flaming oil to engulf German landing craft. This was just as well, for they had little else with which to fight off an assault. Most of their equipment had been left behind at Dunkirk. "The defenders share a total of 786 field guns, 167 antitank guns, and 259 inadequate tanks, enough for two divisions against the forty German divisions waiting across the Channel," Donovan wrote to Bill Stephenson.

On the Norfolk coast Donovan fell in with 60-year-old Col. Eric Bailey, who in his younger years had been a British agent in Central Asia and minister plenipotentiary to the king of Nepal. Bailey led the guerrilla force that the British were training to defend every coastal village. The villagers had dug an observation trench overlooking the beach. As Donovan watched, Bailey wrote out a note and stuffed it into a tennis ball. He dropped the tennis ball into a pipe that ran to his command post, situated beneath the village church. Donovan was delighted, and Bailey became his fast friend. Later, as a King's Messenger, Bailey several times carried top-secret dispatches across the Atlantic in Donovan's plane.

"He sighed for the simpler days," Donovan observed. "Rolling tennis balls down drainpipes, waiting to stick a German with a pitchfork, struck him as healthier than being stuffed into the gun turret of a bomber to be ferried back and forth."

Donovan observed the formidable Spitfires in combat and concluded that since British planes and pilots were both superior to the German attackers, it was most unlikely that the Luftwaffe, despite its overwhelming strength, could sweep the RAF from the skies. The large number and wide dispersal of British airfields also made it hard for the Germans to wipe out the RAF on the ground. On a previous visit to Britain, Donovan had heard of work on a secret death ray. Now he discovered that the so-called death ray was actually radar. Donovan met Sir Robert Watson-Watt, radar's inventor, and he toured coastal radar stations that tracked approaching German air flotillas. Knowing when and where the enemy would strike made it possible to save both British aircraft and gasoline. One by one, Donovan learned the answers to the lists of questions given to him by key government officials in Washington.

On one day Donovan talked to author George Orwell about how British social institutions were standing up under the strain of war. On another he went down to the Thames bank to watch schoolboys experimenting with a new type of floating mine, designed by the distinguished professor J. B. S. Haldane to blow up German landing craft. The explosives, said Haldane, were "detonated when the action of the water dissolves the retaining pin—a cough drop."

Donovan visited defense plants and military training centers, and he learned what it was like inside a shelter during an air raid. Once as he checked into a provincial hotel, German planes came roaring over the city. The raid caught Donovan in a hotel corridor marching along behind the 11-year-old bellboy, who was pulled lopsided by his bag. The boy struggled ahead despite the bombardment. A terrific blast nearby shook plaster and dust down into the hall. The boy glanced at Donovan and stood erect despite the weight of the bag. "Those Huns can't even drop a bomb straight," he said, and there was such cool assurance in his tone that Donovan for the moment forgot the acres of smashed buildings that he had seen in English cities.

"Here, let me carry that bag, son," he said to the boy.

"No, sir!" the lad replied. "I started carrying this bag, and I'll finish carrying it. I'll get stronger as I go, and I'll never quit."

When the raid was over, Donovan sat in his hotel room and thought about his trip. He couldn't get a British youngster to accept help in carrying a heavy bag, but he knew that America would not be turned down if it offered help to the badly hurt British people. What kind of help was needed most? To Donovan it now appeared that the gravest danger came not from air attacks or the threatened invasion but from the mounting submarine warfare that was choking off vital supplies. If America could transfer its overage destroyers to the British Navy, this would probably be the most valuable aid the New World could give to the Old.

Bill Donovan detested Joe Kennedy for his mean spirit and crabbed nature. The more he learned in Britain, the more his contempt for the ambassador's lack of objectivity and integrity mounted. As for Kennedy, he was angry that his first direct word of Donovan's presence in London came from Edgar Ansel Mowrer. When Kennedy understood that Mowrer was working for Donovan, he snarled, "We don't need a newspaperman to make this investigation for the government, and it is most embarrassing to me. I think he should be recalled off the complete assignment."

Kennedy proved ineffective in opposing Donovan. He soon found that although he may have been close to Chamberlain and the Cliveden set of British appeasers, Churchill had no time for him at all. Finally early in August Donovan called on Kennedy. "American policy is to help in every way we can," he bluntly informed the ambassador, "and it doesn't help these people any to keep telling them that they haven't got a chance." Kennedy kept his temper because he understood now that Franklin Roosevelt stood behind Donovan, and he feared that one of Donovan's recommendations upon returning to Washington would be that he be fired.

As Donovan went about his investigations, Mowrer was making his own. At first he stayed at the Hyde Park Hotel on Knightsbridge Road, but then he moved in, as he said, "believe it or not, with Nancy Astor who was trying to compensate for the Cliveden set by cooperating with a notorious antagonist of the Führer."

"I scattered out and saw what I could," he said later. "I had lunch with Winston Churchill, and I went out and inspected tanks. My wife's family is English so through her we saw a great many English people."

From time to time, Mowrer told Allen Dulles, he and Donovan met at Claridge's to exchange information and ideas.

> We both acted independently, covered as much ground as we could, and pooled our information and conclusions. I was delighted to see that we had reached the same understanding.
>
> At the end of the thing, why Donovan and I found the contrary of the reports that had been coming from the American Embassy in London. I understand we were agreed that the English under Churchill were going to fight and if they were beaten by any chance they would then try to carry on the fight from Canada or such places having sent the fleet ahead of them. This Churchill told me specifically, and one had to believe Churchill when he said something!

"Worked till six-thirty on a list of things which Donovan promises to take up with Roosevelt and Knox and Stimson," Military Attaché Raymond Lee wrote in his journal on August 2.

> His time here is getting short as the British are starting a plane to New York via Foynes and Newfoundland tomorrow and offered him a seat. We have never really checked together, as I told him I would rather he made his own conclusions while here and then we could compare notes. So all of us went to Claridge's and had breakfast with him this morning, and talked from 8:15 till 10:30. A lot of ground was covered in free and frank discussion; everyone had a chance to advance his conclusions and recommendations and to ask questions. At the end Donovan said that he had learned so much and was so anxious not to forget many of the matters we had discussed, that he would greatly like to take a list of them along, together with references to the cables and dispatches in which these topics had been very fully treated. His object is to have these reports of ours brought out for consideration by the decision-makers in Washington. What greatly pleased me was that our feeling in the office is pretty uniform about things and what Donovan has found by talking to an extraordinary list of well-posted people, from King and Churchill down, agrees with our conclusions and is not at all defeatist. He gives odds of 60–40 that the British will beat off the German attack.

Donovan spent his last evening in England at Braddocks, the home of Rear Adm. John Godfrey, at Seven Oaks in Kent, within easy driving distance of London. The two intelligence masters sat up until 2:00 A.M. talking as much about America's need for a modern intelligence service as they did about Britain's desperate plight.

"He then told me what he intended to report to the President," said Godfrey after the war.

> One of his first tasks would be to urge the appointment of a "sensible Ambassador," and of someone who could travel backwards and forwards ("a sensible Colonel House") and keep the feelings of each country fresh in the minds of the other country's rulers. The need was for someone who could readily detect all the various ways by which the two countries could concede to each other and co-operate, whilst insisting and explaining to each other the prickly matters, where national sovereignty and too peremptory demand for concessions should be avoided. His answers to the questions "were we in earnest about the war and were we worth supporting" were, "definitely, yes," and in this respect one must regard his influence as decisive, as Kennedy and others had been feeding the President very different information. Donovan also took back with him definite proposals regarding the following matters, concerning all of which he considered that the USA should help us in every way: a. bomb sights, b. flying boats, c. fifty destroyers, d. squadrons of Flying Fortresses with if possible pilots and certainly mechanics and technical maintenance staff, e. twenty-five [pounder] and 105 mm guns, f. motor boats—released

from US Naval service, g. all surplus material including Lee Enfield rifles, h. use of American airfields for training Canadian, Australian, and British pilots.

In addition, he urged full intelligence collaboration and the placing at our disposal of reports by US Consular officers, especially in French ports, direct liaison between myself and the United States DNI [Director of Naval Intelligence], and the establishment of safe and direct methods of communication. In the sphere of technique and material, Donovan said he would be able to smooth out difficulties, as he had among his clients and his clients' relatives, such a large number of industrialists of all sorts, many of whom were carrying out contracts for the British Government.

It was obvious that we had a good friend in Donovan and one who had the ear of the President and knew how to work with the British.

In the morning Godfrey reported to Vice Adm. Tom Phillips on his evening with Donovan, who forwarded his account to First Sea Lord Sir Dudley Pound, who handed it to Churchill with the notation, "This is very satisfactory."

That afternoon Donovan went to Poole, on the English Channel near Southampton, to board the flying boat *Clare* for the long flight to America. The flight was to be the first British transatlantic passenger service in aviation history. In order to make the long hop, the plane was fitted with extra fuel tanks. The only other passengers, British aircraft manufacturer Charles R. Fairey and Geoffrey Cunliffe of the British Air Ministry, were already aboard the four-engined Caledonian flying boat, which had been painted with green and blue patches to camouflage it from German Messerschmidts. Just before he went aboard, Donovan was handed a note from Brendan Bracken, minister of information.

> There may be no luxurious Claridge's to house you during your next visit to London. When you return you will see a poorer England, but you will either look upon the battered relics of a race which never surrendered, or a people which, against great odds and having paid a heavy penalty for neglecting their defense, triumphed over the most bestial tyranny the world has ever known.
>
> These issues will be settled before I have the happiness of meeting you again. Perhaps we shall never meet. But in parting from you I ask leave to thank you for all you are trying to do for this little island of ours.

Captain J. C. Kelly-Rogers taxied out into the Channel to commence his takeoff. Once the *Clare* was airborne, a squadron of Spitfires zoomed up to escort it as far as Ireland, where it landed on the Shannon River at Foynes. Aboard the plane Donovan talked to the other passengers and, among other books, reread a life of Admiral Nelson, making mental notes about his strategy in the Mediterranean, which in the light of the Italian declaration of war seemed pertinent indeed.

Over the Atlantic the pilot turned the radio off, and the plane observed radio security until the following morning when it was approaching Newfoundland. At 10:00 A.M. on August 4 the *Clare* landed at Botwood and then flew another six hours to Boucherville Island near Montreal, where it set down on the St. Lawrence. The other passengers left the plane at Montreal, and Donovan was the only passenger when the flying boat circled La Guardia Field twice in the dying sunlight before gliding in for a landing on the seaplane basin. When he stepped out of the plane onto the pier, Donovan was met by a handful of reporters from the New York newspapers and two FBI agents.

"They're friends of mine," Donovan assured the reporters, who asked him if he were in trouble with the FBI for traveling on the plane of a belligerent power in violation of the Neutrality Act. "I have a special passport."

The reporters wanted to know what he had been doing in England. Donovan said that he had talked with Hugh Gibson, London representative of the Paderewski Fund for Polish Relief, of which he was the chairman. Had he discussed with London officials the idea of delivering overage U.S. destroyers to Great Britain? He denied this, but he admitted that he had been on a mission for Colonel Knox.

"Was the mission a success?"

"Colonel Knox will have to decide if my mission was successful."

Donovan left immediately for Washington.

19

Back Door to the White House

COLONEL KNOX had a chance to decide on the success of Donovan's mission the very next morning, when Donovan made an oral report. Edgar Ansel Mowrer had flown back from London a few days earlier than Donovan, and that evening both Mowrer and Donovan were Knox's dinner guests. Assistant Secretary of War Robert Patterson, Gen. Sherman Miles, James Forrestal, admirals Harold R. Stark and Walter Anderson, and John O'Keefe, Knox's secretary, were also guests. Donovan and Mowrer had a chance to talk at length about the situation in Great Britain.

Washington buzzed about Donovan's mission. At his press conference in Hyde Park, New York, on Tuesday morning, August 6, a correspondent asked President Roosevelt, "Could you tell us, Mr. President, what the mission was that Wild Bill Donovan went on to London?"

"You will have to ask the Secretary of the Navy and Wild Bill," replied Roosevelt.

"We asked Wild Bill," said the correspondent.

Roosevelt flashed a jaunty smile as his only reply.

Donovan spent the day briefing cabinet officers and key senators and congressmen. That evening he dined with Secretary of War Stimson. "In the evening we had Bill Donovan and Patterson and his wife at dinner at Woodley and Donovan told us at length of his recent trip to England to find out the real situation there," Stimson entered in his diary.

> This was taken on the instance and at the expense of Frank Knox. It was a very interesting story, for Donovan had come into contact with all the chiefs of the British Army; had been taken all over their country and had gone up and down the Islands, so that he knew everything that an outsider could learn. He described the morale as very high now and his final summary was that if an attack was made now, the British would probably win. On the other hand, the greatest danger in the future, as he sees it, will be the letdown which will come if no attack is made and the long boring days of winter set in. In such case he fears that while the British will increase their munitions, they will lose their personal morale, and that an attack in the Spring might have more chance of success. He laid special emphasis on the home defense units which had been

created out of older men, and men who had had experience in the last war. He also laid stress on the tremendous part that women were taking in the Army, as well as in the general defense plan. All driving of motor cars and apparently of motor trucks is being done by women. He emphasized Britain's need of destroyers and he spoke especially of her need for 250,000 more Enfield rifles for the home defense force that I have just mentioned.

Roosevelt held another press conference at Hyde Park on Thursday. He was preparing to take a train up to Portsmouth, New Hampshire, where he was to inspect coastal defenses before boarding the presidential yacht *Potomac* to visit naval installations at Boston, Newport, and New London with a stop-off at Nahant Cove in Massachusetts to see his youngest grandchild. Knox was to be a guest on the cruise.

"Has Secretary Knox arrived yet?" asked a reporter.

"No, he is coming up this afternoon," said Roosevelt, "and we will have a full shipload. Oh, I will tell you who is coming up with him and going to be on the train and going down on the *Potomac:* Bill Donovan, so he can tell me what he found on the other side when he went over. . . . He will get off the boat tomorrow afternoon. There is no bunk for him."

"Can you give us any indication of the nature of Donovan's mission abroad?"

"I cannot, and he won't tell you." Roosevelt changed the subject and ended the conference.

Knox and Donovan joined Secretary of Commerce Harry L. Hopkins and the President at Hyde Park about 6:00 P.M. on Friday, August 9. They found Roosevelt delighting in the company of a brand new acquisition, a scottie dog named Fala. They drove with the President to the Hyde Park railroad station, where they boarded the presidential car. Donovan reported to the President about his trip to England as the train rumbled up through New England. When Roosevelt went to bed, the others took up the problem of Joseph Kennedy and also discussed whether the United States should supply weapons and equipment to the British. Donovan advocated the appointment of an ambassador "who would go back and forth across the Atlantic and keep the two countries in touch; someone who could detect ways of making concessions without condescension, while insisting on explaining prickly matters of sovereignty and protocol." After Knox went off to his stateroom, Donovan and Hopkins talked until dawn. Donovan warned Hopkins that the Germans might strike toward Suez through French North Africa.

As Donovan wrote to Britain's Menzies, he emphasized to the President that the English "were strong, determined and would hold out."

He told Roosevelt that if Britain were invaded it would fight, but that it could not fight without American help. He urged that the immediate transfer of overage destroyers to Britain must be made to keep open the lines of communication across the Atlantic. He also proposed that the Sperry bombsight be given to the British and that the production of flying boats and Flying Fortresses be increased. America, Donovan told the President, should establish training schools for Australian, Canadian, and British pilots. Donovan reported to Admiral Godfrey and Sir Cyril Newall, British chief air marshal, that the President was very receptive on all scores.

"Not only did Mr. Roosevelt accept Donovan's appreciation of our war effort," Godfrey later wrote, "but he approved in principle the supply of material on a large scale, which developed into 'Lease Lend' and later full alliance."

Donovan made it clear to the President that the "United States should start preparing immediately for a global war." In the words of Allen Dulles, "He particularly stressed the need of a service to wage unorthodox warfare and to gather information through every means available. He was convinced that America's military planning and its whole national strategy would depend on intelligence as never before and that the American intelligence setup should be completely revamped."

In the months to come Donovan discussed this idea at length with Knox, Stimson, and Attorney General Robert H. Jackson.

Shortly after noon, Donovan boarded the *Potomac* with the other members of the presidential party and continued his briefing of the President. Then he went ashore to return to Washington, where other leading members of the administration awaited him. On Saturday President Roosevelt and Secretary Knox gave another press conference.

"Have you and Mr. Knox anything to say about Donovan's mission to Europe?" a reporter asked the President.

"May I answer that question?" inquired Knox.

"Yes," said the President.

"He went over as my eyes and ears to see what he could find," said Knox.

"Anything to say, sir?" the reporter asked Roosevelt.

"Well, you see it is his mouth," said Roosevelt.

"Your eyes and ears and Colonel Donovan's mouth?" asked the baffled reporter.

Donovan spent Sunday with Gen. Robert E. Wood, the leader of the America First isolationists, to assure him of England's will and ability to repel a Nazi attack. Wood was Franklin Roosevelt's bitter political antagonist, but Donovan reasoned that as a prominent American he was entitled to know the truth about the situation across the Atlantic.

On Monday Donovan briefed some influential senators and congressmen on his trip to England. Henry Stimson wrote in his diary:

> In the evening I attended a dinner given by Senator Burke—the sponsor of the Selective Service Bill in the Senate—with a number of Senators and Congressmen to listen to Bill Donovan on the results of his recent trip to Europe and containing his views on the necessity of the bill. It lasted until nearly midnight and the Senators were very interested and keen in their questions. I spoke. Patterson spoke. And Donovan spoke. Among others, Senator Barkley, Senator Connolly of Texas, Senator Minton of Indiana, Senator Hill, Senator Schwartz, Senator Thomas of Utah, Senator Gurney, Senator Austin, Jim Wadsworth, and Assistant Secretary Patterson, and several others were present. It was encouraging to me to see their interest and they all seemed to think the bill would finally pass in some fairly good form.

The mood in Washington when Donovan returned from abroad had been one of black pessimism. Donovan had a sanguine effect on the capital. "Colonel Donovan almost single-handed overcame the unmitigated defeatism which was paralyzing Washington," said Walter Lippmann.

"I think that so far as the restoration of morale here was concerned the trip was worthwhile," Donovan wrote to Kirk in London. "I found that in general the morale was pretty low and there was a feeling of helplessness insofar as England was concerned."

"The back door of the White House was opened to him," said journalist Frederic Sondern, Jr., "and he took full advantage of it."

Donovan urged upon Roosevelt his plans for irregular warfare—propaganda, sabotage, underground resistance. "Above all," he told Roosevelt, "it would be necessary to know everything about the war potentialities of every country which might become involved in the conflict. That would take a centralized, powerful intelligence agency capable of making a complete picture of any situation anywhere in the world when the President needed it."

Roosevelt agreed with Donovan, but he felt that the political situation within the United States would not yet permit the establishment of such an organization. He explained to Donovan that he had a campaign to fight in the fall.

The President also agreed with Donovan that the transfer of 50 overage destroyers to the United Kingdom had great meaning beyond their military value. It would assure the British that America understood their danger and would not allow the German conquest of Britain without taking action. It would also warn the Germans that America had taken alarm and would oppose their march toward world conquest.

"The last week has been engaged with trying to get U.S.A. up to the point of sending us the destroyers," wrote Lord Lothian in his journal on August 16. "I think the trick has been done. At least the President told me on the telephone this morning that he thought it was. Donovan has helped a lot and Knox."

Eleven days later Roosevelt was far less certain. He told Donovan that he expected to lose the election on the destroyer issue but felt it had to be faced. Donovan argued that from a legal viewpoint Roosevelt need not obtain congressional approval to trade the 50 elderly destroyers to Britain in exchange for 99-year leases on British bases in Bermuda, the Caribbean, and Newfoundland. Roosevelt maintained that what might be legally possible was not politically possible.

"Congress is going to raise hell about this," Roosevelt told his secretary Grace Tully, "but even another day's delay may mean the end of civilization."

Roosevelt drafted his historic message to Congress in late August. To his relief Wendell Willkie, the Republican candidate for president, agreed not to make the transfer of the destroyers a campaign issue. Donovan's friend George Bowden, later to be an OSS man, drew up the bill that made the transfer of destroyers possible. Now it was up to Congress.

One pretext for Donovan's trip to England had been an assignment to investigate the German fifth column. When he finished briefing administration leaders, senators, and congressmen about the situation in England, Roosevelt and Knox urged him to collaborate with Edgar Ansel Mowrer on a series of newspaper articles alerting America to the danger of the fifth column.

"I lived at that time on 30th Street in Georgetown," Mowrer said after the war. "Donovan lived on R Street just off 30th. I saw him fairly often during the following year. He is one of these 'come to breakfast' boys. And I not being an early riser preferred having my appointments somewhat later in the day. I was so startled."

Startled or not, Mowrer found himself at working breakfasts with Donovan. Donovan supplied much of the information for the articles. Some of his information had come from German officers whom Donovan had known from World War I and the early trips he had made to Europe in the aftermath of the war. Mowrer did all the writing. Donovan agreed to share the by-line only when Roosevelt insisted upon it. Frank Knox wrote an introduction to the articles: "They are designed to make Americans fully conscious of methods used by the totalitarian powers, so that, if or when such methods are used here, they will instantly be recognized for what they are and their effect nullified. I regard defense against possible enemy propaganda as second only to defense against enemy armaments."

The three major American news agencies distributed the articles, and they were printed in pamphlet form by the American Council on Public Affairs under the title "Fifth Column Lessons for America."

"The masterpiece of the Fifth Column was unquestionably the French debacle," asserted Donovan and Mowrer.

> Here everything that Hitler promised came to pass with almost mathematical precision. He did not strike until he was in touch with certain important Frenchmen who were ready to treat with him.
>
> What happened to the French officers? Simply this: for the most part they had ceased to believe in freedom, democracy, or any of the slogans which alone could galvanize the entire country.
>
> While not exactly pro-Fascist (and certainly not pro-German), they were hostile to the Third Republic; many had come to believe that an authoritative regime like that of Italy or Germany was really preferable. It would, they thought, save the position of the privileged classes and really save France from the disagreeable necessity of defending itself. If there was to be a war, then let it be against the Bolsheviks. In other words, at least half and perhaps a majority of influential French citizens had come to believe what Hitler wanted them to believe.
>
> For years his agents in France, Friedrich Sieburg, the author, Otto Abetz, pro-French consuls like Nolde and many others, had "worked" the French leaders. When necessary, they were assisted by beautiful women: the Baroness von Einem, the Princess von Hohenlohe and others of lesser brilliance. They "got in" with certain of these leading Frenchwomen, who at the moment of defeat, exercised such a devastating influence on certain French statesmen. They went everywhere, saw everybody, came to know everything, dipped into French politics through scandalously venal French newspapers. To the weak and cynical they preached defeatism; to the unsuccessful, hatred of the Jews; to all, the possibility of living on good terms with Germany if only France would break relations with the Bolsheviks and "money-minded" Britons. During the appeasement period the Germans were actually aided by certain members of the British Embassy in Paris. Not until two months before the outbreak of war did anyone dare to take action against the numerous German agents—and then the vacillating Daladier talked big and did little.

The Nazis had already fostered a fifth column within the United States. Many pro-Nazi Americans took angry exception to the series of articles, and when they broke cover to challenge Donovan and Mowrer, the FBI and military intelligence were able to identify them for arrest if war broke out with Germany.

During the next several months detailed reports came by special couriers from England as British officials answered the lengthy questionnaires that Donovan had left behind. Donovan received these at his New York law office and distributed them to the appropriate officials in Washington. A full year before President Roosevelt appointed him coordinator of information, he was gathering information from overseas sources for the President and his cabinet.

The Century Group was a coterie of leading citizens who believed that the United States must prepare itself for an almost inevitable war with Germany. Donovan was a member, and upon his return from England, the group arranged for him to make a national radio address on behalf of selective service. It was decided that he should speak from Chicago, in the heart of the isolationist Midwest. On Friday, August 16, Donovan went to the midwestern city, checked into the Blackstone Hotel on Michigan Avenue, and went over his notes. He spoke Saturday evening at 8:15 over the Mutual Broadcasting System. The address was actually made from the home of Albert Lasker in the North Shore suburb of Lake Forest, over a telephone line to radio station WGN. At the last minute WGN, which was fully owned by archisolationist Col. Robert R. McCormick, itself refused to broadcast the talk, but the rest of the nation heard it.

Donovan admitted that if Hitler won in England, he still might not attack the United States. "But let us weigh against this the price of unpreparedness in the face of a threat which turns out to have been a real threat," he said. "We have seen other nations pay that cost—the nations of Europe that have fallen." He argued that unpreparedness would be a gamble with the freedom of future generations, a gamble the current generation had no right to make.

He concluded that in World War I, he had seen untrained boys sent into battle and suffering excessive casualties.

> Those of you who were in France can confirm out of your own knowledge and experience. I remember at the battle of Château-Thierry in July 1917, we had suffered heavy losses. These losses were made up while we were on the march to the battle of St. Mihiel. We were given untrained or half-trained replacements. Some of these men had never worn a gas mask; some had never opened the bolts of their rifles; they had never been in a detachment larger than a corporal squad.
>
> And yet, within eight days, they were to be thrown into the first major offensive of the American Army. These men had to be trained while we were advancing to the front by night marches that lasted from darkness to dawn. The only opportunity of training these tired men was to take them from the period of noon until nightfall and to give them in a few hours what should have been given them in months of training. That is what comes of starting training men after war begins and not before. The casualties resulting from that kind of unnecessary wastage of human life eat ultimately into the social life of a nation.

Donovan demanded "a fair chance for his life" for an American soldier and argued that "natural leadership and primitive military skills" were not enough in modern warfare, where tightly coordinated movements of mechanized units and sophisticated weapons were used. The volunteer system must give way to universal selective service.

"While it is absolutely true that if you want to fight, you've got to be strong," he told his fellow countrymen, "it is equally true in this world of today that if you want peace, you've got to be stronger still—and it is because I am for peace that I am for conscription."

The next morning Donovan left for California, where he was trying a law case. Upon his return to Washington he appeared before both houses of Congress to discuss the Burke-Wadsworth Selective Service Training bill in the light of his findings in England. His remarks were based upon his experience in World War I and his observations in embattled Britain, and they swung undecided legislators behind the bill, which was passed a few weeks later.

Donovan was convinced that the United States could not escape war with Germany. He did not think he could urge that young men be drafted into the armed forces without volunteering for active service himself, and he talked to Stimson about a command in the army. "I intend to go with the troops and as it looks now I shall probably spend the winter in Alabama training a division," he wrote to Lord Vansittart.

Despite his involvement in the vital national decisions of the summer of 1940, Donovan managed to continue his law practice. He was in Wyoming trying a case when he received a phone call from Frank Knox. "I am just on my way to maneuvers of the fleet; do you want to come with me, because I would like you to tell the admirals something about yourself."

Donovan finished his legal argument and went to Treasure Island Naval Base in San Francisco Bay. There he met Secretary Knox, his naval aide Capt. Mort Dale, his secretary John O'Keefe, and Adm. Charles Cooke, commandant of naval air in the Atlantic. In the morning the group was to fly to Pearl Harbor in a new navy PBY. It was the first PBY flight over such a distance, and extra tanks of fuel were placed on board. Destroyers and cruisers were stationed every 250 miles along the route to effect a rescue if the plane went down. The navy was taking no chances with the VIPs from Washington.

"When we went to bed in the admiral's quarters," said O'Keefe in recalling the occasion, "we were told that the weather in the morning promised to be too foggy to fly. We'd have a knock on the door at 4:00 A.M. if we were going to take off."

The knock came at 4:00 A.M., and the PBY, heavy with extra gasoline, lumbered into the air. It barely managed to lift over the Golden Gate bridge.

"It was freezing cold in the plane," noted O'Keefe. "Then when a crew member attempted to fix the heating system, a fire broke out. He grabbed a fire extinguisher and put out the flames."

The PBY reached Pearl Harbor without any more trouble.

"I went out with the fleet for three weeks," Donovan said later, "and I never knew there were so many admirals in our country. I had a little of the advantage of it because on coming back from England, I had just reread the life of Nelson, so I proceeded questioning some of those gentlemen on the Mediterranean, and after that I felt more strongly that that was the place that would have to be watched, because Gibraltar, Malta, Cairo, were hooks upon which history was going to be hung."

Donovan and Knox cruised first aboard a heavy cruiser, then a light cruiser, a destroyer, a battleship, and finally the aircraft carrier *Enterprise,* in order to get an impression of the combat readiness of the Pacific fleet. When it came time to leave the *Enterprise,* the members of the official party took off their suit coats in order to slip on Mae West life jackets and parachutes. They climbed into two-seater open-cockpit pursuit planes behind the pilots and stowed their coats behind their seats. Donovan's plane was next to last to take off. O'Keefe, who was in the last, watched Donovan's plane go roaring down the deck and lift up into the air. "Donovan's coat blew out of the cockpit, landed on the end of the deck, and flipped off into the sea," related O'Keefe. "The sailors tried to fish for it, but it sank out of sight. Donovan lost his wallet containing $400 and a watch that he always carried. The crew chipped in to buy him another watch, which was inscribed to him from the men of the *Enterprise.*"

The planes flew to Pearl Harbor, where they landed. "If we can do this," said Donovan, "the Japs can do it too."

Upon his return to Washington, Donovan gave a lecture at the War Department. He stressed the importance of the Mediterranean in the strategy of the war in Europe and said that in talking to the admirals of the Pacific fleet, "I found out that none of us really knew much about what was east of the Strait of Gibraltar or what the situation was there."

Donovan had scarcely returned to Washington when Chief of Staff Gen. George C. Marshall asked him to make a tour of the nation's mobilization centers. With the enactment of the Selective Service Act, the country was gathering its manpower. By March 5, 1941, more than a million soldiers were expected to be under arms, including 375,000 Regular Army, 245,000 National Guardsmen, and 600,000 draftees under the Selective Service Act. Marshall wanted Donovan to observe the preparations being made to train the draftees. The two men conferred on October 1.

"What can we do for these men in the way of arms and equipment?" asked Donovan. "Have we the means with which to train them? Have we the basic weapons, the use of which they must learn? In other words, is it worthwhile to bring these men into service now? Can we give them the instruction they need?"

Colonel J. L. Collins of Marshall's staff and Donovan flew to Barksdale Field, Louisiana, so that Donovan could meet with the officers conducting the Louisiana maneuvers that were to test the readiness of the Regular Army. Donovan found Lt. Col. Dwight Eisenhower performing as chief umpire of the war games. The contending sides were attempting to find their way through Louisiana swamps and forests with the aid of Standard Oil road maps, and there was confusion everywhere.

When the war games ended, the top officers met in a large tent for dinner and a critique from Colonel Donovan. Donovan, who had seen the finely honed German and Italian war machines in Ethiopia and Spain and on maneuvers in Bavaria, found some things to admire in the U.S. Army's performance but much more to lament. Such officers as Eisenhower and Mark Clark who were present took his remarks to heart. There was no doubt at all that the outspoken hero of the World War and perennial observer of foreign military operations knew what he was talking about, but the top brass, perhaps for this reason alone, resented what he had to say.

Donovan and Collins flew to Randolph Field, San Antonio, on October 5, where they watched demonstrations put on by Latin American officers in school at nearby Fort Sam Houston. They observed the U.S. Army preparations for training the draftees not only at Fort Sam Houston but at Fort Sill in Oklahoma, Fort Knox in Kentucky, and Fort Benning in Georgia. Upon his return, Donovan informed General Marshall of what he had learned.

"On the score of sound doctrine and the imparting of that doctrine I am much encouraged," Donovan wrote to Edward Stettinius when he returned to New York on October 10. At the same time he noted, "We are not equipped to go to war. There are many shortages. We still need large quantities of new types of antiaircraft guns, artillery, aeroplanes, tanks, as well as ammunition. And it will take us some time to get them. We do have the basic arms and the basic equipment to train the 1,200,000 men we are to have in service."

"As to a possible war," he wrote to Gen. Robert E. Wood,

> I think all of us ought to resist getting into any war (even though we know someday we must get in) until we are ready. As a result of my trip with the Navy and now my inspection of Forts Benning, Sam Houston, Sill, and Knox, I do not see how we can possibly be ready before a year and, perhaps more accurately, a year and a half. I am in favor of holding off the danger of war by whatever means is possible until we can be ready. If it is necessary to supply England even to a greater extent to do that, I am for doing it. We have just been caught in a spot where we are not wholly master of our destiny and we have got to fight for time until we can regain that mastery.

November 1940 was a hectic time for Donovan, as reported in the newspapers. "Recently, Colonel Donovan has been in and out of Washington much of the time," wrote James L. Wright to Alfred Kirchhofer.

He has been in conference with Secretary of War Henry L. Stimson. He has had luncheon with General George Marshall, chief of staff.

On Wednesday, he arrived by plane from Indianapolis at 5:30 in the morning to have breakfast at that early hour with Secretary of the Navy Frank Knox, Admiral Ernest J. King of the General Board of the Navy, and with Rawleigh Warner of Chicago.

When he wasn't working on America's military preparedness, he was making speeches explaining the plight of Great Britain and the part he feels the United States should play in this world crisis.

"During this period, Donovan badgered anybody who would listen to his views on the situation in Europe," remembered Jim Murphy. "Hull, Welles, Stimson, Knox, all listened to Bill Donovan, whether they wanted to or not."

Donovan at least had one thing to be happy about. On October 16, Joseph Kennedy cabled Franklin Roosevelt and asked to be relieved of his post. He cited his trying experiences in London during German air attack. The same day he telephoned Under Secretary of State Sumner Welles and said that regardless of what he heard from the President, he was coming home. For three months he had been ignored by Roosevelt, who had sent Donovan to London without telling him in advance and who was not giving him any information whatsoever on the destroyers-for-bases deal. Roosevelt accepted his resignation, but upon Kennedy's return home asked him to keep his own counsel until after the election. Kennedy was furious with Roosevelt, but out of party loyalty and out of fear for what the President, who could be ruthless in politics, might do, he acquiesced.

"You will either go down as the greatest president in history or the greatest horse's ass," he told Roosevelt in Washington after the President's November defeat of Wendell Willkie.

"There is a third alternative," Roosevelt replied. "I may go down as the president of an unimportant country at the end of my term."

Kennedy joined the vociferous opposition to the Lend-Lease arrangements with Britain. On December 1, President Roosevelt called Bill Donovan to the White House again. For the man he called "my secret legs," he had in mind a mission that promised to be even more significant than the last.

20

Fifty-Trip Ticket on the Clippers

WHEN DONOVAN ARRIVED at the White House, Roosevelt proposed that he undertake an urgent mission of the utmost secrecy and importance. The President told him he was to go abroad and "collect information on conditions and prospects" and, "more importantly, to impress on everyone the resolution of the American government and people to see the British through and provide all possible assistance to countries which undertook to resist Nazi aggression." Donovan was to undertake a critical diplomatic task under cover of what was an equally vital intelligence mission.

"His directive was a broad one," said Conyers Read, "so broad that it did not indicate with any precision where he was to go. Evidently he was expected not only to investigate but also to recommend a course of action for America. The President suggested that he should find occasion en route to confer with General Weygand and explore with him the possibilities of some form of Franco-American action in North Africa."

Donovan looked forward to seeing his old comrade-in-arms Gen. Maxime Weygand. As early as August he had been arguing that it was important for the United States to arrive at an agreement with the French to protect American interests in North Africa. He expected the Mediterranean to become the next arena of battle between the Axis powers and Britain, and he believed that both France, even if it had been defeated, and the United States must play a role.

The assignment did not begin in the White House. Weeks before he heard from the President, Donovan had talked to Hull, Stimson, and Knox about a far-ranging journey to Europe and the Middle East. He had discussed such a trip with British Security Coordinator William Stephenson, and on November 27 Knox had brought it up with Lord Lothian, the British ambassador. Knox and Stimson had consulted with the chief of Naval Intelligence, Adm. Richmond K. Turner, and with Maj. Gen. George V. Strong, head of the army's war plans division. Intelligence officers in both the army and navy immediately began to joust with one another and with civilian authorities to see who would control Donovan's mission. They might have spared themselves the struggle, because it was Roosevelt himself to whom Donovan was expected to report. Neither army nor navy nor, for that matter,

J. Edgar Hoover was given any true idea of the singular importance and nature of Donovan's assignment.

As soon as the President summoned Donovan to the White House, Stephenson cabled Churchill: "Impossible over-emphasize importance of Donovan mission. He can play a great and perhaps vital role. It may not be consistent with orthodox diplomacy nor confined to its channels." Stephenson also informed Sir Stewart Menzies:

> Donovan exercises controlling influence over Knox, strong influence over Stimson, friendly advisory influence over President and Hull. Being a Republican, a Catholic, and of Irish descent, he has following of the strongest opposition to the Administration. It was Donovan who was responsible for getting us the destroyers, the bomb sight, and other urgent requirements. There is no doubt that we can achieve infinitely more through Donovan than through any other individual. He is very receptive and should be made fully aware of our requirements and deficiencies and can be trusted to represent our needs in the right quarters and in the right way in the USA.

During the first few days of December 1940, Donovan hurried about Washington conferring with administration leaders in preparation for his trip abroad. The day after he met with Roosevelt, he spent the morning with Secretary of War Stimson. He left Stimson a trifle bewildered and at the same time envious. "Colonel Bill Donovan came in this morning to tell me about the new mission which he is going on for Frank Knox and which is approved by the British Government," Stimson wrote in his diary. "His description of it made my mouth water. He is going over to take another look around and see what is really up—what the chances are. He hopes to get to Gibraltar and Malta and I think Syria and Egypt—or else it was Greece and Egypt—and then he hopes to get down into Central Africa and to meet General Smuts of South Africa, coming up to see him. He has his eye on Weygand and is generally trying to get a look round to see."

Each person Donovan talked to got a different impression of what he was going to do abroad, and all sorts of rumors raced about Washington, tumbling over each other, contradicting one another, and mystifying the press. The navy brass was upset by his mission. On November 2 Winston Churchill had asked President Roosevelt for U.S. Navy protection for convoys, and one of Donovan's assignments from the President was to find out how necessary this might be. Naval Intelligence was in the process of negotiating an intelligence agreement with British Naval Intelligence and did not want Donovan making any commitments for the U.S. Navy to shepherd shipping through the Nazi submarine packs until the promise of such help had been used to extract advantageous terms from the British.

As the day drew near for Donovan's departure, Washington intelligence officers discussed various ideas for Donovan's cover. Some thought he should travel abroad in a naval plane; others thought he should travel incognito in a commercial aircraft. Donovan laughed at the idea that he should carry a false passport and employ an assumed name. He thought it totally ludicrous that he should attempt a disguise and travel by some roundabout way. Such cloak-and-dagger arrangements were bound to be penetrated and were completely unnecessary.

On December 5 at 5:30 A.M., Donovan breakfasted with Knox, after which Knox left for the Panama Canal on an inspection trip and Donovan left for New York, where he bade Ruth good-bye and packed his suitcase for a long trip.

The morning of Friday, December 6, the Bermuda Clipper waited at its pier in Baltimore while passengers fumed. At last at a few minutes before noon, a cab dashed up to the terminal, and a well-dressed man, his hair graying at the temples, got out carrying a briefcase. He was called Donald Williams on the passenger list, but waiting reporters took one look at his briefcase, which bore the initials WJD, and readily identified him as William J. Donovan. Donovan did not appear surprised or discomfited when he was recognized. He had already had press contacts in Washington spread the report that he was on his way to Africa, Greece, and Spain, but he had kept secret the actual destination of his trip and its true purpose as well as the date and place of his departure. Now he wondered who exactly had leaked information that resulted in reporters waiting for him in Baltimore.

The *New York Times* reporter also noticed that Donovan spoke to two other passengers, one a Mr. Desgarges, a French citizen, which raised the possibility that Donovan might indeed be on his way to see Maxime Weygand to "induce the French military leader to cast his lot with the anti-German forces in North Africa." Donovan also greeted a Mr. O'Connell. Actually, Desgarges was a French intelligence officer and Mr. O'Connell was Bill Stephenson.

When asked about Donovan's trip, State Department officials confirmed that he was heading across the Atlantic on another mission but insisted that the department knew nothing of its purpose. They even declined to say whether he was traveling on a regular or a diplomatic passport, and they refused to discuss Donovan's destination, "pointing out that passport information was always kept confidential."

Westbrook Pegler observed in his next column, "Our Colonel Wild Bill Donovan seems to have a fifty-trip ticket on the Clippers, which he must use up in a certain time or forfeit the remainder."

By that time, Donovan was safely in Bermuda and waiting for the Atlantic Clipper from New York. When the seaplane took off from the La Guardia basin on December 7, it was fully loaded, but reporters learned that some passengers would leave the plane in Bermuda to make room for Bill Donovan and a party to fly the Atlantic to Lisbon. The *New York Times* also learned that five U.S. Army officers on an undisclosed mission were aboard the Atlantic Clipper and were among the nine passengers booked through to Lisbon.

The army officers, who avoided press cameras, were actually a party of intelligence men headed by Lt. Col. Vernon S. Pritchard. They had been sent by General Strong, ostensibly to help support Donovan in his mission, but actually to make a separate study of British military installations. The army feared that Donovan would report favorably on British preparations and urge the President to give England more military aid. The delegation was instructed to return home with a negative report on the British so as to strengthen the hand of U.S. Army brass, who wanted to give priority to building up American armed strength before attempting to arm the British. The men also were told to learn all they could about British radar and fire-control methods, which appeared to be far in advance of those employed by the U.S. Army.

The Atlantic Clipper arrived in Bermuda at 2:00 P.M., on schedule, but bad weather in the Azores held it up there. Donovan and Stephenson looked in on the British mail censorship unit in Bermuda. The Atlantic Clipper had brought a maximum mail load of 12,000 pounds, the largest shipment of letters and packages ever carried across the Atlantic on the Clipper. All of this mail had to be studied by the British censors before the plane could be cleared for takeoff. Donovan was delighted with Nadya Gardner, the sharp-witted, beautiful Englishwoman whose job it was to fish in the mail for letters that German agents in the United States might be sending to their spymasters in Germany, or vice versa. He was particularly delighted at one of her intercepts, a letter to Reinhard Heydrich from a New York City agent, which proved that Heydrich was spying on his country's own spies. The delay lengthened as the censors struggled with the vast piles of mail.

"The two men had to spend eight days in Bermuda where Stephenson must have spent much time showing Donovan the intelligence operations that took place in that vital air and water link between Europe and the Americas," said Thomas Troy of the Central Intelligence Agency. "All kinds of British authorities checked the passengers, goods, publications, and mail that funneled through their hands."

Finally on December 13, the flying boat carrying Donovan and the oddly assorted group of intelligence men took off. The Clipper landed at Lisbon late on December 14.

"I am hoping to go to London," Donovan confided to an American journalist who was at the pier to meet the plane.

Donovan's hopes proved to be justified, and the next day a British flying boat took him to Poole. From there he went by train to London's

Waterloo Station, where Captain Kirk, the U.S. Navy attaché, and Brigadier General Lee, the military attaché, met him. Several British officials were on hand too, and they drove Donovan to Claridge's, where a comfortable suite awaited him despite Brendan Bracken's gloomy prediction upon his departure from Britain some four months before.

Donovan found the British in a jubilant mood. Their troops in North Africa were pursuing a much larger Italian army, which was in full retreat. The English also were cheered by the Greek victories over the Italian invaders in Albania. There were even Christmas decorations here and there in London, despite the German air attacks. By late fall of 1940 the Germans had given up trying to sweep the RAF from the skies and had commenced the night bombing of British cities.

Vernon Pritchard and his group went about their affairs, and Donovan saw nothing of them during the remainder of his mission. On the evening of December 17, Donovan went to see Lee at his home. "As soon as I got home from the office Wild Bill came in to talk," Lee wrote in his journal.

> He said when he got home from his last trip he told General Marshall and the Secretary of War that, in his opinion, the Military Attaché and his officers were the only people in the Embassy who were making up their own minds about things here without reference to Kennedy's pessimism. He then went on to make a few scathing remarks about Kennedy and the damage he was doing at home. Apparently Kennedy has infected Wall Street with his pessimism and has also succeeded in poisoning the minds of the admirals of the Navy.
>
> His (Donovan's) present mission is here in England, and I think is more or less a general survey, after which he is to go out through the Mediterranean. He does not say that he is going to Vichy or to see Weygand, but I have a notion that he will do both.
>
> One of the things he said which pleased me was that my despatches to Washington were so good that I should be careful to save them because I should write, since I had a real gift for it. I told him that I thought that I would have a file of the despatches, but whether I wrote anything about them would depend first on whether I had the time and second, on whether this whole affair turned out to be as historical as it promised to be.
>
> After a good deal of talk which involved discussing possible theaters in which the United States might take part, and some of my plans for the remodeling of the world after the war is over, and the necessity of getting the right sort of men to do the job (to which he replied that at the present time in the United States they were only to be found in the Army and the Navy) he made off for a dinner engagement.

The next day Donovan lunched with Churchill at Number 10 Downing Street. Reporters who kept their vigil outside the building spotted Donovan upon his arrival. They demanded to know what the smiling presidential agent had in mind. "I can't say anything about

Grayson M.P. Murphy, with whom Donovan sailed on a fact-finding trip to Europe in 1920. Murphy, who had also served in the Rainbow Division, was one of Donovan's earliest acquaintances in America's informal intelligence community.
(American Red Cross)

Donovan, candidate for governor of New York in 1932, and his wife, Ruth, pose for a photograph designed to win votes. Politics brought the Donovans together in a traditional public display of family solidarity.
(Buffalo and Erie County Historical Society)

Herbert Hoover (left) and William Donovan. The two men saw their friendship ripped apart by political controversy in 1929, when President-elect Hoover yielded to anti-Catholic and Prohibitionist pressures and denied Donovan the attorney generalship.

(Buffalo and Erie County Historical Society)

William Stephenson, the British superspy Intrepid, was among the first to recognize the value of Donovan's remarkable experiences and abilities. After establishing the office of British Security Coordinator in New York in June 1940, he campaigned to make Donovan the director of an American centralized intelligence agency.

(Sir William Stephenson)

Right: A jaunty Donovan returns to New York on August 4, 1940, from a presidential mission to England that was to decide whether the United States would help Britain fight on against Germany or would give Britain up for lost and prepare for the expected Nazi attack on the Western Hemisphere.
(Buffalo and Erie County Historical Society)

Below: In June 1941 Eleanor Roosevelt (with Donovan) spoke to the President about the need for an American intelligence service and urged that Bill Donovan be put in charge.
(Buffalo and Erie County Historical Society)

Top: The Hotel Palacio in Estoril, Portugal, was a haunt of spies during World War II. In March 1941 Donovan met there with Averell Harriman (in a room checked carefully for listening devices) before continuing across the Atlantic to report to FDR on his mission to the Balkans and the Mideast.
(Portuguese National Tourist Office)

Bottom: Donovan (at right, hat in hand) reviews Bulgarian cadets in Sofia on January 22, 1941. Later that morning he tried to talk King Boris out of his alliance with Hitler.
(Buffalo and Erie County Historical Society)

why I am here," he replied, "but please don't make me mysterious or important."

During lunch Churchill stated with customary eloquence that the United States and the United Kingdom must together defeat Hitler. Donovan kept to the instructions given to him by Franklin Roosevelt. He informed Churchill that the United States and Britain must help each other in this crisis in history in a "relationship of mutual selfishness."

The prime minister told Donovan he was convinced that, the Nazi-Soviet Nonaggression Pact notwithstanding, the Germans would attack Russia in May. Donovan saw that his trip into the Mediterranean must include an effort to create a Balkan entente that would stand up to German intentions in the area and, if all went well, throw off the Nazis' timetable so they could not attack the Soviets until later. The more the Germans delayed invading Russia, the greater the chance that they would not be able to complete their conquest before the severe northern winter entrapped their armies.

Churchill promised Donovan his complete cooperation. "We will give you the best man in the cabinet secretariat, who has been present at meetings of the Joint Board and Combined Arms, to go with you," Churchill told Donovan.

The best man in the secretariat turned out to be Lt. Col. Vivian Dykes, assistant secretary to the cabinet. A message went from the British government:

> Colonel Donovan is visiting the Mediterranean as an observer for President Roosevelt with whom he has great influence. He is a lawyer who has made a close study of military affairs and is one of our best friends in USA. He proposes to visit Gibraltar, Malta, Crete, Egypt and the western desert, Palestine and Greece. His object is to study and report to the President on our manned [*sic*] situation in Mediterranean, but his terms of reference are very wide. The Prime Minister directs that every facility should be afforded to Colonel Donovan who has been taken fully into our confidence. He will be accompanied by Lieutenant Colonel Dykes, Royal Engineers, of the Cabinet Secretariat.

Donovan studied not only the military situation but the entire complex of forces—political, economic, social, and psychological—which together made it possible to predict the outcome of a campaign. That morning he had turned over a list of questions concerning British tactics and the operations of the mechanized forces to the American Adm. Robert Ghormley, at the U.S. Embassy. A second list that Donovan gave to Ghormley asked for answers to theoretical questions as to what the British would do in this or that contingency. It fell to Raymond Lee to obtain answers to those questions. By that evening he had some of the responses, which he brought to Donovan at Claridge's about seven o'clock.

"I found him with Helen Kirkpatrick, the newspaperwoman," Lee wrote in his journal. "I think she is rather clever but she is far from being as attractive and alluring as she thinks she is. She was trying to get a story out of him but he was not giving her any. They talked about Kennedy and both of them ripped him up the back, and I didn't think I needed to contribute to that. Donovan knows much better how to deal with the press than Kennedy ever did, for Kennedy used to get very much excited and go on saying things which were not at all what he had in mind to say."

When the newspaperwoman had left, Lee showed Donovan some cables that he had sent to Washington. At the time, British and American representatives were preparing to meet in Washington for staff talks. Admiral Stark and General Marshall felt that the British might intend to pay too much attention to their immediate problems and not enough attention to American interests. If they did, the forthcoming talks would be meaningless. Lee's cables dealt with the British delegation to the staff talks and British instructions to their delegates.

Lee's journal went on: "He [Donovan] said that at lunch today Churchill had given him information that instructions to the delegation would be very wide open and that they were to approach every question with a completely open mind, to lay their proposals before the United States for the decision of the United States."

"In England I was given access to the various studies made of the different theaters of war," Donovan said later. "I went through many parts of the country not only to see the effects of bombings, but to see how factories were run, to observe how the activities of peace and of war went on together, and to look with wonder at the way the people went about their daily tasks as if no pall of war lay over them."

There was much to accomplish in London before Donovan could set out for the Mediterranean. As an intelligence agent, he lived by the maxim "You can find out anything you want to know about anybody in the world if you really want to." With Churchill's active support, Donovan set about finding answers to the questions he had about the United Kingdom. Members of the press considered Donovan both "mysterious and important" and did their best to catch up with him as he went about England. The usually fruitless pursuit of the enigmatic Donovan led one reporter to observe that he was "a man who moved so fast he created the myth that he often left one morning and returned the previous afternoon."

Donovan inspected British ordnance, shipping, signal corps, and maintenance depots. He saw firsthand the striking improvements in British preparations to defend their island if the Nazis attacked. When a *New York Times* reporter caught up with him on December 20, he said, "When I returned to the United States last August after a previous visit, I said I found the British 'resolute and courageous.' Now I would add, 'confident.' " Donovan said he thought Great Britain would win the war. This upset some British leaders who feared that if the American people believed Donovan they might think Britain was so certain to win that America need not help.

Menzies saw Donovan to brief him about Britain's intelligence operations and explained Ultra to him, thus confirming what Donovan had guessed on his earlier trip. In this way Donovan became the first American to be told about the British secret cryptanalytic success upon which so much high-level intelligence was to depend during the remainder of the war.

Donovan traveled to Coventry to see the devastation brought by German bombers. Not only the press but also German intelligence attempted to shadow Donovan in London. He lost his tail of German agents by the simple expedient of switching taxis.

On the morning of December 24, Donovan phoned Lee and said he would like to see both Lee and Admiral Ghormley before he left London on the day after Christmas. When the three men got together at Donovan's rooms at Claridge's, they had, in Lee's words, "so much to talk about that we really did not get anywhere." The principal subject was Ireland. Most Irishmen sympathized with Great Britain, but some were such Anglophobes that they were working for a German victory. Churchill was negotiating with Irish Prime Minister Eamon de Valera to cut off Irish assistance to Germany and to obtain bases to help protect Atlantic shipping against German depredations. There also was the very real likelihood that a German strike at the British Isles would not be aimed directly at England but would first attack Ireland so as to divide the British strength.

"It seems that Dulanty, the Irish High Commissioner here, has been after him [Donovan] to go over and pay a visit to De Valera," Lee reported in his journal.

> Donovan said that if De Valera invited him and did so publicly, of course he would be delighted to go over at once. Dulanty had no such invitation to convey, so Donovan declined to have anything to do with it. He asked me if I thought he was correct, and I said yes, that the Irish question had been so badly bungled in the interchange of speeches between Churchill and De Valera that the best thing to do was to let it cool off for a while. I said, of course, Churchill is a man upon whom great responsibilities are resting and he is very worried about the way the war is going, and especially the attacks on British shipping in the Atlantic. His speech about the bases had been hasty and ill-conceived, in my opinion, but De Valera's answer to it was even more hasty and more badly conceived, for

De Valera showed a streak of temper and implied that Churchill had made many threats and statements which had not been made at all. Donovan said that as far as he could see the increasing economic pressure upon Ireland would operate to bring them around. Ninety percent of the people in Ireland, according to Dulanty, had been enthusiastic in their support of Great Britain until this interchange of speeches had been made. Now they were not so much so but if they began to have to go without fruit and supplies and feed for their cattle, it might make them take a little sober second thought. If it were only possible to ignore these three million malcontents who call themselves Irish, it would be a great help. They do more to stir up strife, misunderstanding, and trouble in the world than any other three million people alive. Donovan, in spite of his Irish name and ancestry and the fact that he commanded the Fighting 69th, does not seem to have any particular fondness for the Free State.

In Washington at this time, President Roosevelt also was fuming over the Irish question, and he discussed with aides the possibility of asking Bill Donovan or perhaps even Joe Kennedy, two of the most prominent Irish-Americans, to go to Dublin to try to persuade the Irish that their stubborn policies were apt to betray them as well as the British into the hands of the Germans.

If Roosevelt intended to send Donovan to Ireland, he did not move fast enough in alerting him to the mission. The President's "secret legs" spent Christmas in London, but at two in the morning of December 26 he boarded a British flying boat with Vivian Dykes. The plane lifted off the dark Channel waters and flew into the night. Donovan had completed the first phase of his mission, and his reports to Roosevelt and Knox on the situation were already speeding by air and cable across the Atlantic. Now he was embarked on the real business of the journey.

Later in the day of his departure, the American press in London discovered that Donovan had gone. When they demanded to know where he was going, his friends would only admit that he was bound for an undisclosed destination. They asserted that "Colonel Donovan had not left for Ireland, the United States or the Continent, but was making a private trip." Some journalists, knowing of his appreciation for the fair sex, accused him of a holiday season dalliance in a secluded English country house. Everyone wondered where he would surface next.

21

Playing for Time

AS DONOVAN WAS FLYING southward along the blacked-out coast of Europe, the British commander-in-chief of the Mediterranean fleet was pondering a message from Admiral Godfrey, a message William Stephenson was instrumental in persuading Godfrey to send: "Donovan got us bombsights, destroyers, and other urgent requirements. We can achieve more through Donovan than any other individual. He can be trusted to represent our needs in the right quarters and in the right way in USA."

On his Mediterranean journey Donovan was to fly in British bombers and use British base facilities. For all effects and purposes he was now Churchill's as well as Roosevelt's confidential agent. When his plane touched down at Gibraltar, the key to the Mediterranean, Donovan inspected the British fortifications and gazed 6 miles across the bay to Algeciras, the Spanish port from which the German spymaster, Adm. Wilhelm Canaris, in his turn often peered at the Rock through field glasses from his customary hotel, the Maria Cristina.

Donovan later told the Union League of Philadelphia about his visit to Gibraltar: "There I saw how strongly fortified was that historic rock. I learned there, too, of a proposed and possible German intention of seeking to seal up the Strait of Gibraltar to prevent the passage of British ships, and to do this by striking from Spain." If Germany wanted to go into Gibraltar, he commented,

> it isn't necessary for her to take the Rock of Gibraltar itself. That has been given tremendous strength in the last six months. They had, while I was there, a Canadian detachment of miners that were widening the galleries, projecting the fortifications, they had additional troops in there, but they all admitted that if the Germans can get in position across the bay in Spain, or if they are able to get into Morocco and move into Gibraltar, catch Gibraltar in reverse, that a denial of the use of the harbor to the British will be sufficient to prevent in any practical way, excepting by some night movements, of the use of the Strait of Gibraltar.

At Gibraltar, Donovan also observed how the British kept up tradition even in the face of modern war. He and U.S. Adm. James Fife were both dinner guests of the governor of Gibraltar that night at the Rock. When the entire company of about 15 had been seated, Fife recalled, "There was this very colorful ceremony of the drum major coming in, followed by a small troop of men bearing a pillow on top of which was the key to the gate to La Linea. They paraded around the table, as I recall, three times, and then deposited the key in front of His Excellency, the Governor, to indicate that the Rock was secured for the night."

Donovan and Lieutenant Colonel Dykes of the cabinet secretariat flew east along the British lifeline to beleaguered Malta. Early in the 1930s fascism had taken root among the Maltese, but Donovan now found that persistent Italian air raids had destroyed any pro-Italian feeling there might have been on the three islands that made up the British bastion.

"You will remember the Italian claim that Malta would fall within two weeks," Donovan reported later to the War Department. "Malta, however, still endures after something over 120 bombings and is still serviceable as a repair base for cruisers and destroyers."

Donovan went to sea with a British squadron to learn firsthand how the Royal Navy convoyed merchantmen past threatening Italy. "Any movement of convoy through the Mediterranean is a major operation," he said. "I have seen a rendezvous in the ocean where Admiral Somerville will go out with his force and take it in during the night and, getting through the Strait, carry it as far as Malta, and there at Malta that convoy is picked up by [Admiral] Cunningham and carried on to Alexandria."

On Tuesday, January 7, 1941, Donovan and Dykes reached Cairo and were given comfortable rooms at the British Embassy. On Wednesday Donovan conferred with Bert Fish, the U.S. minister in Cairo, but he spent most of the next several days with British leaders, including the commander-in-chief in the Middle East, Gen. Archibald Percival Wavell, with whom Donovan struck up an immediate friendship. Both men had been through the thick of World War I fighting, and Donovan was greatly impressed by the man he described as "a slight fellow with only one eye. He is a very inarticulate man except that he gets bursts of speech after some days of depression, but he writes exceedingly well." By the time Donovan reached Cairo, Wavell's greatly outnumbered forces had already defeated the Italians in Ethiopia and were dealing them blows in the Cyrenaican Desert west of Cairo. Wavell's brilliant strategy and leadership were bringing disaster to the plans of Marshal Rodolfo Graziani, an old acquaintance of Donovan, to cut through Egypt to the Suez Canal. Donovan also saw a great deal of Air Marshal Sir Arthur Longmore, head of the British air forces in the Near East, Vice Air Marshal Sir Arthur Tedder, and Adm. Sir Andrew Cunningham, who commanded the fleet in the eastern Mediterranean.

"Wavell is all that you hear said of him," said Donovan in a War

Department lecture upon his return to the United States, "and Cunningham is even more than they say. They are both very able officers, and both standing up against superior numbers, conditions that are almost overwhelming, in a remarkable way."

Donovan learned that Wavell was confident of victory in the desert but was greatly worried about German forces that were massing in Romania for an advance through Bulgaria to attack Greece. On the day after Donovan's arrival, London informed Wavell that the only succor England could give Greece had to come from North Africa, and on January 9, Air Marshal Longmore was ordered to withdraw three squadrons of Hurricanes and at least one squadron of Blenheim bombers from action against the Italians and send them to Athens. Donovan was at British headquarters as additional messages arrived from London requiring Wavell and Longmore to dispatch important parts of both their air and ground forces to Greece. On January 10 Wavell showed Donovan a message from Churchill:

> Our information contradicts idea that German concentration in Romania is merely "move in war of nerves" or "bluff to cause dispersion of force."
>
> Destruction of Greece would eclipse victories you have gained in Libya and might affect decisively Turkish attitude, especially if we had shown ourselves callous of fate of allies. You must now therefore conform your plans to larger interests at stake.
>
> Nothing must hamper capture of Tobruk but thereafter all operations in Libya are subordinated to aiding Greece.
>
> We expect and require prompt and active compliance with our decisions for which we bear full responsibility. Your joint visit to Athens will enable you to contrive the best method of giving effect to the above decisions. It should not be delayed.

Although Donovan declined to talk to the press in Cairo, news reports speculated that he would furnish the U.S. government with a firsthand account of the situation in the Middle East and North Africa. Other stories suggested that he was training to become the new U.S. ambassador to the Court of St. James and that he would be sounding out Gen. Maxime Weygand on the possibilities of French forces in North Africa eventually reentering the war on the side of Great Britain. Actually, Donovan did strike up an old acquaintance ship in Cairo, with French Gen. George Catroux, who drew up an estimate of the situation for Donovan to transmit to Weygand. Catroux assured Donovan that Weygand hoped for a British victory but was afraid to take action in North Africa for fear that if he did, the Nazis would occupy all of France. As early as December 1940, when Donovan was still in Lisbon, German intelligence had reported to Berlin that the main purpose of his mystery trip was to bring French troops in North Africa and the Middle East back into the war. On December 10, the German government asked the Vichy government to refuse Donovan admission to any French territories.

Donovan obtained Wavell's permission to go into the Libyan Desert to see the fighting, and on Saturday, January 11, he set out for the front. Five years before, Donovan had been in that very area with the Italian troops; now he was with the British soldiers as they launched their last attacks on his old acquaintances. Jogging in jeeps across the desert sands, Donovan stretched out his sleeping bag beneath the stars at night and learned from the British Tommies what it was like to fight a Sahara campaign.

"I was with the troops at the taking of Bardia and the attack on Tobruk," he said in his speech to Philadelphia's Union League,

> and the surprising thing about that—I see now it is beginning to come out and I can speak of it—is that in that whole advance the British had no more than 30,000 troops. . . . With the 30,000 troops they took something like 150,000 prisoners, and it must not be deduced from that that it was so easy. The difficulty was not lack of bravery of the Italians— true, of course, they did not have their heart in it—but the trouble was in the generalship, and that generalship manifested itself in the setting up of a lot of little maharajahs, medieval style, because these towns you see on the map—Bardia, Tobruk, and Bengasi—are simply a group of houses on the desert, with the exception of Bengasi, which is quite a community. The British made the desert their ally; the Italians looked upon it as an enemy and they locked themselves up in these little fortresses and permitted themselves to be surrounded.

Donovan described what it was like as he came up to the front, just before the attack on Tobruk. "When you are driving an automobile on that desert on a moonlight night, where the sky and desert meet and where you cannot tell exactly where you are," he said, "it is perfectly understandable that any roving column from the enemy can pick you up. I was really scared to death, because I thought that would happen to us all the time, and it is particularly true when you are on the defensive."

In the desert Donovan talked to captured Italian soldiers. Officers whom he had once known as the cocky conquerors of Ethiopia were now bedraggled in defeat. From them he drew information that helped him to assess the Italian war commitment. Both the British and American governments very much wanted to know just how much heart the Italian people had for the war. Donovan became convinced that Italy would quit Germany's side as soon as Mussolini could be removed, but that the dictator's overthrow would take many more defeats and probably an invasion of the Italian peninsula.

Back in Cairo, Donovan continued talks with British leaders. He collected information from confidants. He spoke not only with the British but also with Arabs whom he had met on his visit to Egypt in 1936. He conferred with executives of the Jewish underground in Palestine, who pledged to support the British against the Germans. A sophisticated Zionist intelligence network was in place throughout the Middle East, and its Cairo representatives agreed to keep Donovan informed about political, economic, and military developments. The Jewish leaders promised to cooperate with the Palestinian Arabs until the Germans were defeated, but they warned Donovan that the Grand Mufti of Jerusalem and his extremists were working for a Nazi victory.

On Thursday, January 16, Dykes and Donovan flew over the Aegean Sea to Athens. Axis chancelleries speculated on what Donovan's mission meant, and the Axis and pro-Axis press commented on it. The *Bucharest Tageblatt* suggested that "a secret meeting between the enigmatic Donovan and the Egyptian Sphinx would be in order." Lincoln MacVeagh, the American minister to Greece, reported to Franklin Roosevelt about Donovan's three-day visit. "He did a grand job," wrote MacVeagh. "He flew over from Egypt at about the same time as General Wavell, and stayed at the British Legation with the General, but I had him to lunch with the King and introduced him to the Premier."

Donovan spent considerable time with Premier John Metaxas, the veritable dictator of the country, and Gen. Alexander Papagos, the commander-in-chief who was Metaxas's chief of staff. At the British Legation the British military delegation kept Donovan abreast of negotiations with the Greeks. Metaxas declined the offer of British troops to help the Greek soldiers who were still driving back the Italians on the Albanian front, but he welcomed whatever arms and supplies the British could provide to strengthen the forces preparing to defend Macedonia against a probable German assault. It was Metaxas's position that any British military assistance short of overwhelming strength would merely goad the Germans into action. Only supplies and military aid on the scale that America alone could provide would secure Greece against Germany. Donovan carefully noted exactly what supplies and equipment would most help the Greeks.

Greek friends told Donovan that Adm. Wilhelm Canaris, chief of the Abwehr (the intelligence service of the German General Staff), had also recently been in Athens, as Hitler's envoy. Metaxas was friendly toward Britain and had no illusions concerning the fate of Greece if Germany invaded, but at the same time he believed Canaris was a friend of Greece and had agreed that he mediate the differences between Germany and Greece. Canaris had promised Metaxas not only a guarantee of Greece's prewar frontiers but also the annexation of all

Albanian territory conquered by the Greek Army. In exchange, Greece would assist Germany in its plans for the Balkans and the Middle East.

Donovan soon discovered that Canaris had assigned a team of top agents to monitor his movements in Athens. This did not prove to be any serious problem. What he did not know was that the Germans had broken the American diplomatic code and were able to read the messages sent by cable from the American Legation in Athens to the State Department in Washington. Every message was scrutinized by the research office in the Schillerstrasse in Berlin and then passed on to the foreign ministry and to Hitler. Fortunately, Lincoln MacVeagh's letter to Roosevelt of January 19 went by diplomatic pouch and was not read by the Germans. In it MacVeagh explained Donovan's evaluation of the situation in the Balkans:

> The most outstanding developments from this point of view are the coming of German air forces to the Mediterranean and the subsequent visit of General Wavell to Athens. In the former connection, it seems that Germany has decided to take over Italy's job of pressing on Britain's life-line in this section of the world, and if so, a move on her part to Salonika would make sense as a step toward securing bases in the Eastern Mediterranean to supplement those she now has in southern Italy and Sicily. Thus, new weight is given to the Greek Premier's opinion, which I have already reported, that a German drive southward from Romania may be expected soon. On the other hand, British strategy must not only be prepared to meet this threat, but has always contemplated forming an Eastern Front, if possible, in order to extend and exhaust the enemy within the circle of the blockade. Consequently, immediately after expelling the Italians from Egypt, General Wavell has come to Athens not only to discuss with the Greeks the problem of supplying their army, but to seek their aid in the prompt preparation of Salonika for action against Germany, either defensive or offensive, as circumstances may dictate. At the same time, a British Military Mission now in Turkey is trying to influence that country to enter the war on Britain's side without further delay.
>
> German forces in Romania are increasing, though perhaps not to the extent alleged by British propaganda, and General Wavell's mission, while disappointing so far as concerns insuring immediate and adequate supplies to the Greek Army, has overcome part of Greece's natural caution regarding giving provocation to Germany to set these forces in motion. The British argument in this connection seems to have been that in dealing with the Dictators it is no use not provoking them, since they will follow in any case what they conceive to be their interests, and if no provocation exists, will invent it, as Italy has so recently done with Greece; and that consequently the best policy is to "fear God and take your own part" rather than to fear Hitler and neglect opportunities.

MacVeagh also told Roosevelt that Donovan "was planning to go to the Albanian Front, but the British Minister and General Heywood, Chief of the British Military Mission here, were anxious to rush him up to Sofia and Belgrade without delay, believing that the present moment is truly critical and that he might help to give the leaders in those capitals a very timely steer."

Donovan had come to the conclusion that if Greece and Turkey would unite against the Germans, the other Balkans might join them in an alliance, and Hitler would not dare to attack. If he could help to create such an alliance, he could balk Hitler's plans or at least upset the German timetable of conquest. Churchill had told him in London that Hitler was planning to invade the Soviet Union in May. He could not do this with impunity while the potentially hostile Balkans lay behind him. Perhaps it would be possible to prevent an invasion of Russia or at least delay it into the summer.

On Saturday, January 18, Donovan boarded the Sofia train, shadowed by German agents. In his briefcase he carried documents that detailed British military plans for massive support to Bulgarian resistance to a Nazi invasion. Another paper purported to show huge American military aid. Neither document was authentic. They had been created in a house on Jarvis Street in London where British intelligence technicians fabricated papers intended to mislead the enemy.

As he traveled northward through Thessaly and across Macedonia to Bulgaria, Donovan had time to speculate on the situation. The British had given up Bulgaria to the Germans, but he was not so sure. He would do his best to persuade King Boris III to reconsider his position. Donovan arrived in Sofia the next day and went directly to the U.S. Legation, where Minister George Howard Earle was to be his host for the stay in Sofia. By order of the government, no mention of Donovan's arrival was made in the Sofia newspapers. The government press department also issued an order barring anti-American articles and cartoons, which had been running during the previous month as Bulgaria's leaders attempted to prepare their country for adherence to the Axis.

Donovan discussed the precarious Bulgarian situation at length with Earle, a close friend of Franklin Roosevelt who had become an intimate of King Boris. Earle, a former governor of Pennsylvania, was a canny observer who acted the part of a brash American. He rarely let a chance to abuse the Nazis go by, and once in a Sofia nightclub when the Germans present asked the band to play the "Horst Wessel Lied," he retaliated by demanding that the band give equal attention to the British by playing "Tipperary." This started an old-fashioned bar brawl. When he caught a German spy in the legation, he personally beat a full confession out of him. Earle's current girl friend, a beautiful Hungarian dancer, was a spy for the Abwehr and the Sicherheitsdienst, both German intelligence organizations, and the minister knew it. Donovan listened to Earle's description of the girl with lively interest, and he thought of his briefcase with its documents.

On Monday morning Donovan called upon Bulgarin Foreign Minister Ivan Popoff, and in the afternoon he was received by Premier Bogdan Philoff. The National Assembly was in session, and all day long delegates talked excitedly about Donovan's confidential mission to their country. It was rumored that Donovan had brought a personal letter from President Roosevelt to the king. Democrats, who opposed the German domination over their country, took heart and told other delegates that perhaps the nation was moving too rapidly into the Axis camp. The government should wait until it was learned what Donovan told the king.

Donovan did not limit his talks to officials. He already knew a large number of Bulgarians, some of whom he had met as long ago as 1916, when they came to Vienna to discuss with him their nation's sanitation problems while he was with the War Relief Commission. On Tuesday, January 21, he lunched with Earle, the British and Turkish ministers, and the Bulgarian war minister, Theodoro Daskaloff. That night the British minister gave a dinner party in his honor so that he could meet other key members of the diplomatic community in Sofia.

On Tuesday the Sofia press had suddenly discovered Donovan's presence in the city, and prominent front-page announcements of his arrival were printed together with brief comments emphasizing that Colonel Donovan was one of Roosevelt's closest military advisers. Beyond that the government, and Donovan too, maintained a discreet silence as to his movements about the city and the purpose of his visit. By Tuesday evening Donovan was convinced that the Bulgarian leaders with whom he had been talking were simply waiting for the German takeover.

King Boris III might be another matter. Since 1938 Germany had enjoyed a strong influence on the Bulgarian government. Bulgarians realized that the Romanian cession to Bulgaria of the southern Dobruja during the previous September had been due to German pressure, and Hitler was promising still more land at the expense of Yugoslavia and Greece. Nonetheless, Bulgaria had not yet joined the Berlin-Rome Axis, and Donovan knew that the king was the final authority in the nation.

On Wednesday morning Donovan reviewed the cadets at the Bulgarian military academy at the invitation of the academy commandant, General Nihoff. Then he went to the Royal Palace at eleven o'clock to see the king. He was outspoken in warning the monarch about the danger of collaborating with Germany. He reported to Roosevelt that the king replied, "I must not run the risk of having my country overrun without first attempting to reduce the shock."

"Of course, I understand," said Donovan. "But your difficulty is that in Hitler you are dealing with a man who has never kept his word."

The king shrugged his shoulders. Donovan, unperturbed, suggested a less inflammatory policy. "Germany is still uncertain as to what you will do in the event that she demands passage through your country," he said, "but if a decision is forced and you are no longer able to delay, you will then permit Germany to come through, although you will not participate with her."

King Boris looked Donovan straight in the eye. To the American his smile seemed to suggest that the king loved his people and would protect their interests. There was little more Donovan could do, but before taking his leave, he said, "I wish you would tell me of your meeting with the officers who were involved in the conspiracy to kill you."

The king told how the conspirators had burst in on him at 2:15 in the morning and remained with him until 6:00 A.M. Boris had watched the slow hands of the clock moving toward the dawn, conciliating, granting concessions to their demands, fighting for time with the belief that "conspiracy is strong in the dark but as daylight comes its strength is diluted."

"I now understand your whole manner of dealing with Hitler," Donovan said when the king had finished. "That you are seeking by gaining time, to dilute the force of his demands. I hope you are right about this, and that your attempt to deal with him in this way will not meet the fate of others."

When he left Boris, Donovan was convinced that the king was still uncommitted and that there might be some hope for denying Bulgaria to the Nazis. Concerning the king he wrote in his diary, "I should say that he is idealistic, so much so as to have an overbelief in the virtue of peace; that he is honest, shy; but I fear he has been so successful in maneuver that he places too great reliance upon it, even when the time has been reached when decision and not maneuver is essential."

Donovan did not appreciate that the king was neither shy nor honest. He did not know that Boris was in regular touch with Admiral Canaris. On January 22, the German ambassador phoned Berlin to report that Donovan had told the Bulgarian foreign minister that the United States would not allow Great Britain to be defeated. The next day a phone call from a German agent to Berlin reported that he had "told Boris that Franklin Roosevelt would give aid to Greece in the war against Italy." Then only a few days after Donovan visited the Royal Palace, King Boris met with Twardovsky, head of the cultural department at the German Foreign Office.

"The King spoke derisively about the visit of the American Colonel Donovan," reported Twardovsky, "who demonstrated to him once more how politically naive the Americans really are. Donovan has not the faintest notion of the political conditions and history of the Balkans, nor do these matters seem to interest him in the least. Donovan had asked him to remain neutral, to resist by force of arms any attempt by Germany to move troops through the country, and to put his reliance in the liberality of England and America. To him, the King, this send-ing of emissaries and all the talk of these gentlemen were evidence of American weakness. If America were strong, she would act and not threaten."

Before quitting the legation for the Royal Palace, Donovan had left his briefcase in his bedroom. While Donovan was with the king, Earle entertained his Hungarian girl friend at the legation. When Donovan returned, Earle, anxious to hear about the audience with Boris, spir-ited her off upstairs. While the two men were conversing in the draw-ing room, the woman slipped into Donovan's room, picked up the briefcase, and went off with it to Gestapo headquarters.

Donovan's bags were packed and had been brought down to the door so that he could go to the train station that afternoon and catch the Simplon Orient Express for Belgrade. When he went to his room, he discovered that his briefcase was gone. Although the case contained documents, letters of introduction, his diplomatic passport, and a few hundred dollars, he was not really dismayed. When Donovan told him of the loss, Earle immediately phoned Bulgarian authorities, who promised to have the police investigate the presumed theft. Donovan then phoned U.S. Minister Arthur Bliss Lane in Belgrade and asked him to make necessary entry arrangements with Yugoslavian author-ities so there would be no delay when the Orient Express reached the Yugoslav border.

The Germans now saw fit to put their propaganda machine into action against Donovan. Ian Fleming of the intelligence division of the British naval staff (who was later to create the fictional spy James Bond), sent the following transcript picked up by British Broadcasting Company monitors of a German broadcast on January 24, 1941: "Colo-nel Donovan, shortly before his departure from Sofia, the capital of Bulgaria, discovered that he had lost his passport and other papers. It is now known that he lost his passport, important notes, dollars and paper money, and some letters from the White House during a tour of nightclubs in the Bulgarian capital." A second broadcast on the same day stated:

In war, England employs the notorious method of letting others fight for her. Why shouldn't she attempt the same in the field of propaganda? They have asked a certain gentleman on the other side of the Atlantic to oblige them by touring the countries in southeastern Europe with a view to furnishing information. Maybe those who dispatched this emissary have banked on certain circles which today still look up to the United States in respectful veneration. Credentials and a passport with a recommendation from Washington are thought to make more attractive the mission on which Mr. Donovan is engaged. We hold that the loss of his passport does not necessarily mean that his information tour has failed, as he did not miss the opportunity of carrying out the most searching studies of Sofia by night. In any event, however, we strongly doubt that the information collected during his nightly tour of Sofia will constitute a contribution towards . . . [a few words inaudible in the transmission]. We can, however, offer Mr. Donovan some comfort; the prospects of his tour of southeastern Europe have not been changed through the loss of his passport.

That Donovan and Earle were together suggested still another propaganda broadcast to the Germans. German-controlled Radio Paris announced, "The U.S. minister in Bulgaria, Earle, started a scandal in a Bulgarian nightclub. Under the influence of drink, the Jewish and Masonic minister fought with peaceful customers. The day before, at a reception held at the Soviet Legation, he had been hopelessly drunk. It may be significant that it was in the company of this drunkard that Colonel Donovan lost important diplomatic papers."

At the Sofia railway station the westbound Simplon Orient Express chuffed restlessly, waiting for Donovan and Lieutenant Colonel Dykes. Passengers grew worried because it had been announced that this train would be the last from Sofia to cross the border into Yugoslavia. The border was to close that evening to further traffic, and all train schedules had been suspended. Only travelers bearing diplomatic passports were to be admitted into Bulgaria. Tensions were mounting, and a German invasion was feared. The police were making a last frenzied search for Donovan's briefcase, but they could not find it. When Donovan arrived on the station platform, reporters buttonholed him and begged for a statement.

"I am leaving Bulgaria with the most pleasant impressions of this small but wonderful country," he said, "of this hard-working and progressive people and their kind-hearted, democratic, and sincere king." Donovan was still without his passport when he climbed aboard the train and settled down in his compartment for the journey to Belgrade, Yugoslavia.

As the train rolled toward the border, Donovan thought about Bulgaria's vulnerable situation. It was apparent that the Germans had already filtered in, he later told the War Department. "They were occupying the northern hills of Bulgaria, as watchers against the expected attack of the British against the Romanian oil fields, and as you go through the streets you trip over the number of Germans who were there on ostensibly economic missions. It was very clear after leaving Bulgaria to see that when the German knocked, the Bulgars would let him in."

Donovan also observed how a powerful military apparatus could win battles without firing a shot. "I saw the Nazi military machine at work, seeing how it was used, not for fighting but for intimidation—to impose upon weaker countries Nazi economic and political philosophy. It was just as it used to be in our high school books, where we read that the soldiers of ancient days prepared for the taking of a city by first undermining its walls. This modern Nazi warfare is carried out in the same way. And this I saw with my own eyes and at close hand— how the advance was made in southeastern Europe by political sapping and disintegration."

The Yugoslav and Turkish ministers to Bulgaria were also on board the train, and they joined Donovan for dinner. As they enjoyed the sumptuous cuisine of one of the world's most celebrated trains, they talked earnestly about the German threat that hung over the Balkans. Could a Balkan alliance of Greece, Bulgaria, and Yugoslavia be created to deter the Germans? Should pro-British Turkey join such an alliance?

Donovan was in Belgrade when the Bulgarian police brought his briefcase to the American Legation in Sofia. They explained to Earle that it had been discovered in a trash can, wrapped in old newspapers. Only the currency was missing.

From January 29, 1940, to April 16, 1942, a ledger was kept in Berlin of all German intelligence reports shown to Hitler to begin his day. At the Führer's insistence Walther Hewel, liaison officer between Foreign Minister Joachim von Ribbentrop and Hitler, started each morning's briefing with the latest report on the activities of Colonel Donovan. Hitler, doubtless regretting the occasion nearly 20 years earlier when he confided in the man who would become America's intelligence chief, exploded with rage at every Donovan success and chortled with glee at Donovan's frustrations. Hitler was delighted when he learned that a quick-witted Abwehr agent had made off with Donovan's briefcase, and Canaris congratulated his woman in Sofia.

The documents in Donovan's briefcase portraying British and American plans should Germany invade Bulgaria were of seeming great importance to the German high command. Their contents were radioed in secret code to army commanders and to key German diplomats. The British, listening at their cryptanalysis center at Bletchley Park, in turn read the German messages and had reason to congratulate themselves and that extraordinary agent and diplomat William J. Donovan. The Germans had taken the bait. Dr. Joseph Goebbels was delighted to announce in Berlin that Donovan had lost his papers because he "got himself into a state of complete drunkenness." Both the British and the Germans were very happy about the same event.

British intelligence reports say of Donovan's stay in Sofia: "He did not dissuade the Bulgarian leaders from their pro-German policy, but he did implant in their minds a measure of doubt as to the wisdom of that policy. In result, they hesitated before implementing their proposed intervention on Germany's side, which would have allowed German troops unrestricted passage through their country. Mr. Churchill had intimated that he would be content with a delay of 24 hours. Donovan secured a delay of eight days."

22

Mediterranean Intrigue

LATE ON WEDNESDAY, January 22, 1941, Arthur Bliss Lane, American minister to Yugoslavia, waited in the railroad station in Belgrade. After Donovan had phoned him early that afternoon from Sofia, Lane had contacted Yugoslav officials, who had cleared Donovan's way through the border checkpoint. As soon as the Orient Express eased to a halt, Donovan stepped onto the station platform.

Back in Washington, Cordell Hull had opposed Donovan's mission because he thought that any U.S. involvement in the Balkans would be dangerous. He also considered Donovan's heady mixture of intelligence, intrigue, and diplomacy to be unbecoming an American official. Many of the American diplomats stationed in the Balkans shared the secretary of state's views, and Arthur Bliss Lane was one of them. It had not helped matters when Lane learned that Donovan was coming to Belgrade, not through U.S. diplomatic channels but through the British Legation. It was also disquieting to Lane that Roosevelt, Churchill, and Donovan cloaked the entire mission in mystery while at the same time employing contrived leaks to the press to put psychological pressure on Axis agents, diplomats, and policymakers.

Lane took Donovan to his residence, where Donovan briefed him for several hours on the situation in Bulgaria, British strategy, and how the United States might act in the region. Lane had a message for Donovan that had just arrived from President Roosevelt. The President urged his confidential emissary to let Yugoslav leaders know that "the United States is looking not merely at the present but to the future, and any nation which tamely submits on the grounds of being quickly overrun would receive less sympathy from the world than a nation which resists, even if this resistance can be continued for only a few weeks."

Until he reached Belgrade, the British had been making arrangements for Donovan, but now Lane took over. Thursday proved to be a strenuous day. First of all, in the morning Lane took Donovan to call on Prime Minister Dragisha Cvetković. The prime minister and Foreign Minister Alexander Cinkar-Marković had already decided to throw in their lot with Germany. They had been to Berchtesgaden to see Hitler and had agreed to join the Axis. Donovan's appearance in Belgrade was upsetting, but Cvetković appeared friendly and cordial. He assured Donovan that the Germans would not invade the Balkans. Hitler, he said, had no immediate designs on either Britain or Turkey but would strike next at the Soviet Union. Cvetković explained that the Serbian part of the Yugoslav population would reject any alliance with the Axis, but the Croats, for their part, would oppose siding with the Allies. Donovan contented himself with telling the prime minister what President Roosevelt had to say about nations that did not stand up to Hitler.

At noon Donovan and Lane were at the American Legation for a press conference. Donovan began by telling the correspondents that he would not discuss details of his European trip. The *New York Times* man wrote:

> Told that the Axis press was attacking his mission as "typical American interventionism," Colonel Donovan replied, "No comment." The Colonel chatted easily with the Yugoslav and foreign journalists, but avoided all questions relating to his visit.
>
> The disappearance of his diplomatic passport in Sofia yesterday was explained by Colonel Donovan as an unaccountable loss.
>
> "It simply disappeared some time before I boarded the train," he said.
>
> He denied that his briefcase, luggage, and documents were stolen at Sofia, stating that his luggage was all intact.
>
> "As for documents," he added, "I carry them up here," and tapped his forehead.

Donovan hurried away from the press conference to lunch with Prince Paul, the regent for 17-year-old King Peter. Donovan told the prince of Roosevelt's view. Prince Paul commented that his country might resist the Germans but that he distrusted the intentions of the Bulgarians, and his own countrymen were hopelessly disunited. The Serbs, Croats, and Slovenes were at loggerheads.

"I talked with Prince Paul, and it was very apparent that he was in difficulty," Donovan said in a speech made after he returned to the United States. "He was working for the unity of his people and he said, 'If the German comes in and attacks us, then we will fight.'

"I said, if they go into Bulgaria and are on your flank, what will you do?, and he said, 'Then we can do nothing, because Croatia will not be with us.' So there was a man attempting to get unity of his people, not being able to get it because at the crucial moment [he] would find that disintegration he feared, and upon that Germany played."

There was no real possibility of Yugoslavia's joining a Balkan entente. At least the regent maintained that his country would remain neutral at all costs and that he would refuse German demands for war materials, bases, and the passage of troops through Yugoslav territory.

Donovan assured the prince that if the Yugoslavs let the Germans cross their boundaries without opposing them, the United States would not intercede on their behalf at the peace conference that would occur after the Allied victory. Donovan was impressed by Prince Paul.

From his audience with the prince, Donovan drove out to Avala, where he placed a wreath at the Tomb of the Unknown Soldier, and then met with the Croat leader Vice-Premier Vladko Maček, back in Belgrade.

"If the German asks to pass through freely, we will not permit it," Maček told Donovan.

Maček reported that German soldiers were massed on the northern border but Yugoslavia hoped to forestall an invasion until ready to resist effectively. It would help, he said, if a Russian-German conflict broke out, and this was imminent.

Each of Donovan's presumedly secret conversations with Yugoslav leaders was passed on in one way or another to German intelligence. On January 30 a report to Berlin contained details of Donovan's talk with Maček. Donovan was reported as saying that "the Balkan states and Turkey were aware that American aid to Great Britain would be decisive. No one should be taken in by German propaganda. America would support Great Britain."

Donovan's conversation with Prince Paul was also reported to Berlin, and Smiljanović, the Yugoslav secretary of state for foreign affairs, informed the Vichy French chargé d'affaires that his government's true policy toward Donovan's mission was to play for time. Vichy let Berlin know. German agents tracked Donovan on his travels around Belgrade to be sure that informants among the Yugoslavs reported on every interview.

Late on Thursday afternoon Donovan met with Foreign Minister Cinkar-Marković, who attempted to break the appointment. He was pro-Hitler, and he had no stomach to talk to the American emissary. When a smiling Donovan walked unannounced into his office, the foreign minister judged that this genial American scarcely could be the dangerous agent that his friends in the German Abwehr portrayed, and he relaxed and was genial in return. Only when Donovan had gone did he begin to fear what the Germans would think when they discovered he had been talking to the American. It was Cinkar-Marković who issued an order censoring all mention of Donovan's presence from Belgrade newspapers. The less said about the American the better.

That evening at Lane's house the American minister and his guest dined late and then played poker well into the night. In the morning Donovan and U.S. Military Attaché Col. Louis L. Fortier went to the War Ministry to see Gen. Peter Pesić, the minister of war; Gen. Peter Kosić, the chief of the general staff; and Adm. Julian Luteroti, chief of naval operations. Donovan inspected the general staff school and the military academy. He visited the military academy, Donovan later explained to the War Department,

> because I wanted to see the quality of men who would be the leaders of these fighting forces. I went through the academy in Belgrade with three or four of the younger generals who in the last war had been subalterns, and the thing that struck me and made me wonder—there was always different thought between the soldier and the politician. The soldier was for standing up for his country and the politician was hoping something would turn up and make it unnecessary to face an issue, and that is what struck me about the soldiers there. We went to this little room that was set apart as a kind of a sanctuary, and in that room was an easel, and on the easel was a map of old Serbia, and on the map there were blue lines indicating the position that the Serbian Army had held during the advance of the Germans in the last war, and they pointed out with pride the fact that they had held their army intact even though they had been driven out of their country and even though they had to remain outside of that country for three years before they ever returned, but they were used to that and they didn't fear it.

Donovan observed officers engaged in a study of map problems and fortifications, watched a gymnastic drill and a fencing demonstration, and listened to a chorus of young officers sing marching songs.

He lunched that day with British Minister Ronald Campbell and his aides, and had a press meeting with American reporters. Then he slipped off to a clandestine meeting with Gen. Dušan Simović, commander of the air force. Throughout Europe Donovan already had a network of informants, and Belgrade friends told him that Simović and a handful of patriotic army officers were planning to obstruct the surrender of their country to Germany. Donovan always believed he had escaped the Abwehr surveillance on his trip across the Danube River to the air force headquarters at Zemun, but German intelligence records show that Canaris's people tracked him to his destination. Simović told Donovan that he believed concessions to Germany would be deadly and would destroy Yugoslavia's chance to resist invasion. Certainly the Yugoslavs, tough mountain people with a knowledge of every pass and crag, would be able to make their rugged terrain an ally. Donovan and Simović talked over Simović's plans for a coup d'état against the government of Prince Paul. The patriots would strike as soon as the government signed an agreement with the Axis and would place royal authority in the hands of 17-year-old King Peter, who agreed that Paul had outlived his usefulness. Before he left for Belgrade, Donovan watched flights of Yugoslav Bristols, Blenheims, and trainers maneuver overhead.

Donovan was back at Minister Lane's residence for a late dinner party. He briefed naval and military attachés so they could send his reports to Washington by diplomatic pouch, safe from Axis surveillance. He was able to furnish them with a probable timetable for Hitler's move into the Balkans. He said nothing to the minister about what he had learned from Simović. Lane cabled Hull that Donovan and he had been assured by Prince Paul and by Prime Minister Cvetković that the Yugoslavs would not permit the passage of German troops or war materials through their territory and would resist aggression. When the intercept of the cable was placed before German leaders in Berlin, they had reason to be satisfied. Apparently Donovan had learned exactly what they wanted him to learn. They had no inkling of the plot to overthrow the pro-Axis government, which Donovan had wisely kept to himself.

It had been announced that Donovan would leave the next morning by train for Salonika, Greece, but instead he secretly went to the airport long before dawn and flew in a private airplane. Plans for his flight were closely guarded until he had safely passed over the Greek and Italian fighting front and landed in Greece. "It is understood," said a *New York Times* telephone dispatch, "United States and Yugoslav authorities concealed this information to prevent any possible effort to intercept his airplane during his flight over belligerent zones."

The political climate had shifted dramatically in Greece since Donovan's departure for Sofia, and German intelligence at least was attributing much of the change to him. The Germans believed Donovan had persuaded Premier Metaxas to agree to British plans for the defense of Greece. British troops would land at Salonika when German forces moved into Bulgaria, which must be considered a clear indication that an invasion of Greece was intended.

Donovan met again with Greek leaders on January 27 to discuss what American supplies might be needed for the defense of Greece. Some months later, after the outmanned Greek Army had been overrun by German troops and the British had evacuated the forces they had sent there, armchair generals in the United States laid the blame for the British military failure on interfering politicians in London. Churchill, they claimed, had forced a resisting Wavell to send troops to Greece. Donovan, however, said Wavell himself had favored military aid to the Greeks. "I happened to be with General Wavell the night it was discussed," Donovan remarked before the Union League of Philadelphia,

> I had been at dinner with him, and he showed me a paper he took out of his dispatch case. . . . That paper constituted his appreciation of the situation, and that appreciation set forth possible German intentions . . . to come down and try to get Salonika as a means of protecting her

flank in the event of any action she wanted to take in the Aegean and . . . to deny to the British the use of Salonika as a jumping-off trench. And to do that she also had to do the job that Italy had been unable to do, and that was to mop up Greece.

Wavell set forth all of that, and then he set forth the necessity of putting in six divisions. But he didn't have the shipping to do it—and through all I say, you will see that the whole strategy of England is limited by the lack of shipping, just like the strategy of Germany is dictated by the need, or her fear of the need, of getting her job done before the weight of our support can be felt. And so Wavell decided to put in two divisions, New Zealand and Australian, and one armored division, and to let Salonika go, withdraw from the Bulgarian frontier and take the heights by mountain routes. . . .

From Salonika Donovan went to the Albanian front, where Greek and Italian forces had been fighting since late October. He spent about seven days at the front, accompanied by a young Greek lieutenant and four Greek privates. They traveled by automobile along precipitous mountain roads, and more than once Donovan was "scared to death," he told his Philadelphia audience.

> You would have these drivers who were always eager to discuss political questions, who knew more about the Roosevelt-Willkie campaign than I did, and the driver [would] round these hairpin turns, in the left hand a cigarette, swinging it around as we hugged the mountainside, and his right hand off the wheel pounding the knee of the second driver to emphasize his remarks. I went around more hairpin turns without any hand on the wheel than I have ever done at any other time. Now those men, they talk about those things. Maybe they talk about it too much, but one thing that I found, they weren't ashamed to talk about it, and they weren't afraid to die for it. . . . These boys fought with a rock for a parapet and a mule [for transportation] and a gun for a weapon, and that is one thing that was brought home to me there: If you are going to have mechanized equipment, you have got to have the best. The second best is no good, because if you have the second best against the best, you are apt to rely upon it, and if you rely upon it you get overwhelmed.

One day Donovan said to his Greek companions, "Now here you boys have done pretty well against the Italians, but how about the Germans? You must know that they are going to come here and drive down into Salonika."

"Well, what difference does it make how big they are?" replied a young soldier. "If you want to be free, you got to fight them."

From his observation of the Greeks fighting Italians in Albania, Donovan drew an important principle of modern warfare. "The more we become mechanized, the more important it is that we go back with our men and try to exercise the primal virtues," he later said in a War

Department speech. It was possible, he said, to become overly mechanized. "Then your legs are just something you stand on when you get out of an automobile. I think the British are coming to realize this. They now see that they . . . have to come to the methods the underdog uses—the principle of guerrilla warfare. In addition to their commandos, they have organized units among themselves and their different allies for the purpose of carrying fear into the heart of the enemy by getting behind [his] lines."

Donovan was already seeing the necessity of creating an American bureau that would provide not only strategic intelligence but also men who would be trained in what Churchill called "ungentlemanly warfare."

After his trip to the field, Donovan returned to Athens for a quick round of meetings with British and Greek officials. On January 29, while Donovan was with the Greek Army in Albania, Premier Metaxas had died suddenly. His successor, M. Korysis, was less resolute, but he assured both Donovan and the British that Greece would resist any German aggression, although shortages of transport and artillery ammunition would limit the resistance to a delaying action. Lord Forbes, the British air attaché in Athens, volunteered to fly Dykes and Donovan to Istanbul on Thursday, January 30, but a severe storm postponed the flight for one day. On Friday the plane landed at the Istanbul airdrome, where Donovan was met by the U.S. naval attaché to Turkey, Comdr. Richard B. Tuggle. Tuggle drove Donovan to the American Consulate General to meet with members of the British military mission to Turkey. When Donovan took the 6:30 P.M. train for Ankara, Tuggle accompanied him.

The next morning Donovan arrived in Ankara. His host, American Minister John Van A. MacMurray, was not entirely happy about Donovan's presence there. MacMurray wrote to Hull that Donovan's visit was "a matter of very considerable embarrassment to me in my relations with both the Turks and the British, by reason of my being altogether in the dark as to what it was about."

MacMurray had discovered that the British ambassador and the Turkish president, premier, and foreign minister all knew more than he did about Donovan's mission. On Sunday Donovan lunched with Britain's Ambassador Sir Hugh Knotchbull-Hegessen, who informed him that Churchill had just sent a message to President Ismet Inönü asking that Turkey permit the RAF to station ten squadrons of fighters and bombers in Turkey. Once the planes were positioned in Turkey, Churchill could threaten that if Germany marched on Bulgaria, the RAF would bomb the Ploesti oil fields on the Romanian Black Sea coast, from which Germany drew most of its petroleum.

On Sunday evening Donovan dined with a group of Turkish officials and army officers whom he had met since arriving on Saturday. Then on Monday he met with Premier Refik Saydam as well as the foreign minister, the defense minister, the minister of national defense, and the chief of the General Staff. He saw every Turkish leader of consequence with the exception of President Inönü, who had gone to the Bulgarian border to inspect Turkish Army preparations for a possible German and Bulgar invasion. Donovan informed the leaders that American war production would be in full swing by September. If Greece and Britain could hold out for six months, he said, American assistance would reach them.

Turkish sources told the *New York Times* correspondent that Donovan's "resolute presentation of the position of the United States in this struggle of the free nations against dictatorships is everywhere remarked to have had tremendous effect, stiffening resistance to Germany in the Balkans. No less encouragement has been given by his practical inquiry into just what military aid these countries hoped had been sent direct from the United States to various areas where the struggle against Nazism is in progress or is likely to be taken up this spring."

Donovan noted in his journal that Britain did not have the strength to protect the Balkans from Hitler, and Turkey knew it. The Balkans required a military shield behind which they could unite, and the United States alone could provide such a shield. From Ankara, Donovan advised Roosevelt by confidential messenger that only American armed intervention could prevent the Germans from seizing the area. Roosevelt had little choice but to ignore Donovan's advice. America's potential strength was enormous, but the armed forces presently ready for action could not begin to prevent a German takeover, and the American public was still divided as to the seriousness of the Axis threat. Later Donovan said of the Turks, "I found that Turkey, although not equipped with modern arms and not prepared to carry on an offensive at this time, was an ally of Britain and proud too of the fact that Turks would be the defenders, as they express it, of the Gate."

He also learned a great deal from the Turks about what might happen when Germany attacked Russia. "Russia is scared to death of her," he reported in a speech a few months later. "The only thing I know about Russia is what the Turks told me, and Turkey says Russia is not much better in her army than she was at the end of the war with Finland. There has been some improvement, but nothing to speak of. The Turks feel that the aim of Germany, with her sixty divisions in Poland and her twenty-five divisions in Romania, is to strike at the Ukraine, and in doing that, to try to encircle Russia by getting through the Dardanelles. They believe, too, in Turkey that it is the intention of Germany to strike through Turkey into Iraq." The Turks left Donovan with the impression that if Bulgaria would resist a German incursion, they would step in and assist Bulgaria. But if Bulgaria did not resist, they told Donovan, they did not have the power or the equipment "to stick their neck out."

Donovan learned from Turkish sources that "with the activities of the Germans with the Arabs in Iraq, in Persia, and in Syria, Turkey may feel herself surrounded and may find herself helpless. It may be that the Germans will attack in Syria, get in the rear of the Turks, because it must be remembered that the whole theory of the offensive of Germany is to outflank, take a country not only for the acquisition of that country itself, but to take it because it puts it on the flank of the next country it wishes to dominate."

On Monday evening, February 3, Donovan and Tuggle went to the railroad station to catch the train to Beirut, from where they would go on to Jerusalem. In Beirut, Donovan hoped to see French officers loyal to his old friend Gen. Maxime Weygand, who were with the French Army of the Near East, camped outside Beirut. He also hoped to talk to Gen. Henri Dentz, the French high commissioner. It was not to be.

"There was a dramatic incident in Ankara station Monday," reported the *New York Times* correspondent by telephone, "when Colonel William J. Donovan, President Roosevelt's special envoy in Europe, was to have left by train for Palestine via Syria.

"While he was there with his party waiting to enter the train, a secretary of the French Embassy arrived and informed him that a telegram had just arrived from Vichy saying that under no conditions was Colonel Donovan to be allowed to go through Syria. Colonel Donovan had already received his visa, and this was canceled. No reason was given for this attitude."

Donovan and his party boarded another train that took them to Adana in southern Turkey, from where Lord Forbes flew them in a British military plane to the island of Cyprus. Donovan and the others spent Wednesday at Nicosia on Cyprus and then flew to Jerusalem on Thursday. There, American Consul General George Wadsworth, an old college friend, helped Donovan interview the Grand Mufti of Jerusalem, an Arab leader who was outspoken in his support of Hitler and who was attempting to cultivate a Nazi movement among the Arabs. Donovan discovered that most Arabs, being devout Moslems, were not attracted to the errant religious leader's pro-German speeches.

"In Palestine," said Donovan later, "I saw battalions made up of companies of Jews and of Arabs together, their political differences submerged in the need of a common defense."

When a handful of newspapermen caught up with Donovan in Jerusalem, as the *New York Times* correspondent put it, "the American observer today affably declined once more to reveal the impressions of his journey so far as political matters were concerned or divulge his destination, but he did not deny the possibility that he might go back to London before returning to America."

Donovan posed with journalists for the photographers and remarked that his last visit to the Holy Land had been in 1923. When his attention was called to the previous week's Berlin and Rome broadcasts charging he was giving gratuitous advice to the Balkan states and urging them to resist Axis pressure, he said with a chuckle, "Pity I hadn't heard the broadcasts. Why are they worrying about an ordinary American citizen traveling around with his bags?"

Then he pointed to Wadsworth, who was standing nearby. "There's your story," he said. "George and I were both born and grew up together in Buffalo, New York. We served together in Washington. You can call my visit to Palestine, reunion in Jerusalem."

Donovan made a side trip to Baghdad to talk to the premier of Iraq and to meet with Arab friends. In Baghdad, as everywhere else, he took time to get in touch with perceptive individuals whom he had met over the years. Somebody once called these men and women Donovan's moles. Many had climbed high in their own nation since he had first met them as young officers or as students, and now they were ready to help him set up an intelligence network.

He returned to Cairo on Friday, February 7. Abwehr agents checked his arrival and reported to Berlin that after staying only one night in the city, he departed for the Libyan front. Before leaving Cairo, Donovan met with Australian Prime Minister Robert G. Menzies, who had come to Egypt to learn details about British plans to deploy an Australian division in Greece.

"I saw the American unofficial ambassador, Colonel Donovan, in Cairo after his return from the Balkans," Menzies cabled to Acting Prime Minister A. W. Fadden in Canberra, "and he has stressed to the President of the United States the importance of the formation of a Balkan front."

Donovan had indeed cabled a dispatch to Roosevelt, and it covered far more than the Balkan front:

> Deterred by the magnitude of her task, Germany may abandon the attempt at invasion of England and, while continuing to strike at British shipping, may gamble on overrunning in a short war not only all the Balkans but Turkey as well. Russia's fear of this German encirclement may give us the one chance of securing her support. Germany deals with all theaters of operations as constituting one strategic front from the Atlantic to the Pacific, of which the Mediterranean from Spain to the Black Sea is an integral part. Whatever she does in one theater has its intended repercussions in another. For example, she may induce Japan to strike in the Far East simultaneously with any offensive she may make in the West.

On Monday, February 10, he was in Alexandria to visit the British eastern Mediterranean fleet, which had returned to its base after a running battle with Italian ships and German planes. The British were still convoying ships through the Mediterranean despite the Axis efforts to prevent them. Donovan found the British Navy willing to undertake transporting troops from Alexandria to Greece even if very little air cover was available. The Luftwaffe was known to have positioned a powerful striking force. Donovan delayed his departure from Cairo to confer with Anthony Eden, the new British foreign minister, who flew in from Gibraltar and Malta on February 19. They met at the British Embassy.

"After supper I had some talk with the ambassador, read the telegrams from home and finally had a discussion with Colonel William Donovan," wrote Eden in his memoirs. "He had been touring the Balkans for the United States government and was able to give me a firsthand account of recent developments. His blunt speech in those countries had been useful and I was grateful to him for waiting several days to see me. I asked him to send the President a message emphasizing that any action we might take in the Mediterranean would overstrain our shipping resources and inviting him to help if he could."

The day after he talked with Eden, Donovan filed a confidential report to Franklin Roosevelt. He said that the British should hold on in the Balkans to keep Hitler from invading the United Kingdom. He identified new German secret weapons as "huge land mines parachuted upon square-mile areas and self-propelled barges of soldiers three lines in width, guarded by submarines and canopied by an armada of planes."

Two days later, Eden had another long talk with Donovan. They discussed both the Turkish and the Greek situations. Eden explained that Turkey was Britain's traditional ally but that the needs of Greece were great. Since Britain did not possess enough strength to help both countries at the same time, which should it favor? "My frank reply was," Donovan said, "that I thought they should supply Greece for reasons moral, psychological, and military. If you abandon your tactical position now in your salient in Greece, I doubt if you can ever get it back. You can always go from there to Turkey, but once you leave, I don't see how you will ever get back."

Donovan's views on the critical importance of the Mediterranean in the future conduct of the war intrigued British leaders, as they were to fascinate War Department officials when he reached home in March.

> When you look at your map, try to look at it this way. Don't look upon the Mediterranean as a great arterial highway running from east to west, but draw a north and south axis, and then you see the Mediterra-

nean as a great no-man's-land between two lines of trenches, the northern line of trenches being the European continent as a theater of operation, a great strategic area running from Spain to the Black Sea. . . . On that line up to this moment, the Germans had domination excepting for one little toehold that the British had and which they tried to hang on to, and which was an important justification for their making the fight they did, apart from any moral obligation which they felt very strongly to go to the aid of their fighting ally. Now the southern line of trenches runs along the African continent, in which the British have a strong position in the Suez and west of it, but also where the Germans had an ever-widening salient, actually through that which was held by the Italians and potentially that which would come from the disintegration of the French Empire in North Africa.

What Germany was seeking to do in the fight between the two is shipping demoralization of the Mediterranean. What Germany was seeking to do was to seal up the Mediterranean, and she is trying to do that by closing the Suez and the Strait of Gibraltar, and then having sealed it up, would seek to mop it up by establishing her air bases on that three-pronged position of the Dodecanese and Sicily.

Donovan traveled by plane from Egypt to Malta and Gibraltar on Monday, February 24. The next morning he took the train through Seville to Madrid, where he arrived during the night. Hitler was pressuring Spain's dictator, Francisco Franco, to enter the war on the side of the Axis. American Ambassador Alexander Weddell had quarreled with Ramón Serrano Suñer, the pro-Hitler foreign minister, and for several weeks there had been no communication at all between the U.S. Embassy and the Ministry of Foreign Affairs. Donovan impatiently let the ministry know he would not be put off by any minor diplomatic storm. The morning after his arrival he met with Sir Samuel Hoare, a special British ambassador. Hoare wrote in his journal, "I have had a most interesting morning's conversation with Colonel Donovan. He struck me as first-class in every way, mentally, morally, and physically."

Donovan listened attentively to Hoare, who had been stationed in Spain's capital for nine months. Hoare wondered whether the Monroe Doctrine might be extended to Spain, which was clearly important for America's defense. He suggested that the United States should take the Spanish peninsula and the coast of Northwest Africa under its special protection. He further pointed out the importance of Spain in the strategy of the war. "From the point of view of the United Kingdom, the Spanish Peninsula is practically our only gate left in Europe," he told Donovan, "and the closing of the Strait of Gibraltar would greatly lengthen the war and add to our problems. If we could have a friendly Spain, it would give us the chance of a future offensive."

Hoare admitted that "some would say that the position is hopeless. If things go badly for us in Greece, there will be many people here who will resign themselves to German domination."

Franco, Serrano Suñer, Gen. Juan Vigon, and several of the generals, Hoare told Donovan, were "mesmerized by the size of the German military machine" and expected Germany to win. "Franco and Serrano Suñer also believe that a British victory would mean the end of all dictatorships in Europe, their own included."

Hoare urged that Roosevelt be advised to encourage Latin America to pressure Spain to stay neutral. The combined New World could play an important role in Spain. "If we can keep the peninsula out of the Axis," he concluded, "we frustrate Hitler's effort to conquer all Europe and we keep Spain and Portugal in the orbit of the oceanic powers, the United States and the British Empire, and prevent them being absorbed into Hitler's bloc."

Donovan did not see Serrano Suñer and Franco until the last day of February. Knowing that the United States alone had the oil that Spain needed, Donovan decided to take a hard line. "To both he spoke with almost brutal frankness," reported Hoare. "Serrano Suñer in particular he treated as if he were a prisoner in the dock. Using all his forensic ability he went through a long indictment that omitted nothing in the charge sheet, and left the minister almost speechless with fury. The minister's reactions were what might have been expected. His resentment against the United States became even more bitter than before."

Donovan argued for Spanish opposition to a German takeover, but Serrano Suñer shut off further discussion by saying that the Germans would easily win the war. He hoped for German victory, for then Spain would get Gibraltar and recognition of her claims in Africa. Nevertheless, Spain would "remain aloof" from the struggle "until its honor, interests, or dignity were in question."

Donovan's hectoring attitude toward the foreign minister was calculated to draw indiscretions from the choleric Spaniard, and Donovan was able to report what Serrano Suñer believed would be the results of a German victory in Europe:

> The self-appointed destiny of the German race is to create a new Europe and a new world under Nazi domination. The thirty or forty states which composed Europe and Africa and Asia were too many states. It was necessary to have a single center of European ideology, European military strength, European commercial planning. Force is the basis of all social relationship. Conquered nations and conquered areas must be reduced to a state of permanent inferiority as has already been done in Czechoslovakia and Poland. The German race is the master race.
>
> Only certain parts of the conquered territory, as was explained to me

by Mr. Suñer, the Spanish foreign minister, are to be incorporated into the larger Germany. The areas not so included would be governed by local Nazi leaders and grouped around the Reich in a colonial pattern, their production and their labor contributing to the improved standard of living of the master race, while being forced to reduce their own. Labor unions will be abolished. Anti-Semitism enforced.

"For myself the talk was a tonic," Hoare wrote of Donovan's interview with Serrano Suñer in his journal, "as it showed President Roosevelt's keen interest in the affairs of Spain.

"Most important of all, the world of Madrid soon heard of the strong line that Colonel Donovan had taken and concluded from it that, so far from the war being ended, a new chapter was soon to begin with the formidable participation of the United States."

The night after Donovan met with Serrano Suñer and Franco, the Spanish dictator wrote a letter to Hitler declining to enter the war. Franco did not mention Donovan by name, but Hitler had no difficulty in realizing exactly who had pressured him into turning down Germany's invitation to join the battle.

In subsequent talks Donovan found other Spanish leaders not so certain of a German victory. He stressed how American aid could prevent Hitler from exploiting shortages in Spain to draw the nation into the war. Donovan reported that many of the Spanish generals opposed the Falangist leaders' conviction that Germany would win the war and rejected the idea that Spain should remain faithful to the Nazi cause.

On the first day of March, Donovan flew to Lisbon, where he talked for an hour with the premier of Portugal, Antonio de Oliveira Salazar. Salazar listened to Donovan with apparent favor, and Donovan went away thinking that he was "one of the best intellectually of the statesmen of Europe, who does not want Germany to win but who fears that she will." As for Salazar, he was skeptical of Donovan because he suspected the United States of being interested in making the Azores into a strategic American base. He confided in the Italian ambassador that Donovan lectured him "like a schoolmaster" and had "quizzed him about his ideas on the future of the world and so on."

The ambassador reported to Rome, and Rome shared the impression with Berlin. Oswald Baron von Hayningen-Hesse was also in Lisbon during Donovan's brief visit, and he passed on to Berlin information he picked up about the Donovan–Salazar meeting.

By that evening Donovan was in Seville, from where he went to Gibraltar. On Monday, March 3, he arrived in London. When the British press cornered him at the railroad station, he replied only, "I do not think there is anything to say." The following day Churchill took him to see the king at Buckingham Palace so the sovereign could hear his report and express Britain's appreciation for his remarkable mission.

Donovan had adroitly represented both his own country and Great Britain. That evening Donovan and American Ambassador John G. Winant dined with Churchill.

According to Thomas Troy, Donovan "briefed and was briefed. He was asked to go before the joint board and discuss the hard decision to aid Greece. He went to lunch with the War Cabinet and with the chiefs of staff. He was thoroughly briefed on the organization of SOE [Special Operations Executive] and visited some of its training establishments. With the director of censorship he discussed the problem of getting control of enemy communications. With Britain's home security chief he went into the problem of frustrating Nazi efforts to subvert Allied and neutral seamen in American ports."

Churchill and Donovan had long talks at Downing Street and at Chartwell. According to William J. Casey, they "found themselves in tune in boldness, in imagination, in openness to new ideas, in readiness to innovate and to act. . . . Churchill saw that Donovan returned with a thorough knowledge of the intelligence service which England had developed over five centuries and of the way Britain was nourishing resistance in the occupied nations of Europe pursuant to Winston Churchill's dramatic order to 'set Europe ablaze.' Out of this perspective and knowledge came the OSS."

"During his last few days in London, Colonel Donovan spent much time in gathering together supplementary reports on the Mediterranean theater," wrote Conyers Read.

> He also fortified himself with further material based upon British war experience. More particularly he pursued his study of psychological warfare and of guerrilla operations. He had noted the efficiency of German sabotage and secret intelligence in the Mediterranean theater and he made it his business to find out all he could about British efforts in those directions.
>
> It was at this time also that he secured a description of the organization which was responsible for the conduct of sabotage in enemy-occupied areas and for the supply of resistance groups. In detail he sought to answer such questions as these: How did the British recruit their personnel? What were their plans? In what walks of life are the best men found? In business? Law? Diplomacy? What sort of special training has proved necessary? With what other government agencies has it proved desirable—and possible—to cooperate particularly closely? How was security—secrecy—best maintained? Has any attempt been made to coordinate all British military and other intelligence and if so what has been the result of the attempt?

Donovan interrupted his investigations on March 8 to make a quick air trip to Dublin and back at the request of Roosevelt and Churchill. The threat of an invasion of the British Isles had receded, and there was less concern that the Germans might strike at Ireland, but it was as critical as ever that the Irish allow Great Britain to use their ports to counter the German submarine menace. During lunch with Prime Minister Eamon de Valera and the cardinal from Northern Ireland, Donovan was incensed when the prelate remarked that he did not see much difference between a Nazi victory and British dominion, and he blistered the churchman with his opinion of the anti-British myopia shown by some Irish. De Valera would not make a commitment to the Allied cause.

Not long afterward, Australian Prime Minister Menzies arrived in Dublin to see De Valera. "The people of this 'distressful country,'" he wrote in a memorandum, "or at any rate those who govern it, are in a state of exaggerated self-consciousness. They are not very realistic in their approach to the problems of the war. They are ready to take offense. They resented the fact that Colonel Donovan's visit was only for a couple of hours. They feel, and I think with some justification, that their point of view has been either not examined or impatiently examined. These comments are specially true of De Valera himself."

Churchill was pleased with Donovan's trip to Dublin, and he cabled Roosevelt, "I must thank you for the magnificent work done by Donovan, in his prolonged tour of the Balkans and the Middle East. He has carried with him throughout an animating, heartwarming flame."

When Donovan had completed briefing British leaders concerning his trip through the Balkans and the Middle East and had gathered the answers to his questions, he flew to Portugal. There on Friday, March 14, he rendezvoused with Averell Harriman, who had crossed the Atlantic on his own mission on behalf of the President. The two presidential envoys chatted at the Hotel Palacio in Estoril, which Harriman characterized as a "nest of spies." Pinto, the concierge at the Palacio, remembered the conference. "All the Allied agents stayed at the Palacio," he explained years later. "The Axis agents stayed at the Hotel de Parque, which is just across the gardens. The waiters, chambermaids, busboys, pages, porters, bartenders were all on somebody's payroll. When an agent went into the casino, he didn't go there to gamble; he went there to place an undetected phone call to Switzerland, another nest of spies." Even so, one Berlin agent always concluded his phone conversations with, "Good-bye. Good-bye also to my British friends, wherever you are!"

In this environment Donovan and Harriman spoke softly together in a room that had been checked carefully for bugs. Lloyd V. Steere, a U.S. Department of Agriculture expert, joined the discussions to report on the condition of Britain's farms and how the United States could integrate its own food production into the British supply picture. Then

Harriman flew off to England, and Donovan, after a night's sleep and a round of conferences, continued by Yankee Clipper over the South Atlantic route to the United States.

The day after St. Patrick's Day he stepped out of the Clipper at La Guardia. He was almost expansive with the press at the pier.

"I've been a good many miles—about 25,000. I have seen a lot of warfare and I've seen too how important the administrative and maintenance side of war is," he said, "and from all I have learned, I hope I'll be able to give information of value to our country."

When a reporter remarked that Secretary of the Navy Knox had said Donovan was traveling at his own expense and had no official status, Donovan replied, "The secretary does not need corroboration." Donovan left almost immediately for Washington, and the next morning while he, Harry Hopkins, and Frank Knox ate breakfast with the President, Donovan made the first of a series of oral reports to Roosevelt. Conyers Read summarized this report:

> So far as the Mediterranean is concerned, he was most intent on pointing out both the dangers and the opportunities to America in the French position in Northwest Africa. He thought that it ought to be exploited; that the Arabs and the French in North Africa distrusted the imperial pretensions of the British and that French officialdom had not forgotten the destruction of the French fleet by the British at Oran. Nor had they forgotten the abortive effort of De Gaulle, assisted by the British, at Dakar. On that account Donovan insisted that in any American military operation in Northwest Africa, psychological or otherwise, the British should play a definitely subordinate part and De Gaulle should be omitted altogether. Donovan was, however, definitely of the opinion that any operations in that quarter should be supported by some French general whom the French themselves would respect as a leader.
>
> The point upon which Donovan, in his report to the President, laid greatest emphasis, was the enormous importance of psychological—or as the British called it, political—warfare in the current struggle. He dwelt at some length on German techniques, emphasized their success and insisted that the United States should make ready to fight with the same weapon.

Roosevelt left that afternoon for a trip to Florida, and Donovan's time with him was cut short. "This period of time was totally inadequate to convey the full meaning and significance of what he had learned on the mission," asserted William R. Corson in *The Armies of Ignorance.*

> But then as now, the White House palace guard—in this case in the person of Hopkins—acted to hoard the precious commodity known as the "president's time" for their own purposes. The impact of Donovan's conclu-

sions and recommendations was thus greatly lessened. As a result, Donovan's shortened remarks were later damned with faint praise by others in the administration, and his ideas were put down on the spurious grounds of his being overly pro-British. It was a bum rap, and although Donovan was permitted to take to the airways in a coast-to-coast radio speech to describe in highly sanitized terms what he had seen and concluded, the administration ascribed no real urgency to his recommendations. To be sure, the decision to convoy protection assistance was soon forthcoming, but scant credence was given to Donovan's recommendation that the United States go all out to give the British the means to attack and knock Italy out of the war.

Donovan was discovering the frustration that most American agents at all levels experience. The Washington bureaucracy was—as it still is—a labyrinth through which its inhabitants picked their way with great care, and everything that came to their attention was considered and weighed in terms of how it affected the political situation at hand. Hopkins was only doing what comes naturally to any man who has survived in the American political jungle long enough to become an intimate of a president. Even with Europe on fire, politics in Washington went on as usual.

Time magazine was far more glowing about Donovan's trip. "Colonel Donovan had been on an assignment that any professional reporter would have given his left leg to get. He had been in England under bombardment, in North Africa with the British Empire Forces, in the Albanian Mountains with the Greeks. He had inspected ordnance, shipping, signal corps, maintenance depots. He had slept in sleeping bags on desert sands, on the jogging backs of mules. He had talked to kings, prime ministers, generals, admirals."

Time observed that no newspaper had gotten Donovan's story. "A good soldier first, Colonel Donovan reported first to his Commander-in-Chief, Franklin Roosevelt."

23

The Intelligence Proposal

AFTER LEAVING the President, Donovan discussed his trip with Frank Knox and then telephoned Secretary of War Stimson. Stimson and Donovan met in Stimson's office. "We talked for an hour or an hour and a half, and it was very interesting," wrote Stimson in his diary. "He has played quite an important part diplomatically in the situation during his trip, and he and I stood over the map for a long time talking only in the way in which two old friends who are interested in military affairs can do it." The situation in the Atlantic was particularly black, Donovan told Stimson, and the United States should begin soon to convoy British shipping.

Later in the day Donovan briefed high-ranking navy officers, and on the next morning at Stimson's invitation he talked to the military brass at the War Department. Donovan chronicled his trip in detail and again emphasized the importance of protecting British shipping so that Lend-Lease supplies would reach England.

"I thought," he said, "that if . . . [the British] ever hoped to defeat the German Army, they could not do it in France, where she could get her full strength but that they would have to pull her off base where she would have to fight in a more constricted way and therefore she could be trimmed down to their size; and I thought England would have to take the initiative in a new theater of operations which would be the Mediterranean."

In the days that followed, Donovan shuttled back and forth between New York and Washington. He discussed his findings with Secretary of State Hull and other key State Department officials, Chief of Staff General Marshall, and Chief of Naval Operations Admiral Stark. He dined with the Senate and House Military Affairs committees. Then he dropped out of sight to prepare a nationwide radio address, which had been decided upon at the White House breakfast. He spent Sunday evening, March 23, with poet Archibald MacLeish, at the time librarian of Congress. The next morning MacLeish wrote to Donovan:

> I have thought a great deal about our conversation of last night, and the more I think about it, the more I am convinced that my first reaction was the right one. This speech should be in form and manner what it actually is—a report to the people of the country by one of their fellow

citizens, a soldier, who has just returned from a trip through the asbestos curtain and back and who is talking to them about the things he has seen and felt and heard. What you did last night was exactly that, and what I would like to hear you do would be the same thing again. In other words, I wish you would walk up and down your room and dictate a speech that would sound like your last night's talk—about the best talk I have heard in my life.

On Tuesday, March 25, Donovan, Stimson, and Knox, as well as General Marshall and Admiral Stark, held a conference with the heads of the British air, land, and sea services. The British were at first reluctant to admit their nation's dire predicament. "We finally got the Englishmen talking frankly and fully about the situation," noted Stimson in his diary. "They agreed, each one of them, that they could not, with their present naval forces, assume the entire escort duty that is required to protect the convoys of munitions to Great Britain. They also agreed and admitted that the food shortage in Great Britain was becoming alarming. We discussed some interesting points about methods of convoy; posts from which the patrolling airplanes should be sent out. I was interested to hear Admiral Stark say that in his opinion the most important part of our work was to get at once into the convoying."

The next day Donovan broadcast his report to the nation over all three networks. His speech was a call to arms.

> I have been given an opportunity to study at first hand these great battles going on in the Atlantic and in the Mediterranean, in Africa, in Greece, and in Albania. From my observations I have been able to form my conclusions on the basis of full information. These conclusions I will submit to my country for its use in furtherance of our national defense, an essential part of which is our policy of aid to Great Britain.
>
> We have no choice as to whether or not we will be attacked. That choice is Hitler's and he has already made it, not for Europe alone, but for Africa, Asia, and the world. Our only choice is to decide whether or not we will resist it. And to choose in time; while resistance is still possible, while others are still alive to stand beside us.
>
> Let us keep this in mind. Germany is a formidable, a resourceful, and a ruthless foe. Do not underrate her. If we do, we deceive ourselves. Her victories have brought her new military and industrial strength. She got the jump at the start of the war and has kept it; but not yet has she made a full test. And until this test comes, it is better not to overrate her. But her greatest gains have been made through fear. Fear of the might of her war machine. So she has played upon that fear, and her recent victories are the product.
>
> But we must remember that there is a moral force in wars that in the long run is stronger than any machine. And I say to you, my fellow citizens, all that Mr. Churchill has told you on the resolution and determination and valor and confidence of his people is true.

Donovan informed the public of his conviction that assistance given to England under the Lend-Lease bill "is going to mean nothing in winning the war unless the goods we produce and ship reach their destination. Are we going to deliver the goods? This question must be answered now. Are we prepared to take the chance? For there is a chance. There is a danger, and whatever we do we must recognize that the danger of attack exists."

What Donovan told the American people was much the same thing he had told the leaders of every nation in the Balkans. The response from the isolationists was bitter. He was vilified not only by Goebbels and the German propaganda machine but by newspapers and magazines in the United States as well. Donovan struck back over the next few months in speeches throughout the country.

While the public storm raged, Donovan made a significant report to Knox and Stimson:

> Although the commandos in Britain are somewhat similar to the independent company of the days of the Black Prince, the modern unit had its origin as a result of the Battle of France. In June, 1940, Britain did exactly the same thing that the Boers, Pathans, Afghans, and Arabs have done when they had suffered a hard blow from a powerful force. Britain withdrew her army within her own country and waited for the enemy to come in and fight. The Imperial General Staff recognized that under such conditions in South Africa, the northwestern frontier of India, Mesopotamia, and Palestine, such a movement would have been a signal for a guerrilla band to embark upon a war of attrition. With these lessons in mind, the Imperial General Staff made its first task after Dunkirk the creation of a special force of British guerrillas.

At the end of March, Donovan urged President Roosevelt to consider the advisability of developing a commando force in the United States. He pointed out that the Germans were "big league professionals" in orthodox war and that America had only just begun to rearm and was still a "bush league club." Donovan believed it would take at least two years to raise, equip, and train an army that could hope to beat Germany in a straight fight. America, Donovan told the President, must "play a bush league game, stealing the ball and killing the umpire."

At the same time, he urged Roosevelt to undertake psychological-political warfare, sabotage, and special intelligence operations to be combined with a guerrilla operation under a unified command. "Donovan saw all these instruments as part of an integrated whole," wrote Allen Dulles, "and he presented a plan for an organization which would create and direct them."

Donovan had crystallized his thoughts about the type of organization he believed would serve the United States against Germany and its allies. Roosevelt was convinced that Donovan, who alone among his advisers had seen the war at first hand, was right, but he was held back from taking action by his political fear of the isolationists. Donovan's plan leaked to Brig. Gen. Sherman Miles, assistant chief of staff for intelligence, who on April 8 wrote to General Marshall: "In great confidence ONI [the Office of Naval Intelligence] tells me that there is considerable reason to believe that there is a movement on foot, fostered by Col. Donovan, to establish a super agency controlling all intelligence. This would mean that such an agency, no doubt under Col. Donovan, would collect, collate, and possibly even evaluate all military intelligence which we now gather from foreign countries. From the point of view of the War Department, such a move would appear to be very disadvantageous, if not calamitous."

The inherent tendency of a bureaucrat to protect his own bailiwick and his customary way of doing things had come into play. Just back from his close-up look at the agony of the Old World, Donovan might be concerned with ways in which Hitler could be defeated, but army and navy intelligence officers were just as concerned about how Donovan's radical new ideas would affect their established organizations and their own careers.

On March 25, the day before Donovan's nationwide speech, the Yugoslavs Cvetković and Cinkar-Marković signed the Axis Pact in Vienna. That night young King Peter was taken for a middle-of-the-night auto ride and agreed to claim his throne. Simović and a group of officers rallied around the young king and overthrew Prince Paul. The Yugoslav people responded with patriotic fervor to the king's disavowal of the German alliance.

Hitler was both astounded and angry. He was furious with German intelligence for not warning him of the impending Yugoslav coup d'etat, and he blamed the entire upset on William J. Donovan. On April 6, German soldiers invaded both Yugoslavia and Greece in what Goebbels's propagandists called Colonel Donovan's War. The campaign was short and brutal, since the Greeks, the Yugoslavs, and the British Expeditionary Force put ashore in Greece were poorly equipped and outnumbered. On April 27, the Germans raised the swastika over the Acropolis.

In the United States the isolationist press picked up Goebbels's charges that Donovan had instigated the Yugoslav uprising and therefore made it necessary for Germany to attack the Balkans. Donovan characterized the charges as "poppycock and tripe" during an interview by newspapermen in Chicago.

"The statement that I had the ear of the President is also wrong," he said. "I do not have the ear of the President."

When reporters remarked that German broadcasts had labeled him

Washington's number two agent provocateur, he blandly asked, "Who is number one, I wonder?"

That same day in Chicago, Donovan spoke before a Chicago Council on Foreign Relations luncheon at the Palmer House. He told his audience that Germany had to win the war in 1941 or not win at all.

> This year is going to be a bad year. Germany is making every possible effort to end the war this year and for a very obvious reason. Her resources are under strain. Her lifeline is oil. And the comfortable limit of that supply cannot be based beyond next year.
>
> But it is not only because Germany is under economic strain now and will face economic disaster in the future that I tell you the war is not lost. There is an additional factor. Germany is a totally militarized state, and like all totally militarized states, her military power is at once her strength and her weakness.
>
> In a totally militarized state the army is the nation—materially and psychologically. So long as the German Army is everywhere victorious, Germany is great, powerful, and apparently irresistible. But it is equally true that the moment the German Army is not everywhere victorious, Germany is no longer great, is no longer powerful, but is on the contrary in the greatest danger. Her strength is her vulnerability, for the German nation has no other spirit, no other force than its army. And the army, though it may be everywhere successful for a time, will not be everywhere successful always.
>
> Defeats will come, perhaps this year, certainly next, and when they come, the disintegration of Germany will be as sudden and complete as her present power seems perfect and impervious.

Donovan also urged that the United States convoy shipping to Britain.

"Should we convoy now?" a Chicagoan asked.

"I think we should have begun convoying yesterday," he said.

Donovan's denials that he was responsible for Donovan's War failed to convince many people. His assertions seem particularly hollow in view of Winston Churchill's later remark that Donovan's visit to Yugoslavia alone resulted in a disastrous upset for Hitler's timetable of conquest. Churchill pointed out that short-lived as Yugoslavia's resistance was, it was enough to postpone by at least five weeks Germany's planned assault on the Soviet Union. This undoubtedly contributed to the final German catastrophe in Russia.

Under the auspices of the Fight for Freedom Committee, Donovan went on a speaking tour through the Midwest and to San Francisco. The committee scheduled his appearances in cities where Charles Lindbergh, the aviation hero turned isolationist leader, had just spoken. On May 22 Donovan went to Atlantic City to debate the University of Chicago's Robert M. Hutchins over a national network. The subject of the debate was "Should America Enter the War Now?" Donovan's firsthand knowledge of events across the Atlantic proved an overwhelming strength in his speeches and in the debate.

Archibald MacLeish helped Donovan draw together ideas for the debate with Hutchins. "Yes, we should have been in the fight long ago," stated Donovan's notes.

> Men of the type of Hutchins are those who have weakened American resolve and have kept us from assuming our moral responsibilities by fanning to flame the smoldering embers of selfishness and fear. They have built up a false hope in the hearts of many people that we can hide from a revolution. They have misled the country concerning our self-sufficiency in case of a Nazi victory and the possibility of retaining any of our present standards. They have willfully ignored the true meaning of democracy in proclaiming that we can lose what is really a spiritual conviction by fighting to defend it. They have fallen even lower in the moral scale by their presumptuous demand that we make America perfect before we dare help our neighbor.
>
> What does Hutchins think an attack consists of? We have been attacked in the sense that everything we believe in is being torn down before our eyes—we have German agents among us preaching just what Hutchins preaches; dividing America; telling us our democracy is worthless and so forth. We have full knowledge of the way they plan to bring about our capitulation by economic pressure, false promises, and the help of our Hutchins, Lindberghs, Hoovers, Wheelers, Nyes, et al.

On June 8, Donovan boarded a plane and happened to sit down next to educator Eugene Grassman, who was too busy preparing a speech of his own to talk to him. When they left the plane in New York, they waited together for their bags. Donovan told Grassman about his findings in Europe and concluded, "The battle will be won here. This is the real seat of the struggle. If they can divide our people and keep us out, the English won't have much chance. But if we are solid and stick and get in and produce as we can, we will win."

Donovan made dozens of speeches while at the same time quietly helping to shape his country's intelligence plans. His speeches further incensed the German government. "We hate the Knoxes, Frankfurters, Morgenthaus, and that 'smart aleck' Donovan, but we also know that the great majority of American people do not think their way," a spokesman said. "These gentlemen and their ilk make themselves self-appointed enemies of the Axis and indeed, one might say, of the European continent, but with the American people we have no quarrel. Obviously the prognosis of these gentlemen regarding the indubitable efficacy of American aid to Yugoslavia and Greece has been proven so wrong and Donovan proved such a nincompoop that they must befuddle the American people with vocal strength rather than logic."

President Roosevelt listened with careful interest to Bill Donovan's views on an integrated intelligence service for the United States. Writing about the intelligence problem that Roosevelt confronted in the spring of 1941, Conyers Read said:

> Anywhere from two million to ten million words of strategic information were pouring into Washington every day in reports from all sorts of observers all over the world. Army (MIS) and Navy (ONI) Intelligence, the FBI, the diplomatic and consular services, the Departments of Commerce and Agriculture, Treasury, the Immigration Service, the Coast Guard, and many others received these reports. There was, however, no adequate system for correlating this enormous mass of information, for supplementing it or for analyzing and presenting it in readily comprehensible form to the men who were supposed to base their decisions and actions upon it. A very considerable proportion of this great mass of material went to the President himself—so much of it that he could not possibly read it all, still less digest it.

Roosevelt appointed a special cabinet committee made up of Stimson, Knox, and Attorney General Robert Jackson to study the intelligence problem. They asked Bill Donovan to present his ideas, which he did without delay. He also discussed his intelligence proposals with John G. Winant, ambassador to Great Britain; Winant in turn took them up with the President. While the cabinet committee was working with Donovan, FBI Director J. Edgar Hoover and General Miles of Army Intelligence were embroiled in a jurisdictional battle over intelligence operations. Their battle complicated matters still further. In early June the cabinet report favoring Donovan's ideas reached Roosevelt. The President, who was exasperated by the intransigence and narrow-minded bickering of Miles and Hoover, decided that an integrated strategic intelligence service was long overdue.

That spring of 1941 Bill Stephenson was blunt in his discussions with Bill Donovan. The two men met often in Stephenson's apartment in New York's Hampshire House overlooking Central Park. There they talked about America's intelligence needs. Britain would share its intelligence reports with the United States, Stephenson said, but could Britain be counted on to tell America everything if the interests of the two nations should diverge? Why shouldn't America pull its own weight in the vital field of intelligence and special operations? He explained to Donovan how his work as the British Security Coordinator in New York was complicated by the confusion and jealousies among the overlapping intelligence agencies in Washington with which he had to deal. These agencies were as much concerned with their prestige and selfish interests as they were in doing the job that Donovan more than any other American must know so badly needed doing. Stephenson demanded to know what the United States would do if it had to go to war without a modern intelligence service. Later, after Donovan's death, Stephenson wrote, "I had discussed and argued with him the necessity for the United States government to establish an agency for conducting secret activities throughout the world—an agency with which I could collaborate fully by virtue of its being patterned in the matter of coordination functions after my own organization. Early he agreed in principle."

Donovan, although no friend of Hoover's since their first days together in the Department of Justice, gave J. Edgar and his G-men grudging admiration; but particularly after his last fact-finding trip into the Balkans and the Middle East, he realized that Stephenson was right. The FBI and the other conflicting agencies could not give the United States an intelligence apparatus that could compete against the Abwehr. He not only had lunch with the cabinet committee to talk about the problem, but he used every opportunity to urge the President to establish a central intelligence authority at once.

One day as Donovan talked to the President, Roosevelt remarked, almost as if the thought had just occurred to him, "We have no intelligence service." Donovan realized that it was just a question of time before FDR would take the necessary action and that most likely he himself would be asked to create the service.

During late spring the British and Americans cooperated in intelligence matters as best they could. Donovan persuaded Roosevelt to approve an arrangement by which Stephenson was to work closely with the FBI on counterespionage within the United States. Urgent positive intelligence was to be given immediately by Churchill to the President over a direct line that had been established between the two leaders. On less urgent matters Stephenson and Donovan were to be the go-betweens. All of these arrangements were kept secret from Secretary of State Cordell Hull and Foreign Minister Anthony Eden, who were considered too bound up in diplomatic protocol to be of any use.

From his headquarters in the International Building at Rockefeller Center, Stephenson mounted a campaign to persuade Roosevelt that America needed an intelligence organization of its own and that Donovan was the man to direct it. Then on May 25, Admiral Godfrey came from London, bringing with him his personal assistant, Ian Fleming. Dressed in blue suits of conservative cut, they stepped off the Yankee Clipper in New York posing as two British businessmen. To their discomfort as they came ashore, they saw a parcel of press photographers waiting on the pier. They were only partly relieved when they learned that the press reception was not for them but for Madame Schiaparelli, whose svelte charms were soon being photographed for the evening papers. (That night Admiral Godfrey and Commander Fleming appeared in the background of newspaper photos of the chic Frenchwoman arriving in New York.) They went from La Guardia to Bill Donovan's apartment, where they stayed during their visit to New York.

Godfrey and Fleming were presumably in America to establish better liaison between British Naval Intelligence and the FBI and ONI, but they soon found themselves balked by Hoover's intransigence and the complete disarray of American intelligence. Stephenson had no difficulty enlisting Godfrey and Fleming in his effort to convince Roosevelt to establish a unified intelligence service.

On Sunday, June 1, Bill Donovan drove a car up to a side street at Rockefeller Center; Bill Stephenson stepped out of a doorway and slipped into the seat beside him. The two men drove north across the border into Canada. That night at Dorval Airport, Montreal, they climbed into the gun turret of a brand new B-24 bomber that was being flown to Scotland. Late on Monday they landed at Prestwick and boarded the night train for London. The blacked-out train traveled at a crawl and had to stop several times because of German air-raid alarms.

In London, Donovan conferred with British leaders. Then on Friday, June 6, he and Stephenson were driven to Woburn Abbey on the Duke of Bedford's estate where security men, dressed as gamekeepers, kept away the curious from the small group who had masterminded the Ultra secret. Donovan found himself in the drawing room with Britain's top intelligence leaders.

"Gentlemen," said Reginald Leeper, chief of British Political Intelligence, when everyone was gathered in the room.

> I have been authorized by the prime minister to reveal to you a piece of secret information which has been known to Mr. Churchill and the chiefs of staff for several weeks. He permits me to tell you—and you only—in order that we may concert our plans, that Hitler is to attack Soviet Russia. The actual invasion is expected around the middle of June. The estimate is Sunday, the twenty-second, which is to say two weeks and two days from now. You will not make notes of what I tell you, nor can you prepare any specific action until the day itself. You are each responsible for sections that will come into play when the Germans move.

Not many in the room believed that the Germans would achieve complete surprise in their attack. Donovan was not so sure. In any case, Stephenson and he returned to the United States immediately after the meeting. When Donovan reported to Roosevelt that the British did not intend to share their intelligence discovery with the Soviet Union, he said, "Stalin might have faced reality. But the British regard the whole Bletchley apparatus as far too secret. They feel they can use their information to gain advantage in other ways."

"Colonel 'Wild Bill' Donovan was, at the outset of the war, a hero in search of a role," commented CIA historian Thomas Troy. If America went to war, what was the role to be? He had been considered a possible secretary of war, had worked for draft legislation, helped Knox settle into his job as secretary of the navy, been instrumental in arranging for the transfer of aged American destroyers to the British Navy, and fought for U.S. naval escorts for British-bound shipping. There had been speculation the previous December that he might be named U.S. ambassador to Britain. He might head a bureau for what Roosevelt called "constructive counterespionage work" or head a "sort of ballyhoo committee" on behalf of the administration's foreign policy. He might head the national savings bond drive. Donovan had already undertaken two of the most important diplomatic and intelligence missions ever given to an American citizen.

During his last interview with Stimson before leaving for London on December 7, 1940, Donovan had brought up the possibility that he might be given a military command in the field. The World War I hero wanted very much to join the fray. Stimson noted that Donovan said that what he would like more than anything else was "the toughest division in the whole outfit."

As early as April 1, 1941, news reports indicated that Donovan would be named to administer the Lend-Lease Act. Donovan merely smiled when reporters asked him to verify this or that rumor as to his future.

In late May Roosevelt asked him to draw up a proposal for psychological warfare and the development of intelligence. Donovan set about drafting a memorandum. Ian Fleming was then a house guest in his Georgetown home. Never loath to suggest in later years that he had played a significant role in the founding of the OSS, Fleming was fond of showing off a .38 Police Positive Colt revolver bearing the inscription "For Special Services." The weapon, he claimed, was given to him by none other than the American master spy, Wild Bill Donovan. Fleming never spelled out exactly what the "special services" were, and hardly anybody believed him. In fact, Donovan did give the pistol to Fleming, and Fleming's services were considerable.

Sitting down with pen and paper in Donovan's home, Fleming drafted ideas that Donovan was to consider as he prepared his memo. Fleming suggested that although the United States was presumably neutral in the war, American officers at embassies and consulates should carry out clandestine intelligence work. Secretaries, assistant attachés, cipher clerks, and technical advisers could all help, in collaboration with British agents. They could train with the British Secret Intelligence in England. "These U.S. officers must have trained powers of observation, analysis, and evaluation," wrote Fleming, "absolute discretion, sobriety, devotion to duty, languages and wide experience and be aged about forty to fifty."

According to Fleming, the new U.S. intelligence might concentrate in Stockholm to gather information about the German Navy and in Istanbul to learn what Russia's intentions might be. Before the United States withdrew its diplomatic representatives from Axis nations, it should infiltrate agents bearing neutral passports. American secret intelligence, said Fleming, "should be under the protection of a strong government department and it should be insured by every means possible against political interference or control. Furthermore, it should not be controlled by the FBI, which has no conception of offensive intelligence and is incapable of a strategic mentality."

Some intelligence experts say that Fleming even wrote the memorandum that Donovan was to take to the White House. This is far from the truth, for Donovan called upon his own experiences dating back to his days in the Siberia of Admiral Kolchak. He had a firsthand familiarity with British cloak-and-dagger experience long before he met Fleming. He had long been aware of how Washington bureaucratic and political connivance so often inhibited action. He discussed his report with Secretary Knox, Secretary Stimson, Assistant Secretary of War John J. McCloy, Ambassador Winant, playwright and Roosevelt speech writer Robert Sherwood, and Vincent Astor to get their ideas. He told journalist Wallace R. Deuel that he "talked to everybody who would listen." He appreciated the expertise of a highly capable English agent, but Fleming was hardly Donovan's ghostwriter.

In later years Donovan paid tribute to William Stephenson's contributions to his thinking, saying, "The proposals for the establishment of a service for strategic information, including political, military, and economic intelligence submitted to the President in June, 1941, were to a great extent based upon ideas, appraisals, and experiences of Mr. Stephenson, learned from thorough and detailed discussions with him and his staff."

On June 10, 1941, Donovan submitted to the President a document entitled "Memorandum of Establishment of Service of Strategic Information." "Strategy without information upon which it can rely is helpless," Donovan advised Roosevelt.

> Likewise, information is useless unless it is intelligently directed to the strategic purpose. Modern warfare depends upon the economic base—upon the supply of raw materials, on the capacity and performance of the industrial plant, on the scope of agricultural production, and upon the character and efficiency of communications. Strategic reserves will determine the strength of the attack and the resistance of the defense. Steel and gasoline constitute these reserves as much as do men and powder. The width and depth of terrain occupied by the present-day army exacts an equally wide and deep network of operational lines. The "depth

of strategy" depends upon the "depth of armament." The commitment of all the resources of a nation, moral as well as material, constitutes what is called total war. To anticipate every intention as to the mobilization and employment of these forces is a difficult task. General von Bernhardi says, "We must try by correctly foreseeing what is coming, to anticipate developments and thereby to gain an advantage which our opponents cannot overcome on the field of battle. That is what the future expects us to do."

Although we are facing imminent peril, we are lacking in effective services for analyzing, comprehending, and appraising such information as we might obtain (or in some cases have obtained) relative to the intention of potential enemies and the limit of the economic and military resources of these enemies. Our mechanism of collecting information is inadequate. It is true we have intelligence units in the Army and Navy. We can assume that through these units our fighting services can obtain technical information in time of peace, have available immediate operation information in time of war, and, on certain occasions, obtain "spot" news as to enemy movements. But these services cannot, out of the very nature of things, obtain that accurate, comprehensive, long-range information without which no strategic board can plan for the future. And we have arrived at the moment when there must be plans laid down for the spring of 1942.

We have scattered through the various departments of our government, documents and memoranda concerning military and naval and air and economic potentials of the Axis, which, if gathered together and studied in detail by carefully selected trained minds, with a knowledge both of the related languages and techniques, would yield valuable and often decisive results.

Central analysis of this information is as presently important for our supply program as if we were actually engaged in armed conflict. It is unimaginable that Germany would engage in a seven-billion-dollar supply program without first studying in detail the productive capacity of her actual and potential enemies. It is because she does exactly this that she displays such a mastery of the secrecy, timing, and effectiveness of her attacks.

Even if we participate to no greater extent than we do now, it is essential that we set up a central enemy intelligence organization, which would itself collect either directly or through existing departments of Government, at home and abroad, pertinent information concerning potential enemies, the character and strength of their armed forces, their internal economic organization, their principal channels of supply, the morale of their troops and their people, and their relations with their neighbors or allies.

For example, in the economic field there are many weapons that can be used against the enemy. But in our Government these weapons are distributed through several different departments. How and when to use them is of vital interest, not only to the Commander-in-Chief, but to each of the departments concerned. All departments should have the same information upon which economic warfare could be determined.

But there is another element of modern warfare, and that is the psychological attack against the moral and spiritual defenses of a nation. In this attack the most powerful weapon is radio. The use of radio as a weapon, though effectively employed by Germany, is still to be perfected. But this perfection can be realized only by planning, and planning is dependent on accurate information. From this information action can be carried out by the appropriate agencies.

Donovan maintained that the central intelligence agency should be responsible directly to the President, with an advisory panel to consist of the director of the FBI, representatives of Army and Naval Intelligence, and other officials concerned.

"The basic purpose of this Service of Strategic Information," he concluded, "is to constitute means by which the President as Commander-in-Chief and his strategic board would have available accurate and complete reports upon which military operational decisions could be based."

While Donovan was working on his report, Admiral Godfrey was unsuccessfully attempting to make an appointment to see the President. When Arthur Sulzberger of the *New York Times* said that he could arrange for Godfrey to meet with Mrs. Roosevelt, the British intelligence officer agreed that this was the next best thing. Sulzberger phoned the White House and made the necessary arrangements. On the very day that Donovan sent his report to the President, Mrs. Roosevelt welcomed Godfrey to dinner at the White House, and in the presence of two aides listened to what he had to say.

Suddenly the President rolled his wheelchair into the room. The man who had seemed impossible to see was in a puckish mood.

"Hello, Admiral," he said. "How did you come out?"

Godfrey replied that he had come out on the Clipper via Bermuda.

"Oh yes, those West Indies Islands; we're going to show you how to look after them, and not only you but the Portuguese and the Dutch!"

Godfrey had little choice but to laugh. The Roosevelts and the admiral went into the drawing room, where they watched a movie on snake worship in Laos. When Mrs. Roosevelt remarked that it was getting time to go to bed, the President wheeled his chair into the oval room. He waved Godfrey into the chair that Lincoln had preferred when he occupied the White House, and sat behind his desk. The President reminisced about his stay in London in 1917, when he was the under secretary of the navy, and the admiral, realizing that now was the right time to get to the point, explained from one navy man to another exactly why America had to have a unified intelligence service and why it must have it soon. Roosevelt listened intently.

Up until this evening Roosevelt had been considering Donovan for a variety of other key jobs in the administration, all dealing with the war. While pushing the President to establish a central intelligence agency Donovan, characteristically, had refused to push himself as the essential director. Talking with Admiral Godfrey, Roosevelt decided to establish the agency and to make Donovan its director. In the morning he directed his secretary, Grace Tully, to inform his appointments secretary that he wanted both Donovan and Benjamin Cohen, counsel for the National Power Policy Committee, to see him before Cohen left on a trip to England. Cohen had drafted many executive orders for the President, and FDR now had in mind a particularly momentous paper.

At 12:30 P.M. on June 18, Frank Knox, Donovan, and Cohen met with the President. After a discussion of the intelligence confusion that existed in Washington, the talk turned to Donovan's proposal, which Roosevelt accepted in principle. To the dismay and surprise of the others present, Donovan suddenly said that even if the President were to ask him, he did not wish to serve as director. Roosevelt was not deterred. Donovan later told Stimson that he agreed to accept the President's appointment only when it was understood that the new organization would be "essentially and entirely civilian" and that he would report directly to the President. He consented to the military rank of major general simply to accommodate the President, who had suggested it. The President and Donovan agreed that there would be nothing in writing pertaining to the secret activities, as Donovan reminded Roosevelt later, "especially about the use of radio in the procurement of vitally needed information."

On the cover sheet of Donovan's original memorandum Roosevelt wrote a note to the acting director of the Bureau of the Budget, John B. Blandford, Jr.: "Please set this up confidentially with Ben Cohen—Military—not OEM. FDR."

Explained Thomas Troy: "The 'confidentially' probably referred to the use of secret funds, and vague language in laying out the new organization's purpose and functions. 'Military' meant that Donovan would be a major general. 'Not OEM' meant that he would not be bracketed with the numerous new war agencies under the OEM [Office for Emergency Management] umbrella, but would report directly to FDR."

As soon as he left the President, Donovan got in touch with William Stephenson in New York and informed him that he was to direct the new American strategic intelligence service. "You can imagine how relieved I am after three months of battle and jockeying for position in Washington," Stephenson immediately cabled London, "that our man is in a position of such importance to our efforts."

The next day Cohen and Budget Bureau aides began to draft the order to establish the "Service of Strategic Information." The work went ahead without a hitch, and the order establishing the new agency might have been issued weeks before it finally came out, but Military Intelligence now entered the picture. Both Knox and Stimson had been pleased by the President's intentions, but General Miles, chief of Army Intelligence, was greatly disturbed. He had shown concern early in the spring when he first had an inkling of Donovan's plans. Now on June 24, Army Chief of Staff Marshall, who had been infected by Miles's fears, thundered into Stimson's office, which was right next to his own in the old Munitions Building on Constitution Avenue. General Marshall, wrote Stimson in his journal, angrily branded the plan "an effort to supplant his responsibilities and duties in direct connection with the Commander-in-Chief," which was a clear indication that Marshall saw himself losing out in the military politics of the summer.

War Secretary Stimson attempted to placate Marshall by partially agreeing with him. Later, after Ben Cohen brought the draft in for him to consider, Stimson recorded in his journal that he studied it with a jaundiced eye before finally giving Cohen his response:

> [I told him that] I thought it was such bad planning from the standpoint of military administration that I should not favor it unless Donovan was kept in a purely civilian capacity; that I disapproved wholly of having him made a Major General simultaneously with the assumption of the position. The proposed draft was full of language treating the function as if it were a military one. I told Cohen that this plainly resulted in giving the President two Chiefs of Staff; one, the regular one, and one, an irregular one, because no military man could go to the President with military information without giving at the same time some views in the nature of advice based upon that information. I told Cohen that I thought the thing might be worked out if the Coordinator were kept purely as a civilian. I told him also that I was a friend of Donovan's and that I sympathized with his ultimate ambition to get into the fighting if fighting came, and that I would have no objection to recommending him at that time as a Major General; but that I was wholly against combining in his person the function of being a Major General and being a Coordinator of Information.

Donovan had anticipated this reaction from the military bureaucracy and had attempted to keep the new agency out of the hands of the military and to avoid assuming military rank himself. Cohen had no choice but to agree with Stimson and to take out the paragraphs giving a military aspect to the proposed coordinator of information (COI). The Budget Bureau worked on the paper too, and revisions followed revisions. Donovan consulted with Stimson and with Knox.

On June 24, President Roosevelt held a press conference.

"Mr. President, there have been reports that Colonel Donovan has been given a high position in the military intelligence, or will be given," a White House correspondent said.

"I read that too in the paper," remarked Roosevelt. "I have had nothing come to my desk on it."

The President was being honest. He had spent the last week in June at Hyde Park while in Washington Stimson and Marshall backed and filled. On June 22, as Donovan had told Roosevelt would happen, Germany attacked the Soviet Union. The intensified war in Europe had something of a sobering effect on the military careerists who felt challenged by the proposed COI. Assistant Secretary of War McCloy, General Marshall, and Secretary Stimson argued over the details most of July 2. Marshall, just as irascible as ever, sketched a diagram that showed COI reports going through military and naval channels to the President. In this way General Miles could control what Roosevelt was given. The next morning Donovan went to see Stimson and McCloy at 8:30 to try and set the matter to rest.

When Donovan explained that the military title was Roosevelt's suggestion and that he himself had proposed in the first place that the new agency be entirely separate from the army and navy, Stimson and McCloy judged him fair-minded. Stimson offered to make Donovan a major general any time he wanted to take up a military command; in fact, he could command the 44th Division, but military rank could not go with the directorship of the COI. Donovan admitted that he planned to "make something real" of the COI, but that later he might indeed want to take a try at a command since he had some ideas on guerrilla warfare that needed testing.

Then McCloy took out Marshall's diagram showing the channels through which intelligence would be submitted to the President, and it was Donovan's turn to be angry. Finally a compromise was reached. As a rule, intelligence would go to the President through channels, but Donovan could also submit important reports directly to the President because, as Stimson wrote in his diary, "of the relationship necessary to his position and the President's temperament and characteristics."

Now that the War Department agreed to the COI proposal, Donovan could go to the Bureau of the Budget to meet with Cohen and Blandford and his aides to finish a revised draft. There were still more anguished hours ahead before the army would agree to the revisions, but on July 3, the document was placed on the President's desk. The plan, which J. Edgar Hoover was to label Roosevelt's Folly, now awaited the President's signature.

On July 6, the *New York Times* ran an article under the headline, "Col. Donovan, Who Studied Nazi Espionage, Is Slated for a Big Post, Capital Reports." The article speculated that Donovan was to head a new antispy agency. On July 10, the *Times* ran a second article, saying that Donovan would soon be named the coordinator of intelligence information. His nomination would be sent to the Senate the next day, and Roosevelt would soon issue an order establishing the new office, "the functions of which have been outlined in a formal order," and which "is without precedent in the government's operations."

> Donovan would be accountable only to the President. Heretofore, intelligence reports had been reaching the White House in the form of short digests of long, original reports. Sometimes these lend themselves to easy coordination, but more often it is understood, the varying emphasis placed by observers on related incidents suffers in the digesting, since each digest is prepared by an official necessarily preoccupied with the special interests of his own department.
>
> It will be the primary task of Colonel Donovan, therefore, to take original reports and analyze them in relation to each other, in a manner impossible at present, simply because there is no agency of the government with the freedom from other routine necessary to this task.
>
> The new office, incidentally, is being created with the approval and general cooperation of the various intelligence agencies which will feed reports into it.

The approval of the various intelligence agencies was not exactly enthusiastic, and their cooperation promised to be dilatory, but the *New York Times* was essentially correct. On July 11 President Roosevelt signed the COI order, and the White House announced the new agency to the nation.

> The President today, as Commander-in-Chief of the Armed Forces, appointed William J. Donovan Coordinator of Information.
>
> In his capacity as coordinator Mr. Donovan will collect and assemble information and data bearing on national security from the various departments and agencies of the government and will analyze and collate such materials for the use of the President and such other officials as the President may designate.
>
> Mr. Donovan's task will be to coordinate and correlate defense information, but his work is not intended to supersede or to duplicate or to involve any direction of or interference with the activities of the General Staff, the regular intelligence services, the Federal Bureau of Investigation, or of other existing departments and agencies.

Originally, White House Press Secretary Steve Early had planned to release an additional statement that "Mr. Donovan may from time to time be requested by the President to undertake activities helpful in the securing of defense information not available to the government through existing departments and agencies." Early, it is said, deleted this statement to avoid confusing the issue, and therefore much of the scope and true purpose of the COI was not announced. The Executive Order designating a coordinator of information did not mention subversive operations, guerrilla warfare, or psychological warfare, except as might be included in the terms "supplementary activities." Donovan also had insured, for all effects and purposes, that he should report only to the President, that the President's secret unvouchered funds could be employed, and that all departments of government would be instructed to give him the materials he asked for.

Orally, so as not to stir up a hornet's nest in and out of the administration, Roosevelt had given Donovan responsibility to carry on political warfare against the enemies of the United States. He had told Donovan that there were four things that he required of him: (1) Plan his strategy with the Chief of Staff; (2) Accept guidance from the White House on aims; (3) Find out who in the government was planning postwar policy; (4) Have control of short-wave stations to be sure they said what needed to be said.

Donovan soon discovered that there were enormous obstacles to meeting the requirements of all four points imposed by the President.

PART THREE

Wartime Spymaster

1941–1945

24

Donovan's Brain Trust

DONOVAN DID NOT WAIT for Roosevelt's public announcement of the COI to begin his work. He asked for space at the Bureau of the Budget and was assigned a minuscule office. There was one telephone for Donovan and his first few assistants, and it was on his desk. Everybody scrambled for it when it rang.

Henry Field, then curator of anthropology at the Field Museum in Chicago, recalled that it was late in May when Donovan invited him to breakfast at his Georgetown home. At first Donovan questioned Field about his travels and experiences in Europe and the Near East, particularly the latter. He asked searching questions. The two men pored over a Bartholomew map that Field had brought as they considered problems from the Suez Canal to Iran.

As the clock struck eleven, Donovan suddenly changed the subject. "The President is going to appoint me coordinator of information reporting directly to him," Field recalled Donovan saying. "He finds that the flow of documents is too large for him to read. When he asks for special information on a problem, the reports from many branches of the government require analysis and condensation. He wants me to set up an organization to do this for him. I have authority to employ anyone. I want you to help me to set up the Near East division. Can you start right away?"

"I'm afraid not, Colonel."

"But I have here a letter of authorization from the President." Donovan tapped the inside pocket of his suit; his temper seemed to be rising.

"Colonel, I cannot accept because I am already working for the President."

Donovan's eyes showed surprise. Then he smiled. "I did not know that. In that event can you work part-time for me? I will give you an office in COI."

"May I write a memorandum to the President for instructions?"

"Yes, and I will speak to him about you today. I hope you can start to make a plan for Near East division this evening. Now I have to go. Thank you for coming to see me. I want you on my top team."

That evening Field started to draft a plan. Shortly thereafter, he received a telephoned answer to his memorandum to Roosevelt. The President ordered Field to work part-time for Donovan.

During June and early July, Donovan recruited aides and made plans wherever he happened to be. In New York he worked out of his law office on Wall Street and his Beekman Place apartment; in Washington, out of his law office in the Bowen Building on 15th Street and his Georgetown home. He recruited at cocktail parties, in offices, at military bases. He pressed his law partners, his assistants, and his friends into service. Since there was no time to make exhaustive security checks, he turned to the people he knew best, for both their outstanding abilities and their unquestionable loyalty.

One of his first assistants was Jim Murphy, who joined Donovan to help protect him from political treachery (as Murphy put it later, to "keep the knives out of his back"). "I phoned the Colonel," he said. "If he was going to be involved, I wanted to be with him. I met him on a Saturday morning and just went to work. I worked right through the first weekend."

For two weeks Murphy could not get back to his law office to finish up his own affairs. He had no title and was given no pay, but he interviewed job applicants and took care of Donovan's correspondence, which swelled daily in volume and contained information of a highly confidential nature.

Others of the first COI men were suggested by the President. One of these was Robert Sherwood, playwright and presidential speech writer, whom Donovan picked in June to head up the Foreign Information Service. Sherwood had been planning his staff for a month before the actual order establishing the COI was issued. Among his recruits were Stephen Vincent Benét and Thornton Wilder. In June Donovan also talked to Elmo Roper, nationally known for his public opinion surveys, and asked him to work with the chiefs of the various divisions in setting up their organizations, beginning with the propaganda branch. Roper's job thereafter would be to visit each branch in succession to check on its operation. In this way Donovan tried from the start to establish and insure organizational efficiency.

On June 23 Donovan signed up Thomas G. Early, secretary of the Civil Aeronautics Board, and put him in charge of administration. Then on June 29 Donovan paid a call on Archibald MacLeish to arrange for a Research and Analysis section at the Library of Congress. MacLeish pointed out that a mine of data was in the library in books, magazines, newspapers, and maps, if it could be exploited by research scholars familiar with such sources. He offered the facilities of the Library of Congress and suggested some scholars who might be willing to help. In fact, many new employees of COI (and later OSS) initially went to work in an annex of the library, the only place they could sit and be usefully employed in reading, pending completion of their security clearances. Not only was there a vast intelligence lode buried in the library, but it seemed particularly valuable to Donovan since it could readily be mined without risking a single secret agent.

When Steve Early announced the formation of the COI on July 11, Donovan moved into rooms 246, 247, and 248 in the baroque old State Department Building on Pennsylvania Avenue, next to the White House. He borrowed the furniture from other more established branches of government. On July 12 a mail carrier turned up at the building's front desk with a registered letter for Colonel Donovan.

"Donovan?" said the guard. "I don't know of any Donovan." He sent the letter back to the post office. The COI was appropriately launched on its mysterious course.

Early in August the COI moved to the Apex Building at Pennsylvania and Constitution avenues near Capitol Hill, where it occupied 32 rooms and soon was spilling out into the halls as Donovan expanded the organization. The fateful Sunday of December 7 was still almost four months away.

The rapid growth of the COI was viewed with alarm by Washington rivals.

"It would be of help to us if we knew exactly what picture the President had of Bill's functions," complained Adolph Berle, who had charge of the State Department's intelligence functions. J. Edgar Hoover, jealous of his own prerogatives as director of the FBI, expressed his displeasure at the COI. Navy and army brass hats were offended at the idea that a mere reserve officer such as Donovan had been put in charge of the fledgling intelligence apparatus. The chief of Army Intelligence (G-2) refused even to speak to Donovan and communicated with him only through an intermediary.

"The old army and the old navy were not ready insofar as their G-2 sections were concerned for the new kind of war that was being forced upon them," observed Air Force Gen. H. H. Arnold. "The G-2 men could not see over the hill to the necessity of establishing an agency for securing the new kind of information needed."

Even across the Atlantic, Raymond Lee at the American Embassy in London heard of the bureaucratic war in Washington. FDR's adviser Harry Hopkins, in the British capital on a presidential assignment, rang up Lee on July 21. Hopkins, according to Lee, reported that Donovan was encountering tremendous opposition in trying to put over his intelligence idea, that he was "in a frightful row with Stimson and Knox and Marshall and Stark. Hopkins's recital of how the thing was bungled with everyone at loggerheads is an illuminating commentary on how affairs are conducted in Washington."

The acerbic Secretary of the Interior Harold Ickes shared Hopkins's view. On Friday, July 25, Ickes had lunch with John J. McCloy. "He told me that the War Department had blocked the plan of the President to make Colonel Donovan a major general in charge of all intelligence work in the government," Ickes noted in his diary. "Donovan retains his rank of colonel and has been appointed coordinator of the intelligence services. When we run into a jam in Washington we appoint a coordinator and usually he has a great deal of trouble doing anything in the way of coordinating."

The Treasury's intelligence people cooperated with the COI in good part due to Secretary of the Treasury Henry Morgenthau, who pointed out that Donovan had seen more of the war in Europe than anyone else "by about a thousand percent."

"That is all good preparation for Washington," observed an assistant. When Morgenthau asked what he meant, the assistant replied that the new COI director "ought to be at home in all the fighting that is going on."

"Well, he is a fighter, don't worry," commented Morgenthau

Unlike his opponents in the bureaucratic wars, Donovan was concerned only with getting the COI into action as fast as possible. He understood fully how rapidly world events were rushing to a climax. On July 14 Lee wrote to Donovan:

> There have been rumors, based chiefly on the authoritative sounding surmises of American columnists, that you were to turn into a super-super intelligence man, but the State Department radio confirms it only today.
>
> I'm extremely gratified that something is finally going to be done to consolidate or to collate all the information which reaches Washington by way of a dozen different channels. It is certain that what is reported by the State Department, the army, the navy, and a number of other agencies would make a definite and fairly accurate picture, if properly fitted together. If this is not done, then prodigious decisions will be taken in the light of only a part of the information which is available in Washington.
>
> This may not be fatal as long as we have enough money, men, and material to operate on a wide and wasteful margin, but as that day passes we will be confronted with the responsibility of making only accurate decisions—or else. In that situation we want to weigh and act in the light of every scrap of information we can secure.

In shaping up the COI, Donovan, according to writer Jay Robert Nash, "was everything that Hoover was not. He hated bureaucracy. The chronic paper shuffling, memoranda, and tedious documentation that were a part of all government work bored and enraged him. Donovan preferred to give his orders verbally. He was a conversationalist."

According to Jim Murphy, in those early days of the COI Donovan never even glanced at an organizational chart. For several months he and his staff worked without budget or finance of any kind. There was not even a payroll officer, and nobody got paid. "We thought we'd eventually get our back pay," Murphy remembered after the war, "but most of us never did."

The Bureau of the Budget had first estimated that the COI would be able to get along on an annual budget of $1,454,700. The money was to be taken from the President's Emergency Fund of $100 million. Budget Director Harold D. Smith provided $450,000 for Donovan on July 21 to get the COI started. In the light of COI's clandestine role, the funds were to be unvouchered. This did not mean that Donovan did not insist on strict accounting.

"I may not have to account," he told William Langer when Langer became director of the Research and Analysis branch. "Everybody thinks the COI is wonderful. But once the war is over, there will be criticism, there will be inquiries, and I want every penny accounted for." He brought in the head of a big insurance company to oversee all the finances.

Despite Donovan's careful accounting procedures, the budget people were resentful. Budget Director Smith's resentment mounted when, in September, Donovan put in a request for $10 million for the first year's operation. From the start he had no intention of operating a small agency confined to sifting through other agencies' reports and correlating them for the President. Week by week the COI grew at a pace that astounded the intelligence services of both friendly and hostile nations.

Roosevelt had written to Donovan on July 23, "In your capacity as Coordinator of Information, which position I established by Order of July 11, 1941, you will receive no compensation, but shall be entitled to actual and necessary transportation, subsistence, and other expenses incidental to the performance of your duties." Until April 1942, when he was named a brigadier general, Donovan drew no pay. When Roosevelt asked him to submit an expense account, he asked for $1,000. The Treasury told him he had to itemize the account, and Donovan withdrew it, never to submit it again.

On May 20, Roosevelt had set up the Office of Civilian Defense (OCD). One of its purposes was to maintain domestic morale and disseminate information to the nation. Now his advisers suggested that the new COI might impinge upon the functions of the OCD; therefore, on July 14 Roosevelt directed that the OCD confine its morale functions within the United States while the COI was to undertake the responsibility for international broadcasts.

The first of the COI overseas broadcasts took place on July 14, only three days after the agency was established. Fernard Gustave Auberjonois, the chief of the National Broadcasting Company's French division, presented a program on the anniversary of the storming of the Bastille. The program opened with the pealing of Philadelphia's Liberty Bell and the playing of "La Marseillaise" and featured addresses by William J. Donovan and actor Charles Boyer. Over the next few months COI experts under Sherwood and Donovan created a special program service to be beamed across the Atlantic by the radio broadcasting companies' overseas transmitters.

"The COI," said *Washington Star* writer Blair Bolles, "is the seat of the American radio-propaganda drive for the airwave invasion of Europe. It arranges broadcasts to South America for offsetting the Axis propaganda barrage against that part of the world. It directs psychological inquiries into the inner meanings of German shortwave broadcasts."

German propaganda broadcasts quickly took up the challenge from the COI. The spokeswoman "Jane Anderson" announced:

> Roosevelt has made the innovation of harnessing the American Secret Service to propagandists under a renegade Irishman named Donovan, who prepared for his job by visiting a chain of embassies and the night-clubs of the Balkans.
>
> Highly remunerative experts prepare for the White House each day a report distilled upon the short-wave stations of the universe and from this compilation the Donovan radio is fed so that the larvae lies for the perjuring of world opinion is vomited further from the entrails of this mechanized machine in an avalanche of hatred and vituperation to which Dante might have dedicated with fervor a choice spot in his immortalization of the hell pits of the earth.

Once the COI was launched, a series of Wednesday lunches was held in the Round Table Room at the Library of Congress. COI men from the Apex Building and the Library of Congress annex met and discussed the intelligence questions that Donovan put to them. During the early days of the COI, the Willard Hotel was the after-hours hangout of Donovan's men and women, and Donovan and MacLeish often met there for lunch. With the German war machine slashing deep into the Soviet Ukraine, it was critical that they determine what routes could be used for delivering Lend-Lease aid to Russia. This became one of the first urgent assignments handed to Research and Analysis (R&A).

"The high-level decision had been made, but how and over what terrain (in addition to the sea route to Murmansk) was this possible?" remembered Henry Field.

> Professor Gerald T. Robinson (Columbia University) was given the R&A assignment. After two day and night sessions, the report was ready for typing. The maximum security precautions were arranged. Each typist

copied every third page to prevent continuity of copy. Every desk was four feet apart to prevent even far-sighted reading. Four armed Marines stood guard pacing up and down and across each line of desks. Two Marines collected carbons and recopied pages for the Marine-guarded incinerator. No typist could bring a handbag into the room. Sandwiches and coffee were brought in at noon. A police matron accompanied any typist to and from the washroom. Maximum security prevailed.

About 12:30 Professor Robinson left for luncheon. Walking down the slope toward "Q" Building, the Professor was in an elated frame of mind. The report would be finished in a couple of hours. As he walked in the sunshine, he swung his tightly rolled umbrella.

Suddenly, he noticed [on the ground] fragments of paper, all torn, some charred, some partially burned. When he pierced a torn fragment with his umbrella, Professor Robinson was horrified to find it was a piece of his precious report. Security had been perfect except for the unscreened chimney above the incinerator. An updraft had carried hundreds of pieces skyward to fall on the bushes and ground. . . .

The professor ran back to the South Building. Marines were rushed to throw a cordon around the area and to pick up every fragment.

At about the same time that Donovan directed R&A to study routes to Russia, he asked Roosevelt what he considered the most necessary intelligence. The President replied that it was critical to know the intentions of the Japanese in Indochina and Thailand. Donovan began at once searching for an American scholar who was an expert on Southeast Asia. When Archibald MacLeish, Mortimer Graves of the Council of American Learned Societies, and informants at the University of Pennsylvania, and at Yale, Harvard, Princeton, and Chicago each suggested the name Kenneth Landon, Donovan set about locating Landon.

Kenneth Landon then was a professor of philosophy at Earlham College in Indiana. That July he was vacationing with his wife and children at Gull Lake in Michigan.

"I received a message that I should go to the country store," recalled Landon, whose wife, Margaret, wrote *Anna and the King of Siam.* "There was a call from Washington." Landon went to the phone, and a voice at the other end identified the caller as Donovan. "I'd never heard of him," said Landon. "He said the President wanted me in Washington right away. It was about a three weeks' job. When Donovan announced that I would be paid $15 a day or $50 a day, I don't know which, since it was a bad connection, I decided to go. Both amounts were much more than a professor at Earlham earned."

Landon left his wife and children at the lake and took the train to Washington, where he checked into COI's offices in the Apex Building. "There was the receptionist, two secretaries and me," he remembers. "The next day I went to the office, and when I swung open the door, it hit somebody. It was a tall young man."

"Good morning, sir," the young man said. "My father sent me over to see whether I can help out."

It was Capt. James Roosevelt. Donovan had put him to work probing other government agencies for facts required for COI reports. Most of the agencies were touchy about giving out information, but when the President's son inquired, their touchiness vanished. Young Roosevelt used his clout with the White House staff too. When, on July 23, he telephoned the White House to ask Maj. Gen. Edwin M. Watson, FDR's appointments secretary, about a letter that "Colonel Donovan had written to the President, suggesting returning our consuls from Germany and Italy," he was given the information he needed.

At COI headquarters Donovan briefed Kenneth Landon as to the vital importance of information about Southeast Asia. Landon was handed the key to a cabinet that was labeled "Southeast Asia Intelligence." He opened the first three drawers and found them empty. The fourth drawer contained an envelope marked top secret. He opened the envelope with some trepidation and discovered inside two articles, both of which he had written. At that point he fully understood the staggering dimensions of his new job.

In August the COI chief decided it was important to know what the Japanese were planning. Donovan knew that Hitler wanted Japan to join the war, and he had received alarming information through Japanese connections that dated back to his mission to Siberia in 1919. Donovan asked Edgar Ansel Mowrer to go to the Orient as soon as possible. Mowrer would presumably be writing articles for the *Chicago Daily News,* but actually he was to learn everything he could about Japan's intentions.

"My job was to cover what we would now call Main Beat," Mowrer said after the war. "I intended to get to Tokyo at the end. I went to the Philippines, to Saigon, Hanoi, Batavia [Djakarta], Singapore, Bangkok, Rangoon, over the Hump by air to Kunming up to Chungking."

Mowrer's next stop was Hong Kong. "This was three weeks before Pearl Harbor, and I sniffed the air and said to myself, 'I'm not going to Tokyo.'" Instead he went to Manila, where he had an interview with General MacArthur. In MacArthur's office he met an American businessman. About nine o'clock that evening, as Mowrer was returning to the Hotel Manila from dinner, he met the same man in the lobby. Mowrer attempted to brush past him to the elevators.

"Come over and have a drink," the businessman called.

"No, I don't think I will," replied Mowrer. "I am going to try to get a couple of hours of sleep. I have to get up at 1:00 or 2:00 A.M. or some such ghastly time. I am going to get a plane."

"Well, don't do that. You can sleep on the plane anyway. Please sit down. I want to talk to somebody."

Mowrer thought this curious and sat down.

"You know, I want you to do me a favor when you are in San Francisco. Call up my daughter and tell her I love her. You see, I shall never see my daughter again."

"Why not?" asked Mowrer.

"You know, the war is coming," said the businessman. "The Japanese fleet, so help me God, has gone sailing east. I think they are going to attack us, and if they do they will certainly occupy the Philippines; and we will all be taken prisoner, and I have a hunch I will never see my daughter again."

Mowrer had questioned scores of experts on Japan, including General MacArthur, during his trip, and this man was the only person who anticipated an attack on the United States. On the flight home Mowrer stopped off in Hawaii, where he called on Adm. Husband Kimmel, commander of the Pacific fleet.

"I told Admiral Kimmel what this man had told me, and he pooh-poohed it," said Mowrer.

Back in Washington Mowrer met with army brass, whom Donovan had called into conference at COI headquarters, to report what he had learned. He told the officers that most of the people he had seen thought "that the Japs were going to do something soon. . . . Most believed that they were going to attack Russia, whereas a few believed they were going to attack south, the Dutch Indies and Singapore; but [I told them] that I had met this one freak who had said what they were going to do; and I remember afterwards that [the army officers] sort of looked at each other knowingly." Mowrer made a written report of his trip, finishing it in November. Washington officials who saw it gave little credence to the fears of a businessman whose main concern was to send a message to his daughter.

Another early COI man was Turner McBaine, a San Francisco lawyer. McBaine was upset about giving up his law practice for government service. "Forget that," Donovan told him. "You'll learn more in a couple of years here than if you stayed practicing law."

McBaine asked what Donovan wanted him to do. "I want you to go out and go up and down Constitution Avenue and Pennsylvania Avenue and go into buildings and ask them what they are doing," said Donovan.

"At the time new agencies were being spawned at the rate of two or three a week by FDR," said McBaine years later. "I went out and did what he told me to do. The government manual was hopelessly behind. I made a survey of all those organizations. I had a fantastic lesson in bureaucracy. I came back and told him everything."

McBaine was particularly impressed with one "hard-driving young man, who assured me he was the biggest man in the entire government. He controlled the central purchasing of office supplies, and he could always threaten to cut off the paper supplies from a balky bureaucrat."

One agency that McBaine overlooked was the Office of the Coordinator of Inter-American Affairs (CIAA), directed by Nelson Rockefeller. One day an angry Nelson Rockefeller strode into Bill Donovan's office. The CIAA had an information program that Rockefeller told Donovan was now being superseded by that of the COI. Donovan pointed out that the President certainly knew his own mind and that Rockefeller's service should be incorporated into the COI. Rockefeller stomped out of the office. He returned in a few days and insisted that he be allowed to keep his information service in Latin America.

"You know, Jimmy was talking to his father," Donovan said, "and the President told him he believed the whole information set-up ought to be taken over by one office. So, I think there will be a transfer of the Latin American information program from your office to ours. Jimmy will tell you about it." James Roosevelt's office was right down the hall.

"I'm not interested in talking to Jimmy."

Donovan called James Roosevelt into the room anyway to confirm that he had indeed talked to his father about the matter the previous day as the Roosevelt family cruised on the yacht *Potomac*.

"Did you remind the President of the executive order which he signed creating the CIAA and giving it authority over its own information program?" demanded Rockefeller.

"No, I didn't mention that," said Roosevelt.

"Bill, I don't think it is fair to the President to present this thing to him from only one side, simply getting him to agree to a principle without discussing the problems and the agencies involved. I think we ought to go together to see him and work it out," said Rockefeller.

"No," said Donovan. "The President has made a decision and that's that."

"All right," replied Rockefeller. "I want to make it clear that I don't feel it is in the interest of the President. But if you want to take unilateral action, I want you to know that I will follow the same procedure."

Rockefeller returned to his own office, telephoned the White House, and learned that the COI had indeed won authority over his information program. He dispatched Anna Rosenberg, a good friend of Roosevelt, to the White House to see the President. Another Rockefeller advocate, John Hay Whitney, also saw the President that day. Whitney's wife, Betsey, had once been married to James Roosevelt and was still a favorite of the President. FDR had invited the Whitneys to dine with him that night, and Jock Whitney was certain that he would be able to put in a good word for Rockefeller. But when the Whitneys arrived at the White House, they discovered that a smiling William Donovan was also a dinner guest. Somebody had sent the President a gift of wild duck and it had become a trifle tainted from lack of refrigeration. Whitney and Donovan gingerly sampled the fowl, which FDR pronounced to be delicious. Neither Whitney (who would later serve in the OSS in France with valor) nor Donovan could mention the subject that was uppermost in both of their minds.

Perhaps Anna Rosenberg's intercession was decisive. In any event, the next morning FDR issued an order keeping the CIAA's information program out of the COI.

The antagonism between Rockefeller and Donovan lasted until Pearl Harbor. Then Rockefeller called on Donovan and shook his hand. "Seems to me, it's about time to bury the hatchet. We're on the same side in this war."

"I guess you're right," said Donovan.

The two men became staunch friends.

On July 31 Donovan appointed Dr. James Phinney Baxter III, president of Williams College and distinguished historian, to be the director of R&A. Donovan hired Douglas Miller, author of *You Can't Do Business with Hitler,* who had served in the Berlin Embassy from 1928 to 1939, and John Wiley, former minister to Austria, Estonia, and Latvia. He persuaded Calvin Hoover of Duke University to come to Washington, as well as Edwin Earle of Princeton. He brought geographers, historians, economists, and psychologists into what Washingtonians called Donovan's brain trust.

"Geography," Donovan remarked to President Roosevelt, "has been neglected in this country's policy planning. Close study of geography is invaluable in outguessing the enemy. The Nazis make what they call 'Geopolitics' a vital arm of military policy. Their Geopolitical Institute is an integral factor in the development of that policy."

Every day brought new faces to the Apex Building. There was socialite William D. Whitney, picked by Donovan to set up a London office because of his English connections, and there was Colonel G. Edward Buxton, a friend from World War I days whom Donovan made assistant director of COI. "Ned Buxton was Colonel Donovan's right-hand man," said Henry Field. "His cool, calm New England horse sense proved an excellent foil for the Irish temperament and impetuousness."

"Ned," said Atherton Richards, another early COI man, "was a bulwark of loyalty, who gave Donovan freedom to move around the world, knowing that Buxton would never undercut him."

Kermit Roosevelt, grandson of President Theodore Roosevelt, recalled how he ended up in the COI. "I had been teaching in Pasadena and had been researching the propaganda techniques in the English Civil War. I had written a paper on what kind of clandestine organization the United States should have if war came. I was driving across country and stopped to admire the Grand Canyon the day Germany invaded the Soviet Union. War seemed imminent. When I reached Washington, I told my cousin Joe Alsop, the columnist, about the paper. 'Don't publish it,' said Alsop. 'Send it to Bill Donovan.'"

Roosevelt sent his paper to Donovan, who immediately telephoned him.

"Don't publish this," he said. "Come and work for me instead."

Donovan hired Roosevelt in mid-August of 1941, and the new recruit found himself working side by side with Ralph Bunche, a bright young black, in R&A.

James P. Warburg, banker and political writer, turned up at COI and so did *Chicago Daily News* foreign correspondent Wallace R. Deuel and *New York Herald Tribune* foreign editor Joseph Barnes. The recruited turned recruiters, and they brought in a constantly growing roster of men and women, including Thomas A. Morgan, president of the Sperry Corporation; Estelle Frankfurter, sister of Supreme Court Justice Felix Frankfurter; and the Hollywood film director John Ford.

"Write me a memo on how you can be of service to this organization," Donovan told promising applicants who came to see him, "and if I agree with you, you're hired."

David K. E. Bruce, the lawyer-diplomat who would become OSS chief in Europe, watched Donovan assemble the COI with considerable amazement. "All were fish in his net," Bruce said. "Ornithologists, anthropologists, college professors of every category, safecrackers, paroled convicts, remittance men, professional wrestlers and boxers, circus stars, code experts, military characters, nightclub frequenters, and a miscellany of others, including in the majority ordinary citizens, were jumbled together in what, organizationally, appeared to be chaos."

Donovan was accused by some of hiring too many rich men and by others of hiring too many Reds. In defense of the former, he said, "These Wall Street bank and corporation lawyers make wonderful second-story men." In defense of the latter, when he was told one of his people had been on the "honor roll of the Young Communist League," he replied, "I don't know if he's on the Communist honor roll, but for the job he is doing, he's on the honor roll of the COI."

Wrote William R. Corson, "Donovan was more than equal to the challenge of breathing life into the Coordinator of Information's office. His basic approach, which today stands almost as a classic model in how to create a new government agency, was premised on the need to get the right people for key positions—delegate authority to them, and thereby force positive decisions on their part."

Donovan had told the President that he was going to give him a young organization, and he did recruit a high proportion of young men and women. All over the world he knew talented young people, and he took them into the COI. One such person was actor Sterling Hayden, who had sailed around the world with Donovan's son, David. On September 15, Hayden informed Paramount that he was sick of acting and went to Washington to see Bill Donovan. Donovan sent him to Great Britain, where he found himself undergoing commando training with the Argyll and Sutherland Highlanders. Colonel Edward G. Young, the Highlanders' commanding officer, asked him when he arrived at camp, "What have you been doing recently?"

"Well, sir, this is going to sound kind of strange," Hayden replied, "but a few years ago Colonel Donovan suggested I go out to the West Coast and become an actor."

"Go on."

"I guess it had something to do with my being able to use the acting thing as a cover in case we got in the war."

Hayden trained with the British commandos but unfortunately tore the cartilage in his knee and injured his spine when parachuting from a Sterling bomber. This mishap interrupted his COI career, but in time Donovan dispatched him to Cairo under the assumed name of John Hamilton.

The young men and women of the COI and the OSS believed in Donovan with a fervor that was to lead to great deeds of derring-do and adventure.

"When I went into William Donovan's intelligence service, it was less than two months old and consisted of approximately one hundred people," recalled former OSS member Caroline Bland.

> In the intervening thirty-three years, I have forgotten details of the tremendous experience that followed, just as I was supposed to do. We were not allowed to keep diaries. I never would have violated the rules and I felt the responsibility of secrecy.
>
> Practically nobody remembers now what a fantastic job Donovan accomplished in creating OSS out of nothing. He gave the United States the first real intelligence service of our history. There was no precedent. There was no time for perfect organization, the job just had to be done, and all the individuals doing it, however successful in previous pursuits, were novices in this. It was very challenging.
>
> OSS was the most wonderful place to be young! We young ones had everything—belief, enthusiasm, opportunity, victory. Life rushed on in excitement and in confidence that we were a special group of colleagues with an important mission for our country.

By the end of August 1941, Donovan and his burgeoning crew moved to the limestone and brick buildings just deserted by the Public Health Service at 25th and E streets. The structures were sequestered behind a wall, which provided security. A visitor walked up a steep driveway from the entrance on 25th Street to be confronted by uniformed guards, their automatics snug in shoulder holsters. The Central Building with its Greek pillars became the Administration Department, and there Donovan had his office.

Most of the animals kept by Public Health researchers in the South Building for experimental purposes stayed on for some months. They coexisted with the eminent professors and scholars that Donovan installed in the building as the nucleus of the Research and Analysis section.

"The question arose," said Murphy, "of whether we should put the monkeys on the payroll—if there was ever going to be a payroll."

Some of the monkeys had little chance to make the payroll, as Walt Rostow, later to have a distinguished career in government, was to discover when he arrived at work for the first time. "Out on the steps, on a lovely morning," he recalls, "were Donovan and Jimmy Roosevelt. Smoke was coming from a chimney. Laboratory monkeys, which had been involved in research on syphilis, were being incinerated." Rostow was given a very aromatic welcome to the cloak-and-dagger world of the COI.

Nazi propagandists, learning about the circumstances of the world's newest intelligence organization, lampooned it as "50 professors, 20 monkeys, 10 goats, 12 guinea pigs, and a staff of Jewish scribblers."

It appeared that the Public Health people would never move their animals out of the top floor of the South Building. Then Donovan himself forced the issue. He complained that an infected monkey had bitten a secretary and neither she nor the other women would enter the building until the animals were moved out. The animals left.

The R&A section soon resembled a Who's Who of American intellectuals. In time Donovan managed to house most of his 2,000 research analysts in an old apartment house at 23rd and E streets, Northwest, a State Department annex building, but there was a spillover, not only into the South Building but also into some gray frame temporary structures erected behind the old Heurich Brewery at the end of Rock Creek Drive. This entire complex could be addressed at 2430 E Street.

Growth continued although civil service regulations of the time meant that even top experts hired by the COI could be paid only $8,500 a year. Donovan took up the matter with FDR, who ruled that the COI was not subject to civil service regulations and could pay any wage it wished. Salaries went up instantly, and what was more important, salaries were at last being paid.

It did not take the press long to analyze Donovan's plans for R&A. "What he is aiming at," wrote Ernest K. Lindley, "is an American counterpart of Prof. Haushofer's Geopolitical Institute in Berlin. This organization was the source of much of the Nazi grand strategy and of many of the tactical instruments for furthering it, ranging from the concept of German 'lebensraum' through the hate campaigns against the Poles."

Donovan's R&A staffers worked feverishly in the months before Pearl Harbor. They perused everything from works of scholarship to French railroad timetables. They scrutinized what they called "Aunt Min" photos, snapshots collected from all over America that showed Aunt Min or another family member posing before anything from the railroad station at Munich to a highway viaduct in Sofia. Sometimes it was hard to see around Aunt Min to the valuable piece of intelligence in the picture, but special photo equipment helped to clarify the details.

British Security Coordinator William Stephenson commented that it was "the most brilliant team of analysts in the history of intelligence." McGeorge Bundy, who was to become president of the Ford Foundation and President John F. Kennedy's special assistant for national security, remarked, "A special area of powerful professional connection between higher learning and government is the field of area studies. It is a curious fact of academic history that the first great center of area studies in the United States was not located in any university, but in Washington, during the Second World War in the Office of Strategic Services. In very large measure the area study programs developed in American universities in the years after the war were manned, directed, or stimulated by graduates of the OSS—a remarkable institution half cops-and-robbers and half faculty meeting."

At first, James Phinney Baxter presided over this assortment of historians, political scientists, psychologists, cartographers, economists, and sociologists, who spoke some 40 languages and had been attracted from some 40 universities. Baxter, a highly respected scholar, was a superb leader, and he left his imprint on R&A when ill health forced him to resign. Possibly his greatest contribution was the selection of his successor. One day he telephoned William Langer, the Harvard historian, and persuaded him to drop everything and come to Washington to talk to Bill Donovan.

From the start Langer was attracted to both Donovan and the job, but he was not certain he could succeed in such a difficult undertaking. A year or so earlier he had suffered a mysterious disability. Langer had always been a gifted public speaker, but suddenly he developed an acute fear of audiences. It was all he could do to address his students at Harvard. One of his responsibilities as chief of R&A would be to brief such high-level officials as the Joint Chiefs of Staff. How could he ever do it?

Langer sat down with Bill Donovan in his office and told him of his problem. It was embarrassing to be a world-famous scholar and to be afraid of speaking to a crowd. Donovan nodded sympathetically. "Bill," he said, "I don't believe you have any conception of the severe handicaps most men suffer from, but they still get the job done. I believe you can do it." Langer had an overwhelming sense of the sympathy that emanated from Donovan, and he accepted the position. His subsequent lectures to top government officials were to prove not only significant but dramatic and exciting.

Donovan and Langer became fast friends, and they often break-fasted together at Donovan's Georgetown home. They talked about everything imaginable. When Langer remarked that the savants in R&A were feeling frustrated because they were not able to publish the results of their studies, Donovan observed, "You academics are like a bunch of chorus girls. You've got a fine pair of legs, and you want to show them." One Sunday morning during breakfast, Langer mentioned that Thucydides had written "quite a lot about guerrilla warfare." Donovan was fascinated. He had his chauffeur drive them from bookstore to bookstore looking for one that stocked a paperback copy of Thucydides' book.

Under Langer, R&A continued its growth, and its chief's friendship with Donovan helped to wed its research to the more active field work of the COI and its successor, the OSS. In time R&A was called upon not only to do research but also to test information from secret agents in the field, assess its accuracy, and fit it into a jigsaw puzzle made up of geographical, economic, political, and military factors. R&A experts not only prepared reports for the President and the Joint Chiefs of Staff but also suggested to the OSS's Secret Intelligence branch what important gaps in knowledge needed to be plugged.

"This piecing together and appraisal of strategic information is the most ambitious and expert intelligence operation of its kind of which there is any knowledge," reported Wallace R. Deuel. "It is General Donovan's—and his agency's—first and most important contribution to the theory and practice of strategic intelligence operations."

During World War I, Langer had been a Marine sergeant. The experience, said Henry Field, "gave him the ruthless quality necessary to whip together in short order a working team of prima donnas used to the tranquillity of their ivy-covered towers. . . . In COI four distinguished professors might find themselves in a small room, each ordered to complete a different report within a few hours and forced to type [the reports] themselves. Many quit under the pressure. In time the results were superb. The shakedown cruise lasted but a few weeks. Those indisposed returned home. The rest became a great team, inspired by Langer and super-inspired by Colonel Donovan."

Walter Langer was as distinguished a psychoanalyst as his brother William was a historian. In August 1941, convalescing from a double hernia operation in a hospital and thoroughly bored, Walter read in a newspaper of the new COI, one of whose functions was to organize and conduct psychological warfare. "It was the psychological warfare part that caught my attention," Langer wrote later. "I had never concerned myself with the problem of psychological warfare, but I had served overseas during World War I and had been far from impressed with our blatant psychological warfare endeavors. Psychological warfare, it seemed to me, should be much more than a constant repetition of fabricated atrocity stories which are designed to prove that the enemy were all 'bad guys' who had to be eliminated so we 'good guys' could live in peace."

Langer launched a tirade at his wife, who finally said, "Why tell me about it? Tell Colonel Donovan!"

> So, on the spur of the moment, I dictated a letter to Colonel Donovan covering the range of topics I had been mulling over. Then, having disgorged my sentiments on the subject, I felt that I had done my duty, and the rest was up to him.
>
> My evaluation of the situation proved to be completely erroneous. Scarcely had I returned to my home and begun to "toddle" when I received a call from Washington informing me that Colonel Donovan was very much interested in my views and inviting me to have breakfast with him a week hence. I was flabbergasted both by the invitation and his interest in what I had written. Taken off guard, I accepted, without stopping to consider my physical condition. When I informed my doctor of what had happened, he insisted that I was in no condition to make the trip and urged a postponement. I was adamant, however. I had inadvertently put myself out on a limb and the least I could do now was to follow through as best I could. With great reluctance, he finally consented to the trip, providing I observed a number of restrictions.
>
> I arrived at the Donovan home at the appointed hour, and during a delicious breakfast that lasted almost two hours, we discussed many of the points I raised in my letter. I was pleasantly surprised to find that the colonel was well versed in psychoanalytic theory and much impressed with the possibility of making use of it in a psychological warfare program. This, of course, made it much simpler for me to explain what I had in mind. The discussion, consequently, progressed from generalities to more specific topics and finally the morale of our young men.
>
> The enthusiasm that preceded our entry into World War I was clearly absent. Across the nation there were more and more rallies and demonstrations condemning the war in general and, more specifically, our possible involvement in it. Many of the sentiments that became so vocal and violent in the late 1960's were smoldering at that time. Why this drastic change in attitude? How would the young men who would be called upon to fight respond if this country were drawn into the war?
>
> "What light could psychoanalysis shed on these pressing problems?" Colonel Donovan asked. "And how would you go about getting it?" . . .
>
> I replied, "I have had several patients, mostly college students, in whom this antiwar attitude was manifest and I am sure that every other analyst in this country has had some experience with cases of this type."

[Langer proposed enlisting the aid of psychoanalysts across the country to make a study of the psychological factors underlying these attitudes.]

"That sounds very interesting," replied Colonel Donovan, "but since all of these patients are presumably neurotic, it would throw little light on the psychology of the normal young men of this age. What we want to know is how the cross section of young men would react in the event of a draft."

"I think you will find, Colonel," I answered, "that the neurotics in any culture at a given time are not different from the average in kind, but in degree. The cultural pressures have had, for one reason or another, a more telling effect on them than they have had on the average. If this is true, the neurotic presents us with a magnified picture of what is going on in the culture and affords us the opportunity of exploring in detail the underlying factors that are involved."

"Very good," replied Colonel Donovan. "How soon can you come to Washington and get the project under way?"

Within a month study groups were functioning across the nation. The study provided a fascinating insight into the young men of America in 1941, but it was outmoded when the Japanese attacked Pearl Harbor and changed the social and political climate of the nation in one short hour of violence.

Millard Preston Goodfellow, World War I war correspondent and later president and publisher of the *Brooklyn Daily Eagle* and the *Pocatello* (Idaho) *Tribune,* had served as a volunteer with the Boys' Clubs of America for more than 40 years. He had become a senior director. Late that summer of 1941, his old friend Bill Donovan asked him to come to Washington and help with Donovan's shadowy COI. Goodfellow played an unaccustomed role for a Boys' Clubs director. He was made deputy director of special activities. Donovan coined the name Special Activities Goodfellow to differentiate that group from Special Activities Bruce, which was headed by David Bruce. Bruce was to concern himself with intelligence, and Goodfellow was to be in charge of clandestine warfare and sabotage. Bruce, who eventually became one of America's most distinguished diplomats, later wrote about the COI and the OSS:

[Donovan's] mandate was almost unlimited in the field of clandestine activities. Nor did any chief ever as readily respond to such a challenge. Something had to knit together beings so disparate, recruited for tasks so indefinite. The polarization came from one individual—Donovan. In the midst of the gravest preoccupations, with a task so comprehensive as, at times, to appall his subordinates, the general remained unruffled, calm to deal with the exigencies of worldwide covert operations, but able to turn what seemed an equal concentration on the marital, or extramarital problems, the health or illness, the financial tribulations or any other concerns of those who worked for him.

Around the world Donovan's "moles," recruited over the years on his countless trips abroad, began to report to the Secret Intelligence branch. On August 6, he outlined to the Bureau of the Budget his plans for peacetime and wartime operations. While America was still at peace, Donovan's agents would go about their missions in the Axis countries of Germany, Italy, and Japan, and would make intelligence use of "strategic listening points" at Lisbon, Stockholm, Geneva, and Shanghai. His counterintelligence agents, to be called X-2, would function in the United States, South America, and neutral Europe, and also in the Soviet Union and the United Kingdom.

When the COI first began to submit reports to the President, Donovan announced that he wanted to read everything. By the time the OSS had completed its wartime work, even the speed-reading Donovan would have had to spend eight hours a day, six days a week for 16½ years to read the reports his agents and researchers had assembled. Donovan's reports to the President alone, which are contained among the Roosevelt papers at Hyde Park, total 7,500 pages. They all begin, "My Dear Mr. President," and they all are signed, "Bill."

25

COI Sets Up Shop

THE PRUSSIAN GENERAL and military writer Friedrich von Bernhardi defined intelligence as "unmasking the enemy's intent."

"It is more than that," said William J. Donovan, writing in *Life* magazine. "In this imperfect world, as yet ruled by power and swept by passion and ambition, a nation's foreign policy is successful only to the extent that it is conditioned at all times by the true intent of its enemies and friends. If the purpose of a potential enemy is unmasked in time, the war may be averted. If we Americans, for example, know and are able to evaluate properly the comparative resources, production, manpower, and political outlook of a neighbor, we should be able to measure the friendship or enmity of that neighbor. If we know the true state of morale of our allies and the structure of their economies, we can plan our own security with confidence."

When he established the COI, President Roosevelt had announced that "Mr. Donovan's task will be to coordinate and correlate defense information, but his work is not intended to supersede or to duplicate or to involve any direction of or interference with the activities of the General Staff, the regular intelligence services, the Federal Bureau of Investigation, or of other existing departments and agencies."

"Having stated what Colonel Donovan is not," said Blair Bolles in the October 5, 1941, *Washington Star,* "the White House has never bothered since then to state what Colonel Donovan is."

Even before the COI was officially announced, Donovan forwarded the first of his top-secret reports to the White House for the President's eyes only. From the start, he sent these reports by messenger to Grace Tully, FDR's secretary, and she saw to it that they were handed to the President. Donovan's approach was first to create a flow of information from R&A to the President and other top officers of the government, and then to concentrate on collecting and analyzing secret intelligence. Still, some of the earliest dispatches came from secret agents in the field.

Donovan believed that a man was not completely an intelligence officer until he had been behind enemy lines. "Gentlemen, have you ever been behind enemy lines?" he would sometimes ask a group of staff members who were assessing a sheaf of intelligence reports.

"You can find out anything you want to know about anybody in the world if you really want to," Donovan was fond of saying, and he meant what he said. He also believed that an intelligence organization must not be bound by the laws of probability, but instead by the laws of improbability. "This is no place for a guy bound by the law of averages," he told federal judge Hubert Will, one of his aides. "The unlooked-for, even antic event must be anticipated and understood just as quickly and deeply as the expected, rational event. We must be governed as much by inspired illogic as logic."

To Donovan, intelligence was truly believable only if it could be corroborated by a number of sources. Then it could be seen from more than one viewpoint and given proper perspective.

Mussolini scoffed at Donovan's fledgling COI. "The Americans have the best intelligence system in the world," he said, "because nobody has been able to discover it."

Even as Mussolini was making his quip, Donovan's agents were infiltrating his government. One of Donovan's first informants on Italian affairs, during the summer of 1941, was Count Carlo Sforza, an anti-Fascist statesman who had left Italy in 1929 to oppose Mussolini from voluntary exile. Sforza came to the United States in 1940. Donovan went to see the count in his home at 131 East 93rd Street in New York from time to time to obtain the latest secret information from Italy. Franklin Roosevelt, who had a fine appetite for intrigue, had made the initial contact with Sforza and introduced Donovan to him.

Sforza felt it was the duty of every Italian patriot to fight Hitler and to free Italy from the rule of his accomplice Mussolini. Sforza cooperated with Donovan's COI, and his friends in Italy became Donovan's agents. Because the count was a leading member of one of his nation's proudest and oldest aristocratic families, he knew men who were high in Italian government, the professions, and commerce. Added to these people were Donovan's own high-ranking friends in Italy, many of whom he had come to know during the Italian invasion of Ethiopia. These were people who secretly opposed the brutal attack on Haile Selassie's virtually defenseless kingdom and who considered that the only honorable future for their country depended upon the defeat of Mussolini and his removal from office.

The intelligence services of the U.S. Army and U.S. Navy became part of Donovan's sources. "The United States has never been quite so innocent as it has sometimes pretended to be about spies," commented White House correspondent Jonathan Daniels. "Before World War II we had sent out some very zealous naval and military attachés, some of whom, fortunately, had done more than watch military parades and attend Embassy teas in full uniform. But when war came and Donovan began to train his men for the wonderful jobs some of them did in dangerous territory, the discovery was suddenly made that what spies got in danger was no more important than information we had collected—or should have collected—before the fighting began."

Donovan fumed at the shortcomings of armed forces and State Department information, but he made the best of it. "The armed services had never devoted any considerable attention to political, economic, and psychological problems," reported a Donovan aide, Wallace R. Deuel.

> They were primarily interested in information about the armed forces of other countries. Yet these other types of information were now urgently needed. They could only be gathered and appraised by the most highly qualified experts. The armed forces did not have enough of such experts, nor could they recruit them.
>
> Moreover, the ideals and traditions of the services were marked by a directness of thought and conduct that were ill suited for some of the most important of all intelligence operations. A certain number of professional officers, in fact, looked down on irregular undercover warfare as a dirty business altogether unbecoming an officer and a gentleman.

Much of the intelligence the United States had been receiving from military and naval attachés also ceased by autumn 1941. "After Europe was overrun by the enemy," said Donovan, "our State Department found itself cut off from most sources of information and dependent largely upon what friendly governments chose to provide. We had only the intelligence gathered by other arms. We had no way of telling when information was planted or where rumor originated."

At least the State Department was cooperative with the COI. "Sumner Welles was then under secretary of state, Roosevelt's closest contact in Cordell Hull's rather inert State Department," recalled Ray S. Cline, who served Donovan faithfully throughout the COI's period of mushrooming growth, "and he undertook to work in reasonable harmony with COI and later with OSS. He reached an understanding with Donovan, on August 10, 1941, conceding to the new agency responsibility for the collection of economic information and other related data overseas and levying on it requirement for reports and studies on foreign countries of foreign policy interest. The coverage was not to include Latin America, where not only J. Edgar Hoover but also Nelson Rockefeller, Coordinator of Inter-American Affairs, were already active."

Donovan, the master spy, particularly valued the critical intelligence being provided during the summer of 1941 by William Stephenson, a close personal friend and the principal agent in North America of America's closest ally. As a confidential OSS paper indicated, in July 1941 "arrangements were made by Mr. Stephenson to provide the General [Donovan] with a regular flow of secret information from sources available to his own organization, including highly confidential British censorship material not normally circulated outside British government departments."

On August 9 Stephenson reported to London that Donovan's office was already functioning. He set up a Washington branch of the British Security Coordinator (BSC) to keep in constant touch with the COI, and Donovan set up a COI office in New York to keep in close touch with the BSC. Donovan established other offices in New York too. The Foreign Information Service (FIS) opened at 270 Madison Avenue on August 1, staffed with journalists and radio broadcasters under Robert Sherwood's direction. The FIS produced special programs that were beamed overseas by American broadcasting companies and relayed by BBC transmitters. The Foreign Broadcast Monitoring Service was soon transcribing Nazi propaganda transmissions and hurrying them to Sherwood's staff. The FIS was able to put its response on the air before Goebbels's propaganda had a chance to sink in.

Reports reaching the COI from both covert and open sources were employed in preparing the broadcasts. "The facts go first to the President and heads of departments," journalist Thomas M. Johnson reported. "Then such of them as are not too secret go into the second barrel of Donovan's double-barreled job, are let out over the world in the best way to aid democracy and injure dictatorship. In such a cause are needed devotion, a touch of ardent imagination, with the fundamental, the unvarnished truth. For though the bursting charge be propaganda, it must be propaganda in the true and American sense of that much misunderstood word, which really means not lies and distortion but the propagation of the faith."

James L. Wright, writing in the *Buffalo Evening News,* summed up Donovan's concept of the role of the FIS: "Just as Nazism seeks to undermine each country before it physically attacks it, so in Col. Donovan's judgment, the Allies must confront Nazism with a psychological offensive of their own. He believes that can be made to reach the Rhine and beyond, that there can be a constant hammering of Adolf Hitler's home front."

Ned Buxton and Bill Donovan had also struck upon the idea of debriefing refugees from Europe as they arrived in New York, and on August 25, a small Oral Intelligence unit began operations in Manhattan.

In August Donovan asked Stephenson to make available to his staff "the services of experienced officers of his own organization to assist in laying down the framework of the COI headquarters and field establishment." Donovan's calendar of appointments and telephone calls from August 18 to America's entry into the war shows that the two men were in touch on 36 occasions. The British assistance proved invaluable as, according to OSS man Carleton Coon, the Harvard anthropologist, Donovan modeled the OSS on the British SOE, which, just two years before, Colin Gubbins had in turn modeled on the Irish Republican Army.

After the war Stephenson remarked, "If Donovan had not been able to rely upon BSC assistance, his organization could not have survived. Indeed, it is a fact that, before he had his own operational machinery in working order, which was not until several months after Pearl Harbor, he was entirely dependent on it." Stephenson claimed too much for British support during the early days of COI, but there is no denying that without the assistance of British intelligence, the COI would have found its growth more tortuous and much slower.

British intelligence might be cooperative, but Donovan found that the British Foreign Office could be just as prickly as the U.S. Department of State. "In relation to shipping equipment to the U.S.S.R.," remembered Henry Field,

> the question came up about road conditions and capacities across Afghanistan. Since this was considered a "British sphere of influence," General Donovan requested the latest handbook or handbooks. He was sent a series, obviously out of date, with the statement that these were the latest available. I could not believe this. COI, London, reported the same lack of detailed information.
>
> Just at this time General Donovan asked me to brief Mr. Mauran from Providence, who was leaving shortly for Cairo. I suggested that Mr. Mauran try to obtain the code numbers of any British handbooks on the Near East while in Cairo. He returned to Washington in about three weeks with a splendid list, including Afghanistan. Donovan then requested the latter by number from London. The cabled answer said that this handbook and others were available to COI in the British Mission on nearby Pennsylvania Avenue. Here, upon request by number, I was given the Afghanistan handbook. The keeper of this safe had been instructed not to release a handbook to anyone without the correct number. In this large safe lay many important documents now available to COI through Mr. Mauran's research in Cairo. Mr. Mauran, who died very shortly thereafter from a virus picked up in Egypt, rendered special service.

The pulling and pushing between the FBI, the ONI, G-2, the State Department, and the COI over the gathering of intelligence continued unabated.

"FDR's way of operating Washington was like a boxing free-for-all," observed Turner McBaine. "Put a bunch of pugilists in the ring and let them slug it out. The winner was the last guy left standing. Donovan flourished in this environment. He rose to the top and became the confidant of FDR."

While the bureaucratic battle of Washington raged over the form and substance of American intelligence, the British agent Bickham Sweet-Escott, in London, received a message from Bill Stephenson in New York that "it was going to be a long time before Donovan's position in Washington was clearly defined." Sweet-Escott wrote after the war: "The American system of government at this point was well described by an American friend of mine, who used to say of it that 'there is a lot of noise on the stairs but it is a long time before anyone comes down.' It was a system which encouraged Great Debates about American secret activities."

Atherton Richards once remarked, "Bill Donovan's method of running an organization is like pouring molasses from a barrel onto the table. It will ooze in every direction, but eventually he'll make it into some sort of pattern."

The pattern was not always obvious to the naval commander who found himself countermanded by a corporal, since Donovan delegated authority based on ability and not rank. Nor was it evident to William Langer, who went to Washington to head R&A and found another man in his spot. "He can be the director, and you can be the chief," Donovan said.

As did Roosevelt, Donovan often appointed men with overlapping authority and let them compete to get the job done. He assigned unimaginative aides to watch over his woolliest idea men. "A man with a plan for a bomb that he is going to steer to its target with his feet should be put to work," he said, "but somebody has to keep an eye on him."

Donovan, by his own admission never much of an organization man, refused to respect the table of organization and the chain of command established by his aides. His executives, recalled one aide, "would walk into Donovan's office with dozens of charts, charts for the budget, charts for the administration, charts for the various divisions. Donovan would glance at them, smile at them, approve them with a mild wave of the hand, and then he would have another idea, and he would forget them completely." Since many of his top aides were either corporate attorneys or executives, they struck upon the notion of organizing the COI as a holding company. Donovan burst out laughing at the very idea. He much preferred to run affairs on a person-to-person basis. The kind of organization that emerged sometimes seemed to be no organization at all, but it proved amazingly practical in the world of espionage and subversion. At the same time Donovan was a stickler for security.

"At the first organization meeting which I attended Colonel Donovan laid down a few basic security regulations," recalled Henry Field.

Since very few of us had any security training, each of us was to work as a small cell, communicating any details of our work within COI to the fewest possible number of people. Only the Director, Ned Buxton, and a few administrators would be kept informed of progress. The minimum of interoffice discussion was to be allowed.

The first team of U.S. specialists in all fields was to be assembled in COI. Permission must be granted to discuss any project with anyone outside each individual cell. However, with the assemblage of such a staff, almost any question could be answered. For example, specialists on geography, geology, anthropology, oceanography, meteorology, politics, history, photography, and photo-interpretation were immediately available or could be brought to Washington for immediate consultation.

In conclusion Colonel Donovan emphasized the fact that since COI was to become the key intelligence organization for the President, foreign spies must be expected to infiltrate. He added that the best he could expect with FBI clearance and all possible unusual precautions, would be at least one brilliant spy per five hundred personnel—hence the cellular structure. Any unusual questions asked by a member of COI staff must be reported at once to the Security Division. Hence I never knew what my neighbors were doing; I presume this was mutual. Security officers mixed with the staff in eating places nearby, often encouraging indiscreet talk. On three occasions I reported questioners, two of whom turned out to be security officers. As far as I know my cell members never broke security, a tribute to their loyalty and FBI and COI clearance.

By September, Donovan's COI was making striking progress in secret intelligence. General Miles of G-2, who had opposed Donovan in order to protect his own clandestine intelligence operations, now changed his mind. On September 5, he wrote to General Marshall:

The military and naval intelligence services have gone into the field of undercover intelligence to a limited extent. In view of the appointment of the Coordinator of Information and the work which it is understood the President desires him to undertake, it is believed that the undercover intelligence of the two services should be consolidated under the Coordinator of Information. The reasons for this are that an undercover intelligence service is much more effective if under one head rather than three and that a civilian agency, such as the Coordinator of Information, has distinct advantages over any military or naval agency in the administration of such a service.

The navy held out a little longer. Wallace B. Phillips, who commanded a Naval Intelligence unit in New York City, at first refused to turn over his operation to the COI. When Donovan implied that he might inform the President of the navy's reluctance to close up shop, Alan G. Kirk, now an admiral and chief of Naval Intelligence, decided to give in too. On October 10, Donovan was able to tell Roosevelt that, with the approval of the secretaries of war and the navy and the joint action of G-2 and ONI, "there was consolidated under the COI the undercover intelligence of the two services."

The FBI still remained hostile toward the COI. "The Abwehr gets better treatment from the FBI than we do," Donovan remarked to Allen Dulles.

There was no question in Donovan's mind that the United States was coming closer and closer to war. "One morning in late September, Donovan summoned me to his office," said Kermit Roosevelt. "Pearl Harbor was still three months away, but he was absolutely certain that somehow we would be drawn into war. I shared his feeling."

As Roosevelt was leaving, Donovan called him back. "Kim," he asked, "what do you think of happenings in Iran? That's going to be an important part of the world for us." Roosevelt recalled what occurred next:

> At that point, I must admit, I had very little to contribute on Iran. I knew roughly where it was but little more. So I said, safely but noncommittally, that "it looks serious." That was satisfactory for the moment. As soon as I was out of his office, I looked up Iran in an atlas and an encyclopedia. Thereafter I kept myself better informed.
>
> One thing I did immediately after the Donovan interrogation; in addition to consulting the atlas and encyclopedia, I visited a colleague at the Library of Congress. Ralph Bunche, later under secretary general of the United Nations, was already doing research work for the COI, and was well able to answer my questions.
>
> Ralph was a quiet, studious-looking black gentleman who received me with appropriate gravity.

"Kim," he began, "I take it I'm to start from scratch."

Roosevelt nodded, and Bunche gave him an erudite lecture emphasizing, as Roosevelt remembered, the point, "Don't ever confuse Iranians with the Arabs. They don't like it."

When new recruits reported to the COI, they often looked forward to their first meeting with the director with considerable trepidation. The reputation of Wild Bill Donovan, dauntless hero of World War I, prepared them for a formidable, perhaps even violent individual. "I'm afraid I disappoint people," Donovan confided to the writer Thomas M. Johnson, "for really, my ideal isn't 'Wild Bill' but another Irish character called 'the real McCoy.' I prefer facts to fireworks."

The truth of the matter is that Donovan also had a penchant for fireworks, and by August he was already planning to organize operational groups to fight guerrilla warfare.

"I took Bill Donovan to lunch with me at Woodley," Henry L. Stimson wrote in his diary on August 13, "and had a good talk with him about his proposed guerrillas: I think there is a good deal in this proposition, because we are likely to need that kind of fighting in any South American jungle country that we may have to go into to prevent the Germans from getting a foothold."

COI reports indicated that German agents were infiltrating both Brazil and Argentina and that Allied defeat in Europe would inevitably lead to trouble in South America. Donovan was equally concerned in August about Japanese movements in the Orient. On August 16, T. V. Soong, Chinese minister of foreign affairs, came to see him, to explain China's grim situation. Soong hoped that Donovan would use his influence with the President to obtain fighter aircraft for China. Soong described the overwhelming air assault the Japanese were making on Chungking, China's wartime capital.

Without planes the Chinese could not fight off the bombers over the city or exact retribution by bombing the bases from which the raiders came. "It is perfectly clear," Soong told Donovan, "that the purpose of this bombing is to finish the 'China Incident' before Japan moves in other directions—by demonstrating to the people of China the difference between reality and hopes of the last fourteen months that American assistance would be effective."

Soong noted that, in light of deliveries of aircraft being made to Russia, the Chinese felt their resistance was "just a pawn in the calculations of other democratic powers. Japan is being furnished the materials with which to destroy us in order to relieve the British from attack in the south and maybe even the Russians from attack in the north.

"Remember, Colonel," concluded Soong, "that we have proved that we can fight longer than any other people who are fighting on the democratic side—that given the arms we can really finish the job. We have stuck for five years. Please help us stick now."

Donovan assigned James Roosevelt to urge the Chinese case with such Roosevelt aides as Harry L. Hopkins, and he reported to the President in detail.

In the meantime the structuring of the COI continued. The first meeting of the Board of Analysts was held at 2:40 P.M. on September 10 in James Phinney Baxter's office. Plans were discussed for two large rooms "open only to the President, the Cabinet, Colonel Donovan, and the Board of Analysts." One room was to hold a strategic map of the world, depicting the American defense posture; the other would contain graphic charts "portraying aspects of national defense."

"Mr. Baxter reported," said the minutes of the meeting, "that Colonel Donovan has noted that any secret agents sent into the field by us must be given in advance the most careful set of instructions."

The board dealt with such mundane problems as the routing of top-secret material and the decisions that "Secret material will be placed each night in the central safe, which will be time locked." The projects already under way included: "(1) a general picture of the situation in regard to Japan; (2) a study of our exposed flank in South America, in case we should be drawn into the war; (3) a study of our exposed flank in West Africa; (4) a study of the strategic distribution of Russian war industries."

The meeting adjourned at 3:55 P.M. after deciding that from then on the staff would meet daily at 9:30 A.M.

Donovan continued his recruiting. On September 11, John Ford, 46 years old and at the height of his career as one of Hollywood's most talented directors, finished a film, *How Green Was My Valley,* and left for Washington on the Union Pacific streamliner, ostensibly to join the U.S. Navy. When he reached Washington, Ford checked into the Carlton Hotel where, for the next four years, room 501 was to be his home.

"It was a tiny broom closet of a room," he reminisced, but this scarcely mattered. Ford, in the words of his grandson Don, "had been scooped up, not by the navy but by one of the most dynamic, mysterious, and visionary men in the first half of the 20th century—William J. 'Wild Bill' Donovan." Ford was to organize the Field Photographic branch, and he immediately sent for some of the top cameramen in Hollywood. They set up quarters and a mess and established their shop in the South Building at 25th and E. The laboratory and studio were in the basement.

Ford was to report directly to Donovan. He came back from a meeting with the COI director and told his crew, "We're going to be involved in a hell of a lot more than photography."

Their first assignment was to make a film report on the condition of the U.S. Atlantic fleet, which was escorting convoys from the United States to Iceland. On October 21, Ray Kellogg left for Iceland by boat to shoot the documentary. When the film was finished Donovan screened it for the President as a new type of intelligence report.

Autumn 1941 was a seminal period for the COI. Donovan arranged with the Council on Foreign Relations in New York to consider questions of national import, which he would from time to time pose, and he talked with lawyer-diplomat John Foster Dulles about organizing "a group to study and make suggestions with reference to various phases of the international situation." He persuaded the adventurous members of the Explorers Club in New York to contribute information garnered on their expeditions to odd corners of the world, any one of which could become a cockpit of war.

In 1940 Donovan had engaged the Arctic explorer Vilhjalmur Stefansson as an adviser on a proposed development of oil in the province of Alberta along the Athabasca, Slave, and Mackenzie rivers. The entire project depended upon the construction of an oil pipeline, and

Donovan had attempted to get Roosevelt's approval of the undertaking, which he was confident would greatly strengthen America's military position. On October 28, 1941, Donovan wrote to Stefansson: "I would like very much to discuss with you the possibility of the establishment of a center of Arctic studies. It does seem to me that in connection with my task it would be most desirable to have, in one place, geographical and meteorological information bearing on the Far North."

Stefansson, who had sizable research facilities at his disposal, readily agreed to cooperate, and Donovan went to New York to work out the plans. He was convinced that the Arctic would play a signal role in the war with Germany. If military aid was to be carried safely to the Russians at Murmansk, Allied shipping in the North Atlantic would have to follow the Arctic pack ice to stay as far as possible from German submarines and bombers based in Norway.

From Donovan's point of view, probably the most valuable part of Stefansson's studies would relate to Japan, not Germany. When Hitler and Stalin signed the Nazi-Soviet Pact in August 1939, Donovan realized that the way was opened for Hitler to attack first Poland and then the West without fear of an assault from the Soviet Union. At the same time he recognized that the pact also forced the Japanese to delay their own military adventures in Asia because the Soviet Union remained in a strong position to balk them. Thus, when Hitler attacked Russia on June 22, 1941, it was apparent to Donovan that Japan was now free to move in Asia and that war with the United States would almost certainly result within the year.

Within a month after the German blitzkrieg into Russia, Japan invaded Indochina. Roosevelt warned the Japanese government against its policy of military expansion, placed an embargo on oil shipments, and froze Japanese assets in the United States. When Gen. Hideki Tojo replaced the moderate Prime Minister Prince Fumimaro Konoye in October, it confirmed Donovan's belief that before Japan would abandon plans to conquer East Asia and the South Pacific it would launch an attack on both the United States and Great Britain. Oil embargoes and frozen assets would only goad the Japanese into action.

When war came with Japan, the Aleutians and Alaska would be open to attack, and Donovan told Stefansson that a military road must be built across Canada into Alaska as soon as possible. Stefansson was to study the route. Alaskan and Aleutian weather would also be critical. The Soviet Union, said Stefansson, controlled most of the important stations for forecasting the weather of mainland Alaska, the Bering Sea, and the Aleutian Islands, as well as portions of the North Pacific. Soviet reports would also help to improve the forecasting in the Yukon Territory, British Columbia, and the U.S. Northwest. Donovan and Stefansson discussed how the Soviet Union could be persuaded to share weather information with the United States while denying it to the Japanese. "We would have to agree with the Soviet government upon some secret code, and upon changes of code as frequent as seems necessary," said Stefansson.

On November 17, Donovan reported his arrangements with Stefansson to the President.

> In accordance with your instructions, I have talked with Dr. Vilhjalmur Stefansson. He is ready to make available to us his services, as well as those of his staff, which would include the use of his 15,000 volume library and extensive files. His field would be all of Alaska; Canada north of 60 degrees; all of Greenland; all of Iceland; the Scandinavian countries and Finland north of 60 degrees; the shores of Hudson Bay, and Labrador as far south as Hamilton Inlet. He would also cover Okhotsk Sea, Bering Sea, Hudson Bay, the North Atlantic, and the entire Polar Sea with its islands.
>
> Dr. Stefansson would attempt to supply any kind of information from the geographic area described, including not merely sciences like geography and oceanography, but information regarding such things as religion, language, clothing, food, economics, etc.

Donovan pressed Stefansson for answers to puzzling questions. Stefansson wrote to him: "Yesterday you expressed interest in the double situation (a) that the Germans used glaciers for airplane landings in northern Norway and (b) that the possibility of glacier landings was apparently unknown and undreamed of by those British who were in that part of Norway." Stefansson had turned up Peter Rhodes, a *Chicago Daily News* correspondent, who had been in northern Norway at the time and who could give Donovan information.

By the end of November, the Center of Arctic Studies was a reality, and it was to have an important influence on the conduct of the war with Japan, which was by then little more than a week away.

President Roosevelt continued to find domestic political problems blocking his path. It was certainly in America's interest to supply the Russians to help them blunt the German invasion, which was sweeping ahead on all fronts. Nevertheless, many Americans were outraged that their country should support the Red dictatorship, which to most people seemed little better than those of the Nazis and Fascists. In this instance, the Pope in Rome also feared that U.S. assistance to Russia would only strengthen Communism. Donovan's agents sought information that would help Roosevelt placate both American voters and the Pope. They found it in Russia, where Polish captives of the Soviets were forming to fight Hitler. Corroboration came from Jan Ciechanowski, Polish ambassador in Washington, in a letter to Donovan on September 27:

I am very glad to be able to tell you on the basis of information just received from London that the enthusiasm of the Poles in Russia actively to resume the fight against Hitlerite Germany is so great, that the Polish Army in Russia will be virtually an army of volunteers. Great numbers of Poles of military age apply daily demanding to be enrolled immediately in the Polish Forces, thus swelling the ranks of units which are being formed from our regular soldiers who had been interned in Russia.

The Polish Government is confident that it will be able to put in the field very shortly an army of well over 100,000 men, provided they can be supplied with the necessary material and equipment from Great Britain and the United States. I hear that two divisions are already formed and the third is nearing completion.

What will interest you especially, I am sure, is that the U.S.S.R. has— in the same way as in the case of our army in Great Britain—granted us full rights of an independent National Army, giving it likewise the right of opening its own schools, full cultural freedom, and freedom of worship for both Christians and Jews. We have already got our own Catholic military chaplains.

In the long tide of history, the Russian assurances proved to be illusory, but for the moment, Donovan's report on the Soviet show of tolerance of the Catholic and Jewish faiths allowed Roosevelt to send supplies to the Russians with political impunity.

The consolidation of G-2 and ONI intelligence operations under the COI was reported to the President on October 10. Donovan accompanied his memorandum on the subject with a secret intelligence plan for North Africa. His lengthy trip through the Mediterranean earlier in the year had left him convinced of the pivotal nature of the area, and in September he had put R&A to work on in-depth studies of North Africa. Now he was making plans for intelligence operations. On the same day that Donovan sent his report to Roosevelt, he established a section labeled Special Activities–K and L Funds, which was intended to carry out espionage, subversion including sabotage, and guerrilla warfare.

To Donovan modern warfare seemed to call for three phases of softening up the enemy before an attack in force was made. First, secret intelligence was to infiltrate and discover any information that must be known in order to pave the way for the second phase, which was sabotage and subversion operations. Resistance groups and guerrilla or commando operations were to follow. All of these activities required different techniques and training, but Donovan saw them as tightly related, one preparing the way for the next. "As a concrete illustration of what can be done," Donovan told FDR, "we are now planning to deal with a very present problem in North Africa by setting up at once a wireless station in Tangier and having stationed there an assistant naval or military attaché who can unify the activities of the vice-consuls [actually 12 COI agents] in North Africa and stimulate efforts in the selection of local agents of information."

On the day before he reported to the President, Donovan had appointed Lt. Col. Robert A. Solborg to head Special Operations. Solborg had been born in Warsaw, the son of a Polish general in the service of the Russian czar. He himself had served in the Russian Army. When he was seriously wounded, he was assigned to the Russian military purchasing mission in New York City. With the outbreak of the Russian Revolution, he became an American citizen by joining the U.S. Army. Later he was a military attaché in Paris and then became an executive of Armco Steel Company, for which he traveled throughout Germany and North Africa. Solborg had carried out intelligence missions successfully, first for the British and then for the American G-2. Donovan ordered Solborg to organize his Washington office and then travel to London to get the advice and assistance of British SOE in establishing COI's Special Operations. He was to report directly to Donovan.

At about this same time, Donovan had to ask Roosevelt to be more specific about the role of the COI. The original order of July 11 had been kept vague on purpose. Now, on October 21, Donovan wrote to the President, "While originally we both considered it advisable to have no directive in writing, it now seems necessary to do so to avoid misunderstanding with other departments."

Donovan had already selected Wallace B. Phillips as chief of the COI's Secret Intelligence unit. He had headed the ONI's secret intelligence and by October was already reporting to Donovan on the activities of the 12 vice-consuls in North Africa. The vice-consuls were presumably checking up on American supplies sent to the region, but actually they were observing German and Italian activities. "The main problem," Donovan said after the war, "was to take care of the intellectual side—getting data on the railroads, tides, and any other details that would affect the getting in of arms and other military equipment."

On November 17, Donovan made Phillips director of Special Information Service, which was tantamount to heading up Secret Intelligence (SI).

Donovan also took steps to establish a COI office in London. On October 24, President Roosevelt wrote to Winston Churchill by diplomatic pouch, "Colonel Donovan tells me that he has had most helpful cooperation from the officers of His Majesty's Government who are charged with direct responsibility for your war effort. In order to facilitate the carrying out of the work of the Coordinator with respect to Europe and the occupied countries, I have authorized Colonel Donovan to send a small staff to London." Donovan already had chosen William D. Whitney to be chief of the London bureau, and Whitney was soon off to his new post.

In October and November, Donovan was a frequent caller at the

White House. He breakfasted with the President, and he dined with him. Whenever he went to the White House, he took with him information of great import and also little tidbits that entertained FDR. On October 21, Donovan gave Roosevelt a Nazi map that, he explained, the British had "purloined from a German courier." The map showed South America as it would be restructured after the German conquest. Roosevelt was fascinated and a few days later made it public as proof of Hitler's baleful ambitions. That same day Donovan explained again to the President his concept for an American commando unit of some 2,500 men, talked about John Ford's movie-making for the COI, and showed FDR an article from the German press entitled "The Jew-Roosevelt Names War Maker Donovan as Super-Agitator." Both men chuckled over what they considered a piece of unintended German drollery.

Some of Donovan's meetings with FDR were more significant. On November 13, he informed the President about a secret protocol to the Japanese-Indochina Treaty, and on November 17 they discussed not only Donovan's report on the Center of Arctic Studies but also a clandestine expedition to Central Africa, ostensibly to study the great apes, but actually to observe German spies at work in the area.

Often, early riser that he was, Donovan arrived in the morning before the President got out of bed to begin his official work day. On Friday, November 28, War Secretary Stimson had reason to complain about this. "G-2 had sent me a summary of the information in regard to the movements of the Japanese in the Far East, and it amounted to such a formidable statement of dangerous possibilities that I decided to take it to the President before he got up. I had some difficulty getting in because he had already given an appointment to Bill Donovan, but I persisted on it and finally got there."

Roosevelt had already heard Donovan outline the increasingly dangerous developments in the Pacific. Stimson recorded in his diary what followed: "He [Roosevelt] branched into an analysis of the situation himself as he sat there on his bed, saying there were three alternatives and only three that he could see before us. I told him I could see two. His alternatives were—first, to do nothing; second, to make something in the nature of an ultimatum again, stating a point beyond which we would fight; third, to fight at once. I told him my only two were the last two because I did not think anyone would do nothing in this situation, and he agreed with me."

Before Stimson arrived the President had confided in Donovan that "it was difficult now to find a formula in dealing with Japan." He approved plans Donovan showed him for checking into America's West Coast defenses.

By the end of November 1941 the COI was functioning well. General Strong, soon to become head of G-2, thought perhaps it was working too well, and he began to make political moves to block its growth. On December 3, he succeeded in winning White House approval for a Joint Army and Navy Intelligence Committee, which was to receive Donovan's reports. Donovan was to serve on the committee. The idea was to prevent the free-wheeling Donovan from consolidating his position as America's master spy. Julius C. Holmes, who became the executive secretary for the committee, later observed, "The Military Intelligence leaders all looked on Donovan like the fox in the hen house who was intent on usurping their 'hens' in pursuit of intelligence for someone's organization other than their own." Obligingly enough, Donovan at first sat in with the committee, but he continued to send his reports directly to FDR and to the British when he felt it served America's interests.

American naval cryptographers had solved the cipher machine that the Japanese used to encipher their diplomatic communications. The resulting intercepts were given the code name Magic. Washington knew that the Japanese were planning a major assault somewhere in the Pacific, but when the intercepts indicated that a huge striking force of carriers had set sail for a secret destination, the U.S. Navy assumed that it was bound for the Dutch East Indies. The navy, complacent in its overwhelming strength, did not alert either its commanders at Pearl Harbor or Manila, for surely the Japanese would not dare to risk complete disaster in a head-on collision with U.S. might.

The Japanese had sent Saburo Kurusu as a special envoy to Washington, and he was now negotiating with Secretary of State Cordell Hull. Donovan determined to find out what was going on behind the Japanese move, and he believed that Kurusu was the man who might tell him. It was Ferdinand Lammot Belin, a former ambassador to Poland and a millionaire industrialist, who suggested a way to reach Kurusu.

Kurusu's wife, Alice, was an American woman from Chicago, where Kurusu had served in the Japanese consulate for six years. When, in 1930, he was stationed in Peru, he had made close friends with Americans living in Lima. Among these was the diplomat Ferdinand Mayer, a Hoosier from Indianapolis, who before retiring had served the United States in Japan, China, Germany, and then in Peru. Mayer and Kurusu had gotten along very well, and now Belin, in turn a close friend of Mayer, was urging Donovan to bring the 59-year-old diplomat out of retirement. Perhaps Kurusu, known during South American days for his pro-American sentiments, would talk to his old friend Mayer. Donovan approved the idea, and Belin got in touch with Mayer.

On Saturday morning, December 6, Mayer breakfasted at Belin's Evermay estate in Georgetown. James Dunn of the State Department was also present. He agreed that Kurusu seemed to have something on his mind that he was not expressing in the talks with Hull. Mayer picked up the phone and called the Japanese Embassy.

A hostile crowd had formed in front of the Japanese Embassy on Massachusetts Avenue. Kurusu was watching the Americans outside when he was called to the phone. It was Ferdinand Mayer, who said he wanted to see him. Kurusu replied that he would be happy to see Mayer but "would hate to inconvenience him," since there was an angry crowd outside. From the sound of Kurusu's voice, Mayer realized that the Japanese diplomat was "quite overwhelmed and in the deepest sort of despair."

At 11:00 A.M., Mayer arrived at the Japanese Embassy. He shook hands with Kurusu and talk turned to old times in Chicago and Lima. Kurusu then indicated that he was anxious to discuss his present mission but, as Mayer later reported, he kept "repeatedly turning his head to see if anyone were approaching."

Finally Kurusu whispered, "Fred, we are in an awful mess. In the first place, I was delayed in coming on this mission through an attack of conjunctivitis when I could neither read nor write. This complicated the situation because time was running out, from the point of view of restraining the military element, and it had been planned that I should have left for the United States in August or September."

Kurusu told Mayer that the Japanese government had yielded to the military and given the go-ahead for the invasion of Indochina as the "least harmful alternative." He went on to express his chagrin at the Japanese embroilment in China, the mounting disenchantment with the Nazi partnership, the arrogant behavior of the Germans in Tokyo, and the extreme danger of war between his nation and the United States. He himself opposed the war because he was certain Japan would lose, but he commented that "hotheads could upset the applecart at any time."

As they parted, Mayer asked Kurusu to dine with Belin and himself at eight. He walked out of the Japanese Embassy onto Massachusetts Avenue, where traffic was moving as if nothing whatsoever were going on. It was a strange, unreal world that he hurried to discuss at Evermay. Nothing came of Mayer's talk with Kurusu. It was already too late.

26

Conducting Ungentlemanly Warfare

ON SUNDAY, DECEMBER 7, the New York Giants were playing the Brooklyn Dodgers at the Polo Grounds. In the second quarter the Giants were trailing 7–0. Bill Donovan, a football fan since his boyhood on the Buffalo waterfront, grumbled to his friends; he was not at all satisfied with the performance of the Giants. The Dodgers had just driven again to the Giants' four-yard line when the public-address system cut through the noise of the screaming crowd.

"Colonel William Donovan, come to the box office at once. There is an important phone message."

After shoving his way through the crowd to the box office, Donovan heard James Roosevelt's excited voice on the phone. Roosevelt told him that the President wanted to see him at once. The Japanese had attacked Pearl Harbor, and the first thing the President had said when the dread news reached him was "Phone Bill Donovan." He was to go to La Guardia, where an air force plane was waiting to fly him to Washington. Donovan rushed by cab from the Polo Grounds to the airport, joining Vice-President Henry Wallace, Postmaster General Frank Walker, and presidential adviser Judge Samuel Rosenman for the flight.

At the capital, Donovan conferred briefly with Roosevelt and hurried to COI headquarters. He was already there when Turner McBaine arrived.

"Stark horror filtered through the COI as the magnitude of what had happened became clear," McBaine recalled.

Donovan called McBaine into his office. "You're from San Francisco," he said. "Do you know the name of the admiral in charge of the naval district there? Get him on the phone and find out what's going on there. The President wants to know."

McBaine, who had just been given an ensign's commission, was stunned by the chief's order. Military communications to the West Coast had failed, and for all Washington knew the Japanese were about to land in California. McBaine went into the room next to Donovan's office and rang the long-distance operator. She informed him that all long-distance phone service was suspended in the emergency.

"I had a hell of a row with the telephone operator," said McBaine.

"I cussed her. I told her that I was calling on the direct order of Colonel Donovan. She never heard of either the Colonel or the COI."

Finally McBaine got through to Adm. John Greenslade in San Francisco.

"Admiral Greenslade," answered a gruff navy voice at the other end of the continent.

McBaine, knowing that admirals do not take kindly to being called by lowly ensigns even in a national emergency, mumbled through his rank but managed to pronounce "McBaine" firmly enough and very distinctly said, "calling for Colonel Donovan at the request of the President."

"Who?" demanded the admiral.

McBaine repeated his performance. It wasn't until his third try that Greenslade understood and gave him his anguished report.

"It was already three to four hours after the attack, and he hadn't heard from anyone in Washington," recalled McBaine. "The problem was in Washington. Only officers of a certain rank were supposed to call the head of a naval district. Since all the top-ranking officers were away from Washington on the weekend, only junior officers were on watch. Since nobody had enough rank to call with impunity, nobody had called. The President had been forced to turn to Donovan for information."

Admiral Greenslade explained that he had ordered submarine nets at Tiburón, Mexico. There had been bogies on the radar. What planes did he have to defend San Francisco? Virtually nothing. When Greenslade had finished his gloomy report, McBaine asked him to wait just a second and stepped into Donovan's office.

"You've got to go into the other room and thank him," he told Donovan. Donovan did so and left immediately to see FDR.

William Langer and his wife had spent the afternoon at the Corcoran Art Gallery. As they drove home, they heard the newsboys hawking the terrible news. Dropping his wife at his house, Langer continued on to COI headquarters. By that time Donovan was back from the White House, and the COI staff had gathered.

"With the utmost gravity he gave us a full report of the catastrophe," recalled Langer, "and the American losses in men and material. None of us needed to be told that thenceforth all efforts on our part would have to be redoubled."

The phone rang. It was Robert Sherwood, who was at the White House helping Roosevelt draft his speech declaring war on Japan. Donovan and Sherwood discussed the points the President might make in the address to the Congress.

Nelson Poynter, who had left the editor's chair of the *St. Petersburg* (Florida) *Times* to work for Donovan, was with him throughout the evening. "We were grabbing bulletins, all the information we could from Honolulu and the Philippines, and Donovan leaned back to appraise our situation, and he said, 'Nelson, we've been hit awfully hard. We're going to have to fight guerrilla warfare until we can rebuild our strength.'"

Donovan had seen Britain, stunned by Dunkirk, prepare for guerrilla warfare as its only option in the face of an enemy who possessed overwhelming strength. Now the United States, shattered by the Japanese strike at Pearl Harbor and the Philippines, had to resort to guerrilla warfare to hold off the enemy. It was going to be a long war.

Late in the evening Donovan received a phone call from correspondent Henry J. Taylor at the U.S. Legation in Lisbon. He had heard about the attack on Pearl Harbor from the barber at the Hotel Palacio. News of the Japanese blow had swept through the Lisbon listening post of spies soon after the planes first came out of the dawn. Taylor had rushed to the legation to see U.S. Minister Bert Fish.

"All we know is from Vichy," said Fish.

"Fish and I agreed that I would place a priority telephone call to Washington to Col. William J. Donovan," recalled Taylor. "And Bill Donovan's weird transatlantic words ricocheted back to me over a wavy circuit—weird words, dreamlike and wild."

"Out of the west at 7:55 this morning," said Donovan. "Could anybody believe it?"

Taylor recalled having stood with Donovan at Pearl Harbor and observed the mighty battle fleet, now blasted to the bottom.

"The casualties were high—dreadfully high," Donovan's eerie faraway voice was saying.

"Bill Donovan's voice wound down like a ghostly echo," remembered Taylor. "The connection broke; the circuit was lost."

This was the first direct word from Washington to Europe as to what had happened in the Pacific. Hitler and Mussolini and their sympathizers gloated over their ally's incredible victory. The mighty New World nation that Donovan had portrayed on his mission to the Balkans and the Middle East as readying its colossal power to come to the aid of freedom had instead stumbled blindly into war, its armed forces suffering a terrible defeat from which it would seemingly need years to recover. By that time the European dictators had good reason to believe they would have long since won the war.

The White House appointment book for December 7 shows that the CBS correspondent Edward R. Murrow and Col. William Donovan arrived to see the President at exactly midnight. A delegation of key senators and congressmen and the vice-president had been there a little earlier; Under Secretary of State Sumner Welles was just going out as Donovan and Murrow came in. Murrow left at 12:05, but Donovan stayed until 2:00 A.M. The President and his intelligence chief talked about the attack and what it meant to America's capacity to wage war. Donovan explained his own war strategy and pressed for an American commitment to guerrilla warfare. The failure of military intelligence to define clearly Japanese naval movements, coupled with the astounding lack of preparation by the Pacific command, had led to the worst defeat America had ever suffered. Later Donovan said:

> Before World War II we in America assumed we didn't need intelligence about other nations. As a result, when war came, we found that we were ignorant of what was going on in the world. We had to depend on allied and friendly governments for our information. Even then we were unable to make use of the information we obtained, because the various documents and reports on the enemy were scattered through various agencies of the government and had not been brought together and analyzed to give us the information we needed. Only later, during the investigation of Pearl Harbor, did we find out that in December 1941 we had information, which if properly mobilized and interpreted might well have disclosed to us what Japan intended to do.

Just before Donovan left the White House on that night when the radio still crackled with new details of the disaster and intimations of further Japanese moves, the President talked about the importance of the COI. "It's a good thing you got me started on this," he told Donovan.

December 8, the day FDR signed a declaration of war against Japan, was a frantic day at COI.

"Everyone I saw and worked with at headquarters," said Kay Halle, a Cleveland radio broadcaster who had joined the COI, "felt a strong sense of mission—a fire in the belly."

Mrs. Atherton Richards, wife of Donovan's visual reports director, had long ago scheduled a dinner that evening in honor of the COI director. Bill Donovan attended but was silent. Another guest, Arthur Krock of the *New York Times,* kept going to the phone throughout dinner. "My God," he said after one phone call. "Ninety percent of the fleet has been sunk at Pearl Harbor."

The diners were stunned. They asked Krock for more details. Donovan remained silent. He left the party early to return to his office. One guest caught him at the door and asked whether he thought Krock's estimate of the Pearl Harbor tragedy was correct.

"Arthur has excellent sources of information," Donovan said and hurried down the steps to his car, which whisked him away to COI headquarters, where he spent another long night studying the latest reports of the Japanese attack. Japanese torpedo planes and bombers had sunk the battleships *Arizona, California, West Virginia,* and *Oklahoma.* The *Nevada* lay beached in sinking condition, and the *Tennessee, Pennsylvania,* and *Maryland* were badly damaged. Three cruisers had been hit and four destroyers sunk. Other ships had been sent to the bottom or damaged. Several thousand Americans were dead or injured. The only bright spot was that Japanese planes had left untouched the workshops and drydocks. Donovan believed this meant that repairs to the damaged warships could be started at once.

Donovan sorted out the facts from the rumors, analyzed the information now coming in from secret sources in Europe, Asia, and elsewhere, and sought to learn where the Japanese might strike next and what their great victory might mean to the war in Europe. What effect could it have on the sensitive Middle East, on the battle positions in North Africa, on the Russian front? (A few days later, on December 11, America would formally enter the struggle in Europe, declaring war on Germany and Italy after they declared war on the United States.)

On Tuesday, December 9, Roosevelt ordered Donovan to coordinate all North American intelligence agencies, including the recalcitrant FBI. The lesson of Pearl Harbor was fresh in his mind: The welter of conflicting intelligence agencies had contributed to the tragic unpreparedness in the Pacific. But when J. Edgar Hoover refused to cooperate with Donovan, Roosevelt backed off and on December 23 lamely reaffirmed the authority of the FBI. A week later he sent another directive to the attorney general, Sumner Welles at the State Department, Army Intelligence, and Naval Intelligence, stating, "On December 23rd, without examination, I signed a confidential directive. . . . I believe that this directive interferes with work already being conducted by other agencies. In view of this, please meet together and straighten out this whole program and let me have whatever is necessary by way of an amended directive."

Japan may have dealt the United States a disastrous defeat, but during the gloomy holiday season of 1941 the intelligence services were engaged in angry infighting. It was not until January 6 that the principals met in the attorney general's office and agreed that the President's December 23 directive would stand. Donovan's agents were not to operate in the Western Hemisphere unless they informed the FBI first and even then they were not to operate under cover. J. Edgar Hoover had reason to be content with the arrangement.

Donovan issued a special order to all branch officers: "It is hereby ordered that no member of the Coordinator of Information will carry on any activity within the continental limits of the United States of America."

John Ford received the order at Field Photographic branch, and he called in Robert Parrish and Bill Faralla, then first-class petty officers. He told them to take a prototype Cunningham combat camera and test it. Ray Cunningham, a technician at the RKO studios, had modeled it after a captured German camera for Field Photo. It featured a 35-millimeter Eyemot-type mechanism mounted on a 200-foot magazine on a .30-.30 rifle stock. To operate it the cameraman simply pulled a trigger. Ford rose from his desk, spit accurately into a box of sand in the corner of his office, and carefully lit his pipe.

"I want a complete photographic report on the old State Department Building next to the White House," he ordered. "Cover it from all angles, from the street and from the tops of the surrounding buildings. If anyone asks you what you are doing, show them your COI cards and keep shooting. Don't take any crap from anybody. Just do your job."

Parrish and Faralla, wearing their naval uniforms, took their camera into the hospital across the street from the State Department Building. As they climbed out onto the roof, a head nurse stopped them. Faralla showed her his card.

"Oh, yes," she said, impressed. "COI. Okay."

The two men set up their tripod, snapped on the telescopic lens, and aimed what appeared to be a machine gun. A U.S. Marine sergeant appeared on the roof of Old State. He waved furiously. The Field Photo men made a movie of two marines unconcernedly playing cards on a box they'd set up between them. They photographed a World War I machine gun that was covering the White House. They panned back to the State Department roof just in time to film six marines with rifles running into position, dropping down and aiming their weapons right at the cameramen. A gust of wind blew the marines' cards off of the roof so they drifted down onto the White House lawn. The Field Photo men got a dreamy shot of the fluttering cards and then surrendered. It was good training in combat photography. The marines took them to a lockup in the subbasement of Old State, where they were kept for 42 hours until Donovan sent Tom Early to vouch for them. The Field Photo branch had set a standard for COI and OSS men to follow. Their chief might obey what they considered directives forced upon him by rival agencies, but they would show what was often to be an antic disdain for them.

Donovan was in a ferment of intelligence activity. With the declaration of war, long-range strategic intelligence had to be deemphasized in favor of urgently needed tactical intelligence. The day after FDR's address declaring war, Donovan already had overseas reports on how the speech was received in various European countries. He provided the President with reports on conditions in Germany and on the disillusionment of the Slovaks with the Axis cause, and news of Japanese submarines lurking off the Mexican coasts and of the presence of mysterious Japanese-constructed airfields in Mexico.

David Bruce recalled Donovan in this time of stress. "His imagination was unlimited. Ideas were his plaything. Excitement made him snort like a racehorse," Bruce said later. "Woe to the officer who turned down a project because, on its face, it seemed ridiculous, or at least unusual." Donovan would gaze at him with an expression of such stoic sorrow that the officer would never want to offend his chief again.

Colonel Wally Booth arrived from Puerto Rico for duty with the COI. Donovan called him into his office. "Wally, you speak Spanish, don't you?"

"Yes, sir."

"The British have informed us that the Germans are going to come down through Spain early next summer to take Gibraltar. I want you to go to Spain and find out what is going on," said Donovan.

Booth stared at Donovan with some disbelief at the thought of the sensitive and urgent mission suddenly handed to him.

"You'll be back from Spain in 90 days," Donovan reassured him.

Booth left for Spain a few days later. He did not return for two and a half years.

Donovan's agents already in the field were providing important information, which he sent on to the President. Whitney in the London office reported from British secret sources on the situation in France, where Adm. Jean Darlan, commander-in-chief of the French Navy, had become vice-premier and cabinet leader in Marshal Pétain's Vichy government. Donovan told the President, on December 15, "Although Darlan prefers to remain on the fence he has compromised himself with Germans and has not convinced them of his own sincerity. Full collaboration must come if Pétain can be got around. Believe Pétain must surrender as he has always done when faced with ultimatum. Certain the Germans will occupy French North Africa to prevent British coming from east and shut off Americans from west. Division equally of opinion on whether Spain will be used or whether will enter by Bizerta and convoy from Marseilles if Tunisian Straits are closed."

Donovan informed Roosevelt on December 16 of "a theory that one reason for the failure of the Germans in Russia is the lubricants they use in their mechanized equipment. These lubricants are the product of the Romanian wells. By reason of the cracking process in Romanian plants there is left a residue of paraffin. When these lubricants are used in the machines in this intensely cold weather, it is like putting ice in the gears. I am having those familiar with the subject here on Thursday, and our economists will develop it at that time."

J. Edgar Hoover would fume if he knew that the COI had invaded his Western Hemisphere domain, but Donovan already had put a man in Rio de Janeiro. That agent provided his chief with vital information on Brazil's intentions. The pro-Axis Integralists were well financed and were gaining in popularity. "There have been signs of activities and meetings of known German agents," Donovan told Roosevelt on

December 17. "The Integralists are also active, although there is no actual indication of immediate action by them. There is also the impression that several German air pilots are standing to for some job."

Donovan also stated that "a declaration of war or severing of diplomatic relations with the Axis powers is considered as most improbable. The Minister of War wishes to preserve neutrality, and vigorous anti-Axis policy could probably produce an army revolt.

"The Minister of War could count on a considerable section of the Army to follow him, and according to information from reliable sources, on the bulk of the Air Force also."

On December 21, Donovan had more to say about the Japanese threat to the West Coast. He had top-secret information from Vicente Lombardo Toledano, president of the Confederation of Laborers of Latin America, and Dionicio Encina, secretary-general of the Communist Party of Mexico.

> There is a strong possibility that the Japanese have hidden bases for small submarines and airplanes in Lower California. There are probably no more than 1,000 Japanese on the Peninsula, but enough to do considerable damage. The current immigration of the Sinarquistas [members of a fascist movement in Mexico], allegedly Axis stooges, accompanied by at least one known German agent, represents an added threat.
>
> The Mexican armed forces are totally inadequate to patrol the Peninsula and its waters. However, a Mexican fishermen's cooperative union which has a concession to fish in the Gulf of California can be used to obtain information on Japanese activities in the Gulf, and peasant unions can be used to obtain information about activities on the Peninsula itself. Their information would be most reliable.
>
> The most important organized anti-Axis forces in Mexico are (1) the Confederation of Mexican Workers, 800,000 membership, and (2) the Communist Party, 5,000 to 10,000 membership. That latter, though small, has a highly developed information service.
>
> Though traditional "anti-Yankee" feeling is widespread among the people, anti-Axis sentiment on the part of organized labor and peasant movements is far stronger. With the cooperation of labor and peasants, a majority of the Mexican people could be organized into a powerful anti-Axis front.
>
> The Confederation of Mexican Workers and the Communist Party will cooperate with the United States on condition that the American Government does not support any reactionary Catholic political action or influence directly or indirectly.
>
> In view of the fact that Japanese submarines may already be based along the coast of Lower California, the element of great urgency is present. May I, therefore, have your instructions with regard to enlisting the services of the fishermen's cooperative union and peasant unions in an endeavor to ferret them out?

> We have just received a mass of highly confidential material on Mexico
> which is being processed and will be made available to you at the earliest
> possible moment.

Donovan was also experimenting with visual reports. When he learned that some Washington officials feared Japan might try to take the Panama Canal, he dispatched John Ford and a film crew to make a motion-picture report on the canal's defenses. Ford and two Field Photo cameramen, Al Jolkes and Al Zeigler, flew down to Panama on December 30 and photographed key defense installations over New Year's weekend. They hurried back to Washington, where Ford rushed the "Canal Report" through editing so that the film, complete with narration, could be shown to Roosevelt just a few days after New Year's.

Bob Parrish of Field Photo was present at the screening at the White House, and he reported that FDR was "very pleased not only with the film, but with the ability of the COI to cut through red tape and give him accurate reports on what was really going on. No army or navy unit could have made such a report. By the time it got through channels, all the flaws in the canal's defenses would have been covered up."

Donovan was also pleased with the "Canal Report," and he next gave Ford orders to make a top-secret film report on the Pearl Harbor attack. Donovan was determined to find out who had been at fault in the disaster. He soon discovered that the navy was far more interested in covering up than in discovering how such a thing could have happened. Secretary of War Stimson was also uncooperative and warned the COI director that he would insist upon seeing the film before it could be released. Donovan ignored the army and navy's opposition and sent Gregg Toland and Ray Kellogg by plane to Pearl Harbor.

The Field Photo team was brash and arrogant in Hawaii. They took pictures of salvage operations, obtained footage of the Japanese attack from private sources, and restaged the attack with miniatures. Ford himself flew out in mid-February to check on progress. He tried to bring the nearly completed film back to Donovan so that Donovan could show it to the President, but the navy managed to confiscate the film and lock it up in a vault.

Donovan's concerns during the first month of American participation in the war ranged as far away as China, where he was endeavoring "A. To organize Mongol guerrillas to break the present Japanese control in that area, B. To organize a revolt in Manchukuo and Korea, C. To operate guerrilla bands in China proper." Preston Goodfellow, deputy director of special activities, reported to Donovan that there were problems. The COI must obtain the cooperation of the Chinese government and arrange the delivery of ammunition and supplies despite the fact that "trucks presumed to be engaged in delivering war materials to Chungking are only operating at twenty percent capacity, the remaining eighty percent being used by the Soong family for their own purposes." Also, an agreement would have to be entered into between the Chungking government and the Communists, and "the attitude of the Russians would also have to be taken into consideration as they exercise considerable influence in Mongolia."

Donovan's plans for China would have to wait because the most urgent theater of COI operations was North Africa. On December 22, Donovan informed Roosevelt:

> That as an essential part of any strategic plan, there be recognized the need of sowing the dragon's teeth in those territories from which we must withdraw and in which the enemy will place his army; for example the Azores or North Africa. That the aid of native chiefs be obtained, the loyalty of the inhabitants be cultivated. Fifth columnists organized and placed, demolition material cached; and guerrilla bands of bold and daring men organized and installed.
>
> That there be organized now in the United States a guerrilla corps, independent and separate from the Army and Navy and imbued with a maximum of the offensive and imaginative spirit. This force should, of course, be created along disciplined military lines analogous to the British Commando principle, a statement of which I sent you recently.

Winston Churchill was staying with Roosevelt at the White House. The President showed the prime minister Donovan's memo. The next day FDR told Donovan that he approved the unprecedented COI action. "I want you to take this up with Mr. Churchill and find out whom we should work with in England toward this end," he ordered on December 23.

On the day after Christmas, a glum Christmas for the Donovan family and much of America, Ruth's mother died. Franklin Roosevelt wrote Bill Donovan a note of sympathy. Donovan had always liked his mother-in-law, but he had little time for grief. Since Patricia's death, he had given less and less time to his family. Now he scarcely saw Ruth, who stayed either in the New York duplex or on the Massachusetts coast. Even when Donovan found it necessary to go to Manhattan, he now occupied a suite that he kept at the St. Regis Hotel. The plight of the country preoccupied him, and his mind was busy with the comings and goings of his agents, their deployment around the world, and the fascinating and often highly significant reports that came back to him in one clandestine way or another.

New Year's Day of 1942 was just Thursday, January 1, as far as Bill Donovan was concerned. He brought General Marshall plans as to how the COI might work in the Azores and the Cape Verde Islands in support of American military action. Marshall approved Donovan's plans but asked him to coordinate his Azores project with the British and to discuss the Cape Verde situation with Gen. Joseph Stilwell. Stilwell came to see Donovan the next day, and on January 3 Donovan reported to President Roosevelt on their meeting. He described COI action in the Cape Verde Islands in three stages:

"1. A plan of short-wave penetration. This we would work out by trying to have it reach its climax on 'M Day.'

"2. The ascertainment of detailed information on particular parts of the territory that he [Stilwell] had in mind.

"3. The preliminary installation of a group that would be able to strike at the moment he would designate."

Donovan also proposed a team of COI geographers, photographers, radiomen, and analysts to work with Stilwell's staff "and have the psychological and political preparation go hand-in-hand with the military." As it turned out, the United States never carried out the military action contemplated in either the Azores or the Cape Verde Islands, but the proposal provided Donovan and his COI with a dress rehearsal of their role in the forthcoming North African landings.

Ever since his trip to the Mediterranean the previous year, Donovan had been certain that North Africa was to be a strategic battleground in the war against the Axis. In Cairo, Donovan had met Marine Lt. Col. William A. Eddy, who was the naval attaché at the U.S. Legation. Eddy, who walked with a limp from a World War I wound, had been born in Syria, the son of missionaries, and spoke faultless Arabic. He was former chairman of the English department at the American University in Cairo, where he had introduced basketball to the Egyptians. Eddy had returned to America to become president of Hobart College, in upstate New York.

"I'm out of love with teaching," he explained to the college trustees. "I want to be a marine." Eddy resigned from Hobart, but he didn't explain what kind of marine he intended to be. Donovan had persuaded him to join the COI and picked him to spearhead the COI penetration of North Africa.

Donovan asked Navy Secretary Frank Knox to make Eddy the naval attaché at Tangier, where no naval attaché had ever been stationed, and on January 3 Eddy left for North Africa. He was to preside over the Twelve Disciples, an intelligence network already in position.

The COI had not yet been established in December 1940, when Franklin Roosevelt asked Robert D. Murphy, counselor of the U.S. Embassy in Vichy, to look into the French situation in North Africa. Murphy did so after conferring with Donovan, who was about to leave on his critical mission to Europe and the Middle East. Charles de Gaulle gibed at Murphy as "long familiar with the best society and apparently inclined to believe that France consisted of the people he dined with in town" but conceded that he was "skillful and determined." Tall, stoop-shouldered, and appearing anything but a soldier or an agent, Murphy went about his mission. He negotiated an agreement with septuagenarian Gen. Maxime Weygand, the Vichy governor of North Africa. The United States was to ship such things as tea, sugar, cotton, and enough fuel oil to enable the French to retain the loyalties of the Arabs.

Twelve U.S. control officers were to be stationed in Algeria, Tunisia, and Morocco to see that the supplies did indeed go to the Arabs and were not diverted for the use of Vichy's German overlords. The control officers were to be designated vice-consuls, but in fact they were to be COI agents. An intercept of German intelligence reports indicated that their cover did not exactly mislead the Germans. "We can only congratulate ourselves on the selection of this group of agents who will give us no trouble," said the German report. "They are totally lacking in method, organization, and discipline. The danger presented by their arrival in North Africa may be considered nil."

The Twelve Disciples were not impressed with themselves either. One of the 12, Kenneth Pendar, a young archaeologist from Harvard, later remarked, "We flew over to drop like so many Alices into the African wonderland."

Alices or no, the 12 went to work, and their intelligence reports proved of great value. Donovan advised Roosevelt that the United States must seize French Africa to make a German invasion impossible. "The next war move of the German armies may well be the attack on Great Britain," Donovan told FDR on December 13, 1941, "or it may be the occupation of Spain and Portugal with the consent of those countries and the passage to Africa of large forces that will make impossible the sending of anything more than a token army by the United States to Africa."

He also urged, "Immediate reinforcement of the North Africa Army by American air and ground troops seems the only move which could retrieve the situation. Double thrust at Africa under present circumstances would almost surely succeed."

Donovan had a high regard for De Gaulle and the Free French movement, but he was convinced that De Gaulle lacked sufficient support both in France and in London and Washington. Just before Churchill arrived in Washington to meet with Roosevelt at the end of December, Donovan suggested to FDR that he talk with the prime minister about "the deplorable condition of the whole Free French movement in this country and inquire into the advisability or possibility of getting out of France, some leader, perhaps like Herriott." Donovan believed that a French leader other than De Gaulle must be found to oppose the Axis in Africa and support the British and Americans.

During the last days of December, Roosevelt and Churchill discussed how this might be done. They mulled over British and American combined action in North Africa. Their decision to prepare for Operation Torch—the invasion of North Africa—created a significant role for the COI, which was given the responsibility for secret and subversive activity. At the time Donovan and the COI were under attack from the traditional U.S. intelligence establishment. Donovan was locked in battle with the American military for what Roosevelt called "operational elbow room."

"Our whole future," Donovan informed his staff, "may depend on the outcome of Torch and the accuracy of our intelligence estimates."

With the aid of William Stephenson, Donovan arranged for the cooperation of British Intelligence in Tangier and at Gibraltar. Both British Secret Intelligence (SI) and Special Operations (SO) directed by Col. Brian Clarke at Gibraltar, were placed under COI jurisdiction. Eddy was to report to both London and Washington.

Tangier in January 1942 appeared much like any other North African coastal city. It rose white and gleaming in tiers beside a pellucid bay, and the land about it was tawny as an African lion. There were the usual Medina—the old walled Arab quarter—and the European quarter with broad streets, but otherwise Tangier was a very different sort of place. Located on an inlet of the Strait of Gibraltar, it had always played such a strategic role in the history of the Mediterranean that although the rest of Morocco was a French protectorate, Tangier itself had been officially designated an international zone by the Tangier Convention of 1923. In June 1940, the Spanish had seized the zone, but it was still a place where anything could happen without causing so much as a lifted eyebrow, and it was the most critical intelligence cockpit of North Africa. Spanish authorities looked on the often comic espionage interplay with a mixture of cynicism and bemused lack of comprehension.

Eddy established COI North African headquarters in Tangier. He set up a secret network across North Africa with the assistance of Robert Murphy and the Twelve Disciples so that intelligence information from all of the American listening posts could be concentrated in his office for field analysis and then transmitted to London and Washington. The COI stations were assigned code names: Casablanca became Lincoln; Algiers, Yankee; Tunis, Pilgrim; Oran, Franklin; Tangier, Midway. The Midway transmitter was set up on the roof of the U.S. Consulate. Soon it had to be moved because the wife of the consul, who knew nothing of Eddy's sub rosa life, complained that a mysterious tapping from the roof kept her awake at night. The transmitter was moved in the dark of night to a winepress overlooking the airfield.

"Tunis has transmitted valuable information to Malta regarding the departure and course of ships carrying war materials to the Axis in Libya," was one of Eddy's reports to Donovan.

During the next few months several of the original Twelve Disciples returned to America, and Donovan replaced them with new agents. One of the replacements was Donald Q. Coster, who had been captured by the Germans in 1940 while driving an American Field Service ambulance for the French Army. He had been repatriated to the United States and joined the COI. On a Sunday afternoon Donovan called him into his office. Lincoln needed replacing. "You are going to Casablanca," he said. "It's the most important place in the world at the moment."

Donovan invariably made a man going into the field feel he was undertaking the most important mission of the entire war. Coster blinked.

"French Africa will be invaded one of these days by either the Germans or ourselves," continued the COI director. "You are to help prepare for either eventuality. We must know the German plans."

"Yes, sir."

"A German Armistice Commission is in Casablanca enforcing the terms the Nazis imposed on the French in 1940. You might try to make them believe that, if and when we invade, we will come in through Dakar. I'll leave the method of doing that up to you."

Coster swallowed hard.

"And you'd better stop by London, Lisbon, and Gibraltar to pick up what information you can from British Intelligence. That's all," concluded Donovan. A few days later, Coster left on his mission.

Special Operations chief Robert Solborg returned to Washington from England, where he had spent some time at the British guerrilla school outside London.

Donovan had Eddy heading secret intelligence in North Africa, and now Solborg was to open up an operations and espionage center in Lisbon. Solborg was to contact the French and Arab undergrounds, coordinate his activities with those of the British, and establish secret communications with Eddy and his agents in North Africa. Solborg set up his center in Lisbon, an enclave of agents and double agents in neutral Portugal, and began recruiting.

"The plan involves organization of groups to receive and hide material, which will be supplied them directly by ship from us by road and train from Tangier and Casablanca," Solborg reported to his chief on February 6, 1942. "A group of operatives will be supplied by the British together with equipment to organize and direct the subversive parties I shall put at their disposal in Morocco."

Supplies to assist the Arab underground were to be landed near Agadir and Fedala. Eddy went to Gibraltar to confer with Viscount

Gort and British SI to insure their cooperation, and to Lisbon to work out arrangements with Solborg. At the same time, Eddy was plotting to bribe members of the elderly bey of Tunis's family to carry out a palace revolution and remove the pro-Vichy bey from office. When Eddy told Donovan he needed from $20,000 to $30,000 to "do the trick," Donovan sent $50,000. When it came to buying a palace revolt, an agent could not go hat in hand to his work. Donovan later dropped the plan because it promised to stir up more problems than it would have cured.

Donovan had more than his share of problems in Washington. He and Bob Sherwood, his FIS director, no longer saw eye to eye. Donovan wished to channel information efforts to soften up enemy resistance and to include black propaganda techniques when desirable. Donovan's black propaganda would encompass distortions of truth and even outright lies, while Sherwood saw the FIS as a medium for providing the warring world with accurate news. On February 11, the first Voice of America broadcast was made from New York.

"That night Colonel Donovan paid one of his rare visits to 270 Madison Avenue," remembered actor John Houseman, who worked for Sherwood. "He appeared unannounced in the cramped studio where we were broadcasting—in evening dress with two generals. They listened for two or three minutes, nodded, and departed in silence."

"The Battle Hymn of the Republic" opened the broadcast. "Today and every day from now on we shall be speaking to you about America and the war," an announcer said. "Here in America we receive news from all over the world. This news may be favorable or unfavorable. Every day we shall bring you this news—The Truth."

There was nothing in what the announcer said with which Donovan disagreed, and later Sherwood was to show an aptitude for black propaganda that belied his apparent adherence to "the truth and nothing but the truth" in broadcasting. It was simply that both Donovan and Sherwood were as strong-willed and individualistic as they were gifted, and they no longer could get along together within the COI. Both had back-door access to the White House, and in late winter and spring of 1942 they fought an internecine war over whether the FIS should continue as part of the COI or be established as an independent agency.

"Now that we are at war, foreign propaganda must be employed as a weapon of war," Donovan told Roosevelt.

> It must march with events. It is primarily an attack weapon. It must be identified with specific strategic movements often having within it the flavor of subversion. To do this kind of work effectively it must be allied with the military services. It must be to a degree informed as to possible movements. The more closely it is knit with the intelligence and the physically subversive activities of the Army and the Navy, the more

effective it can be. In point of fact the use of propaganda is the arrow of initial penetration in conditioning and preparing the people and the territory in which invasion is contemplated. It is the first step—then fifth column work—then militarized raiders or "commandos" and then the invading divisions.

Donovan also found himself under new attack from the military brass, who thought of the COI as a fly-by-night civilian outfit trying to horn in on the war. Donovan continued his recruiting, and the COI drafted plans for intelligence and clandestine activities in support of Allied military operations in North Africa as well as in Asia. But Donovan's military critics were inflexible.

"Donovan did a fine job of recruiting able men for our operation, but he had gotten a cold shoulder from the military services. Not a single project had been approved," Preston Goodfellow said of the early months of the war.

When it was learned that Joseph Stilwell had been made Chiang Kai-shek's chief of staff of Allied forces, Goodfellow asked Donovan to let him make staff studies for an intelligence and irregular warfare operation in Burma and submit them to the general. In early February Goodfellow was called to Stilwell's office. The general liked the project; he would give his go-ahead to COI. When a jubilant Goodfellow returned to the COI office, he decided not to tell anybody, including Donovan, until he had the approval in writing.

Goodfellow lived on Q Street in Georgetown, close to Donovan's house, and the two men often walked home from the office together. That afternoon Donovan telephoned Goodfellow and asked him to walk with him. They strolled down Pennsylvania Avenue in the wintry dusk.

"Never did I see Donovan so low in spirits as on that walk," Goodfellow said after the war. "I had decided to await formal acceptance by General Stilwell before saying anything to Donovan about it. But when I reached his home, I weakened. On the promise by Donovan not to mention to anyone my advance information, I told him we were going to get approval of the Burma operation."

Donovan brightened at once and invited Goodfellow into the house for a glass of sherry. They talked for an hour. Then Goodfellow went home, knowing he had not seen the last of his chief for the night. Donovan went to bed but, as usual, he read much of the night, first one book and then another, placing the half-read volumes face down on the bedside stand and on the bed around him. His mind teemed with plans for Asia. Finally he could stand it no longer and telephoned Goodfellow.

"He phoned me three times that night," Goodfellow remembered, "the last at 3:00 A.M."

"You're not in bed, are you, Preston?" he asked on the last call.

"No, I'm sitting here waiting for your call," replied the sleepy deputy director.

"Well, get your pants on and come over here. I want to talk more about Burma."

Goodfellow walked to Donovan's house, and they talked until dawn. Goodfellow reiterated his request that Donovan keep the matter to himself. Donovan was convinced that Stilwell's approval was an important break in the military's hostility toward COI.

In the morning at the regular staff meeting, Donovan called on each aide for his report. At last, when all the aides had been heard from, Donovan announced, "Gentlemen, I have reason to believe that our Burma show will be approved. I want all the Far East studies and operational plans speeded up—those for China, Thailand, and other fields."

"Of course, everyone went out of that meeting jubilant and got busy," Goodfellow remembered. "Three days later the staff study came back from General Stilwell. It was disapproved."

When Goodfellow brought the news to his chief, Donovan was icy.

"Preston, your intelligence was a little faulty," he said.

"No, it wasn't. Let me have that study, and I'll find out what happened."

Goodfellow went directly to General Stilwell's office. He knocked on the door. "Come in," said Stilwell.

"General," said Goodfellow at once. "I had something to do with the secret Burma operational study, and I came to ask you what is wrong with it."

"Not a thing," replied Stilwell.

"Then why the disapproval?"

"It's the officer you put in charge. That man, if sent out to blow up a bridge, would blow up a windmill instead and come back with an excuse."

"General, I don't know this officer. I went to the adjutant general and asked for the name of a senior Regular Army officer—one who knew the Far East and, if possible, had an Oriental language. The officer's name came up. He not only had all the qualifications I requested, but had been on your staff. So, General, why don't you name the man?"

Stilwell wrote a dozen names on a pad of paper. He crossed them off one by one until there were two left.

"Get either of these two men and your project has my approval."

Back at COI headquarters, Goodfellow discovered the first man on the list was in Texas. "I went after him first because of his seniority," said Goodfellow after the war. "He died the day before I got to him."

The second man was Capt. Carl Eifler, who was brought to Washington from Honolulu. Eifler was to head Detachment 101 in Burma, first of the COI groups to go into the field.

Donovan was now certain that the future of the COI rested with the military. With the first meeting of the Joint Chiefs of Staff (JCS) on February 9, he urged the President to place the COI under the JCS. The support of the JCS could help Donovan to ward off the attacks from within the COI being prepared by Robert Sherwood and from without by Adolph Berle in the State Department.

"Due to your continued support and confidence we have been able to set up for you an instrument of modern warfare which if left unimpaired would mean for you a weapon of combined operations which will be able to stand against any similar weapon of the Axis," he wrote to the President. "In doing this we have not usurped the functions or impinged upon the demands of the Army, Navy, or State Department."

On March 30, Donovan urged Roosevelt to sign an order to place the COI under the JCS. "I hope that you will approve the order," he said. "It exactly conforms to your original directive to me, both in name and function—but which was finally modified at the instance of the Army and Navy. The present proposal comes at their instance. The services now seem to have confidence in our organization and feel that we have in motion certain instrumentalities of war useful to them."

Even as he attempted to create a closer working relationship with the army and navy, Donovan had to ward off their attacks, sometimes providing high comedy. When Donovan and an admiral were guests at a formal dinner party, the admiral remarked that the COI was "a Tinker Toy outfit, spying on spies."

"I don't know, Admiral," said Donovan. "I think that we could get your secret files and blow up your ammunition dump on the other side of the river before midnight."

The admiral burst out laughing. Soon afterward Donovan excused himself from the table, presumably to go to the washroom. He telephoned his headquarters and within an hour several high-ranking navy officers showed up at the Navy Building demanding to see the admiral. The sentry saluted and said the admiral was not in.

"Then," said one, "we'll wait in his office."

Once inside, the officers went to work. One, a safecracker, opened the admiral's safe and removed its top-secret contents. Then the party left and drove to the ammunition dump, where they dressed down the officer of the day for not demanding their security clearances at the gate. When the OD left in relief, they planted dummy dynamite tubes. They sent the admiral's top-secret files and a report on their activities to Donovan at the dinner party. As the party was breaking up, Donovan handed the admiral his files without comment and explained where he could find the dummy charges at the ammunition dump.

Sometimes a hostile admiral or general would come to see Donovan at COI headquarters. If the visitor began to get troublesome, the director would call in Donald Downes, one of his aides. Downes had worked with the British in the Mideast and could spellbind listeners with his tales of derring-do.

"Tell them about your experiences in the Mideast," Donovan would ask him.

After Downes told a few intriguing stories that gave his listeners an insight into how a top agent worked, they would go away in a happier frame of mind, perhaps even admitting that there might be something to this intelligence business after all.

Despite its troubles, the COI continued to grow. Donovan recruited a leading ornithologist to solve the bird problem on Ascension Island. Birds nesting on the runway had flown into the propellers of landing DC-3s and brought them crashing to the earth. The ornithologist lured the birds to the other end of the island, where they were not a menace. Donovan persuaded specialists from other government departments and agencies to join the COI. He signed up such socialites as Raymond Guest, who was to carry out a dangerous P T boat mission across the English Channel, and Jock Whitney, who was to work behind the German lines in France. He also recruited as agents the chef of the River Club and the bartender of the Yale Club in New York, together with bullfighter Sidney Franklin, wrestler and Notre Dame fullback Joe Savoldi, Detroit pitcher Tommy Bridges, and Boston catcher Moe Berg. He took in some avowed communists and laughed when a congressman called him up and berated him for it. "They are great at sabotage," he explained.

He interviewed Charles A. Lindbergh for a job. "Donovan was very pleasant and said he would have me, provided it would be satisfactory to the President," Lindbergh later said. But Roosevelt didn't want any part of the aviator hero who had done so much to balk his country's war preparations, and Lindbergh did not join the COI.

One day a celebrated mathematician had an appointment with Donovan. "I know, General Donovan, that you take a dim view of astrology and at one time so did I," he said. "But I can assure you that it is not a pseudoscience; there is something to it, and I am prepared to prove it and to show you how the war can be won with it. I want nothing for myself and I think I can demonstrate with only a small amount of money to cover expenses that very remarkable things can be deduced about the plans and the fate of men whose date and hour of birth can be precisely known. This, of course, would have very enormous implications with respect to Hitler."

"But look, how would one know the date and hour of Hitler's birth?" Donovan asked. "Even his parentage is in doubt."

"In the case of Hitler," continued the mathematician confidently, "these time elements can be more precisely ascertained than even in your case or mine. This is true because we know certain events in

Hitler's life with great precision. We know the date and hour that he became chancellor of Germany; we know the hour that he invaded the Ruhr; the moment he invaded the Rhineland; the time he invaded Czechoslovakia, Austria and Poland. These are fixed points on the chart and by simply extrapolating backward in time, we can arrive not only at the date and hour of his birth but at the precise instant that he first saw light. Then having determined the circumstances and the conjunction of the planets at his birth, we extrapolate forward and find out every decision he will make in the future."

"This is perfectly wonderful," observed Donovan. "How much did you say it would cost?"

"Well, only enough to hire an actuary, a second-class astronomer, and maybe two or three clerks for a matter of a month or so. I would think that $25,000 or $30,000 would cover the bill."

"Fine," said Donovan. "It is precisely what my office should do, but I must observe protocol very strictly or we could not exist, operating as we do between the military and the White House. Put on your hat and coat, sir, and go get the secretaries of war and navy to ask me to act on this, and my office will take it from there."

As the mathematician left the office, Donovan called after him, "And be sure to get it in writing."

In North Africa Col. A. S. Van Ecke, a curt Dutchman who had served in the French Foreign Legion, was plotting with other French officers to revolt against Vichy. Bill Eddy drew up a list of munitions and armaments the French would need if they were to strike, and on March 3 he submitted it to Donovan. Knowing that American arms and supplies were being concentrated in the Pacific, where the Japanese advance was still unchecked, Donovan could only cable Eddy, "The supplies requested appear to be enormous and quite out of proportion to the projected operations."

Donovan once said that he preferred a lieutenant who disobeyed intelligently to a colonel who obeyed without thinking. Eddy was a lieutenant colonel who disobeyed his chief. He fired off a reply to Washington urging that the French North African underground be given all the support possible since it was the only source of opposition to the Axis.

"We will not find such leaders elsewhere," Eddy cabled Donovan, "and we dare not lose them now. They are taking all the risk; and they will receive, distribute, and use the supplies, every step being taken with the threat of execution as traitors if they were uncovered. The least we can do is to help supply them on their own terms, which are generous and gallant."

Donovan could not respond quickly to Eddy's appeal, since it came at a time when Robert Sherwood, Archibald MacLeish, and Budget

Director Harold Smith were trying to persuade President Roosevelt to have the COI dismantled. The information services would be assigned to a new agency headed by Sherwood and MacLeish. Other COI functions would be given to other agencies, and Donovan, it was felt, could be made happy with some sort of intelligence function.

On March 19, Sherwood sent the President a "personal and confidential" letter in which he claimed to speak for Donovan. "Bill himself would be overjoyed to be ordered to service with the Army and Navy," he wrote, particularly if the President "made it known to Bill that this service was of a special, secret and even mysterious nature. Bill would be especially happy and his personal prestige would be undamaged."

Roosevelt appeared to agonize over his decision, but he had already come to the conclusion that if the COI were to be placed under the JCS, the FIS must be separated from it. The President had no intention of allowing the nation's information services to become subordinate to the military. Donovan still struggled for the preservation of the COI as he had conceived it, but Roosevelt had already decided that Sherwood was right.

Donovan, embattled as he was, somehow managed to keep the COI moving at high speed. In the course of his law practice, he had met a talented Chicago attorney named Arthur Goldberg—later a Supreme Court justice and U.S. ambassador to the United Nations—who had built quite a reputation as a labor lawyer. George Bowden, another Chicago lawyer and a close friend of Donovan's who had helped to draft the legislation permitting the President to send the overage destroyers to Great Britain, listened to Goldberg describe how labor in Europe, even in Germany, was solidly anti-Fascist and would provide the Allies with a valiant underground movement. Bowden urged Goldberg to get in touch with Donovan.

"Early in 1942 I sent Donovan a note," said Goldberg. "We had important allies who were ideologically against Hitler, and they occupied strategic positions. Workers loaded ships. Railroads were manned by workers. Laboring men and women who could help the Allied cause."

Donovan, who once remarked, "Half an hour spent with the brakeman of a freight train running into Occupied France would produce more useful information than Mata Hari could learn in a night," immediately telephoned Goldberg. He asked him to go to New York to set up the Labor Desk for the COI. "We'd be more free of bureaucratic restraint and have more contact with refugees from Europe," Goldberg explained. "We had five people in our group."

Goldberg and his aides interviewed working people and labor leaders who were refugees from Europe, and filed valuable reports with Donovan. They also made plans for a future intelligence penetration of Europe, including Hitler's Reich, by labor people. European Social Democrats, Goldberg reported, were promising sources for intelligence and future anti-Nazi action. Dr. Heinrich Bruening, a Social Democrat and one of the last German chancellors before Hitler came to power, was in New York, and Donovan arranged a conference with him for April 1 in New York. Since Donovan wanted to talk with Bruening about creating a German resistance movement, he asked John Wheeler-Bennett, a British expert on German politics and military affairs, to sit in on the meeting.

Donovan's chauffeur picked him up at his Georgetown home shortly after midnight on April 1 and drove off to catch the 1:05 A.M. train to New York. Suddenly a car lunged out of a side street and hit Donovan's limousine in the side. The impact threw Donovan against the wall and struck both knees a sharp blow.

Donovan refused to go to the hospital although the old World War I injury to his right knee was hurting fearfully. He boarded the train, and as it sped to New York, a porter soaked Pullman towels in cold water and applied them to Donovan's swelling knees. From Pennsylvania Station he was driven to his apartment at the St. Regis Hotel. In the morning the meeting with Dr. Bruening took place. Donovan made no mention of his injury, but he did drink two stiff brandy-and-sodas. The talk with Dr. Bruening went well, and when the former chancellor left, Donovan was able to turn over the task of forming a German anti-Hitler movement to Allen Dulles, whom he had put in charge of the New York office, and Goldberg.

For the next six weeks he was confined to his apartment at the St. Regis. Roosevelt sent him a sympathetic letter, and on April 14, Donovan wrote to the President, "As Grace probably told you, I was ready to return when a blood clot, from which knee they do not know, settled in my left lung and after a few uncomfortable days is now in process of absorption. The doctors assure me that it will not be long before I shall be completely well. In the meantime, through direct connection with my office I am able to continue the supervisory, if not the active, part of my job."

Donovan directed the COI and his battle with Washington rivals from his bed. His enforced absence from Washington proved to be a great advantage to his opponents. If there had been any doubt as to what was to happen to the COI, Donovan's midnight auto accident settled it. Roosevelt was tiring of the question. On Thursday, April 30, Adolph Berle lunched on trout and eggs Benedict with the President, and noted in his diary, "We reverted then to the subject of political warfare. I asked whether he had finally come to an arrangement on the Donovan outfit. He said that, as I perhaps knew, he had been trying to get a brigadier generalship for the Colonel; after which he was thinking of putting him on some nice quiet, isolated island, where he could have a scrap with some Japs every morning before breakfast. Then he thought the Colonel would be out of trouble and be entirely happy. The rest of us would have to be re-integrated somehow."

After his return to Washington Donovan made one more effort to keep the COI intact. The Joint Chiefs of Staff helped him to argue his case. Some Washington friends warned Donovan about voluntarily seeking to have the COI report to the JCS. On May 15 Donovan went to see Roosevelt. The President told him that "we'd better stay clear of JCS. They'll absorb you."

"You leave that to me, Mr. President!" said Donovan.

After the war he told an interviewer, "I knew the rumors that were going around that JCS wanted to get us under their control and then tear the agency apart piece by piece and scuttle me, but I explained to Roosevelt that the JCS were the ones who would win the war, so that was the place for the agency to be."

Roosevelt saw his way out of his dilemma. He could separate the FIS from the COI and then place the latter under the JCS. His decision to do so seemed inevitable, but on June 8 Donovan made one more effort. He wrote to FDR:

> It is curious to note that at the very moment when the British are beginning to come to centralization of the various activities we already have under one tent, we have many theorists who, because of a false logic, are seeking to break up our own efficient centralization. The separation of our foreign service is the beginning, and I do hope for the sake of the war effort, you will not permit it to go farther. I say this frankly because you know that if you feel my usefulness here is ended, you have only to tell me so. I know very well that with the assistance of men of brains and character who have been with me, we have built up a real wartime service for you. I would not want to see it broken up without calling it to your attention. Whatever your decision is, we will implement it loyally and efficiently.

Donovan was not at all sanguine about his prospects. He dined with OSS woman Margaret Griggs Setton that night. Afterward they drove back to COI headquarters in Donovan's limousine.

"We may fall," he said, "but we will fall forward." Donovan also said "he would take the case to Congress if Roosevelt took the organization from him," Mrs. Setton recalled later.

Two days after his memorandum to the President, Donovan together with Jim Murphy and Preston Goodfellow went to New York. They picked up William Stephenson and continued to Montreal, where, on the next day, they caught a British plane for England. It was now crucial that an agreement be negotiated with the British on how COI's Special Operations could work with the British equivalent. On the day that Donovan arrived in London, Roosevelt finally acted. His Executive Order 9128 consolidated "certain War Information Functions into the Office of War Information," (OWI) and his Military Order of June 13, 1942, established the Office of Strategic Services (OSS), and abolished the COI. Elmer Davis was to head the OWI. Robert Sherwood would direct the FIS and report to him. The OSS was to be headed by William J. Donovan and was directed "to collect secret intelligence, to prepare intelligence appreciations for the Joint Chiefs of Staff, the planning and execution of secret operations, and the training of personnel for 'strategic services.' "

The President explained that strategic services included "all measures (except those pertaining to the Federal program of radio, press, published and related foreign propaganda activities involving the dissemination of information) taken to enforce our will upon the enemy by means other than military action, as may be applied in support of actual or planned military operations or in the furtherance of the war effort."

On June 15, James L. Wright of the *Buffalo Evening News* went to the White House to talk to Press Secretary Steve Early about Donovan.

> He told me that the Army did not want him [Donovan], but that he thought the President would make the brass hats take him. Of course, the President could make them do that. I told Steve the President had volunteered to me that he was going to appoint Bill a brigadier.
>
> "I still think you will see him in uniform," said Steve, "but right now I do not see the appointment in the works, and I have not talked to the President about it.
>
> "I think," continued Early, "we now have Bill in the right spot. He loves intrigue and the infiltration ideas. He lives in that atmosphere, and we had to get him out of where he was in order that Robert Sherwood, who could not get along with him, might have a free hand in the development of his foreign propaganda."

Donovan heard the news from Bill Whitney, his London bureau chief. He was determined to establish his own secret intelligence overseas and to pool intelligence with the British SIS and to create a partnership with the British SOE. The way was now open for the OSS's two most dramatic roles in World War II, the imaginative collection of intelligence and providing resistance leadership. At the same time Donovan was equally determined to have R&A continue to gather intelligence from open sources and to further Morale Operations' use of black propaganda to undermine the enemy's resistance, although this was inevitably to bring the OSS into collision with the new OWI. X-2 was to carry out OSS counterespionage work. Peter Tompkins, an OSS agent in North Africa and Italy, summed it up by saying that Donovan had been given the job of "subverting governments, sabotaging industry, smuggling bombs and explosives, setting up clandestine radio nets, organizing parachute drops and submarine voyages, falsifying documents, developing secret inks and poisoned pills."

27

OSS Goes to War

ONE OF DONOVAN'S FIRST steps as OSS chief was to reassure Winston Churchill about the role of America's new intelligence service. Then, on June 16, Donovan appeared before the British War Cabinet. According to the presiding officer, Field Marshal Sir Alan Brooke, chief of the Imperial General Staff, Donovan explained in some detail "the organization of their Secret Service."

While Donovan was speaking to the War Cabinet, his aides were developing joint plans with the British SIS and SOE. Subject to the approval of Donovan and Colin Gubbins, head of SOE, the two staff groups divided up the world into areas of responsibility. India, for example, was to be a British sphere, although the OSS would send liaison officers to New Delhi. China, on the other hand, was to be an American domain. While SOE was responsible for most of Europe, the OSS was to be in charge of North Africa, Finland, and in time Bulgaria, Romania, and the northern part of Norway. Neither the British nor the Americans sitting around the table in London on June 16 wanted any part of the South Pacific because that meant conflict with Douglas MacArthur, who claimed with considerable vehemence that he had the intelligence situation in that region well under control. In cases of joint responsibility the British and Americans agreed to keep closely in touch. Donovan and Gubbins approved the arrangements, which were to survive substantially intact to the end of the war.

Lord Louis Mountbatten, chief of Britain's Combined Operations, was present when Donovan spoke to the War Cabinet. He and Donovan had discussed the British and Canadian preparations for a commando raid on German-held Dieppe, France. When Mountbatten offered to let Donovan see a dress rehearsal, Donovan accompanied him to West Bay, Dorset, where the two men sat on an upturned fishing boat at the break of day and watched the commando assault forces storm ashore. Donovan, who was contemplating OSS operational raids on places as far removed from one another as Norway, the Southwest Pacific, and Mindanao in the Philippines, watched with intense interest and asked Mountbatten searching questions.

Donovan also persuaded the British to allow OSS men to study sabotage and subversion in British schools. The British and American

intelligence chiefs agreed to share gadgetry that each developed, ranging from new enciphering devices to plastic explosives. At the end of
June Donovan returned to Washington, where he found the OSS carrying out all the functions of the COI with the exception of information
responsibilities, which now were under the OWI. There were conflicting directives emanating from the White House and the Joint Chiefs
of Staff as to how the OSS would work with the JCS, but these did not
deter Donovan.

On July 6 he wrote to Gen. Sir Archibald Wavell, who had been
sent to India as commander-in-chief, that he had managed to persuade
the JCS to "do something which has never been done in our military
history. That is to take in as part of their organization a civilian unit.
There had been great neglect of the new elements in modern warfare,
and we have succeeded in getting them set up and all under one tent,
including special intelligence, special operations, and psychological
warfare."

First, Donovan had to reorganize the London office to reflect the
changes in Washington. Bill Stephenson had convinced him that it was
essential to separate Special Operations from Secret Intelligence, and
on his last visit to London, Donovan had ordered that this be done.
When London bureau head Bill Whitney refused to accept his chief's
decision on the subject, Donovan removed him. Now he offered the job
to William Phillips, who had been the U.S. ambassador to Italy.

"It was early in July, 1942," Phillips later wrote, "that I received a
cable from Colonel William J. Donovan, asking me whether I would
head his new London Office of Strategic Services. Actually, I knew next
to nothing about the OSS except that it had been created by the President, about a month earlier. Before replying definitely I wrote to the
President that I would not accept it without his approval, and received
a telegram from him saying that he was 'delighted with the idea.' "

On July 3 Donovan invited Phillips to one of his sumptuous Georgetown breakfasts and discussed the matter at length. "My old Foreign
Service friend, Hugh Wilson, former Ambassador to Germany, and now
an important member of the OSS was the only other guest," wrote
Phillips. "I felt at once drawn to the Colonel. His knowledge of world
affairs, his contacts with the State and War Departments, his immense
vitality and conviction that OSS would play an important role in our
military program convinced me that here was a man after my own
heart; I accepted his offer with enthusiasm."

Donovan told Phillips that he had plans for enlarging the OSS
London office, then housed in the U.S. Embassy, and had taken a building on Grosvenor Street. "He thought that it would be desirable for me
to have an office in the Embassy as well as in the new building; on the

theory, I supposed, that my connection with the Embassy would add to the prestige of the OSS set-up," recalled Phillips.

From Donovan's house the three men drove to OSS headquarters, where Donovan showed Phillips around and introduced him to his top aides. After a week of consulting with aides on secret intelligence, secret operations, and research and analysis, Phillips boarded a Pan-American Clipper on July 18 to fly to England. In London he found there were three OSS branches in the Grosvenor Street office corresponding to the three branches in Washington: "SI, Psychological Warfare, and another . . . more terrible line of activity connected with secret demolition in enemy territory before the arrival of our armies." Phillips, whom Roosevelt gave the rank of minister, also made contact with foreign governments in exile; as he put it, "mostly foreign ministers, who had their own secret intelligence sources from behind the lines."

"We had no problem in integrating the OSS activity with similar British activities," said Phillips. "We found nothing but the most welcome response. Immediately, I was invited to luncheons and dinners to meet the members of their various staffs. These were always pleasant occasions and helped to bring OSS into personal touch with their organizations."

Donovan threw himself into psychological warfare preparations. In the reorganization he had emerged as chairman of the Joint Psychological Warfare Committee (JPWC) under the JCS. "For Donovan PW [psychological warfare] was an old weapon," wrote Thomas Troy, "as old as the Trojan horse, the paint on Indians' faces and the whispering promoted by Richelieu beneath the walls of La Rochelle. Basically it was any weapon or tactic, outside organized military action, that undermined the enemy and his will to resist."

Donovan particularly admired author Edmond Taylor's *The Strategy of Terror,* and he brought Taylor into the OSS to draft a program. Taylor presented his ideas on June 30, and Donovan had them in mind when, on July 8, he chaired the first meeting of the JPWC. Donovan explained that psychological warfare as conducted by the OSS would include "genuine propaganda insofar as it affects military strategy, the spreading of rumors, black leaflets and black radio, partisan bands and underground political groups, sabotage, and propaganda in combat zones aimed against enemy forces." During the summer of 1942, he worked diligently with the committee, and on September 7 the essence of his beliefs was embodied in a definition of psychological warfare that was to dominate American policy during World War II.

Donovan learned with regret that the OWI was not interested in continuing Walter Langer's research into the problems of domestic morale and overt psychological warfare. "Colonel Donovan, however, still had faith in the worth of the psychoanalytic approach," said Langer. "Not long after the creation of the new Office of Strategic Services, he suggested that I set up a Psychoanalytic Field Unit in Cambridge, Massachusetts. This would not only be close to my home, but it could also make full use of the Harvard University library and draw on the talents of many experienced psychoanalysts."

On July 9, Donovan outlined the "functions, conception, organization, and operations" of the OSS to the JCS. It was a far-ranging memorandum that described, among other things, the intelligence teams already in the field. The director of the OSS described the overseas offices in such capitals as London, Cairo, Chungking, and Lisbon. He told of the OSS agent "traveling through French Equatorial Africa and the Belgian Congo with instructions to report on the state of mind of native and colonial leaders and report on any evidence of Axis activity," and of the agent in Iran who "was instructed to report on the developments of military interest in Iran, and keep this office advised as to the state of the relationships between the native population and the British and Russian troops."

Another agent, an Armenian-born American citizen, worked in Russian-occupied Iran, Turkish Kurdistan, and the Caucasus. Donovan had instructed him "to secure information of military and political interest such as the strength and disposition of troops and airfields and the movement of the naval and commercial vessels in the Black Sea." There was an agent in Nigeria checking on Axis activities and another in southern Palestine observing the attitude of the Bedouins toward the British. In Portugal, OSS agents were locked in a battle of wits with their Axis counterparts, and in South Africa agents were looking into the activities of German Intelligence. There were OSS men in Sweden, Spain, Syria, Turkey, Afghanistan, and Liberia.

Donovan told the JCS about his special agent in the province of Hatay, Turkey, who was investigating secret enemy activity in Alexandretta and establishing a network of subagents in Turkey and Syria "with a view to obtaining information in the event that this region is overrun by Axis troops." OSS agents were working with Gen. Draža Mihajlović in Yugoslavia and had infiltrated into Romania, where they sought out possible air targets and assessed the effects of air raids.

He spoke of still other agents preparing to go to Japanese-occupied China "to report on Japanese military and naval activities" and to India and Ceylon "to establish an intelligence network which could function in the event that India and/or Ceylon were occupied by enemy forces."

"In an eager, somewhat frenetic effort, Donovan put his men in the field," said OSS man Ray Cline, "and set up the first large-scale professional U.S. espionage network ever to operate abroad. To a great extent, however, collection work became mixed up with the quite different behind-the-lines work of OSS's covert paramilitary action teams. Espionage agents often ended up in contact with internal political or guerrilla resistance forces, and paramilitary teams often ended up sending back useful intelligence, particularly tactical military data."

Bickham Sweet-Escott, a British agent, visited the OSS headquarters. He observed:

> Donovan's intelligence section had made some progress by the summer of 1942. It was under the immediate control of one of the most charming and certainly one of the most able Americans I have ever met, called David Bruce. . . . He was surrounded by a galaxy of talent which seemed to expand daily, but then included Whitney Shepardson, Paul Vanderstricht, Russell Doensch, and Henry Hyde. The operations division, with which I had to deal, had lagged behind, perhaps because the conception of secret operations was harder to grasp than that of secret intelligence. Its commander was a professional army colonel called Goodfellow assisted by one of the Vanderbilts, who was a commander in the U.S. Navy. Below these two there was a small group of men which then included Jimmy Lawrence, Warwick Potter, and John Bross. New faces appeared daily.

Donovan himself said of this period when the OSS was rapidly expanding overseas:

> In the OSS we quickly learned that you can't collect all of the information needed in war by sitting in Washington. And you can't deliver your information to the man who needs it from a Washington desk. So OSS headquarters were established in every theater, in England, North Africa, Switzerland, and Sweden, from which we sent agents and guerrilla fighters into occupied France, Belgium, Holland, Germany, Austria, Yugoslavia and Italy—and on the other side of the globe we operated in Siam, China, Burma, and Indochina. That was an effective wartime intelligence system. Information gatherers and fighters behind enemy lines, and scholars placed all the way from Washington to the front lines. Men who could interpret the information received and gave it to the official or commander who needed it.

Donovan now reported to the JCS, whom he furnished with a torrent of information from his agents abroad. "Donovan also sent his reports directly to FDR even after it was decided he should report to the Joint Chiefs," said Charles Bane, an OSS man who was charged with delivering top-secret "eyes only" reports directly to the President.

At OSS headquarters Donovan was a typhoon of activity. He briefed agents and special operations teams before they went overseas. "He made me feel," said one agent who went on a hazardous mission into the Balkans, "as though it was all going to be perfectly simple. He talked to me quietly for half an hour, and I walked out of his office convinced I could do the job."

"Everything seemed planned so well, that if you got hurt it was your own damned fault," remembered another OSS man, who served in Southeast Asia.

Invariably, Donovan finished his talk with the man he was sending into danger by saying, "Believe me, I wish I were going with you."

"In view of his fantastic record for bravery in World War I, no one doubted he meant it," observed OSS man John Beaudouin.

Donovan's preference for action overseas infected the young men of the OSS, and they resented being kept in Washington when there was a world of adventure awaiting them abroad.

Sam Schreiner, later to be an editor of *Reader's Digest* and a novelist, first joined the OSS as a courier for J. Freeman Lincoln, who in peacetime wrote sea stories. To Schreiner and countless other young men, Lincoln became the Great Emancipator not because of his name but because, as Schreiner put it, "he freed us from slavery by arranging that we escape Washington and go overseas."

In the OSS there was indeed a world of adventure. Count Ilya Tolstoi, grandson of the great Russian novelist, and Lieutenant Brook Dolan were dispatched by Donovan to follow the old caravan route across Tibet to see if it could be used as an overland supply route from India to China. After experiences that seemed to come from the pages of fiction, they arrived at Lanchow, China, on July 4, 1943, bringing not only economic, political, and topographical data, but a presentation scarf, a framed picture of the Dalai Lama, four tanghas of piece brocade, three old coins, and some old and new Tibetan stamps as gifts from the regent to the "King of the United States." Donovan arranged for Goodfellow to present the gifts to the "King" at the White House, much to Roosevelt's delight.

Other OSS men of Detachment 101 penetrated into the Burma jungles behind Japanese lines to contact Zhing Htaw Naw, leader of the Kachin tribes of the remote interior, and to establish a formidable guerrilla force that played a critical role in the defeat of the Japanese in Southeast Asia. Nicol Smith and 21 young Thais infiltrated into Thailand, where Smith was secreted by the Thais in a palace close to Japanese headquarters. He radioed vital intelligence information gathered for him by a network of Thai agents.

In Asia the OSS had much to contend with. There were the machinations of China's Tai Li, Chiang Kai-shek's director of the bureau of investigation and statistics. According to an OSS intelligence report from London, Tai Li was the "head of an intelligence organization modeled on the German Gestapo and . . . has strong German sympathies." There was a German intercept system based in Shanghai.

And there was the problem of stationing agents in such places as Manila, Hong Kong, Singapore, Korea, Manchukuo, and even in Tokyo itself.

"The operators in the most dangerous places use a very ingenious adapter," Al Lusey, who had been a foreign correspondent for Globe Wireless in Shanghai, reported to Donovan from Chungking. The adapter "is plugged into the final amplifier stage of an ordinary medium band broadcast receiver. With this adapter they reckon to develop about ten watts of power. The message is sent out two or three times. The agents use one of several Japanese ciphers. The preamble of the message is in Japanese Kana code so that the messages will attract a minimum of attention. The message from Tokyo night before last contained the information that two of their agents had been caught and executed—they tell me that makes six in two weeks they have lost."

From all over the world such messages flowed in to Donovan, making his late-night reading anything but dull. He passed on everything of importance to a fascinated FDR.

Donovan studied reports, presided over meetings, and found time to step into the telephone room to tell the operators, "Without you girls, what would I do?" The Message Center was situated in the basement just beneath his office, and he would sometimes let himself in with his own key at 3:00 A.M. and hand the navy code clerk on duty a sheaf of messages. "Sailor, will you get this out for me top priority quickly," he would direct.

He was always good-natured and friendly to the cryptographers at work in the Message Center. "Several times he took a few of us out for a beer at a local tavern," recalled Leonard Laundergan, who at the age of 20 worked in the Message Center, enciphering and deciphering secret messages.

Elizabeth Sipe and Anne Boyd, young OSS women, finished lunch at the 1925 F Street Restaurant one noon that summer and were preparing to walk back to the OSS when the democratic OSS chief invited them to ride back in his limousine. "He was absolutely charming the entire way," Elizabeth Sipe recalled. "We were so thrilled." Donovan, always appreciative of feminine charms, doubtless enjoyed the ride as much as the girls did.

Sometimes at an OSS party, in the hall, or in an office, his eyes would meet those of an attractive OSS woman. "Their eyes would just seem to click," remembered one OSS woman, "and Donovan and the girl would somehow go off together."

Today most women who served in the OSS at headquarters or in the field where Donovan traveled so incessantly say that many other OSS women had affairs with the general, but they never admit that they themselves did. With Ruth almost constantly in New York, Bill

Donovan felt free to enjoy the company of some of the most engaging and talented young women in Washington.

Although he could not straighten out his own marital difficulties, Donovan attempted to solve those of his staff. James Donovan (who was not related to his chief) and John English and their wives shared a large house in Virginia. Donovan's wife was of English ancestry and English's wife was of German descent. English complained to Donovan one day that the two wives were quarreling.

"You can't put a German girl and an English girl in one house and expect them to get along," said Donovan. "You're just fools."

Donovan found time to be concerned about the fate of May Emereine, a typist whose husband was a short-order cook in a diner in Kansas.

"She met the driver on a Washington bus," remembered Margaret Griggs Setton, who directed the Central Intelligence files. "May lived with the driver, which was difficult from an OSS point of view. One day she came to me and said she was pregnant. I had dinner with Donovan, and I told him about her. He liked to hear about his people's problems."

"Tell her to get a divorce from her husband," said Donovan. "Then marry her driver."

He made arrangements for his law firm of Donovan and Leisure to take care of the divorce proceedings. Donovan held off the OSS security investigation until her divorce was final because he knew she'd fail to pass the check and would be fired.

"She got her divorce," recalled Mrs. Setton, "but she would bicker with her driver. She went to Baltimore and had an abortion. Donovan was horrified, but he still stuck with her. Finally the typist married her driver, but then went back to Kansas to live with her former husband."

After his auto accident, Donovan gave up squash for a time and boxed daily with a fighter who had joined the OSS. Still, he put on weight, and when OSS woman Betty McDonald drafted a book about the OSS and referred to him as "penguin-shaped," he called her into the office where he had been giving her manuscript a security check. He read the offending passage out loud to her. "May the Lord forgive you for this," he said.

Freeman, Donovan's black chauffeur, was known for his discretion and his complete loyalty to Donovan. One day Bill Langer and Ed Mason stepped out of the Administration Building to take a cab to a meeting of the Joint Chiefs of Staff. They saw Donovan's limousine waiting outside the building. "Freeman, General Donovan is supposed to be at the Joint Chiefs of Staff," said Langer.

"Where the general is, is where the general wants to be," opined Freeman. "Where the general is supposed to be is no mind."

Donovan thought nothing of keeping the brass waiting. Once, while an aide fumed, knowing that he was due at the War Department for a high-level meeting, Donovan talked to a "nondescript little man with a foreign accent." A half hour later he explained, "That man is going to jump into Berlin pretty soon. The meeting isn't going anywhere; it can wait."

On the way from his Georgetown house to headquarters, Donovan would sometimes ask Freeman to stop the car. He'd jump out and hike through Rock Creek Park to the office, or, if there was insufficient time to go the entire way, he'd ask Freeman to pick him up again on a certain corner along the route. His staff was appalled at how few hours he slept at night, and amazed by his ability to catnap for ten minutes in the car and be ready to take on the world.

"It was something about his metabolism that gave him such furious energy," says Jim Murphy, first his executive assistant and then later chief of Counterintelligence (X-2).

One day Murphy tore out a magazine article on metabolism. He handed it to Donovan. "You're not like the rest of us," he said.

It did him little good. Donovan phoned him late that night to ask a question. He drove everybody around him unmercifully, but was at the same time considerate of other people's feelings.

"I'd been particularly driven," remembered Murphy, "and I was staying at his house. He came into my room late at night and handed me a beat-up book of Greek history."

"I want you to read this," Donovan said, pointing out a passage that explained how Alexander the Great drove his subordinates to accomplish an essential purpose.

"General Donovan himself was a mobile unit of the first magnitude. Space was no barrier to him—the Sahara Desert was a little stretch of sand, the Himalayas were a bank of snow, the Pacific was a mere ditch," said one awed member of the OSS assessment staff.

> And, what is more, time was no problem. Circling the globe, according to good evidence, he would catch up with Time and pass it. No one was at all surprised if he left one morning and returned the previous afternoon.
>
> The General's triumph over the two fundamental dimensions of our universe is certainly the leading reason why OSS men, seen or unseen, were operating on most of the strategic surfaces of the earth.
>
> But more elementary than this—for none has to explain why he was inclined to fly about the way he did—was General Donovan's power to visualize an oak when he saw an acorn. For him the day was never sufficient unto itself; it was always teeming with the seeds of a boundless future. Like Nature, he was prodigal, uncontainable, forelooking, and every completed project bred a host of new ones. His imagination shot ahead, outflying days and distances, and where his imagination went, there would his body go soon afterward, and at every stop, brief as it

might be, he would leave a litter of young schemes to be reared and fashioned by his lieutenants and transmuted finally into deeds of daring. This is the key to the problem. It explains why OSS undertook and carried out more different types of enterprises calling for more varied skills than any other single organization of its size in the history of our country.

He was called a Renaissance man by some and "a character left over from the days of the Condottieri of 15th century Italy" by Calvin Hoover, the Duke University savant who served in the OSS. According to Hubert Will, another aide, Donovan "deliberately moved fast and kept a number of people involved in his undertakings. He didn't tell a lot to any one of them."

Donovan told General Wavell that he welcomed the loss of the information activities, now in the OWI, because it meant he could see more of the war. Beginning that summer of 1942, he went off to the battlefronts and to OSS outposts all over the world. His aides were accustomed to being hauled out of bed in the middle of the night to be told they were leaving with him in a few hours for London or Chungking. R&A researchers in the South Building would peer out the windows and watch Donovan being driven up to his headquarters in the building next door.

"When a couple of days went by without him putting in an appearance," recalled geographer George Beishlag, "we suspected he was off on a trip."

By the end of 1942, Donovan drew up guidelines, based upon his observations of the British commandos in June, on how to organize "operational nuclei for guerrillas operating behind enemy lines."

"Recruiting," said Donovan later, "was accomplished with the cooperation of the War Department. All men had to be volunteers for 'extra hazardous duty behind enemy lines,' had to volunteer for parachute training, have language qualifications for the particular group they were joining, and had to have basic military training. High mental and physical standards were also invoked."

When Donovan encountered a young man he considered promising, he recruited him on the spot. "We need young people like you with imagination and daring," Donovan told Manly Fleischmann of Buffalo. "Nine of our people were shot in Greece just yesterday."

Fleischmann avowed that he was not "as excited as the general over the prospect of being shot at," but he accepted a navy commission and ended up running a spy net in Burma.

OSS recruited safecrackers, college boys, steel-mill workers, economists, scions of old-line American families, and recent immigrants from Europe. "Let me say a word about these men," Donovan declared after the war. "They were all Americans. Many of them are of French, Italian, German, Siamese, Chinese origin. But now all Americans. We had often been told by our Allies that this mixture of nationalities in America was a weakness and could be penetrated and exploited by our enemies. But we did convert that so-called liability into a great asset. Only the American melting pot could mobilize such a body of experts in the knowledge of other countries, and we did it to the great advantage of our war effort."

Donovan had a particular belief in the value of refugees. Riding on the train from New York to Washington, he told Ladislas Farago that he had been reading Arthur Koestler's *Scum of the Earth*. Donovan commented on how foolish nations were to refuse new citizens who were fleeing from oppression.

"I will never make that mistake," he said. "Every man or woman who can hurt the Hun is okay with me."

President Roosevelt initiated one of the OSS missions in 1942. On June 24, he gave a White House dinner for young King Peter of Yugoslavia. FDR toasted the king and paid tribute to Draža Mihajlović, who was leading his guerrilla bands, or Chetniks, against the Germans. Before King Peter left the White House that night, the President asked him to get in touch with Bill Donovan, who would arrange for supplies and an OSS officer to be sent to Mihajlović. King Peter and Donovan met upon the OSS director's return from London at the end of June, and they conferred frequently over the next several months in Washington and New York to work out plans for OSS support of the Chetniks. Donovan placed OSS men with Mihajlović.

Later Donovan also put Louis Huot, a sometime *Chicago Tribune* reporter, ashore from an OSS maritime unit in the Adriatic. Huot was taken to headquarters of the Partisans, the communist resistance fighters led by Josip Broz Tito. "Here was no simple warrior," Huot reported of Tito, "no primitive leader or fighting man. He might be that, but he was much more besides. Thinker, statesman, artist, he appeared to be all these, and soldier as well; and there was a light in his face that glowed and flickered and subsided as he talked, but never went away—a light that comes only from long service in the tyranny of dreams. Whatever this man might be and no matter what he signified, here was a force to reckon with, a leader men would follow through the very gates of hell."

For the time being Donovan gave support to both the Chetniks and the Partisans, but there was no denying that in his view Tito was bound to succeed where Mihajlović, who sent negative messages imploring him for help, was bound to lose.

Donovan's life was more kaleidoscopic than ever. His mind teemed with ideas on how to gather vital intelligence. It was important to learn the strength of German combat manpower. "We found that small-town newspapers carried obituaries of German officers killed in action," Donovan said.

> We knew that, as in all armies, there was a fairly constant ratio of enlisted men to officers killed. By underground means we obtained small-town newspapers. We read them carefully. By 1943 we were able to make an estimate of the strength of the German army that turned out to be curiously exact.
>
> A question of high priority through the war was German tank production. We sent some of our economists into the battlefield to examine captured German tanks. Each tank carried a factory serial number. These numbers, we knew, ran consecutively in every factory and never varied. When we collected enough numbers, which meant several thousand, we were able to estimate tank production.

In one way or another, according to Donovan, the OSS learned such information as the first confirmation of the existence of German submarine oil tankers together with the first photograph of such a tanker refueling a submarine at sea, the conversion by the Germans of captured Russian locomotives from wide to standard gauge, and the first description of the new two-man Italian assault boats designed to operate either on or below the surface to attach mines to ships at anchor.

John Ford returned to Washington from an overseas assignment, and Donovan immediately informed him that "something big was going on in the Pacific." Navy cryptographers had broken Japanese Adm. Isoroku Yamamoto's messages, and it appeared that the Japanese were trying to draw the remainder of the U.S. fleet into a battle. Ford had scarcely unpacked his bag when Donovan told him to repack and head for the Pacific. There Ford and Bob Parrish filmed the epochal Battle of Midway.

As soon as the film had been edited, Donovan arranged for a private showing at the White House for the President and his family and close friends. When Donovan discovered that Ford had taken a sequence showing James Roosevelt, who had left the OSS to be with the fleet, he directed that this be included in the screening. The President and Mrs. Roosevelt, James Roosevelt, Harry Hopkins, and Adm. William Leahy were present. As the dramatic battle scenes unfolded before them, FDR and Hopkins talked and made jokes until, during the memorial scene at the end, the picture of the President's son came on the screen. Roosevelt paused in mid-story and paid close attention. When the lights blinked on at the end of the film, he was white-faced with emotion. His wife was sobbing.

"I want every mother in America to see this picture," the President said to Leahy.

Donovan was pleased with Ford's success. He ordered 500 prints of *The Battle of Midway* made and screened throughout the nation.

28

Prelude to Torch

ON APRIL 17, 1942, French Gen. Henri Giraud dropped a rope from his window in the impregnable German castle of Koenigstein near the Czech border and climbed down it to freedom. Some say a French patriot had smuggled the rope to him inside several cans of ham; others say that members of the German underground were responsible. In any case, Giraud slipped through Germany, hiding during the daytime, and escaped into Switzerland and then to unoccupied France. Giraud soon broke with the aged Vichy leader Marshal Pétain, and when OSS emissaries contacted him at Lyon, indicated that he might be willing to come to North Africa to lead a revolt against the Nazi-dominated government.

William Eddy reported the development to Donovan. Giraud might be the heroic French leader who could weld together the Gaullists and other patriots in North Africa. Robert Solborg took action. He flew from Lisbon to London and went to see De Gaulle to enlist his support for Giraud as the leader of the rebellion being plotted in North Africa. Solborg reported to Donovan that he had sounded out De Gaulle regarding Giraud and found that the Free French leader was enthusiastic. Giraud, said Solborg, was the one man under whom De Gaulle said he could work.

Solborg flew back to Lisbon. Donovan had told him emphatically to keep out of Africa, emphasizing that to go there would jeopardize the security of the entire local OSS network. Solborg, however, convinced that he was playing a vital role in the negotiations to bring the French North African troops into the Allied camp, went in early June to Casablanca, where he met with Bob Murphy and Jacques Lemaigre-Dubreuil, emissary of Giraud.

"The African Army on the whole dislikes the British," said Lemaigre. "Too much blood had been shed fighting them at Mers-el-Kebir and in Syria and at Dakar. All of this may have been necessary for the British, but it was humiliating and costly for France."

Lemaigre told Solborg that most Frenchmen considered De Gaulle a British puppet. Yet almost all Frenchmen were pro-American. Henri Giraud was the French leader who could accomplish the job De Gaulle could not. Lemaigre agreed to go back to Lyon and urge Giraud to come to North Africa as soon as possible.

"The plan briefly is that the general would assume command of French forces in North Africa and would issue orders to receive our task force without opposition whenever the opportunity arises," Solborg reported to Donovan.

Solborg was elated, but on June 15 he was dismayed. A cable came from Donovan, then in London, stating, "It was agreed between us that no activities were to be carried on in North Africa. You are directed to stop immediately whatever you may be doing, go to Lisbon and await orders."

Donovan had a high regard for De Gaulle, and he learned from Free French London sources that De Gaulle had actually said only that Giraud was a good soldier. Donovan also was receiving intelligence from France and through London sources that the growing French underground was more likely to support De Gaulle than Giraud. Solborg's activities threatened to compromise the Allies' political options in North Africa. More important, Donovan knew that Solborg had long been identified by enemy agents in Lisbon as an OSS man, and he feared that his presence in North Africa would now jeopardize the security of the entire network so laboriously established by Eddy.

In addition, Murphy was already working on the Giraud connection. With the Russians in dire straits and the Japanese continuing their advance in the Pacific, the plans for Operation Torch were lagging. The new OSS, moreover, had been placed under the Joint Chiefs of Staff, and Donovan, who now had to create a good working relationship with the generals and admirals, scarcely needed Solborg's freewheeling actions to embarrass him. It was hardly the time for Solborg to make a sweeping OSS commitment to Giraud for action in North Africa.

Solborg flew back to Lisbon and then, without orders, crossed the Atlantic to Washington to confront his chief. Donovan, faced with such insubordination, was furious. He refused even to see Solborg, and Solborg could only bombard him with messages.

"No promises were made, nor hopes held out to the French in North Africa," he wrote. "The general with whom I have been negotiating represents today the highest authority, overshadowing that of Weygand, De Gaulle, and everybody else. He is a fighting general and a true and patriotic Frenchman." Solborg's fierce insistence that he was right could lead to only one end. Donovan ordered him dropped from the OSS.

At the start of his ill-fated enterprise, Solborg had hoped to discuss the situation with William Eddy, but Eddy was not in Tangier when he arrived. Disturbed at the skimpy supplies reaching the French and Arab undergrounds in North Africa from the United States, Eddy had gone to Washington to see Donovan. Eddy outlined the extent of OSS intelligence and the size of French and Arab resistance groups, first to Donovan and then on June 10 to the Joint Chiefs of Staff. The JCS was impressed. Increased support would have to be immediate to be effective, since French Premier Pierre Laval was already replacing every pro-Allied Frenchman he could discover in North Africa with a German sympathizer.

When William Eddy returned to Tangier on July 11, he discovered that he had apparently been all too right. Two weeks before, Vichy police had arrested 300 French patriots in Morocco for forming a secret organization antagonistic to the French state. An OSS report from Tangier dated July 11 indicated that plans to sabotage Vichy French resistance to U.S. troops and to propagandize on behalf of the Allies had been leaked to the authorities. Prodded by the Germans, the Vichy police had sprung into action. The fascist Partie Populaire Française was also reported to be getting ready "to act as key men at strategic points in the event of an American invasion of this territory."

Eddy realized that Anglo-British action in support of the hard-hit French underground in North Africa was urgently needed. He flew to London to meet with Ned Buxton, Donovan's assistant director. Hoping for military assistance in obtaining supplies for the French, Buxton gave a dinner party and invited Gen. George V. Strong (the OSS's nemesis in Washington, who had just been made chief of Army Intelligence), the redoubtable Gen. George Patton, and Air Force Gen. James Doolittle.

Wearing his marine uniform decorated with five rows of World War I ribbons, Eddy limped into the room. "I don't know who he is," remarked Patton, "but the son-of-a-bitch's been shot at enough, hasn't he?"

Strong knew well who he was and began the conversation with the warning that if the OSS intelligence was wrong, many American lives would be lost in the invasion. Undisturbed, Eddy gave a factual, point-by-point analysis of the situation in North Africa. He presented a mass of details about the French underground, its leadership, organization, and possibilities. "If we sent an expeditionary force to North Africa, there would be only token resistance," he concluded.

Even Strong was impressed and agreed to pass on Eddy's analysis to those of Eisenhower's staff planning Torch. From then on the French underground in North Africa was taken into account in preparations for the invasion.

"Donovan was included in on all the details of our Torch operation," said Gen. Mark Clark. "Before we went into North Africa, Donovan kept us briefed about his intelligence findings in Europe."

Eddy returned to Tangier with promises of support for the French. On August 3 he cabled Donovan, "There will be no problem at all about reception of the merchandise, since our partners practically control the Province of Oran, as well as other sections of the coast. All they ask is an early delivery to reassure both sides that the traffic can flow."

On July 23 Franklin Roosevelt and Winston Churchill had made a historic decision to launch the Torch attack on North Africa as soon as possible after October 30. The JCS accepted the OSS recommendations for cooperation with the French underground, but objected to staff talks with the resistance leaders for fear that vital information about the timing of the invasion might leak out.

It was time for Bob Murphy to report back to Washington. He crossed the Atlantic and on August 30 met with General Marshall, Admiral Leahy, and Adm. Ernest King. After briefing them about the critical situation in North Africa, he hurried to Hyde Park, where Franklin Roosevelt told him about the plan for the invasion. Roosevelt, deciding that Murphy must also brief Eisenhower and his staff, dispatched him to London. Murphy traveled incognito as Lieutenant Colonel Mc-Gowan. "No one," observed General Marshall, "ever pays attention to a lieutenant colonel."

Murphy flew the Atlantic but finished his journey by train. Eisenhower's aide, Comdr. Harry C. Butcher, met him at the railroad station and whisked him in a staff car to Ike's secret headquarters, conveniently located on a golf course outside London. Eisenhower was completely won over by Murphy's report, but Murphy was not completely won over by Ike. He noted that when it came to talking about North Africa, "Eisenhower and some of his officers had mental pictures of primitive country, collections of mud huts set deep in jungle."

On his way back to Casablanca, Murphy boarded a plane in Lisbon and discovered that most of the passengers were French and German members of the German Armistice Commission, which was supposed to enforce the terms of the Franco-German Armistice in North Africa. The Americans and commission members repeatedly toasted one another with champagne.

"Our groups are prepared to destroy key power stations, tunnels and bridges connecting Morocco with Algeria," Eddy reported to Donovan, "and they are prepared to isolate from reinforcement the Port of Fedala and the Port of Lyautey. These preparations were in anticipation of Axis aggression and will presumably not be necessary if we occupy the territory first.

"It is, of course, in general true that we can count on the submission or active support of the French Army as we must also count upon the determined resistance of the French Navy and of the aircraft under the navy's control."

Admiral Darlan had been made chief of the French armed forces when Pierre Laval replaced Pétain as premier of Vichy France, and

OSS agents were convinced that the navy would remain loyal to Darlan even if the army in North Africa did not.

OSS arms now began to move to the French Resistance. From American stocks in the Gibraltar arsenal, Sten guns, .45 pistols and ammunition, explosives and flares were taken across the Strait of Gibraltar to the British Legation at Tangier. At night they were removed to the U.S. Legation and from there smuggled through the Spanish zone to Casablanca. A Riff, or Berber, leader who had a large cache of hand grenades left over from the Spanish Civil War presented them to OSS agents. They were packed in cartons labeled tea and sugar and loaded on muleback for transport through Spanish Morocco to an OSS agent waiting at the border. Donovan, until now generally stingy with funds, made available $2 million to finance the OSS operations.

The day of invasion was nearing. Donovan went to London on September 10 to confer with SOE head Gubbins. The American and British chiefs agreed that SOE and the OSS would work together under OSS direction to achieve the following tasks: "(A) During the assault: 1. light beaches; 2. neutralize batteries; 3. put out infrared detectors. (B) Safeguard dock installations from Arab destruction. (C) Sabotage enemy air forces by any means. (D) Temporarily block roads and rails. (E) Damage French naval forces if they resist. (F) Provide guides for forces after landing."

Before returning to Washington, Donovan discussed the Torch plans in detail with Eisenhower, General Clark, and Bob Murphy. He made arrangements for William Phillips to serve as a liaison officer between Ike and the OSS. Phillips grimaced when Harry Butcher of Eisenhower's headquarters presented him with a lengthy message from G-2's General Strong in Washington, who spelled out directives from the JCS that were bound to hamper the OSS in its preparations for the North African landings.

Donovan sent the agreement with SOE to Eddy. Eddy shook his head over it. There was no danger at all from the Arabs, who, far from causing trouble for the invading forces, were ready to assist in any way possible. If ordered to do so, Eddy's North African OSS apparatus could carry out all the actions that would be required during the assault. OSS teams could also block roads and rails and sabotage enemy air forces. The SOE was not needed.

On September 23 Clark sent more detailed instructions to Murphy for Eddy's information. One hour before the assault on Algeria a number of coast defense batteries were to be destroyed or put out of action. The batteries, near Algiers, were listed and described. The D day instructions for Eddy continued: "Break electrical connections between infrared detector stations and coast defense batteries. Seize Blida and Maison Blanche airdromes and destroy French planes. Secure and immobilize tanks. Seize and preserve intact the main civil broadcasting station, also the main telephone and telegraph exchanges. Prevent destruction of cables, main power stations and docks. Provide guides for Algiers. Prevent damage to key road and railroad bridges and tunnels. Arrange, insofar as consistent with maintaining secrecy, for seizure or neutralization of German and Italian Armistice Commissioners."

Eddy and Donovan offered solutions to some problems, but Eisenhower's staff turned them down, perhaps out of queasiness. A Frenchman whose son the Germans had murdered in Paris had made detailed preparations, with Eddy's help, for the assassination of German military personnel, most of them Gestapo officers, who were stationed in North Africa. When London headquarters refused to approve the plot, Eddy made a new proposal. A black African waiter who spoke Oxford English and quoted Shakespeare at length, to the delight of the people he waited on, was an OSS spy. At the strategic moment he would drop Mickey Finns into the drinks of the Germans, thus incapacitating them during the invasion.

OSS agents reported to London on the conditions in the harbors of North Africa and on the beaches. A constant watch was kept on the German and Italian Armistice commissions. "The Germans in Fedala and Casablanca now keep their effects ready packed and have been trained to clear from the hotels, complete with baggage within 15 minutes," one report indicated.

The OSS, despite the attitude of the State Department, still was plotting to increase Arab support for the Allied invasion. The Riff leader, Abd-el-Krim, was to be spirited from his exile on Reunion Island, a French possession in the Indian Ocean, about 420 miles east of Madagascar, and Allal-el-Fasi was to be brought from Brazzaville on the Congo River in equatorial Africa. They would lead a Moorish revolt against Spain if the Spanish assisted the Axis. Carleton Coon and Gordon Browne negotiated for the OSS, but they gave up on the project lest they arouse suspicions of the impending invasion.

There were last-minute requests from Eisenhower's staff in London. What were the Italians in Libya planning? Donovan's agents reported they were getting ready to attack. Five thousand troops had been flown to Libya, and Italian destroyers were bringing more. Could a reliable pilot be found to take the Allied fleet to the Algerian beaches? Chief Pilot Malverne of Port Lyautey was the man, and Eddy knew he was hiding in Casablanca. Two OSS men met Malverne at his house and devised a hiding place for him behind some gasoline drums in a trailer. They covered him with a Moroccan rug and a canvas tarp, which they battened down tightly. With the trailer bouncing behind their venerable Chevrolet, the OSS men undertook to smuggle the pilot past the French and Spanish border officers.

"We'd better check Malverne again," one man would say to the other from time to time. They'd stop the car and lift up an end of the tarpaulin to see how he was doing.

"Not dead yet," Malverne would reply, although fumes from the gasoline drums were seeping into his hiding place.

The French border presented no problems, but getting through the Spanish post was not so easy. One OSS man lifted a portion of the tarpaulin so that the Spanish officer could see the gasoline drums. Meanwhile the officer's dog was sniffing at the front of the trailer, where Malverne lay hidden. The other OSS man quickly took a can of meat from his lunch box and opened it for the dog. The Spaniard was delighted at the generosity of the Americans, and he waved them to get back into their auto and drive on. From Tangier, Malverne was flown to Washington. He was to pilot the first American destroyers into his home port.

General Eisenhower realized how essential it was to make certain of the assistance of the French Army during the landings in North Africa, now only a few weeks off, but he was afraid to let the French know when and where the troops would come ashore. That British Army and Navy units were taking part was also necessarily top secret. Eisenhower gave General Clark, commander of the U.S. Fifth Army, the task of meeting with Giraud's North African representative, Gen. Charles Mast, to work out a better relationship. They met on Cherchel Beach, 75 miles west of Algiers, with OSS and French representatives on the night of October 21.

A few weeks later the vast armada of Operation Torch was nearing the Strait of Gibraltar. It was a time of rumors. Eddy instructed two young Austrian anti-Nazis to go to Casablanca and offer to spy for Gen. Theodor Auer of the German Armistice Commission in North Africa. The Austrians dined openly with American consular officers to demonstrate how capable they would be of gaining access to U.S. secrets. Auer was delighted. The Austrians fed him accurate but unimportant information about American plans, which could be easily verified. Once they had gained Auer's confidence, they let him know that there was an Allied invasion fleet nearing Africa and that the blow was to fall at Dakar on the Atlantic coast of French West Africa. This interesting intelligence was flashed to Germany, and the German high command ordered submarine and fleet units to meet in the Atlantic close to Dakar.

Eddy's men also planted a report that the civilian population of the island of Malta was approaching starvation and that a huge fleet of Allied ships was on its way with urgently needed supplies. This rumor, prevalent in North Africa, may have reached the German command and may be the reason Abwehr strait-watchers let the Allied flotilla pass them by without raising the alarm.

At midnight on November 8, the BBC in London announced mysteriously: *"Allo Robert, Franklin arrive!"*

Robert stood for Robert Murphy; Franklin for Franklin Roosevelt. OSS men knew that the attack was about to begin, and the French and Arab undergrounds struck.

"Allo Robert, Franklin arrive!" came the strange message over and over. French resistance groups sent up flares over the beaches to guide the landing craft ashore. Guides waited on the beach to welcome the first men, who began to wade ashore at 1:30 A.M. The password was "whiskey." The answer was "soda."

In Algiers an Englishwoman had shown the conspirators a hidden entry in her villa garden that led to secret passages beneath the ancient city. They had last been used by the Barbary pirates. The French patriots ran through the passages to points where their maps showed vital telephone and cable lines could be cut. That night they could hear the Vichy sentries on duty in the admiralty above them as they cut the lines. The telephones of the city went dead.

Eddy was in Gibraltar with General Eisenhower acting as the OSS liaison officer with the commander-in-chief of the invasion force. Murphy and the other Casablanca OSS men and underground leaders were assembled in José Aboulker's apartment. A radio was operating in the bathroom to keep them in touch with Eddy and the fleet. The unusual gathering of men in the apartment attracted the attention of a Vichy sympathizer, who informed the police. The chief of the political police decided to check on the mysterious group in person. Once inside the apartment, he found a gun pointed at his head. He submitted to arrest in the name of the French people.

There came a knock on the door. A young priest, the Abbé Cordier, stood there. It was his duty to cut the lines of the main French Army telephone station, but the night watchman had a German shepherd that made his approach impossible. Aboulker gave the Abbé the poison he needed to deal with the dog.

In Algiers several hundred boys, members of the OSS-directed Chantiers de la Jeunesse, seized key positions in the city for the Allies. They had few arms because most of the inadequate OSS weapons supplies had been given to older and presumably more dependable underground groups. The Chantiers held out against overwhelming police fire, expecting the American Army to come to their aid momentarily. Unfortunately, U.S. troops missed the target beach and made their landing 4.5 miles farther away than expected. They became lost on the dark roads. By the time they reached Algiers, 13 hours behind schedule, most of the boys were dead and the positions had to be captured all over again.

In Morocco the underground seized the Vichy governor. Pro-Allied

French Army units and the underground went into action, but in Morocco the Allied forces also missed their landing, and before they could reach the city, Vichy troops had arrested the pro-Allied army commander. Everywhere Allied troops blundered and moved ahead so slowly that their friends in North Africa were overwhelmed by French forces faithful to Vichy. What might have been a peaceful invasion turned into a bitter struggle in which both French and American soldiers and sailors were dying.

In spite of the blunders at the start, the Allied invasion of North Africa proved successful. It showed that the decision to strike at Africa before Europe had been a sound one, since the green troops and confused planning most likely would have failed against the European bastion. Donovan's OSS was "blooded" in North Africa. At the same time his agents and operational teams were continuing to move into the field. Allen Dulles was now Donovan's man in Switzerland, from where he was ordered to penetrate the Reich and discover the opposition to Hitler. From the Cairo base, agents were intriguing, according to a JCS directive, "from the eastern boundary of Italy to and including the Middle East as far as the western boundary of India; and in North Africa from the eastern boundary of Tunisia to and including Ethiopia; and islands adjacent to all countries included." Agents of OSS Detachment 101 were now established at Nazira, in Assam, India, and were making their initial probes behind the Japanese lines in Burma. On November 10, at President Roosevelt's press conference, a reporter asked, "Mr. President, is Bill Donovan's work still a secret?"

"What?" asked the President in feigned surprise.

"Is Bill Donovan's work still a secret?"

"Oh my, yes," replied Roosevelt. "Heavens, he operates all over the world."

The President and the White House correspondents laughed together.

Even while the OSS was bringing to life Donovan's ideas of a coordinated intelligence and special operations effort to assure the success of Allied arms in North Africa and also to function throughout the world, Donovan had been forced to spend long hours every day dealing with the jealous and obstructive admirals and generals in Washington. All of this proved as disturbing to General Marshall as it did to Donovan. On December 23, 1942, Marshall looked back over the year and the great contribution the OSS had made to the victory in North Africa. He wrote to the OSS director, "I cannot let the holiday season pass without expressing my gratitude to you for the cooperation and assistance you have given me personally in the trying times of the past year.

"I regret that after voluntarily coming under the jurisdiction of the Joint Chiefs of Staff your organization has not had smoother sailing.

Nevertheless, it has rendered invaluable service, particularly with reference to the North African Campaign." The balky Joint Chiefs of Staff were at last prepared to give Donovan and his men the "elbow room to operate in" that Roosevelt had requested a good nine months before.

Donovan had reason to be pleased with the way things stood in December 1942. His OSS had proven its worth, and Ruth was now living with him in Washington. David was away in the service, and David's wife had also moved into the Georgetown house. Bill Donovan's friend Alexander Woollcott, recuperating from an operation, was contemplating a visit. Donovan always found Woollcott's irrepressible chatter stimulating.

"Of course you would be more than welcome to be with us," he wrote to Woollcott with some satisfaction. "You know, of course, that now besides Ruth, I have my daughter-in-law and my granddaughter there. I hope they would not bother you. You could have the room on the top floor, and we could take good care of you if you wouldn't be annoyed by a child."

29

Professor Moriarty Joins the OSS

"YOU'RE MY EVIL GENIUS," Donovan once told Stanley Lovell. "I promise you that you'll never be killed, for I'll need you in the next story just as Conan Doyle needed your counterpart in his next novel."

Lovell, of whom Franklin Roosevelt remarked, "You're either a Down East Yankee or you've got a case of adenoids," was indeed a Down East Yankee, as well as a chemist and inventor, and Donovan placed him in charge of the OSS Research and Development branch.

R&D was charged with creating everything from improved radio transmitters and receivers for the use of agents and field stations to inventing a new kind of explosive. Carleton Coon, the anthropologist turned OSS man, might fashion explosive horse and camel turds to use against Rommel's tanks and personnel, but it was up to Lovell to invent the plastic explosive in the first place.

Lovell began his Washington career in the laboratory of Dr. Vannevar Bush, director of the office of scientific research and development. One day Bush asked his assistants what they would need if they were to be put ashore in a rubber raft in the dark of night on an Axis-held coast with orders to destroy a radio installation defended by armed guards, dogs, and searchlights. Lovell replied that he would want a silent, flashless Colt automatic, a submachine gun, or both. He would pick off the first sentry with no sound or flash to explain his slumping to the ground. When the next sentry hurried to his aid, Lovell would pick him off too. The reply was scarcely original, but Bush informed him that he had won the contest. He told him he should report to an office at 25th and E that evening.

Lovell stepped out of a cab at the corner where E ends at 25th. He walked up the hill into the 25th Street cul-de-sac and turned in at a gate. Going around a brick building, he found himself in a quadrangle with flowering trees and shrubs. He entered the pillared building dead ahead and walked down a narrow hall to a room at right angles to it. He was told to wait. He studied a 500-year-old map of the world—on which Africa was labeled Terra Incognita—hanging on the wall.

A stocky man with mischievous blue eyes strode into the room and held out his hand. "You know your Sherlock Holmes, of course," he said. "Professor Moriarty is the man I want for my staff here at OSS. I think you're it."

"Do I look to be as evil a character as Conan Doyle made him in his stories?" Lovell asked.

"I don't give a damn how you look. I need every subtle device and every underhanded trick to use against the Germans and the Japanese—by our own people—but especially by the underground resistance groups in all occupied countries."

Stanley Lovell moved into a minuscule office in the basement of the South Building. From his fertile imagination and the minds of his assistants were to flow a freshet of devices and tricks to serve OSS personnel and the patriotic undergrounds in Europe, North Africa, and Asia. Lovell and his staff produced false passports, identification papers, ration books, currency, and letters. They learned to combine the precise paper fibers with the proper invisible inks, trick watermarks, and special identification chemicals to frustrate even the closest scrutiny. The Bureau of Engraving and Printing proved helpful, and Frank Wilson, chief of the Treasury Department's Secret Service, also provided technical assistance so Lovell could develop invisible inks that would stand up to simple iodine tests and more sophisticated tests.

Donovan posted guards around the R&D laboratory for two reasons: to keep away other OSS people on the supposition that if they didn't know what was going on they could scarcely tell anybody about it, and to guard several patriotic if unprincipled counterfeiters who had been released from prison by the President to serve the OSS. FDR found it hard to believe that the counterfeiters would stick to counterfeiting for the OSS. He feared that if given a chance, they would very likely start turning out illegal U.S. currency.

"If the Secret Service picks up anything counterfeit that originated in your shop," the President told Donovan, "we're closing you down."

Invisible inks for secret messages, cameras camouflaged in matchboxes, a candle that was half wax and half explosive, and shoes with hidden space for messages all came out of the laboratory of Professor Moriarty. As each gadget was created, it was put to work in the field. Allen Dulles in Switzerland contacted the Bally Shoe Company in Schoenewerd, a small town some 25 miles from Zurich. Bally's salesmen were persuaded to help the OSS, and as they traveled through Germany and Occupied Europe, they carried messages written on paper or cloth and inserted in place of a shoe's bottom filler. The shoe sole, following a technique worked out by R&D, was laid over the message, stitched in place, and beveled, its edge stained and set.

When Lovell heard that an OSS spy captured in the lobby of the Adlon Hotel in Berlin might have escaped had he been able to create a distraction, he put together a small but mighty fireworks device. Pull a tiny wire loop, and the device gave a startling imitation of a bomb falling with a spectacular roar. It was so distracting that Lovell named it for Hedy Lamarr, the glamorous movie star of the time.

Bill Donovan took Lovell with him to one of his periodic lectures to the Joint Chiefs of Staff on August 28, 1943. Donovan explained Hedy to the top brass. Then he went on talking about other matters as Lovell pulled the ring and slipped Hedy into a metal wastebasket. The fearful sound of a bomb descended on the meeting. Two- and three-star generals and admirals rushed for the door as a mighty roar ended Hedy's performance. Donovan surveyed the nearly empty room.

"Professor Moriarty, we overdid that one, I think," he observed.

The inventions multiplied. There was the pocket incendiary, invented by Dr. Louis Fieser of Harvard, that was about the size of a pencil eraser, and there was an incendiary case filled with napalm with a delayed ignition that could be set for any period of time from 15 minutes to three days. It could be made to resemble anything from a suitcase to a box of crackers. "Beano" was a grenade that looked like a baseball and was named for the game played at carnivals. "Casey Jones" was a small explosive box with a permanent magnet on one side so it could be stuck to the iron or steel undersides of a railroad car.

One of R&D's other inventions was a silent and flashless pistol, carried by OSS agents. It and an equally silent, flashless submachine gun were invented by Professor Gus Hammar of the University of Washington, Dr. Robert King and Gordon Ingram of American Telephone and Telegraph Research, and John Sibelius of Hi-Standard Manufacturing Company. Lovell gave one of the first pistols to Donovan.

"Get me another, Stan," he said. "I want to present one to President Roosevelt."

Donovan obtained a small duffel bag filled with sand and, placing it in a corner of his office, practiced shooting the pistol into it. One day he went to the White House to call on the President. The pistol was in his shoulder holster, and Donovan toted a bag full of sand in his hand past the Secret Service guards. Sitting in a corner of the office as FDR finished dictating to Grace Tully, Donovan fired a clip into the bag of sand.

When FDR's secretary left, Donovan handed the gun to the President with a handkerchief wrapped around the barrel. "Mr. President," he said, "I've just fired ten live bullets from this new OSS silent and flashless pistol into that sandbag over there in the corner. Take the gun by the grip and look out for the muzzle, as it's still hot."

The President was shocked. No man who holds the awesome power of the presidency does so entirely without fear of assassination. He put the gun down on the desk. "Bill, you're the only black Republican I'll ever allow in my office with a weapon like that," he said.

Roosevelt appreciated how valuable the weapon would be to OSS agents. He showed the gun to visiting admirals and generals and sent it to Hyde Park, where it is now in the custody of the Roosevelt Museum.

Other inventions included exploding limpets that could be affixed to the side of a ship by OSS frogmen, a submersible canoe, an arrow gun, and a confusion bomb that was dropped over Europe. This bomb ticked frightfully but contained only a cheap clock, a radio, a speedometer, a thermometer, fuses, valves, and whatever else might be handy when it was assembled.

R&D did not contain the only OSS men with inventive minds, and Donovan was willing to talk to anybody who had an idea. John Shaheen, after the war an international financier, was long on ideas. One day he went to Donovan and proposed a gliding bomb that he himself offered to guide to its target. He would ride the bomb and alter its course by shifting his weight from side to side. Shaheen confidently expected to escape annihilation by spreading a parachute and floating away to safety just before the bomb hit. Donovan gave him a go-ahead on the project. Probably a cat saved Shaheen from his moment of truth. Other OSS men were simultaneously working on having a cat guide a bomb to its target, and they decided against risking Shaheen's life since a cat has nine. The OSS cat-guided bomb also failed to make it out of the laboratory.

OSS proved to be the breeding place for what has been accurately called the battiest weapon of the war. It all got started when Dr. Lytle S. Adams, a Pennsylvania dentist, went exploring in a much larger cavity than he was accustomed to—Carlsbad Caverns, in New Mexico. The bats winging from the cave at sunset fired Adams's imagination, and he saw in the little mammals a way to win the war. Why not tie incendiaries to their wings and release them over Japan? The bats would fly to the nearest Japanese houses and attach themselves to the eaves, and the flammable structures would go up in flames. The dentist sent his suggestion to Eleanor Roosevelt, who passed it to her husband, who sent it to Donovan, who saw merit in it. John Jeffries was dispatched with a team of OSS men to Carlsbad Caverns to capture bats. Louis Fieser set to work designing an incendiary for the bats to carry. Despite the effort put into the project, Stanley Lovell would gladly have forgotten about it, but at a staff meeting Donovan demanded to know what was happening. Franklin Roosevelt had been needling the OSS director about the progress with the bats. Lovell's men put tiny metal bands around the bats and soldered the newly developed mini-incendiaries to them.

But the bats never saw action in Japan. When, during a test, they were released from planes over an abandoned mining town in the American West, they tumbled helplessly to earth, unable to take wing at the plane's speed. Some survivors showed definite Axis sympathies by setting fire to an American airplane hangar and a U.S. general's command car.

Lovell's staff also produced the L (lethal) tablets that OSS men, including Donovan, carried to take if captured. Chemists also concocted K tablets, which knocked a person out for several hours. There were hollow clothing buttons in which messages could be hidden. At first the button tops were made to unscrew by turning counterclockwise. When the Germans discovered this, Professor Moriarty reversed the thread so that the buttons unscrewed clockwise. The harder the Germans tried to open a suspect button, the tighter they screwed it shut.

George Kistiokowsky was the OSS explosives expert. He invented an explosive that could be mixed with water or milk, kneaded into dough, raised with yeast or baking powder, and baked into biscuits. Lovell named the flour-like powder Aunt Jemima.

Lovell, John Jeffries, and Donovan took a quantity of Aunt Jemima to the OSS explosives proving range at the Congressional Country Club to see how effective it would be. General Marshall went along for the demonstration. Molded and patted into dough, the explosive was placed beneath a large section of armor plate. There came a mighty bang, and chunks of steel flew into the air. One smashed through the shatterproof windshield of General Marshall's car. Another whizzed past Donovan's head and plunged into a tree behind him. Donovan didn't flick a muscle. "What's next on the program?" he asked.

Aunt Jemima was packaged in Chinese flour bags, and Carl Eifler, Detachment 101's commander, took it with him to China, where it was put to work. OSS men in the field added a time-delay detonator to Aunt Jemima and blasted a Yangtze River bridge.

While R&D was designing the gadgets for OSS agents and resistance fighters to use in the field, Donovan was establishing camps at which his people could be trained for their tasks. The first OSS men were taught in England or at Camp X, a British-Canadian school of unorthodox warfare established by Bill Stephenson on the shores of Lake Ontario near Oshawa, Ontario. There British, Canadian, and in time American experts taught courses in lock picking, safe blowing, second-story entry, the planting of explosives and incendiaries, the use of radios and listening devices, and codes and ciphers. By March 1942 Donovan had established Area B in the Catoctin Mountains of Maryland, 65 miles northwest of Washington. It was just over the mountain from Franklin Roosevelt's Shangri-La, which today is known as Camp David, renamed by President Eisenhower for his grandson. OSS established other training camps close to Washington, and Donovan took pride in showing cabinet officers, generals, and admirals how OSS agents were trained.

James F. Byrnes, then head of the Office of War Mobilization, told of a presidential visit to Shangri-La in July 1943 that turned out to be something other than peaceful for him and his wife. FDR brought the Filipino mess boys from the presidential yacht and plenty of good food. He also brought some prints and pictures and his stamp collection. The President and his valet hung pictures in the cabin, and then FDR worked on his stamps with the good company of Fala, his dog. All was serene.

Mr. and Mrs. Byrnes and Bill Donovan were guests of the President. Donovan invited the Byrnes to go with him to visit the nearby OSS camp. "When we arrived," wrote Byrnes,

> the Chief [Major Fairbairn] had his men running along a narrow board about fifty feet from the ground; it was supposed to represent a housetop. If they slipped, they fell into a net. After watching this and similar stunts, we went into a house where, accompanied by one of the recruits, we walked through a hall about four feet wide and dark as melted midnight. Suddenly the floor beneath us dropped about six or eight inches and in a split second there appeared ahead of us the figure of Tojo. While off balance the recruit fired from the hip, hitting the papier-mâché Tojo in the head. Then in short order Hitler appeared and was got rid of the same way, and the recruit earned a rating for good marksmanship.

Donovan and Byrnes brought Fairbairn back to Shangri-La with them, and he enthralled the President with his "repertoire of stunts and stories, and by his assortment of trick weapons."

Once he had his training camps functioning, Donovan turned his attention to improving the selection of personnel for OSS. Harry Murray, John Gardner, and James Hamilton, the prominent San Francisco psychiatrist, were asked to establish a psychological testing program. "The old man looked at me with his blue eyes and said, 'I want it done in a month,'" Hamilton recalled. "'You will get the best people from the army and from civilian life. You'll get an estate in the country, and I want it done in a month.'"

At the OSS "assessment school," psychological tests screened individuals who might have Axis sympathies, could not withstand frustrations, could not hold their liquor, or had other characteristics that would limit their effectiveness. Van Halsey, who assessed OSS personnel for overseas duty, found he could learn what he needed to know from the answers men and women gave to these questions: What experience made you feel like sinking through the floor? What things do you dislike seeing people do? What would you like to do if you had unlimited means? What would you teach your children? What would push you into a nervous breakdown? What moods and feelings are most disturbing to you and how often do you have them?

As the OSS grew, the psychological testing program became more and more sophisticated. After the war it was studied by the psychology profession for its groundbreaking contributions to the knowledge of behavior in given situations. The OSS had made considerable progress since the early days of the COI, when a recruiter once asked a friend, "Have you met any well-adjusted psychotics lately?"

OSS testing established what types of personalities made the finest agents. A spy is a peculiar sort of person. He must be secretive by nature but open in manner. He must be well balanced and normal in most respects or he cannot gather and accurately rate information. He must be able to stand up under loneliness and the ever-present fear of discovery. He must keep cool in a crisis.

The first months of 1943 saw a bitter dispute between OWI chief Elmer Davis and Donovan as to who should be responsible for psychological warfare abroad. Donovan, convinced that psychological warfare must be integrated into his overall plans for the completion of the conquest of North Africa as well as for the "softening up" of Italy (the next target for Allied arms), felt that Davis should confine his efforts to keeping the American public informed of the progress of the war. Robert Sherwood, who headed the OWI's foreign information service, told reporter friends that if Donovan obtained control he would quit his post. He had had enough of his former chief's freewheeling ways.

"We are not press agents for the government," asserted Davis. "We expect to set forth the difficulties with which both the military and civilian branches of the government are faced, and their shortcomings as well as their successes."

Donovan had no quarrel with this policy when applied to the American public, but he argued that American information services abroad should "adjust to military strategy." He proposed to plant stories and rumors that would cripple the enemy and help the United States. Both Donovan and Davis proved to be formidable bureaucratic combatants in the service of their conflicting views, and it became evident that only Franklin Roosevelt would be able to settle their differences. Donovan, who was supported by the JCS, urged War Secretary Stimson to intercede with the President.

"Both of these functions," Stimson wrote to FDR in February, "are definitely weapons of war." Donovan and Davis differed, said Stimson, "as to the scope and jurisdiction of their separate duties. As the head of the War Department, I am in the position of the innocent bystander in the case of an attempt by a procession of the Ancient and Honorable Order of Hibernians and a procession of Orangemen to pass each other on the street. I only know that every Army commander in a foreign theater, if the present difficulties persist, will be subject to great embarrassment and danger to his operations."

General Marshall was outspoken in his support of Donovan's OSS. He felt strongly that Sherwood's staff had seriously impeded Eisenhower's political negotiations before and during the North African invasion as well as ongoing military operations. OWI's efforts simply were not coordinated with what American arms had to achieve, and Sherwood had followed his own political predilections regardless of their effect on events in the field.

"How Mr. Sherwood operates has long been one of Washington's mysteries," editorialized the *Washington Post*.

> He has a large staff of ideologists who seem to be well versed in the Four Freedoms, but not so well endowed with the common sense to apply their learning and enthusiasm with prudence and knowledge of local situations, and not so well grounded in the technics of psychological warfare. At any rate, the Joint Chiefs of Staff feel with General Eisenhower that their work has furnished less aid than hindrance in the prosecution of our military operations. Hence they have requested that Mr. Sherwood's agency report in future to Col. William J. Donovan's Office of Strategic Services, which is under the Joint Chiefs of Staff. The directive has set off a jurisdictional dispute of some magnitude.

The dispute became more complicated on February 18, when Davis, who was lunching at the White House with the President, brought Donovan's old foe General Strong of G-2 into the fray. Davis urged that Strong be called to the White House to give his views on the OSS-OWI controversy. Roosevelt summoned Strong, who appeared within the hour. Listening to Davis and Strong's combined arguments, the President decided that propaganda operations should be put under the OWI, and for good measure, to silence JCS support for Donovan, that the OSS should be transferred to the War Department where, for practical purposes, it would report to G-2.

Some observers of Roosevelt's wartime Washington believe that Harry Hopkins had been warning Roosevelt and the Democrats of the political danger of Donovan's undoubted ambition, charismatic personality, and allegiance to the Republican Party. Others say that Strong and Davis changed Roosevelt's mind. In any case, the directive that Strong prepared that day amounted to the dissolution of the OSS. He gave it to General Marshall for his approval the next day. "All this of course was quite out of channels," remarked Thomas Troy. "The G-2 chief, used by the OWI director, was instructed by the President to draft an order abolishing a JCS agency! It was also productive of much high-level scurrying, chattering, and rumoring, all at a feverish pace."

Major General Joseph T. McNarney, who as Marshall's deputy chief of staff was the JCS's link to the White House, asked Donovan to come see him on February 20. He bluntly told Donovan that Roosevelt had decided to put the OSS under G-2. If Donovan would go along willingly with this move, Roosevelt would make him a brigadier general.

"Frankly I was shocked as hell," Donovan recalled after the war.

> The OSS had proved itself in North Africa, and we had our agents out all over the world. We had already earned the respect of both our allies and our enemies, and the President of the United States was going to destroy us for what were his own private political reasons. What began as a difference of opinion between Roosevelt's crony Sherwood and General Eisenhower had involved both the OSS and the OWI in an angry showdown. Davis intemperately had brought G-2 back into the picture in an attempt to find an ally wherever he could, regardless of the consequences to the war effort and American security.

Donovan talked with his key aides. James Grafton Rogers, a Yale law professor who had taken Edmond Taylor's place as the OSS psychological warfare chief, had a gloomy conference with Donovan. "Bill and I agreed," wrote Rogers in his journal, that "we must resign. He is to write a letter of protest, try to see the President as a last resort. We could neither of us live under General Strong."

"Bill Donovan troubles me," added Rogers in a few days. "He is so honest, so aggressive, so scattered, so provocative. Day by day I see him getting near elimination because he excites anger. But he has taught Washington the elements of modern warfare, and no one else has even tried."

People at the JCS told Donovan "to sit tight and wait," but on February 23, Donovan wrote a letter to Roosevelt, who had agreed to see him.

> During these past months I have hesitated to encroach upon your crowded days. This course (however excellent the motive) has perhaps failed to keep you aware of the manner in which we have been endeavoring to fulfill the responsibilities you gave us.
>
> I would like to tell you about these activities. Though I have seen articles in the press to the contrary, this organization has no quarrel with OWI. It is not true that we have in any way invaded the province of OWI.
>
> We do not duplicate their activity in the open propaganda assigned to them by your Directive. We do not possess either equipment or personnel to do such work. In fact, we have not thus far even secured all the equipment necessary to operate in the field of black subversion—an arena in which OWI has always disclaimed any interest.
>
> I suspect that confusion has arisen because the word "psychological"

has been given different meanings by different American and English agencies. The U.S. Chiefs of Staff have used the word in the general sense employed by the German and other Continental armies as applying to all unorthodox methods. They call this weapon of warfare psychological only because of the effect produced rather than as a description of the means employed.

In the subversive field of unorthodox warfare we do not impinge upon the assigned functions of any other agency. The Joint Chiefs made a thorough inquiry into our organization and issued a Directive clearly limiting our duties within our assigned field.

I have heard that a suggestion has been made that you consider transferring this Agency to the War Department. This would, in my opinion, disrupt our usefulness. You early recognized that this work could not live if it were buried in the machinery of a great department. You saw that it must have elbow room and made us an Agency of the Joint Chiefs of Staff.

The Joint Chiefs should have every facility which can effectively aid them. We are prepared to act for them in unorthodox warfare through a far-flung net of organizers and agents throughout the theaters—except for the moment in the South Pacific.

Our connections with underground channels will, as has already been demonstrated, count heavily when invasions are ready.

To disrupt such plans at this moment would, I believe, be a valuable gift to the enemy.

I hope you will examine the situation and ascertain the truth.

I anticipate the privilege of talking with you soon.

Donovan had good reason to be alarmed about the future of the OSS. The directive drafted by Strong was now on the President's desk awaiting his signature. Realizing that one of Roosevelt's motives in moving against him was political, Donovan called in Ernest Cuneo, the OSS liaison officer with both J. Edgar Hoover and Bill Stephenson. Cuneo was a Democratic stalwart with top-level connections in the administration.

"I went into action," Cuneo said. "I phoned the White House time and again. I asked that the directive be taken off the President's desk. They wouldn't do it. I told them to at least put it on the bottom of the pile of work awaiting Mr. Roosevelt's attention. This at least was done."

"He won't reach it until 4:00 P.M.," Cuneo was told.

In this way Cuneo gave Donovan six precious hours in which to mobilize aid from the JCS. Support was swift and vociferous. For once the top admirals and generals, appreciating what OSS had accomplished, spoke up on Donovan's behalf. They also helped by describing Davis and the OWI as unrealistic, uncooperative, and troublesome. Listening to the angry reaction from the JCS, Roosevelt took the directive off his desk. The JCS now set about drafting a new directive that would eliminate the area of conflict between the OSS and the OWI.

On March 9, President Roosevelt issued Executive Order No. 9312. It placed full responsibility for foreign propaganda activities under the OWI. The OSS was to keep the responsibility for propaganda activities behind enemy lines. Nothing was said of removing the OSS from the Joint Chiefs of Staff to place it under G-2. As was the case with many of Roosevelt's directives, the order left plenty of room for bureaucratic maneuvering and confusion in the future, but the OSS survived. On March 15 Donovan, Davis, and OWI Associate Director Milton Eisenhower lunched together. Their conversation was amicable as they explored ways in which the two organizations could cooperate. It seemed to all three men at the table that perhaps the true enemy was in Berlin, Tokyo, and Rome, after all.

There were to be renewed attacks on the OSS by General Strong, but for now Donovan had good reason to be satisfied. He tore up his letter of resignation. At last the OSS had a clear-cut status in the Washington bureaucracy, a standing without which no government agency can expect more than an ephemeral life, regardless of its contributions to the public good.

30

Partners with the Resistance

"THERE ARE TWO sides to covert activities," OSS man George Bowden once remarked, "blowing up a bridge or watching what goes over it. Some people would rather blow the bridge up, and at times Donovan got on that side of the fence."

Certainly Bill Donovan never forgot his own experience as an infantry officer in World War I, and throughout his years as director of the OSS, he felt a lively sympathy for the guerrilla warriors he sent to fight behind the enemy lines. On four separate occasions—in Sicily, Burma, Normandy, and the south of France—he joined in the fray, even though to have been captured would have risked betrayal of some of the Allies' deepest secrets.

Early on, COI-OSS cast its lot with native resistance movements. Before the Allied invasion of North Africa, Carleton Coon and Bill Eddy had contacted the most powerful Moslem leader in northern Morocco, known by the code name Strings, and a tribal chieftain in the coastal mountains of El Rif known as Tassels. Tens of thousands of Arabs, responding to the call of holy men and sheiks, worked for Strings. According to Kermit Roosevelt, agents "penetrated areas forbidden by the French authorities to the general populace" and cooperated with "farmers and shepherds who relayed pertinent items of intelligence in comparative anonymity."

Tassels commanded a guerrilla force of Berbers in the Atlas Mountains. These guerrillas set the pattern for OSS clandestine forces, which in time were to be deployed behind the lines in Asia and on the continent of Europe.

"Marshal Pétain required ten months and a force of 150,000 men and thirty batteries of 65-millimeter mountain guns to put down the Abd-el-Krim insurrection of 1925-28," Donovan told Roosevelt. Now the Berbers were working for the OSS. The Arabs of North Africa also proved outstanding intelligence agents.

In Spanish Morocco, Arabs reported the actions of German submarines lurking in secret bases fashioned out of coastal caves. When Gen. Erwin Rommel threatened to break out of Tunisia and invade Morocco, an underground Arab army of 80,000 men waited to fight him. The signing of the North African Armistice on November 11, 1942, passed control of French North Africa west of German-occupied Tunisia to the

Allies. From that time on Donovan's Arab guerrillas and intelligence forces operated out of Algiers.

In 1943 Donovan made frequent and usually unheralded visits to the OSS headquarters in Algiers to meet with North African OSS men and with Arab and French resistance leaders. He would stay at the St. George Hotel, set among gardens high on a hill overlooking the bay, and entertain a constant stream of visitors, both Europeans and Arabs of both sexes. Often after a long flight from London he would have a masseur work on his body while he read reports and listened to the radio. OSS man Peter Mero, who was stationed in North Africa, once arrived at the hotel only to have Donovan, who was being massaged, give him a look that clearly meant he was to say nothing of importance since the masseur was unreliable. Mero had to wait, making small talk until the man had left, before he could say what he really had on his mind.

Usually Donovan would visit OSS headquarters, which was nearby. Charles Taquey was waiting in Algiers to be sent on a clandestine mission into Sardinia when Donovan arrived at headquarters. "There was a WAC called Mousie," Taquey said. "Glasses, cute little nose. She was elected to be Bill Donovan's secretary in Algiers. Donovan demanded that she bring him all the reports, all the telegrams that had been dispatched or received at the outpost since his previous visit. She obliged. Donovan studied each dispatch and then remarked to Mousie, 'Now I'm going to scare everybody.'" He did exactly that, and OSS Algiers redoubled its efforts.

William Rader, the San Francisco photographer who had opened an OSS photo laboratory in Algiers to process film smuggled out of enemy-held country, remembered several such visits. "Bill Donovan was a dangerous man to know," he observed. "If he really liked you, he'd pay you the compliment of having you dropped into Sicily, Sardinia, Corsica, northern Italy, southern France, or someplace else like that."

One of the men at OSS Algiers whom Donovan took a fancy to was Stuart Hughes, grandson of Chief Justice Charles Evans Hughes and the scholarly director of R&A's field base in North Africa.

"Since Hughes was doing brilliant work for R&A," Rader said, "Donovan conceived that he would do even more brilliant work behind the lines in northern Italy, even though he could scarcely speak ten words of Italian."

Hughes was nonplussed. Swept up as he might be in the whirlwind of Donovan's sense of mission, he was at the same time unable to see how he could function successfully in enemy country.

"We hid Hughes in my photo laboratory until Donovan had left for Cairo," recounted Rader. "I'm confident we saved his life. Donovan found somebody else he liked enough to drop into Italy."

As the British and American armies fought Rommel's troops for

Tunisia, OSS agents cooperated with the British SOE to penetrate German lines for tactical intelligence. In Tunisia the OSS discovered that because they were allies of the French, they did not have the friendly collaboration of the Arabs they had previously enjoyed. Now they were perceived as too close to the colonial masters of North Africa. Some OSS agents resorted to a hostage system to obtain necessary intelligence about the Germans.

"We found that when we entered a distant village where loyalty was wavering," reported an agent, "we would take the eldest son of the most important man and hold him pending his father's arrival. The old man inevitably came with gifts, demanding his son. He was sent back to get good information of enemy positions, and when he came the second time his son was released if the information was satisfactory. This use of hostages was our chief source of intelligence aside from the work of our own patrols."

Rommel's Afrika Korps had fallen back onto the Tunisian peninsula with Montgomery's British Eighth Army in pursuit. The British First Army joined the attack on the German positions from the west, but the Germans were able to repulse the combined attacks because they had been reinforced from Italy and were in very strong positions. When the U.S. Second Corps attempted to join the action, Rommel's counteroffensive in February resulted in a major American defeat at Kasserine Pass. It appeared in the spring of 1943 that it would be a good number of months before the Germans could be routed from Tunisia.

"Meantime, U.S. forces had captured documentary material from the Germans in Africa," said Whitney Shepardson, a top Donovan aide. "G-2 immediately took charge and sent the material to London where they came to conclusion that they lacked language competence. Transported all of it in boxes to OSS, top floor of Grosvenor St. headquarters. There R&A appraised it, and to their amazement, came upon entire plans for interior defense of position Rommel was holding. Transferred this to G-2 and Rommel's position was taken."

By May 6 the city of Tunis fell to the British, followed the next day by Bizerta. Hitler gave orders that his troops should fight until the last. They did continue firing until their positions were overrun, although toward the end most of the soldiers deliberately fired into the air in a bizarre attempt to appease the victors. Ironically, the last Axis troops to surrender to the Allies were Italian. Organized resistance ended on May 13, while in Washington Roosevelt and Churchill were meeting in a conference code-named Trident to plan for the invasion of Italy and to decide what to do about the situation in the Balkans.

When Donovan went to Algiers, more often than not he continued on to Cairo, where, as Sterling Hayden remarked, OSS was situated in a villa that seemed a "bastard version of the Taj Mahal." Broad verandas overlooked a shady lawn surrounded by a high wall. A formidable wrought-iron gate kept out unwanted visitors. Within the building, houseboys padded about ready to bring a cooling drink or a snack. In almost any place in the world where OSS had an outpost, it could be counted on to be the most comfortable and luxurious quarters available.

Donovan's arrivals in Cairo were just as traumatic for the staff as were his appearances in Algiers. "I was at work in the message center, and finally got a message deciphered," remembered a cryptographer. "It announced that 109 [Donovan's code name] was due to arrive at four that afternoon and expected to be met at the airport. I glanced at my watch and saw that the General's plane had already landed. I locked up the message center and was taking the message up to the station chief when who should I encounter on the steps but 109 himself. He had beat the message to Cairo."

Adolph Schmidt had opened the Cairo post, from which he exercised responsibility for the east coast all the way to Mozambique, where Leopold Wertz, German vice-consul in Lourenço Marques, operated an espionage ring extending into South Africa. OSS Cairo was also concerned with operations in the Middle East and the Balkans.

Donovan found much to occupy him in Cairo. He kept an eye on how Reza Shah in Iran was plotting to turn his country into a Nazi satrapy and on the intrigues of the Grand Mufti of Jerusalem on his friend Hitler's behalf. He consulted with his Cairo chiefs on what might be done for Allied pilots shot down in attacks on Romanian oil fields at Ploesti and what the latest intelligence from the Greek underground portended. Greek resistance was divided. On one hand Napoleon Zervas, bearded and patriarchal, led the republican and monarchist force. The combined democratic and communist guerrillas were dominated by the Reds, following much the same pattern as was being demonstrated by Tito in Yugoslavia and by Enver Hoxha in Albania. There were nationalistic slogans to broaden the base of support, but all the key positions went to trusted communist lieutenants.

Agent Stallion in Syria, who had set up a net of 60 subagents, could always be counted upon to provide some nuggets of useful information about the continuing collaboration of the Vichy French and the Germans in Syria. It was Stallion who first informed Donovan that the French were refueling Italian submarines operating in the eastern Mediterranean.

Yugoslavia was one of Donovan's headaches during the spring of 1943. At a conference in Washington in 1942, Donovan and King Peter had discussed sending U.S. supplies to Yugoslavs who were fighting the Germans. Constantine Fotić, the Yugoslav ambassador, was pressing Roosevelt for delivery.

"The Yugoslav Minister is most anxious (a) that we get forty tons of concentrated food now in Cairo delivered (I suppose by air to Yugoslavia) and (b) that we establish definite liaison with Mihajlović," Roosevelt wrote to Donovan on May 10. "I understand British contacts are in effect and that they have ten officers in Yugoslavia. We should not cross wires with them but the Ambassador thinks it would be good if we could get one officer into Serbia."

The next day Donovan replied,

> On May 4, 1943, our representative in Cairo cabled that (a) the distribution of food has definitely been planned and will be carried out when arrangements are completed with the Theater; (b) that the Theater Commander has been requested to requisition approximately 284 tons of dehydrated food, at present in the possession of OSS, in this country. We can have the food as soon as this requisition has been approved.
>
> Two OSS representatives left yesterday for Cairo by air, one of whom is to establish liaison with General Mihajlović in Serbia, and the other to be attached to the Partisans. Each of these men is fully trained in Intelligence and Subversive activities, is a qualified radio operator, and has the necessary language qualifications.

The two OSS men Donovan had sent to Cairo were George Musulin and George Wuchinich, Americans of Serbian descent. With their foreign backgrounds, they represented the kind of Americans Donovan felt could be most effective in Occupied Europe.

The food in question was packed in special containers, each holding ten packages of five pounds each, and wrapped in Yugoslav colors. A message from Franklin Roosevelt in Serbian in each package greeted Mihajlović and his Chetniks, wishing them luck and concluding with recipes for preparing the food. The concentrated food was shipped to Egypt to be dropped to Mihajlović just as Donovan had said it would be, but the Chetniks were fated never to try the recipes provided by the President of the United States. People on Malta were near starvation, and British authorities in Cairo sidetracked the food intended for the Yugoslavs and sent it to the beleaguered island. What the Maltese thought of the supplies, wrapped in Yugoslav colors with instructions in Serbian, is unrecorded. What the Chetniks thought of not receiving the provisions they desperately needed is mercifully unrecorded as well.

Donovan always found his visits to Cairo stimulating, not only because of the intrigues his people were carrying on there but because a blond girl of exceptional beauty vied with a redhead of comparable good looks for his off-hour attention.

Gerhard Van Arkel remembered a visit that Donovan made to Algiers on his way back from Cairo. "We'd taken a villa," Van Arkel said. "The French landlord had ripped out tiles, light bulbs, and the plumbing except for two sinks in the bathroom. We gave Donovan a bedroom opposite mine. In the morning I went into the bathroom to shave and Donovan was shaving at the other sink. A ship had recently exploded in the harbor and smashed all our windows, and a cold wind was blowing through the room. Our furniture was a shambles, we were eating C rations, and the rain had almost washed me out of bed during the night."

"How was Cairo?" Van Arkel asked 109.

"Just like here," he huffed. "Too damned much luxury." Coming from the sybaritic Donovan, the response miffed Van Arkel.

There were other OSS posts in Africa for Donovan to visit from time to time. At Dakar in French West Africa, two OSS officers were working in close liaison with the French Deuxieme Bureau, checking on subversive activities along the coast to the south. From Accra, other agents were presumably checking on Axis diamond smuggling.

Adolph Schmidt was the OSS man given the task of looking into the smuggling. "When I left for Accra, I was told I'd have secret instructions awaiting me there," said Schmidt. "The Congo was a source of uranium, and Donovan had heard that it was being diverted to Europe. Were the Germans working on an atom bomb?"

At Accra Schmidt learned he was to proceed to Leopoldville (Kinshasa) under cover of trying to look for diamonds being sent secretly to Germany. Actually he was to search for evidence of uranium smuggling. Schmidt was not to tell the Belgians, who controlled the Congo, of his mission.

"In Leopoldville I discovered that industrial diamonds were going overland to Addis Ababa from where the Italians were sending them on to Germany," said Schmidt, "but I found no evidence of the diversion of uranium to Germany." Other OSS agents discovered that diamonds were being mailed to the Germans by disloyal Belgians in what appeared to be Red Cross parcels.

On February 17, 1943, the Joint Chiefs of Staff sent President Roosevelt the nomination of William Donovan to the grade of brigadier general. It was added that "it will be necessary to issue an order by direction of the President that he is to continue as Director of the OSS, inasmuch as there are new officers in the Planning Group of the OSS who will be senior to him."

Roosevelt acted on the nomination, and Donovan the civilian became Brigadier General Donovan. OSS staffer Arthur Robinson recalled the first time he saw Donovan in uniform.

> The Director had a regular staff meeting in the mornings for all department heads. It had been quite informal, with attendees coming early, getting a cup of coffee, and sitting on the big table, in lounge chairs, etc.,

and chatting until the Director arrived to open the meeting. On the first day the General was in uniform, it was business as usual. When he arrived and went to the head of the conference table, the others finished their conversations and took their time taking their seats. He thereupon chewed them out for not coming to attention when their Commanding General entered the room, told them not to let it happen again. The others were shocked, of course, and sat silently.

John Ford had been making a night of it. He walked into the silent meeting. Dark glasses hid his bloodshot eyes. He took a seat.

"Commander, if you can see well enough, we can get started!" barked Donovan.

"General," replied Ford, "I can see one thing; you've got a ribbon for the Congressional Medal of Honor on the wrong place on your uniform."

The tension was broken. Everybody laughed, including Donovan, and the OSS got back to work as usual despite the fact that the director was now a brigadier general. From then on Donovan wore his full uniform, which he had tailored at Brooks Brothers, whenever he went to meet with the JCS.

"Even though he was the most decorated U.S. officer in World War I," recalls John Beaudouin, "he wore on his uniform coat only the Medal of Honor. The officers he was confronting in the Joint Chiefs were covered from collarbone to breastbone with 'fruit salad'—except for the Medal of Honor."

Shortly after he went into uniform, Donovan summoned Walter Langer to Washington for a conference. They talked about routine affairs.

"What do you make of Hitler?" Donovan suddenly asked. "You were over there and saw him and his outfit operating. You must have some idea about what is going on."

Donovan then elaborated on his own impressions of Hitler, which he had first gained 20 years before in a Bavarian village *Weinstube*. Remembered Langer:

> I had to confess that although I had given the subject some serious thought on various occasions, the psychology of Hitler and his hold on the German people were still a complete mystery to me. He assured me that I was not alone in this respect, and I gathered from the subsequent conversation that there was a wide divergence of opinion among our top policy makers concerning Hitler and his relationship to the German people. It was the General's view that we should have something more reliable to guide us than what the German propaganda machine and foreign correspondents were feeding us.
>
> "What we need," the General said, "is a realistic appraisal of the German situation. If Hitler is running the show, what kind of a person is he?

. . . What is he like with his associates? What is his background? And most of all, we want to know as much as possible about his psychological make-up—the things that make him tick. In addition, we ought to know what he might do if things begin to go against him. Do you suppose you could come up with something along these lines?" . . .

I pointed out that the value of such an undertaking would be highly uncertain since, to a large extent, we would have to glean our information from the literature. The literature, although extensive, was mostly unreliable, and it was difficult, at this time, to know how much pertinent material it would reveal. Furthermore, I pointed out, neither psychological nor psychoanalytic techniques were designed or readily adaptable to such an enterprise. But General Donovan was not one to be deterred by such considerations.

"Well, give it a try and see what you can come up with," he said. "Hire what help you need and get it done as soon as possible. Keep it brief and make it readable to the layman."

Langer got up to leave, but Donovan was not finished. "Remember, we'll be face to face with Hitler at the peace table," he said.

"You'll never meet him at the peace table," Langer remarked with certainty.

In May 1943, Donovan had good reason to wonder about the mind of Adolf Hitler and his hold on the German people. Early in the month, Donovan had received an incredible report from Arthur Goldberg in London. "I met Samuel Zygelbojm, the representative of the Jewish Board in the Polish government-in-exile in London," recalled Goldberg. "Zygelbojm gave me the first fully documented proof of the Nazi death camps. Late in 1942 there had been stories from refugees who had managed to escape the death camps, but there had been no supporting evidence. Now I was given pictures and affidavits, overwhelming evidence of the terrible horrors at the heart of Hitler's Reich."

Zygelbojm, a socialist labor leader before the war, begged Goldberg to do something to stop the extermination of a whole people. At least, he argued, the Allies could bomb the camps so that the Germans would understand that the Allies knew the camps existed. If innocent Jews were to die in the Allied attack, it would be tragic; but they were going to die anyway, and in the bombing some of their Nazi murderers would die too. Other Germans might be warned that if their country lost the war, there would be retribution for their inhumanity.

Goldberg promised to inform Washington. He sent a detailed report, complete with the affidavits and grim photos, to Donovan.

"Donovan forwarded the report, together with the documents and pictures, to Roosevelt," stated Goldberg. "He asked that the U.S. Air Force bomb the death camps. 'No,' replied Roosevelt. Donovan informed me that President Roosevelt was strongly of the mind that our planes could not be diverted from the attack on Hitler. This was senseless, since some of the targets being struck were only five miles away from the camps."

Goldberg invited Zygelbojm to dine at Claridge's on May 11. During dinner he told the Jewish representative of the President's decision. The next day Samuel Zygelbojm died of an overdose of pills, his response to the President of the United States.

Although Donovan's principal concern in 1943 was with the Mediterranean, he managed to fly on from Cairo to New Delhi and to Kandy, Ceylon, to keep abreast of developments in Asia. On January 11, 1943, he called Col. Nicol Smith into his office and pointed to a map of Thailand. "Here we have an area of more than 200,000 square miles with not a single Allied agent. We need weather information for the 14th Air Force in Yunnan and the 10th in Burma; we also need information on troop movements across this vast country, and we need much more than that." Stilwell and British commanders in Southeast Asia had informed Donovan of their urgent need for information on the Japanese strength in Thailand, the location of Japanese installations so they could be bombed without injuring the Thai population, whether there was a Thai underground, and if it would be possible to rescue Allied prisoners of war who had been captured during the triumphant Japanese advance through the region.

"How are we going to get in there?" asked Smith, who had recently returned from a mission to France.

"You're going to get in there. I know you don't know anything in particular about Thailand, but you are the best man for the job."

Donovan knew that Smith was the son of a wealthy San Francisco family who had lived a life of adventure since the age of 17, when he had run away from a boy's school in Switzerland to go down the Danube River on a raft. In the years just before Pearl Harbor, Smith had traveled over the Burma Road to write a bestselling book. His perceptive reports from Vichy had impressed the OSS chief. Donovan pressed a button on his desk, and Douglas Diamond, the officer in charge of special funds, entered the room.

"Doug has $500,000 for you," Donovan told Smith. The money was from the Free Thais in Washington, who, at the urging of Preston Goodfellow, had unfrozen $11 million in funds to help drive the Japanese out of their country.

"You can't go to the Army Quartermaster and outfit a secret Thai force. You'll have to do your shopping at Abercrombie and Fitch," observed Donovan.

Diamond handed Smith ten checks for $50,000 each.

"You're a little bit startled?" blandly inquired Donovan with a slight glint in his eyes. "You'll manage the assignment."

Smith took the money to the Bank of New York, where an old friend was a vice-president. The bank officer warned him that unless depositors kept a minimum of $300 in an account, they would have to pay a fee of five cents on each check. "And with what amount do you propose to initiate your account?" he finished.

"Fifty thousand dollars. Next week I'll wish to deposit an equivalent sum, and by the end of the year will probably make it half a million."

Having, as he put it later, "rippled the world of finance," Smith proceeded to start shopping for arms for 20 Thais, all of them students in America, who were to go with him to Thailand.

Kenneth Landon briefed Smith on the intricacies of Thai politics and advised him as to which political leaders might be trusted. Then Smith and his Thais left for India, where they trained at Detachment 101's forward base at Nazira, Assam, and then infiltrated into Thailand.

Donovan had reason to be pleased; the reports from the Thai underground proved remarkably accurate. Thai sources provided weather reports, designated bomber targets, and gave information to help in the rescue of downed air crews and prisoners of war. This might be expected in a nation where the number two man in the underground was the head of the country's secret police. The number one man, who was known only as Ruth, turned out after the war to have been Pridi Phanomyong, the prime minister.

"The Siamese Prime Minister was skilled in this kind of warfare," Donovan said after the war. "He pretended to be pro-Japanese but was really on our side. In his own palace he gave shelter and protection for two OSS men and set up a radio transmitter by which they reported."

Ruth not only contributed significantly to the defeat of the Japanese in Southeast Asia, but after the war he was to prove very helpful to Donovan when he went to Thailand for President Eisenhower on his last important mission abroad.

31

Tangled Webs

LUCKY LUCIANO HOPED for a parole. Toward the end of 1942 his emissaries approached the OSS as well as the Office of Naval Intelligence. If Donovan could arrange his release from prison, Luciano promised, his followers in the Mafia would set up an intelligence apparatus on their ancestral island of Sicily and supply the OSS with information. After all, Donovan had sprung counterfeiters and safecrackers. Why not a godfather?

Donovan recalled all too well his early 1920s crusade against the syndicate interests in western New York, and he refused to make a deal. Neither Donovan nor George White, director of X-2 training and a former narcotics bureau agent, believed they could trust the Mafia because it was a supranational conspiracy without any allegiance to the United States. Other OSS agents were also in touch with Mafia chiefs who had been driven out of Sicily by Mussolini and were hiding in Toronto. But nothing came of these negotiations either.

Someone in Washington dubbed the OSS group that finally did undertake the intelligence penetration of Sicily the Italians in Algiers, probably in imitation of Rossini's opera *L'Italiana in Algeri*. In reality, the Italians were Sicilian-Americans recruited from the Italian neighborhoods of Hartford and Middletown, Connecticut, by a young OSS man, Max Corvo, who was rarely at a loss for words in either English or Italian. Corvo and one of his recruits, a Hartford lawyer named Vincent Scamporino, brought their band to Algiers early in 1943. They placed agents in Sicily, from where the Germans and Italians supported their forces in North Africa. Information began to flow back to OSS in North Africa about Italian troop dispositions and fortifications in Sicily.

By July 9 an Allied invasion fleet had gathered in North African ports. Sicily was to be the target. Navy Lt. Comdr. David Donovan was aboard the flagship *Samuel Chase* in the port of Algiers. Orders to cast off had already been given.

"Hold everything," came a new order. "Some brass arriving from Washington!"

The crew felt the usual annoyance at the arrival of military brass when everybody had the coming battle on his mind. David Donovan, standing at the rail, saw a jeep race onto the pier and come to a squealing halt at the gangplank. He recognized the unmistakable burly figure of his father as he bounced out of the jeep and rushed up the gangplank. After him hurried Ray Kellogg, a Field Photo cameraman. Now that the brass from Washington was aboard, the crew cast off, and soon the ship was on the high seas heading toward Sicily.

The British and American naval guns bombarded the attack points on the south and east coasts of the island. Allied planes roared in to drop salvos of bombs. The landing craft headed for the beach and secured a beachhead. Right after the first wave of landing craft, Bill Donovan, wearing borrowed jungle fatigues much too large for him, climbed into a boat and went ashore to find out for himself how things were going. He soon discovered that OSS agents recruited and trained in the United States could not be counted on for combat intelligence missions; it was necessary to recruit local Sicilians, who understood the terrain and could cross into enemy territory undiscovered. Sicilian-Americans, Donovan's Italians in Algiers, proved to be invaluable, however, since they knew the dialects and could be used as forward interpreters and to recruit Sicilians for OSS work behind the lines.

Captain Paul Gale, later an OSS man, was on the First Division staff of Gen. Theodore Roosevelt, Jr. "Teddy called me and said he had a general officer at headquarters, and he would appreciate my showing him some of the operations," recalled Gale. "Here was General Donovan, ruddy cheeks, blue eyes. We climbed into a jeep. I had a light machine gun beside me on the seat. Off we went. He wanted to go farther and farther."

"General," objected Gale, "we're getting where Italian patrols are active."

"Fine," replied Donovan, his eyes sparkling with pleasure.

The jeep dashed on down the road and into an Italian patrol. The Italians opened up with automatic weapons.

"Donovan got behind my machine gun and had a field day," recalled Gale. "He shot up the Italians single-handed. He was happy as a clam when we got back. I'd been bloodied in North Africa, and I knew this guy was something. We had a hell of a fire fight."

When Gale got back to headquarters, Roosevelt chewed him out without mercy "for getting such an important man into such a bad position."

As for Donovan, he never forgot Gale, and he later lured him into the OSS. In fact, he liked Gale so much that he sent him behind the lines in China with the task of replacing Tai Li's prejudiced agents with trustworthy OSS sources. In China, Gale not only discovered the "sweetheart arrangements between Japanese and Chinese commanders, who took and retook certain towns without a shot being fired to impress their governments in Tokyo and Chungking," but also Chiang Kai-shek's penchant for selling U.S.-supplied arms to the Japanese.

Things were going well in Sicily, and on July 23 Palermo fell to the Allies. German and Italian troops withdrew from Catania on August 5, and 12 days later Messina capitulated. The conquest of Sicily, the stepping-stone from North Africa to Europe, was completed.

Donovan flew back to Algiers with Gen. Albert Wedemeyer. He continued on to Morocco to confer with Gen. Mark Clark at Fifth Army headquarters. The Allied invasion of the Italian mainland was planned for early September, and Donovan assured Clark that the OSS was already at work in Italy preparing the way.

"He was very obviously a can-do sort of fellow," said Clark, recalling the conference. Clark, who had seen firsthand the outstanding OSS counterespionage work done on the Spanish Moroccan border, was enthusiastic about OSS help. He was less enthusiastic about some of Donovan's ideas.

"Donovan wanted the army to land north of Rome and not at Salerno, where he insisted that his intelligence sources made it clear the landings would be bloody," said David Crockett, one of Donovan's aides at the time. "Donovan found Clark to be vain, proud, and superficial," added Crockett, "but he had no alternative but to cooperate with him."

During their conference Donovan and Clark and his G-2 aide, Colonel Howard, agreed to form the 2677th Special Reconnaissance Battalion of the OSS. The 2677th was to be assigned to G-2 at Clark's headquarters. It would, reported Donovan, "brief combat intelligence teams, contact pro-American and anti-Fascist organizations, and recruit likely personnel for informers, coup de main groups, censorship work, guides, interpreters, translators, or leaders to be subsidized."

Donovan was delighted that the OSS was now undertaking to provide not only strategic intelligence about Italy but also behind-the-lines intelligence of immediate use to Mark Clark and his officers. The sweep of Allied arms through Sicily had proved to be a fatal blow to Mussolini's regime. On July 25, as Mussolini left the Royal Palace after a bitter wrangle with King Victor Emmanuel III, police acting on the king's orders seized him. Marshal Pietro Badoglio, Donovan's old friend, was asked by the king to form a new government.

"Badoglio lost no time in letting Hitler know that he would maintain the Axis alliance and that Italian soldiers would fight side by side with the Germans, but at the same time he dispatched secret ambassadors to the Allies to discuss surrender," Donovan said after the war.

As Italian crowds raced through the streets of Rome, smashing statues of Mussolini and chanting "Death to the Fascisti," Hitler had no illusions as to Badoglio's true intentions. The Germans, cursing all things Italian, began to move their troops into strong positions to resist the inevitable Allied attack. Mussolini was bundled off into captivity, and the Italian Resistance prepared feverishly to help the Allies dislodge the German Army. Donovan directed his agents in Italy to establish a working liaison with the underground and to step up the flow of intelligence back to North Africa.

Donovan flew back to Washington to attend an August 19 meeting of the Joint Chiefs of Staff. The JCS listened to his reports and authorized him to test his fifth column techniques in Sardinia. On August 23 General Marshall ordered Eisenhower, "Give Donovan a chance to do his stuff without fear of compromising some operations in prospect. If he succeeds, fine; if not, nothing would be lost."

Donovan was anxious to get back to the Mediterranean, but another critical matter demanded his attention. Earlier in the year, Allen Dulles, code number 110, had informed 109 from Switzerland that "one of my men got dry clothes and a breakfast for a French worker who swam the Rhine to Rehn last night. Told following improbable story. Said he was forced labor guard for cask of water from Rjukan in Norway to island of Peenemünde in Baltic Sea."

Stanley Lovell pondered the report in his South Building cubbyhole. He knew there was a huge hydroelectric plant at Rjukan. The only water worth guarding would be heavy water needed for an atomic explosive. Lovell suspected that the Nazis might be working on an atomic bomb at Peenemünde. He rushed to Donovan's office and threw down a brace of maps on his desk.

"Bill," he said, "this may be vitally important."

One map showed Peenemünde in the Baltic; the other showed the northern coast of France. On the latter Lovell had drawn in the locations of curious ski-like runways, with odd curved twists at the ends, that Allied planes had photographed. From west of Boulogne to south of Cherbourg, these strange runways seemed to be aimed at the British cities of London, Bristol, Birmingham, and Liverpool.

"What do you mean?" asked Donovan.

"This little French workman has told us where the German heavy water comes from," explained Lovell, "but vastly more important, where the German physicists are working to make a bomb employing nuclear fission. It all adds up perfectly."

"Adds up to what?"

"To a catastrophic Nazi victory. This explains the ski sites. The Germans are going to attack Britain from those odd-looking launching sites with a secret weapon."

As it turned out, Lovell was wrong in several important respects. Subsequent OSS reports showed that the heavy water was not going to Peenemünde at all; instead, the ships the French captive worker had guarded were taking the water to Wolgast, where it was unloaded and shipped by rail to the Kaiser Wilhelm Institute in Berlin and other places where atomic experimentation was going on. The heavy water had nothing to do with Peenemünde, but neither Donovan nor Lovell knew this. Donovan ordered Lovell to fly to London and brief the OSS European chief, David Bruce, about his suspicions.

According to Lovell, Bruce immediately met with Lord Portal of the Royal Air Force and Gen. Carl Spaatz of the U.S. Air Force. The RAF took to the air en masse on August 17, 1943, and attacked Peenemünde in one of the war's most devastating raids. A thousand Germans, many of them scientists and technicians, died in the attack, and the mysterious facilities on the island were obliterated. There was no atomic research on the island whatsoever, but the attack knocked out the experimental plants developing the V-1s and V-2s, delaying the appearance of these rockets over Britain until June of 1944.

MacArthur had refused to cooperate with Donovan in the South Pacific. Major Charles A. Willoughby, MacArthur's intelligence chief, claimed that

> Wild Bill Donovan's Office of Strategic Service operatives had a fixed idea that they were arbitrarily kept out of MacArthur's Southwest Pacific Theater. Actually, MacArthur had to go along without the help of the Office of Strategic Services, because he couldn't afford to wait for it. Unlike the war in Europe, the United States war in Asia was a "shooting war" from the start. Where the OSS in Washington had time to gather information about North Africa, about the soft underbelly of Europe in general, long before a single landing craft or soldier was ever risked in battle, MacArthur had to improvise with the Japanese breathing down his neck. He couldn't sit back and ransack libraries, even assuming the data was there; he had to have his reports from a 3,000-mile battle arc long before Roosevelt had even given Bill Donovan his basic directives on Europe.

Donovan certainly did not look at it that way. To him MacArthur was a monumental ego who insisted upon "keeping everything in his theater under his thumb." He had attempted to win favor with MacArthur at the time of his Bataan stand by stating in a national radio address, "General MacArthur—a symbol for our nation—outnumbered, outgunned—with the seas around him and the skies above controlled by the enemy—fighting for freedom." On April 26, 1943, he had sent Lt. Comdr. William McGovern to brief Vice-Adm. William Halsey, commander of the U.S. naval forces in the South Pacific, and persuade him to adopt Donovan's way of thinking.

"Donovan wanted to send OSS teams into the Philippines to organize resistance much as we were already organizing the resistance in Burma," said McGovern. "There were other parts of the South Pacific

On July 11, 1941, President Roosevelt established the Office of the Coordinator of Information (COI), making Donovan its chief. When the COI was transformed into the Office of Strategic Services (OSS) in 1942, Donovan continued as America's wartime intelligence master.
(National Archives)

Perched on the corner of his desk, the OSS director confers with top aides. Behind the men is the map that Donovan studied as he pondered reports from the field.
(Coburn Allen Buxton)

THE WORLD

Above: The limestone and brick buildings at 25th and E streets that served as COI/OSS headquarters after August 1941.
Left: Donovan (center) and OSS men and women share a moment of relaxation at OSS headquarters in China.
(Howard Lyon)
Below: The walled-in OSS compound near Kunming, China, was a world away from Washington, but it was in daily communication with the capital.
(Howard Lyon)

The St. Regis Hotel in New York, where Donovan kept a suite during the war. William Stephenson and William Donovan, the two great Allied spymasters, celebrated VE day together in Donovan's St. Regis apartment.
(Sheraton Corporation)

This wartime photograph shows Donovan as the charismatic leader that most former OSS personnel remember. Donovan dispatched his agents on extraordinary missions all over the world as if he were merely sending them on errands. To him, said one OSS staff member, "the Sahara Desert was a little stretch of sand, the Himalayas were a bank of snow, the Pacific was a mere ditch."
(U.S. Army Photograph)

Donovan never lost his taste for field experience and frequently dropped in at OSS bases around the world to see for himself how things were going.
Opposite page: Ray Peers, commander of OSS Detachment 101 (beside Donovan in jeep), meets his chief at a landing strip in Assam, India.
(Lt. Gen. W. R. Peers/ 101 Association)

On one of his busiest trips, late in 1943, Donovan (shown above talking with jungle priest Father James Stuart) traveled behind enemy lines in Burma to meet Kachin resistance leaders; then flew to Chungking to confront the duplicitous spymaster Tai Li; and went to Moscow to talk to NKVD chiefs.
(101 Association)
Left: At Kunming, Donovan visits a parachute riggers' loft to see the chutes upon which an agent's life might depend.
(Howard Lyon)

Above: Lord Louis Mountbatten (left), supreme allied commander for Southeast Asia, confers with Dr. Cora DuBois, chief of Research and Analysis for Detachment 404, and Col. John Coughlin, 404's commander.
(Byron Martin)

Left: Knowing in the summer of 1945 that the United States had the means at hand to end the war with Japan, Donovan journeyed to Hsian in North China to consult OSS agents and Nationalist Chinese leaders about possible Soviet and Chinese Communist moves when Japan was defeated.
(Elizabeth Heppner McIntosh)

Above: In Hsian, Donovan assembles a knot of OSS officers to talk over the potential problems of postwar Asia.
(Elizabeth Heppner McIntosh)
Left: Donovan reviewed guerrilla fighters in China. One Washington officer who accompanied him objected to the OSS director's unmilitary appearance.
(Howard Lyon)

Left: Donovan and Allen Dulles (right) end a conference in Berlin shortly before the Nuremberg trials commence.
(Bernard Gelman)

Below: Robert Sherwood towers over Donovan, Ned Buxton, and Sir William and Lady Stephenson as in November 1946 "Big Bill" presents "Little Bill" with the Presidential Medal for Merit. President Truman, who was seated just off camera, insisted that Donovan have the honor of making the ·presentation.
(Sir William Stephenson)

On January 11, 1946, President Truman awards Donovan an Oak Leaf Cluster to the Distinguished Service Medal. When asked by the President whom he wanted at the White House ceremony, Donovan said he would prefer to come alone.
(Lt. Gen. W. R. Peers)

During the postwar years, Donovan actively supported European unification. Here Donovan, chairman of the American Committee on United Europe, is flanked by Joseph H. Reitinger, secretary-general of the European movement (left), and Thomas Braden, director of the Committee for United Europe.
(National Archives)

OSS man Guy Martin,
Gen. George C. Marshall, Donovan, and
Walter Lippmann gather at the first
George Polk Memorial Award Dinner. In
1948 Donovan investigated the murder
of CBS news correspondent George
Polk in Greece.
(Byron Martin)

The caisson carrying the
body of William J. Donovan
enters Arlington National
Cemetery, where he was buried
with full military honors on
February 11, 1959.
(Buffalo and Erie County Historical Society)

where the OSS was ready and able to play a major role in the defeat of the Japanese, but neither Halsey nor MacArthur would listen. MacArthur never was willing to forget that Donovan was the only American soldier who emerged from the World War I fighting in France with more medals and fame than he did."

Donovan informed MacArthur of McGovern's mission, and received a courteous invitation to come and visit the South Pacific himself. On August 27 Donovan wrote to MacArthur, "I was in the Sicilian operations, and I am going back to Europe whatever else may happen. After that is over I am planning to go out to the Far East, and I wanted to let you know that I will then take advantage of your kind offer and stop for a day or two in your theater.

"I have been doing some work with Mountbatten, and he is really a cooperative fellow. I hope that some time you will see him."

At the Quebec Conference in August, Lord Mountbatten was made supreme allied commander for Southeast Asia. FDR and Churchill informed him that his appointment was top secret. Mountbatten went back to his room at the Château Frontenac. "I drew up a chair, sat down, took a blank sheet of paper and began to write down all the things I would have to do," he told his biographer Richard Hough. "Before I had even finished, there was a knock on the door. It was Bill Donovan, head of the OSS."

"Let me be the first to congratulate you on being appointed supreme allied commander, Southeast Asia," said Donovan.

"I don't know what you're talking about. Why do you come barging in here talking complete nonsense?" said Mountbatten. "Anyway, I'm much too young—halfway down the captains' list."

"You can't fool me," continued Donovan. "Why do you think we're here? I've got spies everywhere. I know that the PM and the President have offered you the job."

"Well, supposing you're right, why do you come and worry me about it?" Mountbatten asked.

"Because I want your permission to operate in Southeast Asia."

Mountbatten informed Donovan that Stilwell was already there and suggested that Donovan ask Stilwell.

"That bastard won't let me operate with him," complained Donovan. "He's a prejudiced old son-of-a-bitch. But you've been working with SIS and SOE, so you know what we're all about."

"Are you any good?"

"You bet we're good."

"Then I'm going to test you." Mountbatten decreed that Donovan must get him two of the best seats for *Oklahoma!*, the hit musical then playing in New York.

"Goddamn it, that's impossible!" exclaimed Donovan. "There are absolutely no seats for six months. How do you expect me . . . ?"

"No seats for *Oklahoma!*, no operations in Southeast Asia."

A few days later Donovan met Mountbatten in New York. Donovan had tickets for the best seats in the house and two of the prettiest girls the city had to offer for the evening. After the show, the party went to a nightclub.

"On the way out, in the foyer, there were a couple of photographers," recounted Mountbatten. "By this time Bill thought he was in. But I said, 'If those photographs are published, not only are you out, but I'll probably be out, too.' "

In a flash, two men suddenly appeared and hustled off the photographers. Donovan was in.

Donovan believed that Mountbatten's gifts for public relations equaled MacArthur's and that Mountbatten was also a strategist of great talent. It seemed to Donovan that the two commanders of adjoining theaters should work in close collaboration. He intended to visit both MacArthur and Mountbatten at their command posts as soon as possible.

By the end of August Donovan was back in Algiers, where he set up an office at OSS headquarters. There were only a few days remaining before the Allied forces embarked for the assault on Salerno, and he wanted to make certain that the OSS did its work with the Italian Resistance well. First, he wanted to take advantage of Marshall's request to Eisenhower that he be given "a chance to do his stuff" in Sardinia and, for good measure, Corsica.

Donovan and Bill Eddy, then the OSS chief at Algiers, asked an operational group instructor who had just arrived from the States to come and see them in the morning. This was Serge Obolensky-Meledinsky-Meletzky, a Russian prince who, his hyphenated name reduced to a relatively simple Obolensky, had long been a fixture of international café society. Obolensky had been a czarist officer and had been given exacting OSS training. When he strode into the office for the interview, Donovan sized him up shrewdly. Donovan needed a brave man—the mission he had in mind was bound to be dangerous—but he also needed a man accustomed to dealing with people of high station.

Donovan explained the mission. Within a few days the Allies were going to land at Salerno. On the flank of the movement across the straits were the islands of Sardinia and Corsica, garrisoned by some 270,000 Italian and 19,000 German soldiers. These must be overcome if the invasion were to be successful. An OSS team must jump into Sardinia and deliver a letter from Marshal Badoglio to General Basso, commander of the Italian troops on Sardinia. In the letter General Basso was ordered on behalf of the king to join the Allies and neutralize the Germans on Sardinia. When Donovan had finished explaining the situation, both Eddy and he directed meaningful looks at Obolensky.

"Do you want me to volunteer?" Obolensky asked.

"Well—certainly," replied Donovan.

"I'd be delighted. When does the mission leave?"

"Tomorrow."

Obolensky asked to pick his team.

"Yes, you should take two radio operators and an interpreter," said Donovan. "You've got one radio man who came over with you, and we'll give you another radio operator from here."

The OSS team jumped from a British Halifax bomber into a stretch of sand dunes between Cagliari, Sardinia's largest city, and the highest hill on the island. They avoided German patrols and bluffed both Italian and German officers. General Basso agreed to "abide by the orders of the king." The Germans fled Sardinia for Corsica. The British Eighth Army made the initial Allied landings on Italy's toe on September 3, and on September 9 the U.S. Fifth Army hit the beaches at Salerno.

Donovan sent two OSS teams ashore with the American troops. A British motorboat put one team, code-named MacGregor, on the beach near Paestum. Headed by John Shaheen, his mind still concocting extraordinary stratagems and plots, the team included Marcello Girosi, later to be an Italian motion-picture producer, Henry Ringling North of the Ringling circus family, and most important, Peter Tompkins. The other team, led by Donald Downes, waded ashore with the soldiers. Their assignment was to provide combat intelligence, since the Fifth Army G-2 badly needed OSS assistance. Downes set up headquarters at Amalfi in what had been a monastery, and his 90 agents began to collect valuable information about the German positions.

The various OSS men went about their business with dispatch. North went from jail to jail liberating political prisoners as the Fascists and Nazis fled. Shaheen tried fruitlessly to reach the Italian Navy's high command to arrange the surrender of the fleet to the Allies, a task that, ironically enough, had already been accomplished.

Just across the bay from Naples (which was still occupied in force by the Germans) lay Capri, seemingly untouched by the war when the MacGregor team arrived there. A resort of the wealthy since the Roman Emperor Augustus gave it to his "most pure and beautiful daughter Julia," Capri seemed as preoccupied with its indolent life as in prewar days. Donovan arrived at OSS headquarters at Amalfi on September 30 and crossed to Capri to see how the MacGregor team was doing.

"Dressed in a field uniform, his pale blue eyes matching the ribbon of his Congressional Medal of Honor, he looked older than when he had recruited me in Washington the week of Pearl Harbor," said Tompkins.

Henry Ringling North explained what the MacGregor team had been doing. "He charged me to requisition Mona Williams's villa and safeguard it against pillage and plunder as Mona was a dear friend," remembered North. "With the constant weight of his vital responsibilities in the midst of war, Bill found time for acts of friendship and consideration." North arrived at the villa just as Count von Bismarck ran out the rear entrance.

Tompkins undertook to explain to 109 something of the intricacies of Italian politics. He finished by taking him to see Benedetto Croce, whom British SOE officers had rescued from his villa at Sorrento, behind the German lines. The great Italian philosopher and historian had lived in his native Naples throughout the Fascist period and never once let his public opposition to Mussolini's regime waver nor allowed himself to be intimidated by the Fascists. History to Croce was the creation of the present and not a record of the past. Since it also was the act of thinking, it became a philosophy.

Croce talked to the young American OSS man and his chief. Long considered a royalist, Croce told Donovan that the king of Italy had been discredited before the Italian people by his cowardice in failing to oppose Mussolini. Donovan asked if Badoglio was popular with the people of Italy.

"What is being popular?" asked Croce in return. "Who is popular in Italy today? Obviously nobody."

"The people," he said, "had been annoyed with Badoglio because once the Fascist regime had been overthrown he had not immediately made peace with the Allies and got rid of the Germans. But the real culprit was the king. I've been working very closely with the group in Italy which has been trying to get the king to throw out Mussolini and make peace with the Allies. Even before the Allied landings in North Africa, Badoglio was the man this group had decided to use. But the king was like a Sphinx and could not make up his mind." Croce proposed that Donovan form a legion of Italian volunteers to fight for Italy, since he was convinced they would never be willing to take up arms on behalf of the king.

In later years Donovan commented that those few hours on Capri with Benedetto Croce were a landmark in his life. "He seemed so sane in a world that made no sense at all," Donovan said.

When Donovan was finished talking with Croce, he boarded a P T boat and crossed to Salerno, where he conferred with Gen. Mark Clark about his findings. Clark listened but, preoccupied with the immediate problems of his command, did not take Croce's plans for a legion of Italian volunteers seriously. The plan never got beyond OSS circles.

The next morning the attack on Naples commenced. Five additional OSS teams sailed into the harbor of the city in fishing boats. German shore patrols drove off two of the boats with machine-gun fire, but the other three landed with arms for the underground. The OSS men organized the Resistance and led them in forays against the Nazis. Their agents infiltrated through the German lines to bring the Allies reports of conditions in the city. When on October 1 the vanguard of the British and American soldiers entered Naples, the OSS men and their underground friends welcomed them with bottles of Chianti.

Downes and Tompkins were in the forefront of the Allied entry into Naples. They spotted a four-story palazzo on a back street, ousted the Fascist manufacturer who lived in it, and made it OSS headquarters. On October 13 the Badoglio government declared war on Germany. Donovan, still in Italy directing the OSS operational groups and intelligence net, came to the crumbling palazzo in Naples to talk with Tompkins. Donovan decided to send Tompkins into Rome, where he was to handle partisan and intelligence activities. Above all, Donovan wanted to keep the Italian monarchists, democrats, and communists united against the Germans, not fighting one another. He began to study Italian. When Rome fell to the Allies, Donovan thought it might be advisable to move his own headquarters from Washington to the Italian capital, from where the OSS intelligence offensive into Europe could be masterminded.

He might have his eye on an OSS headquarters in Rome, but it was now critical for Donovan to return to Algiers. On September 8 the Italian government had surrendered, and the Maquis—guerrilla fighters in the French underground—on Corsica had risen against the Germans. OSS agents with the Maquis had flashed the word to Algiers, and the French command in North Africa was sending an expeditionary force to Corsica to help. It was up to Donovan to send along an operational group of 32 men to assist the French. He also selected a demolitions expert and a few SI officers as well as OSS-trained Corsican agents. The OSS men left with the French troops aboard a French naval vessel and landed at Ajaccio, Corsica, on September 17. Donovan soon dispatched an R&A group to form a complete OSS field unit, representing the three major branches of his organization. He instructed his men that from Corsica they would carry out maritime operations against both the coast of Italy and southern France.

Anthony Scariano was one of the OSS men Donovan sent to Corsica. The OSS set up its headquarters at a villa on the coast and from there began to put operational groups into Italy. "We used P T boats," recalled Scariano. "It was a risky business because we had not yet gained air supremacy."

To Scariano's amazement Donovan appeared at the villa one day while the island was still being secured. He demanded to be told in great detail exactly what each of the teams was doing. Then he relaxed and became jovial.

"We talked about politics," said Scariano, who was a budding Democratic leader back home in Illinois. "I listened. The only drawback was that he was a Republican."

Donovan's trips to the Mediterranean almost always included a stop in London, where he kept close watch on David Bruce's efforts to strengthen the OSS-SOE partnership. Combined teams of OSS, SOE, and French resistance personnel were trained at Jedburgh in Scotland to be sent into France. Realizing that the war for Europe would be won or lost in France, Donovan wanted to be certain that the OSS had effective intelligence and resistance support for the Allied landings he knew must eventually take place. The London office had a huge job to recruit agents, authenticate and train them, and send them into France. And communications with agents in France were a very precarious business. John Bross in the OSS London office recalled Donovan's frequent visits.

"He'd barge into town, and there'd be daily breakfasts at 7:00 A.M. at Claridge's," he remembered. "He'd have a German grammar in one hand and a list of people he wanted to see in the other."

Both King Peter of Yugoslavia and King Michael of Romania stayed on the floor at Claridge's where Donovan kept a suite. Donovan usually conferred with the two kings when he was in town. He saw Eisenhower as well, invariably urging him to support the OSS in its role with the French Resistance. The British should not be given the entire responsibility for working with the French, argued Donovan, and Eisenhower should support the OSS and the Jedburgh teams.

Whether he was talking to King Peter in London, Ambassador Fotić in Washington, or his station chief in Cairo, throughout the summer and autumn of 1943 Donovan kept up his interest in events in Yugoslavia and Greece. In both countries the war with Germany continued to be obscured at times by the conflict between royalists and republicans on one hand and the communists on the other. Donovan tried to avoid the political rivalries in the Balkans. He dropped a key agent to Tito, and to General Mihajlović he dropped Walter Mansfield, one of his law partners. Anxious to "embarrass the Germans on their Mediterranean front," General Marshall became convinced that the warring factions must settle their differences.

Describing a meeting with Col. Truman Smith, Marshall said, "I commented that apparently we needed another Lawrence of Arabia, and he thought that that was exactly the point; some man to go in there in the effort to influence these people for the time being. Offhand I proposed that we might send General Donovan."

Admiral Leahy thought the idea of sending Donovan to the Balkans was a good one. Leahy mentioned it to Roosevelt, who thought it a splendid idea but felt it would need to be cleared with Churchill.

On October 20 Roosevelt sent a message to Churchill.

The chaotic condition developing in the Balkans causes me concern. I am sure you are also worried. In both Yugoslavia and Greece the guerrilla forces appear to be engaged largely in fighting each other and not the Germans. If these forces could be united and directed toward a common end, they would be very effective. In the present confused condition, the only hope I see for immediate favorable action is the presence of a "Lawrence of Arabia." The only man I can think of now who might have a chance of success is Donovan. I do not believe he can do any harm and being a fearless and aggressive character he might do much good. He was there before and is given some credit for the Yugoslavs entering the war against the Germans. If we decide to send him in, all agencies of ours now working in the Balkans should be placed under his direction and the resources we put into this effort should be at his disposal. I understand that your General Gubbins is now in the Middle East. Donovan could consult with him en route.

I feel this is an urgent matter. If you are inclined to agree to my idea, I will discuss the possibilities with Donovan at once.

Churchill did not agree, and Donovan did not go to the Balkans, but the OSS continued to operate in the region. He sent his men into Bulgaria and Romania as well as into Greece and Yugoslavia.

In the fall of 1943 Gen. Leslie Groves, head of the Manhattan Engineer District, came to see Donovan. He explained the critical nature of the atomic research that he directed, and he requested that the director of the OSS present him with an atomic spy, a man who would be "trustworthy, intelligent, and courageous."

"Donovan gave him Moe," stated William Casey, later to direct the CIA.

"Moe" was Moe Berg, Boston Red Sox catcher, "the nation's most intellectual athlete" and an OSS man. He had already undertaken several missions for Donovan. In mid-October Donovan sent him to Norway. The Rjukan plant, which was producing heavy water, had been damaged by Norwegian saboteurs. Word had reached Donovan that the plant was back in operation. Berg was to enter Norway and determine whether this was true.

Berg left immediately for England. A U.S. Air Force plane took him aloft over Norway and dropped him to the Resistance, who spirited him into Oslo, 75 miles from Rjukan. In the Norwegian capital, Berg met with patriotic Norwegian scientists who told him that at least half of the production of the plant had been restored. Furnished with accurate figures, Berg went to a remote airfield controlled by the Resistance and took an American plane back to England. When Berg brought Donovan his report, the OSS director passed the information on to Groves. The JCS ordered an air strike on Rjukan, and the plant was destroyed.

On October 23, Donovan was advanced to the grade of major general. Two days later he furnished the President with a memorandum as to what might be done with Axis war criminals. "You might think it advisable to consider the possibility of having as a term of your unconditional surrender a refusal to conclude an Armistice unless and until there should be turned over to the United States war criminals in areas held by the German armies," he suggested. "I have prepared a partial list of present German officials in that class of criminals, and will see whether other names might be included."

Then he was off again on a trip to the Middle East. Donovan was already looking forward to the end of the war. In Algiers he talked with Arthur Goldberg and Gerhard Van Arkel, who were carrying out a mission for the OSS labor desk.

"He took Art Goldberg and me aside after dinner," said Van Arkel. "I want you guys to draft me a statute for a postwar intelligence agency," Donovan said. "One: It should be small. Two: Limited to intelligence. Three: Super secret."

Donovan left for Cairo, where he attended the Cairo Conference at the request of President Roosevelt. Roosevelt, Churchill, and Chiang Kai-shek were meeting on the Nile to discuss operations in China. Roosevelt received Donovan's reports on the situation in the Far East and promised Chiang Kai-shek strong support in his effort to drive the Japanese out of his country. The OSS would play its part in China, and Donovan was to go there as soon as possible to make necessary changes in his Chinese connections. When the conference concluded, Roosevelt, carrying an additional sheaf of OSS reports dealing with conditions in Europe and the Middle East, left with Churchill for Teheran, where on November 28 they were to begin a historic meeting with Stalin. At the same time that the President departed for Teheran, Donovan left for India and China.

32

Behind Enemy Lines

"BILL DONOVAN IS the sort of guy who thought nothing of parachuting into France, blowing up a bridge, pissing in Luftwaffe gas tanks, then dancing on the roof of the St. Regis Hotel with a German spy."

That is what John Ford told people he talked with in India during the summer of 1943. Donovan had sent him to Southeast Asia to make a motion picture about Lord Mountbatten in the hope that Mountbatten's staff might then cooperate more fully with the OSS. At the same time Ford was to try out a new Mitchell 35-millimeter motion-picture camera to make a photographic survey for the Intelligence Documentary Photographic Project, which Donovan had established. Field Photo men called the project Ippy Dippy Intelligence.

Donovan was convinced that OSS Detachment 101—which by then had successfully organized the Kachin people of the North Burma mountains into units of guerrilla fighters working as much as 250 miles behind the Japanese lines—held the key to Allied victory in Southeast Asia. At the Quebec Conference, Franklin Roosevelt and Winston Churchill had made historic decisions about the war in Asia, and had given the OSS an important role to play. The new supreme allied commander in Southeast Asia was Lord Mountbatten. Because of his experience as head of the commandos, Mountbatten could easily envision an important role for Donovan's OSS in both Burma and China.

Donovan had become worried by reports that the redoubtable commander of 101, Carl Eifler, had received serious injuries on an aborted attack on Ramree Island on the southern Burma coast. Donovan asked Duncan Lee, a young law partner and aide, to make a tour of inspection in Asia to report on OSS readiness to further Mountbatten's plans. Lee was also to evaluate Eifler's ability to stay in command.

In early November Duncan Lee flew into Chabua, India. That evening at 101's forward base at Nazira, Assam, Lee attempted to question Eifler. "When you come from the general with low rank on your shoulders and try to tell a full colonel what to do, you're in trouble!" Eifler shouted at Lee. "If Donovan has something to say to me, let him come and say it."

Chastened by Eifler's explosion, Lee flew on to China, where he had a critical message to deliver to the commander of OSS Detachment 202. Then he returned to Washington. Donovan listened to Lee's report with dismay. He had a high regard for Eifler, and now it appeared that he would have to fire him. He set out for Asia.

John Ford had decided to include the dramatic story of the Kachin resistance to the Japanese in his film about Mountbatten. He had sent Field Photo cinematographers into Burma with the OSS guerrillas. Ford briefed Donovan in Calcutta, and he was with Donovan when 109 flew to Chabua. Carl Eifler met Donovan's transport plane at the airport there. Donovan was courteous and soft-spoken, but Eifler noted that there was an icy glint in his eyes. Eifler carried 109's bag over to the De Havilland Moth, a light plane of 1925 vintage that belonged to Detachment 101. Donovan got into the passenger's seat, and Eifler took the controls. They flew over the jungles of Assam to Nazira.

During a tour of the secret OSS base on a British-owned tea plantation, Donovan was impressed by how much 101 was doing with so little in the way of logistical support. He went into the message center and sent off messages to Washington urging that more personnel, equipment, and money be made available to the unit.

Eifler led Donovan into the war room at headquarters. The general glanced over the seven maps hanging on the wall, each indicating a separate plan for the deployment of OSS teams in Burma. He sat down on a bamboo chair.

"Well, Eifler," he said at last. "What are you doing?"

"General Stilwell told me he might want to approach Burma in seven different ways," replied Eifler. "I was supposed to organize each one of them, and I did."

Donovan continued to study the maps. His voice was still gentle when he spoke.

"That's what I mean about you, Carl," he said. "You are too god-damned ambiguous about organizing. What do you mean by organizing seven different eventualities?"

Eifler fought down his anger. "Sir," he said, "would you like to go behind Jap lines and find out for yourself?" He knew he had thrown down a challenge Donovan could not refuse.

Donovan smiled genially. "When do we leave?"

"First thing in the morning, sir."

As a rule even 101 men did not fly into the hidden bases in Burma, and yet Eifler was daring Donovan to do just that. Japanese Zeros ruled the skies over Burma, and if Donovan, who carried the secrets of the Allied high command in his brain, were captured, it could be a disaster of staggering proportions. Could Donovan, whose battlefield bravery had made him a national symbol for courage, disregard a direct challenge? Eifler found a certain black humor in the situation. Surely once he was behind Japanese lines, Donovan would find out just how much Eifler and his men had accomplished. As an experienced field commander, Donovan would recognize how remarkable a fighting organization the OSS-led American-Kachin Rangers had already become.

Eifler intended to fly Donovan to an OSS outpost at Nawbum, Burma, called Knothead (after the sobriquet of its commander, Vincent Curl), situated some 150 miles behind Japanese lines and about 275 miles southeast of Nazira. Since the venerable De Havilland Moth could not carry enough gasoline to make the round trip, arrangements had to be made for the Air Transport Command to drop a quantity of gasoline to Vincent Curl so Eifler and Donovan could refuel for the return to Nazira. Eifler also informed Knothead that he was bringing 109 in to see him. He set up a radio signal with Curl, which would be flashed to Nazira when the plane had landed safely at Nawbum.

Nicol Smith was training his Thai guerrillas in the jungles of Assam for the infiltration of Thailand, and that night he was Donovan's roommate. Smith was puzzled. Why was 109 risking not only his own life but the secrets he carried in his head? "General," he finally asked, "aren't you risking your life?"

"Everything is a risk," replied Donovan. "My boys are risking their lives every day."

Donovan did not tell Smith, but he was carrying one of Lovell's L pills. Although filled with deadly potassium cyanide, the capsule was insoluble and could be put into the mouth without danger. It could even be swallowed and it would pass harmlessly through the digestive tract. But let it be chewed and the result was almost immediate death. An OSS man who anticipated danger was taught to hide the capsule beneath his tongue, ready for use in case he faced torture.

Smith spent a sleepless night worrying about Donovan who, he said, "slept like a babe." In the morning 109 handed his wallet and identification papers to Smith for safekeeping. "If anything goes wrong, it'll be just as well if I'm incognito," he said.

"That's an understatement, General."

After breakfast Eifler handed a parachute to Donovan. Donovan refused. "I'll ride the plane down if we crash," he said. "I can't afford to be captured."

"General, if we land within 15 feet of the enemy, I will bring you back," said Eifler. "Please put on your chute."

John Ford and a Field Photo crew were standing by, and they photographed Donovan strapping on his chute. Eifler and Donovan put goggles on their foreheads, and donned aviator caps, looking "like a couple of well-fed pilots out of *Wings*," as 101 man Vince Trifletti put it. It all seemed like a Hollywood set with Ford directing a movie.

Then the moviemaking ended, and the two men were in the plane, bouncing down the strip out among the tea bushes. On the way over the Naga Hills separating India from Burma, Eifler flew low over the treetops to hide from Zeros. Finally, at Nawbum, the Moth circled what appeared to be a small village in a long, narrow clearing in the jungle. Kachins dashed out of hiding and dragged simulated huts off what was revealed as a landing strip.

"The strip ran up the side of a hill," Eifler said afterward. "It was short, but gravity helped us to slow down before we reached the far end."

"On that day I lived about five lives," Curl remembered. "The plane rolled to a halt, and Donovan and Eifler got out. I'd met the general in Washington, and he strode right up to me and gave me a real hug. It seemed just as natural seeing him in the middle of the Burmese jungle as it had to see him behind his desk."

Eifler was right. Donovan was indeed a field man, and he watched with professional approval as the Kachins rushed the mock-up huts back into position and rolled the plane into a jungle hiding place. He checked the defenses of the outpost and inspected the smiling young Kachin soldiers who, as Eifler said, "were scarcely as tall as their rifles were long." In Washington Donovan had read reports from 101 about the remarkable Kachin leader, Zhing Htaw Naw. Zhing Htaw Naw proved to be a slight brown man, erect and smiling.

"His eyes alone gave away his penetrating intellect," Donovan said later.

Zhing Htaw Naw bowed his head in the Kachin show of respect and courtesy. Vincent Curl had told him that the leader of the OSS world-wide was coming to visit Knothead, but Zhing Htaw Naw met 109 as an equal. During the next several hours Donovan questioned every man in camp, but Zhing Htaw Naw most of all. Father James Stuart, a Catholic missionary among the Kachins, acted as his interpreter.

Zhing Htaw Naw told 109 about his people and their fight against the Japanese. He put his arm around Vincent Curl's waist. "He is the life blood of our people," he said.

"Zhing Htaw Naw is my buddy from the inside out," responded Curl.

Donovan regarded the American and the Kachin standing together with their arms around each other's waists, a visual embodiment of the American-Kachin partnership. He was confident that this partner-ship would play an important role in the Burma campaigns to come. When it was time for Donovan and Eifler to leave, Donovan clapped Eifler on the back. Eifler could see he was impressed.

The Kachins brought the Moth out of hiding and cleared the strip.

"Rev it up all you can and then take off," Curl told Eifler after the two men climbed into the plane.

The Kachins held back the plane as Eifler revved up the engine. When he signaled, they gave it a push, and the Moth jounced down the field, as Eifler later said, "like a tumblebug. We were taking off down-hill, and we gathered speed slowly because of Donovan's weight."

Eifler himself was a big man, and the light plane, unable to gain speed, bumbled down the strip toward the wall of trees at the far end. Suddenly Eifler cut the plane at a sharp angle to the left, where the forest canopy was lower, and roared over the nearby river.

"We haven't got the power on the nose of these planes that we should have," remarked Donovan to Eifler as the plane banked five feet over the river's brown flood.

John Coughlin, another top OSS man with 101, had returned to Nazira from a trip to find that Donovan was behind the lines with Eifler. He never expected to see either Eifler or Donovan alive again. That night, as the OSS men celebrated the safe conclusion to the flight to Knothead, Coughlin took Donovan aside.

"General, what were you thinking about to go in there with Carl?"

Donovan always was ready to listen to his men's criticism. "I had to," he replied.

"You should have considered more things than your damned honor. If I'd been here, I would have reminded you of every one of them."

Donovan smiled. He felt buoyed by his firsthand impression of the OSS men in the field and their Kachin friends, and he now knew exactly what Detachment 101 would be able to offer Gen. Joseph Stilwell, who was waiting for him in China. He spent much of the evening playing bridge with one of Nicol Smith's young Thais.

Donovan flew in the Moth to Chabua in the morning and took off in another plane for Kunming. John Ford and cameraman John Pennick flew with Donovan, as did the young Thai bridge player. The Thai came along to entertain Donovan at cards on the long flight over the Hump, and Ford, who knew Maj. Gen. Claire Chennault, commander of the 14th U.S. Air Force, was making the trip to introduce Donovan to Chennault's Flying Tigers. Detachment 202 must live up to the commitments 109 had made for it at Cairo. Donovan was concerned, for he had sent representative after representative to China only to have each one fall under the sway of the Chinese intelligence chief, Tai Li.

Tai Li, one of the 20th century's remarkable spymasters, curiously enough was described by some OSS men as stocky and by others as slender. At least all agreed he was short. Unsmiling, he had all the inscrutability attributed to the Orient, but when he smiled he showed an impressive amount of gold bridgework and revealed a sunny innocence that contradicted his malign reputation. His eyes were black and piercing. He usually wore a khaki whipcord suit with a high collar buttoned up to the neck. He believed the less Donovan's OSS knew about China, the better.

Captain Milton Miles, who had replaced Al Lusey as Donovan's man in China, had become Tai Li's close friend, or so it appeared. On April 15, 1943, Far East OSS Chief Miles, Donovan, Chinese Foreign Minister T. V. Soong, Navy Secretary Frank Knox, and Tai Li had met in Washington to establish the Sino-American Special Technical Cooperation Agreement. The agreement pledged that China and the United States, "animated by mutual desire to annihilate the common enemy and achieve military victory," would work together in the fields of intelligence and clandestine warfare. SACO, as the organization came to be called, was meant to end the conflict between American and Chinese intelligence. Donovan had made Miles his coordinator for the OSS in the Far East, but he had become disillusioned with his ability to work out any useful relationship with Tai Li. While Miles was in Washington for the SACO meetings, Donovan invited him to dinner at his Georgetown house and drew him out about his attitudes and plans. His remaining confidence in Miles dwindled, and he decided to send Richard Heppner, another Donovan law partner, to China.

"The OSS is the only institution that is run by its own inmates," said Miles, and returned to China. Heppner arrived in Chungking presumably to assist Miles. Actually Donovan had intended from the start that Heppner should replace him. Heppner and Miles failed to get along, and Tai Li obstructed both of the rival OSS leaders. By late summer 1943, when OSS agents found proof that Tai Li was withholding most intelligence of value and was contributing virtually nothing of importance to the SACO undertaking, Donovan decided that the agreement must be dissolved. The OSS should instead cooperate in China with Chennault's 14th Air Force. Agents would work in the field to discover enemy troop concentrations and supply dumps that might merit 14th Air Force attacks.

The intelligence situation in China became critical when Roosevelt, Churchill, and Chiang Kai-shek held their Cairo meeting beginning on November 23, 1943. Tai Li must not be allowed to obstruct the flow of intelligence about China, and as Donovan flew over the Hump he had every intention of forcing a showdown.

Donovan left his companions in Kunming, where the OSS had an important base, and flew on to Chungking, arriving on December 2. Ed McGinnis, an OSS man who was later to be sergeant-at-arms of the U.S. Senate, accompanied Donovan to a dinner given in 109's honor by T. V. Soong.

There were 20 men seated at two tables, ranging from U.S. Ambassador Pat Hurley and Gen. Albert Wedemeyer to Donovan and Tai Li. Pat Hurley distinguished himself by drinking too much of the Chinese orange wine, which Tai Li usually enriched with a discreet addition of knockout drops, and made a speech in which he blearily announced that there were two men seated at the table who should be the chief executives of their respective countries—the great citizen soldier William J. Donovan and T. V. Soong. Donovan proposed a toast to Tai Li, while privately observing that Tai Li had the earmarks of "a mediocre policeman with medieval ideas of intelligence work."

Oliver Caldwell, an old China hand and an OSS man, was also present. As the dinner, course after Chinese course, ran on into the night, Caldwell listened to "toast follow toast, one *gombei* leading to another, until most of the Chinese and Americans alike were tipsy. Only Donovan and Tai Li drank little or nothing and remained cool and collected. The two great spymasters competed in charm, each smiling and urbane, each so very agreeable. Butter would have melted in their mouths."

Then, to Caldwell's amazement, Donovan bluntly informed Tai Li that if the OSS could not perform its mission in cooperation with him, then the OSS would operate separately.

"If OSS tries to operate outside SACO," said the smiling Tai Li, "I will kill your agents."

"For every one of our agents you kill," replied Donovan, "we will kill one of your generals."

"You can't talk to me like that," said Tai Li.

"I am talking to you like that," said Donovan evenly.

The OSS chief smiled, but a chill that even the most besotted diner soon recognized settled over the room. The party broke up, and Donovan went to OSS headquarters for the night. The next day Donovan and Tai Li met privately. Donovan made certain that the Chinese intelligence chief understood he would not allow any interference with the OSS.

Donovan next descended upon Milton Miles. Miles attempted to pick up the argument where it had been left in Washington the previous summer. Donovan demanded that SACO make sweeping changes to assure OSS control. He asserted that Miles had hurt the OSS by turning over both large sums of money and hard-to-obtain equipment to Tai Li while believing the glowing reports that the Chinese were forever passing on to their American colleagues in SACO. Miles, who had painstakingly negotiated the SACO agreement signed in Washington, shouted, "I don't agree with writing one thing and doing another. I quit!"

"You can't quit," Donovan replied. "You're fired."

Donovan ended OSS participation in SACO and immediately set about establishing a new relationship for OSS with the 14th Air Force. John Ford took Donovan to see Chennault, and 109 made arrangements to have OSS agents brought into China as members of the 5329th Air and Ground Forces Resources and Technical Staff, AGFRTS, which OSS men soon were calling Agfarts.

When Donovan was finished in China, he flew back to Chabua to pay another visit to Carl Eifler. He found Eifler very ill. The 101 commander could not sleep at night and would not take the medicine prescribed by doctors at the 20th General Hospital at Ledo. The pain in his head had become severe. Donovan felt he had no choice but to relieve Eifler of command. On December 11, he placed John Coughlin in command of Detachment 101, but on December 17 Coughlin turned over the command to Ray Peers.

Before leaving Washington on November 11, Donovan had met with Franklin Roosevelt to tell him of his plan to go to Moscow to establish an OSS mission in exchange for an NKVD mission in the American capital. In 1942 Russia had made large additions to its embassy and consular staff, an indication that they were increasing their espionage in the United States. Donovan reasoned that an agreement between the OSS and the NKVD would not enable the Communists to learn more than they were in a position to learn already. If Russia and the western Allies were to work well together to defeat Hitler, they must share essential intelligence. As things were, British and American commanders had to rely on intercepted German battle messages to discover the positions of the Red Army. The Soviets were constantly demanding of the Americans and British both their war plans and estimates of Axis strength, but they were totally unwilling to share any intelligence with the West.

On November 22, Donovan, then in Cairo, had sent a top-secret report to his OSS headquarters in Washington "for distribution among those people who are discreet and who should have the information." It dealt with conditions inside the Soviet Union as a basis for the Kremlin's decisions on the conduct of the war. Donovan considered the possibilities that the Soviets might help the United States fight Japan, but "until Germany has been completely defeated, they will not attack Japan or give us bases." With intriguing insight, Donovan wrote:

> On the subject of the postwar world, they assume that they will have the Baltic states; that the states adjoining Russian territory will not be set up as anti-Soviet buffer states but as friendly to Russia as to Great Britain; also that the Dardanelles will be internationalized. A "Cordon Sanitaire" will not be tolerated. They want Polish and Finnish governments set up which are not anti-Russian. They may be willing to negotiate boundary questions under these circumstances. They desire an accepted position among the nations of the world and expect to be conferred with on all international questions that arise whether it is an Arab or South American problem. They want to secure all the above on a friendly basis but failing this they will employ whatever tactics necessary to attain these ends.

Roosevelt approved Donovan's plan to go to Moscow. John R. Deane, secretary to the Joint Chiefs of Staff, was made part of Donovan's mission. Deane and Donovan met in Cairo to plan the trip, and Deane went on to Moscow. Two days before Christmas Donovan's plane set down in Moscow on an airport runway where the snow was already piled deep. Skies were gloomy, and he shivered, accustomed to the Mediterranean world's warmth. Both Deane and Ambassador Averell Harriman were at the airport to welcome him.

"I was never more pleased to see anyone," Deane noted in his journal. "We were all feeling a little sorry for ourselves at being in the bleak cold atmosphere of Moscow so far from home. His coming was a breath of fresh air from the outside world, and he was none the less welcome because of the case of Scotch whisky which he brought to brighten my Christmas. We had been old friends in Washington and had fought several battles together against some of the Washington agencies which were jealous of OSS achievements. As secretary of the JCS, I was well aware of the strength of the organization which Donovan had created and had some appreciation of its capabilities, and apparently the Russians had too."

Harriman immediately took Donovan to see Foreign Minister Vyacheslav Molotov, who set up a meeting for him with the NKVD. The headquarters for the NKVD was at 2 Dzerzhinsky Street in two buildings that had been joined, their facades combined in such a way that they seemed to be one. One of the buildings was actually the Lubyanka, a prison for political offenders, and the other was a ponderous stone structure that had housed the offices of an insurance company in czarist days and later became a hotel. On December 27, Donovan, Deane, and the Russian-speaking Charles Bohlen as interpreter went to the headquarters of the NKVD, where they were taken down several bleak halls to a conference room.

Donovan made a quick appraisal of the smiling Russians, who he was certain were making a similar appraisal of him. In the conference room, one chair was placed in such a fashion that whoever sat in it would have to look into a strong light. It was an old police trick. Noticing at a glance the chair that the Russians evidently hoped he would take, Donovan willingly passed up several other chairs to take his seat in it.

"I'm ready for the fifth degree," he remarked as he looked into the bright light.

Lieutenant General P. M. Fitin, head of the Soviet External Intelligence Service, wore a Soviet uniform with the blue piping of the Red police. Quiet and cordial in manner, he had long blond hair and blue eyes, and appeared to be a most agreeable spymaster. His colleague was Maj. Gen. A. P. Ossipov, head of subversion in foreign countries, a man with a sallow complexion and a threatening manner. Ossipov spoke excellent English.

In response to Fitin's questions, interpreted by Ossipov, Donovan gave the Russians an outline of OSS activities, describing the kinds of agents employed and in what countries they were active. Fitin was interested in how the OSS introduced agents into enemy territory, their training and equipment, and where they were trained. Donovan gave candid replies. He told about the OSS suitcase radios and plastic explosives, and concluded by saying that he would be willing to appoint an OSS officer to be his liaison with Moscow. Donovan also said he would welcome a Soviet liaison officer in Washington.

Fitin thought the arrangement could be useful. "If the NKVD is about to sabotage a German plant or railroad, it would be good to let the OSS know," he said.

Smoothly and with the same smile that had wreathed his face from the start of the interview, Fitin now wanted to know if Donovan had some other more devious reasons for coming to the Soviet Union. Donovan withered him with a look so contemptuous that no denial was needed.

Both intelligence chiefs relaxed. They agreed that OSS man John Haskell would represent Donovan in Moscow and NKVD man Col. A. G. Grauer would be the NKVD deputy in Washington. Each would have a staff of assistants.

Donovan was anxious to leave Moscow so he could get to Italy for the Allied landing at Anzio, scheduled for late January. When he got back to the U.S. Embassy, Ambassador Harriman offered to send him out of Russia in the four-engine plane that the United States kept at the Moscow airport for Harriman's use. Of course, the Russians had to give permission. It was agreed that Bohlen, who had been recalled by the State Department, would accompany Donovan as far as Cairo.

To the Americans' chagrin, Molotov refused to allow Donovan to fly in the plane. "It is only for the use of the ambassador," said Molotov.

Harriman insisted that Molotov's attitude was unfriendly and detrimental to the Allied war effort, but Molotov was adamant. On the other hand, he would be more than pleased to make available a Soviet two-engine plane to fly Donovan out of Russia.

"This was an empty gesture," Donovan said after the war. "A small plane like that had little chance of making it through the furious storms then sweeping Russia. Molotov was merely trying to throw his weight around. He wanted me to understand fully that he was the boss."

"Averell, you leave this to me," Donovan is quoted by Bohlen as saying, "and I will show you how to deal with the Russians."

Donovan explained that he would take direct action. According to Bohlen:

With me along as interpreter, Donovan and Harriman's pilot went to the military airfield where the plane was stationed. We arrived at about 11 o'clock at night and were met by a Soviet armed guard. Following Donovan's instructions, I explained that he was an American general and wished to see the officer on duty. After some fumbling around with the telephones, a frightened sentry led us to the officer of the watch, a thin-faced young captain. Donovan explained the mission. He said it was an unfriendly act not to permit an American pilot to see the weather report and that he, as an American general, must insist. The captain was much concerned about a derogation from his orders, but General Donovan's importunities wore him down, and he and our pilot went into the weather room and looked at the forecast for the following couple of days.

The weather report was bad, and there was no possibility of flying that night. The Americans returned to the embassy. "You people in the State Department just aren't tough enough," said Donovan as they drove back into Moscow. "You have no knowledge of how to deal with the Slavs. You see the results which we achieved by direct action."

The next morning Harriman was informed that the Soviet authorities had moved his plane from the military field to the civilian field so that they could strengthen their control over it.

For 11 days Harriman and Molotov wrangled. There was nothing to do but to fly in the Soviet plane. The year 1943 came to an end, and a glum Donovan spent the New Year at the embassy. On January 6, Donovan and his party got up at six in the morning and drove in subzero weather to the airport, where they got ready once again to board the plane. A two-engine plane would have to land in Baku, Astrakhan, or Stalingrad to refuel on its way to Teheran over the only routes safe from German attack. Weather was severe in all of these places, and Donovan and his party once again returned to the U.S. Embassy. Donovan and Harriman had breakfast and discussed the situation.

That afternoon Harriman saw Molotov again, and at last the Soviet foreign minister gave Donovan permission to fly in the embassy plane. Donovan flew off over the storm to Teheran, finally on his way back to Cairo.

A *New York Times* correspondent who had caught up with Donovan in Moscow filed a brief dispatch. In it he reported that Harriman described General Donovan's visit as the "natural result of the Teheran conferences."

The dispatch concluded, "Nothing was given out concerning whom he saw."

33

"The Wine Is Red"

ON HIS WAY to Italy, Donovan stopped at OSS Cairo, code-named Gustav, and sent a message to Washington telling of his successful visit to NKVD headquarters.

"He became the only Western intelligence man ever to go into the Lubyanka and emerge alive," said one OSS man.

Donovan had hopes of Soviet cooperation, particularly in the Balkans, where OSS and NKVD agents were encountering one another. "At the same time it now would be possible to judge from how well the Soviets cooperated on intelligence matters as to how well they would cooperate after the war was over," he observed.

Donovan also brought back a virus from wintry Moscow, and he became increasingly ill as he flew to the OSS base at Caserta, Italy. At Caserta, completely exhausted, running a high fever, and delirious, he went to bed.

"I don't trust doctors," he told David Crockett. "I don't like doctors, and I'm too busy to be ill."

Crockett sat by 109's bedside all night. In the morning Donovan did go to the OSS hospital. When Donovan arrived, OSS medic Constantin Bertakis was "in a squatting position administering first aid to an Italian child with injured legs," as Bertakis remembered.

"The first glance was convincing," he said. "This is the General. Impulsively I stood up, and before my right hand could reach my eyebrow for a military salute, the General extended his arms toward me, saying, 'Continue your work, Sergeant.' Hastily I completed my salute and turned toward my little patient."

Donovan refused treatment until the child was attended to. He stayed in the hospital for two days. There was still a little more than a week to go before the Allied assault at Anzio. The American and British advance had been stalled for months at Monte Cassino by Field Marshal Albrecht Kesselring's formidable Tenth Army. By landing at Anzio the Allies intended to outflank the German positions, and Donovan was anxious for his OSS agents to contribute the intelligence needed for victory.

As soon as he could leave the hospital, Donovan appeared without warning at the OSS palazzo in Naples. There he joined the OSS men for fettuccine made of powdered eggs and washed down with splendid wines from a Fascist industrialist's private cellar. He glanced at the gilded mirrors reflecting the candlelight and with typical courtesy declined to be seated at the head of the well-set table.

"You're the host," he said to Peter Tompkins, who was in charge of the mission. "I'll sit at your right."

When coffee was served, Donovan explained to Tompkins his next assignment. Tompkins was to contact the OSS team already in Rome and, working with the Italian underground, sabotage German defense efforts while preventing Kesselring's forces from destroying either basic utilities needed for the life of the city or its art and historic treasures. Donovan gave Tompkins the code name of Pietro and had him flown to Corsica in his own plane. From there Tompkins was taken in a rubber boat to the mainland at Fossa del Telefone and smuggled into Rome by car just a few days before the Anzio landings. He contacted the Italian underground.

On January 21 the British and American troops stormed the Anzio beaches. On the next day Donovan watched from a P T boat as an OSS team went ashore with the Rangers.

"He sat on the deck of the P T boat in a director's chair," said Mike Jimenez, an OSS man assigned to Donovan, "and watched the landings as if it was a Fourth of July celebration. The flak from the fleet anti-aircraft guns was pinging all around him during the incessant German air attacks. I hid in a torpedo tube."

"He was talking to a hard-bitten lieutenant beside him when the German shore batteries opened up," said another OSS man. "Everybody jumped behind what little protection the boat afforded, but not Bill. He just stood there looking at the shore."

Donovan turned to the lieutenant who had ducked down on the deck of the boat. "Lieutenant, what do you suppose is the caliber of those shells?"

Once the OSS men were ashore they ran into total confusion on the beaches. The commanders had been slow in getting the men moving off the beach, and as a result, the Germans were able to forge new defenses in hills overlooking the Allies and mount a deadly counterattack. John Croze, leading the OSS team ashore, desperately needed information about German troop movements. He raised Tompkins, by then in Rome, and Tompkins turned to the Italian Resistance for help. OSS Radio Vittorio in Rome flashed information to the OSS men on the beach about the route the German reinforcements were taking and correctly predicted that the German counterattack would come from Albano, not Cisterna.

"Messages from Vittorio were decoded and passed to G-2 on the beachhead as soon as they were received," said Kermit Roosevelt. "Since one of the sources was an Italian liaison officer in Kesselring's head-quarters, much of the information from Vittorio was of great value in supplying data on the movement of German troops."

The OSS men on the beach infiltrated through the German lines and returned with other combat intelligence. The log of the USS *Biscayne* for January 22 indicates that "at 0937 Generals Lemnitzer, House, Donovan, and Alexander came aboard to join the conference," which was being held by Allied leaders. While the generals talked, "the USS *Portent* hit a mine and sank at 1010 approximately two miles off the beach. Survivors were taken to various units of Task Force 81, forty of them being brought aboard the *Biscayne* for medical treatment, food, and survivors' clothing."

At 1300 generals Clark, Lemnitzer, Donovan, House, and Alexander left the ship. As they disembarked, the Luftwaffe swept in for the attack.

"Donovan found the situation frustrating," said Ned Putzell. "He went ashore with General Clark and observed the turmoil on the beach. He contacted an OSS team on the beach to be sure that they were doing a good job. Richard Kelly, head of SO, and an OSS colonel were with Donovan."

"The general had no use for the colonel, and he was exasperated by his officious conduct on the beach," said David Crockett. "When it was time to go back to the ship, there was not enough room on the P T boat to take everybody."

"You stay, Colonel," said Donovan, "and give me reports every day on what's happening. It'll be a good experience for you."

He waved his fingers tauntingly at the colonel as the boat put out to sea.

While German firepower slaughtered Allied soldiers on the beach at Anzio, Donovan loaded a new team of OSS agents into an amphibious landing craft and ferried them to Pontevecchia, to the north. Their assignment was to do all they could to help the men who were dying on the beach, in what the onetime commander of the Fighting 69th knew was a costly military blunder. The Allies had landed with relative ease, but bungling and indecisive commanders had failed to get the men into the interior quickly enough to elude the deadly German counterattack.

From Pontevecchia, Donovan and Mike Jimenez went to Corsica, where OSS man Anthony Scariano welcomed them to his villa. They sat over dinner and talked.

"Some generals regarded OSS as a nuisance," said Scariano, who listened to 109's angry complaints about the stupidity of the Allied commanders at Anzio. "They were so used to warfare by the books that

Donovan's approach to warfare seemed too unorthodox. They were not cooperative, but when they let Donovan know they needed something, they always got it."

Donovan concerned himself with deploying his agents with the Maquis and with the Resistance in the north of Italy. Then he returned to Washington.

On February 10, J. Edgar Hoover sent the following confidential message to Harry Hopkins at the White House:

> I have just learned from a confidential but reliable source that a liaison arrangement has been perfected between the OSS and the Soviet Secret Police (NKVD) whereby officers will be exchanged between these services. The OSS is going to assign men in Moscow and in turn the NKVD will set up an office in Washington, D.C.
>
> I wanted to bring this situation to your attention at once because I think it is a highly dangerous and most undesirable procedure to establish in the United States a unit of the Russian secret service which has admittedly for its purpose the penetration into the official secrets of various government agencies.

Hoover also informed Attorney General Francis Biddle of his discovery. Hopkins showed Hoover's message to Roosevelt, and the President reversed his previous position, notifying Donovan that the NKVD would not be welcome in America. On March 16, 1944, Roosevelt sent a telegram to Ambassador Harriman in Moscow instructing him to hold off on the intelligence liaison arranged by Donovan. Harriman was shocked at the sudden shift in policy, and demurred, but on March 30 Roosevelt telegraphed again. The exchange between the NKVD and the OSS must not take place because of domestic political considerations. It was an election year, and Roosevelt knew full well that J. Edgar Hoover was capable of making a public furor over the plan. Donovan was angry. He believed the United States was losing a magnificent opportunity to penetrate the Kremlin. He knew that the Soviets had long since penetrated Washington, and felt sure that America would have gained much more than the Russians from an exchange of intelligence liaison officers.

Although he appeared to have abandoned the plan, Donovan continued to talk to the NKVD. The OSS was intriguing to separate Bulgaria from the Axis, and Donovan needed Soviet cooperation. Roosevelt understood this and supported him. Donovan sent a message to Cairo on March 2:

"We have today been directed and authorized by high authority to empower and instruct the so-called Jadwin mission to inform the Minister of Bulgaria that the representatives of the three Allies are prepared to confer in Cairo with a fully qualified Bulgarian mission. The

OSS mission is directed in the same manner to accept any answer the Bulgarian Minister may give and relay it through OSS channels to Washington as quickly as possible."

The OSS plot progressed in both Cairo and Istanbul in the spring of 1944. Lieutenant General Fitin in Moscow had transmitted valuable information on the situation in Bulgaria to Donovan, and on March 31 he in turn sent the NKVD OSS reports from Bulgaria, including a report from Karl von Kelokowski, a German agent who had defected to the OSS. Major General John Deane, chief of the U.S. military mission in Moscow, acted as intermediary.

"Kindly convey my thanks to our Russian friends for the prompt fashion in which they responded to our request," wrote Donovan to Deane.

Later in the spring Soviet intelligence helped OSS agents in Bulgaria to blow up two railway bridges across the Maritsa River, blocking the shipment of chrome to German factories. At the same time Donovan's agents were letting him know that the Soviets often hindered more than they helped.

In early 1944 the OSS collaborated with the State Department in developing a new series of maps that would be useful in intelligence work, and on March 27 Donovan reported to the President on OSS progress in photo interpretation.

"Some of it," he told FDR, "was carried on in the field with your son Elliott's North African Photo Reconnaissance Wing.

"The principles have other uses than photo interpretation. For example, they provide a new method of underwater depth determination, a means for enabling pilots to make accurate estimates of the sizes of ships they sight and a method which enables a person with no knowledge of perspective to draw panoramic field sketches and perspective target maps in a fraction of the time formerly required by trained personnel."

The OSS was bound to be a chaotic sort of place, and this exasperated some of the business executives whom Donovan brought into the operation. One day in the spring of 1944 Donovan asked Atherton Richards, "What changes do you think I should make in the OSS?"

"Run it the way I used to run the pineapple company," replied Richards, who had come to the OSS from the presidency of Hawaiian Pineapple.

Donovan knew that some of his staff were restless, but he was not prepared for what happened in early April. A group of top aides, including Larry Lowman, John Magruder, and Ned Buxton, stopped him in Union Station, Washington, as he and assistant Ned Putzell were catching a train for the West Coast.

"This junta tried to dethrone the General," said Putzell. "They tried to tell him that he shouldn't be running the OSS. They accused him of lack of administrative ability. There were problems in the office, and he was running off in different directions."

Donovan listened to the rebellious men, and his eyes flashed anger.

"We were en route to an important meeting with MacArthur," said Putzell. "I was the only one with him on the train, and it was a tough damn trip. Donovan felt that they were so very unfair. They had accused him of lack of administrative ability, and he was always off putting out more fires in the different theaters of war while trying to expand operations."

Putzell and Donovan met MacArthur in Honolulu on Easter Sunday. Once again, MacArthur was as charming as could be but was not willing to call upon the OSS for intelligence and irregular warfare assistance.

When the two men returned to Washington, Donovan acted as if there had been no encounter at the railroad station. After the war, he said, "I was hurt, but then I realized that they were good men who honestly believed that you could run the OSS as if it were the Columbia Broadcasting System or a textile company. They went back to their jobs, and I went back to mine."

On April 28 Frank Knox died. Donovan lost one of his dearest friends, a man who had come closest of all the leading Americans of the time to sharing his own view of life. Donovan and Knox, each in his own way a disciple of Theodore Roosevelt, had come a long way together. Now Donovan had no choice but to continue on alone.

Donovan had to find time to monitor what the OSS was doing in the Balkans, in Asia, in Scandinavia, and in such remote places as Kurdistan and South Africa. But during the spring of 1944 most of his attention was directed toward Normandy. Donovan's agents entered France through the Pyrenees and slipped ashore from submarines or fast P T boats. In one month alone 52 agents jumped into France; seven suffered injuries when they plummeted to the earth, injuries ranging from broken ankles to a broken back. Other agents managed to cross the closely guarded border from Switzerland, and they even crept into France from Germany. Some 375 American and more than 500 French OSS agents were working in France during this period, sheltered by a network of friendly houses and underground hideouts throughout the country where they could eat, sleep, and set up their secret radios.

OSS spies were everywhere. They identified the crack Panzer Lehr Division deployed in France when it was supposed to be on the Russian front, and Eisenhower was able to bring the weight of a top American division against it. An OSS team working near Le Bourget Airport, near Paris, obtained the plans of two secret war production plants. Allied planes targeted one of them, an explosives factory, and leveled it, and a week later blew up the other, a refinery making oil for aircraft and submarines.

At first the OSS role in the French Resistance was restricted to supplying arms and materials and a few agents to work under French and British orders. In 1943 the OSS intensified its air drops of supplies and sent agents into France in large numbers. OSS dropped 20,000 tons of ammunition, weapons, and food to the Resistance. In September 1943, the OSS and SOE together dropped 5,570 containers of arms to the French fighting against Hitler, and in most months preceding the Normandy invasion they dropped at least 5,000 containers of arms.

In time there were 90 Jedburgh teams in the field in France, each made up of an OSS agent, a British SOE agent, and a member of the French Resistance. Each group of three Allied officers and a radio operator worked with units of from 30 to 50 resistance fighters. Equipped with jeeps, bazookas, and heavy machine guns—all dropped from Allied planes—the Jedburgh teams soon became a major factor in upsetting the German defense plans. They were trained so that basic 32-man units could quickly break into eight-man units, each self-sufficient and cross-trained so that every man was equally at home with espionage, explosives, medical care, or a rifle. Of the 90 OSS men parachuted into France in these teams, 53 were decorated for their valor, an unfortunately large number of them posthumously.

Late in May, as the Allies moved their great armada into position for the cross-Channel invasion by which they intended to wrest control of the Continent from the Nazis, Donovan drove the OSS hard to collect every scrap of hard intelligence that would make Allied success more certain. Paul Ludington was working the graveyard shift at the Reproduction branch of the OSS in the basement of the South Building.

An officer dashed down the stairs, Ludington later recounted. "He told me to unlock certain rooms. That the General would be down in a minute. Before I was through unlocking the doors, the General and four of his staff officers came down. They worked rapidly all night getting papers ready. The General was busy arranging his briefcase and filing the papers and maps they were printing. They worked steadily until about 4:30 in the morning. I learned that the General was leaving on a plane to fly to Europe to report to General Eisenhower before the invasion. I was to tell no one."

When Donovan arrived in London, he conferred with David Bruce and other London people. Then he went to brief Eisenhower. OSS agents throughout France were alerted to act. David Bruce and SOE chief

Gubbins called on French Gen. Marie Pierre Koenig and asked if he had any objection to sending a message to the Maquis for a general rising. Koenig had no objection, which was just as well since the message had already been sent.

"The wine is red," announced the BBC, thus giving the code instruction for the Resistance to strike. All over France and in the Low Countries, men, women, and children and their OSS and SOE friends blocked highways, dynamited bridges, destroyed German supplies, and ambushed German columns.

Donovan and Bruce sailed from Plymouth with the Allied fleet shortly after midnight on June 6.

"I went over in the *Tuscaloosa,* which was the flagship of Admiral Deyo," Donovan reported a week later to Franklin Roosevelt.

Donovan and Bruce watched the attack from the *Tuscaloosa,* with Donovan sitting beside the ship's big guns and munching apples. Then about three in the afternoon, both men took a launch over to the *Bayfield,* an ammunition ship, where OSS man Bob Thayer was giving an intelligence briefing. Thayer, who was in touch with the OSS agents working behind the German lines, was able to report on the activities of the French Resistance. Shortly afterward, Donovan and Bruce went ashore onto Utah Beach to contact OSS agents.

"I was pretty nervous about the whole affair," Bruce said later.

> Perhaps it was my nerves, or my own clumsiness, but I almost killed Donovan. A German plane came swooping down to strafe us, and trying to get away, I plunged right into Donovan, the edge of my steel helmet cutting him just below the jugular vein. He spouted blood, and I thought he was a goner.
>
> Despite the blood pouring out, Donovan insisted it was only a superficial cut. He said we had to push inland and make contact with our agents. We got to an American battery captain who stopped us, but then saw Donovan's Congressional Medal of Honor ribbon, and waved us on. He was still bleeding.
>
> We saw no agents but we did run into a German machine-gun nest. We hit the dirt and burrowed in. Donovan told me that we could not be captured. We knew too much. He asked me whether I was carrying my poison pill. I admitted I was not. Donovan said that was all right, he had at least two on him and would give me one. But, when he searched his pockets, he could not find them. Then he remembered that he had left them in his medicine cabinet in the bathroom back at Claridge's Hotel in London.

"David," said Donovan, "if we get out of this alive, please call Gibb, the hall porter, and tell him to warn everyone not to touch the medicine in my bathroom."

Then he added, "Ah well, no matter for the pills. If the Germans take us, I'll shoot you first as your commanding officer, then I'll shoot myself, so there's nothing to worry about."

Fortunately, Allied troops arrived and silenced the German guns. Donovan and Bruce were able to contact OSS agents with the Resistance. Ignoring the injury to his neck, Donovan explored the entire battlefront, observing the Allied operations with a professional eye. Then he returned to London and called together the OSS staff.

"His staff meetings were all very much to the point—brief," said W. C. Reddick, who was in charge of documentation, counterfeiting, and clothing agents appropriately for their missions. "I recall the one he called just after his landing with the invasion of France. His account was graphic. Told it more like an athletic event."

One London staffer asked if the troops were scared. "Hell, yes," answered Donovan. "You could smell them!"

President Roosevelt had asked Donovan to make a thorough report on how well his generals and their forces were doing. On June 14, by then back in Washington, Donovan wrote to FDR:

> Having just returned from the beachhead in France, I hope that you might find it of some interest to get certain conclusions based on my observations there.
>
> 1. The success of the landing as a whole shows certain fundamental weaknesses in the basic German position. These weaknesses are not only psychological; they are material and physical. It was clear that the Germans had neither the resources nor the capabilities to meet the attack at every possible landing beach. We talked to prisoners at the Utah Beach. One of them, a captain of the regular service, said that he was overwhelmed when he saw the ships coming in and then felt that he wanted to be identified with a movement that seemed so powerful and so efficient.
>
> 2. The presence of so many foreigners in the German forces was indicative of the same kind of difficulty that Napoleon had in Russia, as well as at Waterloo. Many of the Poles in the ranks of enlisted men were looking for an opportunity to escape.
>
> 3. All these various elements of disintegration, spiritual as well as physical, might result in a speedy breakup of the whole German defense if we can sustain an accelerated military pressure.
>
> 4. After the initial landing, we lost our momentum. If it is not regained and reaccentuated, there can be a recoalescing of the elements that make for disintegration.
>
> 5. Everything that I saw made clear that the Germans no longer have an Air Force that belongs in the Big League. They were able to have bombers over us at night and to send over some fighter bombers in bombing missions during the day, but our intelligence showed us that planes hurriedly brought in from Germany were in a very poor state of serviceability.

6. Also, the E-boats which attacked us were, like the planes, not the operations of a great power.

7. One thing that struck me was the very slow reaction of the Germans in counterattack. To me that seemed due to the measures of the Resistance Groups, but, more important, to the work of our Air Corps in the destruction of bridges and oil installations. Our intelligence showed that the present German needs for oil are 1.2 million tons. General oil shortage has not yet impaired mobility of ground forces in N.W. Europe. Constriction of mobility has been due to improved tactical bombing program—bridges, supply dumps, motor transport. However, strategic attack on oil target system could readily reduce output to 600,000 tons per month. With activity in East and West available enemy reserves could bridge the gap for two or three months at the most. This makes oil targets almost a front line target.

Two things particularly impressed me from our side. They were the following:

A. The tremendous effect that the radar countermeasures had in giving us initial advantage. I saw for myself the effect of jamming guided missiles and the detection of attempted countermeasures by the enemy.

B. The tremendous development in precision firing of our naval guns. The navy guns performed the duties not only of field guns but of railroad guns. It is in reality like corps artillery. I think it is probably true that never before has it been attempted to silence with naval gunfire so elaborate a system of coast defenses as here. After the first day the great block of firing was on targets requested by Signal Force Control Parties both to break up threatened counterattacks and to prepare the advance of our troops. The *Nevada,* operating close inshore and threatened by a great number of small and medium batteries, performed with the·greatest gallantry and effectiveness. She succeeded, with her fourteen-inch main battery, in breaking up a serious counterattack which was forming the night of D day north of Carentan, consisting of armored troops and artillery.

All of this demonstrated to me the tremendous strides that have been made which are scarcely appreciated by those who have not observed closely the new equipment and technique of naval gunfire. With the excellent fire control and navigation equipment, not only can the naval forces be used as artillery in placing troops ashore but for protecting them from enemy artillery while expanding the beachhead and assisting them in all defenses until they are beyond range.

In a few days Donovan went to the White House to elaborate on his report to Roosevelt. He had been highly critical of the U.S. landings at Anzio, but he could report that things had gone much better in Normandy.

The same day that Donovan reported to Roosevelt about D day, the President asked for his opinion of De Gaulle. Was he the indispensable French leader he claimed to be, or were there possibly others in France who might have as much or more influence with the Resistance? On the morning of June 15 Donovan and Stimson met to discuss the subject.

"The President last night told me that he had got his information from Donovan about there being a number of other organized Resistants," Stimson wrote in his diary. Donovan told Stimson that he had heard from Allen Dulles and others that, on the whole, De Gaulle was the symbol of the Resistance. However, the French distinguished between De Gaulle as a symbol and as a politician; he did not have the political power he thought he did. Donovan suggested that Eisenhower invite De Gaulle to confer about who should be established in each section of France as it was liberated. Stimson thought it an interesting idea, and he passed it on to General Marshall in London.

Donovan had already prepared a memorandum for the President on his thinking about the De Gaulle question, but now he decided not to send it. He explained to Roosevelt,

> Before I sent it Mr. Stimson called me, and since talking with him I have torn up that memorandum. In view of the questions raised by Mr. Stimson, I think it my duty to tell you what I said to him concerning my position.
>
> I told him that our intelligence clearly showed that there were many people in France, particularly those in the Maquis resistance groups, who did not like the Algiers set-up. I said also there were many who did not look with favor upon De Gaulle as a political figure. However, I told him that in view of the present situation, there were many in the resistance groups, whatever their view of De Gaulle as a political leader, who thought it advisable to have him in France now as a symbol of resistance.
>
> Mr. Stimson then asked me my opinion as to what should be done regarding De Gaulle's claim that his committee should be recognized as the provisional government. I told him that I thought it was right to refuse the demand of the De Gaulle committee for recognition as the provisional government unsanctioned by the approval of the people of France. I did say, however, that there was danger then in France, as well as in England, it would be made to appear that it was your dislike of De Gaulle that prevented this recognition and that this should be avoided. In reply to Mr. Stimson's request for my suggestion, I said the following: We should keep in mind the admonition of Mr. Justice Holmes that "the elements need eternal repetition." Occasion should be taken now to clearly set forth the manner in which we would deal with the liberated areas.
>
> In doing that I thought we ought to put the military situation at the forefront and full recognition should be given to De Gaulle as a military leader under Eisenhower. This was particularly necessary since already formal recognition had been given to General Koenig as the leader and representative of the resistance groups at our High Command. Having given this recognition to General De Gaulle and making the fullest use of him as a symbol of resistance, it could then be stated that General

Eisenhower would consult with him as to the selection of individual administrators in the various regions. This consultation would not carry with it his recognition as head of a provisional government. . . . Such a position would appeal to the ultimate logic of the French people, and they are the ones whom I think you would wish to address. We thus clearly define the distinction we make in De Gaulle as a political and military leader; and while we recognize him in his military capacity, we leave it to the French people to determine his political position.

By July 4 Donovan could tell Roosevelt that his OSS teams were infiltrating at will through the German lines. "Before D day in France, I favored placing our espionage and intelligence people forward with corps and division," he informed Roosevelt. "Instead it was decided to leave them back with army, which was the British plan. My objection to this plan was based on experience with former landings that there would be fluidity coming from the campaign, thus enabling us to infiltrate our agents. I talked to General Bradley at the beachhead on D plus 1 and was able to get some of our men ashore."

Now Donovan was receiving detailed reports from his men in Normandy. The OSS French agents and French Resistance had become virtually the same. Donovan was able to give Roosevelt the following observations on the progress of the fighting:

> Axis troops do not fight as hard as in Tunisia and early Italian campaigns.
>
> Foreign levees in German units surrender easily, but are being told they will be shot by Americans.
>
> Most divisions on north and northeast front of beachhead are now less than one-half normal strength.
>
> They have not seen one German plane in daylight. Luftwaffe attacks beaches regularly one hour after dark, flak very heavy—enemy damage to us usually nil. Our planes everywhere.
>
> French report most German soldiers rarely discussed future, but implied they expected war to be lost eventually ever since last year.
>
> German prisoners not as fine type nor as arrogant as in early days in Tunisia, Sicily, etc. Most seem happy to be captured and out of it.
>
> German Army morale definitely weaker—absence of Luftwaffe a constant blow to their confidence.
>
> Guts of our paratroopers and assault troops tops. G.I.s fought like demons. Where bodies our airborne troops found isolated, frequently surrounded by six or more dead Germans.
>
> Mechanical equipment captured such as radio-controlled small tanks (doodlebugs) etc. all show fine workmanship—no deterioration electrical and mechanical parts. Excellent strong night flares—very bright.

OSS agents inside Germany were sending Donovan other intriguing reports, which he shared with FDR. On July 6, he told the President,

The Japanese Army and Navy, as well as the Foreign Office, are still endeavoring to persuade Germany into a separate peace with the USSR. Early in June, General Arisue recommended this move during a talk with the German military attaché in Tokyo. In the opinion of the Japanese, the war's center of gravity has moved to the western front and thus the USSR and Germany should come to terms so that a common front may be made against the western nations. The trip which Malik, the Soviet ambassador to Japan, made from Tokyo to Moscow on June 20 at the behest of the Japanese Foreign Office was for the purpose of sounding out whether the USSR would agree to negotiate a settlement of the Pacific war. Japan is looking ahead to a defeat of Germany and thinks that the USSR will not want to face the United States and the latter's allies all by herself. Japan is ready to make very great concessions to the USSR and cooperate with her as an ally. Shigemitsu, the Japanese foreign minister, denied up to June 8 that any arrangements existed between the USSR and Japan. He even refused to admit that Japan was shipping supplies to the USSR, which is a fact confirmed by information which came to Berlin via Switzerland.

The Soviets, the Nazis, and the Japanese were in a swirl of secret diplomatic negotiations. Donovan knew that a major function of strategic intelligence was to supply the President of the United States with knowledge of what a presumed friend such as Stalin was actually attempting to do, as well as with information about the intrigues of avowed enemies. At the same time, the OSS had to provide tactical intelligence to those Allied armies already fighting in France and those planning still another landing in the south of France.

Collecting military intelligence and assessing the morale and attitudes of French civilians, Donovan's agents kept him informed as to how the war was proceeding in France. The first OSS man in the south of France was Pierre Martineau, who jumped to the French Resistance with his radio operator, a young Pole named Janyk. As the Germans recognized that another Allied landing was likely to be made on the Mediterranean coast, they moved crack Waffen SS units into the area where the Resistance was active. Martineau and Janyk reported the troop movements to Donovan. The OSS dropped a quantity of a secret incendiary called Firefly to the Maquis. When OSS agents disguised as French workmen gassed up the German trucks and tanks rumbling down to the coast, they added Firefly. The trucks and tanks burst into flames when they were some distance down the road, creating chaos in the long line of vehicles. The Germans soon moved in two additional squads of Sicherheitsdienst and Gestapo to tighten the security on the coast. Several leaders of the French underground were caught by the Gestapo, as well as OSS man Martineau, but Janyk continued to send out information on German movements.

Among other OSS agents in southern France were René Dussaq,

the Hollywood stunt man, and Joseph Le Fou (the Fool), whose sister had been raped by the Germans and who now took pleasure in killing the enemy with his bare hands. Moe Berg, the erstwhile baseball player, had finished his work in Italy. Now he was posing as an entomologist behind the German lines.

Another OSS man, Geoffrey Jones, was flying to Algiers before going into France. "Someone told me that the man sitting opposite me was the baseball star Moe Berg," he said. "I looked him over and when I saw his wristwatch, in spite of myself, I started to laugh. Naturally, he wondered what I was laughing at, but then when my watch caught his eyes, a big grin spread over his face too. Although no one was supposed to know that we were secret operatives, all of the graduates had been issued the same kind of special watch. The OSS might as well have hung tags around our necks."

Presumably both Berg and Jones removed their watches before dropping into France. Jones had gone to school in Caen as a boy, and when the Allied invasion force swept ashore it landed only a mile and a half from where he had lived on the outskirts of St.-Tropez. Jones and his Maquis knocked out a radar installation at Fayence with small mortars and cleared fields so that Allied gliders could land. When coded instructions came over the BBC that the landings would be made on August 15, Jones was ready.

Donovan arrived in Naples in early August and proceeded to the OSS villa on Capri, where he met Colonel Toulmin, chief of the OSS mission in Cairo, and Colonel Huntington, who was to head the American military mission to Tito. On August 11, Tito arrived with Brig. Fitzroy MacLean of the British SOE. Tito brought along his enormous Alsatian dog, which was kept outside while Tito talked with the British and American intelligence leaders.

According to a report to Franklin Roosevelt, Donovan informed Tito that an OSS rescue and intelligence team had been dispatched to General Mihajlović. At that time Tito nodded his head and voiced no objection. He did say, however, that the men might not have such a good time with Mihajlović and suggested that their names be given to him so he could advise his troops to protect them in the event of trouble. Donovan was pleased with this response, for he was anxious to keep OSS men with both Mihajlović and Tito.

"We get valuable information from both of the Yugoslav leaders," he later told Ned Putzell. "No intelligence is worth a hoot unless it is unprejudiced. It is necessary to see it through more than one eye."

When the serious talk was completed, tea was served in the heirloom set belonging to Donovan's friend Mrs. Williams, who owned the villa. Tito's dog leaped into the room. His enormous tail, wagging with delight, brushed the tea things off a serving table onto the floor, where they landed with a crash. Donovan surveyed the debris sorrowfully, as well he might; after the war Mrs. Williams sued the OSS for the damage to her treasured tea service. She also complained that the contents of her wine cellar had disappeared.

"Anybody who thinks she can hide liquor in wartime is daft," observed Henry Ringling North.

On August 15 Donovan was again aboard the *Tuscaloosa*, this time for the Anvil-Dragoon landings in the south of France. He had a jeep and his driver, Sergeant Buda, aboard so he could explore the enemy positions with more mobility once he got on land. Donovan had every intention of driving all the way to Paris. About the same time that he went ashore with Gen. Alexander Patch's Seventh Army, a fresh OSS team landed from another ship.

"Seeking out his OSS team," said Allen Dulles, "he found them upset because they had landed on one beach, their equipment on another, and no available transportation."

Donovan listened to their gripes. "Any man who can't get transportation somehow doesn't belong in this outfit," he announced with a smile, "and I'll fire the first man caught stealing a car."

OSS man Bob Thayer was also at St.-Tropez with two French officers. Donovan suddenly appeared in his jeep. "I want to borrow one of your French officers," he told Thayer. "I want to go to Paris."

"You can't get into Paris," said Thayer.

"It's all right," Donovan said. "I've got my people spotted around. I want a naval officer to see me through. I'll be gone for three days."

One of Thayer's officers got into the jeep with Donovan, and they were off. He was indeed back in three days.

"You were right," said Donovan. "We were almost ambushed."

According to Thayer, Donovan tried to reach Paris three separate times. He was determined to be there when the underground French Forces of the Interior (FFI) rose in revolt, and his agents had informed him he had better hurry. OSS man Gerald W. Davis was with an operational group element that made the first contact with the Third and Seventh armies in the vicinity of Lyon. Later he wrote:

> It was mid-morning on the day before Paris fell at Field Headquarters of Third Army. The 11th SF [Special Forces] Det. HQ tent flap was thrown back and, unexpectedly, in came General Donovan followed by Ernest Hemingway [then a war correspondent]. They were both almost boyishly exuberant. General Donovan announced that they were on their way to Paris and wanted a briefing. I outlined the friendly and enemy dispositions and the Paris FFI conditions as we knew them and recommended a road route to Paris. As they were about to depart in their jeep (with General's two stars), Hemingway asked me if I could find a submachine gun for himself. I cocked an eye at Donovan, and he nodded. I gave

Hemingway a Madson, my personal arm, and two clips of ammunition. Off they went as though to a picnic—on their way to participate in the liberation of their beloved Paris—Donovan in the right front seat of the jeep—Hemingway perched on the back like a full-sized toy bear holding the Madson on his lap.

With Sergeant Buda at the wheel, Hemingway and Donovan worked their way past the forward assault elements of Gen. Philippe Leclerc's First Armored Division, which had been given the task of liberating Paris. They crept forward through the outskirts of Paris, engaging German patrols with machine-gun fire when they encountered them, and were among the first Allied soldiers to pass beneath the Arc de Triomphe.

Donovan and Hemingway gathered up other OSS men who had been living under deep cover in Paris or who were arriving from all directions, and several score of FFI. They decided to liberate the Ritz Hotel. German officers were still packing their bags in the rooms when the unkempt crew, armed to the teeth, burst into the lobby. Charles Ritz was there. The assistant manager rushed to the door to keep the intruders from upsetting the cherished decorum of the hotel. He recognized David Bruce, who was among the OSS men, and Hemingway as prewar guests.

"What are you doing here?"

"We've come with a few guests for a short stay," replied Hemingway.

"What can I do for you?"

"How about 73 dry martinis?" asked Hemingway.

Charles Ritz claimed that it was not martinis but a magnum of champagne that helped the OSS men celebrate the liberation of the Ritz.

"Then there was some rifle firing," Ritz remembered, "and Hemingway rushed up on the roof and fired several bursts from his submachine gun at snipers."

That night Donovan slept in a bed whose sheets were the same ones a German general had slept in the night before.

Among the OSS men now in Paris were William Haines and Walt Rostow, who were interrogating French businessmen involved in the production of German aircraft and aeroengines. "Donovan gathered the OSS personnel in town for a cheerful dinner at a first-class restaurant," said Rostow, "but food was exceedingly scarce. The restaurant supplied champagne and, of all things, corn on the cob—the only time I ever heard of the French serving what they regarded as cattle food. We supplied K and C rations, which the distinguished chef converted into fine fare, subtle sauces and all. A memorable occasion when there was still an occasional shot to be heard around town."

By the time Paris was officially liberated on August 25, Donovan was already in London conferring with King Peter and Prime Minister Subasić of Yugoslavia. The Yugoslavs urged Donovan to use his influence to keep Tito's Partisans from attacking Mihajlović's Chetniks. Donovan reported his interviews to Roosevelt. He also sent him an intelligence report on the situation in Yugoslavia, where the German forces were in retreat and the Russians were advancing toward the nation's borders. He wrote,

> Some of Mihajlović's old followers now consider that it is imperative to alter the movement's attitude toward the invaders and to protect Serbia from attack from beyond its borders. The position of those Chetniks who advocate cooperation with the Germans is strengthened by the fact that the latter may soon be forced to evacuate Serbia. This would be a signal for a show-down engagement between the communists and the nationalists. Mihajlović therefore probably intends to cooperate with the German Army while it is still in Serbia, in order to lessen the effectiveness of Tito's Partisans. By emphasizing the common fight against communism, Mihajlović would obtain as many weapons as possible from the Germans. He feels that he will then be able to take over the German positions easily when the German Army leaves.

34

Preparing for the Peace

ON JUNE 15, 1944, the first German V-1 rocket bomb bumbled through the sky and fell on London with a roar. Donovan's agents had tracked the development of the FZG-76 from its inception at the Research Station at Peenemünde in June 1942, and Donovan knew that mass production of the buzz bomb had begun in March 1944. He also knew that the V-2, the A-4 rocket, was being developed in an underground factory near Nordhausen in the Harz Mountains, and that it would be far more devastating. The question in his mind on June 19 was why the Germans were firing the buzz bomb at southern England. His agents in Germany all reported that most German leaders knew they had already lost the war. Donovan sent the following cable to London:

> Since enemy use of either robot planes or rockets appears to be irreconcilable with good timing or good military judgment, I am looking for some rationalization. Do the Germans believe this attack of sufficient vehemence to be untenable to British-American war effort by the maintenance of suspense and terror? Have you learned that any special explosive is used for the first time in these weapons? If no abnormal explosive is indicated, watch keenly for evidence of the dissemination of any sort of contagion near to places hit. Does wreckage of devices indicate use of gyro? Do robots come over at definite time intervals and how many in 24 hours? Are we using radar defensively? Give appraisal of whole affair. Urgent.

In four days OSS London answered Donovan's questions. Earlier OSS penetration of rocket sites had led to heavy Allied bombing, and the "bombing necessitated entire change of method in launching these craft." Military judgment must have been sidetracked. There was "no evidence of special explosive," and "no evidence as yet of any sort of contagion near place where PAC [pilotless aircraft] hit."

"PAC are robot compass controlled, compass set prior to launching," continued the report. "No change in flight possible. PAC show up on radar."

OSS Bern, Switzerland, was sending Donovan reports from inside Germany. On July 10 Donovan learned of an underground plant south of Kahla, on the railroad line between Rudolstadt and Jena, where "new secret weapons are also produced. In comparison with the V-1 model, the V-2 travels through the stratosphere. It is radio-controlled and is therefore a more accurate weapon. In addition, it possesses a longer range. This new model will be in use by the Nazis within 60 days at the outside." Donovan also learned that the Germans were at work on a still more advanced rocket bomb, the two-stage A-10, which was designed to cross the Atlantic and bombard cities on America's East Coast.

OSS was intercepting German intelligence and diplomatic dispatches, and 109 read with interest a report from German Ambassador Dieckhoff in Madrid, who forwarded information from Spanish sources in London on July 2: "In the last two days, the initial results of the rocket bombing of southern England have become a great deal graver. If this bombing is maintained, it is anticipated that there will be heavy damage and disorder, even though public services have not yet been halted."

Donovan suspected the Germans had come to the mistaken conclusion that their buzz bombs could change the course of the war, and he was able to warn both London and Washington that by the end of the summer a deadlier rocket was bound to cause even more casualties and damage.

"It was all another example of Hitler's irrational behavior," he said afterward. "On one hand, our agents were garnering more and more information showing that Germany had lost the war, but here was Hitler clutching at a last straw."

Much of Donovan's knowledge about what was going on inside Hitler's faltering Reich came to him through Allen Dulles, his man in Bern, who was later to direct the CIA. It was Dulles who first reported on the plot to assassinate Hitler.

"Two emissaries of the conspiring group first approached the OSS representative in Bern in January, 1944," Donovan told Roosevelt.

> The group was then described as composed of various intellectuals from certain military and government circles gathered into a loose organization. The membership was said to be somewhat divided as to a course of action, some holding that Hitler and his cohorts should be made to shoulder all responsibility to the bitter end; while others favored an overthrow of Hitler and the organization of a new government before the fighting stops, which might negotiate peace. The conspiring elements were united in their preference for a western rather than eastern orientation of German policy. In general, they were characterized by their emissaries as well-educated and influential but not rightist individuals; such characterization may have been designed for Anglo-American consumption. The group as a whole apparently maintained its foreign contacts through the Canaris organization [Abwehr].

Donovan assigned the OSS code name Breakers to this group's plan, which called for Hitler's assassination followed by an uprising of the German underground. The underground asked that the OSS cooperate in supplying arms and arrange for American forces to come to its assistance.

"Such action," said Donovan to Roosevelt, "would be contingent upon assurances from Britain and the United States that, once the Nazis had been overthrown, negotiations would then be carried out solely with the Western powers and under no circumstances with the USSR. The essential conservatism of the group's planners was stressed, but also its willingness to cooperate with any available elements of the Left except for the communists. The group expressed its anxiety to keep Central Europe from coming under Soviet domination."

Donovan was surprised when Roosevelt refused to permit him to help the German plotters. "If we start assassinating chiefs of state, God knows where it all would end," FDR told his intelligence chief. "If the Germans dispose of Hitler, that is their prerogative, but the OSS must have nothing whatsoever to do with it." Roosevelt also told Donovan that the United States could not act against the interests of an ally, the Soviet Union. Thus Donovan instructed Dulles not to take any action. "The United States would never act without previous consultation with the USSR," he said.

Soviet victories in the East and Allied successes in France further strengthened the group plotting against Hitler. Early in July it became apparent that the Nazis had become aware of the plot and were taking countermeasures. Reports reaching Donovan said that Heinrich Himmler might well take control; if he did, he intended to negotiate with the Soviet Union. On July 4 Donovan received a report from "a trustworthy source" stating that "a man in a high position in the Foreign Office in Stockholm has claimed that Nazi morale and the German military machine are undergoing a rapid deterioration. This Swedish career diplomat has had experience with Russian affairs; according to him, generals are not politically significant any more. Himmler is prepared to grab the helm, and if he manages to accomplish this, he will attempt a separate arrangement with the USSR.

"In Stockholm our people have reported that it is most probable that one Bruno von Kleist has got in touch with Soviet officials in Stockholm."

The danger that Himmler might seize power caused the anti-Nazi group to strike before they were entirely ready. The attempt on Hitler's life by Col. Claus von Stauffenberg on July 20 during a conference at Hitler's Rastenburg headquarters was made without any support from the OSS and was a fiasco. Donovan and Dulles had followed Roosevelt's orders, and the opportunity to overthrow the Nazi government and rob the Soviet Union of some of the fruits of its approaching victory was lost. OSS agents in Germany reported to Donovan that the Nazis were striking back at the generals who had attempted to kill Hitler.

On July 24 Donovan passed on a report to Roosevelt that stated, "It seems clear now that any prospect of an armed military revolt growing out of the putsch against Hitler has been crushed. I am inclined to believe that the Gestapo probably had a good deal of prior information about some of the persons involved, and were ready to strike and to strike hard. Himmler was probably glad to have the opportunity to do this before the retreating German armies were themselves on German soil, as it is far easier to deal with the Heimatheer than it would be to deal with the troops fresh from the defeats in the east, west, and south."

Donovan also cautioned Roosevelt that

> the next attempt to overthrow the Hitler regime from the inside is likely to come from an eastern-oriented group, possibly after a part of East Prussia is occupied and a German government a la Seydlitz is installed there. It is probable that the failure of [Gen. Ludwig] Beck and his friends [to assassinate Hitler] will still further increase the influence of Russia in Germany and somewhat decrease the influence of the West. Russia has throughout played a more realistic policy in dealing with the internal German situation than has either the United States or England, and it is possible that, from now on, the Seydlitz Committee will increase in importance and have a larger scope of action. This is a development we should not underestimate, particularly now that the western-oriented dissident group in Germany, in and outside of the army, has received a serious if not a fatal setback.

After driving back the Germans from Stalingrad, the Russians had persuaded such captured German generals as Field Marshal Friedrich Paulus and Gen. Walter von Seydlitz to turn against Hitler. Seydlitz became chairman of a Free Germany Committee, which the Soviets expected would not only help defeat Hitler but would also insure Communist postwar domination of Germany.

It was apparent to Donovan that Roosevelt's resolve to be faithful to the Soviet Union, an increasingly faithless ally, was fraught with danger for the future.

A week after the liberation of Paris, Donovan sent a memo to Roosevelt outlining "Future OSS operations in Central Europe." He saw two phases of operations. Of phase one, he wrote:

> The continued resistance of the enemy, in a military sense (though with reduced resources, depleted manpower) up to and within their own borders, with the gradual accent on organized subversion against our Army.
> This will require a reorientation of our thinking. Up to the present we have been operating in enemy-occupied territory. An important factor for

the success of our activities in France was the determination of the resistance groups, as well as their willingness to accept the help and guidance of the British and ourselves in the employment of weapons and tactics within their area against the enemy.

But in enemy territory we will not find (as we have found in France and are finding also in countries like Norway, Belgium, and Holland) friendly airstrips, reception committees, organizers and leaders. On the contrary, we must expect to meet (even though we try to make the enemy population do otherwise) the kind of resistance and the use of methods against us [that] we stimulated against the enemy in territory friendly to us.

In enemy territory, OSS must do with its own force what previously we had had done largely through resistance groups we have organized and trained, and we must place behind enemy lines for operational purposes as we now do for intelligence purposes, men of coolness, daring, and resourcefulness, who fully understand that they must depend upon their own enterprise rather than on support of the inhabitants.

For that reason, SHAPE [Supreme Headquarters Allied Powers in Europe] has accepted the principle we urged of unblocking the joint control of OSS/SOE in such operations and recognizes that to carry on aggressive subversion behind enemy lines we must vest authority in our forward echelons and there must be freedom of action in our movements. But, with our allies, there must be the fullest exchange of information and the constant coordination of activities.

In phase two, Donovan said,

We are inclined to accept the manner of the last war's ending as the pattern for the finish of the present war. But the circumstances surrounding this war give it a characterization different from the last one. It is unnecessary to spell out the difference. We can have no assurance that one day the sound of guns will end and an armistice begin. If the basic assumption be correct, then there can be no armistice and no surrender and no German government left with which the Allies can deal. Of course, with no central government, there would be confusion, but this confusion would give strength to the organized aggressive underground's opposition to the decrees of the Allied Control Mission.

This opposition could take many forms—propaganda, inspiring fear, coercion by passive as well as active means to incite the population against us. We would be obliged to meet it not only with firmness but with skill and ingenuity and comprehension. Countermeasures will need to be employed.

Donovan decided on September 6 to summon Allen Dulles, who would play a leading role in phase one, to a meeting.

"Under orders to return to Washington to report on my two years' stewardship," said Dulles, "I had joined a group of the French underground in a secret retreat in the Rhone Valley between Geneva and Lyon awaiting a clandestine flight to take me to London. As far as I knew, General Donovan was in Washington, and, as far as I knew, he had not the slightest idea where I was hidden. Weather prevented my plane coming from London for several days, and as I was waiting in my hideout, there was a knock on the door in the middle of the night. It was one of General Donovan's aides, telling me that the General himself was waiting for me at the nearest available airstrip south of Lyon, which had just been evacuated by the Nazis."

Donovan had been touring the secret hideouts of Jedburgh teams throughout France. Dulles joined him at the airstrip, and they flew to London. They talked about the attack on Hitler's life and Donovan's plans to penetrate the Reich.

The two men were in London at the Savoy Hotel bar when the first V-2 rockets landed on the city. Donovan had intended to give David Bruce, his London man, another assignment, but talking to Dulles, he realized that Dulles would much prefer to be his man in London and head of the entire European OSS operations. He wanted to keep Dulles in Bern.

"I didn't want anyone to be unhappy over David's replacement," he said to Dulles. "There are lots of guys shooting for the job, good guys with marvelous records—the best men we've got. But they can't see that it isn't the sort of job they're suited for. Just because they're brilliant station chiefs doesn't mean they can handle London—all that administration. Nearly all of them are lousy administrators. They could foul things up at a vital stage in the war.

"So I'm ordering David to stay on, just as I'm asking you to do the same. God knows what would happen if we had a change in Bern at this juncture. We just can't afford to lose you."

Hubert Will flew with Donovan and Dulles across the Atlantic, and he remembered the two men chatting affably and playing not-so-friendly games of bridge. "Donovan bluffed terribly at cards," said Will. "He was my partner, and it was disastrous."

Donovan sent more than 200 agents into Germany between September 1944 and VE Day. Among them were Germans with Social Democrat and labor backgrounds chosen by Arthur Goldberg from among captured German soldiers. Although patriotic Germans, they were anti-Hitler and were anxious to destroy the Nazis so the German nation could be rebuilt on democratic foundations. Other agents were German-Americans. All of them had to be given credible papers and cover stories and dressed in clothing purchased from refugees who had fled the Reich. They contacted the German underground, and gathered information not only about Hitler's faltering war machine, but also about social and economic conditions that would indicate in which direction Germany would go once the war was over.

One agent, Jack Taylor, a California orthodontist turned OSS man, jumped into Austria with three Austrians. He was captured, sentenced to death, and imprisoned at Mauthausen, an extermination camp. A friendly German burned his execution order, and Taylor stayed on in the camp as one of the few Americans to witness the Nazis' savage genocide of Jews. He later assisted Donovan when the OSS chief was called upon to help prosecute Nazi leaders at Nuremberg.

OSS men were everywhere in Europe that autumn of 1944. They were with the Greek underground, with both Tito and Mihajlović in Yugoslavia, and penetrating Romania and Bulgaria. Some agents were among the Polish and French slave laborers in Germany or were passing themselves off as mechanics or salesmen. One agent, Bernard Yarrow, lunched with President Eduard Beneš of Czechoslovakia. Beneš explained that a Danubian confederation would not work out because the Soviet Union opposed it. Beneš believed that the way to stabilize Central Europe was to reach an agreement and a military alliance among Czechoslovakia, Poland, and Soviet Russia. On every question that came up, the Czech president evidenced a pro-Soviet attitude. He reported on his long talks with Stalin and Foreign Minister Molotov in Moscow on the Polish question, which he believed could best be solved by a military alliance with the Soviet Union.

"President Beneš, throughout the whole conversation," Donovan told Roosevelt, "again and again referred to the fact that he is not a communist and never will be, but that his whole pro-Soviet political orientation is motivated by fear and a hope not ever to be faced by another Munich."

It was in Greece and Yugoslavia that Donovan saw most clearly the portents of postwar Soviet policies in Europe. Rivalry between the communist guerrillas and the Greek democrats and royalists burst into civil war as the Germans began to withdraw. The Reds, responding to orders from Moscow, seized whole Greek villages and held men, women, and children hostage, threatening to execute them if the opposing guerrillas or the British moved against them. If there had been Russian troops in Greece instead of British, the country might well have been forced into the Soviet camp, but as it was, the British and the anticommunists soon made it obvious to even the most fanatic Reds that they could not win.

As the German Army withdrew from Greece into Yugoslavia, it found that the Yugoslavs were just as adept as the Greeks at ambushing military columns and demolishing bridges to hamper their retreat. There was the same combination of British SOE and American OSS agents and either communist or anticommunist resistance fighters.

Donovan wished to keep OSS men with both Mihajlović and Tito, but on September 1 Churchill objected. "We are endeavoring to give Tito the support and, of course, if the United States backed Mihajlović complete chaos will ensue. I was rather hoping things were going to get a bit smoother in these parts, but if we each back different sides we lay the scene for a fine civil war. General Donovan is running a strong Mihajlović lobby just when we have persuaded King Peter to break decisively with him and when many of the Chetniks are being rallied under Tito's National Army of Liberation. The only chance of saving the King is the unity between the Prime Minister, the Ban [governor] of Croatia, and Tito."

Roosevelt replied on September 3, "The mission of OSS is my mistake. I did not check my previous action of last April 8. I am directing Donovan to withdraw his mission."

Donovan responded to Roosevelt's orders with a long and intemperate argument against turning Yugoslavia completely over to Tito and his Soviet friends, and he kept his men with Mihajlović until November 1, when he had no choice but to withdraw them. When in September, acting upon Moscow's orders, both Tito and the pro-Soviet Bulgarian guerrillas forced British and American agents to leave, Donovan complained to Lieutenant General Fitin of the NKVD as one intelligence chief to another. OSS agents in Bulgaria had provided a valuable flow of intelligence for Allied use in defeating the Nazis and had rescued more than 300 airmen whose planes had crashed in that country after raids on Romania's Ploesti oil fields. The OSS chief reminded Fitin that the United States and the Soviet Union were supposed to be allies. Fitin withdrew the order requiring the OSS team to leave Bulgaria.

"In order to prevent future misunderstandings, I am sending General Fitin lists of OSS personnel in Bulgaria and Romania as requested by him," Donovan informed Roosevelt on September 29.

"This incident, together with the demonstrated attitude of Tito, shows that the Russians intend to dominate this area and, as Subasić indicates, propose going to the Adriatic. It is apparent that the Russians are going to demand that other governments concerned recognize their primary interest in this area."

Because of his global responsibilities, Donovan could not concentrate on the Balkans, critical as events there might be. There had been an upheaval in China. During the summer the Japanese had overrun U.S. air bases in eastern China. The Joint Chiefs of Staff blamed the disaster on the inferior Chinese troops, and wanted General Stilwell put in command of all Chinese forces. Chiang Kai-shek refused because he blamed Stilwell for the defeats. The Chinese general demanded that Roosevelt recall Stilwell, and in October the salty old officer left China for good. The OSS in China was confronted with a crisis, and Donovan left for the Far East.

Harry Little and Guy Martin were among the OSS men who accompanied Donovan. The party went to London and then flew to Marseilles. While the other OSS men went directly from the airport to their hotel, Donovan stayed behind to follow later in another car.

"Arriving at the hotel," Little said, "we demanded a table for General Donovan and were given the best table in the dining room. We were finishing a splendid meal when Donovan, whose car had broken down, arrived late.

"The headwaiter led him to an obscure table in the corner while we enjoyed what by rights should have been his table. It didn't bother him at all."

Donovan and his party left the next day for Cairo.

"At Cairo we were to leave at 6:00 A.M. the next morning to fly to New Delhi where we were to meet the British viceroy," continued Little. "This ruled out the chance for us young fellows to go nightclubbing in Cairo. We tossed a coin to see who should persuade the General to delay the departure until 2:30 P.M., an hour that would allow for visiting a few hot spots and some sleep besides."

"If we leave at 6:00 A.M. and go straight through," the OSS man who had lost the toss argued, "we'll arrive in Delhi about midnight, a bad time for the viceroy. If we leave here at 2:30 in the afternoon, we'll arrive in Delhi about ten o'clock in the morning, a good time for the viceroy."

Donovan nodded his head in sage agreement, but his eyes twinkled. "Okay, if you fellows want to go nightclubbing, we'll wait until 2:30," he agreed.

Donovan met the viceroy and continued on to Colombo, where he made a surprise inspection of Detachment 404. There he found Erik Lindgren, a Swede who had fought the Soviets when they invaded Finland and now was training jungle fighters to be set ashore in southern Burma and Malaya.

"What are you, a man accustomed to Finnish forests, doing training men for the jungle?" demanded Donovan.

"Jungles are just another forest," replied Lindgren.

"How do you find your way in the jungle?" asked Donovan.

"General, when you step into a jungle, it's like stepping into a closet," said Lindgren, "unless you know how to use a compass."

Lindgren complained that other officers were training their men on a compass course that ran for 3 miles. They always used the same route. "You don't need a compass on that well-worn trail," he said, "and I don't call that training."

Donovan whispered to an aide, and OSS compass training was revolutionized overnight. He went on to inspect the Morale Operations (MO).

"I told him about some of our MO projects: a subversive radio newscast in Thai to Thailand, printing Japanese surrender leaflets, etc.," said Alec MacDonald, who directed the MO team at Colombo.

Donovan opened a door and found Jane Foster and other women on MacDonald's staff blowing up condoms. For once he was disconcerted and irately demanded to know what was going on. MacDonald explained that MO had printed Malay-language leaflets that were to be stuffed into the condoms and then released from a submarine so that they would drift ashore onto the coasts of Indonesia.

"In theory they would be picked up by Indonesian fishermen and villagers and read and circulated," said MacDonald.

The future of the operation hung in the balance while Donovan stared with disbelief. Then he laughed.

"He approved, even applauded Jane's ingenuity, and the team went on with their rather bizarre operation," according to MacDonald.

As for Donovan, he went to Kandy, Ceylon, to see Lord Mountbatten and then toured other OSS operations in Southeast Asia. In Calcutta he met with 101 leaders at the OSS bungalow off Chowringhee Road to talk about the Kachins and their increasingly successful war with the Japanese in Burma.

In Calcutta Donovan sent Guy Martin to scout the city's bookstores for reading material. When he boarded a plane to fly over the Hump to China, he carried four books in each hand so he would have some reading handy. In Chungking he dined with Foreign Minister T. V. Soong, whose relations with Chiang Kai-shek had been strained since June. Chiang had accused the minister of attempting to replace him as the president of China. Donovan's real problems, however, were with the situation of the OSS after Stilwell's departure. In China he checked on the work that the OSS was doing with the 14th Air Force and on the increasing success of other OSS officers in the country.

"We are now collecting a large proportion of all intelligence produced through American sources in the China theater," Donovan told Roosevelt with some satisfaction upon his return to Washington. Donovan was now confident that Detachment 202 in China would be able "to collect information necessary for the defeat of the Japanese enemy and for the making of informed decisions on the ultimate peace settlement in the Far East."

Roosevelt found Donovan's report on the Far East highly significant. Combined with his communications from the Balkans on Soviet activities, it made clear that the United States could not enter the postwar world without a strategic intelligence organization. On October 31 he asked Donovan to draft a plan for a peacetime OSS. Donovan went to work with enthusiasm and submitted his proposal on November 18.

In his memorandum Donovan pointed out that "in the early days of the war, when the demands upon intelligence services were mainly in and for military operations, the OSS was placed under the direction of the JCS.

"Once our enemies are defeated, the demand will be equally pressing for information that will aid us in solving the problems of peace."

To Donovan this meant two things: "that intelligence control be returned to the supervision of the President" and that there was a need for "the establishment of a central authority reporting directly to you, with responsibility to frame intelligence objectives and to collect and coordinate the intelligence material required by the Executive Branch in planning and carrying out national policy and strategy."

Donovan placed coordination and centralization of the proposed authority at the policy level but operational intelligence with the existing agencies. His proposed organization would have no police or subpoena powers and would not operate in the United States. "The creation of a central authority thus would not conflict with or limit necessary intelligence functions within the Army, Navy, Department of State and other agencies."

Donovan felt that Roosevelt should examine whether congressional action would be necessary and urged him to make an "immediate revision and coordination of our present intelligence system.

> [This] would effect substantial economies and aid in the more efficient and speedy termination of the war. Information important to the national defense, being gathered now by certain departments and agencies, is not being used to full advantage in the war. Coordination at the strategy level would prevent waste and avoid the present confusion that leads to waste and unnecessary duplication.
>
> Though in the midst of war, we are also in a period of transition, which before we are aware, will take us into the tumult of rehabilitation. An adequate and orderly intelligence system will contribute to informed decisions.

Roosevelt was greatly impressed but submitted the proposal to the JCS for study. The military examined Donovan's plan with a jaundiced eye. Donovan was caught up in a new round of his ongoing bout with the military intelligence services and J. Edgar Hoover. Nevertheless, he went ahead with his plans for the OSS in the last phase of the war and the winning of the peace to come.

"In late 1944 he sent a man to Cairo to take over the direction of activities at that post," said Allen Dulles, "and gave him oral instructions to the effect that the main target for intelligence operations should now become discovering what the Soviets were doing in the Balkans rather than German activities in the Middle East. The German threat was receding. The Soviet danger was already looming. He realized this but, for obvious reasons, he could not put such instructions in an official dispatch."

35

End of an Experiment

EARLY IN DECEMBER 1944, OSS agents in Germany began to report that the supposedly beaten Germans were grouping for a counteroffensive. Hitler himself was said to have taken command of what was to be a last-ditch attack to defeat the Allies.

"The agents came back and said it would happen," remembered OSS man Vance Vogel, who was stationed with the U.S. Ninth Army, "but General Hodges literally said, 'You're crazy.' "

On the morning of December 16, the agents were proved correct when the Germans struck on an 80-mile front in the wooded hills of the Ardennes and achieved tactical surprise. Two panzer armies cracked the front wide open and drove into Belgium. The Battle of the Bulge had begun. For ten days the German attack made dangerous progress, and the OSS agents in the area were hard put to get reports of value to the OSS liaison officers. Donovan, checking on his OSS groups, appeared at the front lines. He walked into Vance Vogel's headquarters.

"Hi, Vance, how are you doing?" he asked.

"I'd met him only once in a group of 75 or 80 in Washington," recalled Vogel.

Donovan straddled a chair and leaned forward over its back, a genial smile on his face despite the tenseness of the situation.

"For 30 minutes or so I briefed him on our operations," said Vogel. "We'd run over 100 missions out of our unit."

Then Donovan was off to visit another OSS group, then still another. On December 26, the day that the British and Americans halted the German offensive short of the Meuse River, Donovan had dinner with Churchill at Chequers. There was much to discuss concerning the peace, which now seemed only months away.

After he had conferred with OSS London, Donovan flew off on what had become an almost routine inspection of OSS bases in the Mediterranean and Asia. Since he now had his own C-54, which could fly at 210 miles per hour, Donovan was able to include more destinations than before in a given number of days. The Department of State had asked him to assess the Russian losses in the war for the President's information at the Yalta Conference, scheduled to take place on February 4. In Cairo Donovan checked agent sources. The Air Transport

Command had asked that he also gather information about conditions along the routes that the President's C-54, *The Sacred Cow,* and other delegates to the conference would take.

At the same time, the State Department pointedly did not ask Donovan for intelligence information that might have proved critical at Yalta. Donovan had been forbidden to send agents into Manchuria to find out the truth about the Japanese Kwantung Army, which had occupied the province since 1931. "It is terribly easy to go wrong, to make a mistake in high policy because of an intelligence slip-up," said Donovan after the war.

> The appearance of the USSR as a partner of the Chinese in Manchuria was largely brought about by an American policy decision growing out of a fatal gap in intelligence.
>
> In February 1945, at Yalta, Mr. Roosevelt wanted from Stalin a pledge that Russia would enter the Pacific war. At that time the crack Kwantung Army of 750,000 troops was believed by the U.S. chiefs of staff to be based at the Manchurian arsenal. With our own forces about to close with the Japanese on the home islands and, in conjunction with the Chinese, on the continent of Asia, the U.S. high command was anxious to have the Kwantung Army engaged simultaneously by the Russians and thus be drawn away from our proposed battlegrounds. To win the Russians to this plan, Mr. Roosevelt bid high. Did he bid too high? The bargain struck at Yalta was based upon intelligence which we know now was incomplete. The truth about the Kwantung Army is that the best troops had been drawn off to reinforce the Philippines and Okinawa, leaving behind mostly green recruits. When the Russians did in fact invade Manchuria they found a paper army.

From the Middle East Donovan continued to New Delhi, where he rendezvoused with Ray Peers, commanding officer of Detachment 101. Peers briefed him on 101 operations in preparation for a meeting a few days later in Myitkyina, Burma, with Lord Mountbatten and generals Daniel Sultan, Albert Wedemeyer, and Howard Davidson. At Myitkyina the Allied generals sat in Sultan's office and considered what should be done about the serious weakness of the Chinese armies in China. They agreed that the Chinese troops then in Burma should be sent back to China as soon as they had played their part in the capture of Lashio and Mandalay. Donovan and Peers went to Kandy to discuss OSS contingency plans for Asia with John Coughlin, Detachment 404's commander. Together they planned the victory drive of the American-Kachin Rangers, which was to destroy the last important Japanese resistance in Burma.

Donovan flew in a light plane to Ramree Island on the coast of Burma, where a South African motor launch and a U.S. patrol boat had put ashore an OSS operational group to harass the retreating

Japanese. The group's commanding officer, George Bright, and his team were astounded when the plane approached their newly won landing strip. They were even more astounded when the man in the passenger's seat turned out to be Bill Donovan, who wanted another firsthand impression of the war in Burma.

The OSS chief learned much of value in Southeast Asia, but it was in China that Donovan gained the most significant new information. He was first to learn through Chinese sources that the Japanese Kwantung Army had been depleted. From China he sent urgent messages to Washington, but these were discounted by State Department officers who were preparing background papers for the President's use at Yalta. On January 24 Donovan left China aboard his C-54 and over the next two weeks made additional visits to Calcutta, Colombo and Kandy, Delhi, Karachi, Cairo, Casablanca, and Terceira Island in the Azores on his way back to Washington.

Upon returning to America, Donovan caught up on the reports from his agents in other parts of the world. On February 25, he wrote to Roosevelt: "In the course of a search [in Italy] for the official and personal papers of Marshal Graziani (which were found in their hiding place in the Catacombs), our people recovered certain boxes of personal property. This property evidently represented booty taken by the Marshal in the Abyssinian campaign. Of chief interest are the silver service, Coptic cross, and ceremonial garments of Haile Selassie and certain of his chieftains." Donovan wanted Roosevelt to pen a personal note to Haile Selassie, to whom he planned to return his belongings.

The recovery of the emperor of Ethiopia's royal property was just an incident of the day in February 1945, as OSS groups and agents operating at scattered points on the globe sent their reports to Washington. In Switzerland Allen Dulles had received word through Maj. Max Waibel of Swiss Intelligence that the million German troops in northern Italy were considering surrender to the OSS. Dulles kept Donovan in close touch with the negotiations, which he called Operation Sunrise.

The Combined Chiefs of Staff approved Dulles's plan, and a meeting was arranged at Caserta to draw up the armistice. It remained only to inform the Soviet Union, which had long since discovered Dulles's activities through its agents in Switzerland. When Ambassador Harriman told Foreign Minister Molotov in Moscow, the Russian immediately announced that the Soviet Union must send three officers to Bern. Moscow was advised that nothing was to be done at Bern, that the armistice meeting was to be held in Caserta. The Soviets replied that if they couldn't be represented in Bern, they wouldn't go to Caserta either. They demanded that the negotiations be broken off.

Stalin and Roosevelt considered the matter. Stalin accused the United

States of negotiating with Field Marshal Kesselring, in Dulles's words, "to open up the German front to permit the American Army to advance. In return for this military assistance, the United States and Britain had agreed to secure easier peace terms for Germany. In accordance with this agreement, the Germans already had moved three divisions from the Italian front to the Russian front, and the American Army had been permitted to advance in Germany."

Roosevelt was furious at the Russian dictator's Byzantine charges. Operation Sunrise dragged on through March and April, to Donovan's frustration.

Donovan was also encountering frustration at home, where his proposals for a peacetime intelligence agency had run into a storm of opposition. "His plan was beset with conflicting views," said Allen Dulles. "Some in our government would have the new organization report to the Joint Chiefs of Staff—as did OSS during the war—while others preferred it to be under the Department of State. And there was controversy as to whether one individual could or should be responsible for presenting a consolidated view of the intelligence picture to the policymakers, or whether this should be the collective responsibility of the chiefs of all the intelligence services."

The Joint Chiefs of Staff had submitted the Donovan plan to the army and navy for review; both services spiritedly insisted on keeping control of all their intelligence services. The State Department wished to control all political intelligence. Donovan and his OSS aides were confident that with Roosevelt's support they would be able to persuade the armed forces and the State Department to cooperate with a peacetime central intelligence, but on February 9, the roof fell in.

Donovan, still an early riser, got up at 5:00 A.M., stepped outside his Georgetown front door, and picked up a copy of the *Washington Times-Herald*. He found his name in a front-page headline.

"Creation of an all-powerful intelligence service to spy on the post-war world and to pry into the lives of citizens at home is under consideration by the New Deal," began a story by Walter Trohan.

"The *Washington Times-Herald* and the *Chicago Tribune* yesterday secured exclusively a copy of a highly confidential and secret memorandum fron General (William J.) Donovan to President Roosevelt. . . . Also obtained was a copy of an equally secret suggested draft of an order setting up the general intelligence service, which would supersede all existing Federal police and intelligence units, including Army G-2, Navy ONI, the Federal Bureau of Investigation, the Internal Revenue Agency."

Trohan, working for a virulently anti-Roosevelt newspaper that had been a standard-bearer of isolationist feeling in the United States, had found a way to embarrass the administration. Obviously, somebody had leaked the Donovan memorandum of November 18 to Trohan. Donovan telephoned Otto C. "Ole" Doering, his executive officer.

"Ole, I want you to find out who did this and report to me at nine."

There had been five copies of the Donovan memorandum.

"At nine, I was ready," Doering said later. "I told the General that J. Edgar Hoover had personally handed the memorandum to Trohan. Donovan never said a word."

Other sources later implicated General Strong of G-2 in the leak, and Walter Trohan claimed that FDR himself gave him the information. This could hardly have been the case, for FDR was not the sort of politician who willingly handed a political enemy a knife to drive into his back. Roosevelt phoned Donovan on the afternoon of February 9. He directed Donovan to "shove the entire thing under the rug for as long as the shock waves reverberate."

On February 23 Donovan wrote to the President concerning the "deliberate plan to sabotage any attempt at reorganization of this government's intelligence services," saying, "The characterization of the plan as 'Gestapo' is fully refuted by the specific provision in my paper that the organization have no police or law enforcement functions, either at home or abroad. The entire situation is most disturbing because it looks like an inside job or at least, it was abetted by someone on the inside."

Donovan also suggested to the JCS that the "matter be investigated by those who have the power to take testimony under oath," since General Strong and not J. Edgar Hoover might have been the person responsible for the breach of security.

Roosevelt waited until April 5 before he judged the shock waves were no longer reverberating. "I should appreciate your calling together the chiefs of the foreign intelligence and internal security units in the various executive agencies, so that a consensus of opinion can be secured," Roosevelt told Donovan. "It appears to me that all of the ten executive departments, as well as the Foreign Economic Administration and the Federal Communications Commission have a direct interest in the proposed venture. They should all be asked to contribute their suggestions to the proposed centralized intelligence service."

The next day Donovan set about calling the meeting. He asked each of the heads of the executive departments and agencies to comment on the proposal.

"I am hopeful that the meeting can be held immediately after my return, on or about April 25, from a brief trip to Europe," he wrote to Roosevelt.

Allied armies had crossed the Rhine and were throwing a ring of steel around the German Army in the Ruhr. The war was drawing to a close, and Donovan had urgent preparations to make for the OSS role in Europe after the armistice was signed. By the evening of April 6, Donovan had sent letters to all the agencies mentioned by Roosevelt, and at 9:00 P.M. he and John Wilson, a young aide, left for Paris. They arrived the next day and stayed at the Ritz Hotel in a suite that Hermann Göring had favored. Russell Forgan and David Bruce came from London, and other key men from OSS bases on the Continent joined them to attend a conference held at the Hotel Metropole on the Boulevard des Italiens.

"We all know about the Free French," Donovan said when the subject of France came up. "We've been working with them for three years, but we don't know anything about Vichy French. We'll call them the conservatives."

Adolph Schmidt was directed to find out everything he could about the Vichy French, who also must be counted upon to rebuild their nation if France were again to be a great power.

"My plan for a peacetime central intelligence seemed assured, providing the President continued to support it," Donovan said later. "I had nothing to worry about. I went to bed on the night of April 12 confident that things would work out one way or the other. I dropped off to sleep little knowing that Franklin Roosevelt had suffered a massive cerebral hemorrhage and had died just a few hours before."

OSS in Washington sent an urgent message to the Ritz Hotel. Forgan and Wilson received the message and burst into Donovan's room. Told the news, Donovan stared in silence for several moments. "I'm not surprised," he finally said.

He immediately placed a transatlantic call to Ned Buxton in Washington to confirm the circumstances.

"What will happen now to OSS?" Buxton asked.

"I'm afraid it's the end," replied Donovan.

Donovan knew he must hurry back to Washington to meet with Harry S. Truman, the new President, but he first had to give further instructions to his men in Europe. At the time there was much talk about the diehard Nazis forming a redoubt of resistance in the Alps. Before leaving Washington Donovan had reported to Roosevelt:

> The Nazi Party Intelligence Service (RSHA), controlled by Himmler, has absorbed the Abwehr and the two services are being consolidated into an effective tool, which may be used by the underground after military defeat.
>
> Among other things the report indicates that officers for a German resistance army of between 35,000 and 40,000 men are receiving training in resistance methods and guerrilla warfare at special Nazi schools.

There is also evidence of the caching of supplies and that RSHA has issued directions which, although they have not so far related to continuing guerrilla resistance, have directed intelligence, subversion, and sabotage activities.

To disrupt the Nazi redoubt, OSS mission Iron Cross had been created under Capt. Aaron Bank. "The personnel involved were around 150 German POWs, who had been recruited in French POW camps in January 1945, who claimed they were anti-Nazi," said Bank. "I organized and trained them in pertinent aspects of unconventional warfare and parachuting."

The Iron Cross mission was to parachute into the Inn Valley of the Austrian Alps, where the Nazis were expected to make their last stand. Donovan dined at the Ritz with Bank's staff supervisor from OSS Paris headquarters. He approved of Bank's mission. "Tell Bank to get Hitler" were his final instructions.

Donovan also called Adolph Schmidt to the Ritz. "We don't know where the Russians will stop," he said. "I want you to load up with about ten radio sets and put them in plastic material. Take them into Germany to points behind where the Russians are supposed to stop. Bury the radios 20 to 30 miles apart so that they'll be there in case we want to send some people in once they've taken over."

Donovan left for Washington on April 25, and Schmidt and a team of OSS men with their radios left for Germany.

"We had no trouble passing the Russian lines," said Schmidt. "We handed out cigarettes to the Russian troops. We buried the radios 20 to 30 miles apart pretty much along a line."

Even as Donovan flew back to America, patrols of the U.S. First Army were crossing the Elbe River to make the first Anglo-American contact with Soviet troops at Torgau. On the same day, Russian forces under Marshal Georgi K. Zhukov and Gen. Ivan S. Konev surrounded Berlin. OSS agents soon reported that Hitler himself was trapped in the beleaguered city. He had made no effort to reach the Alpine stronghold that OSS agents had feared would create one last obstacle to Allied victory. On April 28 Benito Mussolini and his mistress were captured and put to death by partisans while attempting to flee to Switzerland. Two days later Hitler married his mistress, Eva Braun, and then committed suicide with her in a bunker beneath the Reich Chancellery. Berlin surrendered on May 2, and on May 7 the official German capitulation was signed by Hitler's successor, Adm. Karl Dönitz, at Allied supreme headquarters in Reims.

Throughout Europe OSS men and women celebrated the Allied victory and then went back to work. Donovan had given orders to gather evidence for war crimes trials and to keep a close eye on the Soviets.

OSS teams were among the first to reach Hitler's death camps and discover the grim proofs of genocide.

On May 7 Bill Donovan and Bill Stephenson were together in Donovan's suite at the St. Regis Hotel in New York when word reached them that Germany had signed the peace. The war was over in Europe. "We both let out a shout of jubilation," remembered Sir William Stephenson. "We embraced in a big hug and did a bear dance of triumph."

Big Bill and Little Bill, partners in intelligence who had done so much in the clandestine world of secret warfare to bring about Hitler's defeat, pranced about the room, whooping with boyish delight at the good news. Then they sat and soberly talked about what the future held for American and British intelligence services once the war with Japan was won as well. Already the principal business at hand was the winning of the peace. To Bill Donovan it seemed that critical mistakes had already been made. He knew that the Soviet Union was an untrustworthy ally and that possible cause for still another great war was being created by the subjection of Eastern Europe to Communist rule. The Yalta agreement supposed that the Soviets would permit democratic institutions and free elections in the countries they occupied, but Donovan knew this would never happen.

On the day of Roosevelt's death, Attorney General Francis Biddle, Secretary of State Edward Stettinius, and Secretary of the Navy James Forrestal had been meeting to discuss Donovan's plans for a central intelligence agency and who might direct it.

"It was generally felt that since the new organization would work on a highly secret plane," reported Biddle, "it should start from scratch and be on its own from the beginning. Its functions would not be the detection of crime like those of the FBI but the gathering and weighing of information in the foreign field. These should be separated from any association with criminal investigation."

The three men agreed that Bill Donovan should direct the agency. The discussion was interrupted by a message for Stettinius to report immediately to the White House. He left the meeting but returned soon with the tragic news that Roosevelt was dead. The three men went to the White House together. There was no longer any point in discussing the fate of the OSS until the viewpoint of the new President was made clear.

As for Truman, it was not at all definite that he wanted a central intelligence agency, and certainly not one with Bill Donovan as director. Donovan was among other things a Republican, and a dangerous one at that, who might still become a candidate for the presidency. Truman was dealing with the most urgent problems of his new presidency, and such things as the surrender of Nazi Germany, the development and use of the atomic bomb, and the proposed meeting with Stalin and Churchill at Potsdam all required his attention. He had no time for Donovan and the future of the OSS until May 14, when he noted in his appointment book, "William Donovan came in to 'tell how important the Secret Service is and how much he could do to run the government on an even basis.' "

Donovan found Truman in a puzzled and, to Donovan, a puzzling mood.

"The OSS has been a credit to America," Truman said. "You and all your men are to be congratulated on doing a remarkable job for our country, but the OSS belongs to a nation at war. It can have no place in an America at peace."

Donovan interrupted to aver that the OSS could play an even more important role in the troubled peace that seemed likely after Japan surrendered. The President studied him for a moment and continued:

> I am completely opposed to international spying on the part of the United States. It is un-American. I cannot be certain in my mind that a formidable and clandestine organization such as the OSS designed to spy abroad will not in time spy upon the American people themselves. The OSS represents a threat to the liberties of the American people. An all-powerful intelligence apparatus in the hands of an unprincipled president can be a dangerous instrument. I would never use such a tool against my own people, but there is always the risk, and I cannot entertain such a risk.

Donovan, now angry, argued with the President in favor of continuing the OSS in peacetime.

"Mr. Truman was very quiet, and when I left, there was no question in my mind that the OSS would be dissolved at the end of the war," Donovan said later.

The entire interview could not have taken more than 20 minutes.

Peace was a long way off yet, and Donovan still had the OSS to run. Operation Sunrise had become a perplexing problem. On the day he died, Roosevelt, believing that the angry showdown with the Soviet Union was over, cabled to Stalin, "The Bern incident now appears to have faded into the past without having accomplished any useful purpose." He was wrong. The Soviets were still incensed and seized upon the Dulles negotiations as grounds for suspicion of the British and Americans. Almost a million Germans and Italian Fascists had surrendered through Operation Sunrise, but because of Soviet obstruction their surrender had been put off until only six days before the final armistice was signed with Germany. This had cost thousands of British and American lives, and both Donovan and Dulles were bitter. Donovan, in particular, believed that Russia's ambition to seize as much of Europe as possible had cost needless casualties and prolonged the war.

Now that victory had come in Europe, Donovan did not put Allen Dulles in charge of OSS Europe as most OSS men had expected. Some said Donovan believed that Dulles had mishandled Operation Sunrise; Dulles's supposed failure, it was said, prejudiced Donovan against him. "I thought Allen was a fine operative," said Donovan after the war, "but I did not think he had the organizational skill to handle all of Europe. It is not true that I was soured on Allen because of Operation Sunrise. Both of us knew that the Soviets were to blame for the delays and after them, Roosevelt for attempting to placate Stalin."

Donovan put Dulles in charge of the OSS office in Germany, where Dulles did important work gathering information that Donovan was to use the coming autumn at Nuremberg. On May 2 President Truman had made Associate Supreme Court Justice Robert Jackson the chief prosecutor for the war crimes trials. On May 22 Justice Jackson went to Paris to meet with Donovan and Gen. Edward C. Betts, judge advocate of the European Theater of Operations, to discuss how the trials might be conducted. Subsequently, Jackson asked Donovan to serve as assistant prosecutor, and the two men traveled to Frankfurt, to Switzerland, and back to Paris to consult with OSS personnel who were gathering war crimes evidence. They met in London with Britain's Attorney General Sir David Maxwell Fyfe and the Soviet ambassador so that the Russians would not think the Western Allies were preparing the war crimes trials behind their back.

On July 7 Jackson and his staff accepted Donovan's invitation to fly in his C-54 to Wiesbaden, where they were lodged at OSS quarters. Lieutenant General Lucius Clay and Ambassador Robert Murphy met them at the Fabian Building to make additional plans for the trials. The first question to come up was where the war crimes trials should be held. Murphy suggested Luxembourg, but the others believed that they should take place in Germany. The Russians had made it clear they preferred the trials to be conducted in Berlin, where they had strong armed forces, but the Americans and the British decided on Nuremberg. The city had important symbolism to the Nazis and there was sufficient housing available for the numbers of people who would be involved.

During the summer of 1945, Donovan struggled to keep the OSS together. "We were winding down our operation in Europe," he recounted later, "but we were still adding to our groups working in Asia."

On July 25 Donovan and R&A chief William Langer flew around the world visiting OSS bases. "The trip might have been called The World's Airports by Midnight," Langer told his wife.

The tour included impromptu visits to the Shatt-al-Arab waterway, oil refineries at Abadan, tea plantations in Ceylon, India, and China. Donovan was concerned with the needs of American intelligence in the Middle East now that Japan also was certainly going to surrender within weeks. Throughout July, American B-29s had been raining bombs and incendiaries on Japanese cities. Donovan's agents were reporting that Tokyo was as much as 40 percent destroyed, and other cities were even more seriously damaged. Before he left Washington, Donovan had been consulted about the ultimatum that the United States, Great Britain, and China were preparing to give to Japan. The first atomic bomb had been successfully tested at Alamogordo, New Mexico, on July 16, and the Allies, meeting at the time at Potsdam, had decided to give the Japanese a chance to surrender before being attacked with the fearful new weapon. Their ultimatum, containing no mention of the atomic bomb, was delivered to Japan on July 26 as Donovan and Langer were flying toward India.

Crossing the Arabian Gulf, Langer and Donovan were issued a new type of parachute, which Donovan undertook to explain to his companion. "You pull the right-hand cord, and it opens up," said Donovan. "Just before your feet touch the ocean, you pull the left cord, and it disengages the chute." It was clearly no time to mistake the left hand for the right hand.

In China Donovan and Langer set about a last inspection of OSS posts. Howard Lyon was given the task of driving Donovan around in a jeep with a machine gun sitting at his side in case of need. "The general visited Chinese and American generals, inspected Field Photo laboratory, and parachute drying sheds," said Lyon.

Lyon also found himself strapping on a .45 automatic to guard the entrance to a house where Donovan was staying. The only visitor admitted was one of Donovan's favorite OSS women.

Donovan continued up to Hsian, where he was met by Gus Krause, the OSS commander for northern China. The long war with Japan had exhausted the Chinese Nationalists. Inflation and corruption in the government were fueling demands for military and political reform. From their Yenan base Mao Tse-tung's Reds appealed for revolution. Communist partisans not only were attacking the Japanese but were extending communist control in anticipation of the day when the war with Japan would end and an all-out struggle with the Nationalists could commence. Donovan was with Krause, studying the Chinese situation, when on August 6 news came that the atomic bomb had been dropped on Hiroshima.

"Donovan knew that the bomb was going to be dropped," recalled Krause. "I remember he said, 'It'll stop the war in a hurry.' "

With the explosion of the atomic bomb on Nagasaki two days later, the Russians attacked the Japanese in Manchuria.

"The Japanese had planned to fight a last-ditch battle in Manchuria," said Krause. "There were warehouses by the mile, full of equipment and material. Donovan and the OSS tried to persuade Washington to prevent the Soviets from seizing these vital warehouses, but no, our government was unwilling to offend Old Joe. It wasn't right for America to work against Russian interests. As a result, all of this equipment and material was seized by the Russians and turned over to Mao Tsetung."

Donovan knew he must press for American action in the face of the Soviet move when he returned to Washington.

"He knew he had a difficult problem," said Krause. "The very OSS was about to be dismantled, and he was anxious for it to continue. We were having lots of trouble in China with the damned Russians. They were not only invading Manchuria but had crossed the Great Wall and were advancing on Peking. We had 20 OSS men against a brigade of Russians in our area. They were pushing us around as if we were children."

On his last night in Hsian, Donovan ate dinner in the OSS mess hall. "All of the OSS group was there," remembered Mitchell Werbell. "I was a Second Lieutenant, way below the salt, but after dinner, the general decided to go with me to buy jewels—rubies, Alexandrite, this and that and the other thing."

Everything that Donovan bought, Werbell bought, confident that the OSS chief would certainly know a valuable gem when he saw it.

"I sent my gemstones home with General Donovan," said Werbell, "and he promised to mail them to my wife."

Before his plane took off for the flight back over the Hump to India, the pilot asked Donovan and Langer if they had chutes.

"No," they both replied.

"Anybody have a chute for these guys?"

There was no answer.

"Well, I guess I'll have to fly safely."

In India a Donovan aide bought a beautiful vase for $50. He later had doubts.

"Bill," he said to Donovan, "I think I've been had."

"What difference does it make?" asked Donovan. "It's just as beautiful."

The plane flew on to the Philippines and then to San Francisco. When they landed on August 13, Donovan and Langer discovered that Japan had surrendered. By noon of the following day they were in Washington.

At home, Mitchell Werbell's wife took the stones he had bought to a hometown jeweler. "Why didn't you get more?" he demanded.

Then she took the stones to Tiffany's, where a more practiced jeweler examined them beneath a glass. "You have some very nice pieces of jeep taillight," he said.

"Bill Donovan had a bagful of stones," Werbell observed, "and I had only a few."

The aide who had bought the vase took it to the Metropolitan Museum in New York City.

"It is worth at least two thousand dollars," he was told.

Intelligence reports continued to come in from all over the world, and Donovan went on forwarding the vital information upon which policy decisions might be made to the President. When Donovan paid a visit to President Truman, both men were cordial, but Donovan realized that the termination of the OSS was close at hand. He assured Budget Director Harold Smith that he was liquidating the various overseas operations and that he himself wished to return to private life by the end of the year, or at least by February 1, 1946. Actually, he had no desire whatsoever to return to private life, but he knew the OSS was doomed. On August 25 Donovan wrote to Smith:

> In our government today, there is no permanent agency to take over the functions which OSS will then have ceased to perform. These functions, while carried on as incident to the war, are in reality essential to the effective discharge by this nation of its responsibilities in the organization and maintenance of peace.
>
> It is not easy to set up a modern intelligence system. It is more difficult to do so in a time of peace than in a time of war.
>
> It is important therefore that it be done before the war agency has disappeared so that profit may be made of its experience and know-how in deciding how the new agency may best be conducted.

Men and women began to leave the OSS. On September 13 Donovan brought René Dussaq to see the President in recognition of Dussaq's heroism with the French Resistance. Truman was properly affable, but later in the day he gave the go-ahead to Budget Director Smith to finish off the OSS. Smith reported on his September 13 conference with the President: "I referred briefly to the Office of Strategic Services and to the fact that General Donovan . . . was storming about our proposal to divide the intelligence service. The President said that Donovan had brought someone into his office this morning, but they did not talk about this matter. The President again commented that he has in mind a broad intelligence service attached to the President's office. He stated that we should recommend the dissolution of Donovan's outfit even if Donovan did not like it. I told the President that this was precisely my attitude."

On September 20, Smith was back at the White House. "When I gave the President the order on OSS for his signature," he stated, "I told him that this was the best disposition we could make of the matter and that General Donovan would not like it."

President Truman glanced over the documents and signed the order. How was Donovan to be told? Smith suggested that the President should call him to the White House, but Truman had no desire to confront Donovan. The President directed Smith to deliver the order, but when Smith returned to his office, he was embarrassed at the prospect of taking the order and an accompanying letter to Donovan. So he sent his assistant, Donald Stone.

"The President doesn't want to do it, and I don't want to do it," Smith told Stone, "but because I can, I'm ordering you to do it."

Stone saw Donovan at OSS headquarters. "When I delivered the document," he said, "Donovan took it with a kind of stoic grace. He knew it was coming, but he gave no outward indication of the personal hurt he felt by the manner in which he was informed."

Truman scaled down espionage and covert operations and placed them in a Strategic Services Unit in the War Department. R&A and the intelligence briefing and reports sections were given to the Department of State. All over the world, field operations halted or went awry. Donovan wrote to Arthur Krock of the *New York Times:*

> I called you the other day, but missed you and take this means of saying good-bye, as I am leaving for Germany within a few days. I could not go without telling you how grateful I am for your support in what our outfit tried to do. I think especially of your article which came out the very moment the Budget Director's plan came out, the effect of which is to destroy an intelligence system at the very moment when we need it most.
>
> I do not speak of OSS because I think as I often told you, it is better for that to end its life with the war. I speak of the principle of intelligence. It is strange that at the moment when both the French and the British are modeling their systems upon what we did during the war in the consolidation of functions, that we should go back to the 18th-century idea of having it in a Foreign Office.

Jim Murphy was less restrained. "It was a disgraceful and irresponsible business," he said. "Truman summarily dismissed his only intelligence chief and did not even trouble to observe the customary ritual of sending for him personally."

On September 28, 1945, about 2,000 morose OSS men and women crowded into the Riverside Roller Skating Rink on the Potomac flats below the headquarters buildings. They listened attentively when Bill Donovan stepped to a dais to talk.

> We have come to the end of an unusual experiment. This experiment was to determine whether a group of Americans constituting a cross section of racial origins, of abilities, temperaments, and talents could

meet and risk an encounter with the long-established and well-trained enemy organizations.

How well that experiment has succeeded is measured by your accomplishments and by the recognition of your achievements. You should feel deeply gratified by President Truman's expression of the purpose of basing a coordinated intelligence service upon the techniques and resources that you have initiated and developed.

This could not have been done if you had not been willing to fuse yourselves into a team—a team that was made up not only of scholars and research experts and of the active units in operations and intelligence who engaged the enemy in direct encounter, but also of the great numbers of our organization who drove our motor vehicles, carried our mail, kept our records and documents, and performed those other innumerable duties of administrative services without which no organization can succeed and which, because well done with us, made our activities that much more effective.

When I speak of your achievements that does not mean we did not make mistakes. We were not afraid to make mistakes because we were not afraid to try things that had not been tried before. All of us would like to think that we could have done a better job, but all of you must know that, whatever the errors or failures, you have done an honest and self-respecting job. But more than that, because there existed in this organization a sense of solidarity, you must also have the conviction that this agency, in which each of you played a part, was an effective force.

Within a few days each one of us will be going to new tasks whether in civilian life or in government work. You can go with the assurance that you have made a beginning in showing the people of America that only by decisions of national policy based upon accurate information can we have the chance of a peace that will endure.

It fell to OSS Deputy Director Ned Buxton to speak of Donovan at the farewell gathering.

Let me say as simply as I can that we are very proud to have stood with him at Armageddon. At the outbreak of global war, he was given a fantastic assignment—to create and operate a secret intelligence agency after the enemy had erected its barbed wire and contrived every conceivable scheme to make himself impregnable. The General created the organization; he formulated the program, he devised the tactics; he penetrated the barriers. He personally attended the invasions. . . .

You were a legend of gallant combat leadership in the First World War.

It would seem that a very full and honorable lifetime of unique experience and training had unconsciously prepared you for your role in World War II.

When Buxton finished speaking, the entire audience of 2,000 filed past Donovan so that each could shake his hand. He called them by name, joked with them, and thanked them for their service. Then they all returned to their offices to finish up the last day of the OSS.

It remained for an OSS wag to send out a bulletin to all stations. Its classification was *Arcanissimum,* its number *ultimum.* It was addressed to *Urbi et orbi;* the subject was *Tempora mutantur, nos et mutamur in illis.* Its origin was *E septime circulo* in the theater of war *infernus.* On the face of the message was the sketch of a tombstone inscribed *Hic Jacet Inconsecrata in Terra Infans Illicitus Gulielmi Donovan Intempeste Leortus, Perum Quiden Tarde Occisus, Quem Nomines O.S.S. Nuncupare Solebant Resurgan (??) Natus Est MCMXLI obit MCMXLV Siste Viator, Pro Infelicem, Lacriman Relinquite.*

On the base of the grave marker was imprinted BUY WAR BONDS!

A little pot containing one flower stood before the tombstone.

PART FOUR

The
Cold War
Years
1945–1959

36

Bringing the Nazis to Trial

ONE OF DONOVAN's last acts as director of the OSS was to send a memorandum to all OSS men who were working on war crimes investigations to continue their activities under the direction of the general counsel. At the end of September he flew to Germany to take up his duties as assistant prosecutor.

"We are awaiting the General, who no doubt is busy winding up OSS," General Counsel James Donovan (no relation to William Donovan) wrote to his wife from Berlin. "You probably know that it goes out of business on Oct. 1. So far as I know, however, it's almost a paper change for administrative purposes, and I'll go right on liquidating its affairs for the War Department."

Donovan arrived on October 2 at OSS quarters, which were in a country house in the Wansee Lake region near Berlin which, as James Donovan said, "was strafed by Russian planes but otherwise undamaged." Donovan consulted with his still loyal OSS men. That evening, along with Ambassador Murphy, Donovan looked at a harrowing motion picture that Field Photo had made of the Nazi concentration camps.

In a few days Donovan and his staff left for Nuremberg, which had been badly shattered by British bombing and the siege by the American Seventh Army. "You simply cannot imagine the result," wrote James Donovan to his wife.

> It is the most complete picture of devastation that could be conceived. You stand in the "Grand Hotel" (about 50 percent of which is intact, but frightfully damaged) and so far as you can see it looks like the ruins of Carthage. You can drive for ten minutes in any direction and cannot see a building standing. The damage to London is negligible compared with this. The walled city is simply a huge mass of rubble, twisted steel and great concrete slabs. Parts of the wall can still be seen in places; but very little of it. I cannot believe that this city could be rebuilt in anything less than a century. I think they would be better off to allow it just to stand— and begin to build on another site.
>
> Where the people who survived now live is beyond me. They are fed in bread lines, and you see some walking along the streets in the day, looking dazed and haggard. If we are going to establish in our trial—the main point—that to plan and launch a war of aggression is a crime, punishable under international law, we certainly came to the right place in which to hold the trial.

Hundreds of SS prisoners were working on the Criminal Courthouse to put it in condition for the trial. Bill Donovan's office in the courthouse was directly across from that of Justice Robert Jackson, who was chief prosecutor.

"The prisoners, Göring, Ribbentrop *et al,* are housed in a big jail just behind the courthouse," wrote James Donovan. "From a window across from my office you can look down into the exercise yard and see them walking around. They are not allowed to speak to each other and are under heavy guard."

In Nuremberg Bill Donovan lived in a suburban house that had been unscathed by the war, under heavy army guard. That die-hard Nazis might try to assassinate either Jackson or Donovan seemed very possible. Ruth Donovan and David's wife, Mary, had come to Nuremberg to join Donovan.

One day Adolph Schmidt in Berlin received a message from Donovan to bring some investigation reports to Nuremberg. He drove down from Berlin. "When I walked into the general's residence, Donovan was in the library declaiming in German," Schmidt remembered.

"I never knew you could speak German," Schmidt said.

"Yes, I spent time studying it. I've spent considerable time in Germany over the years. I like the language and the people. I am to be the prosecuting attorney."

"You're going to do it in German?"

"I'm going to do it all in German so the men in the box know just why they're being tried. We'll be the laughingstock of the legal profession if we don't show that this war has been criminally conducted."

Schmidt expressed agreement.

"Jackson is saying that Hitler and his men lost the war, shoot them," continued Donovan. "This won't do. Otherwise, if we lost a future war, our politicians could be shot too."

OSS reports, particularly those from the German underground, provided Donovan valuable information with which to interrogate the captive Nazis. There were extensive reports on the atrocities of the Holocaust and the oppression of slave labor; other documents detailed how various Nazi leaders had stolen art treasures from all over Europe; Field Photo had assembled a collection of photographic evidence of Nazi horrors.

Hermann Göring was second only to Hitler in the Nazi hierarchy, and Donovan spent ten days alone interrogating him. One day he confronted Göring with details of his looting. Göring, who had charged his entire staff with collecting, had assembled a vast store of art objects. He had intended to open a new museum to house the art, according to the report, "either in Berlin or at Counhall, in which case a railroad was to be built from Berlin to bring tourists."

Time and again Donovan accused Göring of kindling the Reichstag fire that had given Hitler the excuse to crack down on the political left and strengthen his hold on the levers of power.

"You must at least be convinced that with death staring me in the face, I have no need to resort to lies," Göring said to Donovan. "I give you my word that I had nothing whatever to do with the Reichstag fire." Donovan was not convinced, but he passed on to other subjects.

"You are walking on the edge of the grave," Donovan told Göring, "and the question is only how you will go in, whether your people will learn that you were a man to be respected for what you did for Hitler or to be despised."

Donovan called on Fabian von Schlabrendorff, an OSS German resistance leader, to help him with Göring. Donovan considered it critical to shorten the trial as much as possible. He was of the opinion that if Göring would assume responsibility as the representative of Hitler for most of the war crimes, his conviction, sentencing, and execution would be quick. Other top Nazis would then be tried, but the rank and file could be turned over to German courts. Donovan believed that if the Germans themselves tried the Nazis, they would share the responsibility for their condemnation and would help to atone for their nation's crimes against humanity. Moreover, it seemed to Donovan that the trials should not be conducted under Anglo-Saxon law but under German law, which the Nazis had violated. Only then would the German people as a whole share in the world's revulsion for the Nazis and prevent the rise of another Hitler in the future. Could Schlabrendorff suggest how he might talk Göring into a deal? After all, the Nazi knew full well that his execution was already a certainty.

Schlabrendorff suggested that Donovan put on full uniform with all his medals in place to visit the medal-conscious Göring and appeal to his sense of honor as an officer and a gentleman. Donovan arrived at Göring's cell in full uniform, displaying his formidable assortment of decorations, and Göring was impressed; here was a man who owned more medals than he did. Göring agreed to the arrangement, and Donovan turned his attention to Rudolf Hess.

"Tomorrow we are going to make a very interesting experiment," James Donovan wrote to his wife on November 7, "and I will write you all about it. Hess has been claiming that his memory is bad and that he suffers from total amnesia. He met Göring in one of the rooms and simply passed him by. Well, we are going to take him in tomorrow and run for him some sound movies of himself when he was at the height of his power, next to Hitler in all Germany. I wonder what will go through his mind when he sees them. We're quite sure—by medical testimony, etc.—that he is a faker. But I'm going to sit there and just watch his reactions."

On the next day Hess, his hands handcuffed to two guards, sat in a projection room and watched newsreels taken during the days of his ascendancy. While he gazed at the screen, Bill Donovan, Jackson, James Donovan, and Russian and American psychiatrists studied him. A shot of a "Party Day" in Nuremberg flashed on the screen while Wagnerian music thundered through the room. On the screen Hitler did a small jig of joy when Hess led the multitudes in a chant of *"Sieg Heil! Sieg Heil!"* Hess sat impassively. When the movie had finished, Col. John Amen, the chief interrogator, asked Hess in a gentle voice, "Do you remember?"

Hess tried to brush his hands across his eyes, but the handcuffs prevented him. "I recognized Hitler and Göring," he finally said. "I recognized the others, but only because I heard their names mentioned and have seen their names on cell blocks in this jail."

"Don't you remember being there?"

"I don't remember. I must have been there because obviously I was there, but I don't remember."

The guards led Hess back to his cell, and the experiment was over.

When Donovan talked to Jackson about the arrangement Göring had agreed to, the chief prosecutor would have none of it. The two men also had sharp differences about legal procedures. Justice Jackson was in favor of employing mainly documentary evidence, whereas Donovan held that the major emphasis should be placed upon the testimony of defendants and German witnesses. Only then, he thought, would the Germans accept the guilt of the Nazis.

Robert G. Storey, the distinguished Texas jurist, was on Jackson's staff at Nuremberg. He said later:

> One of my most embarrassing experiences was to be caught in the middle of the rather tense dispute between Justice Jackson and his associate, General Donovan.
>
> General Donovan was very strong in his belief that a great many enemy witnesses should be used in lieu of documents. He argued that documents would be dry and uninteresting. On the other hand, Justice Jackson and some of us contended that we could not afford to take a chance with enemy witnesses, especially when we had absolute and convincing proof of the guilt of the various defendants through their various documents and admissions.

Jackson and Donovan discussed their viewpoints with Storey in private conversations, and he attempted to reconcile their differences.

"Finally, General Donovan would not yield and neither did Justice Jackson," said Storey. "I was present when the break came."

Donovan argued that "it is not convincing to read in the court long indictments and the exhibits in substantiation." Donovan reminded Jackson that most of the important documents had been provided by the OSS. They had their value, but they could not make up the entire case. "The important thing," he contended, "is to prove German national guilt through the lips of the German leaders who were responsible."

"Bill, you may be right," said Jackson, "and I think I am right, but it so happens that I have the responsibility and I am going to run this case according to my best judgment. I highly respect you, personally and officially, but it is an honest difference of opinion."

"Bob, you may be right, but I believe you are wrong. If that is your final decision, I shall return to the States and withdraw from the prosecution."

Donovan was convinced that Jackson's position was legally and politically unsound. He explained to Adolph Schmidt that he "wanted to make it clear to the German people that the trials were not a retribution but were because of the Nazis' unprecedented outrage against humanity."

"Jackson," claimed Donovan, "was not interested in principles, but he only wanted to execute the Nazis."

Shortly after the trial began, Donovan left for the United States. At his Georgetown home he talked off the record with newspaperman James Wright. Donovan told Wright that he "never was for mass trials, and attempting to hold the German General Staff as a staff responsible for military deeds or misdeeds. He wanted to try individuals and hold them for their individual wrongs."

Donovan said that he was for "sucking Schacht, Göring *et al* into the cases as witnesses, so that the German people would be impressed by the testimony of their own leaders with German national guilt."

Aside from talking to Wright, Donovan kept his peace. Ostensibly he had returned to America because, now that the war was over, his private law practice required his attention. He did not think it appropriate to air his disagreement with Justice Jackson.

Donovan had kept in touch with the men responsible for turning his OSS into the truncated Strategic Services of the War Department, and he had reason to be satisfied with President Truman's choice of his former aide Brig. Gen. John Magruder as the director. Magruder was assisted by Lt. Gen. William W. Quinn, who as the colonel in charge of G-2 of the Seventh Army had worked closely with him during the landings in southern France. Unlike other G-2 officers, Quinn had also listened carefully to OSS reports on the German buildup that led to the Battle of the Bulge, and had, in fact, been awarded the Distinguished Service Medal for his accurate assessment of German intentions as the battle progressed.

"I had been on my way to reassignment to Japan," recalled Quinn.

"I was getting my DSM at the Pentagon on September 30, 1945, when I was handed a note to go and see Gen. Clayton Bissell of G-2."

"You're going over to OSS," said Bissell. "Your orders for the Pacific have been changed. You are to report to General Magruder as his executive officer."

"I don't know anything about it," said Quinn.

"You don't have to. This is by order of President Truman."

During the last days of the OSS, Donovan had received a phone call from President Truman, requesting his views on who might be the director of the Strategic Services Unit (SSU).

"It can't be somebody from the ONI, the FBI, or others who fought the OSS," Donovan told the President. "Put in Bill Quinn."

It was decided between the President and the retiring OSS director that Magruder would be given the job in order to provide initial continuity, but since he was suffering from painful arthritis and wished to resign, Magruder would turn it over to Quinn as soon as possible.

"Donovan had gone to Germany the day before Magruder took over his office," said Quinn. "I'd seen him just before then at a cocktail party in Georgetown. 'If there is anything I can do to help you, just give me a call,' he said."

Quinn and Magruder were astounded at the speed with which Donovan had left the OSS. "You know, it's an amazing thing, that Donovan can walk out and not have the umbilical cord stringing behind him," said Magruder.

Upon his return from Nuremberg, Donovan discovered that the squabble concerning the future of a peacetime central intelligence service to take the place of his wartime OSS was continuing in the Truman administration. At least President Truman had come to a new appreciation of Bill Donovan's contribution to the Allied victory. As OSS sources dried up, the flow of significant intelligence to Washington dwindled. By the end of 1945 Truman found himself increasingly in the dark about what was going on abroad. He determined to award Donovan the Oak Leaf Cluster to the Distinguished Service Medal that he had won in World War I. Donovan was to come to the White House on January 11, 1946, to receive the honor. Most people given such a high award wanted the press and various dignitaries and friends in attendance, but not Donovan.

"When asked what guests he wished to invite, [Donovan] expressed the wish to come alone," Truman noted in his desk calendar.

At 12:45 P.M., the appointed time, on the appointed day, Donovan arrived at the White House. The President presented him the Oak Leaf Cluster and made appropriate remarks about Donovan's great service in "secret intelligence, research and analysis, and the conduct of unorthodox methods of warfare in support of military operations." Donovan was credited with "intelligence and operational aid to theater commanders, the JCS, State Department, and other government agencies."

Donovan had been given new honor by the President for the accomplishments of OSS, but the SSU, which had declined to perhaps a 20th of the dimensions of the OSS, was in trouble. Quinn and Magruder found themselves under heavy attack from J. Edgar Hoover, who claimed the SSU had been infiltrated by the communists.

"The problem became serious," remembered Quinn. "It was a typical J. Edgar Hoover vendetta. SSU had obtained [information showing] the full armaments of the ships of the Soviet Baltic fleet. I went to the admiral in charge of Naval Intelligence with a satchel loaded with the details, but he wouldn't accept the material."

"It is probably a deception," said the admiral. "You're riddled with communists."

Quinn telephoned J. Edgar Hoover. "My name is Quinn," he said. "I'm director of the SSU."

"I know," said Hoover.

"May I come over and see you?"

"What is your problem?"

"I'll tell you when I see you."

Quinn met with Hoover at FBI headquarters the next morning, and he told him of the admiral's remarks. "I want you to vet each of my principal officers," he finished.

Hoover leaned back in his chair. "This is beautiful," he said with satisfaction. "The Donovan days are over."

"Hoover sent me a liaison officer," said Quinn. "In other words he made a real penetration, but he was very nice about it. The FBI began vetting . . . fingerprints, photos, backgrounds. When he was finished, we were in the club. I took the satchel of Soviet Baltic fleet plans back to the ONI, and the admiral accepted them."

Donovan was now engaged again in his law practice, but this did not keep him from following the travails of the SSU with more than passing interest. One day he asked David Bruce and Russell Forgan to meet with him. The men talked over dinner at Bruce's Georgetown home. By now Magruder had resigned because of ill health.

"You've got to help Quinn," Donovan said. "He is getting clobbered, and the concept of central intelligence is at stake."

From that day on, a number of former OSS men met from time to time at the Bruce home and advised Quinn on problems that he chose to present to them. At the same time Donovan also asked Larry Houston to be his go-between with an administration committee working on a new plan for a central intelligence service.

"We'd breakfast at the Metropolitan Club or sit in the garden and talk about things," said Houston.

The OSS might be part of the past, but this did not keep its former chief at home. John B. Okie, formerly of the OSS, who was to work for Donovan again in the forthcoming World Commerce Corporation, remembered a Donovan visit to Europe.

> The General came through Paris after the war and asked me if I would go with him to Baden-Baden to visit General [Lucius] Clay. He wanted to go by car and wanted me to pick him up at the Ritz at 4:00 A.M., which I did. One can imagine that, after a late night, a cup of coffee was at the top of my list. Whenever I suggested we stop for coffee or go to a men's room, the General would ask me one of his simple, early-morning questions to divert my attention from stopping; a question like, "Jack, how do you feel we should organize our intelligence network so as to be in a position to battle all the political and civil brush fires that will be set by the Russians in the underdeveloped countries of Asia and Africa?"

Clay gave a reception and dinner for Donovan, at which there were about ten other guests. Okie was relaxing over a drink at the reception. "After a shower, General Donovan came down and called me away from my hard-earned drink to inquire if I had found out who all the other people in the room were," he recalled, "and why they were there. The General was most disappointed that I did not have a complete list of answers."

Donovan returned from his foray into Germany with a better knowledge of the Soviet attitudes toward their presumed allies. Then on March 1, 1946, he made an impassioned speech before the Overseas Press Club in New York. Truman had announced a new Central Intelligence Group. Donovan pointed out that faulty intelligence had seriously injured the nation in the past, and now he said that the CIG would fail since it lacked both civilian control and independence. The United States must have a coordinated, centralized, and civilian-directed intelligence service that would be independent of other departments. The CIG was responsible to the National Intelligence Authority, which Donovan in a speech on April 10 in New York characterized as "a good debating society but a poor administering instrument."

At the same time that Donovan played an important role in the debate on a peacetime intelligence for America, he directed the new International Rescue Committee, which was formed to aid refugees from Soviet conquest. In addition, together with Edward Stettinius and Sir William Stephenson, he founded the British American Canadian Corporation, with the purpose of starting up commerce and industry in countries devastated by the war or in the path of Soviet subversion. Donovan registered the corporation in Panama to give it certain tax advantages and by April was pressing his associates for action. On April 23, he wrote to Stettinius, "This country has emerged from the war as a dominant economic power. It is the only significant creditor nation and can capture at will almost any export market from which it is not artificially barred. While the movement is temporarily held in check by lack of shipping space and uncertainty as to possible political restrictions in certain areas, soon we shall be exporting in great volume credit, commodities, technique, and specialist manpower."

Donovan also told Stettinius that American business with few exceptions was "unprepared by experience and ill-equipped in personnel to make a complete success of foreign commerce under postwar conditions. The mechanisms and structure of foreign trade are obsolete. They date from clipper ship days and are cumbersome and anachronistic in these days of air freight and radio telephone." Donovan and Stettinius both had farms in Virginia, and during the summer of 1946 they met first at Stettinius's Horseshoe Farm and then at Donovan's Chapel Hill Farm to continue the discussions.

Meanwhile Donovan was establishing a secret office in uptown Manhattan, which he made the center of a private intelligence web. For years before World War II and immediately after the war, he had directed his own agents from his 2 Wall Street law offices, but now he put a brilliant young Armenian refugee at the head of a staff whose responsibility was to keep in touch with undercover representatives located in strategic places. Donovan was no longer director of the OSS, but he had no intention of letting his knowledge of what was going on in the world be reduced to what he read in the newspapers.

Periodically the uptown office would provide Donovan with books, articles, and reports to read. He perused these at his usual breakneck speed, underlining what he considered to be important points that the staff should investigate at greater length. The passages that Donovan marked off were typed on cards and filed in top-secret cabinets. Donovan not only wanted to understand the world around him, but he had decided to write a vast history of intelligence in the western world since the Byzantine Empire.

After the Central Intelligence Agency was created in Washington in 1947, a CIA liaison officer was appointed to maintain contact with the former OSS chief, who in the shadow world of postwar conflict continued to be America's master spy. Top government officials concerned with the conduct of America's foreign policy asked Donovan for his opinions and confidential information, since in many cases he seemed to be better informed than the CIA. Strikingly, Donovan did not tell his law partners of his intelligence network, except Richard Heppner. Heppner, who had served Donovan as director of OSS Detachment 202 in China, acted as Donovan's alter ego in the undertaking. From time to time Donovan met his agents either on his trips abroad or in clandestine rendezvous in New York, Washington, or Chicago.

"On such trips, he had a passion for anonymity," observed one of his agents. "He above all refused to have his picture taken. 'I just want to seem to be an aging little fat man,' he would say."

In July 1946 Donovan visited the Command and General Staff School in an effort to persuade them to "set up a chair on irregular warfare," and he corresponded with Allen Dulles about the safety of former German OSS agents in Berlin in the light of Russian hostility. He involved himself in mining properties in Nova Scotia and considered building hotels, which would be managed by Hilton, in Egypt and Guatemala. At the conclusion of the war Donovan had been awarded a number of honors, including honorary knight commander of the Order of the British Empire, commander of the French Legion of Honor, and first class rank in Thailand's Most Exalted Order of the White Elephant. Now in August, he was retained as legal counsel by Thailand in a border dispute with French Indochina.

By August Donovan also was taking a serious interest in possibly becoming the Republican candidate for U.S. senator from New York. A boom for Donovan for U.S. senator swelled in New York City, and a headquarters was opened in the Hotel Lexington. His supporters ranged from solid Republicans to Eleanor Roosevelt. Nancy Fogarty, who had worked for the OSS in London, was now working for the State of New York, but this did not keep her from volunteering for the Donovan campaign.

"I worked in Governor Dewey's office," she explained. "After hours, I'd go to Donovan headquarters. The women there were nuts about General Donovan. Society ladies would come in after dinner to help out."

Ernest Cuneo had been responsible for swinging Eleanor Roosevelt behind Donovan, and he went to the Donovan Sutton Place apartment to tell him about it. While he was explaining the situation to Donovan, the phone rang.

"It was Tom Dewey," said Cuneo. "He said he would back Donovan if Donovan would back him for the presidency in 1948."

"I don't think you're qualified for president now," said Donovan to Dewey, "and you won't be qualified then." He hung up.

"What job would you like other than being the senator from New York?" Cuneo asked him.

Dewey angrily opposed Donovan, accusing him of being big business and antilabor and antiunion, and when the Republicans met in Saratoga to choose a senatorial candidate, Dewey was instrumental in denying the nomination to Donovan.

Donovan spent many happy weekends at Chapel Hill Farm in 1946. Ruth and he usually stayed in a two-bedroom cottage on the grounds, since David and Mary and their five children lived in the big house. At Easter the five children and their grandfather colored eggs together.

Whenever Bill Donovan arrived at the farm, the children would dash to grab him by the hand and lead him to the stables, where there were ponies to ride. The Donovans were members of the Blue Ridge Hunt Club, and Mary, at least, rode to the hounds on every possible occasion.

The happy family life was tragically marred on New Year's Eve 1946. The hunt club ball that was to take place that night was to be especially lively in honor of Maj. Gen. William J. Donovan, who would celebrate his 64th birthday on the morrow. Preparing for the evening's festivities, Ruth Donovan placed some jewelry in a glass of liquid silver polish in the kitchen. Five-year-old Sheila was playing with the other children outdoors and, feeling thirsty, dashed indoors for a drink. Hastily, she gulped down the glass of what seemed to be water and went into immediate convulsions. The polish contained cyanide of potassium, one of the deadliest of poisons, and Sheila was soon unconscious. David and Mary rushed the child to the hospital in Winchester, 12 miles away, but she was pronounced dead upon arrival. The Donovans insisted that the hunt club ball go on, but the tragedy made it the most cheerless in the history of the club.

37

Donovan's Last Missions

THE BRITISH AMERICAN CANADIAN Corporation, as might be expected of the creature of Donovan, Stephenson, and Stettinius, plunged into developmental projects worldwide. In Guatemala thick stands of white oak were studied as a source of barrel staves for American National Distillers. Representatives explored the prospects of shoe manufacture in Venezuela, where the bottleneck was the lack of tanning facilities for local hides. In Egypt efforts were made to raise the standard of living through such industries as food canning and the manufacture of fertilizers, caustic soda, chlorine, and penicillin. Donovan and Stephenson approached Paul McNutt, who in May 1947 was retiring as governor general of the Philippines, about entering a partnership with BAC to develop industry in the islands. In many cases, former OSS men who were citizens of countries in which BAC had projects acted as principals. Notably, Pridi Phanomyong, who had led the Thai underground in the war, now was working with Donovan again to help create a brighter economic picture for his nation. Prince Waithayakon also was participating.

On September 24, 1947, the British American Canadian Corporation changed its name to World Commerce Corporation. By that time the company was "exporting from the United States heavy machinery, textiles, excavators, earth-moving equipment, motor cars and tractors, fine and heavy chemicals, and certain drugs." It also was importing "botanical drugs in bulk, waxes, gums, seeds, spices, and oils." It was represented in 47 countries.

Not only were Donovan and Stettinius seeing one another regularly on their respective farms in Virginia, but they also met frequently at Stettinius's suite at the Savoy Plaza in New York, where they abstemiously sipped orange juice instead of cocktails at the cocktail hour or breakfasted on bacon and eggs while they made their plans.

"Our purpose," said Donovan, "is to break the logjams that are preventing the renewal of free trade among the nations of the world. Private initiative can achieve more lasting beneficial development in the impoverished nations of the world than can intergovernmental assistance programs. The best way to oppose Communist expansionism is by materially strengthening the challenged societies."

At the same time Donovan favored the program of economic aid to

Europe that came to be called the Marshall Plan. He conferred with George C. Marshall, who had replaced James Byrnes as secretary of state, concerning how U.S. government help might be employed to avert the threatening economic collapse of Europe. Throughout the year Donovan worked for the establishment of a central intelligence organization in Washington. He gave talks, worked through former OSS men who were active with the interim Central Intelligence Group, testified before congressional committees, and otherwise supported the creation of such an agency. When on September 18, 1947, almost two years to the day after his OSS had been abolished, the Congress authorized the Central Intelligence Agency, Donovan was delighted. The new CIA in most important respects followed the blueprint that he had submitted to Franklin Roosevelt three years before. The continued turmoil in the world and the hostile actions of the Soviet Union had convinced most Americans of the need for a central intelligence organization. President Truman had long since come around to that view.

Some of Donovan's friends suggested that he should by all rights be the first director of the CIA, but Truman still did not like him personally, and it was common knowledge that Donovan was not exactly fond of the President. In 1953 Donovan was again talked about as CIA director as an alternative to Allen Dulles, but he was by then 70 years of age and beginning to slow his activities. Even so, a CIA historian noted that "although Donovan was certainly getting on in years, he had a mind which exploded all over the place, whether it was clandestine collection, covert action, or analysis. Bill Donovan would have brought to the CIA the knowledge of certain aspects of the intelligence business that Allen Dulles may have seen and recognized, but never understood."

Donovan may have been slowing down, but in addition to his law practice and World Commerce Corporation activity, he still managed in the postwar years to chair the American Committee on United Europe, which he had formed to bring Europe together as a basis for the reintegration of Germany into Europe and therefore its eventual rearmament.

Donovan's suspicions of the Russians were increased when the Soviets overthrew the government of Czechoslovakia in 1948 to install a puppet Communist regime. He testified concerning the European Recovery Act before the Foreign Relations Committee of the Senate on January 22. Senator Tom Connally asked Donovan to comment on the advisability of a positive approach to rebuilding Europe.

"I think that is right, Senator," said Donovan. "But we do not want to err on the other side and show that we still want to genuflect to appeasement." In dealing with the Russians, said Donovan, it was very important to have their respect.

Donovan, who had early recognized the seeds of World War II, now became an aging Cassandra telling the American people that the Soviet Union's policies were already creating World War III. He told the senators:

> These evidences of Soviet antagonism might have strengthened our understanding of Soviet intentions. But this antagonism should not have caught us off guard. Rather, it should have prompted our leaders to integrate the facts and interpret them, so that the American public could be told what we were called upon to do and why we were called upon to do it. This should have been done long ago. Only now in America and in Europe are we awakening to the existence of the hard fact that the Stalin challenge to our world is indistinguishable from the Hitler challenge— except that the Stalin attack is more thorough and more ruthless.
>
> At the time the proposal of the Marshall Plan became concrete, on December 19, 1947, we learned of the determination of the Cominform to fight it to the death. Our government must have known this just as the man in the street in Italy and France knew that ammunition and supplies were being sent from Russia or its satellite countries to Communists in France and in Italy to be used, if necessary, for the overthrow of the duly constituted governments of these countries.

The European Recovery Act passed and was signed into law by President Truman on April 3. On July 17, Donovan was in Berlin to talk with General Clay about the high-handed Soviet actions there, which had shut off the city from all but air traffic. Donovan recommended to reporters that the United States send a tank column to open the land route to Berlin. "If the Russians are determined to have war," he said, "we might as well have it here as 500 miles farther back."

Later when defeatists argued that his attitude would only serve to make the Soviets behave more savagely, he replied, "If you're afraid of the wolves, you'd better stay out of the forest."

Donovan, himself still very much unafraid of wolves, walked into the forest of intrigue that surrounded the strange murder of George Polk, a CBS news correspondent, in Salonika, Greece. Polk, who was the network's chief Middle East correspondent, was covering the civil war in Greece. The struggle between Greek rightists and leftists had been complicated by the invasion of Soviet-led Bulgarian forces, and the chaotic situation defied easy analysis. Donovan had sent one of his close friends from OSS days into Greece to observe the fighting in northern Macedonia and determine whether Greece had a chance of remaining free of Soviet dominance or would go the way of its Balkan neighbors.

"Providing Greece remains free and democratic, it doesn't matter whether the nation prefers a course to the right or the left," Donovan had instructed his friend. "The real danger to the Greek people comes from across the border. It is important to know whether the Soviets will succeed in taking advantage of the Greek civil war to place the ancient homeland of western democracy under the police surveillance of a Soviet-dominated state."

After two months in northern Greece in the summer of 1947, Donovan's agent was convinced that the Greeks would settle their differences in their own time and that the Soviets and Bulgarians had incurred the hatred of both warring parties except for a relative handful of Greek communists who remained partial to their mentors in Moscow.

"Nobody from the outside is going to conquer the Greeks," Donovan was told, and he acted on this advice, extending activities of the soon-to-be-renamed British American Canadian Corporation into the country with the intention of assisting the Greek economy.

George Polk, considered by his colleagues to be a gifted and objective reporter, set about ascertaining the truth of the situation in Greece. He had published or aired a number of dispatches from Greece that were highly critical of the right-wing government in Athens.

"When a reporter writes this kind of report, he comes under attack by the Royalist right-wingers who are squeezing the country for their own benefit and sending dollars out in diplomatic pouches as fast as possible," Polk wrote to Drew Pearson.

According to *Christian Science Monitor* reporter Constantine Hadjiargyris, Polk said that he had received phone calls naming him as a communist and threatening, "We are going to kill you." Hadjiargyris, a communist agent, may not have reported these calls accurately, but he was at least the man who assisted Polk in his last effort to contact the left-wing guerrillas of Gen. Markos Vafiades. Early in May 1948 Polk, who had been grounded in Salonika when the plane he was taking developed engine trouble, told friends he was going to contact Vafiades. On May 16, fishermen found Polk's body floating just below the surface of Salonika Bay. He was trussed hand and foot with rope, and there was a single bullet hole in the back of his head. Robbery was apparently not the motive. The money was still in his wallet and his wristwatch was on his wrist; but his correspondent's press card had been stolen.

"The autopsy showed," said Leo Hochstetter, a fellow newsman who went to Greece when he heard of Polk's death, "that his lungs were full of water, indicating that he had died by drowning. Presumably the pistol shot had been made after death. His card case was missing, but it later was mailed to the police."

The Overseas Press Club in New York, to which Polk belonged, was outraged by his murder, and Walter Lippmann was directed to form a committee to investigate. Lippmann and Ernest K. Lindley, *Newsweek*'s Washington bureau chief and president of the club, retained Bill Donovan to make the investigation. Donovan, who had close friends from the Greek underground of World War II fighting both with the rightists and the leftists, was in a good position to obtain the facts. He entered the Polk case in June and immediately left for Greece. Secretary of State Marshall cabled the American Embassy in Athens that Donovan had the "blessings of the State Department," and Donovan got in touch with the American ambassador to Greece.

When Donovan arrived in Salonika, James Kellis, who had been the head of the OSS group working in Greece with the anti-Nazi resistance in the north, had joined him. Donovan conferred with C. Moushountis, who was investigating the Polk murder for the General Security Police. Americans with the American Mission for Aid in Greece and the embassy were convinced that the leftists had killed Polk, but Donovan was not at all sure of that. To begin with, Polk's widow, Rhea, a Greek herself, believed that the Greek government was responsible, and Donovan, characteristically, had a high opinion of a woman's testimony. James Kellis was even less certain. On June 18, 1948, he wrote to Guy Martin, who was the assistant counsel to the Lippmann Committee, in Washington, "Up to this moment, I sincerely believed that the Communists were behind the murder . . . now I was not too certain. . . . Many of our officials here were concerned that if the extreme right committed this murder and were discovered, that this may upset our aid program to Greece."

After several months passed, Gregory Stactopoulos, a reporter for *Makedonia,* a daily newspaper in Salonika, confessed to the murder and was tried and sentenced to life in prison. But Donovan's investigators were not convinced that he was even present at the killing. Nevertheless, when Donovan made his report from Salonika on April 21, 1949, he assured Lippmann, "Your committee can be certain that your original purpose has been realized, that no innocent man be framed and no guilty one be whitewashed."

Donovan had, he said, "impressed on Greek officials the necessity of exploring fully the leads which pointed to the Right as well as those pointing towards the Left," but after the Lippmann Committee's report was published, the charge was made that Donovan did his best to block any line of inquiry that would have embarrassed the Greek government. Donovan had undertaken to investigate the Polk case while he was engaged in a number of other important undertakings, which limited the time he spent in Greece. Had he arrived at the truth? He always insisted that he had. Some of George Polk's friends thought otherwise.

"My impression is that Donovan was far too busy and perhaps too innocent of Greek intrigue to do more than hit the high spots," said George Weller, who had lent his only blue suit to Polk when he married Rhea and who had been his best man on that happy day one year before he died.

As a founder of the American Committee on United Europe Donovan was working closely with leaders in Belgium, France, Germany, Italy, Luxembourg, and the Netherlands to bring about European union. On March 29, 1948, Donovan invited prominent Americans to a luncheon at New York's Ritz-Carlton at which Winston Churchill was the off-the-record speaker. Churchill, then out of office, was devoting much of his time to Donovan's committee. He spoke eloquently about conditions in Europe. The committee decided that it could best achieve its goals by working through the Consultative Assembly of the Council of Europe at Strasbourg, and Churchill was entrusted with deciding how the funds the committee had raised were to be used toward this purpose. Donovan and Churchill both believed that the political and economic union of Europe was a prerequisite to restoring European prosperity and security. Donovan chaired another meeting in New York in July and then on August 2 left for Strasbourg to attend the Consultative Assembly. He returned from Europe more convinced than ever that only a united Europe could deter Soviet aggression. On March 3, 1950, Donovan told a House committee, "I believe that we have a stake in Western Europe, one that we must not risk losing because we must wage and win the war in which we now find ourselves, none the less dangerous because it is a subversive and not a shooting war. That is why I believe in the necessity of a united Europe."

Donovan practiced law, but his partners could not help noticing that he no longer made the exhaustive preparations for a case that had so distinguished his work in the 1930s. Nevertheless, when one of his arguments before the Supreme Court did not go well, everyone was complimentary, except for one partner who acidly observed, "You weren't prepared."

The remark made Donovan furious, and the next several times he appeared in court, he was brilliantly prepared. Then his work slumped off again. His energies were failing, and friends noted that he even slept for eight hours at night. Sometimes when a case particularly intrigued him, the old Donovan was still in evidence. In the middle of December 1950 he journeyed first to London and then to Hong Kong with law partner Richard Heppner and Heppner's wife, Betty, to try to prevent the delivery of 71 of Claire Chennault's China National Aviation Corporation airliners to the Chinese Communists. The planes had found refuge in Hong Kong when the Reds took over China, but the British courts threatened to yield to the Communists' demands.

"The issue is drawn," Donovan stated to a group of reporters in Hong Kong, "whether they [the British] are going to support the Communists in their unlegalized position against us, or us in our legal position against them."

The case dragged on in the courts, and Donovan and the Heppners went to India on business. Here again they encountered delays, and they looked for ways to fill their time.

"General, let's go see the Taj Mahal, the most beautiful building in the world," said Heppner, and the three friends went to Agra. As they strolled through the famous mausoleum, Donovan talked about the law case the entire time.

"Gee, wasn't that wonderful?" he commented about the Taj when they returned to their car.

Back in Hong Kong matters remained at a standstill. There was time to spare, and Donovan went sightseeing. He bought a frieze from a Chinese temple and had it crated so he could send it home by air. It turned out to be a masterpiece. Finally, the courts acted. They dismissed Donovan's legal moves, and the case seemed certain to be lost. The battle would have to be carried to higher courts in London.

As he moved about the Far East and Southeast Asia, Donovan's Chinese, Indian, Thai, Burmese, and Japanese friends came to see him, bringing him up to date on what was happening in their part of the world. In Tokyo on his return trip to the United States, Donovan discussed his findings with Douglas MacArthur, commander of Occupied Japan who was also commanding the United Nations forces then engaged in Korea.

On February 12, 1951, Donovan wrote to Secretary of State Dean Acheson and commented:

> Experience would indicate that the Philippines should be considered as a part of a strategic unit which would include the area of the Far East as well as of Southeast Asia.
>
> That our assistance be given the Malay Peninsula because the sea lane between the Peninsula and Sumatra forms the traditional channel between India and the rest of the East.
>
> That Indochina be buttressed because it is the bastion of the Malay Peninsula and of Siam [Thailand].
>
> That while chaos exists now in Burma, that it be reconstituted as a bulwark before India.
>
> That Indonesia be considered as the master key since it is a base not connected with the threatening Asiatic Mainland, yet is backed up by Australia. The Indies secure, would form a protective shield for the Philippines. Formosa would be denied to enemy occupation, and Japan would feel that effective aid was within operable distance.

Donovan anticipated Soviet moves in the area and urged that a "Supreme Commander or High Commissioner with authority and discretion to carry out the political and military policy of the United States" should be designated and "should be authorized and directed to employ such countermeasures as he finds necessary to meet acts of subversion against this area."

Impressed by MacArthur's performance in helping to guide Japan from defeat to prosperity, Donovan had him in mind; but in Washington some people, after reading Donovan's ideas for an American policy in Southeast Asia, immediately thought that the best man for the job would be the former OSS director himself. In making this proposal, Donovan opened the way for his last important service to the United States, a service that was to take him to Thailand, nominally as U.S. ambassador, but in reality with responsibilities going well beyond that office.

Donovan had now become preoccupied with events in Southeast Asia, where a onetime OSS agent named Ho Chi Minh had become disillusioned with America's dalliances with the colonial French and was implementing Soviet policy.

"He was Moscow-trained, of course," said Donovan of Ho, whose wartime reports had been sent to his own desk, "but he might have remained loyal to the West if mossbacked reactionaries had not refused to listen to OSS intelligence on the area concerning the aspirations of the people of the Asian countries. There was a time that Ho asked our OSS representatives for books about Abraham Lincoln and Oliver Wendell Holmes. Why, one of our OSS medics saved his life! He was sick with malaria and dysentery. Then he became our bitter enemy."

Donovan continued his work with the American Committee on United Europe. He assembled statements from 32 leading statesmen in 14 European democracies calling for economic and political integration of the Continent as a practical necessity. Among the leaders who endorsed this viewpoint were Churchill, Vincent Auriol of France, Alcide De Gasperi of Italy, Paul-Henri Spaak of Belgium, and Konrad Adenauer of Germany.

"Only the British Labor Government, the traditionally neutral Swiss, and the Russian-occupied Austrians hold back," Donovan told the press. "Most of the leaders pledge strong support and urge immediate action." Donovan was also able to report that Winston Churchill and the Conservative Party backed the ideal of unity. He threw the weight of his committee behind the French proposal that the "entire French-German production of steel and coal be placed under a joint high authority, within an organization open to the participation of other European nations." He again attended the meetings of the European Consultative Assembly at Strasbourg in 1950. He brought various European leaders such as Robert Schuman, French minister for foreign affairs, and Spaak of Belgium to the United States on speaking tours to help convince his fellow citizens of the need for European unity. Donovan agreed with Winston Churchill when he proposed on the floor of the assembly that the Europeans must establish a European army, and he was optimistic as 1950 drew to an end that Europe might yet become united.

Back in the United States Donovan decided that it was about time he learned to speak French well, and he got in touch with Justin O'Brien of the French faculty at Columbia University, who had served him in the OSS. He asked O'Brien to find a French tutor for him.

"The General speaks some French and wants to improve," O'Brien told prospective tutors. "He has lately even given a speech in French in Lyon, he tells me. Since he is such a dynamo of energy and such a dominant type, he should have someone very good and very sure of himself as a tutor."

O'Brien sent Donovan a bright young linguist named Carl Viggiani, who ended up spending every morning from nine to eleven in Donovan's apartment conversing with him in French. Donovan sent his car for Viggiani each morning and returned him to his home when the lesson was finished.

In July 1952, Donovan went to London to attend the Privy Council concerning Chennault's planes in Hong Kong. Donovan won the case and was jubilant. "This Chennault plane case is the first Cold War victory in the Far East," he wrote to Sen. Tom Connally. "It could be felt all over London.

"Technically this decision applies to 40 aircraft," he said, "but it governs 31 more involved in another suit in Hong Kong, which had not yet reached the Privy Council. Therefore, it passes title to a total fleet of 71 planes with spare parts and appurtenances."

Now Donovan was worried about getting the planes moved from Hong Kong to where they could be "used in ferrying operations and Cold War support all over the world." The planes were at the British military airport on the mainland of China directly across the sea from Hong Kong. "The British and our own people in Hong Kong are afraid they will not be able to protect these planes from Communist sabotage if they have to stay on the field there more than a week or ten days." Donovan urged the British to speed up their legal processes.

During the summer of 1952, he served on the advisory commission of the Citizens for Eisenhower. He also made speeches calling the U.S. policy of containment of the Soviet Union "a futile strategy" that "betrays an ignorance of the nature of the enemy." To Donovan it appeared that the expansion of Communism could not be halted by drawing a political and military ring around the Russians. He likened Communism to a virus that had become endemic in the modern world. Wherever there were poverty and social and political stagnation, Communism would flare up, promising the people freedom and a better life. But it would instead deliver them to Soviet imperialism. The United States and other western nations must, Donovan believed, work to improve conditions throughout the world to prevent new outbreaks of Communism; at the same time captive nations should be encouraged and supported in their struggle against Soviet tyranny.

On October 3, Donovan was happy to receive a letter from Jean Monnet, president of the new European Coal and Steel Community. The Consultative Assembly of the Council of Europe was being called to draft a constitution for Europe. "In this manner," Monnet told Donovan, "we are proceeding to build a United States of Europe. Because Americans understand the importance of this, for themselves as well as for Europe, they have supported and encouraged our efforts. The aid and encouragement of Americans which is marshalled by the American Committee on United Europe has done much to strengthen this great undertaking. Your continued support, now more crucial than ever, will help us greatly to advance toward the full realization of our plans."

"They call me the father of central intelligence," Donovan told a friend when he received the news from Monnet,

> but I would rather be remembered because of my contribution to the unification of Europe. Until the great heartland continent of the West is truly unified there can be no assured future for all of mankind. Today unification is critical because it contributes to the defense of the West, but tomorrow it will be a great source of strength through peace. One day the Iron Curtain will lift and the captive nations of the East will become part of a United Europe. Even Russia, purged by future events of its desire to bully and subdue its neighbors, will be a member, and given the innate genius of the Russian people, a highly respected and valued member. When Europe is truly unified, it will flourish, and Communism will be shown for what it is, not the wave of the future at all, but a dead ideology out of a cruel past which has been employed by cynical masters to control common mankind.

Donovan immediately got in touch with such supporters as Bernard Baruch to raise more funds to support the Europeans in their effort to unite. When Dwight Eisenhower was elected president in November 1952, Donovan was boomed by supporters as a possible secretary of defense. He liked the idea.

"He came to Washington and took a suite," said Guy Martin. "When nobody called him, he became irritated. I told him that he would have to organize a campaign if he really wanted to be secretary of defense. He wouldn't do things that way. He was very destructive of his own interests."

In 1953, the 70-year-old Donovan continued to work for a united Europe, and on April 16, he gave a luncheon at New York's Waldorf Astoria to enable Konrad Adenauer to speak on the subject. That summer Donovan went to Fort Bragg, North Carolina, to see the Tenth Special Forces Group in training. Colonel Aaron Bank, the first commander of the Green Berets, took him into the field to watch his men in action.

"Although it occurred indirectly," said Bank, "there is no doubt that OSS gave birth not only to CIA but also the Green Berets in 1952. All the Green Beret training programs, maneuvers, concepts, and conduct of operations were based on those of OSS. I feel that Donovan should have bestowed upon him the honor and credit for this continuity of the heritage and traditions established through his genius and foresight. Another tribute for his extensive contributions to advance the very important field of unconventional warfare."

Donovan was much impressed by the young men of the Green Berets. In the world of the 1950s and the decades to come, the defense of the western world would in good part depend upon unconventional warfare. The United States must have the means to aid resistance movements wherever necessary without becoming involved in a major military adventure, which would be self-defeating by its very nature.

On July 29, 1953, President Eisenhower appointed Donovan ambassador to Thailand. It was to be his task to evacuate to Taiwan Chinese Nationalist troops who had retreated into Thailand when the communists came to power in China. The soldiers had been attacking the Chinese Reds in Yunnan, and China threatened to invade Thailand to bring an end to the harassment. At the same time Donovan was to make a study of the political, military, and economic situation throughout the nations bordering on China. Donovan immediately got in touch with former OSS people who had remained active in Asia and asked for recommendations. He contacted former agents in the field.

"They're scraping the bottom of the barrel to send out an old guy like me," he told a former guerrilla fighter from Detachment 101 who came to his New York law office in response to his summons.

For a moment he looked his 70 years, but then his eyes twinkled youthfully.

"It is good to have one more challenge to meet," he said.

While Donovan was talking with his old OSS friends, the FBI incongruously was checking his security. In Buffalo an FBI man asked Frank Raichle, Donovan's friend since 1920, whether Donovan's mother and father had been born in the United States. The President might know who William Donovan was, but the Buffalo office of the FBI did not. The Australian foreign minister also knew who he was, and when he heard that Donovan was to be Eisenhower's ambassador in Bangkok, he went to see Gen. Walter Bedell Smith.

"I asked Bedell Smith about General Bill Donovan's appointment as American Ambassador to Thailand," Foreign Minister R. G. Casey wrote in his diary. "As I expected, this was not a chance appointment. He is concerning himself closely with the equipping and training and general strengthening of the Siamese forces. They didn't send such a high-powered man to a relatively small post like Bangkok for nothing. Wherever Bill Donovan goes, something starts to happen."

As would any other ambassador going out to his post, Donovan went to the State Department to meet the Thai political desk officer.

"You'd better find out who's on the political desk," he had been advised by a State Department official. "The political officer can kill an ambassador."

Kenneth Landon was in his office when he heard Donovan's well-known voice in the hall asking to see the political desk officer. He hurried to the door to welcome his old OSS chief. "He fixed me with his blue eyes," remembered Landon, "put his arms around me, and said, 'I'm saved.'"

Donovan might have the friendship and support of the political officer, but Walter Robertson, assistant secretary for the Far East, disliked him. Donovan had shown little patience for the "old China hand" views of Congressman Walter Judd, and Robertson was "Judd's man." One day Donovan walked into Landon's office.

"Kenneth, my boy," he said, "I'm going to Bangkok in just a few days, and I can't get an appointment with Walter Robertson."

"That's outrageous," said Landon. "I'll call his office." When Robertson answered the phone, Landon asked, "What's the problem?"

"Just too busy," said Robertson, and began a tirade.

"I'll let you talk to Bill Donovan!" interrupted Landon, and handed the phone to Donovan, who listened to the angry assistant secretary with a smile on his face.

"Walter, this is Bill Donovan," he finally cut in.

"It was a dirty trick, but Robertson deserved it," said Landon later. "He had to invite Donovan up to see him."

Donovan returned in an hour and gave Landon a bear hug. "I had a very interesting conversation whether he wanted it or not," he said.

Landon went with Donovan to Bangkok, where they arrived in November. Donovan set about the evacuation of the Nationalist troops, which he considered an urgent matter. The Chinese communists had already organized a spurious Thai Autonomous People's Government in Yunnan, and Donovan wanted to remove any pretext for a Chinese invasion. Donovan, Landon, and a small detachment of U.S. Marines went with Thai officials to northern Thailand to arrange for the Nationalist guerrillas to surrender.

"Each group," said Landon, "was to meet us at a certain spot and turn in their weapons."

The first 50 soldiers brought along a 9-by-15-foot portrait of Chiang Kai-shek but not a single weapon. Donovan cabled the U.S. Embassy in Taiwan to get the Chinese Nationalist government to order the men to bring out their weapons as well. Karl Rankin, U.S. ambassador in

Taiwan, did his best to persuade the Chinese Nationalists to send such an order, but he was told that if Donovan did not lay off, they would make public the CIA's involvement with the guerrillas. Rankin cabled Donovan to this effect.

"The Chinese and the Soviets already know," Donovan cabled back, "so keep up the pressure."

Donovan insisted that the soldiers bring out their guns, and from then on they brought out rusty old flintlocks. "They never did turn in their real weapons," said Landon.

Moreover, some of the soldiers themselves never came to the amnesty points where they were to meet Donovan and the Thai officials. In their place they offered boys from Burma's Shan state, whom Donovan rejected at a glance. By patience and determination Donovan was finally able to gather some 4,000 soldiers, about 90 percent of the total. He arranged for trucks to take them to the nearest airport, from where they were flown directly to Taiwan.

"As we hiked along the jungle trails in all that heat from one rendezvous to the next, Donovan walked the legs off of us all, even the young marines," said Landon.

"Uncle Bill, you ought to take it easy," suggested Landon to Donovan. "You're not a young man any more, and you'll die in all this heat."

"What's the matter with that?" demanded Donovan.

Red-faced, perspiring, grown plump instead of stocky, the old hero bridled. He wanted to die in the field, and the jungled mountains of the Thai-Burmese border seemed as good a place as any. When the job was finished, Donovan returned to Bangkok.

Twenty-three-year-old William J. vanden Heuvel, an air force lieutenant, was Donovan's personal assistant. He accompanied Donovan as he now set about strengthening Thailand and making it an integral part of the regional defense. "I had the privilege of sitting in with him at conferences with Nehru, Syngman Rhee, the Generalissimo," he recalled. As Donovan went about his journeys he found himself being tagged by what he at first took to be Soviet agents. Then to his delight he learned that the agents were from the CIA. Allen Dulles apparently did not trust his old mentor.

Ruth Donovan, who in these last years of Donovan's life had drawn close to him again, was with him in Bangkok, and he now showed her the courtly attention and concern that had never failed to win a woman. They enjoyed their time together, and this was to remain so after their return to New York. Their grandchildren came to visit them in Thailand, and so did Carleton Coon.

Coon last saw Bill Donovan alive in Bangkok in 1954. "He and Ruth Donovan and Gordon and Eleanor Browne (also living there) and Lisa Coon and I were about to go riding elephants into a jungle,"

Coon recalled, "to visit a large cave that might have an archaeological deposit on its floor. Bill sent his aide Mr. Rafferty along in his place, because a Donovan grandchild had cut his grandfather's eyeball with a glazed page of the *Saturday Evening Post.*"

The French were at the time fighting the rebellious Vietnamese, and Donovan commented to James Burnham that the fall of Vietnam, Laos, and Cambodia would lead "to the toppling of one after another of the row of dominoes—Thailand, Burma, Malaya, and then next Indonesia and the Philippine Republic right up to New Zealand and Australia."

Taking into consideration geopolitical and strategic relationships, Donovan worked to create a regional system that he still felt must become a "combat theater" under a combined military-political theater command. He had done the intelligence job, but he was now fatigued and not very well, and he no longer had any expectation of becoming the commander of the theater that he proposed. On May 7 Donovan sent his resignation to President Eisenhower.

Eisenhower wrote back on May 26, 1954, that he had "a feeling closely akin to dismay" at the thought of losing Donovan. "Because of the emergency conditions now existing, it is possible that Foster [Dulles, the secretary of state] may ask you to remain for a few weeks extra; however, I assure you that if he does, it will only be for the reason that the situation of the moment is both fluid and difficult. Obviously we need competent and experienced representation in that region.

"In any event, once you return here I shall want to have a talk with you," the President concluded. "Possibly if you cannot be with us longer on a 'full time' basis, there may be some consultative function that would appeal to you."

Donovan returned to the United States in the late spring to talk over the situation with President Eisenhower. He agreed to stay on in Thailand a while longer. "Bill was temporarily in Washington, and had made all arrangements to return to Thailand by way of the Pacific," recalled Tracy Voorhees, a friend who was working with NATO. "I was in Washington, temporarily, and was about to return to my NATO job in Paris. Bill said, 'Well, Tracy, if you are going that way I will go along with you.' So he cancelled all of his reservations to go by way of the Pacific, and went around the world in the other direction as an act of friendship for me."

Donovan stayed with Voorhees in Paris for three days, and when he left, he handed him his black dinner coat. "Tracy, just take this back to America the next time you go, will you? I don't think I will have any need for it in Thailand."

There was a look on his face that suggested he felt he might never have any more need of it.

In Bangkok Donovan threw himself back into his mission, carrying out Eisenhower's new orders. He found himself impatient with the intrigues of the Thai generals and politicians. He spent more and more time with his family or just getting to know the Thai people and their city. One day as Landon and he were driving back into the city, Donovan said, "I want to do something big for Thailand. I want to do something that will help the people. What can I do?"

"Redirect the Mekong across the Khorat Plateau," snapped back Landon. "Build dams, navigation, power, irrigation. You'll really have made an impression."

"You know, that's an idea. I'll go out and survey it."

Donovan sent a series of top-secret reports to Eisenhower covering preliminary investigations of the value of a dam on the Mekong.

"They'll make 150 copies of each report," said Donovan to Landon, "and send one to everybody. In this way the idea will get across. It is important to mark a report 'top secret' to be sure it gets maximum distribution."

In time the Army Corps of Engineers arrived in Thailand to begin work on a great dam, which has indeed provided the Thai people with irrigation water, electric power, and improved navigation.

Eisenhower accepted Donovan's resignation "with extreme reluctance" on September 15, and on October 1 Donovan's law office announced that he was resuming the practice of law. Said *Newsweek* magazine:

> This week Donovan could take a substantial portion of the credit for another achievement—the creation of an anti-Communist bastion in Thailand and the welding of a first-class fighting force in a nation known more for peacefulness than bellicosity.
>
> Donovan stopped Communist infiltration in Thailand. He created an atmosphere of trust toward the U.S. and began operations to help bolster Laos and Cambodia. Donovan's energy and drive captivated the Thai. Despite his 70 years, he moved about the country constantly, getting to know the people. He hustled back and forth between Washington and Bangkok, cutting through red tape to get things done.
>
> Last week, his quiet work paid off. As the Indochinese war limped toward its tragic conclusion, the Thai announced that they would double the size of their training forces and welcome a large American military mission.

Donovan went to Chicago in October 1954 and met with several former OSS men in a suite atop the Conrad Hilton. A violent rainstorm lashed Grant Park below. Gusts of wind rattled the windows as Donovan talked about his mission to Thailand. He spoke of old friends and causes, of strategies that had helped to win the war, of his concern for the situation in Southeast Asia.

"Ho Chi Minh has signed a peace with the French, but it is meaningless," he said. "He will follow the classical Communist doctrine, negotiate when you are weak and the enemy is strong, attack when you are the strongest, but always to wage war. There is no such thing as peace to any Communist unless it is the peace of the grave."

Donovan's face was ashen. His voice had become softer and softer as he talked. He explained in detail his plans for an integrated defense of Southeast Asia.

"It is not essentially a military matter," he said. "It is a political struggle which must be won in the stomachs of the hungry and in the minds of the people. In Washington they think that American military might is the solution to the problem, but any intelligence man knows this is not true."

"General, have you told the President this?" asked a former OSS man.

"I've told everybody I possibly can," he replied, "but the politicians in Washington never listen to any unpleasant truths from abroad that may force them to take action that would be unpopular at home. There is nothing more perplexing than to know what should be done in a critical situation and to have the authority to do the thing in the hands of somebody else who has insufficient background in foreign affairs to make the correct decision."

The night grew late, and the storm mounted in fury. Listening to Donovan, the OSS men realized for the first time that he was an old man and a very sad one.

Nonetheless Donovan still had work to do. He testified before the Clark Task Force of the Hoover Commission, which was investigating the American intelligence establishment, and he became chairman of the National Committee of the International Rescue Commission to help refugees from Soviet-dominated states. In 1956 he went to the border of Hungary to assist the 10,000 Hungarians who had fled their country after Russian tanks put down the Budapest uprising. He raised $1.5 million for the refugees.

"There are two and one-half million refugees in the West who have fled Communist oppression," he wrote in a fund-raising letter. "Each individual is a living witness against the brutality and terror of Communist totalitarianism. In their national committees and governments-in-exile, refugee groups have taken energetic and effective measures of resistance to the Soviets. Their existence is a symbol of successful opposition."

On a day not long after Donovan's return from Hungary, Walter Berry, his secretary, heard him cry out in his office. Berry hurried into the room to find Donovan slumped in a chair, wearily passing his hand over his forehead.

"Are you ill, General?" asked Berry.

"I'm all right, Walter."

But Donovan was not all right. Some months before, at Ruth's insistence, he had gone to see a doctor and had been told that he was suffering from arteriosclerosis. The doctor's advice that he refrain from strenuous work had not kept Donovan from going to Hungary. Now in his office he was having a mild stroke. He would not let Berry send for a doctor. When he felt better, he sent for his car and went home for the day.

Donovan still appeared at 2 Wall Street daily, and on some days his mind seemed as brilliant as ever. On other days he stared uncomprehending at his partners as they explained a legal fine point. He dropped off to sleep at odd moments, and when he walked from the elevator to his car, he leaned on the arm of whoever was walking with him.

On December 12, 1956, sick though he was, Donovan opened a new drive for funds to finance the work of the American Committee on United Europe. "The tragedy of Hungary has shown again the need for such union," he argued. "It proves that Stalin's successors will continue to seek their objectives of force and repression. A united Europe could become a powerful center of attraction for the restless nations of Eastern Europe. Such a union would also be a bulwark against the aggressive designs of world communism."

During the bleak New York months that followed, Donovan kept to his Sutton Place apartment. He rarely went to the office. Then in the last week of March he was overcome with a massive cerebral thrombosis, a blood clot in the brain, and had to be taken to the hospital. Once again he rallied, and he returned to Sutton Place.

"Lying in his bed, he could look out over the Queensborough Bridge," remembered Larry Houston, who spent long hours with his onetime chief. "His clouded mind imagined the Russian tanks were advancing over the bridge to take Manhattan."

When President Eisenhower learned that the man who had been America's master spy seemed near death, he awarded him the National Security Medal, the highest honor a civilian can earn. Donovan became the first American in history to hold the nation's four top decorations—the Congressional Medal of Honor, the Distinguished Service Cross, the Distinguished Service Medal, and now the National Security Medal. Larry Houston made the trip to New York on April 2, 1957, and pinned the medal on Donovan's pajama tops.

"Through his foresight, wisdom, and experience he foresaw, during the course of World War II, the problems which would face the postwar world and the urgent need for a permanent, centralized intelligence function," said Eisenhower's citation. "Thus his wartime work contributed to the establishment of the Central Intelligence Agency and a coordinated national intelligence structure."

Donovan rallied once again. "He is slowly but steadily improving," Walter Berry was able to write on May 17, "and we hope before too long to have him back on the job."

This was not to be. Another stroke further incapacitated him, and in the spring of 1958, at the request of President Eisenhower, Donovan was taken from New York to Walter Reed General Hospital in Washington. On February 8, 1959, at the age of 76, he died.

Of the many tributes received by William J. Donovan in the course of his life of service to his country, that delivered by Ned Buxton at the final gathering of OSS employees in 1945 ranks among the most eloquent and fitting.

> History will know and record only in part the value of [Donovan's] service.
>
> As the perilous years passed, he extemporized; he devised; he asked for the improbable and confidently achieved it. He capitalized on his weaknesses and attacked. Inspired by his personality and his vision, thousands of devoted people took the uneven odds. People of all ages lived or died as duty demanded or circumstances permitted. They killed and were killed alone or in groups, in jungles, in cities, by sea or air. They organized resistance where there was no resistance. They helped it to grow where it was weak. They assaulted the enemy's mind as well as his body; they helped confuse his will and disrupt his plans.
>
> And with it all, the General assembled the brains to evaluate and the competence to estimate the material that flowed back from a thousand vital sources, dealing with the enemy's capabilities and intentions and morale, military and civilian, the bottleneck targets, and the web of diplomatic intrigue. General Donovan, all of us, whatever our role, whatever our individual spot in the pattern of your unprecedented task—we esteem it a very great privilege to have served our country under your banner.

Acknowledgments and Chapter Notes

It would have been impossible to create a faithful account of the life of Maj. Gen. William J. Donovan without the assistance of the intelligence community. I am indebted to the many men and women who not only shared their own recollections and memorabilia of Bill Donovan but who arranged for me to see still other people who knew him. In particular, I want to thank Walter Pforzheimer, Thomas Troy, and Sir William Stephenson. Others who played a cardinal role in my research included: Ray S. Cline, David Crockett, Ernest Cuneo, John W. English, Arthur Goldberg, William J. Gross, Lawrence Houston, Sir Edwin Leather, Sir Fitzroy MacLean, Elizabeth Heppner McIntosh, James Murphy, Hayden B. Peake, Lt. Gen. W. R. Peers, Edwin Putzell, Jr., Frank Raichle, Kermit Roosevelt, Nicol Smith, and Thomas W. Streeter. Geoffrey M. T. Jones, president of the Veterans of the OSS, was helpful and encouraging throughout the work.

Archivists and librarians are an author's best friends. John Taylor, who as Modern Military Archivist presides over the labyrinthine OSS collection at the National Archives, was my research mentor, but I also am greatly indebted to John Barden, St. Joseph's Collegiate Institute; Edward T. Boone, Jr., MacArthur Memorial; Nancy Bressler, Seeley G. Mudd Manuscript Library, Princeton University; Dennis V. Cavanaugh, 101 Association Archives; Rudolf A. Clemen, Jr., American Red Cross Library, Washington, D.C.; Mal Collet, Citadel Memorial Archives; Kenneth C. Cramer, Dartmouth College Library; Joseph D'Addario, Buffalo Cavalry Association; William R. Emerson, Franklin D. Roosevelt Library; Nancy L. Fappiano, Sterling Memorial Library, Yale University Library; Susan Halpert, Houghton Library, Harvard University Library; Paul T. Heffron, Library of Congress; Clyde E. Helfter, Buffalo and Erie County Historical Society; Gregory Johnson, Alderman Library, University of Virginia Library; Kenneth A. Lohf, Rare Books and Manuscripts Collection, Columbia University Libraries; Royster Lyle, Jr., George C. Marshall Research Foundation; Edward Lyon, George Arents Research Library, Syracuse University; I. Frank Magavero, Niagara University Archives; Russell Malone, Special Collections, Northwestern University Library; Dwight M. Miller, Herbert Hoover Presidential Library; Charles G. Palm, Hoover Institution on War, Revolution, and Peace, Stanford University; Paul Palmer, Columbiana Collection, Columbia University Libraries; Mary Jo Pugh, Bentley Historical Library, University of Michigan Library; Jon K. Reynolds, Special Collections Division, Georgetown University Library; Earl M. Rogers, University of Iowa Library; Richard Sommers, U.S. Army Military History Institute; Robert D. Spector, Long Island University, Brooklyn; Arthur Veysey, Cantigny, Wheaton, Illinois; Charles Anthony Wood, Marine Corps Historical Center, Washington, D.C.

Mr. and Mrs. Thomas Carroll of Fairfax, Virginia, assisted my research through a crucial period. My wife, Joan, shared the entire burden of the work. She extended love and understanding throughout the writing of the book and contributed the index. She too knew Maj. Gen. William J. Donovan and joins me in expressing our appreciation for his revelation of details of his life.

The works of all authors cited in the Notes are given with full publication information under those authors' names in the Bibliography. Newspapers consulted are identified in the Notes but are not listed in the Bibliography. The following are the abbreviations used in the Notes:

BCAA	Buffalo Cavalry Association Archives
Buffalo Society	Buffalo and Erie County Historical Society
Hoover Institution	Hoover Institution on War, Revolution, and Peace
Hoover Library	Herbert Hoover Presidential Library
Marshall Foundation	George C. Marshall Research Foundation
PAA	Politischen Archiven des Auswartigen
Pforzheimer Collection	Walter Pforzheimer Collection on Intelligence Service
RFAC	Rockefeller Foundation Archives Center
Roosevelt Library	Franklin D. Roosevelt Library
ULPA	Union League of Philadelphia Archives
USAMHI	U.S. Army Military History Institute

Prologue

Page 2: Interview with Houston.
Page 3, lines 5–26: Interview with McIntosh.
Page 3, lines 27–44: Interview with Crockett.
Page 4, line 15: Pforzheimer Collection.
Page 5: Poem, dated June 2, 1959, given to author by Coon.

Chapter 1. The Boy from the Irish First Ward

The account of Donovan's life in Buffalo is in the main drawn from his own recollections.
Page 10, line 24; page 12, line 29: Interview with Kathleen Donovan.
Page 11, line 10: Graham.
Page 14, line 43; page 20, line 20: Mary Duggan interviewed by McIntosh.
Page 17, line 34: Interview with Irene Murphy.
Page 17, line 43: Nardin Academy Archives.
Page 19, line 35: John J. Barden to author.

Chapter 2. Donovan the Young Lawyer

Page 21, line 7: Niagara University Archives.
Page 22, line 2: On June 4, 1901, Donovan's oration, "True Manhood," won second place in the second "Complimentary to Professor Egan" contest. The 18-year-old stated: "There has come into the hearts and minds of men a fatal moral lethargy, the destroyer of all pure thought, the breeder of wickedness. Wrapt in the pleasing dream of self-complacency, the young men of today care not for duty, religion, virtue. They look upon them as empty phantoms which are soon forgotten in the bright sunshine of life's pleasures. Enveloped in the mists of admiration and self-glorification and dazzled by the glare of wealth, they grope their way blindly on, pursuing, revering, adoring their gods—wealth and notoriety."
Page 25, line 14: Alpheus Mason, 92.
Page 25, lines 18–28: Jackson E. Reynolds interviewed by Dean Albertson, June–August 1949, Oral History Archives, Columbia University Libraries.
Page 26, lines 2–14: Freidel, *FDR: The Apprenticeship*, 74.
Page 26, line 31: Even in his first year of law practice Donovan showed an interest in public service. W. A. King of the *Catholic Union and Times* wrote to Republican leader Edward H. Butler, "I presume you are the object of numberless importunities

to use your all-potent influence to 'place' ambitious young men when the Republican victories are secured by the November elections. I beg, therefore, that you will give kindly thought to the 'good word' I wish to say for my young friend William J. Donovan, who aspires to a post in the District Attorney's office. Perhaps you know of young Donovan, but you cannot possibly know him as I know him, for I have watched him through his every upward step from his school days through St. Joseph's College, through Columbia University, and so far in what promises to be a brilliantly successful legal career. In college, he was always a leader, and carried off enough medals and honors for oratory and scholarship to turn the head of one less well-poised. His course at Columbia was no less marked by success, and his fine muscle and good-fellowship earned him a place on its football team. Leaving college, he buckled down quietly to the study and practice of law, and in the short time he has been at it has given evidence of those qualities that ensure him the reward of patient and persistent application, combined with brilliancy of intellect. Mr. Donovan is a splendid type of the young Catholic professional man whose success can be lauded by his fellows, and he is certain as time goes on to gather around him a circle of earnest friends whose chief desire will be to see him achieve the destiny which his gifts entitle him to.

"With good brain, good looks, good judgment, he does not feel that he 'knows it all,' and is just the kind of man that *you* are known to favor. If through your good offices he succeeds in his present desire, I predict that you will always be glad that you helped to give him a start." King to Butler, Oct. 2, 1908.

Pages 28 ff.: Donovan's Troop I experiences are chronicled in the BCAA.

Chapter 3. Relief Mission to Europe

Page 36, line 10: This telegram, as well as other telegrams and correspondence between Donovan and Greene and with other personnel of the War Relief Commission that are quoted in this chapter, is in the RFAC.

Page 37, line 44: Beck, 176.

Page 39, line 3: "My job was to keep the back of the United States against that door and hold it open. It was not always easy. I was obliged to make protests, remonstrances, and polite suggestions about what would happen if certain things were not done." Van Dyke.

Page 40, line 17: Lithgow Osborne, then a young diplomat assigned to the embassy in Berlin and later Franklin Roosevelt's ambassador to Norway, taped his impressions of Donovan as he then appeared in Germany. He remembered him as "an extremely agreeable and pleasant young Irish-American who had come up the hard way. I don't know whether he married the boss's daughter, but he married into one of the old families in Buffalo." Osborne interviewed by Wendell Link, Oct. 29, 1952, Oral History Archives, Columbia University Libraries.

Page 40, lines 18–24: Dr. Sareyko to author, May 5, 1980, PAA.

Page 41, lines 11–15: Donovan diary, June 10, 1916, RFAC.

Page 43, line 4: "The Rockefeller Commission, however, up to the time I left Germany, did continue to carry on some measure of relief and succeeded in getting in condensed milk, to some extent for the children of that unfortunate country," wrote Ambassador Gerard about the work Donovan had begun. "I wish here to express my admiration for the work of the Rockefeller Commission in Europe. Not only were the ideas of the Commission excellent and businesslike, but the men selected to carry them into effect were without exception men of high character and possessed of rare executive ability." Gerard, 299.

Chapter 4. Joining Up with the Fighting 69th

Page 44, lines 3–12: Horne, 871.

Page 44, lines 13–28: Herbert Mason, *The Great Pursuit*, 222.

Page 45, line 5: When asked why his men called him Galloping Bill, Donovan replied, "The boys called me that because I drove them hard. I knew if we went to France, it would not be a cavalry war, and I was determined to have my unit physically fit." "Wild Bill Donovan, War-Time and Peace-Time Fighter."

Page 45, lines 17–32: *Rio Grande Rattler*, Vol. 1, No. 17.

Page 46, line 18: Donovan's snarled accounts were the subject of correspondence between Warwick Greene and the Commission for Relief in Belgium. Warwick Greene to the Commission, Sept. 23, 1916; William Roland to the Commission, Oct. 2, 1916, Hoover Library.

Page 46, line 35: Buffalo Society.

Page 47, lines 10–19: "An Account of the Mexican Border Service, Troop I, 1st Cavalry, N.G.U.S.," BCAA.

Page 47, line 22: In the Buffalo Cavalry Association's Club Room in the Connecticut Street Armory, Bill Donovan's portrait hangs among others of Troop I's commanding officers. A McClellan saddle like the one Donovan used is kept in a place of honor. A rack contains the sabers of each of the troop's commanders. A card explains that one of the sabers was carried by Bill Donovan, but General Hogan explained that this is not so.

"He came into the armory one day," he told the author, "and discovered that his saber was missing from our collection. My saber was handy, and I suggested that we put it up on the wall and attribute it to him. Bill grinned and approved of the idea."

Page 47, lines 26–29: Duffy, 24.

Page 47, line 34: In the decades to come, the Captain William J. Donovan Trophy was given to men of Troop I "To encourage good performance." "Trophies were awarded to outstanding individuals for shooting. The trophy was purchased by Captain Donovan and awarded to the squad which performed best each year." BCAA.

Page 47, lines 34–40: Army Times, *The Daring Regiments*.

Page 48, lines 18–25: Martin Hogan, 5.

Page 49, lines 1–19: Theodore Roosevelt, 1195.

Page 49, lines 26–30: Corey Ford.

Page 50, lines 1–8: Interview with Cassidy.

Page 50, lines 26–31: Berry, 330.

Page 51, lines 18–23: Flick, 86.

Page 52, lines 11–19: Theodore Roosevelt, 1236. Ironically, this letter was delivered to Archibald in France by Mrs. August Belmont, Donovan's friend of amateur theatrical days. She was there to get background for training Red Cross workers.

Page 52, lines 37–44: Woollcott, 47.

Page 53, lines 17–22: Flick, 161.

Page 53, lines 36–44: Howe.

Page 54, line 5: "Major Donovan's War Diary."

Page 55, lines 5–8: Freidel, *Over There*, 87.

Chapter 5. Rehearsal for War

Page 59, lines 4–9: Berry, 316.

Page 59, lines 14–16: USAMHI.

Page 59, lines 23–27: Flick, 162.

Page 59, lines 32–40: Lenahan journal (*I Remember—I Remember*), 54, USAMHI.

Page 60, lines 34–37: Martin Hogan, 35.

Page 63, lines 1–3: Frazier Hunt, 72.

Page 63, line 21: "The rest and the food were not only needed by ourselves but also by our 'cooties' boarders, who had become mighty scrawny on the poor entertainment that we had been able to furnish them on the rationless hike. With the return of better times, the cooties became more active." Martin Hogan, 47.

Page 65, line 6: Oliver Ames letter home, Jan. 27, 1918.

Chapter 6. A Wood Called Rouge Bouquet

Page 68, lines 12–17: Raymond Tompkins, 63.
Page 68, lines 18–23: *Rainbow Reveille*, May–June 1935.
Page 68, lines 32–38: Berry.
Page 71, line 24: Brigadier General Michael J. Lenahan remembered, "On the afternoon of March 8th, while I was attending a theatrical performance staged by some French soldiers at Bonamenil, I was informed of the loss of the 1st platoon of Co. 3, 165th Inf. A direct hit by a projectile fired by a German minenwerfer had struck a dugout occupied by Lt. Norman and 22 of his men in Rouge Bouquet. All were killed and buried in the dugout. I left immediately on horseback for the scene but was met by Father Duffy who was returning. He said there was nothing anyone could do—the men were buried under 20 to 30 feet of earth. He had given general absolution on the spot. Such a catastrophe was depressing for everyone." Lenahan, 56, USAMHI.
Page 72, lines 11–14: Duffy.
Page 72, lines 21–24: Freidel, *Over There*, 129.
Page 72, lines 29–39: Greene.
Page 73, line 6: Harbord, 246.
Page 73, line 25: Kilmer.
Page 74, line 44: "In what other regiment would a commander have dared to publish a soldier's poems at retreat?" asked Col. Frank McCoy, one of Donovan's fellow officers. Reilly, 209.

Chapter 7. Taking Hell with Bayonets

Page 76, lines 23–30: Flick.
Page 78, line 19: Colonel Frank R. McCoy dropped in on Donovan's command post and wrote to Caroline Ames, "I found such interest and keen soldierly spirit that I quickly knew all the men about him." Howe.
Page 78, lines 27–30: Anne Hard.
Page 79, lines 9–12: Berry.
Page 79, lines 32–36: Duffy.
Page 80, line 2: "Toward midnight Chalons was reached," wrote Col. Frank McCoy after the war, "traversed, and the tail of our column passed the regulating point on the dot. The whole of a war-strength division moved through the narrow, dark streets of the ancient town, past the moonlit cathedral, without the confusion or as much jamming as usually takes place during a St. Patrick's Day parade in New York." Reilly, 272.
Page 80, line 32: Lenahan noted in his journal, "About 9 o'clock in the evening of July 14th, I received a telephone message in code, delivered to me personally. Translated it read, 'Execute the order of the General Alert.' I knew then that battle would be on by midnight." USAMHI.
Page 80, line 40: An 18-year-old soldier wrote a letter about the fighting to the *New York Sun*. "It's great sport ducking those shells. They have the cutest little whistling sounds. We don't worry about the ones we hear whistling, because you won't hear the one that's going to get you.

"Fritz isn't particular about the kind he sends over. He mixes them up for you. He gives you grenade shells, high explosives, minenwerfers, and shrapnel all at one time.

"The shrapnel has a nasty habit of taking off an arm or a leg. The minenwerfers are the best of the bunch, though. They come lobbing through the air like a stuffed pig. They dig about 10 feet in the ground before they go off and leave the nicest little hole after they go off." Walter Bryan, July 28, 1918.
Page 81, line 4: "My brigade held what is known as 'second position.' Gen. Gouraud's plan was to abandon the 'first position' just before the attack came; to permit the

Germans to waste their strength on 1st position—when Germans had reached 1st position and felt that they had secured it, they were to be destroyed by our troops by fire action from 2nd position. The plan was successful. When the battle was over, German offensive power had ended." Lenahan, 60, USAMHI.

Page 81, line 42: Howe. Donovan's narrative of the fighting in the following pages is drawn from a letter he wrote to Caroline Ames, contained in this book.

Page 84, line 1: Berry, 325.

Page 84, lines 2–28: Scott.

Page 86, line 7: A corporal wrote "A courteous kindly gentleman and a true soldier" on a wooden cross made from an empty ammunition box and placed it over Ames's grave at Meurcy Farm. Bostonians later gave the name Oliver Ames, Jr., Square to the place where Commonwealth Avenue meets Fenway Park. Howe.

Page 86, lines 16–38: Berry.

Page 88, line 18: Floyd Gibbons, having lost an eye in the fighting and wearing a sling, spoke at Carnegie Hall on September 8. He told his audience that the 69th and the Alabama Regiment had refused to fall back to safety during the fighting. "Wave after wave of picked German shock troops stormed their position, only to be sent scurrying back to their holes. Then the Germans sent low flying airplanes over their lines to rake them with machine-gun fire.

"On the fourth day, when the 69th and the Alabama continued to hold, the French general said, 'Well, I guess there is nothing for me to do but fight the war out where the New York Irish want to fight it." *New York Sun*, Sept. 9, 1918.

Chapter 8. Wild Bill Leads the Charge

Page 89, lines 29–35; page 90, lines 1–4: Army Times, *The Daring Regiments*, 80.

Page 90, lines 20–26: Army Times, *The Daring Regiments*.

Page 99, line 10: By the third morning after Donovan's attack began, the St. Mihiel salient no longer existed. It had been held since 1914. The Germans fell back, believing that they had been struck by two American divisions—the 42nd and the Rainbow. Ibid.

Page 99, lines 30–44: Sweeney, 291.

Page 101, line 26: The Record and Telephone Book of the 149th Field Artillery kept during the battle contains terse details of the struggle. On October 14 at 21:43, the log states, "Gould called, said Col. Donovan wanted barrage along line of German wire, was told the line in on X.286.6, which is just north of line Donovan asks for." On October 15, "Message from Donovan. Order for attack received by him at 12:05. Company's A&C ref. against enemy machine-gun fire, and enfilade artillery fire from left. Long range enfilade fire from both flanks." USAMHI.

Chapter 9. The Men We Left Behind

Page 107, line 15: MacArthur was twice awarded the Distinguished Service Cross, the Distinguished Service Medal, two Purple Hearts, and a number of French awards. He never quite forgave Donovan for eclipsing him in the 42nd Division's roster of heroes. James, 239.

Page 110, lines 25–33: Donovan to Thomas M. Johnson, Jan. 5, 1942, American Legion National Headquarters Library.

Page 110, line 33: Pershing was at the time an active candidate for president of the United States, and the rumors that morale was plummeting in the AEF disturbed him. General Eric Fisher Wood stated, "There was actually a very stormy meeting in General Pershing's office. The call for the Paris Caucus had been issued by Wood, without prior knowledge on the part of General Pershing and his staff. Pershing was furious. He considered this a transgression of his rights. Several of those meeting with the Committee of 20 were called to Pershing's office by orders marked

'Urgent.' Among those present were Roosevelt, Donovan, White, and Wood. These civilian soldiers did not 'knuckle under' to General Pershing. Roosevelt was suave about it. Donovan was brutally frank and said words to the effect that 'the General apparently does not realize that the war is over.' Finally, General Pershing said he would not oppose the Paris meeting." Wood also said that George White was "the real brains throughout the formation of the Legion. Roosevelt, Donovan, Wood, and Clark were all younger than White. Thirty years old or less. They furnished the energy. White was older, a leading statesman in Oregon, the moving spirit of the 'Portland Oregonian,' a respected and valued friend and adviser to Theodore Roosevelt, Sr. He was much looked up to by the others. They willingly accepted the guidance of his snaffle rein. He made the bricks they threw; and indicated what heads they were to be thrown at." American Legion Library.

Page 110, line 39: Donovan chaired the Committee on Permanent Organization. He urged that an Executive Committee be named to go back home and organize the American Legion community by community. Then delegates could meet at another caucus that would have a broader base than the Paris Caucus. "The Paris Caucus."

Page 111, lines 9–13: George White.

Page 111, line 25: *Washington Star*, March 16, 1949.

Page 112, line 17: "There were 615 gold stars on the white banner which led the regiment up the avenue, each star for a valiant comrade who 'went West' in the winning of the decisive fields in France." Hogan, 270.

Page 112, line 22: Kaye, 202.

Page 112, lines 28–31: Corey Ford interview with Vincent Donovan, Dartmouth College Library.

Page 113, lines 7–24: Souvenir of "Father Duffy Day at Polo Grounds," May 15, 1919.

Chapter 10. Siberian Adventure

Page 117, lines 1–16: Graves.

Page 118, line 10: During the decades to come, O'Brian was to combine a distinguished legal career with government service and to carry out confidential intelligence missions, much like Bill Donovan. He would be an important member of the unofficial intelligence community made up of gentleman amateurs. Donovan was also to be part of this elite circle of men who shared their information and insights concerning world affairs and in one way or another kept their government informed.

Page 118: Donovan diary, 1917–1918. The material in the chapter attributed to Donovan is from this diary, which is in the possession of the author.

Page 118, lines 33–44: Diplomatic Section, National Archives.

Page 119, lines 3–5: Ibid.

Page 119, lines 30–37: Graves.

Page 120, line 43: Both historic maps are preserved among Ambassador Morris's papers in the Manuscript Division, Library of Congress.

Page 121, line 29: Reuters Pacific Service also carried a Harbin report on July 15. Its correspondent identified the American general as General Greffs.

Page 122, line 25: Diplomatic Section, National Archives.

Page 122, line 32–44; page 123, lines 1–3: Manuscript Division, Library of Congress.

Page 124, lines 41–44; page 125, lines 1–8: Diplomatic Section, National Archives.

Page 126, lines 17–20 and 27: Manuscript Division, Library of Congress.

Page 128, line 19: Nevertheless, McDonald gave Donovan a sheaf of grim pictures of the corpses left by Semionoff's men. Today these pictures, among the Morris papers in the Library of Congress, serve as reminders of how vicious civil war in Siberia was.

Page 129, line 13: Eichelberger's confidential report details Japanese anti-American propaganda and harassment of American personnel. Graves turned the report over to Donovan and Morris. "Conduct of Japanese in Siberia which would indicate an unfriendly attitude towards the United States," Sept. 22, 1919, Diplomatic Section, National Archives.

Chapter 11. Fact-Finding in Europe

Page 130, line 3: Manuscript Division, Library of Congress.
Page 133, line 8: Flick.
Page 133, lines 20–31: Interview with Buffalo Mayor James D. Griffin.
Page 133, line 33: Donovan continued to take an interest in Siberia. He wrote to Morris, "I attended a dinner the other night and send you a list of those that were most interesting in it. It was a small dinner of only 40 at which the Russian Ambassador, Mr. Root Washburn, the war correspondent, and Russel, a Socialist, spoke. They talked up until midnight, at which time I had to leave to catch a train, but the disappointing part of it was that no one offered any real basis to work upon. The thing that impressed me was that all of them were ignorant of, or else glossed over, the real inefficiency, as was evident to us, of the crowd surrounding Kolchak."
Donovan also informed Morris that he had attended a dinner in New York in honor of Pershing. "There were only 28 people there, and when I sat down and looked them over, the crowd struck me as significant. I immediately jumped to the conclusion that there was an effort being made to launch a boom for Pershing. . . . The man behind the movement is supposed to be Charles Dawes, who is president of a bank in Chicago, and who was a brigadier general in the service of supply abroad. Pershing is now making a tour of the country, ostensibly to inspect the army posts and camps."
Donovan remarked too about "hysteria here in regard to the Reds. Committees of citizens are assembled by government officers, and these citizens go out in automobiles to round up alleged Bolsheviks. Generally they are not furnished with warrants, but a slip of paper saying that warrants are on file in the office of the United States District Attorney, and that no opportunity should be given the suspects of talking with anyone. Some of the methods now used are very highhanded, and there is a general tendency to characterize all kinds of free speech as Bolshevism." Manuscript Division, Library of Congress.
Page 134, line 30: *Chicago Tribune,* June 6, 1920.
Page 135, line 15: Ibid., June 7, 1920.
Page 135, line 35: *Chicago Daily News,* June 7, 1920.
Page 137, line 25: "Our First War Commissioner Dies."
Page 141, line 28: Donovan to Ellis Loring Dressel, Sept. 16, 1920. Donovan wrote, "I was sorry not to see you before leaving. I am particularly anxious that you should know how much I appreciated your fine courtesy while I was in Berlin.
"The information which I obtained chiefly through the facilities that you placed at my disposal has been a great help in obtaining a proper view of the present situation. I am grateful not only for that, but for your kindness.
"I asked Wilson to tell you that I found your organization there not only the most courteous and helpful, but also the most efficient I have seen in any of our legations or embassies."

Chapter 12. Racket-Busting DA

Page 142, lines 23–30: *New York Times,* Sept. 7, 1922.
Page 143, lines 2–8: *Buffalo Courier-Express,* Dec. 21, 1922.
Page 143, line 16: Ibid., Feb. 12, 1922.
Page 143, lines 19–24: Ibid., Feb. 15, 1922.
Page 143, line 26: "Wild Bill Donovan, War-Time and Peace-Time Fighter."
Page 143, line 33: Anne Hard.
Page 144, line 20: Harvard University Library.
Page 145, lines 9–34: Mullany.
Page 145, line 43: Donovan's agent Chung Su was shot and killed in New York's Chinatown a short time afterward during what the newspapers portrayed as a Tong War. Donovan always believed that the killing was a gangland revenge.
Page 146, lines 21–25: Bentley to Hoover, Jan. 18, 1929, Hoover Library.

Page 147, line 18: New York Republican leaders met in Washington on September 13, and picked Donovan to be their candidate at the convention later in the month. *New York Times,* Sept. 13, 1922.

Page 147, lines 20–29: Ibid., Sept. 29, 1922.

Page 148, lines 1–4: Ibid., Nov. 6, 1922.

Page 148, lines 18–27: Hoover Library.

Page 149, lines 12–24: "Town Tidings."

Page 149, line 33: *Buffalo Times,* Feb. 3, 1929.

Page 150, line 8: Interview with Raichle.

Page 150, line 39: *Buffalo News,* Jan. 19, 1923.

Page 151, lines 1–33: The military attaché at the U.S. Embassy in Berlin first suggested to Donovan that he should try to see Hitler. Conversations with Donovan and interview with Putzell.

Page 151, lines 34–39: *New York Times,* April 18, 1923.

Chapter 13. With the Department of Justice

Page 152, lines 21–28: Alpheus Mason, 141.

Page 154, line 23: Wheeler never looked at it that way. In his autobiography he wrote that Eleanor Patterson, then a leading Washington hostess, had "tipped me off that Colonel Donovan, then an assistant attorney general, knew Mrs. Wheeler was pregnant and scheduled the trial so as to coincide with the expected date of the birth. She said the idea was that I would probably ask for a continuance and the government could then drag the case out. But I didn't do so."

Mrs. Wheeler did present her husband with a baby on the very day he was acquitted. The story made the rounds of Washington, and it did Donovan very little good. Wheeler, 241.

Page 154, lines 25–30: Interview with James Murphy.

Page 154, line 35: Donovan sent Mary J. Connor, red-haired, blue-eyed, and beautiful, to break the Chicago kitchen-cabinet rackets since the cabinets in question were shipped across the state line from Indiana to Illinois. Mary Connor was a prototype of hundreds of OSS women to come, and she did her job with efficiency. Shepherd.

J. Edgar Hoover suffered in silence as Donovan dispatched his agents on racket-busting missions. On April 8, 1928, he finally complained to Donovan, "I didn't know even where the accountants or Special Agents were, and it was only after several months that I was able to have orders issued that would at least enable me to know where these men were." Whitehead, 332.

Page 154, lines 35–44; page 155, lines 1–9: "Wild Bill Donovan, War-Time and Peace-Time Fighter."

Page 155, line 9: Shepherd.

Page 155, lines 13–19: Land, 120.

Page 155, lines 19–23: "Wild Bill Donovan, War-Time and Peace-Time Fighter."

Page 155, line 24: A *Saturday Evening Post* writer poked fun at Donovan as "The Nadir of Wildness." He inveighed against misleading nicknames, maintaining that "Wild Bill is a quiet, low-voiced good-looking young man, whose speech, garb, and demeanor are as little deserving of the epithet 'Wild' as were those of the impeccable John Drew in 'The Tyranny of Tears.'" "Who's Who—and Why."

Page 156, line 12: In 1926 Donovan served on the campaign committee of New York Sen. James W. Wadsworth, an old friend. Wadsworth ran on a Wet platform, and this was to make many Dry leaders fear that Donovan, despite his record as a racket-busting DA in western New York, was too Wet for their support. Fausald, 192. The same year Donovan also was talked about as GOP nominee for governor of New York. It was thought that he would help "balance the ticket." *Buffalo Courier-Express,* July 11, 1926.

Page 156, lines 20–21: *Buffalo Times,* March 24, 1925.

Page 156, line 27: Anne Hard.

Page 156, lines 24–35: Donovan in this way helped those who came to be called

constructive cooperationists to avoid unnecessary legal difficulties in efficiently
organizing American industrial activities to meet the challenge of the growing
complexity of the economy. Hawley, 102.
Page 157, lines 1–22: Choate.
Page 157, lines 23–28: Anne Hard.
Page 157, lines 37–44; page 158, lines 1–2: "The Aluminum Case."
Page 158, lines 14–26: Anne Hard.
Page 158, line 35: "Town Tidings."
Page 158, lines 38–42: Choate.
Page 159, line 6: The University of Notre Dame gave Donovan an honorary doctor of
laws and literature degree on May 31, 1925. Donovan went about America making
speeches before bar associations and business congresses on such subjects as cartels
in Europe. Archives of the University of Notre Dame.
Page 159, line 7: On May 23, 1926, 9-year-old Patricia's pony Raggle Tail won the
blue ribbon at the National Capital Horse Show, and her father was the proudest
man in town. *Washington Star,* May 23, 1926.
  Bill Donovan loved both of his children, but he found Patricia the more congenial.
As David grew older, he was anything but athletic, and this dismayed his father. A
schoolmate at the Faye School, Northampton, Mass., which he attended as a boy,
remembered him as "rotund, diffident and laboring under the burden of having a
great father. Donovan's macho image didn't help him a bit." Interview with Welles.
Page 159, lines 9–15: Manuscript Division, Library of Congress.
Page 159, lines 16–19: Donovan telegram to William Howard Taft, Aug. 17, 1927, and
Taft to Donovan, Aug. 18, 1927. Manuscript Division, Library of Congress.
  Bill Donovan was a great party favorite in Georgetown. He could play the piano
and sing Schubert or Brahms lieder. But not all his neighbors approved of him.
Mabel Willebrandt, who was an assistant attorney general, remarked that he "uses
gate-crasher tactics but makes himself so pleasant people are rather glad he crashed
in." Willebrandt to Hoover, Hoover Library.
  Throughout the 1920s and early 1930s Donovan, together with Kermit and
Theodore Roosevelt, Jr., Suydom Cutting, and Roy Chapman Andrews, the explorer,
was a member of an informal club called the Room. The room in question was a
hotel room in New York City kept expressly for meetings of the club. "All we needed
to do," explained Dr. Andrews, "was to call the others and say, 'Meet me at the
Room,' and we'd all rendezvous at such and such a time. We discussed everything
from international affairs to personal problems with absolute confidentiality. Sometimes Somerset Maugham was allowed to meet with us. Donovan had a sincerity
and honesty that nobody could corrupt." Interview with Andrews.
  Kermit Roosevelt, Jr., reported that Lincoln Ellsworth and Adm. Richard Byrd
were also members of the Room. Kermit Roosevelt to author, July 17, 1981.

Chapter 14. The Parade Passes By

Page 160, lines 4–5: Frank Kellogg telegram to American Embassy, Paris, March 8,
1928, Diplomatic Section, National Archives.
Page 160, lines 7–12: Charles Dewey to Donovan, April 10, 1928, Chicago Historical
Society Library.
Page 160, line 20: Paul Leverkuehn, a young German, visited Donovan often and told
him about affairs in his homeland. During World War II Admiral Canaris stationed
Leverkuehn in Istanbul, where he continued to give his principal loyalty to Donovan.
Colvin, *Chief of Intelligence,* 181.
Page 160, line 24: One of Donovan's associates was Henry L. Stimson, who was
appointed in 1927 by President Coolidge to arbitrate a dispute over the Nicaraguan
presidency. Upon Stimson's successful return Donovan congratulated him on his
"splendid service in Nicaragua." "To an ordinary citizen like myself," he said, "your
mission seemed not only a difficult one but a discouraging one. Your report is not
only creditable to you but reassuring to the country. Anyone who has followed the

situation will know that you have done a fine job." Donovan to Stimson, June 2, '
1927, Yale University Library.

Stimson replied, "It is very kind of you to send me such a cordial note of congratulation, and I appreciate it very greatly, particularly coming as it does from one who is in a position to know the character of the mission in Nicaragua." Stimson to Donovan, June 8, 1927, Yale University Library.

Page 160, lines 34–35: Hoover to Donovan, July 27, 1927, Hoover Library.

Page 161, line 4: *Buffalo Courier-Express,* Dec. 27, 1927.

Page 161, lines 12–17: Courtesy of Kirchhofer.

Page 161, line 35: In May there was a boomlet for Bill Donovan for vice-president. *Buffalo Truth,* May 5, 1928.

Page 162, line 3: Carol Green Wilson, 172.

Page 162, lines 6–9: Wilbur, 396.

Page 162, line 11: *Baltimore Sun,* Feb. 28, 1929.

Page 162, lines 20–26: Roper, 237.

Page 162, lines 27–37: *New York Times,* Oct. 23, 1928. After the campaign was over some of Donovan's detractors claimed that he had avoided any public speeches for Hoover so as not to offend Catholic supporters of Al Smith. Actually Donovan was listed by the Speakers Commission of the New York State Republican League under the chairmanship of his old Fighting 69th noncom friend, Sgt. Richard W. O'Neill, and he gave several speeches in New York State. Press release of Sept. 15, 1928, Hoover-Curtis Campaign Committee, Hoover Library.

Hoover's friend James H. MacLafferty later wrote, "Personally I give Donovan credit for being friendly to Hoover's candidacy, but I also know, from my own knowledge, and not from Hoover, that Hoover wanted Donovan to go out speaking in the last campaign and that Donovan continually side-stepped it." MacLafferty diary, March 1, 1929, Hoover Library.

Page 163, lines 18–19: *Buffalo Courier-Express,* Nov. 14, 1928.

Page 163, line 31: C. McCall to Hoover, Dec. 3, 1928, Hoover Library. An article in the *Wichita Falls* (Texas) *Daily Times,* Dec. 2, 1928, details the Klan's opposition to Donovan.

Page 163, line 36: Many Prohibitionists advocated the transfer of the Bureau of Prohibition from the Treasury Department to the Department of Justice. When Hoover asked Donovan if he supported this, Donovan replied, "American tradition had followed the Anglo-Saxon practice of separating the office of sheriff from the office of prosecuting attorney. If the District Attorney were to be liquor administrator, no self-respecting lawyer would take the office." Robinson and Bornet.

Page 163, line 37: Even as Hoover was listening to Donovan's critics, he was soliciting Donovan's views on who might fill various cabinet positions together with the reactions of various members of Congress and the public to them. Donovan memo to Hoover, Jan. 3, 1929, Hoover Library.

"There is a very pronounced opposition from our friends in the Southern border states to the naming of Colonel Donovan to a position in the Cabinet," California Congressman W. E. Evans wrote to Hoover. "The opposition is based on two points. First, that he is not in sympathy with the theory and principles of the Prohibition Act. . . . The other objection is on account of his religion, and which I am constrained to say does not appeal to me personally as a valid reason why any man should not be appointed to a public position. . . . It is said that if he is named, the Southern States, which gave you their support, will be disappointed at the very beginning of your administration." W. E. Evans to Hoover, Jan. 22, 1929, Hoover Library.

Page 163, line 44: The Reverend I. M. Haldeman to Hoover, Nov. 14, 1928, Hoover Library.

Page 164, line 2: Myers to Hoover, Nov. 15, 1928, Hoover Library. The Hollywood, California, *Protestant* ran the headline "Rome Demands Donovan in Cabinet" on its front page. The editor sent a copy of his journal to Mrs. Hoover and noted, "Please call your husband's attention to this and oblige." Hoover Library.

Page 164, line 11: At this time newspapers carried articles stating with absolute

certainty that Donovan was to be the new attorney general or secretary of war. *Buffalo Courier-Express,* Jan. 8, 1929.
Page 164, line 28: Courtesy of Kirchhofer.
Page 164, line 38: Hoover Library.
Page 165, line 10: Coded Message No. 51 to Hoover from George Akerson states, "Borah came to see me and of his own initiative said he does not favor Donovan." Hoover Library.
   On February 11, 1929, Mark Sullivan also wrote to Hoover, "Sunday night Borah came to see me. His coming was of his own initiative and everything he said was of his own initiative. He said first his judgment is strongly against your appointing Donovan. He says the Democrats will oppose Donovan's confirmation and he, Borah, as your friend in the Senate, would be embarrassed to defend the appointment." Ibid.
Page 165, lines 11–45; page 166, lines 1–17: Oral History Archives, Columbia University Libraries.
Page 166, line 37: Ickes, 88.
Page 167, line 11: Donovan gave James L. Wright a verbatim account of his conversation with Hoover. Wright to Kirchhofer, Feb. 28, 1929, courtesy of Kirchhofer.
Page 167, line 31: President Coolidge appointed Donovan to the Rio Grande Commission. *Buffalo Courier-Express,* Feb. 8, 1929.
Page 167, line 29: On Feb. 21, 1929, Sen. William Borah dined with Hoover to discuss candidates for attorney general. He opposed Donovan because he said Donovan favored repealing the 18th Amendment. He supported the New York lawyer William D. Mitchell. Hoover was reluctant to throw over Donovan, an old friend, and name Mitchell, who was a Democrat.
   "A few people may grunt and groan about it," said Borah concerning Mitchell's appointment, "but not very loud and it will not cause one vote against confirmation." McKenna, 261.
Page 167, line 42: Later O'Brian remarked that Donovan had taken most of his antitrust division staff with him into private practice. Oral History Archives, Columbia University Libraries.
Page 168, line 29: Some Donovan supporters urged him to take the post of governor general of the Philippines. They pointed out that William Howard Taft had stepped from that job to the presidency, and Leonard Wood had almost done so. Donovan simply replied that he did not seek a political career. *Baltimore Sun,* Feb. 28, 1929.
   Hoover also expressed his surprise that Donovan did not accept the governor generalship. "Hoover marveled at this refusal," wrote MacLafferty in his diary, "because he said he regarded it as a great office and a great stepping-stone for future service. He felt that in making this offer he had fulfilled every or any obligation he had to Donovan. That Hoover regards the governor generalship of the Philippines as an office of high distinction is proven by the fact that John Tilson told me that Hoover had told him that he would have left the secretaryship of commerce to take it, had it been offered to him. I could see that Hoover was ill at ease over the Donovan episode, and he felt that some people would accuse him of being a bigot because he did not appoint Donovan attorney general." Hoover Library.
Page 168, line 38: David Lawrence, in commenting upon the falling-out between Hoover and Donovan, remarked that "Democrats say it is a big political blunder, that Donovan could have been spared the humiliation by being told last November that he wouldn't be chosen and that the omission will be interpreted by Catholics as an emphasis of the coming controversies and a victory for the Klan. . . .
   "Anyway if by 1932 there are adverse political developments for Mr. Hoover, the antagonism awakened by the Donovan incident may have some weight. If he has a successful administration and the country is prosperous, Herbert Hoover's opportunities for re-election are as good as any of his predecessors." *Buffalo Evening News,* March 4, 1929.
   Pollster Daniel C. Roper also speculated on what Hoover's break with Donovan meant to the Hoover presidency. Roper felt that having Donovan in Hoover's cabi-

net probably would have prevented the Bonus March, which did so much to damage Hoover's prestige. Roper, 240.
Page 168, lines 38–42: Cutler, 116.

Chapter 15. Politics and Foreign Affairs

Page 170, lines 1–6: Donovan to Coolidge, Feb. 15, 1929, National Archives.
Page 170, lines 7–32: Interview with James Murphy.
Page 171, line 14: *Chicago Tribune,* Oct. 9, 1929.
Page 171, line 22: *Buffalo Times,* Oct. 9, 1929.
Page 172, lines 19–31: "Donovan took a fortune home, at least $250,000 a year throughout the Depression," stated Richard Greenlee, "but he never had money." Interview with Greenlee.
Page 172, line 34: "Bill was wildly, deliberately extravagant," said Guy Martin. "The best cuisine, the best accommodations everywhere he went, a barber who came to shave him, a private masseur." Interview with Martin.
Page 173, lines 5–14: Interview with O'Brian, Oral History Archives, Columbia University Libraries.
Page 173, line 18: Donovan to Milton Handley, Manuscript Collection, Columbia University Libraries.
Page 173, line 28: Young William O. Douglas went to New York for a couple of days a week to work for Donovan in the bankruptcies investigation. Douglas, 175.
Page 173, line 32: Most New York lawyers were delighted that a man of Donovan's stature would undertake the task, but Louis Brandeis was critical. "How a well-meaning Bar Committee could entrust the Bankruptcy Cleansing job to Donovan is beyond comprehension," he wrote to Felix Frankfurter on April 21, 1929. Brandeis, 380.
Page 174, line 6: In late summer 1930, Donovan flirted with the idea of joining Senator Wadsworth to oppose Hoover within the ranks of the Republican Party, but he backed off from the alliance when his friend Edward T. Clark, who was former President Coolidge's private secretary, wrote, "So far as the President is concerned, it would perhaps create a definite break and completely remove from favor a man who has always been potentially able to come back into power as an advisor or into public life as a candidate. Perhaps certain people would like to see you take a licking so that the country might see that the myth of Donovan's power was exploded." Clark to Donovan, Sept. 9, 1930, Manuscript Division, Library of Congress.
Donovan did challenge Hoover in an attack on the 18th Amendment. In a speech before the New York Young Republican Club at the Lawyers Club, he urged the GOP to face up to the issue that Prohibition simply was not working. U.S. Attorney Charles H. Tuttle, favored to be the Republican candidate for governor of New York in 1930, was present, and he was given a smattering of applause. When Donovan's name was mentioned for the governorship, the audience gave him an ovation. Donovan accepted the demonstration with a jaunty wave of his hand, and Tuttle scowled. Donovan made no effort to obtain the nomination to run against the popular Democratic Gov. Franklin D. Roosevelt, who easily defeated Tuttle to win a second term.
Page 174, line 18: Sometimes Donovan weekended at Arthur Brisbane's Lakewood, New Jersey, estate. On one occasion a fellow guest was Will Rogers, who remarked that "Bill Donovan, the fellow we all thought was going to be attorney general, was there. Nice fellow." Donovan, Rogers, and Brisbane went riding. "You don't suppose I went clear down there just for the horseback ride, do you?" asked Rogers. "I got horses at home, but I can't learn anything riding 'em." *Tulsa World,* April 27, 1931.
Page 174, lines 35–44: Interviews with Putzell.
Page 175, line 4: Interview with Halsey.
Page 175, line 29: After Ruth Donovan stopped coming to Washington except on rare occasions, Donovan charged law partner Richard Maher, who lived next door, with seeing to it that all the household and office bills were paid. Interview with James Murphy.

Page 175, line 30: In July 1929, Ruth was taken seriously ill at Nonquit. A worried Donovan hurried to the summer home and brought her to Buffalo. He interrupted bankruptcy hearings in New York to look after his ailing wife. *Buffalo Courier-Express,* July 21, 1929.

Page 175, line 37: Donovan encouraged his son to sail on the *Yankee.* "David had poor grades at college and jumped at the chance to go," reported Francis S. Kinney, a school friend of David's, who later in life was to win fame as a yachtsman and author on yachting subjects. Interview with Kinney.

Page 176, lines 14–28: Interviews with Mahoney, a close Donovan friend, and Impelliteri.

Page 177, line 2: *New York Times,* June 4, 1931.

Page 177, line 13: Interview with Raichle. Raichle recalled that Donovan "probably traveled to Manchuria over the Trans-Siberian Railroad."

Page 178, line 3: *Buffalo Courier-Express,* Feb. 23, 1932.

Page 178, lines 11–20: *Observation Post,* August 1932. Sculptor Charles Keck created the figure of Father Duffy holding a prayer book against a Celtic cross. The statue in Times Square was dedicated on June 26, 1936. Flick, 169.

Page 178, line 32: Manuscript Division, Library of Congress.

Page 179, lines 2–10: *New York Times,* July 10, 1932.

Page 179, lines 27–40: Ibid., July 30, 1932.

Page 180, lines 11–35: Bernays, 648.

Page 181, line 2: Win with Donovan and Davison Committee papers, Columbiana Collection, Columbia University Libraries.

Page 181, lines 2–6: *New York Herald Tribune,* Oct. 5, 1932.

Page 181, lines 6–26: *Buffalo Courier-Express,* Oct. 6, 1932.

Page 181, line 41: Interview with Lehman, Oral History Archives, Columbia University Libraries. Journalist William Hard presented a picture of candidate Donovan in his article "Dock Yards to Fame": "He is fortunate, to begin with, in having an arresting physical character. When he enters a room, one is instantly, acutely conscious of his presence, for a reason not at all subtle but altogether obvious. He sends out rays of health, happy health, and more. There is discharged from him a sort of electricity of elation. He is not only healthy, and happily healthy, but his nerves seem to be seeking an outlet toward some sort of joyous expression in adventures beyond ordinary chance."

Page 182, lines 1–7: *New York Times,* Oct. 6, 1932.

Page 182, line 14: *New York Post,* Nov. 4, 1932.

Walter Mahoney, who toured New York in 1932 to organize Young Republican clubs in support of Donovan's candidacy, said that Donovan's opponents would tell Catholics that he had left the church. When they talked to Protestants, they claimed he was a rabid Catholic. Interview with Mahoney.

Page 182, line 20: From a leaflet published by the Win with Donovan and Davison Committee.

Page 182, line 26: *New York Post,* Nov. 4, 1932.

Page 182, lines 29–43; page 183, lines 1–10: Win with Donovan and Davison Committee papers.

Page 183, line 12: Donovan also lost a wager on the election. Arthur Brisbane had bet Mrs. Ned McLean, wife of the *Washington Post*'s owner, and Donovan that FDR would carry all but eight states. When only six states voted Republican, Will Rogers remarked about the bet, "I thought Brisbane was crazy, and he was by two states." Franklin Roosevelt, *FDR: His Personal Letters,* 575.

Page 183, line 14: Lehman also remarked to DeWitt Clinton Poole, later chief of the Foreign Nationalities branch of OSS, that Donovan had conducted "the decentest and most clean-cut campaign" he had ever experienced. Conyers Read manuscript, 3, Pforzheimer Collection.

Page 183, line 19: Manuscript Division, Library of Congress.

Page 183, line 21: Ibid.

Page 183, line 29: Yale University Library.

Page 183, line 40: Ironically, Donovan spoke on nationwide radio in March 1934 to mark the 16th anniversary of the U.S. infantry's entry into the front lines in World War I. *Observation Post,* March 1934.

Chapter 16. The Unfolding Crisis

Page 184, line 6: Hugh Wilson, 322.

Page 185, line 18: Later on in 1937, Mannie Marcus, a Washington lawyer and president of the Rainbow Division Association, gave a party in Chevy Chase, Maryland, to which both MacArthur and Donovan came. Ward McCabe, a young guest who later served in the OSS, recalled that "Bill Donovan arrived on time in civilian clothes and was relaxed and pleasant company. MacArthur made a late theatrical entrance in white jodhpurs, white boots, and white gloves." Donovan asked McCabe what he was studying.

"Going into the foreign services," replied McCabe.

"Whatever you do," said Donovan, "remember we're going to be in a war in four or five years, so study everything you can." Interview with McCabe.

Page 186, line 25: Donovan diary in possession of author. The following account of Donovan's trip is drawn from this diary unless otherwise indicated.

Page 188, line 33: Diplomatic Section, National Archives.

Page 188, lines 34–45; page 189, lines 1–19: Hugh Wilson, 322, and Salvemini, 418.

Page 190, line 24: "The trip to Rome and Ethiopia was very important," stated Edwin Putzell. "He [Donovan] talked of it and the lessons it held for him on many occasions, particularly as they bore on the influence of intelligence on the course of world events." Putzell to author, Aug. 23, 1981.

Page 190, lines 40–41: Interview with Jaeckle, New York State Republican leader.

Page 191, line 25: Interview with Guy Martin.

Page 191, lines 37–40; page 192, lines 1–10: *Time,* Oct. 18, 1937.

Page 192, lines 27–38: *Time,* Jan. 31, 1938.

Page 192, line 40: On May 2, 1937, Donovan spoke at the unveiling of the statue of Father Duffy at Times Square, New York. "Father Duffy would have liked this occasion," he said. "He would have liked this multitude of friends gathered here. He would have liked the flashing white sunlight of this day, his birthday. He would have liked the 69th Band swinging up Broadway playing the regimental march 'Garry Owen.' All of this in his honor he would have enjoyed simply and genuinely, because he was so human."

Chapter 17. Contagion of War

Page 195, line 26: Donovan was crossing the Atlantic when the capitulation came. "On the way back on the steamer, we had as fellow passengers Justice McReynolds, former Justice and Mrs. Sutherland, Sir Gerald and Lady Campbell, the former Consul General, Martin Conboy, Col. William J. Donovan, Lord Wright of the Privy Council, and others. During the whole of the voyage we all clung to the radio without any intimation that there was going to be any surrender until the last day when news came in and it was a surprise, I think to everyone," wrote Henry L. Stimson. Yale University Library. Donovan had little to say about his own trip.

Page 198, line 4: Roosevelt Library.

Page 198, lines 20–29: Ickes, 93.

Page 198, line 40: Roosevelt Library.

Page 199, line 3: Franklin Roosevelt, *FDR: His Personal Letters.*

Page 199, line 5: Interview with McGinnis.

Page 200, lines 1–9: Merian Cooper to Donovan, April 23, 1940, Hoover Library.

Page 200, line 10: Hoover and Donovan had first become friends while working during World War I for the relief of Poland. They became friends again in 1940, working together again for the relief of the Polish people. *New York Herald Tribune,* March 24, 1940.

Page 200, line 21: Donovan, "Should Men of 50 Fight Our Wars?"

Page 201, lines 14–23: Telephone interview with Mary Frances Merz, who was Pat Donovan's sorority sister.

Page 201, lines 25–40: Notes from Elizabeth Heppner McIntosh. President Roosevelt telegraphed Donovan on April 9, 1940, "My heart goes out to you in the sorrow which has come to you with such sudden and tragic force. Please accept for yourself and for all who mourn with you an assurance of sincere sympathy and of my warm personal regard."

Donovan replied, "Your warm and understanding message, I deeply appreciate. "That you took the time from many and pressing duties makes me doubly grateful—as it will my wife who is still on a sailing vessel in the South Pacific. You are most thoughtful." Donovan to Roosevelt, April 10, 1940. Both telegram and letter are in the Roosevelt Library.

Page 202, lines 9–16: Albion and Connery, 7.

Chapter 18. Confidential Mission to Britain

Page 203, line 19: When Donovan arrived at the convention, he found many of the delegates up in arms about Stimson and Knox, Republicans, serving in a Democratic president's cabinet. He immediately telegraphed John D. M. Hamilton, chairman of the Republican National Committee, that the convention should approve the appointments. "As a Republican, but most of all as a citizen," he said, "I was greatly disturbed at newspaper reports of delegate reaction yesterday to the Cabinet appointments of Colonel Knox and Colonel Stimson.

"I sincerely hope the convention will take different action. We should, I believe, approve the designations and commend the acceptance of these two distinguished and outstanding men.

"We as a party should recognize before the country our duty to support without imputation of motive, the Commander-in-Chief of the Army and the Navy, who, under the Constitution, faces the duty of preparing our nation for defense. The immediacy of this problem is measured by days, cannot await the outcome of the election and transcends all other questions." *Chicago Tribune,* June 22, 1940.

Page 205, line 17: Baker.

Page 206, line 26: Diplomatic Section, National Archives.

Page 206, lines 27–32: Welles memorandum to Roosevelt, July 12, 1940, Roosevelt Library.

Page 206, line 34: Roosevelt Library.

Page 207, line 24: "Memorandum for Mr. Stettinius, to outline the type of useful information which Colonel Donovan might obtain while in England," July 13, 1940, University of Virginia Library.

Page 207, lines 25–35: Conyers Read manuscript, 6, in collection of the author.

Page 208, lines 4–11: Frank Knox to his wife, July 14, 1940, Manuscript Division, Library of Congress.

Page 208, line 25: Pforzheimer Collection.

Page 209, line 44: Report to the king, July 16, 1940, Pforzheimer Collection.

Page 210, line 12: Conyers Read manuscript, 6, author's collection.

Page 210, line 29: Leutze. Other remarks by Lee are from this journal.

Page 211, line 8: Godfrey, 129, and Beesly, 176.

Page 211, line 22: Transcript of conversation between Mowrer and Allen Dulles, circa 1962, Princeton University Library. Other Mowrer material is from this source as well.

Page 213, line 3: Conyers Read manuscript, 7, author's collection.

Page 213, line 24: William Stevenson, *A Man Called Intrepid.*

Page 217, line 13: Beesly.

Page 217, line 38: Pforzheimer Collection.

Page 218, lines 7–12: Telephone interview with Paul Bewshea, who in 1940 was in charge of Imperial Airways operations in New York and who met the plane carrying Donovan.

Chapter 19. Back Door to the White House

Page 219, line 23: Yale University Library. All other Stimson quotes in this chapter are from his diary.

Page 220, lines 8–24: Franklin Roosevelt, *Complete Press Conferences*, Press Conference No. 668, Aug. 8, 1940.

Page 220, lines 25–30: *New York Times*, Aug. 10, 1940.

Page 221, lines 1–10: Conyers Read manuscript, 8, Pforzheimer Collection.

Page 221, line 4: According to an aide of OSS days, William Langer, Donovan also reported that the dispersal and multiplication of British airfields would save the RAF from the Germans. Langer and Gleason, *The Challenge to Isolation,* 744.

Page 221, lines 10–12: Donovan to Admiral Godfrey, Aug. 27, 1940, and Donovan to Sir Cyril Newall, Aug. 27, 1940.

Page 221, lines 29–39: Franklin Roosevelt, *Complete Press Conferences,* Press Conference No. 669, Aug. 10, 1940.

Page 222, line 19: Conyers Read manuscript, 9, Pforzheimer Collection.

Page 222, line 25: Frederic Sondern, Jr., "Wild Bill Crusades Against Wars."

Page 223, line 5: Butler, 297.

Page 223, line 14: Goodhart.

Page 224, line 3: Donovan estimated that the Nazis had spent some $50 million on the fifth column in France. Felstead, 106.

Page 224, line 38: In the spring of 1941 Spruille Braden, back from a diplomatic assignment in Colombia, breakfasted with Donovan from eight in the morning until noon. Donovan elaborated on Nazi fifth column activities and revealed that he had gotten some of his information from German officers he had met during and after World War I. Braden recognized the seeds of rebellion in Colombia and informed Roosevelt, who scoffed at the idea. Two days later a revolution broke out in Bogotá. Braden, 245.

Page 224, line 42: "I am looking forward to reviewing the material myself with great interest," Stettinius wrote Donovan on Oct. 2, 1940, about the answers to his questions that Donovan had gathered in Britain, "and I shall personally bring it to the attention of the President. Your friends in the War Department and I feel that you have rendered an outstanding service in having made this information available." University of Virginia Library. Donovan had already informed Roosevelt about this report.

Page 225, line 5: Chadwin, *The Warhawks,* 79.

Page 226, line 3: Manuscript of the radio address is in the Fight for Freedom Archives, Princeton University Library.

Page 226, line 22: April 29, 1941, ULPA.

Page 226, lines 23–45; page 227, lines 1–25: Telephone interview with O'Keefe.

Page 227, line 4: April 29, 1941, ULPA.

Page 227, lines 22–26: Lecture, War Dept., Hoover Institution.

Page 227, lines 27–40: Marshall Foundation.

Page 228, line 19: Stimson had hopes of persuading Donovan to help train the draftees. "On my side I put up to Donovan my present plan for a renewal of the Training Camps in September and asked if he would cooperate as the head of one of those camps. He said he would not say no, but he thought that the plans ought to be laid out well in advance, so that people would have time to make their arrangements. He was determined to get into the war some way or other and was the same old Bill Donovan that we have all known and been so fond of." Stimson diary, Aug. 6, 1940, Yale University Library.

Page 228, line 29: University of Virginia Library. Wood, leader of the America First movement, had written to Donovan that "I am going to be on the losing side, but that does not alter my convictions. . . . I want to ask one favor of you, which I want you to bear in mind if the time for action comes. If we go into this war and go into it in an active way, where land forces are engaged, I want to get into the fighting branch of the force. I do not care what the rank is, that is immaterial to me. I began my active career in the fighting end of the army and if war comes, I want to end my

career that way. As I say, the question of rank is entirely immaterial. I think that you will be able to help me." Wood to Donovan, Oct. 3, 1940, Hoover Library.
Page 228, line 40: Hoover Library.
Page 229, lines 22–31: Krock.

Chapter 20. Fifty-Trip Ticket on the Clippers

Page 230, line 9: Donovan himself said that Roosevelt "asked me if I would go and make a strategic appreciation from an economic, political and military standpoint of the Mediterranean area." Speech, ULPA.
Page 230, line 15: Conyers Read manuscript, 11, Pforzheimer Collection.
Page 231, line 17: Stephenson cable to Churchill, and letter to Menzies, Pforzheimer Collection.
Page 232, lines 8–31: *New York Times,* Dec. 6, 1940. *Business Week* speculated that Donovan's mission was tied to increased French resentment of the Nazis, and that he might be going to Vichy to promise France postwar aid in exchange for a little backbone now. "Mystery Mission—and Defense."
Page 233, line 24: *New York Times,* Dec. 8, 1940.
Page 233, line 37: Troy, 37.
Page 233, line 42: *New York Times,* Dec. 15, 1940.
Page 234, line 2: *Chicago Tribune,* Dec. 17, 1940.
Page 239, line 2: *New York Times,* Dec. 19, 1940.
Page 239, line 34: Conyers Read manuscript, 12, Pforzheimer Collection.
Page 241, line 5: *New York Times,* Dec. 21, 1940.
Page 242, line 21: Sherwood, *The White House Papers of Harry L. Hopkins,* 231.
Page 242, lines 30–39: *New York Times,* Dec. 27, 1940.

Chapter 21. Playing for Time

Page 243, lines 1–8: Whiting.
Page 243, lines 14–15: De Launay, 441.
Page 243, line 31: Speech, April 29, 1941, ULPA.
Page 244, line 6: Admiral James Fife, interviewed by John T. Mason, Jr., Oral History Archives, Columbia University Libraries.
Page 244, line 16; page 244, line 35; page 245, line 4: Lecture, War Dept., Hoover Institution.
Page 245, line 29: Connell, 310.
Page 245, lines 37–39: Langer and Gleason, *The Undeclared War,* 376.
Page 246, line 6: *New York Times,* Jan. 12, 1941.
Page 247, line 21: Roosevelt Library.
Page 249, line 17: German agents kept a close eye on Donovan throughout his trip. Friedlander, 187.
Page 249, lines 30–34: *New York Times,* Jan. 21, 1941.
Page 249, line 36: Earle dispatched preliminary cables and finally on January 23 a full report to Secretary of State Hull on the progress of Donovan's mission in the Balkans. The Germans read the cables, but the report got through with full security. Diplomatic Section, National Archives.
Page 250, lines 8–10: *New York Times,* Jan. 22, 1941.
Page 251, line 31: Minister Earle reported to Hull on Jan. 23, 1941, "Donovan's forceful declaration to the king and his ministers that America, exerting all her enormous force will ensure ultimate victory for England has had a tremendous effect." Lane and Petrov.
Page 251, line 36: Donovan wrote to Knox on Jan. 24, 1941, that the king was "idealistic, honest and shy, although somewhat over-confident of his ability to maneuver in a difficult international situation." Ibid.
Page 252, line 14: Twardovsky memorandum, Jan. 31, 1941, PAA.
Page 252, lines 15–34: Lane and Petrov.

Page 252, line 44: "I am sending you a selection of German references over the radio," Fleming wrote Donovan on March 8, 1941. "I dare say there have been others, but the BBC does not monitor all wave lengths infallibly.

"I am very disappointed in Dykes for having led you into such bad company!

"Please don't forget my remedy for all our ills—namely that the man in the street should learn the names of our Dominions and Colonial Secretaries, and forget the name of our Foreign Minister. For the last twenty years the opposite has been the case.

"Don't spend too long in America." Philip Strong papers, Princeton University Library.

Page 253, line 39: *New York Times*, Jan. 23, 1941.

Page 255, line 15: Donovan himself said, "The British felt that at least as a result of these efforts the Bulgarian action was held up for two or three weeks, which gave them a little time." Conyers Read manuscript, 13, Pforzheimer Collection.

Chapter 22. Mediterranean Intrigue

Page 256, line 9: When U.S. embassies abroad and foreign embassies in Washington asked about Donovan's mission, Hull ordered that they be told that Donovan was solely Knox's agent. By sending Donovan on his mission, Roosevelt had circumvented Hull without making a public issue of his differences with his secretary of state, which considering the strength of isolationist critics might have been politically difficult. Lane and Petrov.

Page 256, line 12: Bendiner, 208, and Lane and Petrov, 136.

Page 256, line 18: Lane and Petrov, 136.

Page 257, lines 10–24: *New York Times*, Jan. 24, 1941.

Page 257, lines 25–30: *New York Herald Tribune*, April 2, 1941.

Page 257, line 40: Address, April 29, 1941, ULPA.

Page 258, line 26: On February 14, Cvetković and Cinkar-Marković went to Berlin, where Cvetković told Von Ribbentrop that Donovan "had told him that America would help all countries which resisted the Axis. He had replied that not only the Atlantic Ocean but also a wide strip of European continent separated Yugoslavia from America and her assistance. Yugoslavia felt herself in no way threatened, but maintained cordial relations with Germany and therefore needed no help." Friedlander, 190. Other reports in the PAA detail his visits to Sofia and to Egypt.

Page 260, line 38: When in April Stimson told Donovan that American officers in Washington were saying that "the decision of the British to send troops to Greece was the worst instance of the political element of the government interfering with the military strategy that has happened since General Halleck," Donovan told Stimson that the decision to send British troops to Greece had not been made by the cabinet of Churchill at all but by Wavell himself and that he had been present when it was made. Stimson diary, April 17, 1941, Yale University Library.

Page 262, line 13: Lincoln MacVeagh wrote to the State Department that Donovan had "said he believed that Germany would refrain from making any attack on the Balkans if she were convinced of united opposition on the part of Bulgaria, Yugoslavia, and Turkey, and that despite the forces tending to keep their nations apart, their common desire for American moral support and material assistance might well be sufficient to bring them together should a move in that direction be made by the President." Lane and Petrov.

Page 262, line 27: While Donovan was arriving in Turkey, Frank Knox was defending him before the Senate Foreign Relations Committee. Senator Clark of Missouri demanded to know what his status was.

"He is a private individual, traveling at his own expense," answered Knox. "And he is a darn good observer. He has no official status. He has an itching foot and a love of adventure." *New York Times*, Feb. 2, 1941, and Lane and Petrov.

Page 262, line 32: *New York Times*, Feb. 3, 1941. Lord Halifax wrote to Frank Knox on February 11, "I have a telegram from the FO saying that the British represen-

tatives at Sofia, Belgrade, and Ankara have all reported that Colonel Donovan's recent visits to those capitals and his frank statements to the leading personalities about the attitude of the United States toward the war have made a deep impression on all concerned. All three British representatives have expressed the view that in paying these visits at the present moment and in using the language which he did, Colonel Donovan has rendered a most valuable service to the Allied cause."
Page 263, line 34: The German military attaché in Ankara reported to Berlin that Donovan was "interested in country's roads and ports in view of the events which are going to take place in the Balkans." Report to Foreign Office, Feb. 6, 1941, PAA.
Page 264, line 11: Speech, ULPA.
Page 264, line 28: *New York Times*, Feb. 7, 1941. A French government spokesman in Vichy explained that Donovan had been denied a visa to cross Syria because of "the extremely delicate geographical situation of Syria between British Palestine and Turkey. Colonel Donovan was told he was welcome and free to go anywhere he wanted in North Africa, but in view of the delicate situation in Syria the French government desired to avoid any incidents that might harm our empire, especially as Colonel Donovan was accompanied by Lord Forbes, who is a British citizen. . . . We certainly hope Colonel Donovan will not take the refusal personally as an insult." *New York Times*, Feb. 8, 1941.
In December 1940, Germany ordered Vichy to refuse Donovan admission to any French territories, and on February 2, 1941, the order was repeated because of Nazi fear that Donovan would intrigue against their interests in Syria or North Africa. Record of the meeting of the Subcommission on Political and Military Affairs, PAA.
On February 8, the Portuguese ambassador in London reported to the Foreign Office in Lisbon that Donovan was making a study of the arms needed for an anti-German uprising in France and North Africa. That very day the report was phoned to Berlin. Hitler was sufficiently disturbed that he discussed Donovan's activities with Mussolini.
Page 264, line 30: *New York Times*, Feb. 6, 1941.
Page 265, line 31: Neale, 453.
Page 265, line 44: Roosevelt Library.
Page 266, line 11: "We are expecting Colonel Donovan too in the near future, and he should have a great deal of interest to say about the Balkans, where his talks would seem to have had an excellent effect," King George wrote to Roosevelt on February 14, 1941. Roosevelt Library.
Page 266, line 20: Eden, 226.
Page 266, line 37: Lecture, War Dept., Hoover Institution.
Page 266, line 40: Donovan also developed striking concepts for a "war of movement." "It is my distinct impression that General Donovan's strategic views derived in part from his own World War I experiences and observations from which he concluded that his was no way to fight a war, and began to crystallize and take form during the course of his extended tour of observation through parts of Europe and the Balkans shortly prior to the entry of the United States into the war." Frank G. Wisner to Allen Dulles, Dec. 30, 1954, Princeton University Library.
Donovan also told the President that the British should hold on in the Balkans to keep Hitler from invading the United Kingdom. He said too that the Germans wanted to secure the Balkans to insure supplies of oil, food, and raw materials. "Such a joint venture," he concluded, "would result in economy of time, of force, and of administration." Lane and Petrov.
Page 267, line 32: Hoare, 107.
Page 267, line 44: Winston Churchill had instructed Hoare to give Donovan this message to President Roosevelt. Higgins.
Page 268, line 18: Gallo, 104.
Page 269, line 6: Speech, April 11, 1941, Chicago Council on Foreign Relations.
Page 269, line 24: Langer and Gleason, *The Undeclared War*, 365.
Page 269, line 34: Friedlander, 208.
Page 269, line 38: In his report Hayningen-Hesse referred to "Colonel Donnovan." David Kahn, 469.

Page 270, line 40: Conyers Read manuscript, 17, Pforzheimer Collection.

Page 271, line 18: Neale, 550.

Page 271, line 38: Interview with Pinto. Pinto also remarked, "The British actor Leslie Howard spent his last night on earth here at the Palacio. He left with two British schoolchildren and their nanny who were returning to England. The Germans knew that Howard was a British agent, and they learned of his departure and made certain that his plane was shot down. Others have said the Germans believed that Churchill was aboard the plane, but I've never thought this was their belief."

Pinto explained that "when the Germans spoke in loud voices I knew they wanted to be overheard. When they whispered, they had a secret." When a German agent confided in him, Pinto realized he was planting false information since he believed a British or American agent would soon happen along to pump him. Every day, according to Pinto, a violin and piano ensemble played for lunch and dinner at the Palacio. Every time a known agent entered the room, the ensemble struck up a tune entitled, "Boo, Boo, I Am a Spy."

Page 271, line 40: Harriman and Abel, 21.

Page 272, line 5: *Buffalo News*, March 15, 1941, and *Buffalo Courier-Express*, March 19, 1941. Among the other Clipper passengers were Francis Aiken, Ireland's minister for defense coordination, and Dr. Eelco N. Van Kleffens, the Netherlands prime minister.

Page 273, line 19: "The trip to the Balkans impressed him [Donovan] with respect to the skills of the Germans and their complete infiltration of the area," remarked Edwin Putzell, Jr. Putzell to author, Aug. 23, 1981.

Page 273, line 30: *Time*, March 31, 1941. Journalist Elizabeth Valentine wrote, "On and off during the past year foreign correspondents from American newspapers have found themselves involved in a gopher hunt. The territory was the Near East, the Continent, and the British Isles: the quarry was Colonel William J. Donovan. First spotted nonchalantly boarding a waiting clipper in Baltimore, he later popped up unannounced at 10 Downing Street, and then appeared and disappeared mysteriously all along the line from Cairo to Gibraltar. His comings and goings were always inconspicuous and unheralded, and when nabbed by reporters, he was as affable and enigmatic as a Tibetan lama. Colonel Donovan was on a fact-finding mission for the President—'just having a look around'—beyond this he had nothing to say." Of an interview with Donovan, Valentine wrote, "Directly after saying how-do-you-do-won't-you-sit-down, he begins asking questions; the caller has a fine time talking about himself, leaves in a warm glow, without a scrap of personal information about William J. Donovan."

Chapter 23. The Intelligence Proposal

Page 275, line 7: Manuscript Division, Library of Congress.

Page 276, line 7: *Washington Star*, March 27, 1941.

Page 276, line 27: Conyers Read manuscript, 19, Pforzheimer Collection.

Page 276, line 42: Ibid., 20.

Page 277, line 5: Irving, 41. In his speech declaring war on Yugoslavia, Hitler shouted that Roosevelt had sent Colonel Donovan, "a completely unworthy creature," to intrigue in Bulgaria and Yugoslavia. Bailey.

"The German and Italian radio and press attacked Donovan, Minister Fotitch, and me as instigators of the uprising," said Sveteslav Petrovic. Petrovic, 245.

Page 278, line 2: *New York Times*, April 12, 1941.

Page 278, line 25: Speech, April 11, 1941, Chicago Council on Foreign Relations. After his speech Donovan had a talk with Adlai Stevenson, then a prominent Chicago lawyer who was a leading member of the council. The two men believed that the Chicago Irish might be persuaded to help influence Ireland's government to grant Great Britain naval bases. Adlai Stevenson.

Page 278, line 29: *New York Times*, April 12, 1941.

Page 278, line 39: Donovan also penned a widely read magazine article. "The Nazis have not overlooked their opportunity in our hurried preparations to meet sudden danger," he said. "With the same psychological sabotage they used to 'soften' one European democracy after another before plucking them off by force, the Nazis are offering countless suggestions and innuendoes to persuade us that democracy has made us 'soft'—not fit material to challenge the 'tougher' products of Nazi discipline. "A few months ago I traveled all over the U.S. I visited our training camps. I was with our fleet at sea. Nowhere did I see evidence of softness."

Donovan also wrote, "Although greater brawn is not important in their jobs, some of the finest physical specimens in my regiment during the last war were men from banks, offices, and stores." He concluded, "I would bet on democratic peoples anyhow. I have yet to learn of a strong and enlightened people submitting for long to dictatorship. Nor has democracy ever flourished among the weak. It takes the best qualities of humanity to make democracy possible at all. We have every reason to look upon our trust in democracy as a barometer of our fitness to defend this country." "Who Says We're Soft."

Page 278, line 41: Fight for Freedom Archives, Princeton University Library.

Page 279, line 5: MacLeish to Donovan, May 17, 1941, and Fight for Freedom Archives, Princeton University Library.

Page 279, line 32: Eugene Grassman journal, June 8, 1941, Bentley Historical Library, University of Michigan Library.

Page 279, line 43: *New York Times,* April 26, 1941.

Page 280, line 20: Conyers Read manuscript, 20, Pforzheimer Collection.

Page 281, line 36: Godfrey had discussed the idea of unifying U.S. intelligence with Ambassador Winant in London, and in New York he conferred with Sir William Wiseman, a senior British intelligence man who had served in America during World War I. Both Stephenson and Wiseman talked to Donovan about a central U.S. intelligence, and the British representatives made it clear they felt that Donovan should head it. Beesly, 181.

Page 283, line 22: *Buffalo News,* April 1, 1941.

Page 283, line 24: Conyers Read manuscript, 21, Pforzheimer Collection.

Page 283, line 33: Pearson.

Page 286, line 8: Roosevelt Library.

Page 287, line 2: Roosevelt had considered Donovan for a domestic propaganda role. Henry L. Stimson conferred with the President and noted in his diary, "He had first of all told me that La Guardia had accepted the position of home defense until August and outlined the two committees which La Guardia wishes to create. The second committee—sort of a ballyhoo committee. He was thinking of Donovan, Bill Bullitt, Pat Hurley: hasn't made up his mind. He wants a high-ranking officer to help La Guardia in home defense." "Memorandum of Interview with Roosevelt," May 20, 1941, Henry L. Stimson papers, Yale University Library.

Page 287, line 29: "At a Bureau of the Budget conference regarding a preliminary draft of the proposed order, Colonel Donovan explained that he proposed to set up a service organization which would collect and analyze information for the Army, the Navy, the Federal Bureau of Investigation, and other agencies. For each project, there would be a correlated summary supported by reports from such technicians as geographers, political scientists, and economists. Colonel Donovan wanted the Library of Congress to serve as an instrument for securing the cooperation of libraries and scholars, and he hoped that an FBI man would assist him on the offensive side of his work. He mentioned Robert Sherwood as a type of person who would be used in the overseas information program. While he referred to the President's desire that he set up a committee on the 'Economics of the future,' plans were already far advanced for a separate board of economic defense." Report in the OSS Archives, National Archives.

Page 286, line 42: Hyde, 153.

Page 289, line 2: Franklin Roosevelt, *Complete Press Conferences,* Press Conference No. 750, June 24, 1941.

Page 290, line 23: *New York Times,* July 12, 1941.

Page 290, line 31: "Attached is an Order designating William J. Donovan as Coordinator of Information," stated Harold Smith, director of the Bureau of the Budget in a memorandum to the President dated July 3, 1941. "Pursuant to your instructions, we have worked with Ben Cohen in preparing and clearing this draft which bears the approval of Colonel Donovan, Secretary Knox, and Secretary Stimson. Since the appointment is made by virtue of your authority as Commander-in-Chief of the Army and Navy, it should be issued as a Military Order.

"While both the Army and Navy objected to our original title for Colonel Donovan of Coordinator of *Strategic* Information or Coordinator of *Defense* Information, I think either of these titles is preferable to the one used in the Order as now presented. 'Coordinator of Information' is vague and is not descriptive of the work Colonel Donovan will perform.

"Also attached is a proposed press statement you may wish to issue at the time of signing the Order. We are preparing appropriate letters to the departments and agencies concerned with the subject of defense information, requesting their full cooperation with Colonel Donovan in carrying out his duties." Roosevelt Library.

The Order as signed by Roosevelt read: "By virtue of the authority vested in me as President of the United States and as Commander-in-Chief of the Army and Navy of the United States, it is ordered as follows:

"1. There is hereby established the position of Coordinator of Information, with authority to collect and analyze all information and data, which may bear upon national security; to correlate such information and data, and to make such information and data available to the President and to such departments and officials of the Government as the President may determine; and to carry out, when requested by the President, such supplementary activities as may facilitate the securing of information important for national security not now available to the Government.

"2. The several departments and agencies of the Government shall make available to the Coordinator of Information all and any such information and data relating to national security as the Coordinator, with the approval of the President, may from time to time request.

"3. The Coordinator of Information may appoint such committees, consisting of appropriate representatives of the various departments and agencies of the Government, as he may deem necessary to assist him in the performance of his functions.

"4. Nothing in the duties and responsibilities of the Coordinator of Information shall in any way interfere with or impair the duties and responsibilities of the regular military and naval advisers of the President as Commander-in-Chief of the Army and Navy.

"5. Within the limits of such funds as may be allocated to the Coordinator of Information by the President, the Coordinator may employ necessary personnel and make provision for the necessary supplies, facilities and services.

"6. William J. Donovan is hereby designated as Coordinator of Information."

Chapter 24. Donovan's Brain Trust

Page 295, lines 6–35; page 296, lines 1–2: Field, "Memorandum on Office of Coordinator of Information," manuscript, April 5, 1963. Given to author by Field.
Page 297, line 2: Cline, 36.
Page 297, line 13: The previous tenant was Wayne Coy, FDR's special assistant and executive secretary of the Office of Emergency Manpower. "High Strategist."
Page 297, line 33: Berle.
Page 297, line 34: Arnold.
Page 298, line 9: Ickes.
Page 298, line 18: Morgenthau diary, Roosevelt Library.
Page 299, line 16: Interview with Mrs. William Langer.
Page 299, line 31: Roosevelt Library.
Page 300, line 13: Blaire Bolles, "A Look at 'Invisible' C.O.I.," *Washington Star,* Oct. 5, 1941.

Page 301, line 17: Field, "Memorandum on Office of Coordinator of Information," manuscript, April 5, 1963, author's collection.

Page 301, lines 18–44; page 302, lines 1–18: Telephone interview with Landon.

Page 302, line 25: "With the permission of Colonel Frank Knox, secretary of the navy and owner of the *Chicago Daily News,* I severed my connection with that newspaper for a period of three months, and started preparing myself for a trip to the Far East," stated Mowrer. "It was understood that, although furnished with credentials from the United States Government, I was to show these only when necessary and pass currently as a newspaper correspondent. In the course of my travel I divulged my character as Colonel Donovan's representative to only about a half dozen persons, exclusively British and American, some of whom, like British Minister Duff Cooper, had heard of my trip in advance and promised cooperation." "Final report of Edgar Ansel Mowrer to Colonel Donovan, concerning a mission to the Far East in the Autumn of 1941," Allen Dulles papers, Princeton University Library.

Page 303, line 26: Transcript of conversation between Dulles and Mowrer, circa 1962, Princeton University Library.

Page 303, lines 31–44; page 304, lines 1–4: Telephone interview with McBaine.

Page 304, lines 1–36: Morris.

Page 305, line 42: Interview with Richards.

Page 306, lines 1–13: Interview with Kermit Roosevelt.

Page 307, line 40: Caroline Bland manuscript.

Page 308, lines 12–19: Rostow to author.

Page 309, lines 30–45; page 310, lines 1–15: Interview with Mrs. William Langer.

Page 312, line 15: Walter Langer.

Page 312, line 44: David Bruce letter to the *New York Times.*

Page 313, line 18: Steve Early suggested to FDR, "If you are asked a question about *Colonel Donovan's* organization, the following is suggested:

"Almost every time the government of the United States acts to strengthen its defenses and to increase its efficiency—for the better protection of the people of the United States—it seems that one or two senators immediately label that act in a way that creates distrust, fear and misunderstanding.

"One senator has referred to Colonel Donovan's organization as an Ogpu or Gestapo. That just isn't so.

"Another senator has spoken in a way that leads to misunderstanding and distrust of the 'good neighbor' policy. We intend, however, to carry on—to do our best to strengthen our defenses and give the Government a better efficiency." Aug. 1, 1941, Roosevelt Library.

Chapter 25. COI Sets Up Shop

Page 314, line 13: Donovan, "Intelligence: Key to Defense."

Page 315, line 9: Interview with Will.

Page 315, line 15: Rowan and Deindorfer, 615.

Page 316, line 3: Daniels.

Page 316, line 17: Wallace Deuel, notes for proposed OSS history, manuscript.

Page 316, line 37: Cline.

Page 318, line 3: Hyde. "Mr. William Samuel Stephenson was the earliest collaborator with and chief supporter of the early movement which culminated in the establishment of the Office of the Coordinator of Information," said Donovan. "His early discussions with the Coordinator were largely instrumental in bringing about a clearer conception of the need of a properly coordinated American intelligence service. His wise counsel and earnest efforts helped to consolidate the activities of scattered intelligence units and agencies. He readily accepted this duty of great responsibility to help establish, train, and maintain the personnel to perform the services of the COI and later, the OSS, in order that those services might in themselves stand as exceptionally meritorious to this government and at the same time fit harmoniously into the war plans of the combined Allied cause to the mutually

great benefit of all." "Recognition for award of Distinguished Service Medal," Donovan to the adjutant general, War Dept., May 13, 1943, Hoover Institution.
Page 318, line 34: Field, "Memorandum on Office of Coordinator of Information," April 5, 1963, author's collection.
Page 318, line 42: Interview with McBaine.
Page 319, line 9: Sweet-Escott.
Page 319, lines 17–19: Interview with Mrs. William Langer.
Page 320, line 38: Marshall Foundation.
Page 321, lines 5–29: Kermit Roosevelt, *Countercoup*, 24.
Page 321, line 37: Johnson.
Page 322, lines 5–31: Sherwood, *The White House Papers of Harry L. Hopkins*, 411.
Page 323, lines 8–30: Don Ford.
Page 323, line 31: Donovan's days were hectic. Raymond Lee noted in his London journal on October 31, 1941, that Noel Hall had just returned from Washington. "He went on to discuss Donovan's activities and said that he was attempting to do too much in too great a hurry. He was very amusing in describing a meeting with Donovan, who asks everyone to come and see him. Hall went in to the waiting room where he talked to a secretary who asked him to sit down and telephoned about him. After twenty or thirty minutes Hall, who has the rank of a British minister, bestirred himself and said that he did not want to wait any longer. The man then ushered him into a second waiting room where he went through the same performance once more, and after waiting again complained. This secretary then ushered him into a third waiting room. By this time Hall was on to the curves of Donovan's machinery and simply walked in where he found him with his coat off, surrounded by a dozen men and with Hall the last person in the world he was thinking of. But Bill, who is always equal to the situation, looked up and saw him and shouted, 'Here he is now, exactly the man we want,' and then went on talking about something Hall knew nothing whatever about."
Page 323, line 36: Dulles to Hugh Wilson, Mott Belin, and Fred Mayer, Sept. 15, 1941, Princeton University Library.
Page 324, line 7: Dartmouth College Library.
Page 324, line 10: Stefansson enlisted the assistance of Vice-President Henry Wallace in approaching Roosevelt. Stefansson to Wallace, Nov. 10, 1941, University of Iowa Library.
Page 324, line 25: Stefansson to Donovan, Nov. 13, 1941, Dartmouth College Library.
Page 326, line 18; page 327, line 42: Roosevelt Library.
Page 327, line 31: Donovan, "Intelligence: Key to Defense."

Chapter 26. Conducting Ungentlemanly Warfare

Page 332, lines 30-39: William Langer, *In and Out of the Ivory Tower*, 183.
Page 333, line 41: "The President's Appointments," Dec. 7, 1941, University of Virginia Library.
Page 334, line 18: Donovan, "Intelligence: Key to Defense."
Page 334, line 27: Interview with Halle.
Page 334, lines 31–39: Lombard, 5.
Page 335, line 39: Dec. 23, 1941, OSS Archives, National Archives.
Page 335, lines 41–44; page 336, lines 1–33: Parrish.
Page 337, line 3: David Bruce letter to the *New York Times*.
Page 337, lines 5–16: Interview with Booth.
Page 339, line 3: At 6 P.M. on December 21, Donovan sent the President another memo concerning North Africa: "I talked this afternoon with a man who knows a holy man who he has befriended. My man was a friend of Lyautey and lived there for six years. His friend, the holy man, is very close to the Sultan. He thinks that he would have a reasonable chance of inducing the Sultan to carry out the project we have in mind. He thinks money would not be required, but arms and equipment plus a promise of semi-autonomy.

"Our agent is an Englishman, graduate of Sandhurst, excellent education and experience. Our only chance of getting him in, however, would be under an American passport.

"On the operational side, I would have it handled by our S.O.S. here who will be returning from England where I have had him at the guerrilla school.

"It would be necessary to get our supplies in there at once.

"If you feel that you wish this to be taken up, please let me know as quickly as possible. I think we could work it jointly with the British."

"WJD," penned Roosevelt at the top of the memo, "take up with Marshall & State Dept. FDR." Roosevelt Library.

Page 340, line 6: Hoover Institution.
Page 344, lines 2 and 42; page 350, line 43: OSS Archives, National Archives.
Page 344, line 11: Reader's Digest, "We Were Expecting You at Dakar," *Secrets and Spies.*
Page 345, line 20: Houseman, 36.
Page 346, line 33: Goodfellow papers, 101 Association Archives.
Page 348, line 42; page 349, line 8: Interview with Van Arkel.
Page 349, lines 30–44; page 350, lines 1–21: Strauss.
Page 350, lines 23–31: William Langer, *Our Vichy Gamble.*
Page 351, line 11: Roosevelt Library.
Page 351, lines 19–45: Interview with Goldberg.
Page 351, line 36: Wilhelm, 87.
Page 353, lines 30–35: Interview with Setton.
Page 354, line 1: Roosevelt wrote to Donovan, "I know you are aware of what I am doing in the way of tying all the Information Services together. I am putting the C.O.I. under the Joint Chiefs of Staff under this new Order and you will head up the division to be known as 'the Office Of Strategic Services.'

"I think that Elmer Davis, with his long experience and his genuine popularity in press and radio circles, will be able to tie together the many factors of information in the broadest sense of the term.

"I hope you had a grand trip to London." June 13, 1942, Roosevelt Library.
Page 354, line 27: Wright to Kirchhofer, June 16, 1942, courtesy of Kirchhofer.
Page 354, line 42: Peter Tompkins, *Italy Betrayed.*

Chapter 27. OSS Goes to War

Page 355, lines 23–33: Zuckerman, 157.
Page 356, line 16: Corey Ford papers, Dartmouth College Library.
Page 356, lines 24–43; page 357, lines 1–21: Phillips, 206.
Page 357, line 21: William Phillips interviewed by Wendell H. Link, July 1951, Oral History Archives, Columbia University Libraries.
Page 358, line 7: Walter Langer.
Page 359, line 6: Cline.
Page 359, line 21: Sweet-Escott, 133.
Page 359, line 35; page 364, line 34; page 365, lines 27–42; page 366, line 12: Donovan, "Intelligence: Key to Defense."
Page 359, line 40: Interview with Bane.
Page 360, line 5: Beaudouin to author, March 20, 1981.
Page 360, line 18: 101 Association Archives.
Page 361, line 14: OSS Archives, National Archives.
Page 361, line 24: Interview with Bashor.
Page 361, line 29: Laundergan to author, Sept. 3, 1981.
Page 361, lines 30–35: Interview with Sipe.
Page 362, lines 1–10: Interview with English.
Page 362, lines 11–29: Interview with Setton.
Page 362, line 36: Interview with McIntosh.
Page 362, lines 37–44: Interview with Mrs. William Langer.

Page 364, line 6: OSS Assessment Staff, 10.
Page 364, line 11: Interview with Will.
Page 364, lines 19–24: Beishlag to author, Feb. 14, 1981.
Page 364, line 27: Donovan memo, OSS Archives, National Archives.
Page 364, lines 35–42: Cardinale.
Page 366, line 43: Parrish.

Chapter 28. Prelude to Torch

Page 367, lines 14–31; page 368, lines 1–4; page 368, line 9; page 371, line 22: OSS Archives, National Archives.
Page 369, line 41: Interview with Clark.
Page 372, line 6: Citadel Memorial Archives.
Page 375, lines 24–30: Franklin Roosevelt, *Complete Press Conferences*, Press Conference No. 859, Nov. 10, 1942.
Page 375, line 45: Marshall Foundation.
Page 376, line 17: Harvard University Library.

Chapter 29. Professor Moriarty Joins the OSS

Page 377, line 3: Interview with Lovell. Unless otherwise indicated, the material concerning R & D was obtained during several days spent with Dr. Lovell.
Page 378, lines 20–30: Interview with Putzell.
Page 382, lines 4–28: Byrnes.
Page 382, lines 29–37: Interview with Hamilton.
Page 382, lines 38–46; page 382, lines 1–2: Interview with Halsey.
Page 384, line 22: *Washington Post*, Jan. 21, 1943.
Page 384, line 43; page 385, lines 17–26: Troy.
Page 386, lines 31–56: Interview with Cuneo.
Page 387, lines 1–12: Roosevelt Library.

Chapter 30. Partners with the Resistance

Page 388, line 4: Interview with John Bowden, son of George Bowden.
Page 389, lines 16–25: Interview with Taquey.
Page 389, lines 26–45: Interview with Rader.
Page 391, lines 7–15: Interview with Hart.
Page 392, lines 42–44; page 393, lines 1–10: Interview with Van Arkel.
Page 393, lines 16–31: Interview with Schmidt.
Page 393, line 37: Marshall Foundation.
Page 394, line 14: Interview with Coggins.
Page 394, line 19: Robinson to author, Feb. 20, 1981.
Page 394, line 24: Beaudouin to author, March 20, 1981.
Page 394, lines 25–44; page 395, lines 1–19: Walter Langer, 10.
Page 395, lines 20–44; page 396, lines 1–6: Interview with Goldberg.
Page 395, lines 7–44; page 396, lines 1–22: Interview with Nicol Smith.

Chapter 31. Tangled Webs

Page 398, lines 1–7: Campbell, 175.
Page 399, lines 20–44; page 400, lines 1–2: Interview with Gale.
Page 400, lines 12–16: Interview with Clark.
Page 400, line 21: Interview with Crockett.
Page 401, 12–44; page 402, lines 1–14: Interview with Lovell, and Whiting, 137.
Page 402, line 30: Willoughby and Chamberlain, 144.
Page 402, lines 35–41: Lee, 84.

Page 403, line 4: Interview with McGovern.
Page 413, line 14: MacArthur Memorial.
Page 413, lines 15–45; page 414, lines 1–12: Hough, 166.
Page 416, line 5: North to author, March 29, 1981.
Page 416, lines 6–40: Peter Tompkins, *Italy Betrayed*, 257.
Page 417, lines 36–45; page 418, lines 1–2: Interview with Scariano.
Page 418, line 19: Foster Howe of the OSS London office made arrangements for Donovan to breakfast with foreign correspondents, and sometimes went shopping with him so that he could buy such things as "20 books, 4 wallets and a couple of briefcases to take back to people at home." Donovan did not take notes when he talked to Churchill or Bill Stephenson. "Nobody knew what was said," remarked Howe, "and there never were any cables summarizing the meetings." Interview with Howe.
Page 418, line 40: Memorandum to Gen. Thomas Y. Handy, Oct. 20, 1943, Marshall Foundation.
Page 419, line 17: Marshall Foundation.
Page 419, lines 21–44: Louis Kaufman, Fitzgerald, and Sewell, 165.
Page 420, lines 1–17: Interview with Van Arkel.

Chapter 32. Behind Enemy Lines

Page 421, lines 1–11: Don Ford.
Page 421, lines 24–44; page 422–423: Interview with Eifler.
Page 423, lines 15–33: Interview with Nicol Smith.
Page 424, lines 9–14: Interview with Curl.
Page 425, lines 10–19: Interview with Coughlin.
Page 426, line 5: Marshall Foundation.
Page 426, lines 15–25: Interview with Heppner.
Page 426, lines 34–44; page 427, lines 1–38: Interviews with McGinnis and Caldwell.
Page 427, lines 16–23: Deacon, 289.
Page 428, lines 25–43: OSS Archives, National Archives.
Page 429, line 19: Deane, 50.
Page 429, line 21: Harriman and Abel, 291.
Page 430, line 39: *New York Times*, Jan. 7, 1944.
Page 430, lines 42–44; page 431, lines 1–12: Bohlen, 155.

Chapter 33. "The Wine Is Red"

Page 432, lines 6–10: Interview with Putzell.
Page 432, lines 11–17; page 434, lines 21–28: Interview with Crockett.
Page 432, lines 17–26: Constantin Bertakis to author.
Page 433, lines 17–32; page 434, lines 37–45; page 435, lines 1–3: Interview with Scariano.
Page 433, line 29: Allen Dulles note, Princeton University Library.
Page 435, line 18: De Toledano.
Page 435, line 26: Harriman wrote to Roosevelt, "We have penetrated here for the first time an intelligence branch of the Soviet government, and I am certain this will be the opening wedge to far greater intimacy in other branches if pursued. I cannot express too strongly my conviction that our relations with the Soviet government in other directions will be adversely affected if we close the door on this branch of the Soviet government after they had shown cooperative spirit and good faith." Harriman and Abel.
Page 436, line 13: OSS Archives, National Archives.
Page 437, lines 1–16: Interview with Putzell.
Page 438, lines 30–40: Ludington to author.
Page 439, lines 10–45; page 440, lines 1–8: Interview with Bruce, and Schoenbrun, 408.

Page 440, lines 9–15: Reddick to author.
Page 445, lines 6–22: Interview with Jones.
Page 445, lines 39–41: Interview with Putzell.
Page 445, lines 41–44; page 446, lines 1–6: North letter to author.
Page 446, lines 14–19: Allen Dulles papers, Princeton University Library.
Page 446, lines 20–30: Interview with Thayer.
Page 446, lines 31–44; page 447, lines 1–5: Davis to author, Feb. 19, 1981.
Page 447, lines 15–34: Interview with Ritz.
Page 447, lines 35–44: Rostow to author, May 21, 1981.

Chapter 34. Preparing for the Peace

Page 454, line 31: Interview with Will.
Page 456, lines 41–44; page 456, lines 1–21: Interview with Little.
Page 457, lines 23–40: Interview with Lindgren.
Page 457, lines 41–44; page 458, lines 1–10: MacDonald to author, June 16, 1981.
Page 459, line 40: *Buffalo Courier-Express*, May 5, 1951.

Chapter 35. End of an Experiment

Page 460, lines 5–22: Interview with Vogel.
Page 463, lines 3–9: Tom Braden.
Page 463, lines 31–41: *Chicago Tribune*, Feb. 9, 1945.
Page 466, lines 5–15: Bank to author, Feb. 14, 1981.
Page 466, lines 16–26: Interview with Schmidt.
Page 467, lines 3–20: Interview with Stephenson.
Page 467, lines 22–39: Biddle, 359.
Page 469, lines 41–44; page 470, lines 15–21; page 471, lines 27–44; page 472, lines 1–8: Interview with Mrs. William Langer.
Page 470, lines 23–30: Interview with Lyon.
Page 470, lines 30–44; page 471, lines 1–17: Interview with Krause.
Page 472, lines 19–44; page 472, lines 1–4: Interview with Warbell.
Page 472, line 27: Hoover Institution.
Page 472, line 44; page 473, lines 1–11: Smith journal, Sept. 20, 1945, Roosevelt Library.
Page 473, line 32: Arthur Krock papers, Princeton University Library.
Page 474, line 29: Pforzheimer Collection.
Page 474, line 42: Talk, and the last bulletin of the OSS, Ibid.

Chapter 36. Bringing the Nazis to Trial

Page 479, line 11: Hoover Institution.
Page 479, line 17: The two-and-a-half-hour motion picture was assembled by Frank Capra from raw footage taken at the death camps. OSS man John English, who was present, later led a team that captured the Wehrmacht's film library in an old castle at St. Johannes, near Bayreuth. The OSS men also discovered ten tons of damning Nazi records behind the bricked walls of the castle dungeon. Interview with English.
Page 480, lines 15–30: Interview with Schmidt.
Page 481, line 7: Von Papen, 271.
Page 481, lines 12–34: Von Schlabrendorff, 261.
Page 482, lines 28–41: Storey, 98.
Page 483, lines 21–27: Wright letter to Kirchhofer, Jan. 11, 1946, courtesy of Kirchhofer.
Page 483, lines 34–44; page 484, lines 1–24; page 485, lines 3–30: Interview with Quinn.
Page 485, lines 31–44: Interview with Houston.
Page 486, lines 1–21: Okie to author, March 6, 1981.

Page 487, line 11: Donovan to Stettinius, Jr., April 23, 1946, University of Virginia Library.
Page 487, lines 15–44: Interview with Byron Martin.
Page 488, lines 21–26: Nancy Fogarty also remarked that she "helped Mrs. Donovan with her records. He was not a one-woman man. He respected her, and she thought him a great man. He was going so fast, how could she keep up with him? He was so interested in the world. How could a woman keep up with him?" Interview with Fogarty.
Page 488, lines 26–36: Interview with Cuneo.

Chapter 37. Donovan's Last Missions

Page 492, line 26: *New York Times*, July 18, 1948.
Page 493, lines 40–44: Weller to author, May 15, 1981.
Page 496, line 21: "MacArthur suspected that Donovan was engaged in secret work," recalled Thomas Bland, who was with the CIA in Tokyo. "Willoughby gave a party in Donovan's honor at the Imperial Hotel. I was invited. It was all men, all black tie. Willoughby was trying to tie Donovan into some intelligence operations. I hadn't seen Donovan since the day I left Bern in the war, and I hadn't had any contact with him until this moment. He walked into the room and said, 'Hello, Barney, how are you doing?' It threw Willoughby into a flat spin." Interview with Bland.
Page 496, line 38: Author's collection.
Page 500, lines 37–44; page 501, lines 1–2: Casey, 149.
Page 501, lines 3–44: page 502, lines 7–22; page 504, lines 5–13: Interview with Landon.
Page 501, line 44: A Reuters correspondent was also present, and he reported that "the khaki-clad Chinese soldiers filtered in. They were hungry but fit, wore peaked caps, rolled-up trouser legs, carried blankets and personal gear but no arms. Donovan met the Chinese in Burma and escorted them across the border into Thailand. They flew to Taiwan from the Lampong airstrip." *Chicago Tribune*, Nov. 9, 1953.
Page 502, lines 43–44; page 503, lines 1–4: Coon, 14.
Page 503, line 28: Allen Dulles papers, Princeton University Library.
Page 503, lines 31–44: Hoover Institution.
Page 504, line 15: Eisenhower wrote to Donovan, "In accordance with our understanding I am accepting your resignation as American ambassador to Thailand, to take effect on a date to be determined later. I take this action with extreme reluctance for I am aware of the drive, energy and devotion which has characterized your service.
"Your accomplishments on this assignment reflect a broad comprehension of the complex factors so influential in the molding of our policy toward the free nations of Southeast Asia." Sept. 15, 1954, Allen Dulles papers, Princeton University Library.
Page 505, line 25: Donovan returned to Chicago again in 1956 to address the Chicago-area Council of the American Veterans Committee. "The paradox of our foreign policy is that we have been forced to seek alliances with countries whose interests are not always parallel to our own," he said. "Our alliance with countries like Britain, France, and Holland raises grave doubts in the minds of Asians and Africans who remember these countries as their former colonial masters.
"While we gave material support to the French in Indochina as part of an international defense against the expansion of Communism, we neglected to give proper attention to the needs of the Vietnamese themselves. What we saw clearly as a struggle against Communism, the Vietnamese saw as against a background of a century of French colonial domination." Donovan concluded that the United States must find a method to support free nations of Asia against "a new colonialism—Communist imperialism." *Chicago Tribune*, April 24, 1956.
Page 505, line 40: Donovan to Christopher Emmet, Dec. 12, 1956, Hoover Institution.
Page 507, line 32: Pforzheimer Collection.

Bibliography

Books

Accoce, Pierre, and Quet, Pierre. *A Man Called Lucy.* New York: Coward-McCann, 1966.
Adleman, Robert H., and Walton, George. *The Champagne Campaign.* Boston: Little, Brown, 1969.
———. *The Devil's Brigade.* Philadelphia: Chilton, 1966.
———. *Rome Fell Today.* Boston: Little, Brown, 1968.
Albion, Robert G., and Connery, Robert H. *Forrestal and the Navy.* New York: Columbia University Press, 1962.
Alcorn, Robert Hayden. *No Banner, No Bands.* New York: David McKay, 1965.
Andrews, Peter. *In Honored Glory.* New York: Putnam's, 1966.
Anisimov, Oleg. *The Ultimate Weapon.* Chicago: Henry Regnery, 1953.
Army Times. *The Daring Regiments.* New York: Dodd, Mead, 1967.
———. *Famous Fighters of World War I.* New York: Dodd, Mead, 1964.
———. *Heroes of the Resistance.* New York: Dodd, Mead, 1967.
———. *Modern American Secret Agents.* New York: Dodd, Mead, 1964.
Arnold, H. H. *Global Mission.* New York: Harper, 1949.
Aron, Robert. *France Reborn.* New York: Scribner's, 1964.
Bailey, Thomas A. *Hitler vs. Roosevelt.* New York: Free Press, 1979.
Baker, Roscoe. *The American Legion and American Foreign Policy.* New York: Bookman, 1954.
Barker, Elizabeth. *Churchill and Eden at War.* New York: St. Martins, 1978.
Barron, Gloria. *Leadership in Crisis.* Port Washington, N.Y.: Kennikat, 1973.
Beck, James M. *The War and Humanity.* New York: Putnam's, 1917.
Beesly, Patrick. *Very Special Admiral: The Life of Admiral J. H. Godfrey, CB.* London: Hamish Hamilton, 1980.
Belmont, Eleanor Robson. *The Fabric of Memory.* New York: Farrar, Straus, 1957.
Bendiner, Robert. *The Riddle of the State Department.* New York: Farrar & Rinehart, 1942.
Bentley, Eric, ed. *Thirty Years of Treason.* New York: Viking, 1971.
Berle, Adolph A. *Navigating the Rapids, 1918–1971: From the Papers of Adolph A. Berle.* Edited by Beatrice Berle and Travis Beal Jacobs. New York: Harcourt Brace Jovanovich, 1973.
Bernays, Edward L. *Biography of an Idea: Memoirs of Public Relations Counsel.* New York: Simon & Schuster, 1965.
Berry, Henry. *Make the Kaiser Dance.* Garden City, N.Y.: Doubleday, 1978.
Beschloss, Michael R. *Kennedy and Roosevelt.* New York: W. W. Norton, 1980.
Biddle, Francis. *In Brief Authority.* Garden City, N.Y.: Doubleday, 1962.
Bird, Michael J. *The Secret Battalion.* New York: Holt, Rinehart & Winston, 1964.
Birnbaum, Karl E. *Peace Moves and U-Boat Warfare.* Stockholm: Alnquist & Wiksell, 1958.
Blum, John M. *V Was for Victory.* New York: Harcourt Brace Jovanovich, 1976.
Bohlen, Charles E. *Witness to History, 1929–1969.* New York: W. W. Norton, 1973.
Bowers, Claude G. *My Mission to Spain.* New York: Simon & Schuster, 1954.
Boyle, Andrew. *The Fourth Man.* New York: Dial/James Wade, 1979.
Braden, Spruille. *Diplomats and Demagogues.* New Rochelle, N.Y.: Arlington House, 1971.

Brandeis, Louis D. *Elder Statesman.* Letters of Louis D. Brandeis, vol. 5. Edited by Melvin I. Vrafsky and David W. Levy. Albany: State of New York Press, 1978.

Brophy, Leo P.; Miles, Wyndham D.; and Cochrane, Raymond C. *The Chemical Warfare Service: From Laboratory to Field.* Washington, D.C.: Office of the Chief of Military History, U.S. Dept. of the Army, 1959.

Bryant, Arthur. *The Turn of the Tide.* Garden City, N.Y.: Doubleday, 1957.

Burlingame, Roger. *Don't Let Them Scare You: The Life and Times of Elmer Davis.* Philadelphia: Lippincott, 1961.

Burnham, James. *The War We Are In.* New Rochelle, N.Y.: Arlington House, 1967.

Butcher, Harry C. *My Three Years with Eisenhower.* New York: Simon & Schuster, 1946.

Butler, J. R. M. *Lord Lothian.* London: Macmillan, 1960.

Byrnes, James F. *All in One Lifetime.* New York: Harper, 1958.

———. *Speaking Frankly.* New York: Harper, 1947.

Campbell, Rodney. *The Luciano Project.* New York: McGraw-Hill, 1977.

Casey, R. G. *Australian Foreign Minister: The Diaries of R. G. Casey, 1951–60.* Edited by T. B. Millar. London: Collins, 1972.

Chadwin, Mark L. *The Hawks of World War II.* Chapel Hill: University of North Carolina Press, 1968.

———. *The Warhawks.* New York: W. W. Norton, 1970.

Chennault, Claire Lee. *Way of a Fighter.* New York: Putnam's, 1949.

Childs, Harwood L., and Whitten, John B., eds. *Propaganda by Short Wave.* Princeton, N.J.: Princeton University Press, 1942.

Churchill, Winston S. *The Grand Alliance.* Boston: Houghton Mifflin, 1950.

Clark, Mark W. *Calculated Risk.* New York: Harper, 1950.

Clark, Ronald W. *The Man Who Broke Purple.* London: Weidenfeld & Nicalson, 1977.

Cline, Ray S. *Secrets, Spies and Scholars (Blueprint of the Essential CIA).* Washington, D.C.: Acropolis, 1976.

Codman, Charles R. *Duce.* Boston: Little, Brown, 1957.

Coffman, Edward M. *The War to End All Wars.* New York: Oxford University Press, 1968.

Colby, William, and Forbath, Peter. *My Life in the CIA.* New York: Simon & Schuster, 1978.

Collins, Larry, and Lapierre, Dominique. *Is Paris Burning?* New York: Simon & Schuster, 1965.

Colvin, Ian. *Chief of Intelligence.* London: Victor Gollancz, 1951.

———. *Master Spy.* New York: McGraw-Hill, 1951.

Compton, James V. *The Swastika and the Eagle.* Boston: Houghton Mifflin, 1967.

Conant, James B. *My Several Lives.* New York: Harper & Row, 1970.

Connell, John. *Wavell, Scholar and Soldier.* New York: Harcourt, Brace, & World, 1964.

Cook, Fred J. *The FBI Nobody Knows.* New York: Macmillan, 1964.

Cookridge, E. H. *They Came from the Sky.* New York: Thomas Y. Crowell, 1967.

Coon, Carleton S. *A North Africa Story,* Ipswich, Mass.: Gambit, 1980.

Copeland, Miles. *Without Cloak or Dagger.* New York: Simon & Schuster, 1974.

Corson, William R. *The Armies of Ignorance.* New York: Dial/James Wade, 1977.

Craig, William. *The Fall of Japan.* New York: Dial, 1967.

Creel, George. *Rebel at Large.* New York: Putnam's, 1947.

Cutler, Leland W. *America Is Good to a Country Boy.* Palo Alto, Calif.: Stanford University Press, 1954.

Dallin, David J. *Soviet Espionage.* New Haven, Conn.: Yale University Press, 1955.

———. *Soviet Russia and the Far East.* New Haven, Conn.: Yale University Press, 1948.

———. *Soviet Russia's Foreign Policy.* New Haven, Conn.: Yale University Press, 1942.

Daniels, Jonathan. *Frontier on the Potomac.* New York: Macmillan, 1946.

Davis, Forrest, and Lindley, E. K. *How War Came.* New York: Simon & Schuster, 1942.

Davis, Kenneth S. *Experience of War.* Garden City, N.Y.: Doubleday, 1965.

Dawson, Raymond H. *The Decision to Aid Russia, 1941*. Chapel Hill: University of North Carolina Press, 1959.

Deacon, Richard. *The Chinese Secret Service*. New York: Taplinger, 1974.

Deane, John R. *The Strange Alliance*. New York: Viking, 1947.

deGramont, G. Sanche. *The Secret War*. New York: Putnam's, 1962.

Deighton, Len. *Fighter*. New York: Alfred A. Knopf, 1978.

De Launay, Jacques. *Secret Diplomacy of World War II*. New York: Simmons-Boardman, 1963.

Delmer, Sefton. *Black Boomerang*. New York: Viking, 1962.

Delzell, Charles F. *Mussolini's Enemies*. Princeton, N.J.: Princeton University Press, 1961.

De Toledano, Ralph. *J. Edgar Hoover*. New Rochelle, N.Y.: Arlington House, 1973.

———. *Spies, Dupes and Diplomats*. Boston: Little, Brown, 1952.

De Vosjoli, P. L. Thyraud. *Lamia*. Boston: Little, Brown, 1970.

Diggins, John P. *Mussolini and Fascism*. Princeton, N.J.: Princeton University Press, 1972.

Divine, Robert A. *Foreign Policy and U.S. Presidential Elections*. New York: New Viewpoints, 1974.

Douglas, William O. *Go East, Young Man*. New York: Random House, 1974.

———. *The Court Years, 1939–1975: The Autobiography of William O. Douglas*. New York: Random House, 1980.

Duffy, Francis P. *Father Duffy's Story*. New York: George H. Doran, 1919.

Dugan, James, and Stewart, Carroll. *Ploesti*. New York: Random House, 1962.

Duggan, Stephen. *A Professor at Large*. New York: Macmillan, 1943.

Dulles, Allen. *The Craft of Intelligence*. New York: Harper & Row, 1963.

———. *The Secret Surrender*. New York: Harper & Row, 1966.

Dulles, Allen, ed. *Great True Spy Stories*. New York: Harper & Row, 1968.

Dulles, John Foster. *War or Peace*. New York: Macmillan, 1950.

Dunlop, Richard. *Behind Japanese Lines: With the OSS in Burma*. Chicago: Rand McNally, 1979.

Dupuy, R. Ernst. *World War II: A Compact History*. New York: Hawthorn, 1969.

Dupuy, Trevor Nevitt. *European Resistance Movements*. The Military History of World War II, vol. 5. New York: Franklin Watts, 1965.

Eden, Anthony. *The Reckoning; The Memoirs of Anthony Eden*. Boston: Houghton Mifflin, 1965.

Ehrlich, Blake. *Resistance: France 1940–1945*. New York: New American Library, 1966.

Eichelberger, Clark M. *Organizing for Peace*. New York: Harper & Row, 1977.

Eichelberger, Robert L. *Our Jungle Road to Tokyo*. New York: Viking, 1950.

Elliott-Bateman, Michael, ed. *The Fourth Dimension of Warfare*. Intelligence Subversion/Resistance, vol. 1. New York: Praeger, 1970.

Ellis, L. F. *Victory in the West*. London: Her Majesty's Stationery Office, 1962.

Emmerson, John K. *The Japanese Threat*. New York: Holt, Rinehart & Winston, 1978.

Esposito, Vincent J. *A Concise History of World War II*. New York: Praeger, 1965.

Farago, Ladislas. *The Broken Seal*. New York: Random House, 1967.

———. *Burn After Reading*. New York: Walker, 1961.

———. *The Game of the Foxes*. New York: David McKay, 1971.

———. *Spymaster*. New York: Paperback Library, 1962.

———. *War of Wits*. New York: Funk & Wagnalls, 1954.

Fausald, Martin L. *James W. Wadsworth, Jr.: The Gentleman from New York*. Syracuse, N.Y.: Syracuse University Press, 1975.

Feis, Herbert. *From Trust to Terror*. New York: W. W. Norton, 1970.

———. *The Spanish Story: Franco and the Nations at War*. New York: W. W. Norton, 1966.

Felstead, S. Theodore. *Intelligence*. London: Hutchinson, 1941.

Flick, Ella M. E. *Chaplain Duffy of the Sixty-Ninth Regiment, New York*. Philadelphia: Dalton, 1935.

Flynn, John T. *The Roosevelt Myth*. New York: Devin-Adair, 1956.
Foat, M. R. D. *Resistance*. New York: McGraw-Hill, 1977.
Foley, Charles. *Commando Extraordinary*. New York: Putnam's, 1955.
Ford, Corey. *Donovan of OSS*. Boston: Little, Brown, 1970.
Ford, Don. *Pappy: The Life of John Ford*. Englewood Cliffs, N.J.: Prentice-Hall, 1979.
Foster, Jane. *An Unamerican Lady*. London: Sidgwick & Jackson, 1980.
Fotitch, Constantine. *The War We Lost*. New York: Viking, 1948.
Franklin, Charles. *The Great Spies*. New York: Hart, 1967.
Freidel, Frank. *Franklin D. Roosevelt: The Apprenticeship*. Boston: Little, Brown, 1952.
———. *Franklin D. Roosevelt: The Triumph*. Boston: Little, Brown, 1956.
———. *Over There*. Boston: Little, Brown, 1964.
Friedlander, Saul. *Prelude to Downfall*. New York: Alfred A. Knopf, 1967.
Gallo, Max. *Spain Under Franco*. New York: E. P. Dutton, 1974.
Gerard, James W. *My Four Years in Germany*. New York: George H. Doran, 1917.
Gerhart, Eugene C. *America's Advocate: Robert H. Jackson*. Indianapolis: Bobbs-Merrill, 1958.
Gibson, Hugh. *A Journal from Our Legation in Belgium*. Garden City, N.Y.: Doubleday, Page, 1917.
Glenes, Carroll V. *Four Came Home*. Princeton, N.J.: D. Van Nostrand, 1966.
Godfrey, John Henry. *Naval Memoirs of Admiral J. H. Godfrey*. Vol. 5. London: Hailsham, 1964.
Goodhart, Philip. *Fifty Ships that Saved the World*. Garden City, N.Y.: Doubleday, 1965.
Gordon, David L., and Dangerfield, Royden. *The Hidden Weapon*. New York: Harper, 1947.
Graham, Lloyd. *Niagara Country*. New York: Duell, Sloan & Pearce, 1949.
Graves, William S. *America's Siberian Adventure, 1918–1920*. New York: Peter Smith, 1941.
Greene, Warwick. *Letters of Warwick Greene, 1915–1918*. Edited by Richard W. Hale. Boston: Houghton Mifflin, 1931.
Gregory, Ross. *Walter Hines Page: Ambassador to the Court of St. James's*. Lexington: University Press of Kentucky, 1970.
Gunther, John. *Taken at the Flood: The Story of Albert D. Lasker*. New York: Harper, 1960.
Guttmann, Allen, ed. *American Neutrality and the Spanish Civil War*. Boston: D. C. Heath, 1963.
Hagen, Louis. *The Secret War for Europe*. New York: Stein & Day, 1969.
Haldane, R. A. *The Hidden War*. New York: St. Martin's, 1978.
Hanssen, Hans Peter. *Diary of a Dying Empire*. Bloomington: Indiana University Press, 1955.
Harbord, James G. *Leaves from a War Diary*. New York: Dodd, Mead, 1925.
Harriman, W. Averell, and Abel, Elie. *Special Envoy to Churchill and Stalin, 1941–1946*. New York: Random House, 1975.
Hawley, Ellis W. *The Great War and the Search for a Modern Order*. New York: St. Martin's, 1979.
Hayden, Sterling. *Wanderer*. New York: Alfred A. Knopf, 1963.
Herschmann, Ira A. *Life Line to a Promised Land*. New York: Vanguard, 1946.
Hersh, Burton. *The Mellon Family*. New York: William Morrow, 1978.
Higgins, Trumbull. *Winston Churchill and the Second Front, 1940–1943*. New York: Oxford University Press, 1957.
Hilsman, Roger. *Strategic Intelligence and National Decisions*. Glencoe, Ill.: Free Press, 1956.
Hinton, Harold B. *Cordell Hull*. Garden City, N.Y.: Doubleday, Doran, 1942.
Hoare, Sir Samuel. *Ambassador on Special Mission*. London: Collins Clear-Type, 1946.
Hoehling, A. A. *Home Front, U.S.A.* New York: Thomas Y. Crowell, 1966.

Hogan, Jim. *Spooks: The Haunting of America.* New York: William Morrow, 1978.
Hogan, Martin J. *The Shamrock Battalion of the Rainbow.* New York: D. Appleton, 1919.
Hohne, Heinz. *Canaris.* Garden City, N.Y.: Doubleday, 1979.
Hohne, Heinz, and Zollong, Hermann. *The General Was a Spy.* New York: Coward, McCann & Geoghegan, 1972.
Holborn, Hajo. *American Military Government.* Washington, D.C.: Infantry Journal Press, 1947.
Hoopes, Roy. *Americans Remember the Home Front.* New York: Hawthorn, 1977.
Hoover, Calvin. *Memoirs of Capitalism, Communism and Nazism.* Durham, N.C.: Duke University Press, 1965.
Hoptner, J. B. *Yugoslavia in Crisis.* New York: Columbia University Press, 1962.
Horne, Charles F., ed. *Source Records of the Great War.* Vol. 4. Washington, D.C.: National Alumni, 1923.
Hough, Richard. *Mountbatten.* New York: Random House, 1980.
Houseman, John. *Front and Center.* New York: Simon & Schuster, 1979.
Howe, M. A. DeWolfe. *Oliver Ames, Jr., 1895–1918.* Boston: privately printed, 1922.
Hull, Cordell. *The Memoirs of Cordell Hull.* Vol. 2. New York: Macmillan, 1948.
Hunt, E. Howard. *Undercover.* New York: Berkley, 1974.
Hunt, Frazier. *The Untold Story of Douglas MacArthur.* New York: Devin-Adair, 1954.
Hutchinson, William T. *Lowden of Illinois.* Chicago: University of Chicago Press, 1957.
Hyde, H. Montgomery. *Room 3603.* New York: Farrar, Straus, 1963.
Hyman, Sidney. *The Lives of William Benton.* Chicago: University of Chicago Press, 1969.
Icardi, Aldo. *American Master Spy.* New York: Stalwart, 1954.
Ickes, Harold L. *The Secret Diary of Harold L. Ickes.* Vol. 3. New York: Da Capo, 1974.
Ind, Allison. *A Short History of Espionage.* New York: David McKay, 1963.
Irving, David, ed. *Breach of Security.* London: William Kimber, 1968.
Ivinskaya, Olga. *A Captive of Time.* New York: Warner, 1979.
Jackson, Gabriel, ed. *The Spanish Civil War.* Chicago: Quadrangle, 1972.
James, D. Clayton. *The Years of MacArthur.* Vol. 1, 1880–1941. Boston: Houghton Mifflin, 1970.
Jeffreys-Jones, Rhodri. *American Espionage.* New York: Free Press, 1977.
Johnson, E. A. J., ed. *Power and the Academy.* Baltimore: Johns Hopkins University Press, 1964.
Jones, Richard Seelye. *A History of the American Legion.* Indianapolis: Bobbs-Merrill, 1946.
Kahn, David. *Hitler's Spies.* New York: Macmillan, 1978.
Kahn, E. J., Jr. *Far-Flung and Footloose.* New York: Putnam Publishing Group, 1979.
———. *Jock: The Life and Times of John Hay Whitney.* Garden City, N.Y.: Doubleday, 1981.
Katz, Robert. *Death in Rome.* New York: Macmillan, 1967.
Kaufman, Beatrice, and Hennessey, Joseph, eds. *The Letters of Alexander Woollcott.* New York: Viking, 1944.
Kaufman, Louis; Fitzgerald, Barbara; and Sewell, Tom. *Moe Berg.* Boston: Little, Brown, 1974.
Kaye, Joseph. *Victor Herbert.* Freeport, N.Y.: Books for Libraries, 1970.
Kilmer, Joyce. *Poems, Essays and Letters.* Garden City, N.Y.: Doubleday, Doran, 1943.
Kirkpatrick, Lyman B., Jr. *Captains Without Eyes.* London: Macmillan, 1969.
———. *The Real CIA.* New York: Macmillan, 1968.
Kleber, Brooks, and Birdsell, Dale. *The Chemical Warfare Service: Chemicals in Combat.* Washington, D.C.: Office of the Chief of Military History, U.S. Dept. of the Army, 1966.
Klein, Alexander. *The Counterfeit Traitor.* New York: Henry Holt, 1958.
Knappen, Marshall. *And Call It Peace.* Chicago: University of Chicago Press, 1947.
Knebel, Fletcher, and Bailey, Charles W. II. *No High Ground.* New York: Harper & Row, 1960.

Kose, Toshikazu. *Journey to the "Missouri."* New Haven, Conn.: Yale University Press, 1950.
Koskoff, David E. *Joseph P. Kennedy.* Englewood Cliffs, N.J.: Prentice-Hall, 1974.
Krock, Arthur. *Memoirs.* New York: Funk & Wagnalls, 1968.
Land, Emory Scott. *Winning the War with Ships.* New York: Robert M. McBride, 1958.
Lane, Arthur Bliss, and Petrov, Vladimir. *A Study in Diplomacy.* Chicago: Henry Regnery, 1971.
Langer, Walter C., *The Mind of Adolf Hitler.* New York: Basic Books, 1972.
Langer, William L. *In and Out of the Ivory Tower.* New York: Academic, 1979.
————. *Our Vichy Gamble.* New York: Alfred A. Knopf, 1947.
Langer, William L., and Gleason, S. Everett. *The Challenge to Isolation.* New York: Harper, 1952.
————. *The Undeclared War.* New York: Harper, 1953.
Langford, Earl of, and O'Neill, Thomas P. *Eamon de Valera.* Boston: Houghton Mifflin, 1950.
Leahy, William D. *I Was There.* New York: Whittlesey, 1950.
Lee, Clark. *Douglas MacArthur.* New York: Henry Holt, 1952.
Lerner, Daniel. *Psychological Warfare against Nazi Germany.* Cambridge, Mass.: M.I.T. Press, 1971.
Leutze, James, ed. *The London Journal of General Raymond E. Lee, 1940–1941.* Boston: Little, Brown, 1971.
Le Vien, Jack, and Lord, John. *Winston Churchill: The Valiant Years.* New York: Bernard Geis, 1962.
Lilienthal, David E. *The Atomic Energy Years, 1945–1950.* The Journals of David E. Lilienthal, vol. 2. New York: Harper & Row, 1964.
Loewenheim, Francis; Langley, Harold D.; and Jones, Manfred, eds. *Roosevelt and Churchill: Their Secret Wartime Correspondence.* New York: E. P. Dutton, 1975.
Lombard, Helen. *While They Fought.* New York: Scribner's, 1947.
Lovell, Stanley P. *Of Spies and Stratagems.* Englewood Cliffs, N.J.: Prentice-Hall, 1963.
Lowenthal, Max. *The Federal Bureau of Investigation.* New York: William Sloane, 1950.
McCoy, Alfred W.; Read, Cathleen B.; and Adams, Leonard P. II. *The Politics of Heroin in Southeast Asia.* New York: Harper & Row, 1972.
McCoy, Donald R. *Calvin Coolidge.* New York: Macmillan, 1967.
MacDonald, Charles B. *The Mighty Endeavor.* New York: Oxford University Press, 1969.
McFarland, Keith D. *Harry H. Woodring.* Lawrence: University Press of Kansas, 1975.
McKenna, Marion C. *Borah.* Ann Arbor: University of Michigan Press, 1961.
McLachlan, Donald. *Room 39.* New York: Atheneum, 1968.
Manchester, William. *American Caesar.* Boston: Little, Brown, 1978.
Mangeri, Franco. *From the Ashes of Disgrace.* New York: Reynal & Hitchcock, 1948.
Mann, Peggy. *Ralph Bunche.* New York: Coward, McCann & Geoghegan, 1975.
Manvell, Roger, and Fraenkel, Heinrich. *The Incomparable Crime.* New York: Putnam's, 1970.
Marks, John. *The Search for the Manchurian Candidate.* New York: Times Books, 1979.
Marshall, Bruce. *The White Rabbit.* Boston: Houghton Mifflin, 1953.
Martin, David. *Ally Betrayed.* Englewood Cliffs, N.J.: Prentice-Hall, 1946.
Martin, David C. *Wilderness of Mirrors.* New York: Harper & Row, 1980.
Mason, Alpheus Thomas. *Harlan Fiske Stone: Pillar of the Law.* New York: Viking, 1956.
Mason, Herbert Malloy, Jr. *The Great Pursuit.* New York: Random House, 1970.
————. *To Kill the Devil.* New York: W. W. Norton, 1978.
Matloff, Maurice. *Strategic Planning for Coalition Warfare, 1943–1944.* Washington, D.C.: Office of the Chief of Military History, U.S. Dept. of the Army, 1959.
Mattingly, Robert E. *Herringbone Cloak–GI Dagger: Marines of the OSS.* Quantico,

Va.: Marine Corps Command and Staff Center, 1979.

Mayzisch, L. C. *Operation Cicero.* New York: Coward-McCann, 1950.

Minott, Rodney G. *The Fortress That Never Was.* New York: Holt, Rinehart & Winston, 1964.

Morgan, William L. *The OSS and I.* New York: Pocket, 1956.

Morris, Joe Alex. *Nelson Rockefeller.* New York: Harper, 1960.

Mosley, Leonard. *Dulles.* New York: Dial/James Wade, 1978.

Nash, Jay Robert. *Citizen Hoover.* Chicago: Nelson-Hall, 1972.

Neale, R. G., ed. *Documents on Australian Foreign Policy, 1937–49.* Vol. 4. Canberra: Australian Government Publishing Service, 1975–.

Neumann, William L. *After Victory.* New York: Harper & Row, 1967.

Nevins, Allan. *Herbert H. Lehman and His Era.* New York: Scribner's, 1963.

Ogilvy, David. *Blood, Brawn, and Beer.* New York: Atheneum, 1978.

OSS Assessment Staff. *Assessment of Men.* New York: Rinehart, 1948.

Parmet, Herbert S. *Jack: The Struggles of John F. Kennedy.* New York: Dial, 1980.

Parrish, Robert. *Growing up in Hollywood.* New York: Harcourt Brace Jovanovich, 1976.

Paterson, Thomas G. *Soviet-American Confrontation.* Baltimore: Johns Hopkins University Press, 1973.

Pendar, Kenneth. *Adventure in Diplomacy.* New York: Dodd, Mead, 1945.

Persico, Joseph E. *Piercing the Reich.* New York: Viking, 1979.

Petrovic, Sveteslav-Sveta. *Free Yugoslavia Calling.* New York: Greystone, 1941.

Philby, Kim. *My Silent War.* Great Britain: MacGibbon & Key, 1968.

Phillips, William. *Ventures in Diplomacy.* London: John Murray, 1955.

Pike, James A. *A Roman Catholic in the White House.* Garden City, N.Y.: Doubleday, 1960.

Pogue, Forrest C. *George C. Marshall: Organizer of Victory.* New York: Viking, 1973.

Powers, Thomas. *The Man Who Kept the Secrets.* New York: Alfred A. Knopf, 1979.

Prouty, L. Fletcher. *The Secret Team.* Englewood Cliffs, N.J.: Prentice-Hall, 1973.

Ransom, Harry Howe. *Central Intelligence and National Security.* Cambridge, Mass.: Harvard University Press, 1958.

———. *The Intelligence Establishment.* Cambridge, Mass.: Harvard University Press, 1970.

Reader's Digest. *Secrets and Spies.* Pleasantville, N.Y.: Reader's Digest Assoc., 1964.

Reilly, Henry J. *Americans All; The Rainbow at War.* Columbus, Oh.: F. J. Beer, 1936.

Reston, James B. *Prelude to Victory.* New York: Alfred A. Knopf, 1942.

Roberts, Walter R. *Tito, Mihailovic and the Allies, 1941–1945.* New Brunswick, N.J.: Rutgers University Press, 1973.

Robinson, Edgar E., and Bornet, Vaughn D. *Herbert Hoover.* Stanford, Calif.: Hoover Institution Press, 1975.

Rogow, Arnold A. *James Forrestal.* New York: Macmillan, 1963.

Rolo, Charles J. *Radio Goes to War.* New York: Putnam's, 1940.

Roosevelt, Eleanor. *This I Remember.* New York: Harper, 1949.

Roosevelt, Eleanor Butler. *Day Before Yesterday.* Garden City, N.Y.: Doubleday, 1959.

Roosevelt, Franklin. *Complete Presidential Press Conferences of FDR.* New York: Da Capo, 1972.

———. *FDR: His Personal Letters.* Edited by Elliott Roosevelt. Vols. 1 and 2. New York: Duell, Sloan & Pearce, 1950.

———. *The Public Papers and Addresses of Franklin D. Roosevelt.* Compiled by Samuel I. Rosenman. 1941 vol. and 1942 vol. New York: Harper, 1950.

Roosevelt, Kermit. *Countercoup.* New York: McGraw-Hill, 1979.

———. *War Report of the OSS.* New York: Walker, 1976.

Roosevelt, Theodore. *The Letters of Theodore Roosevelt.* Edited by Elting E. Morison. Cambridge, Mass.: Harvard University Press, 1954.

Root, Waverly. *The Secret History of the War.* New York: Scribner's, 1945.

Roper, Daniel C. *Fifty Years of Public Life.* Durham, N.C.: Duke University Press, 1941.

Rosenstone, Robert A. *Crusade of the Left.* New York: Pegasus, 1969.
Rositzke, Harry. *The CIA's Secret Operations.* New York: Reader's Digest Press, 1977.
Rowan, Richard Wilmer, and Deindorfer, Robert G. *Secret Service.* New York: Hawthorn, 1967.
Salisbury, Harrison E. *Without Fear or Favor.* New York: Times Books, 1980.
Salvemini, Gaetano. *Prelude to World War II.* Garden City, N.Y.: Doubleday, 1954.
Sanborn, Frederic R. *Design for War.* New York: Devin-Adair, 1951.
Scheurig, Bodo. *Free Germany.* Middletown, Conn.: Wesleyan University Press, 1969.
Schoenbrun, David. *Soldiers of the Night.* New York: E. P. Dutton, 1980.
Schuman, Frederick L. *Night over Europe.* New York: Alfred A. Knopf, 1941.
Seth, Ronald. *The Noble Saboteurs.* New York: Hawthorn, 1966.
————. *Unmasked.* New York: Hawthorn, 1965.
Sheean, Vincent. *This House Against This House.* New York: Random House, 1945.
Sherwood, Robert E. *Roosevelt and Hopkins.* New York: Harper, 1948.
————. *The White House Papers of Harry L. Hopkins.* London: Eyre & Spottiswoode, 1948.
Singer, Kurt, and Sherrod, Jane. *Spies for Democracy.* Minneapolis: P. S. Denison, 1960.
Smith, Paul C. *Personal File.* New York: Appleton-Century, 1964.
Smith, R. Harris. *OSS.* Berkeley: University of California Press, 1972.
Snell, John L. *Illusion and Necessity.* Boston: Houghton Mifflin, 1963.
Stallings, Laurence. *The Doughboys.* New York: Harper & Row, 1963.
Stettinius, Edward R., Jr. *The Diaries of Edward R. Stettinius, Jr., 1943–1946.* Edited by Thomas M. Campbell and George C. Herring. New York: New View Books, 1975.
————. *Roosevelt and the Russians.* Garden City, N.Y.: Doubleday, 1949.
Steven, Stewart. *Operation Splinter Factor.* Philadelphia: Lippincott, 1974.
Stevenson, Adlai E. *The Papers of Adlai E. Stevenson.* Vol. 1. Boston: Little, Brown, 1972.
Stevenson, William. *The Bormann Brotherhood.* New York: Harcourt Brace Jovanovich, 1973.
————. *A Man Called Intrepid.* New York: Ballantine, 1977.
Stoler, Mark A. *The Politics of the Second Front.* Westport, Conn.: Greenwood, 1977.
Storey, Robert G. *The Final Judgment?* San Antonio: Naylor, n.d.
Strauss, Lewis L. *Men and Decisions.* Garden City, N.Y.: Doubleday, 1962.
Strong, Sir Kenneth. *Intelligence at the Top.* Garden City, N.Y.: Doubleday, 1969.
————. *Men of Intelligence.* London: Cassell, 1970.
Sulzberger, Cyrus L. *A Long Row of Candles.* New York: Macmillan, 1969.
Sweeney, Daniel J. *History of Buffalo and Erie County, 1914–1919.* Buffalo, N.Y.: Matthews-Northrup, 1920.
Sweet-Escott, Bickham. *Baker Street Irregular.* London: Methuen & Co., 1965.
Swope, Herbert Bayard. *Inside the German Empire.* New York: Century, 1917.
Tansill, Charles C. *Back Door to War.* Chicago: Henry Regnery, 1952.
Taylor, Edmond. *Awakening from History.* Boston: Gambit, 1969.
Taylor, Foster Jay. *The United States and the Spanish Civil War.* New York: Bookman, 1956.
Thorne, Christopher. *Allies of a Kind.* New York: Oxford University Press, 1978.
Tompkins, Peter. *Italy Betrayed.* New York: Simon & Schuster, 1966.
————. *The Murder of Admiral Darlan.* New York: Simon & Schuster, 1965.
Tompkins, Raymond S. *The Story of the Rainbow Division.* New York: Bone and Liveright, 1919.
Troy, Thomas F. *Donovan and the CIA.* Washington, D.C.: Center for the Study of Intelligence, Central Intelligence Agency, 1981.
Truman, Harry. *Memoirs.* Vol. 2. Garden City, N.Y.: Doubleday, 1956.
Truman, Margaret. *Harry S. Truman.* New York: William Morrow, 1973.
Tully, Andrew. *CIA: The Inside Story.* New York: William Morrow, 1962.
————. *The Super Spies.* New York: William Morrow, 1969.
Utley, Freda. *The China Story.* Chicago: Henry Regnery, 1951.

Van Dyke, Henry. *Fighting for Peace.* New York: Scribner's, 1917.
Von Papen, Franz. *Memoirs.* New York: E. P. Dutton, 1953.
Von Schlabrendorff, Fabian. *The Secret War Against Hitler.* New York: Pitman, 1965.
Wallace, Henry A. *The Price of Vision: The Diary of Henry A. Wallace, 1942–1946.* Edited by John Marten Blum. Boston: Houghton Mifflin, 1973.
Ward, John. *With the Die Hards in Siberia.* New York: George H. Doran, 1920.
Warner, Oliver. *Admiral of the Fleet: Cunningham of Hyndhope.* Athens: Ohio University Press, 1967.
Wedemeyer, Albert C. *Wedemeyer Reports.* New York: Henry Holt, 1958.
Westerfield, H. Bradford. *The Instruments of America's Foreign Policy.* New York: Thomas Y. Crowell, 1963.
Wheeler, Burton K. *Yankee from the West.* Garden City, N.Y.: Doubleday, 1962.
White, Dorothy Shipley. *Seeds of Discord.* Syracuse, N.Y.: Syracuse University Press, 1964.
Whitehead, Don. *The FBI Story.* New York: Random House, 1956.
Whiting, Charles. *The Battle for Twelveland.* London: Leo Cooper, 1975.
Whitlock, Brand. *Belgium: A Personal Narrative.* New York: D. Appleton, 1919.
Wilbur, Roy Lyman. *The Memoirs of Roy Lyman Wilbur.* Edited by E. E. Robinson and P. C. Edwards. Stanford, Calif.: Stanford University Press, 1960.
Wilhelm, Maria. *The Man Who Watched the Rising Sun.* New York: Franklin Watts, 1967.
Willoughby, Charles A., and Chamberlain, John. *MacArthur, 1941–1951.* New York: McGraw-Hill, 1954.
Wilson, Carol Green. *Herbert Hoover.* New York: Evans, 1968.
Wilson, Hugh R. *Diplomat Between Wars.* New York: Longman, Green, 1941.
Wise, David, and Ross, Thomas B. *The Espionage Establishment.* New York: Random House, 1967.
———. *The Invisible Government.* New York: Random House, 1964.
Wittner, Lawrence S. *MacArthur.* Englewood Cliffs, N.J.: Prentice-Hall, 1971.
Wolf, Walter B. *A Brief Story of the Rainbow Division.* New York: Rand McNally, 1919.
Wolff, Robert Lee. *The Balkans in Our Time.* Cambridge, Mass.: Harvard University Press, 1956.
Woollcott, Alexander. *While Rome Burns.* New York: Viking, 1934.
Zink, Harold. *American Military Government in Germany.* New York: Macmillan, 1947.
Zuckerman, Solly. *From Apes to Warlords.* New York: Harper & Row, 1978.

Magazines

"The Aluminum Case." *Outlook,* Jan. 20, 1926.
"Balkan Torch." *Time,* Feb. 3, 1941.
Braden, Tom. "The Birth of the CIA." *American Heritage,* February 1977.
Cardinale, Anthony. "The World of Manly Fleischmann." *Buffalo News Magazine,* July 8, 1979.
Chamberlain, John. "OSS." *Life,* Nov. 19, 1945.
Choate, Robert. "Donovan Has Charge of That." *The Independent,* July 3, 1926.
"The CIA: Time to Come in from the Cold." *Time,* Sept. 30, 1974.
"Colonel Donovan's War." *Time,* March 31, 1941.
Cuneo, Ernest. "Mountbatten." *American Legion,* December 1979.
Davis, Forrest. "Secret History of a Surrender." *Saturday Evening Post,* Sept. 22, 1945.
"Diplomacy: It's Donovan Again." *Newsweek,* July 26, 1954.
Donovan, William J. "Fugitives from the Soviet." *Commonweal,* June 8, 1956.
———. "Intelligence: Key to Defense." *Life,* Sept. 30, 1946.

———. "Major Donovan's War Diary." *The Sun Magazine*, Sept. 22, 1918.
———. "Our Stake in Thailand." *Fortune*, July 1955.
———. "Religion: The Need of the Hour." *Niagara Index*, June 15, 1902.
———. "The Schumann Plan: A Blow to Monopoly." *Atlantic Monthly*, February 1952.
———. "Should Men of 50 Fight Our Wars?" *Reader's Digest*, June 1940.
———. "Stop Russia's Subversive War." *Atlantic Monthly*, May 1948.
———. "True Manhood." *Niagara Index*, June 9, 1901.
———. "Who Says We're Soft?" *Reader's Digest*, April 1941.
"Donovan Strategy." *Newsweek*, Nov. 17, 1941.
Dulles, Allen. "The Craft of Intelligence." *Harper's*, April 1963.
FitzGibbon, Constantine. "Spying for the Yanks." *American Heritage*, June–July 1980.
Ford, Corey, and MacBain, Alastair. "Cloak and Dagger." *Colliers*, Oct. 6, 1945.
Hadley, Arthur T. "Complex Query: What Makes a Good Spy?" *New York Times Magazine*, May 29, 1960.
Hard, Anne. "Wild Bill Donovan." *New York Herald Tribune*, March 13, 1927.
Hard, William. "Dock Yards to Fame." *New York Herald Tribune*, Oct. 30, 1932.
"High Strategist." *Time*, Aug. 4, 1941.
"Homes of Washington." *House and Garden*, August 1942.
"Job for Donovan." *Newsweek*, July 21, 1941.
Johnson, Thomas M. "Nailing Nazi Lies." *American Legion Magazine*, April 1942.
Jones, Stacy V. "Who's Going to Spy for Us Now?" *Liberty*, Dec. 15, 1945.
Ledeen, Michael. "Tinker, Turner, Sailor, Spy." *New York*, March 3, 1980.
"Mama Spank." *Time*, Oct. 18, 1937.
Mullany, Harry B. "Smashing the Narcotic Racket." *Buffalo Times*, May 3, 1932.
"Mystery Mission—and Defense." *Business Week*, Dec. 14, 1940.
Naver, Barnet. "Vignette Colonel William Joseph Donovan, Soldier-Lawyer." *Town Tidings*, January 1929.
Observation Post, August 1932, March 1934.
"Our First War Commissioner Dies." *Red Cross Courier*, December 1937.
"The Paris Caucus." *American Legion*, March 1969.
Pearson, John. "Ian Fleming." *Life*, Oct. 7, 1966.
Persico, Joseph E. "The Fearless Yanks Who Spied on Hitler." *Parade*, Feb. 11, 1979.
Rainbow Reveille, July 13, 1923; May–June 1935.
"Resolute Jury." *Time*, Jan. 31, 1938.
Roubatis, Yiannis P., and Vlanton, Elias. "Who Killed George Polk?" *More*, May 1977.
Scott, H. D. "Bill Donovan on the Ourcq." *Rainbow Reveille*, January–February 1935.
Shepherd, William G. "Meet the Colonel." *Colliers*, March 2, 1929.
Sondern, Frederic, Jr. "Our Wartime Spymaster Carries On." *Reader's Digest*, October 1947.
———. "Wild Bill Crusades Against Wars." *Reader's Digest*, August 1940.
"Think V.S.S." *New Yorker*, Nov. 12, 1979.
Time, Oct. 18, 1937; Jan. 31, 1938; Mar. 31, 1941; Oct. 5, 1970.
Tolstoi, Ilya. "Across Tibet from India to China." *National Geographic*, August 1946.
"Town Tidings." *Buffalo Magazine*, January 1929.
Valentine, Elizabeth R. "Fact-Finder and Fighting Man." *New York Times Magazine*, May 4, 1941.
Villard, Oswald Garrison. "Jew and Gentile in New York." *Nation*, October 1932.
"Where Do They Stand Now?" *More*, May 1977.
White, George A. "Cradle Days in the Legion." *American Legion Magazine*, Nov. 19, 1920.
White, Theodore H. "Episode in Tokyo Bay." *Atlantic*, August 1970.
"Whole Bankruptcy Law Wrong, First Searching Study Shows." *Business Week*, April 2, 1930.
"Who's Who—and Why." *Saturday Evening Post*, Nov. 14, 1925.
"Wild Bill Donovan, War-Time and Peace-Time Fighter." *Literary Digest*, May 9, 1925.
"William J. Donovan." *Buffalo Magazine*, January 1929.

Personal Interviews

Chester Allen, Esther Andrews, Roy Chapman Andrews, A. G. Atwater, Thomas Baldwin, Mary Bancroft, Charles Bane, Leif Bangsboll, Paul E. Bashor, Walter Berry, John T. Beaudouin, Paul Bewshea, Edward L. Bigelow, Donald Billman, Thomas F. Bland, Congressman John A. Blatnik, Waller B. Booth, John Bowden, John A. Bross, David Bruce, G. Edward Buxton III, Oliver Caldwell, John Cassidy, Dennis V. Cavanaugh, Chester R. Chartrand, Gen. Mark Clark, Ray S. Cline, Adm. Cecil H. Coggins, William E. Colby, Carleton S. Coon, Mel Corvin, John G. Coughlin, Robert E. Coulson, David C. Crockett, Ernest Cuneo, Vincent Curl, William Cybulski, Luther Dawson, Rene J. Defourneaux, O. C. Doering, David Donovan, Kathleen Donovan, Maj. Gen. William J. Donovan, Thomas Driscoll, Carl F. Eifler, John W. English, Sr., Robert H. Flaherty, Eugene Fodor, Nancy C. Fogarty, Leo Frances, William G. Fuchs, Ets Galassi, Paul Gale, Carroll Garretson, Millicent Amstutz Garrison, Arthur Goldberg, Richard Greenlee, James D. Griffin, Nelson Guillot, Roy C. Hall, Kay Murphy Halle, Samuel Halpern, Van R. Halsey, Dr. James Hamilton, Philip Hardinger, Jan Smiley Hart, Richard Heppner, Roger Hilsman, Leo Hochstetter, Lawrence R. Houston, Foster Howe, Henry B. Hyde, Phil Impelliteri, James Irmiter, Ed Jaeckle, Geoffrey M. T. Jones, Congressman Walter Judd, Francis S. Kinney, Ander Klay, Milton Klein, Gus Krause, Nicholas S. Kudlek, Kenneth Landon, Mrs. William Langer, Erik A. Lindgren, Harry W. Little, Jr., Stanley P. Lovell, Lawrence W. Lowman, Howard Lyon, Turner McBaine, The Reverend Ward McCabe, Edward McGinnis, William McGovern, Elizabeth Heppner McIntosh, Walter Mahoney, Byron Martin, Guy Martin, Sir Fitzroy MacLean, Peter Mero, Mary Frances Merz, Walter Mess, Frank Mogavero, Mel Montgomery, Irene Murphy, James R. Murphy, Paul Nitze, John O'Keefe, George Overton, Lt. Gen. W. R. Peers, Walter Pforzheimer, Pinto, Orlando A. Ponzio, Edwin J. Putzell, Jr., Lt. Gen. William W. Quinn, William J. Rader, Frank Raichle, Virginia R. Renshaw, Atherton Richards, Charles Ritz, Fred Rodell, Kermit Roosevelt, Don Russell, Claude Sainsot, Oliver J. Sands, Jr., Rose Sault, Anthony Scariano, Adolph Schmidt, Margaret Griggs Setton, Maj. Gen. John K. Singlaub, Elizabeth Keeney Sipe, Sen. H. Alexander Smith, Nicol Smith, Edward Snyder, Sir William Stephenson, Thomas W. Streeter, C. Bruce Sutherland, David Talley, Charles H. Taquey, Robert Thayer, David L. Titus, Thomas Troy, Gerhard P. Van Arkel, Vance V. Vogel, Mitchell Warbell, Marilyn Wayliner, Phillip Weld, Benjamin Welles, Hubert Will

Correspondence Received by Author

Herbert Agar, Marguerite Allen, N. F. Allman, H. Amory, Jr., Dorothy May Anderson, Ira Ashley, Jules Weber Aubry, Mary Bancroft, Aaron Bank, John J. Barden, John T. Beaudouin, George Beishlag, Melvin O. Benson, Andrew Berding, Nahum A. Bernstein, Constantin S. Bertakis, Waller B. Booth, Earl D. Brodie, Thomas W. Bullitt, Julia Child, Donald Coers, Harold J. Coolidge, Joseph R. Coolidge, Gerald W. Davis, William W. Downey, John W. English, Edward L. Field, Henry Field, William T. Fitzgerald, Richard S. Friedman, Bernard Gelman, Joseph Gould, George L. Graveson, Roy C. Hall, Douglas Patrick Harper, John H. F. Haskell, John H. N. Hemmingway, Ralph E. Henderson, Robert F. Houlihan, A. S. Jackson, Clifford Kachline, Alfred H. Kirchhofer, Nicholas S. Kudlek, Jacques J. LaFia, Kenneth P. Landon, Mrs. William L. Langer, Leonard P. Laundergan, Paul Ludington, Alexander MacDonald, Laura Hoke McGehee, John W. Mowinckel, James R. Murphy, David M. Nichol, Henry Ringling North, John B. Okie, Paul R. Palmer, Lt. Gen. W. R. Peers, Daniel B. Potochniak, Edwin J. Putzell, Jr., Lt. Gen. William W. Quinn, William J. Rader, W. C. Reddick, Arthur H. Robinson, Kermit Roosevelt, W. W. Rostow, Harriet Sabine, Dr. Sareyko, Bertha Shurtok, S. H. Simpson, Jr., Nicol Smith, Robert D. Spector, Mrs. Alexander Graham Stone, Charles Porter Storey, Thomas W. Streeter, George Weller, Benjamin Welles, Joan G. Whitbeck, G. K. Young

Archives

American Legion National Headquarters Library, Indianapolis
Archives of the University of Notre Dame, South Bend, Ind.
Donovan addresses.
George Arents Research Library, Syracuse University, Syracuse, N.Y.
Manuscript Division: Berlin journal of Lithgow Osborne, Osborne family commu-
nications and writings.
Beaverbrook Library, London
Papers of Lord Beaverbrook.
Buffalo and Erie County Historical Society, Buffalo, N.Y.
Donovan memorabilia; papers of A. Conger Goodyear.
Buffalo and Erie County Public Library, Buffalo, N.Y.
Donovan scrapbooks and Donovan collection.
Buffalo Cavalry Association Archives, Buffalo, N.Y.
Donovan collection and history of the cavalry units.
Chicago Historical Society Library, Chicago, Ill.
Letters and speeches of Charles Dewey.
Citadel Memorial Archives, Charleston, S.C.
Papers of Gen. Mark Clark and Action Report of USS *Biscayne.*
Columbia University Libraries, New York, N.Y.
Columbiana Collection: Donovan files; Herbert H. Lehman papers in Inter-
national Affairs Building; Manuscript Collection; Oral History Archives in Rare
Book and Manuscripts Collection: Interviews with Paul Henson Appleby, Henry
Breckinridge, Luther Harris Evans, James Fife, Alan Goodrich Kirk, Herbert
H. Lehman, Eugene Meyer, John Lord O'Brian, Lithgow Osborne, William Phillips,
Jackson E. Reynolds, Allen Wardwell, John Campbell White, James Thomas
Williams, Jr.
Dartmouth College Library, Hanover, N.H.
Papers of Corey Ford and Vilhjalmur Stefansson.
First Division Museum and Library, Cantigny, Wheaton, Ill.
World War I Collection.
Georgetown University Library, Washington, D.C.
Special Collections Division, Bowen Collection on Intelligence.
William J. Gross Intelligence Collection, Centerville, Ohio
Harvard University Library, Cambridge, Mass.
Houghton Library: Papers of Ellis Loring Dressel, Walter Hines Page, Oswald
Garrison Villard, Alexander Woollcott, Theodore Roosevelt.
Rutherford B. Hayes Library, Fremont, Ohio
Special Collections.
Hoover Institution on War, Revolution, and Peace, Stanford, Calif.
Papers of Herbert Blankenhorn, Oliver J. Caldwell, Claire L. Chennault, Emmett
Christopher, Costa C. Couvaras, James Donovan, Christopher T. Emmet, J. Russell
Forgan, Hermann Göring, Millard P. Goodfellow, Herbert Hoover, Stanley Hornbeck,
David Wooster King, Franklin Anthony Lindsay, John C. Metcalf, Gilbert Stuart,
Gero von Schulze-Gaevernits, Tracy Voorhees.
Herbert Hoover Presidential Library, West Branch, Iowa
Oral History Archives: Interviews with George E. Akerson, Jr., James A. Farley,
Bonner Fellers, Alfred H. Kirchhofer, Sallie MacCracken, Bradley D. Nash; Papers
of American Committee on United Europe, William R. Castle, Herbert Hoover,
James H. MacLafferty, Truman Smith, Robert A. Taft, Walter Trohan, Hugh R.
Wilson, Gen. Robert Wood.
Library of Congress, Washington, D.C.
Manuscript Division: Papers of Joseph and Stewart Alsop, Edward T. Clark, Calvin
Coolidge, Felix Frankfurter, William F. Halsey, Cordell Hull, William E. Humphrey,
Harold Ickes, Frank Knox, Archibald MacLeish, Roland Morris, Harlan Fiske Stone,
William Howard Taft, Henry Wallace.

MacArthur Memorial, Norfolk, Va.
Douglas MacArthur Archives: Personal Correspondence, Chronological File and VIP File; Records of General HQ, Supreme Commander for the Allied Powers, 1945–1951; Records of HQ, SW Pacific Area, 1942–1945.
Robert R. McCormick Library, Cantigny, Wheaton, Ill.
World War I Collection, privately held.
Marquat Memorial Library, Institute for Military Assistance, Fort Bragg, N.C.
Donovan papers; Joseph Freeman Lincoln Collection.
George C. Marshall Research Foundation, Lexington, Va.
Donovan reports and Donovan memoranda and correspondence with George Catlett Marshall.
Minnesota Historical Society, St. Paul
Papers of William D. Mitchell.
Nardin Academy Archives, Buffalo, N.Y.
Donovan memorabilia.
National Archives, Washington, D.C.
Department of Justice Records; Diplomatic Section, papers relating to the foreign relations of the United States; Modern Military Branch, OSS Archives.
New York Public Library, New York
Manuscript and Archives Division.
New York State Library, Albany
Manuscripts and Special Collections: Papers of Herbert Lehman and Alfred E. Smith.
Niagara University Archives, Niagara Falls
Donovan records.
Northwestern University Library, Evanston, Ill.
Special Collections: Franklin Roosevelt Collection.
101 Association Archives, Orange, Calif.
OSS and Donovan materials.
Walter Pforzheimer Collection on Intelligence Service, Washington, D.C.
OSS and Donovan documents and memorabilia; Conyers Read manuscript.
Politischen Archiven des Auswartigen, Bonn, West Germany
Reports to German Foreign Office.
Princeton University Library, Princeton, N.J.
Seeley G. Mudd Manuscript Library: Papers of Bernard M. Baruch, Allen W. Dulles, John Foster Dulles, Fight for Freedom Archives, Arthur Krock, David Lawrence, David E. Lilienthal, H. Alexander Smith, Philip Strong, United China Relief–United Service to China.
Public Records Office, London
Halifax papers.
RAF Museum, Hounslow, Middlesex, England
Special Projects.
Rockefeller Foundation Archives Center, North Tarrytown, N.Y.
Record Group 1.1, Series 100 N; War Relief Commission.
Will Rogers Memorial, Claremore, Okla.
Papers of Will Rogers.
Franklin D. Roosevelt Library, Hyde Park, N.Y.
Donovan memoranda and letters to Roosevelt, OSS reports, Roosevelt papers, including press conferences, memoranda, letters, and reports; Papers of Adolph A. Berle, Francis Biddle, Stephen T. Early, Henry Field, Harry L. Hopkins, Mary Lasker, Henry M. Morgenthau, Samuel I. Rosenman, Whitney Shepardson, Harold D. Smith, Henry A. Wallace, John G. Winant.
St. Joseph's Collegiate Institute Archives, Buffalo, N.Y.
Donovan memorabilia.
State University of New York Library, Geneseo
Wadsworth family papers.
Union League of Philadelphia Archives, Philadelphia
Donovan addresses.

United Kingdom, Foreign and Commonwealth Office, Foreign Office papers, London
U.S. Army Military History Institute, Carlisle Barracks, Penna.
Brig. Gen. Michael J. Lenahan journal, Maj. Hugh W. Ogden diary, 149th Field Artillery Record and Telephone Book, 165th Infantry Field Reports.
University of Chicago Library, Chicago
Special Collections: Papers of Frank Lowden and William Benton.
University of Iowa Library, Iowa City
Special Collections Department: Papers of Henry Wallace.
University of Michigan Library, Ann Arbor
Bentley Historical Library: Papers of Arthur Scott Aiton, Eugene Grassman, Frank Murphy, Alexander Ruthven, G. Mennen Williams.
University of Virginia Library, Charlottesville
Alderman Library, Manuscripts Department: Papers of Edward Stettinius, Jr., Edward Stettinius, Sr., Edwin M. White.
University of Wyoming Archive of Contemporary History, Laramie
Donovan biographical material.
Warren Historical Society, Warren, Penna.
Grandin material.
Yale University Library, New Haven, Conn.
Sterling Memorial Library: Papers of Arthur Bliss Lane, Henry L. Stimson (and Stimson diaries), Samuel Watkins.

Index